Say It Loud!

Say It Loud!

ON RACE, LAW, HISTORY, AND CULTURE

Randall Kennedy

Pantheon Books, New York

Library of Congress Cataloging-in-Publication Data
Names: Kennedy, Randall, [date] author.
Title: Say it loud! : on race, law, history, and culture / Randall Kennedy.
Description: New York, NY: Pantheon Books, 2021. Includes index.
Identifiers: LCCN 2020055460 (print). LCCN 2020055461 (ebook). ISBN
9780593316047 (hardcover). ISBN 9780593316054 (ebook).
Subjects: LCSH: African Americans—Legal status, laws, etc. African
American—Civil rights. African Americans—Social conditions. United States—
Race relations. Racism—United States.
Classification: LCC KF4757 .K46 2021 (print) | LCC KF4757 (ebook) | DDC
342.7308/73—dc23
LC record available at lccn.loc.gov/2020055460
LC ebook record available at lccn.loc.gov/2020055461

www.pantheonbooks.com

Jacket design by Linda Huang

Printed in the United States of America
First Edition

2 4 6 8 9 7 5 3 1

For Mona Simpson

CONTENTS

Preface

The writings that follow are the impressions of a Black/Negro/ Colored/African American law professor born in Columbia, South Carolina, in 1954, four months after the Supreme Court handed down *Brown v. Board of Education*. These essays chronicle people, events, arguments, ideas, and books that over the past quarter century prompted me to put pen to paper.

Three beliefs that are sometimes in tension with one another infuse these pages.

First, racism continues to be a major force in America. Nothing more clearly evidences its menacing influence than the astonishing rise of Donald J. Trump. His election to the presidency in 2016 revealed a prevalence of bias and tolerance for bigotry that many (including me) underestimated, even though an underlying social rot was evident. Dissidents had focused a bright light on racist policing and other wrongs. (See "The George Floyd Moment" and "The Constitutional Roots of 'Birtherism.'") And commentators had noted mounting evidence of racist reaction against President Barack Obama and all that he was perceived as representing. But few anticipated that status anxieties among whites would, when combined with other factors, propel Trump to the presidency given his glaring deficiencies.

The circumstances under which Trump was ousted from power put the United States in a light that is unspeakably sad. Yes, he was defeated; for that the world must be grateful. But the repudiation was by no means overwhelming. Trump attracted the support of almost half of the American electorate (around seventy-four million voters) and deepened the influence of his baleful ethos within an increasingly right-wing and militant Republican Party. That he received as much support as he did should be deeply disturbing given the incompetence of his response to the deadly COVID-19 pandemic, his efforts to sabotage the electoral process, the foolishness of his reaction to ecological threats, the loathsomeness of his personal conduct, his solicitude for tyrants globally, the cruelty of policies he sponsored (the separation of children from their parents pursuant to immigration policy was perhaps the most atrocious), not to mention his indifference to threatened violence by supporters and his incitement of various prejudices. Trump did not create racism, and racism is but one facet of the catastrophe his presidency represents. But the racism he exploited, legitimated, and helped to popularize is an important ingredient in the wicked stew that has poisoned the country. For most of my life I have been an optimist regarding the possibility of creating a racially just republic as part of a broader realization of the promise of America. (See "Shall We Overcome? Optimism and Pessimism in African American Racial Thought.") That hopefulness has been profoundly shaken, though not altogether extinguished, by the Trumpian turn that will shadow the country for the foreseeable future.

Second, there is much to be inspired by when surveying the African American journey from slavery to freedom. Blacks encountering racist impediments have responded repeatedly with brave demands for racial decency and social justice in general. (See "Frederick Douglass: Everyone's Hero" and "How Black Students Brought the Constitution to Campus.") People of every complexion have played a role in that epic struggle and continue to be shaped by it. (See "J. Skelly Wright: Up from Racism," "Isaac Woodard and the Education of J. Waties Waring," and "On Cussing Out White Liberals: The Case of Philip Elman.") Transfixed by impressive figures in that saga, I insist that they be taken seriously, which means acknowledging their vices as well as their virtues. (See "Remembering Thurgood Marshall" and "Derrick Bell and Me.") Victimization does not exempt individuals from moral obligations. Even those enslaved should be held to high moral standards. (See "Should We Admire Nat Turner?") And being on the side of antiracism is no inoculation against error. The thinking and conduct of those challenging injustice must be carefully examined because they, too, like all of us, are prone to narcissism, thoughtlessness, and abuse of power. (See "Black Power Hagiography" and "The Princeton Ultimatum: Antiracism Gone Awry.")

Third, social relations are complex and messy. We protest against the memorialization of figures who propounded antiblack racism while simultaneously celebrating figures who propounded bigotries of other sorts. (See "Race and the Politics of Memorialization.") We urge individuals to be independent while insisting that there are certain boundaries of loyalty that cannot be crossed without incurring the stigmatizing label of "traitor." (See "Policing Racial Solidarity" and "Why Clarence Thomas Ought to Be Ostracized.") We condemn racial discrimination while expressly limiting the power of law to erase it because of our rightful attentiveness to freedom of expression and prudential fear of excessive governmental intrusiveness. (See "Racial Promised Lands?") In the essays that follow, I luxuriate in the messiness. I savor the paradox and irony. I try to share with readers my sense of surprise, ambivalence, and humility while seeking to understand the race line in American life.

Say It Loud!

1

Shall We Overcome?
Optimism and Pessimism in
African American Racial Thought[1]

Take courage . . . ye Afric-Americans! Don't give up the conflict,
for the glorious prize can be won.

—Peter Osborne (1832)[2]

In the quest for equality, black folks have tried everything. We've
begged, revolted, entertained, intermarried, and are still treated
like shit. Nothing works, so why suffer the slow deaths of toxic
addiction and the American work ethic when the immediate
gratification of suicide awaits?

—Paul Beatty (1996)[3]

Within the diverse, always-changing spectrum of black American racial thought can be discerned two broad camps: the optimists and the pessimists—those who believe that blacks are (or can become) members of the American family and those who believe that blacks will always be outsiders; those who predict that we shall overcome and those who conclude that we shall not.

I

The fight at the founding of what became the United States of America made blacks think about and act upon which outcome would offer a better future: a victory for the colonists with their libertarian rhetoric and entanglement with slavery, or a victory for the Crown, which was, in principle, indifferent to slavery but willing to free the colonists' bondsmen as a war measure.

Keepers of African American memory have emphasized the story of blacks making common cause with the rebels, hoping to elicit a recognition of African American contributions to the nation's founding in order to gain better treatment. Consider William Nell's *Colored Patriots of the American Revolution* published in 1855.[4] Nell sought to use the memory of Crispus Attucks and other blacks who fought with the rebels to obtain from whites some measure of respect for colored folks whose forebears had helped the colonies secure independence. It should therefore come as no surprise that Nell ignored the blacks who fled *to* and fought *for* the British. Pessimistic about their prospects in an America ruled by rebellious slaveholders, many slaves deserted their masters, including some of the most eminent of the Founding Fathers. Slaves fled George Washington and Thomas Jefferson, as well as James Madison and Patrick Henry.[5]

The British offered freedom to slaves who took up arms for King George. About fifteen thousand did so, while about twenty thousand fought alongside the colonists. One who joined the British was a New Jerseyan named Titus. When he learned in 1775 of the British proclamation promising freedom in exchange for assistance in quashing the rebellion, Titus headed south to seek liberation. Three years later he returned to New Jersey, bearing the name Colonel Tye and leading a band of fighters who struck fear into the ranks of rebel colonists. We know little about Colonel Tye's motivations. It is certainly plausible, however, that a driving factor was outrage at people like Thomas Jefferson who championed "freedom" while simultaneously endorsing legislation to provide slaves as compensation to colonial rebel soldiers.

After the Revolution, several observers concluded that Euro-Americans and Afro-Americans would never be able to coexist as equals. Thomas Jefferson held this view, declaring, "The two races, equally free, cannot live in the same government."[6] Asked why he disfavored efforts to incorporate blacks into the polity, Jefferson answered,

> Deep rooted prejudices entertained by the whites; ten thousand recollections by the blacks, of the injuries they have sustained; new provocations; the real distinctions

which nature has made; and many other circumstances will divide us into parties, and produce convulsions, which will probably never end but in the extermination of the one or the other race.[7]

Alexis de Tocqueville's prediction was similarly bleak. In *Democracy in America* he forecast that the racial oppression of blacks would remain a salient feature of American society even after the abolition of slavery. "I do not believe," he wrote, "that the white and black races will ever live in any country upon an equal footing. But I believe the difficulty to be still greater in the United States than elsewhere." Why this distinction? In America, he observed, "the abstract and transient fact of slavery is fatally united with the physical and permanent fact of color. The tradition of slavery dishonors the race, and the peculiarity of the race perpetuates the tradition of slavery." Tocqueville believed that slavery had forever poisoned relations between black and white. "You set the Negro free," he writes, "but you cannot make him otherwise than an alien to the European." Furthermore, he maintained that the baleful effects of slavery would persist not only in the South (where slavery was most deeply entrenched), and not only in the Northeast (where abolition gradually prevailed in the three decades prior to Tocqueville's visit), but also in those areas of the country where slavery had never taken root:

> Slavery recedes, but the prejudice to which it has given birth is immovable. . . . [I]n those parts of the Union in which the Negroes are no longer slaves they have in no wise drawn nearer to the whites. On the contrary, the prejudice of race appears to be stronger in the states that have abolished slavery than in those where it still exists; and nowhere is it so intolerant as in those states where servitude has never been known.[8]

An important institutional manifestation of such pessimism was the American Colonization Society (ACS), which sought to send free blacks to Africa. The ACS included among its members scores of prominent figures including James Monroe, Bushrod

Washington, Andrew Jackson, Francis Scott Key, Daniel Webster, and Henry Clay. Most members of the ACS were supporters of slavery and viewed free blacks as negative role models. A few, however, were genuinely sympathetic to free blacks. They championed colonization in part because they hoped it would put blacks beyond the deadening grip of antagonistic whites. In Africa they could rule themselves.

Swayed by this prospect of self-rule, some free blacks were initially drawn to colonization. Its attractiveness waned, however, when free blacks became further acquainted with Negrophobes such as Henry Clay who maintained approvingly that colonization would "rid our country of a useless and pernicious, if not dangerous, portion of its population."[9] After learning more about the ACS, free blacks turned against it en masse, asserting their rootedness in and fidelity to the United States.

A few blacks, however, continued to support colonization. Among them was the remarkable Paul Cuffe. A sea captain, abolitionist, and businessman, Cuffe wanted blacks to return to Africa because he thought that they would never "rise to be a people" until they had their own nation.[10] Another black colonizationist was Newport Gardner, a former slave who had luckily been able to purchase freedom for himself, his wife, and his children. Gardner lived a charmed life for an African American in the early days of the nation, supporting himself from money he earned through music lessons and royalties from musical compositions. He was an officer in the Free African Union Society and a sexton of the First Congregational Church in Newport, Rhode Island. Still, in 1826, at the age of eighty, Gardner felt impelled to immigrate to Liberia, accompanied by two dozen black Rhode Islanders including one of his sons. "I go," he remarked as he boarded a ship, "to set an example to the youth of my race. . . . They can never be elevated here. I have tried for sixty years—it is in vain."[11]

Between 1820 and 1840 as many as ten thousand blacks immigrated to Liberia, Canada, and Haiti. Some who had previously eschewed emigration came to embrace it under the pressure of unremitting Negrophobia. The Reverend Henry Highland Garnet had opposed colonization, ignoring "the harp-like strains that whisper freedom among the groves of Africa . . . while three millions of my country are wailing in the dark prison-house of oppression."[12] By the 1850s, however, he had reconsidered. "My mind of late has greatly changed in regard to the American Colonization scheme. I would rather see a man free in Liberia than a slave in the United States."[13]

Despair was the sentiment from which emigration sprang. It is on vivid display in Martin R. Delany's *Condition, Elevation, Emigration, and Destiny of the Colored People of the United States.* "Our common country," Delany wrote, "is the United States. Here we were born, here raised . . . here are the scenes of childhood . . . the sacred groves of our departed fathers and mothers. . . . [W]e love our country, dearly love her. [But she doesn't] love us—she despises us, and bids us begone."[14]

No act of the U.S. government crystallized more vividly its rejection of blackness than the U.S. Supreme Court's 1857 ruling in *Dred Scott v. Sandford.*[15] The Court held, among other things, that blacks were ineligible for federal citizenship. It concluded that blacks were not a part—and could *never* be a part—of the national political family, that blacks could never actually become African Americans, that all that they could ever be were Africans in America.

Chief Justice Roger Taney's portrayal of a racist Constitution ratified the view of Negrophobes and was lauded by them. There were some racial egalitarians, however, who also agreed with Taney's interpretation descriptively, though they found it to be morally appalling. One was William Lloyd Garrison, the indefatigable abolitionist editor of *The Liberator.* It was precisely because Garrison agreed with Taney's portrayal of the Founders that he scorned the Constitution, deemed it illegitimate, and argued that it ought to be disobeyed or destroyed. The Constitution was, he maintained, a "covenant with death," "an agreement with Hell," a "heaven-daring arrangement" that "will be held in everlasting infamy by the friends of justice and humanity throughout the world."[16]

Frederick Douglass, Garrison's extraordinary protégé, initially echoed his mentor's position. He, too, damned the American government and its Constitution, declaring,

I have no patriotism. I have no country. . . . The only thing that links me to this land is my family, and the painful consciousness that here there are three millions of my fellow-creatures, groaning beneath the iron rod of the worst despotism ever devised. . . . I cannot have any love for this country or for its Constitution. I desire to see its overthrow as speedily as possible, and its Constitution shivered into a thousand fragments.[17]

Abraham Lincoln's assessment of the Constitution was very different: he revered it. But like Cuffe, Tocqueville, Jefferson, and the early Frederick Douglass, Lincoln was a racial pessimist. During his famous debates with Senator Stephen A. Douglas, Lincoln repeatedly eschewed the possibility or advisability of racial equality in America. "I am not in favor of negro citizenship," Lincoln declared on September 18, 1858. In that same debate he averred,

I am not, nor ever have been in favor of bringing about in any way the social and political equality of the white and black races. . . . I am not nor ever have been in favor of making voters or jurors of negroes, nor of qualifying them to hold office, nor to intermarry with white people; and I will say in addition to this that there is a physical difference between the white and black races which I believe will forever forbid the two races living together on terms of social and political equality.[18]

The coming of the Civil War intensified conflict between optimists and pessimists, pitting blacks who were determined to assist the Union war effort against blacks who were determined to avoid being exploited without attaining any enhancement of status—the bitter fate that befell previous generations of African Americans. Exemplifying the optimistic camp was a petition from blacks in Boston to the Massachusetts legislature sent in the spring of 1861 after the fall of Fort Sumter. Wanting to join the war effort, the petitioners requested that the legislature disregard a federal statute prohibiting colored men from serving in state militias. Other blacks, however, balked. Unwilling to fight on behalf of the Union, a black Ohioan remarked,

> If the colored people . . . are ever ready to defend the government that despoils them of their rights, it may be concluded that it is quite safe to oppress them. . . . The truth is, if, in time of peace the fact of our having bled in defense of the country when it was struggling desperately for independence, avails nothing, it is absurd to suppose that the fact of tendering our services to settle a domestic war . . . will procure a practical acknowledgement of our rights.[19]

Other blacks also held back in the absence of a demonstrated change of heart by Union officials. "We are in advance of our fathers," a Negro from Troy, New York, declared. "They put confidence in the word of the whites only to feel the dagger of slavery driven still deeper into the heart throbbing with emotions of joy for freedom. We are not going to re-enact that tragedy. . . . We of the North must have all rights which white men enjoy; until then we are in no condition to fight under the flag which gives us no protection."[20]

Notwithstanding the destruction of slavery, events transpired during the Civil War that reinforced pessimists' intuitions. In cities throughout the North, resentful whites subjected blacks to harassment or worse. For four days in July 1863, blacks in New York City were chased through the streets, beaten, robbed, thrown into rivers, and hanged. A mob torched the Colored Orphan Asylum in Manhattan. Resigned to a continuation, maybe even an intensification, of Negrophobia, one black commented,

> We need have no hope in the present conflict, for the atmosphere of North America is interwoven and vocal with the blasting breath of negro prejudice. It is the first lesson taught by white parents to their children, that the negro is a low, debased animal, not fit for their association nor their equal.[21]

Similarly downcast was a black editor who observed with Tocquevillian gloominess,

> If this war should result in the abolition of slavery, as we hope it may, while it strikes the shackles from the slave, it will not ameliorate the condition of the free black man one iota. . . . [S]o soon as the purposes of the Federal Government may have been served through his instrumentality, [the black man] will be rewarded with a mockery of thanks, and unceremoniously thrust aside.[22]

The fears of pessimists were initially abated by the advent of Reconstruction, which brought about a remarkable elevation in the status of blacks. Between 1870 and 1877 sixteen African Americans were elected to Congress. One, Hiram Revels, served as a U.S. senator representing Mississippi. Eighteen served as state lieutenant governors, treasurers, secretaries of state, or superintendents of education. Six hundred were elected to state legislatures. Mirroring, enabling, and reinforcing these breakthroughs were an array of constitutional and statutory interventions: the Thirteenth Amendment; the Fourteenth Amendment; the Fifteenth Amendment; the Reconstruction Acts; the Ku Klux Klan Act; the Civil Rights Act of 1866; the Freedmen's Bureau bills; and the Civil Rights Act of 1875. Reconstruction, however, turned out to be only a momentary respite. When it was overthrown by ruthless white supremacists, another phase of betrayal and despair descended, giving rise to new proponents of pessimism. Two of the most notable in the half a century between 1880 and 1930 were Henry McNeal Turner and Marcus Garvey.

Henry McNeal Turner was born free but grew up in the Deep South surrounded by slaves. A minister in the African Methodist Episcopal Church, he was also a politician and journalist who briefly thought that racial reconciliation was possible. In an 1866 address to freed slaves, Turner pointed to an American flag and proclaimed triumphantly that while in the past "every star was against us," now things had changed; now "we can claim the protection of the stars and stripes." Blacks, he declared, should "let by-gones be by-gones." Let us show whites we can be respectable, he suggested, "and soon their prejudice will melt away, and with God for our Father we will all be brothers."[23] By 1868, however, his buoyancy had dissolved into disillusionment. After being ejected from the Georgia legislature along with the other blacks elected in the state's first multiracial election, Turner commented bitterly that "white men are not to be trusted. They will betray you."[24] He became an ardent emigrationist who insisted for the remainder of his life that whites would never permit blacks to enjoy independence and dignity as equal neighbors in America. "I do not believe," he declared in 1893, "that there is any manhood future in this country for the Negro."[25] That same year he acknowledged that thousands of fellow blacks "hope and expect better times . . . in this country." But he maintained that he could "see no signs of a reformation. . . . I have no hope in the future success of my race in our present situation."[26] By the early twentieth century, Turner's belief in America's irreparability had hardened. "I used to love what I thought was the grand old flag," he remarked. "But to the Negro . . . the American flag is a dirty and contemptible rag. Not a star in it can the colored man claim. . . . [H]ell is an improvement on the United States where the Negro is concerned."[27]

Marcus Garvey Jr. was a Jamaican immigrant who founded the Universal Negro Improvement Association. He was convinced that the United States was indeed a white man's country that could never satisfactorily meet the cultural, social, and political needs of Negroes. Speaking in 1919, he told his followers,

> If you think that the white man is going to be more liberal to Negroes than they are at present, you are making a big mistake. Every succeeding generation of the white race is getting more prejudiced against the Negro.[28]

Garvey urged blacks to celebrate themselves, to create their own socioeconomic infrastructure, and to create their own government. In America, Garvey declared, "the Negro will never reach his highest ambition."*[29]

---

* Garvey is an endlessly fascinating figure who expressed appreciation for and cooperated with white supremacists who agreed with his depiction of the United States as a "white" nation. In 1922 he met in Atlanta with leaders of the Ku Klux

Two notable figures in the pessimistic tradition during the tumultuous half century following 1930 were W. E. B. Du Bois and Elijah Muhammad.

Du Bois was the most intellectually formidable black activist of the twentieth century. A historian (*Black Reconstruction*), sociologist (*The Philadelphia Negro*), journalist (editor of *The Crisis* during its most impressive days), and man of letters (*The Souls of Black Folk*), Du Bois mined every ideological resource that could plausibly serve to advance the fortunes of African Americans. He coined two formulations that have become canonical. The first was a commentary on the African American condition: "One ever feels his twoness—an American, a Negro; two souls, two thoughts, two unreconciled strivings; two warring ideals, in one dark body, whose strength alone keeps it from being torn asunder." The second was a commentary on the international condition: "The problem of the twentieth century is the problem of the color line."[30] A founder of the National Association for the Advancement of Colored People (NAACP), Du Bois was long an optimist. He rebounded with renewed faith in the possibility of racial progress in the United States despite setback after setback. Late in life, however, he gave up on America. He joined the Communist Party, expressing admiration for the Soviet Union; in 1960 he accepted the Lenin Prize. While he was abroad, the U.S. government refused to renew his passport. He settled in Ghana, passing away in 1963.

The Honorable Elijah Muhammad was the longtime leader of the Nation of Islam (NOI). The scope of his influence was remarkable. He launched (and then scuttled) the career of Malcolm X, directed the spiritual pilgrimage that led Cassius Clay to become Muhammad Ali, and served as mentor to Minister Louis

Klan to discuss their agreement on the need for racial separation. He praised the Klan for "honesty of purpose." He made common cause with the Anglo-Saxon Clubs of America, a group that sought to narrow racial definitions and reinforce prohibitions against interracial sex and marriage. Later Garvey endorsed legislation proposed by the notorious segregationist U.S. senator from Mississippi Theodore Bilbo, who drafted a bill supporting the repatriation of Negroes to Africa. *See* Lawrence W. Levine, "Marcus Garvey and the Politics of Revitalization," in *Black Leaders of the Twentieth Century*, ed. John Hope Franklin and August Meier (1982).

Farrakhan. He saw the American dream as the African American nightmare. At the high tide of the Second Reconstruction, when federal civil rights legislation was in the process of enactment and Martin Luther King Jr. was electrifying the world with lyrical sermons voicing hopeful visions of universal brotherhood and sisterhood, Elijah Muhammad preached that whites are irrecoverably racist, that the United States is doomed, and that blacks can save themselves only by separating from whites. While "integration" was the watchword for Roy Wilkins, Whitney Young, Thurgood Marshall, John Lewis, and other progenitors of the Second Reconstruction, Elijah Muhammad found integration a literally devilish delusion. "We believe," he wrote, "that the offer of integration is hypocritical and is made by those who are trying to deceive the black peoples into believing that their 400-year-old open enemies of freedom, justice, and equality are, all of a sudden, their 'friends.' "[31]

Calling himself the "Messenger of Allah, Leader and Teacher to The American So-Called Negro," Elijah Muhammad declared in *Message to the Blackman in America* (1965) that the NOI "want[s] our people . . . to be allowed to establish a separate state or territory of their own—either on this continent or elsewhere." Explaining himself, Elijah Muhammad wrote,

> Since we cannot get along with [whites] in peace and equality after giving them 400 years of our sweat and blood and receiving in return some of the worst treatment human beings have ever experienced, we believe our contributions to this land and the suffering forced upon us by white America justifies our demand for complete separation in a state or territory of our own.[32]

Sometimes Elijah Muhammad indicated a willingness to allow individuals to determine whether they wanted separation from whites. Hence he declared, "We want every black man and woman to have the freedom to accept or reject being separated from the slave-master's children and establish[ing] a land of their own." Sometimes, though, he was not so permissive: "We believe that intermarriage or race mixing should be prohibited."[33]

Elijah Muhammad and other purveyors of racial pessimism in the 1950s and 1960s voiced their gloomy assessments against the backdrop of the Second Reconstruction's legal reforms. Those advances, however, failed to dissuade a new cadre of intellectuals and activists from voicing the themes of racial pessimism. They refused to accede to narratives of racial redemption notwithstanding *Brown v. Board of Education*, the Civil Rights Act, and the Voting Rights Act. One of their number is Randall Robinson, who founded TransAfrica, a think tank that played a key role in the American antiapartheid movement. In 2001, Robinson sent himself into exile, decamping to St. Kitts. Explaining himself, he echoed pessimistic forebearers: "America. America. Land of my birth and erstwhile distress. . . . My heart left long ago. At long last, I have followed it. Trying my very best, how could I, in good conscience, remain *for* a country that has never, ever, at home or abroad been for me or for mine?"[34]

II

Now let's turn to the tradition of those who believe that despite the gravitational pull of division, degradation, and oppression, Americans shall somehow overcome and create a racially equitable commonwealth. Those advancing this position have often had to do so in the face of excruciating circumstances that seemed to mock their prediction. But they have persisted nonetheless, creating what has been throughout American history the dominant sensibility in black political culture.

The most remarkable racial optimist in American history was also for a time its most compelling pessimist: Frederick Douglass, the runaway slave who became an acclaimed abolitionist orator and writer. Like his mentor, William Lloyd Garrison, Douglass initially viewed the Constitution as irredeemably sinful, the evil memorialization of a dastardly compromise. He thought that a good-thinking, noble-hearted American should do nothing to even implicitly recognize the Constitution as a source of rightful authority. He sought to disassociate himself totally from the contamination of slavery.

Eventually, however, Douglass reconsidered and amended his

interpretation. He came to argue that, far from being pro-slavery, the Constitution was actually antislavery. This evolution in perspective was neither quick nor painless. It proved deeply controversial in abolitionist circles and both reflected and contributed to his estrangement from allies.

Douglass changed his position because he came to think it unwise to cede to the Slave Power a symbol as powerful as the U.S. Constitution. The defenders of slavery claimed that the Constitution was on their side and benefited from persuading others to defer to this claim. In the 1850s Douglass decided to contest their interpretation. Garrisonianism kept its adherents unsullied by rejecting any compromise that embraced America's foundational document. But Douglass came to see that desire for purity as an indulgence—good perhaps for the self-regard of Garrisonians, but bad for the slaves who would suffer even more if antislavery folk really did secede from the Union. Douglass came to see Garrisonian radicalism as a program hindered by a sterile otherworldliness ill-suited for practical action. So Douglass took a different tack. He argued that the Constitution was not wholly evil but internally divided, a product of compromise that contained both good and bad elements.

Douglass argued strenuously that the Constitution could be interpreted to contain antislavery tendencies. Nowhere in the Constitution, after all, was there any express mention of color or slavery.* The preamble of the Constitution refers to "We the people of the United States"—*not* "We the *white* people of the United States." Slavery, moreover, was unmentioned—at least not explicitly. Douglass stressed these omissions. He insisted that the

---

* By contrast, the Constitution of the Confederate States of America expressly mentioned both race and slavery, as in the provision that declared, "No bill of attainder, ex post facto law, or law denying or impairing the right of property in negro slaves shall be passed." The U.S. Constitution did not expressly refer to slavery until slavery was abolished by the Thirteenth Amendment. The Constitution did not expressly refer to race until the Fifteenth Amendment when states were prohibited from denying the vote to anyone on the basis of race (or color or previous condition of servitude). Clearly textual silence about a social condition is no guide as to its actual prevalence. The constitutional breaking of silence regarding race and slavery was indicative of a heightened commitment to addressing racial oppression.

Constitution's dearth of express authority for enslavement permitted or even encouraged the inference that that brutal practice was illicit. Douglass read the Constitution's stated purpose "to form a more perfect Union, establish Justice, ensure domestic Tranquility . . . promote the general Welfare, and secure the blessings of Liberty" as repudiating any practice that subjugated a subset of "we the people." What about the infamous clause pursuant to which, for purposes of determining a state's representation in Congress, a slave amounted to only three-fifths of a free person? Douglass said that that clause was antislavery in tendency because it punished states that permitted slavery by diminishing by two-fifths the representation that would be their due in the absence of slavery. Douglass recognized that slavery existed as a brute sociological fact and that it enjoyed the protection of governmental power. But he insisted that that stemmed only from an improper reading of the Constitution, encouraged by ignorance and tainted by racism and the selfish ambitions of slave masters and their allies.

Other aspects of Douglass's thinking accompanied his belief in the Constitution's redeemability.[35] He eschewed emigrationism, maintaining that America was "home" and that its injustices could be remedied. In 1863, even before the abolition of slavery, he posed the question whether "the white and colored people of this country [can] be blended into a common nationality and enjoy together . . . under the same flag, the inestimable blessings of life, liberty, and the pursuit of happiness, as neighborly citizens of a common country?" He answered, "I believe they can."[36]

Since Douglass's death in 1895, countless devoted optimists have carried on his legacy. James Weldon Johnson—poet, novelist, diplomat, lawyer, and the first black managing director of the NAACP—wrote in 1900 the lyrics to "Lift Every Voice and Sing," a song I memorized as a child when it was commonly known as the Negro national anthem. It has now become part of the hymnal of American patriotic expression. "Lift Every Voice and Sing" acknowledged the brutal racism that confronted African Americans, speaking of a "gloomy past" in which blacks had had to tread through the blood of the slaughtered. But its predominant message is that there awaits for blacks a promising future "where the white gleam of our bright star is cast." Johnson implores his fellow blacks to forever stand "True to our God, / True to our native land."[37]

A. Philip Randolph, the socialist organizer behind the Brotherhood of Sleeping Car Porters, marked the 150th anniversary of the U.S. Constitution by declaring in 1937 that "the Negro peoples face the future . . . resolved to march forward in the van of progress, with hope and faith in the creation of a new and better world."[38] Then there was Mary McLeod Bethune. Born in 1875 to former slaves in South Carolina, she became an educator, founding Bethune-Cookman College, and an activist, establishing the National Council of Negro Women. Bethune developed a close friendship with Eleanor Roosevelt and was chosen by FDR to be the director of Negro Affairs in the National Youth Administration. In a November 1939 radio broadcast, Bethune joined with several others to address the question, "What does American democracy mean to me?" Her remarks describe the privations and mistreatment that blacks faced, noting,

> In the Deep South, Negro youth is offered only one-fifteenth of the educational opportunity of the average American child. The great masses of Negro workers are depressed and unprotected in the lowest levels of agriculture and domestic service, while the black workers in industry are barred from certain unions and generally assigned to the more laborious and poorly paid work. Their housing and living conditions are sordid and unhealthy. They live too often in terror of the lynch mob; are deprived too often of the Constitutional right to suffrage; and are humiliated too often by the denial of civil liberties.[39]

More salient, though, than her note of protest was her note of anticipation. "Democracy is for me, and for twelve million black Americans, a goal towards which our nation is marching. It is a dream and an ideal in whose ultimate realization we have a deep

and abiding faith." She acknowledged that blacks had been terribly mistreated. But she emphasized that in America "my race has
been afforded [the] opportunity to advance from a people 80 percent illiterate to a people 80 percent literate; from abject poverty
to the ownership and operation of a million farms and 750,000
homes; from total disenfranchisement to participation in government; from the status of chattels to recognized contributors to the
American culture." With the prospect of American intervention
in World War II on the horizon, Bethune noted that blacks had
repeatedly fought for the United States even when their government mistreated them. "We have fought for America, with all her
imperfections," Bethune asserted, "not so much for what she is,
but for what we know she can be."[40]

Similarly patriotic and upbeat was Ralph J. Bunche, the distinguished black academic and diplomat who was awarded the Nobel
Peace Prize for his efforts to mediate the conflict between Arabs
and Israelis. "While nothing is easy for the Negro in America,"
he declared in 1949, "neither is anything impossible. The barriers
of race are formidable, but they can be surmounted. Indeed, the
entire history of the Negro in this country has been a history of
continuous, relentless progress over these barriers. Like 'Old Man
River,' the Negro keeps 'movin' along,' and if I know my people,
the Negro will keep on moving resolutely along until his goal of
complete and unequivocal equality is attained."[41] A year later, calling himself an incurable optimist, Bunche returned to this theme.
"Because of its basically democratic nature," he observed, "the
American society affords the opportunity, even for disadvantaged
groups such as the Negro, to aspire for and make progress toward
the good life." Within this democratic framework, he insisted,
"the Negro, because of his persistent struggle, has made progress
and will continue to make progress."[42]

Optimistic, too, was Roy Wilkins. In his 1955 address to the
NAACP as its new executive director, Wilkins vowed that segregationists conspiring to nullify *Brown v. Board of Education* were
doomed. The segregationists, he declared,

> say "never" like the Romans before the coming of Christ;
> like King John before Magna Charta; like the emperors

of France [*sic*] before 1789; like George III of England before the Declaration of Independence; like the Southern plantation owners before the Civil War. . . . We shall never return to bondage, with or without shackles. . . . We shall not—we cannot—fail. We shall, we will, be free men.[43]

The twentieth century's most eloquent and influential expositor of the optimistic tradition was the Reverend Martin Luther King Jr. His hopefulness about America stemmed from a broader hopefulness about humankind. "The arc of the moral universe is long," he famously declared, "but it bends towards justice."[44] Neither naive nor a sentimentalist, King described racial oppression with unsparing directness. Speaking at the March on Washington in August 1963, he observed that the Negro "is still not free," that the Negro "is still sadly crippled by the manacles of segregation," that the Negro "is still languishing in the corners of American society and finds himself an exile in his own land."[45] His "I Have a Dream" oration is beloved, however, not because of its critique of America but because of its claim that things could and would improve. While "America has given the Negro people a bad check which has come back marked 'insufficient funds,' [w]e refuse to believe that the bank of justice is bankrupt. We refuse to believe that there are insufficient funds in the great vaults of opportunity in this nation."[46]

King made what could be taken as a veiled threat: "There will be neither rest nor tranquility in America unless the Negro is granted his citizenship rights" (a muted version of the oft-heard refrain "No justice! No peace!"). But his dominant sentiment was optimism about the American future: "I still have a dream . . . that one day this nation will rise up and live out the true meaning of its creed. . . . I have a dream that one day . . . the sons of former slaves and the sons of former slaveowners will be able to sit down together at the table of brotherhood. . . . I have a dream my four children will one day live in a nation where they will not be judged by the color of their skin but by the content of their character."

Five years later, on April 3, 1968, the night before he was murdered, King again voiced his optimism. He told his listeners to take heart because he knew that, eventually, they would overcome the obstacles they faced. King knew this, he said, because he had been to the mountaintop and glimpsed the promised land, though he might not ever make it there himself.

After King, Barack Obama is the most influential modern exponent of the African American optimistic tradition.* Voicing the "audacity of hope," Obama has constantly stressed his view that all is possible in the United States. "America can change," he insists. "That is the true genius of this nation."[47] There is nothing surprising about this posture; optimism about the American future is virtually obligatory for any politician seeking high political office.† Politicians have made into a cliché the notion of the bright American future. Obama is no different. He portrays the story of blacks in America as a saga that, albeit suffused with tragedy, is nonetheless destined for redemption. He calls slavery "this nation's original sin." But he maintains that from the outset slavery was doomed by the Founders' virtuous ideals. "The answer to the slavery question was already embedded within our Constitution," he declares, "a Constitution that had at its very core the ideal of

---

* A notable precursor among politicians was Barbara C. Jordan, the first African American in the twentieth century to be elected to the Texas Senate and the first African American woman from a southern state to be elected to a seat in the U.S. House of Representatives. In 1976 she delivered a keynote address at the Democratic National Convention. She remarked that her speech was "one additional bit of evidence that the American dream need not forever be deferred." *See* Barbara C. Jordan, Democratic National Convention Keynote Address, July 12, 1976, www.americanrhetoric.com.

† *See, e.g.,* George W. Bush ("The United States has been the greatest force for good in history. [It] provides the single surviving model of human progress."); Jesse Jackson ("America is God's country."); Madeleine Albright ("We are the indispensable nation . . . we see further into the future."); Sarah Palin ("America is a nation of exceptionalism."), quoted in Randall Kennedy, *The Persistence of the Color Line: Racial Politics and the Obama Presidency* (2011), 192. "The mainstream of American politics is defined by a deep faith in the progress story. Only extremists and cranks resist or dispute it." Richard Thompson Ford, "Civil Rights and the Myth of Moral Progress," in *Civil Rights in American Law, History, and Politics,* ed. Austin Sarat (2014), 196.

equal citizenship under the law; a Constitution that promised its people liberty and justice and a union that could be and should be perfected over time." Obama does not explain how it was that so many of the leading statesmen of antebellum America could have overlooked that "ideal of equal citizenship" or why it took a bloody civil war to rid the country of slavery. He prefers to dwell on happier subjects. He places at the center of the national narrative the yearning "for a more just, more equal, more free, more caring and more prosperous America." He repeatedly expresses an "unyielding faith in the decency and generosity of the American people." He speaks with unalloyed earnestness about "the singular greatness of our [American] ideals," about America as a "magical place," about how "no dream is beyond reach in the United States of America," and about how he "will never forget that in no other country on Earth is [his] story even possible."[48]

III

Obama's election to the presidency on November 4, 2008, seemed momentarily to reflect and further beckon fundamental change in the racial habits of America.* Many expressed their astonishment at what they perceived to be a miraculous event that

---

* According to Marcus Garvey, "If the black man is to get all his Constitutional rights in America—then the black man should have the same chance in the nation as any other man to become president." Because he viewed a black president as a preposterous impossibility, Garvey also viewed as a preposterous impossibility the prospect of blacks enjoying all of their constitutional rights. *See* Philip S. Foner, *The Voice of Black America: Major Speeches by Negroes in the United States, 1797–1971* (1972).

There were some observers sufficiently prescient in the later half of the twentieth century to foresee the election of a black president. In 1958, Senator Jacob Javits of New York stated that "the march of progress and world events make it quite possible that a member of the Negro race will . . . be elected to the Presidency . . . by the year 2000." In 1961, Robert F. Kennedy maintained that "there's no question" that a black could be elected to the presidency in the next thirty to forty years. In 1964, Martin Luther King Jr. allowed as to how "we may be able to get a Negro President . . . in twenty-five years or less." Quoted in Kennedy, *Persistence of the Color Line*, 63. *See also* "Obama Proved Them Wrong: Historical Speculation on the Prospects of a Black President," *Journal of Blacks in Higher Education* (Winter 2009/2010).

they never expected to witness. The president-elect was well aware of the momentousness of the occasion and the hopes invested in it. "If there is anyone out there who still doubts that America is a place where all things are possible," Obama declared, "tonight is your answer."[49]

But, alas, the Obama story is hardly one of uncontested triumph for racial equality. True, for eight years the single most important person in America was a black man. Commander in chief of the U.S. Armed Forces, Obama played an instrumental role in opening up the military to people of all sexual orientations. Head of the executive branch, he lifted the economy from the Great Recession and reformed the health-care system through the Patient Protection and Affordable Care Act (popularly known as Obamacare). The nominator of all federal judges, Obama elevated two women to the Supreme Court, one of whom, Sonia Sotomayor, became the nation's first Latina Supreme Court justice. For eight years, the nation's First Family was black.

But for many, the sight of a black family in the White House triggered derangement.

Obama's ascendancy provoked one of the most aggressive, vehement, and consequential political reactions in American history. The backlash featured an unprecedented array of snubs and insults, the rise of the Tea Party and kindred outcroppings of right-wing populism, an openly expressed policy of obstructionism on the part of the Republican Party, and a concerted effort to delegitimize a sitting president. Even late in Obama's second term, after much investigatory ink had been spilled, many Republicans continued to claim that Obama was secretly a Muslim and born abroad. The vilification of Obama tapped into and trafficked in a centuries-old tradition of deriding "uppity" black folk. Polite society would no longer permit detractors to call Obama a "nigger"—at least not on the record. But right beneath the surface a seething resentment, fueled by racial animosity, gathered force.

From the outset of Obama's candidacy, some progressive-minded pessimists warned that his election would generate profoundly negative consequences. They feared complacency. They suspected that the election of a black president would nourish the belief that racism had been vanquished from American life. The most consequential judicial decision that substantiated this fear was *Shelby County v. Holder*,[50] the 2013 Supreme Court ruling that invalidated the formula governing the preclearance provision of the Voting Rights Act. The Court concluded that that formula— keyed to conditions of racial discrimination in the first half of the twentieth century—was no longer appropriate. Stressing the Act's success in facilitating the registration of black voters in the Deep South, the Court denied the reasonableness of continuing to impose special measures on states that had formerly practiced racial disenfranchisement. Skewering the Court's logic, Justice Ruth Bader Ginsburg wrote that "throwing out preclearance when it has worked and is continuing to work to stop [discrimina-tion] is like throwing away your umbrella in a rainstorm because you are not getting wet."[51]

For pessimists, the Obama presidency was never an indication of secure racial progress. Indeed, for them it demonstrated with cruel irony the intractability of antiblack racism. It proved that to rise to the top of American politics, a black politician must be will-ing to limit criticism of the racial status quo to superficial caviling. "There is nothing about a congenitally racist country," Ta-Nehisi Coates writes, "that necessarily prevents an individual leader hail-ing from the pariah class." The office does not care where the leader originates, Coates observes, so long as the leader ultimately toes the established line.[52] Pessimists viewed the Obama adminis-tration as a mere diversification of an undisturbed order in which a relatively small sector of privileged blacks prosper while the con-dition of the black masses stagnates or deteriorates. They found the Obama era littered with bitter incongruity. While *People* mag-azine fawned over a black family occupying the White House, a light-skinned African American boy seriously weighed passing for white to escape the dangers posed by racist policing that subjects black men wholesale to harassment, humiliation, and brutality.[53]

And then came Trump. Yes, he ascended to the presidency in part *despite* (rather than because of) his appeal to racism and related bigotries. A good many voted for him holding their noses, dislik-ing his racism but disliking Hillary Clinton even more. After all, more than six million Obama voters supported Trump in 2016.[54] At the same time, others supported Trump precisely because he is overtly reactionary—"Make America Great Again"—heralding a purported lost glory when gender roles and identities were stable, when Christianity was the unchallenged societal religion, when police malfeasance was patiently accepted, and when an implicit but clear deference to the imagined superiority of whiteness reigned supreme, from immigration policy, to television screens, to Miss America pageants, to universities, to Pulitzer Prize awards. Trump became the most prominent proponent of birtherism— the allegation that Obama's presidency was illegitimate because, in violation of constitutional requirement, he was not a native-born American. Trump declined to repudiate the support of David Duke and other white supremacists. Trump impugned the ability of a Mexican American judge to treat him fairly because of the judge's parentage—a position that the Republican Speaker of the House, Paul Ryan, aptly dubbed a textbook example of racism. Trump continued to elicit and nourish racial resentments after assuming the presidency. Examples include his whitewashing of the violent white supremacists who marched on Charlottesville, Virginia, in the summer of 2017 and his not-so-subtle reelection promise in the summer of 2020 to "save" white suburbia from you know who.

IV

I have long been a racial optimist, even though my father, whom I revere, was a racial pessimist through and through. He had no affection for what he saw as merely a fearsome abstraction—"the United States of America"—and he was convinced that blacks in America would never consistently receive treatment on par with whites. In the 1850s, Martin Delany's experiences with racism prompted him to write, "I have no hopes in this country—no confidence in the American people."[55] My father felt the same way a century later. Born in Covington, Louisiana, in 1917, my father was a smart, resourceful, hardworking, and ambitious man who constantly encountered race bars that bore the cruel message that regardless of his talent and industry many of the things to which he aspired were simply off-limits because of his race. He suffered humiliations at the hands of bigots, and he witnessed numerous episodes in which friends were terrorized without any hint of disapproval from onlooking authorities. My father had a special loathing for police—*all* police—because, in his experience, the main aim of cops was to keep blacks in their "place." He viewed white police with disdain: "You mean to tell me that a white man couldn't do better than become a policeman with all the advantages that white men have in this society?" And he viewed black police with misgiving, suspecting that they were liable to be particularly brutal in their dealings with fellow blacks to show their white peers that actually they were "true blue."

My father did not view the United States as his country or himself as a participant in its governance (though he always voted). He perceived himself to be in the clutches of a large, powerful, sophisticated gang. He followed its demands not out of feelings of civic duty but as a matter of self-defense: he feared punishment and did what he could to avoid it. When I asked him why he enlisted in the army in the 1940s, he said nothing about patriotism. He enlisted, he recalled, in order to eat. I never asked him why he had declined to emigrate abroad. He had, after all, fled the Deep South by moving to Washington, D.C. Why not flee farther? I suspect that he would have told me that he remained in America not out of any sense of national loyalty but only because he knew of nowhere else offering a better deal.

My father was a postal worker who was married throughout his adult life to my mother, a schoolteacher, who loved him. He was often happy, was widely respected in his neighborhood and church, owned a home, and sent three children not only to college (all three attended Princeton University) but to law school as well (one attended Harvard, one Yale, one Howard). Many would say that my father's life exemplified the American dream. But he did not see it that way. He saw himself as one of millions of victims of a gigantic crime that white America refused to satisfactorily acknowledge. He would have been surprised by Obama's electoral successes. He would have been unsurprised by Trump's. He would have said that in elevating Trump to the presidency, white America was simply reverting to form. My father pushed his black nationalist pessimism strongly. But wonderful man that he was, he also left room in the household for disagreement, space that I eagerly seized.

I became a committed racial optimist upon becoming convinced of the strength of the trajectory charted by John Hope Franklin's classic text on African American history—*From Slavery to Freedom.* I learned about the sad fate of Reconstruction and the horrors that followed its downfall. But I took heart from learning about how that tragedy was eclipsed by the wonder of the Second Reconstruction, which propelled the changes that offered to me countless opportunities denied to my father. In 1950—four years before my birth—racial segregation was deemed to be consistent with the U.S. Constitution, and no federal laws prohibited proprietors of hotels, restaurants, and other privately owned public accommodations from engaging in racial discrimination. No federal law prohibited private employers from discriminating on the basis of race against job applicants or current employees. No federal law effectively counteracted racial exclusion from the ballot box. No federal law barred racial discrimination in private housing transactions. By 1970, however, the civil rights movement had transformed federal law. *Brown v. Board of Education* and its progeny repudiated the lie of "separate but equal." The 1964 Civil Rights Act forbade racial discrimination in privately owned public accommodations and many areas of private employment. The 1965 Voting Rights Act provided prophylactic remedies for racial discrimination in voting. The 1968 Fair Housing Act addressed racial exclusion in a market that had been zealously insulated against federal regulation. None of these interventions were wholly effective. All were compromised. But the racial situation in 1970 was plainly better than the one into which I had been born. And the situation improved still further for blacks like me with access to higher education, to affirmative action, and to a new generation of upwardly mobile whites more racially enlightened than their parents.

There were other reasons for my optimism. Although I admired a wide swath of civil rights activists, those whom I most admired—Thurgood Marshall, Martin Luther King Jr., John Lewis—were the most insistent that the American people would be able to overcome the racism that has been implanted in the national psyche. Then there was religion. As a teenager I happily attended Asbury United Methodist Church, where I fell under the sway of a wonderful pastor, the Reverend Frank Williams. At church there was much talk about the need to have faith in the evidence of things unseen. Later, these religious sentiments insinuated themselves into my politics as I came to believe that progressive politics required optimism. Hopefulness became an ethical and political mandate.

Over the past decade I have abandoned much—but not all—of my quasi-religious faith in optimism. I no longer propound the notion of an ethical obligation to be hopeful. Some commend optimism by reference to a supposed inevitability of historical progress and a moral imperative to aid history's path. Proponents of these tenets often speak of wanting to be "on the right side of history." But how can anyone know in what direction history is headed? And, in any event, what does history's trajectory have to do with the morality of conduct? Just suppose it could be shown that, in fact, history is trending toward authoritarianism? Certainly that would not justify embracing tyranny. To the contrary, it would be our moral obligation to stand on the "wrong side of history" and fight against prevailing winds.

Others commend willed optimism, believing that hopefulness nurtures dissent. Because we do not know for sure what the future will bring, they argue, why not do all that we can to improve the odds for a good outcome, including maintaining the morale of those struggling on behalf of racial justice? I propounded that view for many years. But no longer. I now perceive that attitude as justifying well-intended fraud. I concede the considerable power behind the claim that optimism nurtures dissent and that undermining hopefulness risks facilitating resignation. But offering a facade of hopefulness is a manipulation, which is, for me, no longer tenable. If I believe in good faith that a situation is hopeless, I will say so.

Is overcoming racism in America a hopeless prospect? It all depends on what "overcoming" means. One can doom the exercise quickly by creating an unreachable standard of success. If the absence of *all* racism is a requirement, if the removal of *all* scars of past racial mistreatment is a prerequisite, if rigorous racial proportionality in all domains of social life is nonnegotiable, then, no, we shall not overcome—at least not within a foreseeable future.[56]

In an effort to guard my hopefulness, I gave up demanding rigorous racial egalitarianism and settled instead for something less ambitious: racial decency—a society largely free from newly imposed racial humiliations even if the scars of past racial wrongs remain evident. I came to believe that racial decency could coexist with racial difficulties that are still in the process of being resolved and that might withstand complete resolution. I am fearful now for the future of even my reduced ambition.

I take some solace in the extent and tenor of the antiracism that flared so spectacularly in the protests that followed the highly publicized killing of George Floyd in the summer of 2020. Hundreds of thousands of whites joined fellow Americans of all complexions to assert that Black Lives Matter. The geographical dispersion and ideological diversity of white protesters was unprecedented.[57] I take solace, too, in advances made by black folk even in the cold shadow of the Trump ascendancy: the presence of two black senators (Cory Booker and Kamala Harris) in the race for the Democratic Party's presidential nomination; the election of fifty-seven blacks to Congress in 2020, a record number that included the election of a black senator, the Reverend Raphael Warnock, representing Georgia; the emergence of blacks in positions of influence throughout society that sometimes occasion little notice because such breakthroughs have become common— the appointment of a black historian (Lonnie Bunch) to head the Smithsonian; the selection of a black woman (Dr. Patrice Harris) to head the American Medical Association; the appointment of an African American (Lieutenant General Darryl A. Williams) as the superintendent of the U.S. Military Academy; the selection of a black woman (Simone Askew) as the top cadet at West Point; the selection of a black woman (Sydney Barber) as the top midshipman at the U.S. Naval Academy; the leadership of African Americans in big philanthropy (Darren Walker at the Ford Foundation and Elizabeth Alexander at the Andrew W. Mellon Foundation), and on and on.*

---

* In many domains, however, the marginal position of African Americans remains glaring. *See, e.g.,* Denise Lu et al., "Faces of Power: 80% Are White, Even as U.S. Becomes More Diverse," *New York Times*, Sept. 9, 2020.

Then, of course, there was the ousting of Trump. Twenty-eight years had elapsed since the last time an incumbent president was unseated (Bill Clinton over George H. W. Bush in 1992). Only ten presidents prior to Trump have been denied reelection. Joe Biden won in both the popular vote (81,283,485 to 74,223,744) and the Electoral College (306 to 232). In the course of prevailing, Biden not only recaptured traditionally "blue" states (Michigan, Wisconsin, Pennsylvania) that Trump had won in 2016; he also captured a couple of traditionally "red" states (Arizona, Georgia). Optimists would be right to point to the career of Joe Biden as a reflection of both black advancement under American democracy and black contribution to American democracy. Obama elevated Biden to the vice presidency, and Biden's campaign to win the Democratic Party presidential nomination was helped tremendously by the African American congressman James Clyburn, whose endorsement was pivotal in the South Carolina Democratic Party primary. In the general election, Biden was dependent upon a strong showing by black voters—a showing that he received, undoubtedly aided by his running mate, Kamala Harris, the first woman and the first black to serve as vice president.

The triumph of the Biden-Harris ticket permitted the United States to escape the utter ruination Trump's reelection would have entailed. The extent of support that Trump elicited, however, is profoundly disturbing. Again: he received about seventy-four million votes. Despite exhibiting conspicuously gross deficiencies, including obvious and odious racism, he still bested Biden among whites, winning around 58 percent of their votes.[58] The pall cast over prospects for racial reconciliation by strong support for Trump can hardly be exaggerated. The fealty he elicits reveals and reinforces ugly racial attitudes that are considerably more prevalent, deep-seated, and influential than I had recognized, even after decades of studying the race question. I am thus no longer a confident optimist. I feel chastened. True, I continue to decline to embrace despair. Tens of millions of Americans resolutely abjure racism. And for the most well positioned of African Americans, horizons of opportunity continue to widen. On the other hand, it is difficult to envision the effectuation of reforms anytime soon that will effectively treat the injuries of race that are

so glaringly evident and that constitute such a damning indictment of America. I evince hopefulness largely out of habit and a
forlorn yearning on behalf of my children. But I do not expect in
the remainder of my life to glimpse, much less enjoy, a progressive
racial promised land.

2

Derrick Bell and Me

Derrick Albert Bell Jr. (1930–2011) was the first black tenured professor at Harvard Law School (HLS). Celebrated in some quarters as the godfather of critical race theory (CRT) and for renouncing his professorship to protest the absence of a black woman professor at HLS, Bell was an intrepid and influential scholar-activist who deserves careful assessment.[1] I try to offer that along with an account of my relationship with him. Mentor, friend, and adversary, he was a significant presence in my life. We had a complicated association, marked by private amity, public conflict, and, near his end, partial reconciliation.

I

Born November 6, 1930, in Pittsburgh, Bell was the eldest of four children.[2] His father was a mill worker and department store porter, his mother a homemaker. He was the first person in his family to attend college. A participant in the Reserve Officers' Training Corps, he graduated from Duquesne University, then served in the U.S. Air Force, rising to the rank of lieutenant. After his military service, he enrolled in 1954 in the University of Pittsburgh School of Law, the only black student in his class of 140. He excelled despite having to contend with pervasive casual racism. He recalled property classes in which the professor would sprinkle "hypotheticals with 'negras' whose craving for water-melon induced entrance in property not their own."[3] Although he became associate editor in chief of the school's law review, where he published two pieces on antidiscrimination law,[4] his strong record did not elicit much in terms of opportunities for lucrative employment. He recalled having no job offers as graduation approached. "The one large Pittsburgh law firm that invited the top students . . . for interviews was candid: they were, I was told, not ready to hire a black associate."[5]

Bell joined the U.S. Department of Justice, serving briefly in the Conscientious Objector Section before being assigned to the newly created Civil Rights Division. His tenure there was short-lived. Superiors objected to his membership in the National Association for the Advancement of Colored People (NAACP) because the NAACP often participated in litigation in which the Civil Rights Division was also involved. In 1957, Bell resigned rather than accede to demands that he drop his membership.[*] He returned to Pittsburgh, where he worked briefly as the executive director of the local branch of the NAACP. Then, at the invitation of Thurgood Marshall, he joined the staff of the NAACP Legal Defense and Educational Fund (LDF) in New York City.[†] Between 1960 and 1966, working alongside Marshall, Robert L. Carter, Jack Greenberg, Constance Baker Motley, James M. Nabrit Jr., and Michael Meltsner, Bell devoted himself to litigation at the high tide of the Second Reconstruction, participating, most notably, in school desegregation suits and the defense of protesters.[6] It was legal work that sometimes entailed peril. Representing Noelle Henry, the wife of the indomitable Dr. Aaron Henry, a stalwart leader of the Mississippi NAACP, Bell recounts how he slept on a couch in their living room because no hotels nearby accommodated blacks:

---

[*] Was Bell's response justified? I don't know. It would be useful to know whether the standard imposed upon Bell was a standard generally applied.

[†] The NAACP and the LDF are separate organizations. From 1940 until 1957 they were organically linked, with LDF serving essentially as the legal department of the NAACP. In 1957 the two organizations became independent of each other. Their parallel careers have been marked mainly by cooperation, though they have also intermittently suffered through bouts of destructive competition and unseemly resentments. See NAACP v. NAACP LDF, 753 F.2d 131 (1985).

Each evening around dusk, a man would knock and be admitted. He carried a shotgun and sat in a chair beside the large window in the living room and stayed on guard duty until dawn. His presence was both reassuring and a visible reminder that in the Mississippi Delta civil rights activism involved dangers that were more than rhetorical.[7]

On occasion he honed his advocacy in venues beyond the courtroom. The files of Bull Connor's police note that on July 20, 1962, Bell participated in a rally at the Metropolitan Baptist Church alongside the Reverend Fred Shuttlesworth and the Reverend C. T. Vivian.[*]

Throughout his career Bell lauded the heroic persistence of poor, unlettered black folk who challenged the Jim Crow regime despite their glaring vulnerability.[8] He credited people like his client A. J. Lewis, the father of a black elementary school student who, despite retaliation, persisted as a plaintiff in a school desegregation case in Leake County, Mississippi. Lewis was fired from his job the day his daughter enrolled in a previously all-white school. White segregationists also attempted to destroy his house. "Without a commitment from individuals [like Lewis] who were able to overcome fear, discouragement, and defeat after defeat, we civil rights lawyers and our organizations, who take most of the credit for change and reform, could have accomplished nothing."[9]

Bell himself directly experienced segregation's cruel sting. Seeking to worship in a small town in Louisiana during the early 1950s while serving in the air force as a second lieutenant, Bell was consigned to the balcony of a "white" church, where he sat alone, separated by race from fellow Presbyterians. Later he was jailed when he used a phone booth in a "white" waiting room in a train depot in Jackson, Mississippi. Bell knew, however, that the South was not the only region suffused with anti-Negro prejudice:

* As commissioner of public safety in Birmingham, Alabama, in the 1960s, Bull Connor dispatched police to civil rights rallies at which they took notes and produced memoranda detailing what they saw and heard. One memo reports on a speech delivered by a Negro lawyer erroneously identified as "Eric" Bell. *See* Birmingham Police Department Inter-office Communication, July 20, 1962, Birmingham Public Library.

I never shall forget the evening I walked into a downtown [Pittsburgh] bar that did not serve blacks. Several black friends had promised to join me there. None did. As I sat at the bar, some of the white patrons began muttering about the stranger. I heard sotto-voiced calls to "throw the nigger out" and worse. No one said anything to me, including the bartender, who ignored my repeated order for a beer. Finally, discretion gained the upper hand over whatever valor I had been able to muster. I walked out.[10]

Bell left LDF in 1966 to become deputy director of civil rights in the Department of Health, Education, and Welfare (HEW). There one of his major responsibilities was enforcing Title VI of the relatively new Civil Rights Act. Again he felt disappointment in government service: "I found my work neither satisfying nor very productive. It was frustrating to watch racial issues receiving back burner priority."[11]

Bell began looking for a position in legal academia. Initially his efforts were unavailing. He was rebuffed by George Washington University, the University of Michigan, and HLS.[12] He succeeded, though, in landing jobs as the executive director of the Western Center on Law and Poverty and as an adjunct professor at the University of Southern California Law Center. In 1968 he wrote a brief article that presaged themes upon which he later elaborated.[13] One was the limitations of lawyering. "Even our best efforts and programs," Bell lamented, "have failed to enable the poor to climb out of their poverty status and take their place in the mainstream of the society."[14] Another was what he saw as the underestimated malevolence of the forces arrayed against those marginalized in America, particularly poor urban blacks. "For the poor," Bell observed, "the police do not protect, but contain; they do not assist, but rather harass, and their presence in the ghetto is not to keep peace but to maintain control."[15]

Before long Bell began receiving attention from other law schools including HLS as "Black Power" eclipsed "We Shall Overcome" and as rioting engulfed scores of cities. In 1968, Martin Luther King Jr. was assassinated and massive disorder across the country followed, including protests on many campuses. In response, many colleges and universities increased their efforts to recruit black students and instructors.

> Spurred by a new sense of crisis, institutions began recruiting minorities with training and skills previously deemed "inadequate." . . . Major law schools, often pressured both by events and by their slightly increased ranks of black students, joined in this tardy recognition that their self-interest would be served by adding one or two blacks to their all-white faculties.[16]

As Bell remembers it, HLS followed suit, adopting an attitude toward him that was very different from its initial rejection:

> At Harvard, students did not serve on the committee responsible for reviewing applicants for teaching positions. . . . In my case, though, student approval was quite important. During my visit, I was asked to present a lecture to the black student group. . . . [T]he faculty subsequently voted me an offer which the then Dean, Derek Bok, flew to Los Angeles to deliver to me in person. To help persuade me to accept . . . Dean Bok brought with him a representative of the Black Law Students Association (BLSA).[17]

This recruitment experience affected Bell deeply. It impressed upon him the susceptibility of liberal universities to charges that they fail to live up to their preachings. Believing that his own appointment was mainly due to extra-academic force, Bell subsequently sympathized with the deployment of such force throughout his career.

Bell's first stint on the HLS faculty lasted a decade, from 1969 to 1979. He liked the teaching, the writing, the "access to resources, compensation, and prestige that is without parallel in legal education." But he also characterized that period as "tough."[18] From the outset he felt alienated, remarking to a friend,

> I enjoy the company of my colleagues but fear that I shall never become accustomed to the fact that so many of them

really believe that a Harvard faculty position carries with
it a general acknowledgment by the world (and perhaps by
God) of their intellectual superiority and absolute mastery
of the law. It is a most interesting phenomenon and I fear
a manifestation of a most serious ailment which I pray is
not contagious.[19]

From early on he evinced anxiety about his standing at HLS.
Writing to William H. Hastie Jr., an HLS alumnus and the country's first black federal judge, Bell stated, "I am well into my first
year and have noted no evidence that my presence has caused the
walls of this august institution to crumble."[20]

In his initial year of teaching, Bell found himself in the middle
of a dispute between the faculty and black students disciplined
for actions taken to protest the university's hiring practices on
construction and maintenance projects. The students demanded
that the university require that its contractors hire a minimum
percentage of minority workers. To press their point, students
obstructed the office of a dean at the college and occupied the
university faculty club for a day.[21] The law school faculty punished
five students, suspending one for a semester.[22] Bell disagreed publicly with the faculty's decision.

Bell believed that he had to combat a presumption that he was
less capable than white professors:

> There was always the need—especially with first-year stu-
> dents—to overcome their apprehension that because I was
> the one black on an otherwise all-white faculty I might not
> be competent.[23]

Bell maintained, moreover, that this stigmatizing presumption affected blacks as well as whites, averring that "some black
students, were afraid to take my course for fear I would embarrass
them by being less able than the white teachers."[24]

According to Bell, university authorities asked him to develop
a civil rights course and to be a mentor and model for the black
students.[25] He could not help but have been aware that that
assignment was far different from the mission his white peers
were expected to fulfill. The white professors were expected to

be nationally recognized leaders in some field of the law. He, by contrast, seems to have been expected mainly to mollify black students. That awareness became an omnipresent feature of his experience at HLS.

Bell obtained tenure in 1970. Soon thereafter, he published a casebook, *Race, Racism, and American Law,* that was the first "devoted specifically to a study of racism in the law."[26] It featured a photograph on an opening page that captured the spirit Bell sought to inculcate. The photograph pictured the black American sprinters Tommie Smith and John Carlos atop the medal stand at the 1968 Olympics in Mexico City, arms defiantly aloft, wearing black gloves in protest against racial mistreatment.* Bell's pioneering effort brought together a huge amount of material, highlighted overlooked important cases, focused attention on neglected subjects, and peppered readers with provocative questions and hypotheticals.

In 1976, Bell published "Serving Two Masters: Integration Ideals and Client Interests in School Desegregation Litigation" in *The Yale Law Journal.*[27] He argued that because of their attachment to integrationist aims certain civil rights organizations (most notably the NAACP) had lost sight of key realities, including the preferences of their putative clients. He complained that they had failed to appreciate sufficiently that white flight had eclipsed hope of integration in many school districts by leaving few whites with whom blacks could integrate without undertaking busing or some other burdensome arrangement. He also charged that integration-obsessed attorneys had failed to be sufficiently deferential to black parents whose priorities for their children differed from those of their lawyers. Bell contended that champions of African American racial uplift ought not view predominantly black or all-black institutions as illicit or problematic merely because of racial demography. Majority-minority schools had their virtues, he insisted. And in any event, the preferences of black parents and students

* Cropped from the photo was the white silver medalist, the Australian Peter Norman. Displaying solidarity with the Americans, Norman wore a badge, "Olympic Project for Human Rights," that caused him to be ostracized back home. *See* "Peter Norman, 64, Who Shared Podium at '68 Games Dies," *New York Times,* Oct. 4, 2006, www.nytimes.com; Mike Wise, "The Third Man in Mexico City," *New York Times,* Sept. 17, 2000.

were entitled to more respect from their legal representatives. Bell maintained that instead of pursuing at all costs an illusory vision of racially mixed public schooling, those seeking to advance the best interests of black communities ought to seek access to more effective education regardless of the racial makeup of student populations.

"Serving Two Masters" attracted considerable attention, including a combative open letter from Nathaniel Jones, then the general counsel of the NAACP. Maintaining that "the Bell indictment of civil rights lawyers (and the NAACP) fails on several counts," Jones fervently defended his litigation strategy. "Blacks have learned," he wrote, "that 'green follows white.' With desegregation—and white children being reassigned to previously black schools—also came new resources."*

Bell was aware that some liberal activists, including former colleagues within the ranks of the NAACP and the LDF, viewed his article as an unforgivable apostasy. He noted that he had deviated from "the unwritten civil rights Commandment: Thou shalt not publicly criticize [fellow proponents of black racial uplift]."[28] Bell continued, however, to publicly critique the integrationist orthodoxy. He was convinced that "it is out of just such unorthodoxy that effective review of existing policies can take place, and new means and more appropriate policies may be evolved." He lamented that "the dearth of serious writing offering liberal criticism of school desegregation policy constitutes a form of academic abstention that speaks more for the personal discretion of potential critics than the public value of the silence that so many have used as a balm for their growing concerns."[29]

Bell followed "Serving Two Masters" with "*Brown v. Board of*

---

* Nathaniel Jones, Correspondence, "School Desegregation," 86 *Yale Law Journal* 378, 380 (1976). After his stint as NAACP general counsel, Jones served on the U.S. Court of Appeals for the Sixth Circuit between 1979 and 1995. In a section of his autobiography describing their exchange, "Bridging a Gap with the Enigmatic Derrick Bell," Jones displayed an ongoing bewilderment with his adversary's position: "How someone with the impressive civil rights and academic credentials of Derrick Bell could miss the logic, rationale, and reason we were following baffled me." Nathaniel R. Jones, *Answering the Call: An Autobiography of the Modern Struggle to End Racial Discrimination in America* (2016), 143. Jones's inability to appreciate Bell's point replicated Bell's inability to appreciate Jones's point. They argued with the focused zealousness of retained counsel.

Education and the Interest-Convergence Dilemma,"[30] published in 1980 in the *Harvard Law Review*. He argued that *Brown v. Board of Education* and kindred breakthroughs stemmed not so much from enlightenment on the part of white decision makers as from their perception that such reforms would accrue advantages to white America: an improved image useful in the propaganda war for international hegemony; the mollification of restive blacks (without decisively challenging white dominance); and the removal of antiquated racial roadblocks to capitalist modernization. "The interest of blacks in achieving racial equality," Bell declared, "will be accommodated only when it converges with the interests of whites."[31]

That "*Brown v. Board of Education* and the Interest-Convergence Dilemma" is viewed as a pathbreaking scholarly intervention is itself curious. What realist ever doubted that moving a dominant group to reform its ways involved either overcoming that group with force or convincing it that reform would serve its own interests, properly construed? Professor Justin Driver has noted other issues that also ought to concern celebrants of the article.[32] These include Bell's under-theorized handling of the idea of "interest" and the accordion-like malleability of his theory. Bell's formulation is irrefutable. It rationalizes *Brown v. Board of Education* as a triumph for white "interest" just as much as it rationalizes *Plessy v. Ferguson* as a triumph for white interest. A theory so formless should elicit skepticism. Yet Bell's hypothesis of interest convergence has often been uncritically praised and enthusiastically generalized.[33]

Despite placing articles in prestigious law reviews, publishing a casebook, and attaining a full professorship, Bell continued to feel like an outsider at his home institution. "My tenured status," he recalled, "did not entitle me to admission to the Law School's inner circles."[34] Especially nettlesome to him was the fact that no other blacks gained appointment to the full-time faculty until the hiring of C. Clyde Ferguson in 1974.[35]

In 1980, Bell left HLS to assume the deanship of the University of Oregon Law School. Two developments punctuated his six years there. First, in 1985, at the invitation of the *Harvard Law Review*, he wrote the foreword to its annual assessment of the previous year's Supreme Court term. The foreword is probably the

most prestigious venue for an article in legal academia.[36] Bell was
the first African American law professor to occupy that space. He
did so in a unique fashion. In "The Civil Rights Chronicles,"[37] he
enlisted "fantasy to explore . . . racial myths in the hope that resort
to the unreal may lead us toward a realism needed to uncover, at
last, the real content of the racial complexity we call civil rights."[38]
He framed a series of scenes featuring discussions between himself
and a fictional character named Geneva Crenshaw, a civil rights
lawyer seriously injured by racially motivated violence in Mississippi. In one episode, "The Chronicle of the DeVine Gift," a black
entrepreneur helps Crenshaw locate black academics with credentials and skills that enable them to obtain faculty positions at some
unnamed major law school. The seventh of these black academics
is the most impressive of the lot but is denied an appointment
because, in the view of the law school's dean, another African
American appointment will push the school beyond its racial tipping point. Bell has his imagined law school dean say the following
to Geneva:

> We promised you we would become an integrated faculty,
> and we have kept our promise admittedly with a lot of
> help from you. But I don't think we can hire anyone else
> for a little while. I thought we might "share the wealth" a
> bit by recommending your candidate to some of our sister
> schools whose minority hiring records are far less impres-
> sive than our own.[39]

When Crenshaw pushes back against the dean's objection—
"I can assure you that the seventh candidate will be better than
anyone now on the faculty without regard to race"—the dean
seeks to justify his decision:

> This is one of the oldest and finest law schools in the
> country. . . . [W]e want to retain our image as a white
> school. . . . [A] law school of our caliber and tradition sim-
> ply cannot look like a professional basketball team.[40]

Outraged, Geneva decries "the futility of it all" before discussing with Bell a variety of issues, including the many difficulties that

plaintiffs in employment discrimination litigation must surmount, especially in the context of high-status jobs. Invoking a theme that Bell would repeat on numerous occasions subsequently, Geneva remarks that the chronicle of the DeVine Gift "is a nice reminder that *progress* in American race relations is largely a mirage, obscuring the fact that whites continue, consciously or unconsciously, to do all in their power to ensure their dominion and maintain their control."[41]

Second, in 1985 Bell resigned his deanship at the University of Oregon Law School when its faculty declined to extend a professorship to a candidate whom he strongly supported. As he remembered the imbroglio,

> The final straw came when the faculty voted not to authorize me to offer a position to Pat Chew, an Asian-American woman who graduated high in her class at the University of Texas Law School. Chew . . . spoke Chinese and had gained experience through law practice with the many legal problems in doing business with Pacific Rim countries. Both the school and the community would have benefitted from her expertise. In addition, Asians are the Oregon Law School's largest minority group. We had reviewed more than one hundred candidates and listed Chew as our third choice behind two white males with fancier credentials but, as I recall, no practice experience. Both rejected our offers. In an hours-long faculty meeting, a few professors convinced a majority that "we could do better" and urged that we reopen the search. All were aware of my strong support for Chew. I promised to honor the vote and not extend Chew an offer, but told them that I was stepping down so they could select as dean someone whose leadership they were ready to follow.[42]

Bell returned to Harvard, where he spent another five years dotted with controversy, much of which had to do with claims that HLS discriminated against leftists, particularly those affiliated with critical legal studies, racial minorities, and women, particularly black women.[43] In 1990, Bell announced that to protest the absence of any women of color on the faculty, he was going to take an unpaid leave of absence until at least one was appointed. This action attracted widespread praise including an encomium from the first black president of the *Harvard Law Review* and future president of the United States. Barack Obama lauded Bell as the Rosa Parks of legal education.[44]

At the end of a two-year grace period, Bell sought a waiver from a university rule limiting the period during which professors may be on leave. When no waiver was extended and Bell remained absent, Harvard terminated his employment.[45] He subsequently joined the faculty of the New York University School of Law, which served as his institutional base for the remainder of his life, a productive period during which he wrote a series of books— *Faces at the Bottom of the Well: The Permanence of Racism* (1992), *Confronting Authority: Reflections of an Ardent Protester* (1994), *Gospel Choirs: Psalms of Survival for an Alien Land Called Home* (1996), *Afrolantica Legacies* (1998), *Ethical Ambition: Living a Life of Meaning and Worth* (2002), and *Silent Covenants: Brown v. Board of Education and the Unfulfilled Hopes for Racial Reform* (2004).

II

Bell's signature argument in his final quarter century was that racial hierarchy, or, more precisely, white domination, is destined to remain a permanent feature of American life:

> Black people will never gain full equality in this country. Even those herculean efforts we hail as successful will produce no more than temporary "peaks of progress," short-lived victories that slide into irrelevance as racial patterns adapt in ways that maintain white dominance. This is a hard-to-accept fact that all history verifies.[46]

One difficulty in coming to grips with this claim is determining its genre. Is it a polemical gesture that should be evaluated primarily in terms of its effect upon its audience, particularly activists seeking to elevate the fortunes of African Americans? Or is it a social scientific hypothesis that should be evaluated primarily in terms of its explanatory aptness? I shall consider both.

Bell described his permanence of white domination pro-
nouncement as "an act of ultimate defiance." Analogizing fear of
death to fear of never-ending white hegemony, he declared that
"those who conquer their dread . . . are freed to live more fully."
African Americans, he maintained, "must confront and conquer
the otherwise deadening reality of our permanent subordinate status. Only in this way can we prevent ourselves from being dragged
down by society's racial hostility."[47]

Bell has been criticized for positing an analysis perceived to be
dispiriting, even immobilizing.[48] Critics contend that hopefulness
is an essential ingredient for effective protest and that Bell's thesis
is wrong or that his public articulation of it is wrong because that
thesis tends to suffocate hope. I used to voice that criticism.[49] I do
so no longer. I continue to disagree with Bell (for reasons to which
I will soon turn). But I do so no longer on the basis of mandatory optimism. Diagnosticians of society should ply their mission
coldly and clinically. They should not be compelled to minister
to morale. That should be left to coaches, therapists, clerics, or
the like. If a commentator perceives a situation to be hopeless,
he should say so. Some situations *are* hopeless—à la the situation of Jews in Germany circa 1934. The best thing to have done
in that terrible moment was broadcast as loudly as possible that
there was no prospect for a survivable future for Jews in Germany
under Hitler and that Jews should thus flee as quickly as possible.
Unconditional optimism is senseless. If Bell is correct in his reading of the American past, present, and future, then his pessimistic
counsel is sound.

Another reason behind my change is that I am no longer convinced that Bellian pessimism is inevitably debilitating. In *Faces at
the Bottom of the Well*, Bell remarked that for him "the challenge
throughout has been to tell . . . the truth about racism without
causing disabling despair."[50] He sought to do this by proclaiming the virtue of stoicism, though he did not refer by name to
that venerable tradition. Stoics stress mastering oneself regardless of external circumstances. So did Bell. He contended that
struggle against racial injustice is a life-affirming activity in which
one should be involved regardless of outcome. He insisted upon
righteous defiance without expecting to prevail, believing that

resistance alone constituted triumph. He movingly illustrated this perspective by reference to a black farmer who left his fields to join the famous voting rights march from Selma to Montgomery:

> Along the march [the farmer] was asked whether he thought the marchers would be able to win in Montgomery. He responded directly and simply: "We won when we started." The winning was not in Montgomery but in the overcoming of fear and disillusionment. . . . Whatever happened on the road and in Montgomery would not deprive them of their victory.[51]

There is no reason to axiomatically maintain that one cannot be a wise, effective, admirable dissident while believing that one's efforts are doomed. While rising expectation often fuels rebellion, it can also prompt disappointment that exacerbates the hurt that defeat inflicts. An assumption of defeat might serve as a useful antidote to disappointment.

I believe, however, that Bell meant to offer more than a gesture of defiance. He also intended to posit a statement he thought to be accurate about the actual workings of American race relations along the white-black frontier. Let's look again at Bell's thesis that we shall *not* overcome:

> Racism in America is not a curable aberration. . . . [O]ppression on the basis of race returns time after time—in different guises, but it always returns. . . . [R]acism lies at the center, not the periphery.[52]

"Racism," he wrote, "is an integral, permanent, and indestructible component of this society."[53] White society, he asserted, "condemns all blacks to quasi citizenship as surely as it segregated our parents and enslaved our forebears." Blacks remain, he averred, "what we were in the beginning: a dark and foreign presence, always the designated 'other.' "[54] African Americans, he insisted, "will never gain full equality in this country."[55]

Bell left key terms—"racism," "quasi citizenship," "full equality"—undefined. He omitted metrics that could assist in

confirming or rebutting his proposition. He offered no suitable
baseline for assessing whether we are moving forward or backward
or are locked in stasis. He offered no comparisons between the
United States and other divided societies. He was drawn to grand
generalities that crumple under skeptical probing. He wrote, for
example, that "most of our civil rights statutes and court decisions
have been more symbol than enforceable law. We hail and celebrate each of these laws, but none of them is . . . fully honored at
the bank."[56] Yet consider that phrase "fully honored at the bank."
It does suggest a baseline for assessment—perfect enforcement.
But such a standard is utopian. *All* law is underenforced; none is
"fully" honored. Useful to know for purposes of making careful
appraisal is the consequence of a given law and the extent to which
law is enforced. Answers require empirical investigations of the
sort to which Bell paid little attention.

Nor did he show interest in reckoning with analyses that challenged his thesis. The National Research Council's Committee
on the Status of Black Americans published a study, *A Common
Destiny: Blacks and American Society*, that contained information
and arguments highly pertinent to Bell's claim. *A Common Destiny*
was published in 1989, just a few years before *Faces at the Bottom
of the Well*, Bell's fullest elaboration of his permanence of racism
theme. Yet Bell ignored the study, just as he ignored other writings that deviated from his preferred position. *A Common Destiny*
noted the ambiguous place of blacks in late twentieth-century
America. "The status of black Americans today," the National
Research Council observed, "can be characterized as a glass that
is half-full—if measured by progress since 1939—or as a glass that
is half-empty—if measured by the persisting disparities between
black and white Americans since the early 1970s."[57] The council,
in other words, was hardly naive about the racial facts of life in
America, observing forthrightly that "race still matters greatly in
the United States."[58] It recognized that both "fresh" racial discrimination and the vestiges of past racial mistreatment weigh
heavily on blacks. The council also acknowledged, however, that
over the previous half century, along many dimensions, the legal,
political, social, and economic fortunes of large segments of black
America had improved markedly, in some ways dramatically. Bell's

refusal to acknowledge certain obvious progressions discredited his analysis.

When Bell wrote that "even those herculean efforts we hail as successful will produce no more than temporary 'peaks of progress,' short-lived victories that slide into irrelevance as racial patterns adapt in ways that maintain white dominance," he was alluding to the Second Reconstruction, including its most famous judicial ruling, *Brown v. Board of Education*. Bell wrote about *Brown* on many occasions. Over time he became increasingly dismissive.[59] In 1980 he suggested that by offering him a deanship, officials at the University of Oregon had signaled that "the spirit of *Brown* survives."[60] The same year, in "*Brown v. Board of Education* and the Interest-Convergence Dilemma," Bell accorded the landmark ruling considerable praise. "It has triggered," he declared, a revolution in civil rights law and in the political leverage available to blacks in and out of court.[61]

By 2004, his assessment had changed, becoming almost wholly derisive. Those who maintain that *Brown* is a valuable precedent, he remarked, are like "those who hold that the earth is . . . flat."[62] *Brown*, he asserted, "was a disaster for the schooling of black children."[63] It was such a disaster, in his view, that he suggested it might have been preferable for the Supreme Court to have reaffirmed *Plessy* while requiring strict enforcement of separate but equal. *Plessy* at least nominally required equal if separate facilities. *Brown* as elaborated in subsequent case law got rid of the separate but equal formula but replaced it with what Bell deemed to be a mirage—a prohibition on state-mandated segregation that courts eventually interpreted as requiring neither the end of racial isolation nor the end of black schools marked by material deprivation. *Brown* might at one point have contained a potentiality for transformation. But that version of *Brown*, according to Bell, "is truly dead and beyond resuscitation."[64]

Now, it is true that the Supreme Court's most famous twentieth-century ruling has often been excessively inflated and extravagantly praised, thus making it an inviting target for debunking. Some have credited *Brown* with inspiring the civil rights movement. But of course well before *Brown*, A. Philip Randolph, Walter White, E. D. Nixon, Rosa Parks, Bayard Rustin, James

Farmer, Roy Wilkins, Modjeska Simkins, Albert DeLaine, James Hinton, Thurgood Marshall, and many others had already begun to stir the aspirations, build the networks, and hone the skills that were later revealed so magnificently. Some commentators praise *Brown* for its supposed eloquence. In actuality, though, *Brown* is diffident and wan—purposefully so.* Chief Justice Earl Warren wrote privately that he sought to draft an opinion that would be "short, readable by the law public, non-rhetorical, unemotional and above all non-accusatory."[65] He succeeded. But his success came with the price of obscuring the truth about segregation. Bell rightly observes that the Court in *Brown* treats segregation as though it were a policy that "descended unwanted from the skies."[66] The *Brown* opinion manages to invalidate de jure racial discrimination in public primary and secondary schools without castigating the officials behind it. Because Warren insisted upon writing an opinion that was non-accusatory, he omitted a central aspect of the segregation story: the reason why segregationists separated students racially pursuant to the coercive force of governmental power. Perhaps Warren's choice was prudent. Maybe obfuscation was necessary to obtain a unanimous ruling. Perhaps unanimity was essential. But whatever the merits of the judicial strategy, the *Brown* opinion lacks clarity and candor. Missing from the most honored race relations decision in American constitutional history is a forthright reckoning with racism.†

* Noting the "blandness" of the *Brown* opinion, J. Harvie Wilkinson III observes that Chief Justice Earl Warren's most famous judicial declaration "failed to rouse or inspire." It would be more accurate to say that Warren's opinion *declined* to rouse or inspire. The chief justice did not try and fail; he purposefully muted the opinion. Whatever the rhetorical strategy and motivation, *Brown* is written such that a reader expecting to find in it "a Declaration of Independence or Gettysburg Address will likely be deflated." J. Harvie Wilkinson III, *From* Brown *to* Bakke: *The Supreme Court and School Integration, 1954–1978* (1979), 29.

† Compare *Brown v. Board of Education*, 347 U.S. 483 (1954) with *Briggs v. Elliott*, 98 F. Supp. 529 (E.D.S.C. 1951) (Waring, J., dissenting). Judge Waring anticipated Chief Justice Warren's repudiation of segregation in public schooling. Waring's now obscure opinion, however, was far more direct and eloquent. Nothing in *Brown* is as rhetorically strong as Waring's declaration in *Briggs* that segregation in education "can never produce equality . . . it is an evil that must be eradicated. . . . [Segregation] must go and must go now. *Segregation is per se inequality*." *Id.* at 548 (emphasis added).

And then there was the post-*Brown* story: the failure of nerve signaled by "all deliberate speed"; the openly evasive pupil placement laws accommodated by courts; the dilatory tactics pursued by local school boards; the outright lies told by judges; and the threatened and actual racial mistreatment of black children and their parents. Bell lived intimately with these outrages. He was among the lawyers who represented James Meredith, an air force veteran like himself who risked death to attend the "white" flagship university in Mississippi. Bell knew that the board of trustees of the University of Mississippi had perjured themselves by declaring that race had had nothing to do with their decision to reject Meredith's application and that a federal district court judge had deceptively given credence to that obvious lie. He saw parents fired from jobs and evicted from homes simply for seeking to vindicate the rights of their children. He saw white supremacists make black students wait year after year after year to attend schools that under *Brown* they had a right to attend. He might well have been describing himself when he noted that "the still unfulfilled promise of the *Brown* decision deadens and embitters those who remember the sweet sense of liberation and the optimistic expectations generated by that decision. Diehard resistance was expected, but few predicted that persistent opposition would survive the civil rights era . . . and gain strength during the societal frustration of the post–Vietnam War era."[67] The accumulation of these disappointments aggrieved Bell, corroding his willingness to trust those whom he called "the white folks." Recollecting the tragedies he had seen, Bell said to me on more than one occasion, "Randy, the white folks simply don't play fair."

Some *Brown* deflationists have performed a useful service by downsizing the importance of Supreme Court rulings relative to other influences (for example, migration, urbanization, the Cold War), by reconsidering the wisdom of the Court's strategies (for example, "all deliberate speed"), and by demanding an accounting of "the concrete ways in which [*Brown*] mattered."[68] Bell, however, pushed the deflationist argument over the proverbial cliff. To see how this is so requires attending to basic facts.

Prior to the Court's announcement of *Brown* on May 17, 1954, public authorities could and did lawfully separate students on a racial basis. With *Brown* the boundary of legitimacy moved. The Court invalidated the racial policies guiding public primary and secondary schooling in twenty-one states and the District of Columbia. After *Brown*, public authorities could no longer *lawfully* segregate students racially. Many officials continued segregationist practices. But now they could no longer do so legitimately. They had to start lying to cover their tracks.* Prior to *Brown*, with respect to public schooling, federal constitutional law did not prohibit racial segregation, per se; so long as substantial equality was provided to separate schools, segregation could be practiced without apology. *Brown* changed that. The Supreme Court invalidated de jure segregation in public schooling, and there has been no going back on that momentous advance. True, in many locales there is conspicuous racial separateness in schooling, often on account of white flight. But "separateness" is not the same as "segregation." Nowhere now can an official say openly without fear of legal repercussions that he or she is seeking in public schools to educate students of different races separately albeit equally. Any such statement will be immediately attacked, and the spear of that challenge will be, of course, *Brown v. Board of Education*.

De jure segregation affected more than education; it touched all manner of facilities including courtrooms, restaurants, buses, golf courses, swimming pools, beaches, hospitals, taxis, and phone booths. *Brown* itself did not apply expressly beyond schooling. That is why many protracted campaigns were needed after *Brown* to extend the invalidation of separate but equal to other domains. Still, *Brown* constituted *the* centerpiece in all of the subsequent litigation against segregated facilities.[69] *Brown* and its burgeoning progeny did not negate every racist feature of Jim Crow pigmentocracy. But that case law did open up many opportunities for blacks and nullified indignities that had long tormented them. It

---

* A vivid illustration is provided by one of the most famous cases on which Bell worked: the desegregation of the University of Mississippi by James Meredith. Prior to *Brown*, Mississippi officials could openly declare, without apology, that regardless of Meredith's record he lacked the credential most essential for admission: white skin. After *Brown*, Mississippi officials were forced to resort—vainly—to ridiculous lies. *Meredith v. Fair*, 305 F. 2d 343 (5th Cir. 1962), *cert. denied*, 371 U.S. 828 (1962).

threw a pall over *all* segregation laws, encouraging litigation and
other protests that attacked white supremacism on every front. It
is fatuous to deny that *Brown* represents a major accomplishment.*

And what about the Civil Rights Act of 1964 and the Voting
Rights Act of 1965? Are they, too, rightly seen as mere "temporary 'peaks of progress,' short-lived victories"? Prior to Title II
of the Civil Rights Act it was lawful, in jurisdictions without
local or state antidiscrimination prohibitions, for private owners of public accommodations to inflict upon potential customers racial segregation or exclusion altogether. The consequences
for blacks ranged from merely annoying to painfully humiliat-
ing to gravely dangerous.[70] After the enactment of Title II things
changed quickly and dramatically for the better.† Similarly, prior
to the enactment of Title VII of the Civil Rights Act, it was perfectly lawful for an employer in jurisdictions without local or state
antidiscrimination prohibitions to declare openly that under no
circumstances would a black worker be permitted to earn more
than the lowest-paid white worker.[71] After Title VII took effect,
even many recalcitrant racist employers grudgingly got rid of such
Jim Crow arrangements or, upon retaining them, suffered losses
in court. The changes prodded by Title VII, along with kindred
legislative, executive, and judicial reforms, contributed to the
socioeconomic advance of black Americans, particularly those in
the South during the 1960s and 1970s.[72]

Among the initiatives of the Second Reconstruction, the Voting Rights Act produced the clearest record of altered conduct, in
the short run and the long. In 1965 in Alabama, 69.2 percent of
adult whites were registered to vote, while only 19.3 percent of
adult blacks were registered. By 2004, the percentages of black
and white registered voters were roughly equal (73.8 percent of
whites compared with 72.9 percent of blacks). In 1965 in Georgia,
two-thirds of the white population was registered to vote compared with less than a third of the black population. By 2004 the
percentages were about equal. In 1965 in Mississippi, nearly 70

* For additional commentary on these points see "*Brown* as Senior Citizen."

† For additional commentary on this point see "The Civil Rights Act Did Make
a Difference!"

percent of whites were registered, while only 6.7 percent of blacks were registered. By 2004, the percentage of white registered voters had risen by two points, while the percentage of black registered voters had risen by nearly seventy percentage points.[73] Voter registration, of course, is only part of the process of electoral politics. In other areas the story is mixed, featuring a sobering presence of incessant resistance, opportunistic voter suppression schemes, and dubious judicial rulings, most important, the erroneous decision in *Shelby County v. Holder* that has crippled the Voting Rights Act. Complexities abound, but one thing is clear: the narrative of unequivocal, unvarying, inevitable African American subordination that Professor Bell offered is grossly oversimplified.

How did Bell interpret the most dramatic challenge to his pessimism—the election of an African American to the presidency? On the one hand he was elated at witnessing Obama's triumph. He spoke of his "great appreciation for having lived to see a day [he] thought would never come."[*] On the other hand his elation was "diluted by experience"—a history that, viewed properly, counseled caution. Bell noted that despite Obama's outstanding qualities and favorable circumstances—an economic meltdown, John McCain's mismanaged campaign, unpopular wars, an eight-year run of the Bush presidency that had generated a widespread hunger for change—most whites still refrained from voting for the "Yes We Can" candidate. "We should not forget," Bell wrote, "that Obama won only 43 percent of the white vote, even though he was the much superior candidate . . . competing against a party (the Republicans) that had left the country in shambles."[74] Bell

---

[*] Derrick A. Bell Jr., "On Celebrating an Election as Racial Progress," *Human Rights* (Fall 2009). Bell had been deeply gladdened eighteen years previously when Obama was chosen as president of the *Harvard Law Review*, the first black selected to the post. Bell is said to have responded,

> I'm very pleased. . . . I tend to be one who stays in a state of constant pessimistic despair about the chances of America ever doing the right thing as far as race is concerned. Well, I grasp these little indications as a sign that maybe it might work out after all.

Bell's standing with many students at HLS was such that news of Obama's historic election traveled to his home almost immediately. *See* Paul Tarr and John Thornton, "Obama Election Lauded. Coast to Coast," *Harvard Law Record*, Feb. 9, 1990.

warned that Obama's adversaries would deploy time-tested racial ploys to undermine the new president:

> Republicans are trying hard to rebuild the old racial divide-and-conquer strategy. The tactics of division barely masking racism have been successful for hundreds of years. Holding them at bay and enacting policies that help all those in need will not be easy, and may not be possible.[75]

Bell further lamented that if Obama faltered, "those of us who look like him had better prepare to a return to the past."

Here Bell proved to be prescient. He predicted the backlash, the ferocity of which took many—including me—by surprise. That is an important achievement on his part that must be acknowledged. His pessimistic diagnosis can be read as anticipating the Tea Party, Senator Mitch McConnell's obstructionism, and *Shelby County v. Holder*. Attentive readers of his writings would not have been surprised by the Trump ascendancy.

III

Bell is best known for his protest against HLS. He claimed that in making hiring decisions, the faculty discriminated against racial minority candidates, especially women of color. He took a leave of absence to dramatize his objection. When Harvard refused to extend the maximum period it allows for leaves, Bell ended his relationship with the university, though he portrays the university as having fired him.

Bell's anger, distrust, impatience, and revulsion over faculty hiring had deep roots. Writing to Judge Wade McCree in 1971 about the decision of the faculty to refrain from making an offer to a black visiting professor (who subsequently joined the Stanford Law School faculty), Bell declared, "I was extremely disappointed about this decision which means that I shall remain the only black tenured faculty member. . . . As you can imagine, I personally find this both burdensome and embarrassing."[76] In 1973, in correspondence with Clyde Ferguson, before he joined the HLS faculty (becoming its second black tenured professor), Bell wrote, "I am simply not sure how much longer I wish to remain as the sole black faculty member."[77] Seven years later, as he departed HLS to assume the deanship at Oregon, Bell remarked at a farewell dinner in his honor, "My only regret is that I leave Clyde Ferguson the way he found me—alone!"[78]

Although Bell constantly forwarded black candidates to the HLS appointments committee, it declined to extend offers. That he was unable to bring black academics on board with him at HLS pained Bell deeply because he saw the recruitment and advancement of black academics as a major part of his personal, institutional, and political mission. Responding to someone who had written to congratulate him upon receiving tenure, Bell remarked, "It is sad . . . (and more than a little disquieting) that the School permitted so many of its outstanding black law graduates . . . Bill Coleman, Clyde Ferguson, and others, to get away without ever seriously considering [them for] faculty positions. . . . [I]t is obvious that I came along at the right time. I see it as my responsibility to help correct the School's sins of omission by pressuring for as many black faculty as I can."[79]

Throughout his career Bell was critical of the law school establishment and insistent that special efforts be undertaken to open up opportunities for blacks in legal academia. But his approach changed significantly over the years. In the 1970s, during his first decade at HLS, despite his commitment to increasing the ranks of black professors, he was demanding in assessing black candidates; obtaining a recommendation from him was by no means automatic. In 1971 a veteran black civil rights attorney asked Bell for help securing a faculty position. Phillip Areeda, the chair of the Appointments Committee, asked Bell for his impression of the candidate. Bell candidly replied, "Unfortunately, nothing I know about —— leads me to believe that he merits serious consideration by your committee."[80] Later, Bell changed, refusing to do anything other than be a cheerleader for black candidates, believing that any negative comments would tend to be magnified while positive comments would tend to be discounted.

A similar transformation can be seen in Bell's writings. In 1970, Bell penned his first major law review article, "Black Students in White Law Schools: The Ordeal and the Opportunity."

In it he offered an interpretation of the sentiments and strategies of black law students and an assessment of the dilemmas they confronted and prospects they faced. His analysis is complex and searching. He paid heed, as always, to the onerous weight of racial wrongs, noting that racial prejudice, combined with a continuing lack of educational and economic resources, served to curtail the number of blacks who aspired to join the legal profession and to limit the range of success enjoyed by those who somehow overcame these multiple handicaps. But he also recognized that "the outlook ha[d] changed," that "opportunities for black attorneys [had] expanded tremendously." Elaborating, Bell remarked that "the active recruitment of black law students is continuing and indeed is becoming more vigorous as the top schools compete with one another to insure their share of black talent."[81]

In "Black Students in White Law Schools," Bell called attention to external obstacles, but also called attention to internal impediments. "Today's black student," he observed, "finds it impossible either to dedicate himself entirely to his legal studies, or to consider scholastic competition with his white classmates as a valid method of proving his worth." These dispositions, he recognized, subverted "the intensive, purposeful effort needed to succeed in law school. These attitudes are actually detrimental, constituting the most serious deprivation the black student faces."[82] Here Bell spots ways in which victimization reinjures victims, prompting them to victimize themselves. Later Bell constructed one-dimensional portrayals of black students and academics that airbrushed their blemishes (unless they were ideological deviants—that is, conservatives).

Bell's article also addresses the consequences of applying lower standards to black as opposed to white students. He noted a report that "one major law school [had] quietly applied a double standard of grading with black students being passed on an easier scale."[83] Bell objected. "Whatever arguments are used to justify such a policy," he declared, "there is little denying that it robs those black students who have done well of receiving real credit and the boost of confidence that their accomplishments merit. . . . It is also something considerably less than a spur to their motivation to excel during the remainder of their law school careers."[84]

Articulating a perspective that is almost wholly missing in his subsequent, more acclaimed writings, Bell insisted that black students be required to perform on the same basis as their white peers notwithstanding the racist burdens they shouldered. A "laissez faire attitude towards black scholarship," Bell cautioned, "encourages the development of a characteristic often deemed vital to ghetto survival, called appropriately . . . the 'hustler mentality.' Those afflicted with this outlook seek, almost as a lifestyle, to obtain as much as possible with as minimal an effort as possible." Abjuring sentimentality, Bell averred that "racial prejudice has not served to transform its victims into super-beings purged of all human weakness . . ."[85] In other words, blacks, too, have flaws, sometimes glaringly so. These weaknesses may be the consequence of racist mistreatment. But they are weaknesses nonetheless.[86]

By the 1990s, Bell had abandoned mention of academic shortcomings of black students or professors. Instead, he preached single-mindedly that when black students and professors fail to win this or that competition, the overwhelmingly likely reason is not their inadequacy relative to rivals but unfair and misleading standards of assessment. "The standards for hiring and promoting faculty at Harvard Law School," he charged, "erect almost unassailable barriers of class and race" that bear "little correlation to effective teaching or significant scholarship."[87] Addressing the oft-cited notion of a "pool problem"—the idea that there were relatively few plausible minority candidates available for faculty positions particularly at the more selective schools—Bell argued that there was no real difficulty with supply. Competent black candidates with useful experiences abounded, he insisted. The problem resided in the unwillingness of law school authorities to abandon outmoded criteria that prevented the recognition of relevant talents.

Bell's indictment was dismissed by most of his colleagues. There was reluctance, however, to explain the basis of disagreement with him. This diffidence facilitated rumors, misunderstandings, and inaccuracies that seeped into debates that became increasingly acrimonious. Bell and his followers succeeded in embarrassing the law school administration by asserting that the paucity of minority professors revealed a damning judgment on the quality of black lawyers—a judgment that no black lawyers, or notably few, were smart enough to be asked to join the professoriat. The tiny number of blacks on the faculty was turned into a statement that purportedly denigrated the entire population of African American attorneys. As Jesse Jackson declared, speaking in support of Bell's critique, "To say that in 1990 there is no black woman anywhere in America qualified to be a tenured faculty member is both an error and a gross insult to our intelligence."[88] That assertion should have received a forthright response stressing that the demographics of the HLS faculty did *not* "say" what Jackson and Bell claimed. Noting that by 1990 HLS had trained more black lawyers than any school save Howard University, the response should have celebrated the highly impressive black lawyers scattered across the United States who contribute superbly as government officials, entrepreneurs, trial attorneys, counselors to nonprofits, and captains of industry. The response should then have emphasized that for various reasons, including the desire to make lots of money, many outstanding lawyers of all complexions decide that they would rather pursue careers outside the academy. The response should then have pointed out the narrowness of the talents, skills, and propensities that many faculty members *appropriately* prize in fellow academics, including omnivorous curiosity, habitual argumentativeness, analytical dexterity, and a penchant for counterintuitive insight. Many important virtues, including capacities for empathy, generosity, collegiality, and wisdom, often figure negligibly in faculty hiring and promotion. A negative evaluation of a person's likelihood for becoming a preeminent law professor is thus hardly tantamount to a negative evaluation of a person's overall abilities. There are scores of formidable attorneys who have never been invited to join a law school faculty, just as there are scores of estimable law school professors who have never been invited to join law firms or other endeavors. The absence of an offer to join the faculty of HLS should hardly be seen as a stigma.*

---

* Caroline Wittcoff voiced a contrary view. Representing the Harvard Law School Coalition for Civil Rights in its lawsuit against HLS, she charged the law school with having engaged in various forms of unlawful discrimination. Addressing the Supreme Judicial Court of Massachusetts, Wittcoff averred,

Bell attacked what he saw as the law school's misguided elitism. He asserted that there were "dozens" of minority candidates who had performed well in legal academia and would have been excellent hires despite the absence of certain conventional badges of merit, particularly outstanding grades, that HLS valued excessively. But anger made Bell's perceptions regarding hiring sadly unreliable. Denouncing a decision to decline a candidate whom he strongly backed, Bell wrote that "the [HLS] Appointments Committee justified [the candidate's] rejection by pointing to what they regarded as unimpressive credentials and unscholarly work."[89] That characterization was woefully inaccurate. The person to whom he alluded would never have been a visiting professor at HLS if the faculty had believed her credentials to be "unimpressive" and her writings to have been "unscholarly." She was seen as a plausible candidate for a tenured position precisely because her record was impressive. In the end, the faculty refrained from extending an offer. But that decision did not derive from a judgment that the candidate was weak; it derived from a judgment that while the candidate was strong, she was insufficiently outstanding, relative to others, to warrant an invitation to join the faculty. HLS did not and does not content itself with settling for a "performs well" standard. It has sought to hire and promote scholars who will hopefully reach the highest tier of their chosen specialty.

There are numerous considerations brought to bear in making such decisions. These include candidates' academic records (for example, grades, prizes, participation in law reviews), their writings, teaching, standing among peers, collegiality, institu-

---

When students at Harvard Law School sit in the classroom every day for three years and are never once taught by a single woman of color, or Latino, or Asian-American, or Native American, or openly gay and lesbian person, the discrimination that is behind this long history of exclusion sends students a devastating message: that while we are good enough to sit in the classrooms at Harvard Law, we're not good enough to sit on the faculty, and that's a stamping of a badge of inferiority.

Quoted in Eleanor Kerlow, *Poisoned Ivy: How Egos, Ideology, and Power Politics Almost Ruined Harvard Law School* (1994), 110. *See also* Darryl Royster Alexander, "A Rare Gesture of Protest," *New York Times*, April 29, 1990, www.nytimes.com ("The school's familiar response to Professor Bell's protest—it can't find anybody qualified—is one that has long rubbed many black Americans raw.").

tional citizenship, and likely trajectory. Many people—members of the faculty Appointments Committee, members of the faculty, the dean, the president of the university—have a say in the matter. Various decision makers attach differing weights to these considerations. Some attach importance to the subject mastered by a given candidate, favoring those who specialize in a subject for which there is deemed to be an institutional need (while concomitantly disfavoring those who specialize in subjects for which there exists no pressing institutional need). Other decision makers, by contrast, are inattentive to matters of institutional need and focus instead on what they take to be the particular merit of candidates considered separately and discretely, one by one. There is no clear, consistent protocol governing appointments. In Bell's time (and now), the HLS process for appointments and promotions (and that of all law schools of which I am aware) is messy, opaque, ad hoc, and subjective. A faculty resolution in 1986 stated, for instance, that "it is the sense of the faculty that the prima facie scholarship standard for promotion of assistant professors to tenure is the demonstration of promise of excellence in scholarship by means of substantial scholarly achievement of high quality."[90] The vagueness of this proposition puts me in mind of Justice Potter Stewart's quip about obscenity: I know it when I see it.

The subjectivity of the process, in conjunction with the dearth of minority hires, ought to have raised eyebrows and prompted inquiries—and it did. The HLS faculty in the 1980s and 1990s was roiled by debate about standards for hiring and promotion and about decisions in discrete cases.[91] By then, however, Bell eschewed debate, seeing it as a draining, digressive, distracting activity mainly engaged in by those who were either naive, complacent, or racist. Filing a complaint with the U.S. Department of Education against HLS,[92] he inveighed repeatedly against criteria—test scores, grades, law review participation, and similar signals of "merit"—that were, in his view, illicitly exclusionary.[93] Such barriers, he complained, "exclude on the basis of social class, as well as race."[94] But what about a requirement for a high school, college, or graduate school degree? Those markers, too, are far from infallible and fence out sectors of the population that are disproportionately poor and disproportionately people of color.

Are they illegitimate factors to consider in assessing prospective hires for professorial positions?

Courts have responded to disparate impact challenges to university criteria for faculty hiring and promotions by giving academic institutions a much greater degree of deference than that offered to employers engaged in the selection of employees who are deemed to be engaged in more routinized endeavors.[95] One gathers from the tenor of Bell's argument that he objected to such deference. He was convinced that conventional criteria "bear . . . little correlation to effective teaching or significant scholarship."[96] But Bell offered little substantiation for his claim. Without citing corroborating evidence he declared that "outstanding grades are as likely to signal undeveloped social skills as they are the interactional capability good teachers should possess" and that "empathy . . . is often found in people for whom law study was a challenge rather than in those who easily earned high grades."[97] These observations are mere stereotypical put-downs of "nerds." They don't build a case for abandoning widely used, long-established criteria or hint at even a moderately developed alternative regime of selection.

To his credit, Bell eschewed the hubris demonstrated by many people from modest origins who attain upward mobility. He avoided succumbing to the delusion that personal success arises wholly, or even predominantly, from personal virtue. He rejected the widespread fantasy of having made it "on his own" with no help from good luck or social conditions, including protest movements that have made possible the cultivation and manifestations of talents located in previously marginalized groups. Keenly aware of the communal roots of individual flourishing, Bell might have offered a useful antidote to the excesses of meritocratic individualism. But he grossly overcorrected and in so doing excessively demoted individual effort and talent in his portrayal of achievement. Describing his own emergence as a legal academic, Bell attributed his breakthrough not at all to his own labors but to the student dissidents who put pressure on the authorities at HLS. Self-abnegation of this sort had the bad consequence of obscuring the painstaking self-investment that was essential to his accomplishment. His tendency to minimize personal contribution also showed itself in the thinness of his recommendations on behalf of candidates he championed. When asked to react to the news that Lani Guinier had been invited to join the HLS faculty, becoming its first tenured woman of color, Bell said next to nothing about *her* writing, *her* teaching, *her* work as a practicing attorney, *her* promise.* He announced that "it is the Harvard Law School students who deserve credit for this appointment."[98]

While much of Bell's critique invokes disparate impact discrimination—exclusion stemming from negligently designed criteria—he also retained as part of his indictment a claim of disparate treatment discrimination: exclusion stemming from a race-specific intent to bar certain candidates. The writing that best illustrated this feature of Bell's thinking was his allegorical tale, mentioned above, "The Chronicle of the DeVine Gift."[99] In this story, as you will recall, Bell imagines how an elite, predominantly white law school would react to the prospect of hiring a black candidate—the Seventh Candidate—who, if hired, would increase the minority presence on the faculty to 25 percent. Bell creates a white dean who states that the school will not appoint this Seventh Candidate because doing so would, in his eyes, change the racial character of the school to an intolerable degree. According to Bell, the Seventh Candidate's effect on the racial makeup of the faculty would "threaten[], at some deep level, the white faculty members' sense of ideological hegemony."[100] In order to highlight what he perceives as the racism that affects even those institutions formally committed to affirmative action, Bell hypothesizes that the Seventh Candidate has impeccable credentials and is super-

---

* Before her appointment to the HLS faculty in 1998, Guinier was a professor at the University of Pennsylvania School of Law, a lawyer in the Civil Rights Division of the U.S. Department of Justice, and a litigator for the NAACP LDF. She earned her college degree from Radcliffe and her law degree from Yale Law School. She became the focus of national attention in 1993 when President William Jefferson Clinton nominated her to be assistant attorney general for civil rights and then withdrew his support in the face of opposition from conservatives. *See* Randall Kennedy, "Lani Guinier's Constitution," *American Prospect* (Fall 1993); Laurel Leff, "From Legal Scholar to Quota Queen: What Happens When Politics Pulls the Press into the Groves of Academe," *Columbia Journalism Review*, Sept.–Oct. 1993.

qualified by any reasonable standard.* Although Bell criticizes the conventional standards used to identify merit, his main point is a warning that even when blacks satisfy these standards, they can still expect to face discrimination, especially if whites become upset at the prospect of too many successful African Americans.

Fictional in its specifics, this allegory set forth what Professor Bell viewed as a realistic portrait of selective white law schools. Elsewhere he bluntly averred that "qualifications aside, law school faculty [at mainly white schools] consider their schools as 'white schools' and would resist hiring beyond a certain number of even the most qualified teachers of color."[101] At the time he was writing, considerable evidence suggested that few black candidates had attained the distinctions typically required for selection to elite law school faculties—the types of qualifications that Bell conferred upon the Seventh Candidate: super-high grades, law review membership, publications, prestigious clerkships. Indeed, some reports indicated that minority candidates with excellent conventional qualifications were in such short supply that those attaining them became the focus of veritable bidding wars.† Bell sidesteps the issue by recourse to poetic license: he *imagines* a black candidate who is superqualified by conventional measures but who is excluded nonetheless by naked prejudice.

---

* Bell's Seventh Candidate is "exceptionally able" with "impeccable" academic credentials. One of Bell's characters relates that the Seventh Candidate was

> the top student at our competitor school, . . . had edited the law review and written a superb student note. After clerking for a federal court of appeals judge and a U.S. Supreme Court Justice, he had joined a major New York City law firm where, after three years of work they rated "splendid," he was in line for early election to partnership.

Derrick Bell, *And We Are Not Saved: The Elusive Quest for Racial Justice* (1987), 142–43.

† Bell himself documented this response in describing the aggressive recruiting of an exceptional African American prospect by HLS. According to Bell, "When Harvard discovered Scott Brewer, a black who was the editor-in-chief of the *Yale Law Journal* and an outstanding student, [it] acted with as much speed and enthusiasm as anyone—including this critic—could ask." Derrick Bell, *Confronting Authority: Reflections of an Ardent Protester* (1994), 78. *See also* David A. Kaplan, "Letter Calls for Harvard Probe; Academic Freedom in Peril?," *National Law Journal*, Aug. 10, 1987, 28.

Bell eventually came to scoff at those—like me—who explained the small number of black legal academics at selective schools as mainly a function of the small pool of black candidates bearing superlative conventional indicia of achievement and promise. But he made little effort to engage their argument. He seemed to believe that it was self-evidently wrong and unworthy of debate. I wonder how he would have responded to a comparison of Thurgood Marshall's selection process for law clerks and HLS's selection process for junior professors. Justice Marshall hired several law clerks annually. During his first twelve years on the Court he hired only one black law clerk. During the next twelve years he hired six—or seven black clerks out of eighty altogether. The profiles of those he hired were strikingly similar to the profiles of law professors hired at HLS and similarly selective schools. He looked for rarefied grades, membership on law reviews, recommendations from a small number of "feeder" professors and judges, and graduation from an even smaller number of elite schools. Of the seven black clerks Justice Marshall hired, three attended Yale Law School and three attended HLS. None hailed from Howard, his alma mater, or any other historically black law school. Was Thurgood Marshall indifferent to matters of racial justice? Or did his hiring record reveal the consequences of societal racism that had tragically shrunk the pool of minority lawyers who had attained the indicia of merit that he deemed essential for clerks in his chambers?

Even if one believes—as did Bell—that conventional standards governing appointments are inadequate or misleading, it is still important to know why relatively few black candidates excel within those standards. Even if those standards are faulty, they are, nonetheless, influential. This is not to discourage efforts to unmask and reform criteria that fail to accomplish efficiently the purposes they purportedly serve. It is self-defeating, however, to leave unexplored why it is that widely accepted criteria adversely affect large numbers of minority candidates. The "pool problem" has long been in dire need of investigation. It is a subject, however, that Bell in his later years largely avoided.

Others concerned about black scholars and their reception have adopted a different stance. Although the esteemed historian

John Hope Franklin indignantly protested the racist belittlement to which he and other black historians were subjected during the Jim Crow era, he refused to exempt them (or himself) from critical evaluation, even though they worked under the pall of open, unapologetic, invidious racial discrimination. He maintained that even in the midst of injustice black scholars were still free to hone or neglect their talents. Writing about black historians in the 1940s and 1950s, Franklin observed,

> Many black scholars of my own generation were reluctant to prepare the kind of papers that were required for the national professional meetings in my field. One needed only to have attended the black professional meetings to see the difference in quality and the willingness of some black scholars to settle for much less than first-rate papers.[102]

Writing in 1962, the African American sociologist E. Franklin Frazier stated bluntly, "We have no . . . thinkers who command the respect of the intellectual community at large."* More recently, the conservative commentator Thomas Sowell has lamented academic "underachievement" by black students and professors,[103] as has Sowell's ideological opposite, the socialist scholar Cornel West. Echoing themes propounded by Frazier and Sowell, West charges that "mediocrity of various forms and in different contexts suffocates much of Black intellectual life."[104] He maintains

---

* E. Franklin Frazier, "The Failure of the Negro Intellectual," in *E. Franklin Frazier on Race Relations*, ed. G. Franklin Edwards (1968), 273. The Negro intellectual, Frazier charged, "[had] failed to study the problems of Negro life in America in a manner which would place the fate of the Negro in the broad framework of man's experience in this world." *Id.* at 274. Frazier continued, "[The black intellectual] has carried on all sorts of arguments in defense of the Negro but they were mainly designed to protect his own status and soothe his hurt self-esteem." *Id.* at 278; see also E. Franklin Frazier, *Black Bourgeoisie* (1957), 159 ("The lack of interest of the black bourgeoisie . . . in the broader issues facing the modern world is due to the fact that the Negro has developed no economic or social philosophy except the opportunistic philosophy that the black intelligentsia has evolved to justify its anomalous and insecure position.").

that "despite the larger numbers of Black scholars relative to the past (though still a small percentage in relation to white scholars), Black intellectual life is a rather depressing scene."* My point here is not to affirm Franklin, Frazier, Sowell, or West; I suspect that they are all too negative. Rather, my point is to affirm the usefulness of at least posing the questions they ask—questions that consider not only the possibility that certain black scholars are receiving less than their just due in terms of hiring, promotion, and other career-enhancing honors but also the possibility that certain black scholars, in attaining less acclaim than white peers, actually *are* receiving their just due.

Racism and complacency toward it are widespread influences in American life that are highly contagious, deeply destructive, and undoubtedly present in legal academia. But much more than prejudice or complacency within the ranks of university decision makers accounted for the absences against which Bell raged. Competition for entry into the professoriat comes at the end of a series of preparatory stages—elementary, secondary, collegiate, and professional schooling—at which blacks are disadvantaged in comparison to whites. To a large extent, the disadvantage stems from structural inequalities that produce racially disparate circumstances that affect aspirations, opportunities, and achievement. These patterns and their consequences constrict the number of minorities seeking to ascend the academic hierarchy.

Another explanation is that other opportunities lure potential black scholars into career paths that some find more attractive than what is on offer in universities. In the 1980s, Harvard Law School made offers of appointment to John Payton and Adebayo

---

* At another point, West writes,

> There has not been a time in the history of Black people in this country when the quantity of politicians and intellectuals was so great, yet the quality of both groups has been so low. Just when one would have guessed that Black America was flexing its political and intellectual muscles, *rigor mortis* seems to have set in.

Cornel West, "The Crisis of Black Leadership," *Zeta Magazine*, Feb. 1987, 22. "Why," he asks, "hasn't Black America produced intellectuals of the caliber of W. E. B. DuBois, Anna Cooper, E. Franklin Frazier, Oliver Cox, and Ralph Ellison in the past few decades?" *Id.*

Ogunlesi, both of whom embarked instead on highly successful nonacademic careers. Payton became a partner at a major firm and the director-counsel of the NAACP Legal Defense Fund. Ogunlesi, a former Marshall clerk, worked at a major firm before becoming a prodigiously successful banker. HLS and other selective law schools are unable to attract many people of all colors whom they might want to hire. There are those who would prefer to pursue ambitions other than becoming a law professor.

Alongside variables that affect entry into the professoriat are others that affect upward mobility within it. Because of their scarcity, minority academics find themselves beset by greater demands from students (particularly black students) and administrators than their white counterparts. For some, this added burden impedes efforts to produce top-grade legal scholarship. Another factor is self-limitation. "Too often," Professor Rennard Strickland observed, "minority faculty members sell their potential short. We accept [the whites'] stereotype that minority professors are incapable of producing first-rate scholarship. . . . It is far easier to talk about how busy we are, about the great demands on our time, about unfairness, . . . than it is to write books and articles."[105]

A number of explanations thus accounted for the paucity of black professors at many law schools. But Bell's writings increasingly focused exclusive attention on one—racially unfair regimes of selection—while ignoring others. A consequence is that those other impediments have received less remedial attention than they should have.

HLS can rightly be criticized on a variety of fronts. Until 1950 a gender bar rendered women ineligible as students. For decades thereafter, as students and professors, women were subjected to sexist mistreatment. The history of HLS reveals other injustices as well. Ideological repression surfaced in the 1990s when university authorities, concluding that leftist academics associated with critical legal studies exercised undue influence, acted to restrict their numbers.[106] On the racial front, HLS should have done more sooner to bring blacks (and other racial minorities) into the ranks of its faculty. Within the small pool of plausible hires were scholars to whom offers should have been made. There were reasonable grounds for reaching the conclusions the faculty reached.

Still, in retrospect I wish the votes had gone another way. The candidates in question were strong, and a small number of different hiring decisions might well have spared the HLS community untold hours of bitter conflict that could have been put to better use. I regret my own votes in some of those cases. I also regret having failed to repudiate a controversial HLS policy regarding lateral hires—that is, hires of professors visiting from other law schools. Derrick Bell did.[107] I wish that I had. Under this policy an offer to join the HLS faculty permanently could be extended only *after* a candidate had finished her visit, which usually entailed returning to her home institution. The purpose behind the policy was to discourage precipitous faculty decisions. The idea was to force the faculty to slow down when considering a candidate and to make sure that it did so outside the possibly distortive influence of a candidate's presence on campus. On several occasions when students requested that the faculty act favorably immediately with respect to a visiting minority professor, they were told that because of this policy no conclusive hiring decision could be made. The rationale behind the policy was dubious. The faculty routinely made tenure decisions regarding assistant professors who were present on campus. Pressure in cases involving people who had for years been part of the community was usually more intense than pressure in cases involving visitors. Yet nothing required the banishment of assistant professors while their elders determined their fates. Moreover, the policy was by no means ironclad. There were instances in which offers were extended to visitors during their stay at HLS. That these instances involved visitors who were white men exposed HLS, quite appropriately, to charges of hypocrisy and racial and gender bias.

I have had colleagues who were, I think, actively prejudiced along lines of gender and race. The very candidacy of a woman or racial minority seemed to spark their negative energies. Though their number was small, even a marginal vote can matter decisively in a close case. I don't recall an instance in which a decision turned on such a vote. But how can I know for sure? I regret having failed to speak out more loudly about my conviction that the votes of certain colleagues were tainted.

There was, then, some merit in Bell's critique of HLS. Alas, he debased it through exaggeration. His lamentations became parody.

IV

I first met Derrick in 1986 when he returned to HLS following his deanship at Oregon. I had joined the HLS faculty in 1984. When we met, he was fifty-six years old and I was thirty-two. He was a generous senior colleague, unfailingly attentive to requests for feedback on papers and inclined to praise enthusiastically the work of a junior colleague, especially a person like me—a younger black academic. When editors of journals or conveners of conferences asked him for the names of potential contributors, he recommended me on numerous occasions.

We seldom socialized together; I recall few shared lunches or dinners. But we did have one intimate bond: the early deaths of our spouses, both of whom we lost to cancer. My wife, Yvedt Matory, was a surgeon at the Brigham and Women's Hospital who specialized in the treatment of breast cancer, the malady that killed Jewel Bell, Derrick's first wife. Though she was not Jewel's doctor, Yvedt spent a considerable amount of time monitoring Jewel's care, explaining the treatment that she was receiving, discussing alternatives, and being present to lend support. I sometimes joined Yvedt at Jewel's hospital bedside. Derrick appreciated our solicitude. Later, I much appreciated his condolences when Yvedt died and his encouragement in the aftermath of that personal catastrophe.

That connection born of tragedy accentuated the awkwardness occasioned by increasingly bitter disagreements. Initially, as I have noted, Derrick supported me enthusiastically. He believed, he later wrote, that I began my career "with great promise" and he saw me as "a comrade." Then, in his view, I took a misguided turn. He disapproved of the way I came to teach the course on race relations law that he had pioneered, complaining that I had "dropped its advocacy orientation." "Disgruntled students," he noted, complained that I "spent more time challenging and even denigrating civil rights positions than . . . analyzing the continuing practices and policies of discrimination."[108] He also disapproved of what he saw as a disturbing turn in my writing, exemplified by an article that challenged arguments advanced by him, Richard Delgado, Mari Matsuda, and others associated with critical race theory. In "Racial Critiques of Legal Academia,"[109] I questioned two of their key theses. Their exclusion thesis contended that in legal academia the scholarship of professors of color was wrongfully ignored or undervalued. Their racial distinctiveness thesis maintained (1) that minority scholars have experienced racial oppression; (2) that that experience inclines them to view the world with a different perspective from white colleagues; and (3) that this different perspective displays itself in valuable ways in their scholarship. I argued that the CRT scholars had failed to support persuasively their allegation of racial discrimination or their claim that legal academic scholars of color produce a racially distinctive brand of valuable scholarship. Bell urged me to forgo publishing the piece, believing that those hostile to CRT would wield my assessment "as a club to denigrate and even deny tenure to young scholars who dared identify with the new movement."[110] When I declined to follow his advice, Bell reacted by stating publicly that the positive attention my critique attracted "shows that the media is ready to accord Kennedy that special celebrity status available to any black willing to speak for whites . . . who are unwilling to criticize blacks for the record. The list of blacks who achieve renown by serving as racial apologists is already too long. I regret that . . . Kennedy's article is read by so many as an audition to play the role of academic minstrel."[111]

I gather that what Derrick meant by "advocacy orientation" is an attitude of engagement in which the teacher is seeking to change the world, at least a bit, by shaping the perspectives of his or her students. Advocacy orientation is a commitment to challenging injustice and recommending reform. If this is indeed what Derrick meant, I agree with him. Where, then, did we disagree?

Derrick was supremely confident that he knew what policy positions were *the* correct positions to adopt and thus the ones to urge his students to follow. He was so confident that he became impatient with others who lacked his certitude. He displayed this impatience by routinely portraying opponents as racists, naïfs, or opportunists. I lack his certitude and believe that there is good reason to be open-minded about a variety of hotly contested debates regarding race policy. I therefore believe that a well-constructed course on race relations law should provide room for exploration of alternative resolutions to the dilemmas we face.

I suspect that the disgruntlement to which Derrick alluded stemmed from the displeasure of some students who resented taking a class on race relations law in which they were forced to understand and take seriously perspectives at odds with those that they embraced. That I scrutinized those perspectives searchingly and attempted to present opposing viewpoints sympathetically was seen by some students as a betrayal—an opinion that Derrick largely shared.

One might have thought that the author of "Serving Two Masters," which suffered its own confrontation with ideological excommunication, would have understood that determining how best to proceed requires more than an emotional commitment to "doing the right thing." Useful prescription also requires an intellectual investment in figuring out what doing the right thing entails. There are, after all, many areas in which people who are thoroughly committed to advancing the interests of blacks disagree over how best to proceed. Some champions of African American uplift urge rejection of integrationist educational policy. Others counsel pursuing integrationist strategies. Some champions of black advancement argue in favor of seeking better housing and other opportunities by encouraging the dispersal of black ghetto dwellers. Others argue in favor of consolidating the strength of black ghettos and bringing greater opportunities to inner-city blacks where they already reside. Debates rage over whether it is better to elect as many black representatives as possible from majority-black voting districts or to more fully spread the influence of black voters, even at the cost of sacrificing dominance in a certain number of voting districts; whether it is better to invest more in securing public safety in high-crime, majority-minority neighborhoods or to scale back policing given mass incarceration; whether it is better to prefer to place black orphaned children in black adoptive families or to place such children in the first adoptive homes available, regardless of race; whether redistributive reforms primarily animated by a desire to help blacks are best packaged as race-specific or race neutral. These issues are not, forgive the expression, black and white. They are complicated and filled with ambiguity and paradox and should be studied as such.

A second area of disagreement arose from differing premises concerning the normative aims of a course on race relations law. Derrick assumed that its aim should be to advance the interests of black people. As I indicated above, what actually constitutes the best interests of black people is more contested and more difficult to discern than Derrick recognized. But even if a consensus could be reached, major difficulties would still loom over an approach, like Derrick's, which measures the political virtue of any given policy in terms of "Is it good for the blacks?" Blacks, after all, constitute only one portion of the American polity. What is good for that portion will likely often be consonant with social justice. But that need not always be the case. What is most immediately advantageous to blacks might not be what is most immediately advantageous to other groups whose claims are more compelling. When such conflicts arise, I see no reason to prefer what blacks desire.

A good course on race relations law in the United States would show that any group, like any person, is capable of perpetrating racial harms upon others. It would show how people of Chinese ancestry have attempted to deflect anti-Asian animus by scapegoating Indians and blacks;[112] how some Native Americans enslaved African Americans even as they themselves were being cruelly ousted from their lands by Euro-Americans;[113] how people of African ancestry have attempted to escape antiblack animus by scapegoating Native Americans;[114] how Jews have attempted to escape anti-Semitism by scapegoating Negroes;[115] how some African Americans have racially targeted Korean Americans;[116] and how, of course, whites of various ethnicities have attempted to subordinate blacks and other peoples of color. Derrick was really interested only in the last of these topics. When one looks up the key term "racism" in the third edition of *Race, Racism, and American Law*, one finds the following entry: "Racism—See White racism."[117] That remark stems from a theory that racially oppressed peoples cannot be "racist" because "racism" can only be manifested by groups with power. According to this theory, "racism" equals prejudice plus power. Thus, while blacks can be "prejudiced," they cannot be "racist," because they lack the power to effectuate any prejudices they harbor. A good course on race relations law would enable a student to see the speciousness of this theory. Blacks do occupy positions of authority from which they could, if they so choose, use their power to effectuate prejudices. Scores of cities, police departments, military units, prisons, personnel offices, and social service agencies are directed by blacks who, like their white counterparts, make numerous low-visibility, discretionary choices that are routinely granted tremendous deference both within and without the bureaucracies in which they function. For eight years the president of the United States was black!

Beyond the empirical fact that blacks can and do exercise appreciable amounts of power in America, even while they remain targets of racism, is the fact that circumstances can change rapidly, elevating those who have been oppressed and lowering those who have been ascendant. It is important, then, to be attentive to the moral hygiene of everyone, including subordinates. World history shows that persons and groups who have been oppressed are quite capable of visiting injustices on others.

From Derrick's vantage, even worse than my writings and classes were my deviations from Bellian orthodoxy when it came to judging candidates for appointment to the faculty. During Derrick's final stint at HLS, a black candidate would have had to have been blatantly incompetent to forfeit Bell's support, which meant, practically speaking, that he favored *all* black candidates because no one blatantly incompetent would have made it to the floor of a faculty meeting. Indeed, Bell let it be known that, absent extraordinary circumstances, he would never vote against a candidate of color. That stance facilitated his marginalization, guaranteeing that his appraisals would be substantially if not wholly discounted. He never served on the Appointments Committee at HLS, the committee principally charged with identifying professorial prospects and making hiring recommendations to the faculty. I was put on the Appointments Committee the year I received tenure and served on it on several occasions in subsequent years. In assessing candidates, racial minority status figured positively into my calculations, though much less so than Derrick thought appropriate. In a close case, I thought a thumb on the scale was proper, while for him a body on the scale was acceptable.

Already deteriorating, our relationship worsened when Derrick publicly revealed my support for one black woman candidate and my opposition to another.[118] He never requested permission to publicize my positions and was certainly aware that views and votes about appointments were confidential matters that were intended for the eyes and ears only of faculty colleagues. That breach of confidentiality was deeply painful and injected a poisonous distrust into our relationship.

The duty to respect confidentiality can be outweighed, of course, by a countervailing imperative, for instance, the duty to save a life or to expose serious malfeasance. I maintain only that a colleague has a presumptive duty to respect confidential faculty deliberations. Derrick offered nothing that can reasonably be interpreted as an effort to overcome that presumption. He evinced no concern with confidentiality at all. Perhaps his thinking was that he owed no obligation to follow the conventions of what he saw as a rotten institution. Here, however, he was not simply defying an institutional protocol; he was exposing a colleague who had considered him a friend.

Colleagues have suggested that I ought to be angry with Derrick for things that he wrote about me. He once declared, for example,

> It galls me that black scholars who labor in relative obscurity can leap to instant attention and acclaim by criticizing their black colleagues. This happened when Professor Randall Kennedy at Harvard Law School asserted that minority scholars have no special legitimacy in writing about race, and that their scholarship, measured by traditional standards, is flawed.[119]

Some readers of that passage see it as a charge of self-aggrandizing Uncle Tomism. Derrick, however, does not attribute bad motives to me or the others whom he criticizes. He expressly disclaimed making the charge "that black scholars who gain enhanced standing because of the anti-black or anti–civil rights tone of their writing have taken their positions for personal gain." Conceding that "some, perhaps all, [of the people he criticizes] actually believe what they're saying," he objects to "their refusal to come to grips with the effect of their statements."[120] Some readers will pay no attention to Derrick's disclaimer. But that isn't his fault. Furthermore, in my view, motives are a legitimate subject of inquiry. Motives matter. I would evaluate a book differently than I would ordinarily, for example, if I knew that an author was molding his scholarship precisely to nab a plum post in the White House. So I am not angered by questions that focus on whether I have taken positions opportunistically. It is true that some people who articulate views congenial to influential gatekeepers do so strategically to reap premiums in the marketplace of policy analysis, punditry, foundation sinecures, universities, and government.

It is also true, though, that racial advocates of the sort that Derrick exemplifies reap premiums. Derrick himself was hardly a victim of any gulag. He was a tenured professor at Harvard University. He presented his work in the legal academy's most prestigious journals. He was never more of a star than after his highly publicized decision to leave HLS. Upon leaving, he was hardly consigned to the wilderness. He obtained an ongoing visiting professorship at New York University. He sought and received adulation and enjoyed the heady and delicious sense of having acted nobly. He ought not be viewed as a martyr.

I admire Derrick for having had the skill, perseverance, and resiliency to survive and indeed thrive professionally in the HLS of the late 1960s—an institution that was hardly welcoming.[121] He had to contend with university authorities and students who imposed upon him a wholly different set of expectations from those imposed upon his peers. He had to grapple with the lowered expectations of colleagues who doubted that he could become a first-rate teacher and scholar. He had to shoulder the heightened expectations of black students who looked to him for counsel and support and saw him as their ambassador to the university administration. He had to confront what he termed "the perversity of the racial time clock" during a period of racial transition when, in his experience, "the possibility of equal opportunity brought to blacks, who sought it, more frustration than fulfillment."[122]

V

Throughout his life, Derrick seems to have been constantly on the lookout for people to help and causes to promote. In August

1967, he received a letter from Elnora Fondren, who had been a young client of his in an NAACP LDF school desegregation suit in Clarksdale, Mississippi. She told him the good news that she had graduated from high school with honors. She also told him that she was in desperate need of money to purchase winter clothing because she hoped to travel north for additional education. Derrick responded with characteristic bigheartedness. He wrote a memorandum to colleagues in the HEW Office of Civil Rights describing Ms. Fondren and her predicament and eliciting their help. Following through, he sent her a congratulatory letter and check.[123]

Two years later Derrick found himself in the vicinity of Brandeis University in Waltham, Massachusetts. He encountered a man who worked as a cook at the university. The man was running late for various reasons and was deeply worried about showing up tardily. Derrick not only gave this man, a complete stranger, a lift in his car; he also volunteered to vouch for the man. When they arrived at the university, the cook's coworkers and supervisor cruelly belittled him. Derrick responded by writing a detailed account to the university's president.[124] He was subsequently assured that the cook would henceforth be treated appropriately.

Derrick defended, nurtured, encouraged, and inspired scores of students and professors who have generated a steady stream of appreciative testimonials.* Professor Henry McGee Jr. spoke of

---

* While a student at HLS, Barack Obama took no classes with Derrick but was nonetheless moved to write him a note of appreciation. The future president stated that it was Bell's presence that "in large part brought [him] to Harvard in the first place. . . . I was inspired with the belief that . . . I would meet people like yourself who had a commitment to the struggle for equality and the experience and erudition to translate broad goals into concrete practice. . . . I doubt that I could have maintained my moral compass over the past three years had I not had you there, speaking out and challenging the conventions that we all have a tendency to take for granted." Quoted in David J. Garrow, *Rising Star: The Making of Barack Obama* (2017), 446. *See also* Steven W. Bender, "Derrick Bell: Oregon Trailblazer," 36 *Seattle University Law Review* ix (2013); Keith Boykin, "Remembering Derrick Bell," *Huffington Post*, Dec. 6, 2011; I. Bennett Capers, "Derrick Bell's Children," 2 *Columbia Journal of Race and Law* 6 (2012); andré douglas pond cummings, "Derrick Bell: Godfather Provocateur," 28 *Harvard Journal on Racial and Ethnic Justice* 51 (2012); Norman Dorsen, "Tribute to Derrick Bell," 69 *New York University Annual Survey of American Law* 21 (2013); Vinay Harpalani,

how Derrick "was never so busy that he could not extend a help-ing hand."[125] Professor Patricia Williams credited Derrick with being the only reason she completed her course of study at HLS: "He imbued legal education with a sense of purpose and respon-sibility: we weren't there for ourselves alone, but had to live up to a calling."[126] According to Professor Williams, Derrick's "door was always open," and "he made other doors open, too. . . . [He] created family in the unlikely setting of the law school."[127] It was Derrick's encouragement, Williams recalls, that prompted her to become a law professor. Professor Adrien K. Wing described Der-rick as the "replacement for the intellectual and spiritual father that [she] lost at an early age."[128] Professor Cheryl Harris similarly credits Derrick, noting that he inspired her, offered suggestions that improved her scholarship, and assisted her rise professionally. Bell showed, she wrote, "dedication to struggle and a tremendous love of teaching that was contagious. Sometimes we argued . . . [but that] never changed the fact that when we met again, he would still start the same way—'Chile, I've been thinking about you.'"[129]

VI

In the final months of his life in 2011, I spoke with Derrick twice. The first time I called to tell him that I had heard that he was ill, that I was pulling for him, and that I was grateful for all that he had done for me. He discussed his impending end with

"From Roach Powder to Radical Humanism: Derrick Bell's 'Critical' Consti tutional Pedagogy," 36 *Seattle University Law Review* xxiii (2013); Charles R. Lawrence III, "Doing 'the James Brown' at Harvard: Professor Derrick Bell as Liberationist Teacher," 8 *Harvard BlackLetter Law Journal* 263 (1991); Robin A. Lenhardt, "A Legacy of Teaching," 2 *Columbia Journal of Race and Law* 24 (2012); Martha Minow, "Storytelling and Political Resistance: Remembering Derrick Bell (with a Story About Dalton Trumbo)," 28 *Harvard Journal on Racial and Ethnic Justice* 1, 2 (2012) ("No personal action [by Bell] produced more endur-ing effects than his loving mentorship of generations of students."); Peggy A. Nague, "Tribute to Derrick Bell," 36 *Seattle University Law Review* xxxix (2013); Gabrielle Prisio, "Tribute to Derrick Bell," 69 *New York University Annual Survey of American Law* 13 (2013); John Sexton, "Tribute to Derrick Bell," 69 *New York University Annual Survey of American Law* 1 (2013); Adrien K. Wing, "Derrick Bell: Tolling in Protest," 12 *Harvard BlackLetter Law Journal* 161 (1995).

aplomb and declared that he felt himself to be supremely lucky in having been able to marry Janet Dewart Bell, with whom he had spent years of happy, delightful, and productive companionship. A few weeks later he called to ask whether I'd be willing to teach a session of his seminar at NYU Law School. His illness and treatments were preventing him from attending to his classes as fully as he would have liked. Throughout his career, Derrick had been punctilious in the fulfillment of his obligations. It pained him that illness was interfering with what was clearly going to be his valedictory class. I jumped at the chance to participate. I was honored by his invitation and told him so. That was the final time we exchanged words. I taught the seminar a week after he died.

3

The George Floyd Moment:
Promise and Peril[1]

The killing of George Floyd by a police officer in Minneapolis on May 25, 2020, and the ongoing responses to it induce a bewildering whiplash of emotions and impressions.

One is horrified by the videotape of Floyd's demise. He dies beneath the knee of an arrogant police officer who, callously disregarding the pleas of onlookers, nonchalantly crushes and suffocates an unarmed man who had been arrested on suspicion of passing a $20 counterfeit bill. One is terrified by the realization that the gratuitous police violence inflicted upon Floyd was by no means an aberration. Every day in every part of America, people of all backgrounds, but especially people of color, are menaced by poorly regulated police. One is disturbed by the knowledge that, absent the fortuity of the videotape, the circumstances of Floyd's death would have probably been effectively covered up and buried. One is troubled by knowing that even with the evidence at hand, securing a conviction and appropriate punishment is by no means guaranteed; police caught red-handed abusing civilians have frequently escaped accountability.

At the same time, much of the response to Floyd's killing has been remarkable and should be uplifting. People of all races, all ages, all gender identifications, and all party affiliations have raised their voices. Tens of thousands have taken to the streets braving the risks associated with the pandemic and panicky law enforcement. They acted out of grief for Floyd, determined to make sure that the crime inflicted upon him did not go unpunished. They acted out of solidarity with other demonstrators who were mistreated by police. They acted out of revulsion for the antics of President Donald Trump, who, far from displaying any empathy with those devastated by Floyd's death, tried to vilify and intimidate them and appeal to the nethermost instincts of his electoral base. The low point in this effort was the widely mocked photo opportunity in which, having deployed police and National Guard personnel to clear a path with batons, flash-bangs, and tear gas, Trump stood in front of St. John's Episcopal Church across the street from the White House holding aloft a Bible.

The breadth and intensity of the expressions of bereavement, solidarity, sympathy, and demands for reform are what have made this period feel so promising. Organizers hailing from across the spectrum of progressive activism have, to a large extent, conducted themselves admirably, eliciting broad participation and infusing supporters with fervor and resolve. After years of often overlooked work, they have clearly honed their skills and become remarkably effective agitators. These are the organizers, almost all of whom are associated with Black Lives Matter, who are most responsible for drawing and channeling the massed dissent that, persisting and growing day after day, has seized the attention of the nation and the world. An impressive feature of their leadership has been their loud, clear, unapologetic insistence upon *disciplined* militancy. Knowing that looting and random violence are discrediting in the eyes of many people—including African Americans—to whom they want to appeal, they wisely eschewed the hooliganism that right-wing commentators seize upon and exaggerate to besmirch protests that have been overwhelmingly peaceful.

That the influence of the antiracist protest has extended far beyond the precincts of those typically present at Black Lives Matter rallies is substantiated by polling. One survey reports that in the two weeks following the killing of Floyd, "American voters' support for the Black Lives Matter movement increased almost as much as it had in the preceding two years." Another poll found that in the summer of 2020, 76 percent of Americans considered racism and discrimination a "big problem," up twenty-six points from 2015.

Figures that seldom participate in polarizing racial controversies found themselves stepping forward, or being pushed, to take a stand. In a speech to graduates of the National Defense University, General Mark Milley, chair of the Joint Chiefs of Staff, apologized for walking with Trump to the church photo op. He said that his presence "in that moment and in that environment created a perception of the military involved in domestic politics." That was the most publicized portion of his speech and understandably so. Here was the country's top military officer apologizing for being seen with the commander in chief! What received too little attention, however, was the large portion of Milley's speech in which he identified racism, condemned it, specified its legacy in the military, and committed to making the armed forces more racially equitable. He said that he was "outraged" by the "senseless and brutal" killing of Floyd. His death, the general said, "amplified the pain, the frustration, and the fear that so many of our fellow Americans live with day in and day out. The protests that have ensued, not only speak to his killing, but also to the centuries of injustice towards African Americans." Then, displaying the reach of cultural revisionism championed by initiatives such as *The New York Times*'s 1619 Project, General Milley went on to say, "What we are seeing is the long shadow of our original sin in Jamestown 401 years ago. . . . We are still struggling with racism, and we have much work to do. Racism and discrimination, structural preferences, patterns of mistreatment, and unspoken and unconscious bias have no place in America and they have no place in our Armed Forces."

Notable, too, was the statement by the bishop of the Episcopal Diocese of Washington, D.C., Mariann Edgar Budde, who complained loudly about Trump's use of Bibles and churches as props in the service of his right-wing agenda. Disgusted by Trump, she excoriated the president but also focused on key problems that preceded him and that will outlast his misrule:

> It's past time to fix a law that allows police officers and vigilantes to go unpunished for crimes against people of color. It's past time to correct the gross disparities in

health care that Covid-19 has revealed. It's past time to change economic and educational systems that privilege white people.

Even organizations that are normally defiantly immune to antiracist demands have recently succumbed. At the prompting of its only top-ranked black driver, Bubba Wallace, NASCAR banned the Confederate Battle Flag from its events. Wallace now races in a car emblazoned with "Black Lives Matter." Likewise, Roger Goodell, commissioner of the National Football League, flipped dramatically. Previously he threatened or punished players who demonstrated on the field against police brutality. Now he sang a new tune:

> We, the NFL, condemn racism and the systematic oppres-
> sion of Black People. We, the NFL, admit we were wrong
> for not listening to NFL players earlier and encourage all
> to speak out and peacefully protest. We, the NFL, believe
> Black Lives Matter.

In a letter to customers, Bloomingdale's acknowledged that "systemic racism" had been "woven in to the fabric of our nation" but "has no place in our company." Bloomingdale's asserted that it had "zero tolerance for racism" because "Black lives must matter." Similar messages have been prominently displayed by Amazon, McDonald's, even Walmart. Of course, much of this is merely opportunistic branding. If these firms are sincerely committed to social justice, including racial equity, the first thing they should do is offer underpaid labor decent wages and benefits. Their racial justice advertising, however, is significant. It shows the gale-force energy unleashed by the protests. Clearly these profit-maximizing firms are determined to be on what they perceive as the side of these controversies that their most valued customers favor. The advertising is also important because it confers added legitimacy upon the protest.

A great challenge that faces any protest movement is winning victories that can establish roots that enable reformers to with-stand not only backlash but something even more fearsome—the dulling power of inertia. Establishmentarians know that fervor, for all its potentiality, eventually subsides. When the crowds go home, bureaucracies continue to do the prosaic tasks that society requires. It is therefore imperative to reprogram bureaucracies through legislation and similar specific, enduring interventions. The protesters behind the George Floyd moment have succeeded in winning a few such victories. In New York, for example, lawmakers enacted legislation that criminalized the use of choke holds by police and that repeals a policy that kept police disciplinary records secret. Such steps, however, are hardly sufficient. Policing as currently practiced is riddled with still larger problems that need attention. What other reforms are urgently needed?

In his excellent book *When Police Kill*, Professor Franklin E. Zimring argues that fatalities would be substantially diminished if police authorities embraced the belief that the preservation of the lives of civilians is a compelling aim of police policy. Zimring writes that to effectuate that belief, the most important things that police authorities can do are promulgate clear restrictions on the circumstances in which officers are permitted to use deadly force and vigorously enforce those restrictions. Another needed reform is the modification, if not the elimination, of "qualified immunity," a judge-made doctrine that insulates police from liability for violations of civil rights in circumstances in which the precise conduct in question has not previously been declared illegal. The poorly reasoned judicial expansion of qualified immunity has let police off the hook in egregious cases in which culpability is obvious. Another needed reform is the paring of legislation and provisions in union contracts that frustrate efforts to hold police accountable for misconduct. A commonsense proposal for which it is difficult to imagine reasoned opposition is simply requiring data collection to enable the public to know about citizen complaints and the way they are resolved. Businesses constantly audit their agents to determine whether they are interacting properly with customers and potential customers. Police agencies and the officials who oversee them ought to do something similar. There has been a lot of talk lately about police "bad apples." Yet in many locales there exist no protections against police malpractice recidivism. Procedures should be instituted to prevent officers who have been disciplined (or who are facing discipline) in one jurisdiction from moving on, without notice, to another. These are some of the many concrete steps that can and should be taken. Whether these initiatives are put on the path to becoming binding policies will tell us a lot about whether the George Floyd moment will mark a turning point toward effective police reform or instead dissipate with little enduring effect.

The obstacles facing racial justice activists are daunting. Policing in the United States is decentralized with some eighteen thousand police autonomous agencies. We saw how difficult it was to even begin to investigate, monitor, and punish priestly sexual misconduct within the hierarchy of the Roman Catholic Church. Policing the police will be a much larger, hugely more arduous enterprise. Even when ridiculously overprotective laws or policies are pruned away, the essentially sound fundamentals of due process will often make the imposition of accountability hard to effectuate.

Then there is the double sidedness of policing. Police protection against criminality is most needed in the very communities in which uprisings against police authorities are most intense, which highlights the bind in which African American communities have long been stuck. They suffer from legal under-protection (as when officers fail to protect them against criminal misbehavior by fellow officers and others) and simultaneously they suffer from over-policing (as when officers subject them to a type of surveillance and interference that is typically absent from white communities). The situation would be less vexing if one could responsibly demand simply abolishing police. But one cannot responsibly urge that course (though some protesters do). Police are an essential public service that are especially important to the well-being of those without the means to hire private police protection.

The difficulties run deeper still. Passing laws and promulgating new policies, though crucial, are just a beginning; afterward, there remains the difficult task of enforcement. That will turn on political will, which rests on tricky currents of popular sentiment. We need to be careful when deciphering the complexities of public opinion in this massive country of ours. Much attention has been focused upon whites who, prompted by black friends and allies, have enlisted in strenuous efforts to confront their own prejudice, acknowledge their own misbegotten privilege, and subordinate their own vanity in preference to leadership undertaken by people of color who have long been marginalized. The emergence of "woke" white people is something to behold! Although the virtue signaling of some is preposterous and annoying, overall there is much that is encouraging about this development. Never in American history have there been more ordinary white people willing to demonstrate forcefully and publicly on behalf of black people in the teeth of disapproving officials. But we dare not overlook those large multitudes who remain in deep denial about the facts of life in our pigmentocracy. This includes white downwardly mobile working-class people who live in pinched circumstances that make it difficult for them to feel privileged (though in terms of race they are). An upshot of Black Lives Matter is that for increasing numbers of Americans the black victim of police violence is the most salient racial image that comes to mind when considering the relationship between the words "race" and "police." At the same time, across large swaths of America, blackness remains closely associated not with victimization but with perpetration. For many, the face of crime remains a feared black face. That visceral apprehension will, alas, play a major role in ongoing struggles over racial justice in policing and other domains.

4

Isabel Wilkerson,
the Election of 2020, and Racial Caste[1]

Late in her book *Caste: The Origins of Our Discontents*, Isabel Wilkerson recounts a conversation in 2018 with the author Taylor Branch on the state of race relations in America. Branch described the situation as reminiscent of the 1950s on the eve of the Second Reconstruction. Wilkerson countered that the situation was reminiscent of the approximately seventy years beginning around 1880, when white supremacism defied the promised antiracism of the First Reconstruction. Branch's optimism soon waned. He declared that the key question of the moment was, given a choice between democracy and whiteness, how many Americans "would choose whiteness"? Wilkerson writes that "we let that settle in the air, neither of us willing to hazard a guess."

The outcome of the 2020 presidential election offers an ambiguous answer. By selecting Joe Biden and Kamala Harris, the U.S. electorate dodged immediate disaster by depriving Donald Trump of a second term. In a surge of voting, sometimes undertaken at personal risk because of the pandemic and sometimes undertaken at substantial inconvenience because of efforts to discourage participation, many millions chose democracy. There were others, however, quite willing to compromise if not subvert democracy by supporting an incumbent president who openly attacked norms of fair electoral contestation with a campaign of lying, intimidation, and attempted vote suppression. It is sad but true: some seventy-four million voters preferred Trump. A substantial number of them appear all too ready to choose whiteness over democracy.

Wilkerson seeks to reveal the lineage of anti-black racism in America. Hasn't this tragic tale been told at length before? Yes, it has. Winthrop Jordan's *White over Black: American Attitudes Toward the Negro, 1550–1812*, first published in 1968, remains unsurpassed in its analysis of the origins of Anglo-American Negrophobia. And there exists a library of books exposing the centrality of racial slavery, the betrayal of Reconstruction, the depredations of Jim Crow segregation, the resistance to the civil rights movement, and the persistence of the race line. But the educational radiations of even great books fade quickly, while there exists a constant need to instruct newly maturing audiences. The great Samuel Johnson once observed that "people need to be reminded more often than they need to be instructed." *Caste* is an elaborate reminder of things that many Americans of all races would just as soon forget. It is a catalog of racial degradation.

Wilkerson is an accomplished curator of racial wrongs. The offense she mines most deeply is slavery, noting that "the vast majority of African-Americans who lived in this land in the first 246 years of what is now the United States lived under the terror of people who had absolute power over their bodies and their very breath, subject to people who faced no sanction for any atrocity they could conjure." Wilkerson impresses upon readers in vivid detail what slavery meant, showing how "loving mothers and fathers, pillars of their communities, personally inflicted gruesome tortures upon their fellow human beings." She quotes the Virginia General Assembly mandating in 1662 that "all children borne in this country shall be held bond or free only according to the conditions of the mother," a provision that revised the English common law under which children inherited the status of the father. This revision was an acknowledgment of the frequency with which enslaved black women were bearing children fathered by white masters. The revision was also an incentive for sexual exploitation to continue because children born of it enlarged masters' estates. This provision, Wilkerson writes, "converted the black womb into a profit center, as neither mother nor child could make a claim against an upper-caste man, and no child springing from a black womb could escape condemnation to the lowest rung."

The mistreatment of black women under slavery has seldom received the attention it warrants. Abolitionists did focus upon this feature of "the peculiar institution"; it was, for example, an important aspect of Harriet Beecher Stowe's *Uncle Tom's Cabin*. But after the Civil War, when defeated Confederates and their allies succeeded in concocting an influential myth of plantation benevolence, mention of the slave regime's pervasive sexual criminality was resolutely repressed. It remained, however, an excruciating presence in the minds of many blacks. "I hate every drop of the rapist's blood that's in me," Malcolm X declared. This summer, during the George Floyd moment, the black poet Caroline Randall Williams authored a striking column in *The New York Times* challenging the valorization of Confederates by monuments across the country, but particularly in the South. "If they want monuments," she wrote, "well, then, my body is a monument." Damning her white male ancestors, she observed, "I have rape colored skin."

Wilkerson is similarly attentive to the sexual tribulations of black men, particularly their victimization at the hands of those who have believed widespread tales that black men are obsessed with white women and thus threaten the purity of white bloodlines. She describes in detail the lynchings of black men accused of sexual crimes against white women. The most memorable of these, however, involves neither a man nor an accusation of rape. In 1943 in Live Oak, Florida, a fifteen-year-old black boy named Willie James Howard sent a Christmas card to a white girl named Cynthia. When he learned that his card might have displeased the girl, Howard wrote a note of apology in which he said, "I know you don't think much of our kind of people but we don't hate you, all we want [is] to be your friends." The next day, in retribution for this violation of racial etiquette, the girl's father and two other white men dragged Willie James and his father to the banks of the Suwannee River. They "hog-tied Willie James and held a gun to his head. They forced him to jump and forced his father at gunpoint to watch him drown. Held captive and outnumbered as the father was, he was helpless to save his only child." The men who committed this crime admitted that they abducted the boy but claimed that he jumped into the river on his own. No criminal prosecution against them was ever undertaken.

Confronting one of the great mysteries of modern times, Wilkerson asks how it was that the America that twice elected Barack Obama to the presidency could turn around and elect Donald Trump? For her, Obama's election amounted to the "greatest departure from the script of the American caste system." She suggests, though, that there were indications from the start that Obama's ascendancy would prove to be less a harbinger of new possibilities than a miracle with little likelihood of repetition. "To break more than two centuries of tradition and birthright," she observes, "it would take the human equivalent of a supernova." Noting that Obama is the child of a white American mother and a black man born in Africa, Wilkerson hypothesizes that the former president's origin story freed many whites inclined to support him from having to think about commonplace racism or commonplace blacks. White folks, she ventures, "could regard him with curiosity and wonderment and even claim him as part of themselves, if they chose." Even so, only 43 percent of white voters supported Obama in 2008 and only 39 percent supported him in 2012.

In Wilkerson's view, the story of the white reaction that culminated in the election of Donald Trump is largely the tale of a massive racial freak-out. Many whites have been unhinged, she argues, by anxieties over racial status. They fear the demographic transformation that will make them a minority in a few decades. And they resent the emergence of people of color who are sufficiently assertive to proclaim the virtue of being unapologetically black. Many millions of white Americans grew up under the spell of an unspoken curriculum which taught that the United States was a white man's country. For them, the spectacle of a black family occupying the White House was shocking indeed.

Many commentators have struggled to explain why whites of modest means vote for Republican candidates whose pro-rich economic policies seem so apparently at odds with their class interests. For Wilkerson, the explanation is that many of the middling whites who vote for Republicans are not victims of false consciousness but consumers of caste consciousness. In supporting politicians who are either consciously or unconsciously committed to perpetuating the traditional racial pecking order, many whites *are* voting their interests—as they define those interests. The comfort of being ahead of "them," even while sinking, is a sufficient psychological premium that many whites are willing to "forgo health insurance, risk contamination of the water and air, and even die to protect their long-term interest in [America's racial] hierarchy as they know it." That is why, Wilkerson concludes, in "the pivotal election of 2016 . . . the majority of whites voted for the candidate [Donald Trump] who made the most direct appeals to the characteristic most rewarded in the caste system. They went with the aspect of themselves that grants them the most power and status in the hierarchy."

Wilkerson argues that racism is a toxin that hurts not only racial minorities but the entire population. She insists that racism, as much as anything else, accounts for the primitive state of American social welfare policy, vitiating the interracial communal empathy needed to undergird generous governmental supports for those in need. "Caste does not explain everything in American life," Wilkerson observes, "but no aspect of American life can be fully understood without considering caste." It is because of racial caste that "the United States, for all its wealth and innovation, lags in major indicators of quality of life among the leading countries in the world." Infant mortality in the United States is the highest among the richest nations. American women are more at risk of death during pregnancy and childbirth than women in other wealthy countries. The United States has the highest incarceration rate in the world, while life expectancy is the lowest among the eleven highest-income countries (beneath the U.K., Canada, Germany, Australia, Japan, Sweden, France, the Netherlands, Switzerland, and Denmark).

Wilkerson's deployment of the idea of caste, however, sheds little new light on our understanding of racism. She writes that "caste is the infrastructure of our divisions. It is the architecture of human hierarchy, the subconscious code of instructions for maintaining, in our case, a four-hundred-year-old social order." She observes that a caste system "uses rigid, often arbitrary boundaries to keep the ranked groupings apart, distinct from one another and in their assigned places." She posits that in the American caste system "race is the primary tool and the visible decoy, the front man, for caste." She declares that while "caste is fixed and rigid," "race is fluid and superficial, subject to periodic redefinition." These various formulations, albeit initially interesting, do not offer substantial new guidance in exploring the American social landscape.

Nor did I glean much from her comparisons of antiblack repression in the United States and the repression of Jews in Germany and untouchables in India. She portrays these examples of oppression as unique, writing that "throughout human history, three caste systems have stood out. The tragically accelerated, chilling, and officially vanquished caste system of Nazi Germany. The lingering, millennia-long caste system of India. And the shape-shifting, unspoken, race-based caste pyramid in the United States. Each version relied on stigmatizing those deemed inferior to justify the dehumanization necessary to keep the lowest-ranked people at the bottom and to rationalize the protocols of enforcement." I am sure that a rigorous, systematic, comparative study could produce an important payoff. But doing that is a tall order beyond the framework Wilkerson constructs. Her effort at comparison is propelled, she says, by the singularity of these three regimes. To make that claim of uniqueness persuasively, however, one would have had to study many brutally repressive, rigidly hierarchical societies across the globe and over many eras and then make comparisons among them. There is little indication of such study in Wilkerson's volume.

Wilkerson writes that while her book "seeks to consider the effects on everyone caught in the hierarchy, it devotes significant attention to the poles of the American caste system, those at the top, European Americans, who have been its primary beneficiaries, and those at the bottom, African-Americans." What about Native Americans? They are given virtually no attention by Wilkerson. Slavery is frequently called America's "original sin." Yet much of the landmass constituting the United States of America was seized from Indian nations by conquest, duress, and fraud. Indian peoples have been slaughtered, enslaved, detained, removed, segregated, vilified, and subjected to forced assimilation. Academic historians have documented these atrocities; note, for example, the volumes by Benjamin Madley, *An American Genocide: The United States and the California Indian Catastrophe, 1846–1873*, and Jeffrey Ostler, *Surviving Genocide: Native Nations and the United States from the American Revolution to Bleeding Kansas*. Overall, though, the conquest and mistreatment of Native Americans occupy in the American mind nowhere near the saliency of black slavery and antiblack segregation. Even liberal politicians routinely render indigenous peoples invisible with paeans to "pioneers" who "settled" an "empty" wilderness.

While the misery index among black Americans—rates of incarceration, impoverishment, unemployment, risk of victimization by criminality, premature death—is scandalously high, the misery index among Native Americans is just as alarming, if not even worse. Black Americans, though, have been far more effective than Native Americans in publicizing their plight, aspirations, and demands. The ubiquity of Black Lives Matter is a reflection of African American power as well as vulnerability.

Throughout American history, some whites have been willing to subordinate virtually everything—even the survival of their governments—to white supremacy. During the American Revolution, George Washington suggested to his comrades in South Carolina that in order to defeat the British, they might have to arm at least some of their slaves and promise them emancipation as payment for fighting on behalf of the rebels. The South Carolina authorities indicated that they would rather lose to the British than arm their black slaves. During the Civil War, some secessionists begged their new government to arm slaves and promise them freedom in return for fighting on behalf of the Confederacy. But the racism of the Confederacy prevented it from taking this step even to save itself. During World War II, there were bigots who said that they would prefer to see white soldiers die than have them transfused with blood offered by black volunteers. Almost two decades later, the governor of Arkansas closed all of the high schools in Little Rock for a year rather than submit to a federal court decision ordering the continued desegregation of one of the schools. Asked why she supported the governor, even though his policy would cost her educationally, a white teenager responded forthrightly, "I'd rather be stupid than go to school with a nigger."

Racism, then, is obviously a central feature of the American story. But so, too, are alternative and opposing features that Wilkerson slights. One need not avert one's gaze from Thomas Jefferson's wicked hypocrisy to acknowledge the ageless grandeur of his liberatory rhetoric. From Frederick Douglass to Huey Newton, champions of the black freedom struggle have quoted approvingly Jefferson's declaration that "all men are created equal." One need not defend the moral crimes of the Founding Fathers to note that a faction of them did succeed in preventing the nation's founding constitution from expressly embracing or encouraging racial slavery. One need not apologize for the deficiencies of the statesmen who hammered out the Reconstruction Amendments to recognize that they are, as Eric Foner has argued, quite exceptional in world history in the extent and alacrity with which they elevated (male) slaves to citizenship and to full participation in government.

Although antiblack racism has been on vivid and grotesque display throughout American history, it has also been constantly challenged and occasionally overcome. The pro-slavery vituperation of John C. Calhoun was overmatched morally by the abolitionist polemics of William Lloyd Garrison. James O. Eastland's advocacy on behalf of Jim Crow segregation was shamed by the resistance of that remarkable sharecropper Fannie Lou Hamer. The proponents of white supremacism, despite all of their advantages, have often been bested by champions of racial justice: Daisy Bates, E. D. Nixon, Ella Baker, Constance Baker Motley, Matthew J. Perry, Michael Meltsner, Anthony Amsterdam, Jack Greenberg, Julius Chambers, Diane Nash, Julian Bond, John Lewis, and many, many others. An African American was twice elected president of the United States. A black woman has become vice president of the United States. Black voters in South Carolina who would have been barred on grounds of race from participating in that state's Democratic Party primary before 1947 played a decisive role in February 2020 in pushing Joe Biden to the front of the pack in his campaign to be the Democratic Party's presidential nominee. And black voters constituted a strong and essential segment of the coalition that sent Biden to the White House.

On a different front, during the nationwide protests against police brutality in the aftermath of the killing of George Floyd, African American demonstrators were joined by hundreds of thousands of people of various racial backgrounds who insisted as one that Black Lives Matter. Other markers of progress and protest could be pointed to even as we continue to feel the foreboding shadow of Trumpism. Yes, we remain mired in the muck of racial caste. But we are also beneficiaries of antiracist struggles upon which can be built future movements for enhanced racial equity. The struggle for racial decency goes on.

5

The Princeton Ultimatum:
Antiracism Gone Awry[1]

It is no surprise that universities have become targets of the activism erupting in the wake of the killing of George Floyd. University police forces have been implicated in racist malfeasance. Universities oversee labor forces that reflect the class and racial divisions partitioning society at large. Universities are the sites of cultural battles over iconography (Calhoun College at Yale, the Woodrow Wilson School at Princeton, Washington and Lee) and the propriety of taking race into account in admissions. At a time when racial reckonings have visited the NFL and NASCAR, *The New York Times* and *Vogue*, Minneapolis and Mississippi, it was inevitable that they would visit campuses, too.

And they have. Recently, chairs of African American studies departments at Georgetown, Notre Dame, Fordham, and other Catholic universities and colleges asserted that "systemic racism and white supremacy are problems" at their campuses. "Symbolic statements, marches, token town halls, or other typical measures to pacify our campus communities," they warned, are insufficient "while grave inequities persist." A letter to the trustees and president of Dartmouth from professors and staff called for the dismantling there of "structures that implicitly or explicitly work against and devalue Black, Brown, and other people of color." Faculty and staff members at the University of Chicago set forth "a set of specific and immediate actions the [university] must take to begin to repair and redress its long history of willingly enabling and directly contributing to structural racism." If their requirements remain unmet, they said, they will decline to participate in university affairs, urge colleagues at other institutions to boycott the university, and prevent the university from using their accomplishments to launder the "neglect and derision of people of color and scholarship and teaching on race."

The recent upsurge in anti-racist dissent is splendid in many respects, displaying creativity, persistence, and bravery in demanding the redress of long-neglected wrongs. After all, according to virtually every indicator of well-being imaginable—life expectancy, wealth, income, access to education and health care, risk of victimization by violent criminality, likelihood of being arrested or incarcerated—a distinct, adverse gap separates blacks from whites. The dissidents and their allies have refused to allow business to proceed as usual. They have pushed racial inequity to the front of popular consciousness. They have crammed into a couple of months more public education about matters of race than has taken place in years. They have been the heroes of the George Floyd moment.

But being on the side of antiracism is no inoculation against error. An allegation of systemic racism leveled against a university is a serious charge. If the allegation is substantiated, it ought to occasion protest and rectification commensurate with the wrong. If an allegation is flimsy or baseless, however, it ought to be recognized as such. Engaging in the urgent work of antiracist activism should entail avoidance of mistaken charges that cause wrongful injury, exacerbate confusion, and sow distrust that ultimately weakens the struggle.

One might wonder about the need to voice such an obvious observation. But the fact is that laudable protest has been shadowed by a rise in complacency and opportunism. Some charges of racism are simply untenable. Some complainants are careless about fact-finding and analysis. And some propose coercive policies that would disastrously inhibit academic freedom.

These disturbing tendencies are found in the ultimatum delivered in July 2020 to the president of Princeton University, Christopher Eisgruber, in a letter that was signed by about 350 professors, lecturers, and graduate students (on a campus with a faculty numbering around 1,280). The signatories included a number of Princeton luminaries, including Tracy K. Smith (the Pulitzer Prize–winning U.S. poet laureate and chair of the university's Lewis Center for the Arts), Eddie S. Glaude Jr. (chair of the Department of African American Studies), Jhumpa Lahiri (director of the Program in Creative Writing and winner of a Pulitzer Prize for fiction), Paul Muldoon (professor in the humanities and winner of a Pulitzer Prize for poetry), Michael Wood (a professor emeritus of English and comparative literature), and Nell Irvin Painter (a professor emerita of American history).

"Anti-Black racism," the ultimatum reads, "has a visible bearing upon Princeton's campus makeup and its hiring practices. . . . We call upon the administration to block the mechanisms that have allowed systemic racism to work, visibly and invisibly, in Princeton's operations." A long list of demands follows. In order "to become, for the first time in its history, an anti-racist institution," the university is called upon to redress "the demographic disparity on Princeton's faculty immediately and exponentially by hiring more faculty of color"; "elevate faculty of color to prominent leadership positions"; "consider giving faculty of color a full year of course relief to run [faculty-hiring searches]"; "implement administration- and faculty-wide training that is specifically anti-racist"; "commit fully to anti-racist campus iconography"; "remove questions about misdemeanors and felony convictions from admissions applications"; "fund a chaired professorship in Indigenous Studies for a scholar who decenters white frames of reference"; "require anti-bias training for all faculty participating in faculty searches"; "give new assistant professors summer move-in allowances on July 1 that cover rent deposits, first month's rent, and rent and food for the summer." The ultimatum also insists that the university "constitute a committee composed entirely of faculty that would oversee the investigation and discipline of racist behaviors, incidents, research, and publication on the part of faculty."

Should one believe, as the ultimatum charges, that antiblack racism is "rampant" at Princeton despite its "declared values of diversity and inclusion"?

The exploitation and exclusion of African Americans is, indeed, deeply embedded in Princeton's history. Its early presidents were slaveholders who occasionally auctioned their human property. John Witherspoon was a member of the Continental Congress and signatory of the Declaration of Independence who lectured against emancipating slaves and later opposed abolition in New Jersey. The antiblack prejudice of another president of Princeton, Woodrow Wilson, seeped into national policy during his stint as president of the United States. No African American graduated from Princeton until 1947. The university did not hire a tenure-track black professor until 1955. Because of reactionary racial attitudes that casually manifested themselves on campus, Princeton was widely seen as the "southern" Ivy.

Since the 1960s, however, and with increasing momentum, Princeton has persistently made special efforts to recruit, admit, and graduate African American and other minority students. While many have participated in this metamorphosis, no one was more consequential than the late Princeton president William G. Bowen, an impassioned advocate for racial affirmative action as both an administrator and a scholar. His 1998 book (co-written with Harvard University's president Derek Bok), *The Shape of the River*, is an oft-cited justification for race-conscious measures designed to ensure racial integration at selective institutions of higher education. His successors have also been strong proponents of racial affirmative action. A new Princeton is eclipsing the old.

Princeton, moreover, has served as the professional home of a range of distinguished educators of color including Toni Morrison, Kwame Anthony Appiah, Valerie Smith (president of Swarthmore College), and Ruth Simmons (president of Prairie View A&M University and president emerita of Brown University). These are formidable personalities with a demonstrated ability to make known their views. None of them have castigated Princeton in a fashion consistent with the charge that it is a place at which racism is "rampant." When Cornel West retired from Princeton in May 2012, he spoke of having been "blessed" by his association with an institution that had evolved from being known as the northernmost tip of the Confederacy into a community "consecrated by a new legacy."

Obviously, there are differences of opinion among Princetonians of color; some did sign the ultimatum. But if racism is as big and stultifying a presence as the ultimatum suggests, it is a mystery that so many black Princetonians could have somehow overlooked it. If Princeton's racism was as conspicuous as alleged, one would expect the ultimatum's authors to be able to dash off some vivid, revealing examples. Instead, they refer with unsatisfying generality to "micro-aggression" and "outright racist incidents," leaving readers uncertain about what, precisely, they have in mind. To be fair, the authors do get specific with respect to certain matters. They maintain that a "glaring" example of the university's "failure" to elevate more faculty of color to prominent leadership positions is that "never once has the Humanities Council been directed by a scholar from an underrepresented group." The Humanities Council brings together leaders from a wide range of academic departments, fosters interdisciplinary initiatives, and advises the university administration. The letter writers also assert that "the Council's most important outward facing program, the prestigious Society of Fellows, has never once had a director of color."

Assuming the accuracy of these facts, do they make a convincing case of racial "exclusion" in the broader context of racial change at Princeton? No, they do not. The claim of racial exclusion is implausible. For years now, throughout the university, there has existed a self-conscious impulse to promote people of color to positions of leadership. Either today or in the very recent past, black professors have been chairs of the departments of history, anthropology, English, religion, African American studies, and the Lewis Center for the Arts. Black professors have also served as the dean of the School of Public and International Affairs and as the director of the Program in Gender and Sexuality Studies. Scores of scholars of color have been Humanities Council fellows. The general counsel of the university is Latinx. The dean of admissions is African American. The recently retired vice-chair of the university board of trustees, Brent Henry, a black lawyer keenly attuned to matters of racial equity, has been for at least a decade one of the three or four most important figures in the governance of the university. Current or recent trustees include Terri Sewell, an African American member of the U.S. House of

Representatives; Henri Ford, the Haitian American dean of the University of Miami School of Medicine; and Melanie Lawson, a seasoned African American television journalist. These people, all Princeton alumni, are alert and capable and in demand. They are by no means needy. They could associate themselves with any number of prestigious enterprises. They would surely decline to contribute to or be involved with the sort of institution that the ultimatum depicts. Such power and privilege are possessed also by many of the authors and signatories of the ultimatum, which accounts in part for the whiff of bad faith that suffuses this whole affair.

The ultimatum complains that, in its view, past initiatives aimed at enlarging the number of faculty of color at Princeton have "failed" because in 2019–2020 "among 814 faculty, there were 30 Black, 31 Latinx, and 0 Indigenous persons. That's 7%." According to the ultimatum, this "is not progress by any standard; it falls woefully short of U.S. demographics as estimated by the U.S. Census Bureau, which reports Black and Hispanic persons at 32% of the total population." The suggestion that these statistics show racial unfairness in hiring at Princeton is misleading. According to *The Journal of Blacks in Higher Education*, African Americans in recent years earned only around 7 percent of all doctoral degrees. In engineering it was around 4 percent. In physics around 2 percent. Care must be taken to look for talent in places other than the familiar haunts of Ivy League searches. But even when such care is taken, the resultant catch is almost invariably quite small.

The reasons behind the small numbers are familiar and heartbreaking. They include a legacy of deprivation in education, housing, employment, and health care, not to mention increased vulnerability to crime and incarceration. The perpetuation of injuries from past discrimination as well as the imposition of new wrongs cuts like a scythe into the ranks of racial minorities, cruelly winnowing the number who are even in the running to teach at Princeton. The racial demographics of its faculty do not reflect a situation in which the university is putting a thumb on the scale against racial minority candidates. To the contrary, the university is rightly putting a thumb on the scale in favor of racial minority candidates. That the numbers remain small reflects the terrible social problems that hinder so many racial minorities before they even have a fighting chance to enter into the elite competitions from which Princeton selects its instructors. The ultimatum denies or minimizes this pipeline problem.

What I am saying is widely known within the university but largely unspoken because it has become bad manners for a person of progressive inclination to point out obvious fallacies of the sort that damage the credibility of the Princeton ultimatum and similar protests. As everyone knows, some signers of group letters join out of feelings of general solidarity, rather than specific agreement. And peer pressure accounts for the apparent approval of some who actually disagree but want to protect their reputations. But a lack of candor is not limited to some of the dissidents. The evasiveness if not mendacity of administrators is a large part of the problem. They often pander to protesters, issuing faux mea culpas that any but the most gullible observers recognize as mere public relations ruses aimed at pacification. In July 2020, for example, in the course of saluting Black Lives Matter, the board of trustees of Dartmouth stated, "We know there are no easy solutions to eradicate the oppression and racism Black and other students, faculty, and staff of color experience on our campus." The board then proceeded to list several remedial initiatives it was authorizing, none of which, singly or collectively, came close to addressing "the oppression and racism" that it appeared to concede as a major feature of life at Dartmouth. It is easy to see how the disparity in scope between the problem and the response would lead many to conclude that the authorities at Dartmouth did not actually believe their self-criticism. No wonder faculty dissidents responded with demands that the administration "take concrete steps to unravel its built-in structural racism perpetuated through the superficial and short-term fixes that our senior leadership constantly applies to the problem."

Whatever wrongs that universities have perpetrated or neglected to rectify are compounded when university authorities speak thoughtlessly or insincerely about matters that cut so deeply. When a substantial number of professors indict a university on charges of "systemic racism," the president of the university ought to state publicly whether or to what extent he or she agrees with the charge. Bureaucratic obfuscation ought not to be permitted. Neither should silence. Mistaken indictments that are opposed only by conservatives become entrenched and reiterated despite their weaknesses. And people are misled. Minority students who take such indictments at face value—unaware of strategic hyperbole—become overwhelmed by unrealistic fears of encountering racist assessments that will unfairly limit their possibilities for advancement.

Several of the Princeton ultimatum's long, odd list of demands are flagrantly problematic. When the authors say that the university should "consider giving faculty of color a full year of course relief to run [faculty-hiring searches]," they are urging the consideration of something that is both unwise and illegal. The most egregious demand, however, is for a faculty committee to "oversee the investigation and discipline of racist behaviors, incidents, research, and publication on the part of faculty." If adopted, this proposal would throw a pall over intellectual life at the university. An investigatory and disciplinary apparatus for a vice as vague and contested as "racist behaviors" would quickly lead to a level of fear and resentment, inhibition and threat that would poison the community to an extent that is difficult to exaggerate. When apprised of this provision, some signatories hoped that it would silently be abandoned. But not all. Andrew Cole, a professor of English, explicitly defended it. "In a country so embarrassingly incapable of acknowledging its history of racism and anti-Black terrorism," he wrote, "it strikes many of us as a curious indirection to talk about academic freedom when we speak of anti-racism." Starting with the proposition that "racism" is unethical, and that the university prohibits unethical research, Cole concludes that the university has an obligation to root out racist research, racist publication, and racist teaching. Cole's argument is specious. The university's prohibition on "unethical" research applies to research based on fraudulence—for example, a researcher claiming to have tested ten animals when she tested only five—or to violations of protocols guiding research on humans. Determining whether research is "racist," by contrast, takes one into a realm of ideological contestation in which, at a secular, modern research university, there should be no imposition of orthodoxy of the sort that the ultimatum threatens.

Yes, Princeton University does officially endorse certain tenets. It endorses democracy, freedom, the value of truth seeking, and policies that expressly welcome the education of students regardless of race, gender, sexual orientation, or place of birth. So the university does adopt certain political positions. But it does so sparingly, in a minimalist spirit that enables it to host a broad range of scholarly and artistic constituencies, methodologies, commitments, and styles limited only by guild-based conceptions of competency. A professor at Princeton University need not worry about being investigated or disciplined for writing a book propounding the idea that the world would have been better off had England squashed the American uprising in 1776, or that it is preferable to say that "women" get pregnant as opposed to saying that "people" get pregnant, or that abortion is a moral abomination, or that restricting abortion rights is a moral abomination, or that racial affirmative action has been a failure, or that racial affirmative action has been a success, or that it is perfectly appropriate to enunciate "nigger" in full for pedagogical purposes, or that "the n-word" should never be voiced under any circumstances. The horizon of intellectual freedom at the university is gloriously wide open—as it should be.

How would the antiracism committee demanded by the letter decide whether to investigate a complaint? Having investigated and found an infraction, what kind of discipline would it levy? Would a professor be engaging in censurable "racist" conduct if she argued on behalf of broad rights to abortion? Some claim that such a position is antiblack. What about a professor arguing in favor of decreasing the size of police forces? Some argue that that position is antiblack, too, because it could lead to greater vulnerability of black people to violent criminality. What about a professor arguing in favor of freely permitting interracial adoptions? Some insist that such a regime facilitates antiblack cultural genocide. And what about a professor who expresses admiration for the Honorable Elijah Muhammad? After all, the leader of the Nation of Islam taught that whites were, quite literally, "devils." To open the door even a crack to the possibility of "investigations" into such matters under the aegis of the university is antithetical to the freedom essential to intellectuals and artists in institutions of higher learning.

Nongovernmental cultural institutions—newspapers, journals, museums, and so on—are essential, vulnerable, and under attack. This is particularly true of the selective, cosmopolitan research colleges and universities that many on the political right especially loathe. The aspiration of those institutions is to search for truth, cultivate knowledge, and nourish and satisfy curiosities about virtually everything. They fall short, of course, as do all institutions. But nowhere in American society is more of a concerted effort being made to exemplify and respect intelligence, collaboration, and inclusivity. Antiracist activists targeting universities need to be more thoughtful in their condemnations and in their demands.

6

How Black Students Brought
the Constitution to Campus[1]

Black high school and college students in the Deep South brought the federal Constitution to campus. Lawsuits stemming from their campaigns against racism prompted judges to recognize that students at public schools are entitled to rights to due process and free speech. This linkage of civil rights and civil liberties was not unusual. Ardent champions of racial justice have typically been ardent champions of fairness and freedom of expression. The black freedom struggle of the 1960s, for example, prompted not only the emergence of law aimed at undoing racial hierarchy; it also prompted the growth of constitutional doctrines expanding civil liberties.

To protect members of the National Association for the Advancement of Colored People (NAACP) from damaging exposure by segregationists, activists moved courts to recognize organizational privacy (*NAACP v. Alabama*). To shield civil rights attorneys from rules that would have crippled their ability to further their cause through lawsuits, advocates nudged the courts to acknowledge litigation as a form of political expression (*NAACP v. Button*). To insulate news organizations from local officials who loathed publicity that put Jim Crow in a bad light, lawyers persuaded the Supreme Court to transform the law of libel (*New York Times v. Sullivan*). To protect civil rights protesters against hostile authorities, advocates moved courts to craft rules that inhibit the squelching of massed dissent (*Edwards v. South Carolina*).

Student activists contributed mightily to this dual campaign for racial justice and enhanced liberties. A seminal confrontation stemmed from events on February 25, 1960, when twenty-nine students at the all-black Alabama State College participated in a sit-in. Their target was a racially segregated grill located in the county courthouse in Montgomery. Their protest occasioned neither violence nor arrests. Still, when the governor of the state, John Patterson, heard about the demonstration, he "advised" the African American president of Alabama State, H. Councill Trenholm, to consider expelling participants. As governor, Patterson was the ex officio chair of the Alabama State Board of Education. His advice therefore mattered greatly to Trenholm.

On March 4, after additional demonstrations and after having personally warned dissidents to desist, Trenholm sent letters to nine students informing them that they had been expelled. Six of the students challenged the legality of the expulsions in *St. John Dixon et al. v. Alabama State Board of Education*. Their attorneys (a distinguished array that eventually included Thurgood Marshall, Jack Greenberg, Fred Gray, and Derrick Bell) argued that the punishment violated the federal Constitution. They mainly focused on the absence of any notice or hearing.

The federal trial judge presiding over the case was Frank M. Johnson, a white Alabamian who later distinguished himself by safeguarding the rights of antiracist protesters. On this occasion, however, he ruled against them. First, he maintained that "the right to attend a public college or university is not in and of itself a constitutional right." Second, he posited that "the right to attend . . . is conditioned upon an individual student's compliance with the rules and regulations of the institution." A regulation imposed by the Alabama Board of Education declared that "just as a student may choose to withdraw from a particular college at any time for any personally-determined reason, the college may also at any time decline to continue to accept responsibility for the supervision and service to any student with whom the relationship becomes unpleasant and difficult." A related provision stipulated that "acts of insubordination, defiance of authority, and conduct prejudicial to discipline and the welfare of the school will constitute grounds for suspension or expulsion." Judge Johnson saw these terms as having "the effect of reserving to the college the right to dismiss students at any time for any reason without divulging its reason other than its being for the general benefit of the institution."

A splintered panel of the Fifth Circuit Court of Appeals reversed Judge Johnson. Constituting the majority was Judge John Minor Wisdom, the most staunchly liberal of the judges on that court, and Judge Richard Taylor Rives, another strong liberal, who wrote the opinion. Judge Ben F. Cameron, a fervent segregationist, dissented.

The question for decision, Judge Rives declared, was "whether the students had a right to any notice or hearing whatever before being expelled." He and Judge Wisdom concluded that they did. Rives gave short shrift to the right/privilege distinction invoked by Judge Johnson, declaring that even if a person has no constitutional right to pursue a given activity, he does have a right to be free from governmental interference unless it is constrained by due process. The court of appeals similarly dismissed the argument that the plaintiffs had waived their rights by matriculating at Alabama State upon terms to which they had agreed. The state, Judge Rives declared, "cannot condition the granting of even a privilege upon the renunciation of the constitutional right to procedural due process."

Judge Cameron groused in dissent that the court's decision would undercut school authority, subvert student discipline, and make "federal functionaries" into a "gargantuan aggregation of wet nurses or baby sitters." Judges Wisdom and Rives insisted, however, that under the federal Constitution the student protesters were entitled to due process and that under the circumstances due process required notice and some opportunity for a hearing prior to expulsion.

The *Dixon* decision broke with a deeply ingrained judicial tradition of deference to school authorities. Judge Rives sought to obscure the novelty of what he and Judge Wisdom had done. Their innovativeness, however, is highlighted by a ruling announced by another federal court of appeals five months prior to the protests that triggered the *Dixon* expulsions. *Steier v. New York State Education Commissioner* involved a student who wrote letters to the president of Brooklyn College complaining that the school's administration was wrongly dominating student organizations. This student was suspended for six months under a rule requiring students to "conform to the requirements of good manners and good morals." After being readmitted and agreeing to "have a change of spirit," Arthur Steier cooperated with publicizing the news of his suspension and probation in the college newspaper. For this he was expelled. Responding to Steier's assertion of a federal constitutional grievance, federal courts concluded that he had no valid claim. One judge quipped that while the plaintiff was indeed constitutionally free to say what he pleased, he was not entitled to say it as a student at Brooklyn College. After all, the judge reasoned, the student had been admitted "not as a matter of right but as a matter of grace having agreed to conform [to the school's] rules and regulations."

Steier was no outlier. When it was decided, federal case law permitted students to be disciplined, even expelled, on virtually whatever terms school officials determined. It is against that backdrop that *Dixon* is rightly seen as a pioneering ruling.

Dixon, also, highlighted the peculiar position of the black college president. On the one hand, black college presidents exercised powers that were rare for any African American to experience in Jim Crow America, especially in the South. Black college presidents oversaw workforces, dictated the fates of professors and students, associated with some of the nation's most affluent people, and knew, sometimes quite familiarly, major regional and national politicians. At the same time, the all-white boards of education and boards of trustees that selected and supervised black college presidents typically communicated the expectation that these educators would toe the segregationist line on racial politics, or at least prevent open rebellion on campus. Trapped by dependency on whites for financing and other essential resources, black college presidents were victimized by many of the same aggravating racial humiliations visited routinely upon "ordinary" Negroes. Although to students and peers in the world of the black college, President Trenholm was a formidable figure, to white officials he was but another "boy" from whom they could and did demand obedience. When Governor Patterson got fed up with the desegregationist dissent of Lawrence D. Reddick, the chair of the history department at Alabama State College, the governor denounced the professor on television as "a Communist sympathizer and racial agitator" whom President Trenholm should dismiss "before sundown." Trenholm dismissed Reddick just as he expelled the dissident students.

Many observers faulted Trenholm for failing to do more to resist the segregationists. "It is indeed unfortunate," wrote a correspondent from Chicago, "that you have become the hatchet man for the governor of Alabama and expelled those kids." Someone from Philadelphia complained, "The Uncle Toms are supposed to be dead. . . . Does economic security mean so much? How will you face tomorrow?" An observer from Huntsville, Alabama, declared, "We must not jump every time the white man speaks." Writing from Dayton, Ohio, Trenholm's own cousin remarked, "You should have resigned yourself."

Many students, however, recognized Trenholm's vulnerable position and the agonizing compromises that attended it. The same day that Trenholm warned activists to desist from further protest, one of them sent a remarkable petition addressed to the governor—the figure whom they correctly saw as the real power behind the repression. This student, Bernard Lee, was expelled, became a plaintiff in *Dixon*, and subsequently emerged as a key aide to Martin Luther King Jr. Lee's petition reflects the idealism, poise, and boldness that suffused the sit-in movement of the early 1960s:

To the Honorable Governor John Patterson.

We, a united group of students . . . humbly request that you reconsider your order to President Trenholm. This decision is out of tune with the spirit of Americanism. The snack-bar at the Court House is a symbol of injustice to a part of the citizens of Montgomery. It is a flagrant contradiction of the Christian and Democratic ideals of our nation.

We went to the snack-bar not as hoodlums, but
in the same manner and spirit in which other college
students have done in other parts of the country. Our
purpose was to express our resentment of a scheme that
fails to recognize its responsibility to decent and orderly
persons of all creeds, color or nationalities. . . .

Our cause is just. We are asking that you study it with an
open mind and give President Trenholm the authority to
settle this issue with us.
        We are reasonable and considerate. We may be
crushed, but we shall not bow to tyranny.

Although Lee and the other expelled students won their lawsuit, none of them reenrolled. Eventually, though, their sacrifice
did receive a bit of recognition. In 2010, Alabama State University
reinstated the nine and conferred upon them honorary degrees.

Dixon involved college students. What about federal constitutional
rights for high school students? The most famous case recognizing a right to freedom of expression for high school students is
Tinker v. Des Moines Independent Community School District decided
by the Supreme Court in 1969. In *Tinker* a principal suspended
junior high school students who refused to remove black arm-
bands symbolizing protest against the Vietnam War. Noting the
absence of any evidence that the students' symbolic protest caused
any disruption or posed a threat of substantially interfering with
the work of the school, the Court ruled that the principal had violated the young dissidents' First Amendment rights. Writing for
the Court, Justice Abe Fortas declared that neither students nor
teachers "shed their constitutional rights to freedom of speech or
expression at the schoolhouse gate." As is usual, however, the judgment of the Supreme Court represented a ratification rather than
the initiation of a legal proposition. As Justice Fortas acknowledged, courts in the Deep South had previously grappled with the
issue of constitutionally protected rights to freedom of expression
for secondary school students.

In one of the disputes, *Burnside v. Byars*, the black principal
of the black Booker T. Washington High School in Philadelphia, Mississippi, forbade students to wear "freedom buttons"
to school. Emblazoned on these buttons were "One Man One
Vote" and "SNCC," the abbreviation, of course, for the Student
Nonviolent Coordinating Committee. Students who refused to
remove the buttons were suspended. Three challenged the constitutionality of this punishment. They argued that it wrongfully
encroached upon constitutionally protected freedom of speech.
The state contended that the prohibition should be permitted
under the circumstances because it assisted in the maintenance
of proper discipline. Allowing students to wear political buttons
would inevitably result in distraction, thereby undercutting the
school's educational mission.

The plaintiffs lost the first round when a U.S. district judge
declined to issue a preliminary injunction against the suspen-
sions. On appeal, however, the plaintiffs prevailed with the Fifth
Circuit Court of Appeals bestowing upon high school students
a right protected by the First Amendment to express themselves
unobtrusively even against the wishes of school authorities. The
Fifth Circuit thus anticipated by three years the Supreme Court's
Tinker decision.

A third case stemmed from events at South Carolina State
College in Orangeburg. The president of the college was Benner
C. Turner. Born into an affluent family in Columbus, Georgia,
Turner attended Phillips Academy in Andover, Massachusetts,
before attending Harvard College and Harvard Law School. He
served as the dean of the South Carolina State Law School before
being selected in 1950 as the president of South Carolina State
College by Governor Strom Thurmond and an all-white board
of trustees.

Like other African American presidents of segregated black
public institutions, Turner occupied a precarious position. He
served at the pleasure of a political regime committed to the maintenance of white supremacy. Annually he had to beg an all-white,
segregationist legislature for funding. He had to wrest support
from lawmakers who openly and unapologetically favored white
schools over black schools. He had to contend with influential

arbiters of white public opinion who maintained that under segregation race relations were harmonious and that blacks ought to be satisfied with what they had received. "The Negro," the newspaper *The Times and Democrat* announced in August 1955, "has much for which to thank the white race. He has been given, through public monies, a splendid educational establishment in this state."

Under Turner, South Carolina State gained important educational accreditation. He oversaw the building of dormitories, housing for faculty, classroom facilities, and a football stadium and the elevation of faculty salaries and qualifications. In 1950 only two members of the faculty had earned doctorates; by 1967 the number had risen to twenty-seven. At the same time, Turner ran South Carolina State autocratically. According to the historian William C. Hine, Turner "segregated himself from most black people. He had little interest in social activities. He took no part in church, lodge, or fraternity affairs. To some people, he resembled the overseer of a plantation."

The suppression of students and employees of the college, including professors, was a salient feature of Turner's rule. Some contend that his authoritarianism should be understood as a technique that he perceived as needed to protect his institution. He sought, it can be argued, to preempt white extremists who were all too eager to shutter the school by seizing upon provocations—including mere demands for equal treatment—that would alienate white segregationists. There is something to that defense. Turner undoubtedly viewed cracking down on anti-segregationist dissent as a price worth paying for the survival of an institution that contributed significantly to the advancement of blacks. It would be unrealistic, however, to portray Turner's dictatorial ways as stratagems focused solely on the well-being of the college. Turner liked exercising power and disliked being contradicted by those he viewed as subordinates. He suppressed dissidents not only because he saw them as threats to his institution; he suppressed them, too, because he abhorred being challenged, especially by other black people.

In 1956, when the student government president, Fred H. Moore, called a strike to protest against threats to send law enforcement personnel onto campus to quell anti-segregationist activism, Turner (with the board of trustees) retaliated harshly. He expelled Moore summarily and notified fourteen other students that they would be excluded from campus after the end of the school year. Several professors were also sent packing, including the faculty adviser to the student newspaper. Her offense? She had failed, in Turner's view, to be sufficiently rigorous in excluding from the newspaper objectionable commentary. Turner took decisive steps to foreclose that from happening again; he put into his own hands the authority to preclear what was published.

On February 24, 1967, three students—Joseph Hammond, John Stroman, and Benjamin F. Bryant Jr.—received notice that college officials had suspended them for three years for having violated college regulation one: "The student body . . . is not to celebrate, parade, or demonstrate on the campus at any time without the approval of the Office of the President." An unauthorized protest had voiced disapproval of Turner's dictatorial streak. Previously his censorship had been resented but not legally challenged. This time students took South Carolina State College to court and prevailed. Striking down regulation one as an illicit prior restraint on speech and assembly, a U.S. district court judge maintained that "academic progress and academic freedom demand their share of Constitutional protection." Three months later President Turner resigned.

Because of the efforts of activists who demanded rights to due process and freedom of expression as they fought to dismantle Jim Crow pigmentocracy, *all* students and teachers at public institutions came to enjoy an elevated legal status. In 1950 they had been subject to the dictates of authorities uninhibited by federal constitutional restraints. By 1970 they had won judicially recognized rights. Here, as elsewhere, brave souls committed to battling racial oppression widened the circle of freedoms to which all in America can properly lay claim.

7

Race and the Politics of Memorialization

All of the institutions of higher education in which I have been involved have been swept by controversies over memorialization. My workplace, Harvard Law School, dropped its insignia in the face of complaints that that emblem stemmed from the coat of arms of a slaveholding and slave-trading family—the Royalls. Yale University, where I obtained my legal education, removed from one of its residential colleges the name of John C. Calhoun. As vice president of the United States (under Presidents John Quincy Adams and Andrew Jackson), congressman and U.S. senator from South Carolina, secretary of state, and secretary of war, Calhoun was a fierce partisan of the Slave Power who propounded the notion that Negro slavery, far from being just a necessary evil, was actually a positive good. Princeton University, where I received my undergraduate education, has also been the site of controversy over memorialization, and it is there on which I shall focus.

The dispute at Princeton concerned the school's memorialization of Woodrow Wilson, particularly the maintenance of his name atop the Woodrow Wilson School of Public and International Affairs. A student group, the Black Justice League, argued that Princeton ought to rename the school because of Wilson's racist beliefs and actions. It garnered support from many quarters, including the editorial page of *The New York Times*. Those who wanted to retain the name argued that Wilson contributed commendably to Princeton as its president; that his racist views and policies, albeit regrettable, were common failings of his time; that his deficiencies, while important, are outweighed by his record of accomplishment; and that the university's veneration honored not his racism but the positive features of his persona. In 2016, after much discussion, the Princeton administration decided to retain Wilson's name. But in 2020, during the eruption of protest in the aftermath of George Floyd's killing, the administration changed its mind, removing Wilson's name as part of an overall demotion of the former president.*

What should one think about all of this?

First, let's be clear about Wilson. He lived between 1856 and 1924. He was a Princeton undergraduate and a Princeton professor and became the university's thirteenth president, serving for eight years. He raised the university's scholarly standards, hired the first non-Protestants (a Jew and a Catholic) to the faculty, and coined the university's unofficial motto "Princeton in the Nation's service" (which was modified recently with a Wilsonian ring: "Princeton in the nation's service and the service of humanity"). After serving as New Jersey's governor, Wilson was elected in 1912 to the presidency of the United States. In that post, he did some things for which he is widely lauded. He nominated the first Jewish Supreme Court justice, Louis Brandeis. He played a key role in designing and enacting legislation that created the Federal Reserve System and the Federal Trade Commission. After leading the United States into World War I, he joined with other heads of state in seeking to create an international association that could henceforth prevent war. This association became the League of Nations, an innovation for which Wilson was awarded the 1919 Nobel Prize for Peace.

Wilson, however, did other things for which he has been rightly

* Oxford University, which I attended as a Rhodes Scholar, was also buffeted by protests. There the target was a statue honoring Cecil Rhodes that stood outside his alma mater, Oriel College. Rhodes was a mining magnate (he founded the De Beers diamond firm) and a devotee of British imperialism who served as a prime minister of the Cape Colony. While a spirited "Rhodes Must Fall" campaign has demanded the removal of the statue, its fate remains undetermined. I focus on the institutions with which I have had the closest associations. I failed to graduate from Oxford. A member of Balliol College, I was one of those who, alas, contributed to the reputation of Americans as scholastically unserious.

condemned. First, he trampled civil liberties. During World War I
he permitted his postmaster general to deny the mails to dissenting publications. He pushed through Congress the Espionage Act
of 1917 and the Sedition Act of 1918, thoroughly regrettable measures that were used to intimidate and punish antiwar dissidents,
including Eugene V. Debs, head of the Socialist Party. After the
war, Wilson's attorney general, A. Mitchell Palmer, directed notorious raids that violated civil liberties.

It is a second criticism, however, that put the big question mark
over whether Princeton should continue to honor Wilson. That
critique focuses on the fact that the Wilson administration deepened and broadened antiblack racism in the federal government.
Professor Eric S. Yellin writes in *Racism in the Nation's Service:
Government Workers and the Color Line in Woodrow Wilson's America* that the "goal of Wilsonian discrimination was not just racial
separation but the limitation of black people to a controlled and
exploitable class of laborers. It meant channeling civil servants into
a racially tiered system with less mobility and less money." Wilson's administration "combined institutionalized racism with progressive reform in a way that devastated not only careers but also
the very foundations of full citizenship for African Americans. . . .
As Wilson and his managers cut down African American civil servants, they undermined an actual as well as a symbolic black middle
class in the nation's capital and nationalized a white supremacist
social order."

Some scholars contend that Yellin and other detractors go too
far in condemning Wilson. Those with a less damning assessment
note that Wilson's racial beliefs and policies, albeit ugly, were
a far cry from the aggressive Negrophobia of contemporaries
such as James Vardaman of Mississippi and Benjamin Tillman of
South Carolina. Here, however, we need not become too deeply
entangled in historical debate. All serious students of Wilson concede that he viewed blacks as racial inferiors, that he decried the
Reconstruction effort to elevate African Americans to civil and
political equality, and that he did indeed reinforce racial segregation in the federal government. From there the argument of
those who demand Wilson's demotion is straightforward: his racism should disqualify him for memorialization. They insist that to

honor Wilson is to dishonor African Americans, especially those who are part of the Princeton University community.

A common response is to draw up a list of widely esteemed figures, note their failings, and then contend that broadly applying the logic behind dememorializing Wilson would also entail dememorializing scores of others. The assumption is that the audience, or at least large sectors of it, will believe that a blanket dememorialization of white male heroes is too horrible or fanciful for any sensible person to take seriously. If Wilson should be disqualified from honorific acknowledgment, the argument runs, then what about George Washington, Thomas Jefferson, and James Madison—slaveholders all—or Abraham Lincoln, Theodore Roosevelt, and Franklin Delano Roosevelt, all of whom believed in the racial superiority of whites over blacks? The implicit argument is that dememorialization on account of what might be characterized as "regular racism"—the racism common in a particular time and place—would be excessive. It would be excessive because it would entail the dememorialization of many, indeed most, of the leading figures of American and Princeton history.

While many will be swayed by this argument, those who are most adamant in demanding the removal of Wilson's name will be unmoved. The prospect of a wholesale demotion for the Founding Fathers as well as Wilson will suit them just fine. Consider Charles M. Blow's *New York Times* column "Yes, Even George Washington." On the issue of American slavery, he declares, "I am an absolutist: enslavers were amoral monsters." Should Washington suffer the same demotion as Confederates? Blow's response is unflinching: "abso-fricking-lutely!" After all, Washington "enslaved more than 100 human beings," people who could love, laugh, cry, and hurt just like any other human beings.

An alternative approach involves broadening the conversation. All too often only white men are discussed. What happens when racial minorities are among those judged?

Let's start with an African American, born in Princeton, whose application to the university was rejected categorically on account of race by Wilson himself. Paul Robeson became a star athlete and an outstanding student at Rutgers College. He also became an internationally acclaimed singer and actor. He also distinguished himself as a political activist, ardently protesting against racial and class injustice. A number of institutions have been named in his honor, including the Paul Robeson High School of Business and Technology in Brooklyn, the Paul Robeson Malcolm X Academy in Detroit, and the Paul Robeson High School for Human Services in Philadelphia. I suspect that many who demand the dememori-alization of Wilson would be thrilled by the prospect of Princeton memorializing Robeson. What does one do, however, about the following facts? In 1952, Paul Robeson accepted the Stalin Peace Prize and in 1953 wrote a eulogy for Stalin titled "To You Beloved Comrade" in which he praised the dictator's "deep humanity." One might object by saying that the conduct in question by Robe-son was mere gesture that was nowhere near as morally significant as slaveholding or the other misconduct that is giving rise to the reckoning over memorialization. Point taken. Still, by 1952, any educated, politically aware person was on notice of Stalin's mon-strous crimes—the complicity with Hitler in carving up Poland, the waves of purges, forced labor on a massive scale, and the sub-jugation of Eastern Europe. The horrors perpetrated by Stalin continue to haunt millions today. Should Robeson's egregious praise of the tyrant disqualify him from memorialization?

A second figure to consider was born Malcolm Little but became known to the world as Malcolm X. He, too, has been widely honored. There is the Malcolm X Elementary School in Berkeley, California; the Malcolm X Shabazz High School in Newark, New Jersey; the Malcolm X College in Chicago; the U.S. Postal Service Malcolm X postage stamp; and Malcolm X Boule-vard in Harlem. For much of his life as an activist, Malcolm X subscribed to the tenets of the Nation of Islam, which maintained that white people—*all* white people—are literally devils who are irredeemable and who ought to be shunned as fully as possible. In a 1963 interview with the journalist Louis Lomax, Malcolm X assailed black people married to whites, including Harry Bela-fonte and Lorraine Hansberry. He asserted that "only a man who is ashamed of what he is will marry out of his race. There has to be something wrong when a man or a woman leaves his own people and marries somebody of another kind. . . . Why would any black man want to marry a devil . . . for that's just what the white man is." In the last year or so of his life, Malcolm X repudiated some of what he had preached previously. Still, while engaging in the activism for which he is much praised, Malcolm X spouted anti-white sentiment of the sort just quoted. Should he be disqualified from memorialization?

A third figure to consider is the Reverend Fred Shuttlesworth, a co-founder of the Southern Christian Leadership Conference and a key leader of the Alabama Christian Movement for Human Rights. Reverend Shuttlesworth was instrumental in inspiring the movement that overcame Bull Connor and other white supremacists in the extraordinary struggles that took place in Birmingham and other locales in the 1960s. Arrested on numerous occasions, viciously beaten, and twice targeted in bombings, he never relented in his efforts to enlarge the realm of racial freedom for blacks. He, too, has been memorialized. The airport near the city in which he battled most famously was named in 2008 the Birmingham-Shuttlesworth International Airport. In 2004, however, Reverend Shuttlesworth lent his name to a campaign to prevent the city of Cincinnati from passing an ordinance supportive of gay rights. The problem, Reverend Shuttlesworth announced, is gay people's "equat[ing] civil rights, what we did in the '50s and '60s, with special rights. . . . I think that what they propose is special rights. Sexual rights is not the same as civil rights and human rights." Needless to say, gay rights activists were appalled by these sentiments. To them Reverend Shuttlesworth's comments echoed those voiced by some of the racial segregationists whom he had valiantly challenged in previous decades. Given that many people in and allied with the LGBT community find Reverend Shuttlesworth's views deeply distressing, should he be memorialized?

In my view, the line-drawing dilemmas applicable to Robeson, Malcolm X, Shuttlesworth, Calhoun, Washington, Wilson, the Royalls, and others admit of several acceptable conclusions. I have limits to be sure. I think it proper to be intolerant of memorials that lie—including the fraud of nondisclosure. I think it proper, as well, to be intolerant of memorialization that is presently aimed at demeaning people. Beyond that, though, I am open to a variety of outcomes.

Many members of the Harvard Law School community saw

the Royall family crest as an indelibly tainted symbol that insulted
the memory of the enslaved and should therefore have offended
anyone attuned to their plight. These observers urged the university to remove the Royall family crest from the law school's insignia. There is much that is reasonable and attractive about that
position. And it prevailed. Also reasonable and attractive, however, was the dissent voiced by Professor Annette Gordon-Reed.
For her, the most important thing was to "keep alive the memory
of the people whose sale helped found Harvard Law School." She
contended that retaining the shield and "tying it to a historically
sound interpretative narrative . . . would be the most honest and
forthright way to insure that the true story of our origins . . . is
not lost."*

At Yale the authorities decided to remove Calhoun's name
after having initially decided to retain it. His championing of slavery, the university president observed, "fundamentally conflicts
with Yale's mission and values." Moreover, Calhoun had played
no major role in Yale's development, through academic or financial contribution. He was an undergraduate alumnus who became
an outstanding statesman and whose name was chosen to adorn
a residential college in 1931 for now ironic reasons. His name
was thought to be a choice that would arouse no controversy—an
indication of the hegemony of white supremacist values in the
early years of the Great Depression. His name was also thought
to be good for purposes of "diversity": it would reinforce the message that southerners—at least white ones—were welcome.

The president of Yale, Peter Salovey, said that a desire to
avoid erasing history had prompted his initial decision to retain
the Calhoun name: "I was concerned about inviting a series of
name changes that would obscure Yale's past." Explaining his
about-face, Salovey said that Yale had established "an enduring
set of principles" that addressed the problem that had previously
bothered him. Those principles, the product of a committee

---

* Of course, debate will attend all attempts to construct "the true story." Professor Gordon-Reed says that in her "true story" the progenitors of Harvard Law
School are "the enslaved people at Royall's plantation, not Isaac Royall." But
why not Isaac Royall? How can he be rightly erased from any "sound interpretive
narrative" of the origins of Harvard Law School? The true story should include
the enslavers as well as the enslaved.

chaired by the eminent historian and legal scholar John Fabian Witt, proclaimed that "renaming on account of values should be an exceptional event," that "sometimes renaming on the basis of values is warranted," and that decisions to retain or rename "come with obligations of nonerasure, contextualization, and process." In this instance, Salovey concluded, the balance of considerations militated strongly in favor of renaming. That decision seems reasonable to me. It was not, however, the only decision that I find acceptable.

It would have been fine with me had Yale retained the name and used it as the basis for educating people about the substance, implications, and influence of Calhoun's actions and beliefs. Note that in 1973 the first African American faculty member to be appointed as the head of a Yale residential college agreed to do so only if he was named the master of Calhoun College. Professor Charles Davis (a pioneering champion of African American studies) believed that leadership of that college in particular would serve as a vivid refutation and repudiation of Calhoun's racial ideas. Clearly Professor Davis did not believe that the Calhoun name was unalterably insulting; he carried it for years as part of his professional identity. Later, another African American professor, Jonathan Holloway (now the president of Rutgers University), also became the master of Calhoun College.

My attitude toward the controversy at Princeton is similar. I accepted equably the decision by the authorities to retain Wilson's name insofar as they promised to make more salient the racist features of his story. But there were, it seemed to me, good reasons for continuing his memorialization. Most important, unlike in the case of Calhoun, Wilson had played a major role in Princeton's development. His exertions as university president helped to transform Princeton into a first-class research university. The only PhD (thus far) to occupy the White House, Wilson created a presidential record that is marred by racism and repression. Yet it is also distinguished by initiatives, domestic and international, that sought creatively to better social conditions. His example has inspired many people, abroad and in America, especially at Princeton, to deploy knowledge in the service of humanity. Those are the features of his persona that Princeton memorialized.

I am also accepting of the decision to do an about-face for

reasons noted previously: Wilson instituted destructive, white supremacist policies from the apex of American government.

I do not accept, however, all of the arguments invoked to explain the about-face. Justifying his turnabout, President Christopher Eisgruber stated, "When a university names a school of public policy for a political leader, it inevitably suggests that the honoree is a model for students who study at the school. This searing moment in American history [the George Floyd moment] has made clear that Wilson's racism disqualifies him from that role. In a nation that continues to struggle with racism, [Princeton] and its school of public and international affairs must stand clearly and firmly for equality and justice." But Wilson's racism was as clear in the days before Mr. Floyd was killed as in the days afterward. The university had made a considered judgment to retain Wilson's name after thoughtfully weighing the particulars of his wrongs and their social implications.

Why, really, the change of heart? I suspect that the real reason is that dissident opinion on campus was heating up dramatically, that authorities believed it necessary to propitiate the outraged, and that they calculated that an about-face regarding Wilson's name could accomplish that mission at an acceptable cost. If that was the strategy, it was only partially successful. Instead of satisfying a burgeoning anger, the name change might have only emboldened it, encouraging dissidents to make broader demands such as a total overhaul of the university's iconography, removing memorials to all who are documented racists. The logic of that demand is powerful. If the university's position is that Wilson's racism "disqualifies" him from commemoration, it would seem that most of the other figures memorialized on the campus ought to be demoted as well. Why accept the presence of statues of Jonathan Edwards, Samuel Finley, or John Witherspoon—all of whom were slaveholding presidents of Princeton—in light of Wilson's defenestration?

Thus far, I have indicated that I would find a variety of outcomes acceptable. But what outcome would I prefer? I would prefer an outcome based on addition rather than subtraction. More upsetting to me than memorials to the arguably undeserving is the paucity of acknowledgment to those who have indisputably distinguished themselves by remarkable, heroic, and admirable conduct that has received all too little acclaim. I yearn to see more memorials honoring the likes of Harry and Harriette Moore; John Carlos and Tommie Smith; Septima Clark and Daisy Bates; Medgar Evers and John Lewis; John Hope Franklin and James Baldwin; William Julius Wilson and Marian Wright Edelman.

At Princeton, I would have preferred leaving alone the name of the Wilson School (and all of the other memorializations of Wilson) and committing the university to further action along two other dimensions. First, the university should never again be morally and intellectually complacent in its presentation of those whom it chooses to memorialize. It should be transparent, acknowledging openly, candidly, and realistically the sobering mixture of virtue and deficiency that attends the careers of even the most outstanding people. Second, going forward, the university should act quickly and decisively to bestow honor upon admirable (but inevitably flawed) figures who would reflect and inspire the full range of Princeton's multifarious community, particularly those affiliated with groups that have had to contend with persistent prejudice.

I shall conclude on a personal note. I am the child of refugees from the Jim Crow South who settled in Washington, D.C. My father was a postal clerk whose occupational possibilities were narrowed by the legacy of Wilson's segregationism. I came to Princeton largely under the influence of my brother, Judge Henry Kennedy Jr., class of 1970, a graduate of the Wilson School. I am well aware that during his tenure as president of Princeton, Wilson would have undoubtedly prohibited my presence at the university on account of my race. What thoughts and sentiments does that awareness prompt? Three come to mind. First, as a student and then as an alumnus, I never felt burdened by any memorialization of Wilson. One of my favorite professors was the editor of the Wilson papers and a leading Wilson biographer, Arthur S. Link, who described Wilson's racism in detail decades ago in articles and books with which I was thoroughly familiar. I simply chose to avoid interpreting the naming of the Woodrow Wilson School as a racial affront. My choice was by no means singular. I was in good company insofar as a distinguished cadre of antiracist scholars including Toni Morrison, Kwame Anthony Appiah, and Cornel West also appear to have felt no need to protest Princeton's memorialization of Wilson. Morrison, Appiah, and West were certainly capable of calling attention to practices they perceived as objectionable. The absence of their voiced objection is notable. Professor West has subsequently declared his solidarity with those calling for renaming. But previously, including in 1996, when Professor West was awarded and accepted Princeton's James Madison Medal, the public record of which I am aware discloses no condemnation on his part of Princeton's memorialization practices.

Second, upon considering whether to perpetuate the honoring of Wilson's memory, I note that people sometimes change. Perhaps by dint of some miraculous feat of time travel he would apologize now for his racist acts and take delight in the heartening irony that the Wilson Professor of Literature at Princeton was, for years, the esteemed black critic Valerie Smith, now the president of Swarthmore College, and that the current dean of what used to be the Wilson School is also an African American, Cecilia Rouse, a distinguished economist.

Third, if I am wrong and Wilson declined to apologize and change, I hope that I would remain free from any debilitating burden. I hope that upon gazing at his name etched into marble, I would smilingly give him the finger and shout with satisfaction, "Look at me and my people now!"

8

The Politics of Black Respectability[1]

Rosa Parks was not the first African American in Montgomery, Alabama, arrested in the 1950s for refusing to give up her seat on a bus to a white rider. Several others had preceded her. But because of the politics of respectability, she was the person selected to be the face of black suffering and resistance, the emblem of the majestic boycott of 1955–56. Listen to a key organizer, E. D. Nixon, on why he refrained from building a protest around others who had been arrested:

> OK, the case of Louise Smith. I found her daddy in front of his shack, barefoot, drunk. Always drunk. Couldn't use her. In that year's second case, the girl [Claudette Colvin], very brilliant but she'd had an illegitimate baby. Couldn't use her. The last case before Rosa was the daughter of a preacher who headed a reform school. . . . My interview with her convinced me that she wouldn't stand up to the pressure. She was even afraid of me. When Rosa Parks was arrested, I thought "This is it!" 'Cause she's morally clean, she's reliable, nobody had nothing on her, she had the courage of her convictions.

Martin Luther King Jr. reiterated this point. "Mrs. Rosa Parks is a fine person," he declared, observing that he was happy that she would be the community standard-bearer, "for nobody can doubt the height of her character."

At the conclusion of the victorious boycott and lawsuit that got rid of segregated seating, King again displayed awareness of the importance of maintaining an exemplary image and reputation. He and his colleagues in the Montgomery Improvement Association distributed a flyer which stated that victory "places upon us all a tremendous responsibility of maintaining, in the face of what could be some unpleasantness, a calm and loving dignity befitting good citizens and members of our race. . . . Remember that this is not a victory for Negroes alone, but for all Montgomery and the South. Do not boast! Do not brag! . . . If cursed, do not curse back. If pushed, do not push back. If struck, do not strike back, but evidence love and goodwill at all times. . . . If you feel you cannot take it, walk for another week or two. We have confidence in our people. GOD BLESS YOU ALL."

Those who participated in the electrifying Freedom Rides and sit-ins of the early 1960s were given detailed instructions on what to wear (jackets for men and dresses for ladies) and how to act (be courteous and refrain from retaliating even if assaulted). Their leaders, including James Farmer of the Congress of Racial Equality and John Lewis of the Student Nonviolent Coordinating Committee, were doing what many leaders routinely do: packaging their campaigns in ways designed to blunt the opposition of enemies, elicit solidarity from supporters, and induce acceptance from the uncommitted. Recall the dignified black teenagers desegregating Central High School in Little Rock, Arkansas, while bands of snarling, foulmouthed white hooligans sought to torment them. Remember the determined activists demanding service at segregated lunch counters while screaming white thugs doused them with ketchup and mustard. A vivid snapshot is provided by the racist journalist James J. Kilpatrick, who fiercely opposed the civil rights movement yet expressed grudging admiration for the youngsters who carried off the sit-ins with such splendid tact:

> Here were the colored students, in coats, white shirts, ties, and one of them was reading Goethe and one was taking

notes from a biology text. And here, on the sidewalk outside, was a gang of white boys come to heckle, a ragtail
rabble, slack-jawed, black-jacketed, grinning fit to kill. . . .
Eheu! It gives one pause.

The attentiveness to image and reputation that was so central
to the civil rights movement in its most productive phase (1950–
1965) had been presaged by previous efforts. One involved the
Woman's Convention (WC) of the National Baptist Convention, an organization of black churchwomen that did important
work at the turn of the twentieth century following the disastrous
collapse of Reconstruction. The WC established kindergartens,
orphanages, and old folks' homes; conducted training classes for
new mothers; created a school to professionalize domestic service;
offered counseling and comfort to prisoners; provided forums in
which black women shared their impressions about their condition and how to elevate it; and served as the institutional sponsor
for protests against all manner of social vices including the racist
mistreatment of African Americans through lynchings and other
Jim Crow outrages. In her history of the WC, Professor Evelyn
Brooks Higginbotham coined the term "politics of respectability" to describe the WC's outward approach to whites and inward
approach to blacks. According to Higginbotham, that politics
"emphasized reform of individual behavior and attitudes both as
a goal in itself and as a strategy for reform of the entire structural
system of American race relations." Racist dogma portrayed black
women as dirty, dishonest, lazy, irresponsible, and lascivious. By
stressing that black women can be clean, honest, hardworking,
frugal, responsible, and chaste, the WC's "emphasis on respectable behavior contested the plethora of negative stereotypes."
The WC protested against racist limitations imposed on blacks.
But it also stressed blacks' own capacity to better oppressive conditions even under the pressure of racist constraints. A statement
by the executive board of the WC in 1915 is characteristic: "Fight
segregation through the courts as an unlawful act? Yes. But [also]
fight it with soap and water, hoes, spades, shovels, and paint to
remove any reasonable excuse for it."
Stoicism suffused the WC's preachings. It demanded that

blacks resist permitting the cage of segregation from imprisoning their inner lives. "Men and women are not made on trains and on streetcars," declared Nannie Helen Burroughs, the WC's most outstanding leader. "If in our homes there is implanted in the hearts of our children . . . the thought they are what they are, not by environment, but of themselves, this effort [by segregationists] to teach a lesson of inferiority will be futile."

For members of the WC, Higginbotham notes, "respectability demanded that every individual in the black community assume responsibility for behavioral self-regulation and self-improvement along moral, educational, and economic lines. The goal was to distance oneself as far as possible from images perpetuated by racist stereotypes. Individual behavior . . . determined the collective fate of African Americans." The impulse to ostracize blacks who failed to measure up generated harsh judgments. S. Willie Layton, a president of the WC, declared that "bad Negroes have given the race a questionable reputation; these degenerates are responsible for every discrimination we suffer." Nannie Burroughs maintained that the woman who "keeps a dirty home and tolerates trifling shiftless inmates" is "as great an enemy to the race as the man who devotes his life to persecuting and maligning the race."

Higginbotham observes that "the Baptist women spoke as if ever-cognizant of the gaze of white America." Determined to avoid looking bad in front of the white folks, the WC fielded "an army of black Baptist women [who] waged war against gum chewing, loud talking, gaudy colors, the nickelodeon, jazz, littered yards, and a host of other perceived improprieties." Sometimes their efforts were predicated on a belief that blacks needed to elevate themselves to reach parity with Euro-American peers. Higginbotham recognizes, however, that sometimes "the Baptist women's emphasis on manners and morals served to reinforce their sense of moral superiority over whites." Urging blacks to display "proper conduct" on streetcars, the WC observed in 1910,

A certain class of whites have set a poor example for the Negro . . . by making it a point to rush in and spread out, so that we cannot get seats. . . . We have seen our people provoked to act very rudely and to demand seats, or squeeze in, and almost sit in the laps of the "spreaders." Here is an opportunity for us to show our superiority by not squeezing in. . . . Let us at all times . . . remember that the quiet, dignified individual who is respectful to others is after all the superior individual, be he black or white.

Themes sounded by the WC have been echoed time and again, in many quarters of black America, including among leading activists. Thurgood Marshall carefully screened potential clients before agreeing to represent them in the landmark cases that created the legal groundwork for the civil rights revolution. "Mr. Civil Rights" would withhold his services and the backing of his organization, the National Association for the Advancement of Colored People (NAACP), if he doubted the ability and willingness of a person to present a good face to the public in the glare of publicity that accompanied efforts to topple racial segregation. He was similarly calculating in criminal cases. In his role as a campaigner for law reform, Marshall did not proceed as do most conventional defense attorneys. He was not indifferent to the culpability of potential clients. To the contrary, he was keenly interested, often declining to commit scarce resources to the defense of those he deemed unworthy of the investment. He wanted to avoid having the standing of the NAACP belittled by association with incorrigible criminals. He viewed the reputation of his clients, himself, and his organization as important resources in the legal, cultural, and ideological struggle to advance the fortunes of black America.

The effort to present the civil rights movement in a fashion that would generate sympathy and admiration paid off. Segregationists attempted repeatedly to suppress the NAACP by means that had worked effectively to cripple the Communist Party. They tried, for example, to make public employment contingent upon an absence of affiliation with the NAACP. They also tried to obtain NAACP membership lists so that members could be publicly identified and intimidated. Courts, however, thwarted those efforts with decisions that protected the NAACP, validating Marshall's long-term cultivation of its reputation.

Throughout the 1960s decision makers who could have plausibly ruled *against* demonstrators arrested for disorderly conduct and similarly amorphous offenses instead ruled *for* them in part on account of their carefully constructed self-presentation. In Columbia, South Carolina, police arrested 187 protesters who refused to leave the grounds of the South Carolina State House when ordered to do so. Taking care to avoid blocking vehicular or pedestrian traffic, the tightly organized, impeccably behaved demonstrators stood their ground, praying and singing religious and patriotic songs. In *Edwards v. South Carolina*, in an opinion by Justice Potter Stewart, the federal Supreme Court quashed the prosecutions of the demonstrators, concluding that the students were engaged in protected expression displayed in its "most pristine and classic form."

Black respectability politics has continued to be widely championed. A form of it was certainly propounded by my parents, who inculcated in their three children a sense of racial kinship such that, in our dealings with the white world, we were encouraged to think of ourselves as ambassadors of blackness. My parents told us that our achievements would advance the race and that our failures would lower it. They insisted that the fulfillment of our racial obligations required that we speak well, dress suitably, and mind our manners. In our household we felt tremendous pride in the attainments of blacks. We also took personally their disgrace. When scandal ensnared a black lawyer, doctor, or politician, we all felt ashamed, diminished, let down. Similarly, we felt embarrassed when blacks with poor diction and ridiculous comportment appeared on television. We thought that they made all of us blacks look bad. Indeed, we suspected that some whites in the news and entertainment industries preferred to publicize ignorant, silly, or menacing Negroes. We were taught to avoid and look down upon such blacks. We saw them as "bad Negroes" whose antics burdened "good Negroes"—like us.

My parents sternly ordered their children to always be dignified in the presence of white folks so that there would be no opportunity whatsoever for them to put us in racist stereotypical categories. We were told bluntly, "Don't act like a coon." "Don't act ghetto." "Don't act like a nigger."

My parents also told me and my siblings that racism made us

much more vulnerable than our white counterparts to certain sorts of risks and that we would be judged by less forgiving standards. Throughout my years at an elite, predominantly white, private high school (St. Albans), my parents warned me against attending any boisterous parties because if something went wrong, calling for the intervention of police, blacks like me would be the ones singled out for punishment. My parents maintained as well that in competition for advancement I would have to clearly outdistance my white peers. If my father said it once, he said it a thousand times: "Tie-tie, you lose."

My parents never suggested that these circumstances were just; to the contrary, they resented them and abhorred the prejudice and discrimination that littered with dangerous booby traps the pathways trod by their beloved children. They believed, however, that realities had to be faced with clear eyes in order to fashion effective responses. They were under no illusion that strict adherence to their protocols would immunize us completely against the ravages of Negrophobia; they knew of scores of episodes in which "good" blacks, too, fell victim to racism. But they reasoned that their strictures would at least improve our chances of surviving and thriving.

Respectability politics have become a target of derision among some who denounce it as a flight from blackness, an opportunistic gambit, a cowardly capitulation, a futile exercise, an implicit concession that racist mistreatment is excusable unless committed upon a perfect black victim. Michael Eric Dyson has dismissed the politics of respectability as the misguided notion that "good behavior and stern chiding will cure black ills and uplift black people and convince white people that we're human and worthy of respect." Theodore Johnson has asserted that the politics of respectability "is really a coping mechanism. It affirms the inferiority and unattractiveness of black culture." Mychal Denzel Smith has charged that "instead of asking why the options for black survival are so limited, the proselytizers of respectability politics would rather reify the theories of black inferiority that excite the white racist imagination." Ta-Nehisi Coates has called the politics of respectability "one of the most disreputable traditions in American politics," a strategy that is futile insofar as it constitutes "an attempt to raise black people to a superhuman standard," a strategy that is insidious in that "a separate and unequal standard for black people is always wrong," a strategy that is misguided insofar as "white racism needs no verification from black people."

Willing to acknowledge that the politics of respectability might have been necessary in the bad old days when blacks' weaknesses and the naked force of unapologetic white supremacy forced African Americans to swallow their pride for purposes of survival and advancement, detractors see current versions as an impediment to accomplishing valued new goals. They want to show solidarity with blacks who refuse to clean up their language or hitch up their pants notwithstanding the presence of NPR microphones or CNN cameras. They insist that however people speak or act, they are entitled to decent treatment, especially by agents of government, especially the police. They want to stress that there is no escape from racism, because neither a business suit, nor a briefcase, nor crisp diction, nor any of the other appurtenances of elevated status will enable an African American to avoid the racial taxes levied upon blackness.

Given the controversy surrounding it, what should one make of the politics of respectability? First, understand that it is mainly a strategy of public relations. A sound assessment of its deployment in a given instance depends on the goals sought to be attained, the manner in which it is practiced, and the context within which a given struggle is being waged. If you are truly indifferent to what onlookers think about you—if you really have an "I don't give a fuck" attitude toward the world—it makes sense for you to decline to make any of the calculations and compromises that attend the politics of respectability. Most people, however, are and should be attuned to their image. Appearance frequently affects the treatment one receives. Image does not wholly dictate response. But often it makes a difference. This proposition is so obvious as to be banal. Yet some commentators dispute it, asserting that racism is no respecter of respectability. "No matter how angelic their acts," Professor Melissa Harris-Perry has averred, "no matter how appropriate their attire, respectability has never been armor against violence toward black bodies." " 'Acting better,' " Professor Myisha Cherry has declared, "does not bring about being 'treated better.' . . . [F]our girls were in Sunday School when their Birmingham church was bombed. Amadou Diallo did not commit any crime, obeyed the police, yet was shot 41 times by the police."

No one (with any sense) claims, however, that "acting better" *ensures* immunity against racist violence or any other lurking catastrophe. The argument is simply that prudent conduct and sensitivity to how one appears to others improves chances for success in environments peppered with dangerous prejudices. It is unfortunate that safety might require such self-consciousness. It is imperative to reform society such that self-defensiveness of this sort is unneeded. In the interim, though, it is important for blacks to do what they can to protect themselves insofar as they remain burdened by a derogatory racial reputation that has been centuries in the making.

Is it wrong for black parents to deliver to their children the sort of talk that my parents gave to me? Does that talk constitute a form of blaming the victim insofar as it demands young blacks pursue certain actions and avoid certain actions in response to racism and thus implicitly faults young blacks if they decline (or fail) to follow the directives? The argument would run that just as it is blaming the victim to complain about the "suggestive" attire or demeanor of women who are raped, so, too, it is blaming the victim to complain about the "menacing" (or merely "too black") attire or demeanor of African American men who are harassed, assaulted, or killed. Continuing on, the argument would posit that just as the clothing a woman wears ought to be deemed irrelevant to the culpability of a rapist, so, too, should the appearance of a young black man be deemed irrelevant to the culpability of anyone who wrongfully inflicts violence upon him. Alas, this argument is misleading. The point of the parents' talk is not to determine the matter of fault; it is to assist the child in staying clear of a danger even though she or he is completely innocent and even though having to expend energy to avoid that danger is itself unfair. The parents' talk is merely a prudential plea to take reasonable precautions. Following the advice is no guarantee. But it improves the odds. The fact that so many black families engage in such talk illustrates their realistic belief that even though African Ameri-

cans remain hemmed in by unjust discriminations, there is still
something that they can do to better their prospects.

The tone of indignant futility struck by some opponents of
black respectability politics is peculiar. "Black folks," Professor
Brittney Cooper writes, "have already tested out" respectability
politics. "We've been trying to save our lives by dressing right,
talking right and never, ever fucking up since about 1877. That
shit has not worked." One wonders what the professor has in mind.
Is she complaining that even after having practiced respectability
politics, blacks still maddeningly confront racism? If so, I concur.
I disagree, however, if she is saying that the precautions and cultivation of image pursued by countless blacks have not mattered.
By dint of intelligent, brave, persistent, collective action that has
been undertaken at its best with due regard for public opinion,
African Americans have helped to improve conditions such that
people like Professor Cooper are now able to enjoy opportunities foreclosed to an earlier generation of blacks. To be sure, the
self-conscious deployment of black respectability politics has not
banished racism. But it has sometimes bettered the situation and
kept some black people alive when they might otherwise be dead.

It is worth noting the gap separating what many detractors of
respectability politics say and how they themselves behave. Well-
known detractors typically dress to impress—as do most adults on
a regular basis. Whenever people dress to impress, they are engaging in a politics of respectability. They may be contemptuous of
the conformism that demands the donning of certain attire for the
purpose of securing a job, or attaining a promotion, or satisfying
the expectations of a television audience, or obtaining relief for a
client in court. But they don the attire anyway, calculating that the
cost of doing so is overmatched by the potential costs of failing to
do so. Professor Dyson does not wear casual street clothes when
he appears on *Meet the Press*. He dresses up because he is rightly
attentive to his image. He practices the politics of respectability
even as he disparages its practice.

An oft-heard critique of the politics of respectability is that
it wrongly shifts attention from illegitimate social conditions to
the perceived deficiencies of those victimized by those conditions. One errs, however, in making a rigid choice between *either*

outward-facing protest *or* inward-facing character building. *Both* are needed. The achievements of the civil rights movement stemmed from and reinforced the reformation of white America to be sure, but they stemmed from and reinforced the reformation of black America as well.

Jesse Taylor writes that respectability politics assumes that "any bad outcome for black people is the fault of and can only be solved by black people." There are, I suppose, some people who believe that. But such an extreme and silly position should not be permitted to taint the whole camp of those who propound sensible black respectability politics. A sound version does not contend that any bad outcome for black people is their own fault; it recognizes the powerful effect of racism, impoverishment, and other conditions that are largely beyond the control of victims. A tenable version of respectability politics simply maintains that blacks ought to resist compounding the unfair burdens they bear by avoiding self-sabotage and otherwise objectionable conduct.

There are, to be sure, real problems that proponents of a sensible black respectability politics face. What should count as disreputable conduct can be subject to serious debate. Taylor observes that "the saggy pants of today were the backward caps of yesterday, the Afros of the 70s, the jazz music of decades ago." He has a point. Recall that the ladies of the WC "waged war" against jazz, perhaps America's greatest cultural invention. Some proponents of respectability politics have condemned rap, though it, too, is rightly celebrated as a remarkable American innovation.

"Respectability," moreover, has served as a harbor for bigotry or complacent accommodation of it. Certain leaders of the civil rights movement took care to keep Bayard Rustin and James Baldwin at a distance because of their dislike of gays or their desire to prevent homosexuality from being allowed to "taint" the movement's reputation. Distinguishing a prejudice that ought to be disregarded from a judgment that ought to be acted upon can be a difficult endeavor.

Who gives me the authority to distinguish what ought to be ostracized from what ought to be accepted? No one. It is an authority

I assume on my own. When a sufficient number of people concur with my preferences, a societal line is drawn. That line may be contested. But it is drawn nonetheless, and unavoidably so. Taylor may conclude that wearing "saggy pants" ought not be viewed as disreputable conduct. But surely he believes that some conduct ought to be avoided and condemned. What about the kid who ditches the saggy pants altogether and walks around dressed only in briefs or, further, in the nude? At some point, Taylor, too, will demand attentiveness to some zone of acceptable conduct . . . or flee.

Taylor writes that respectability politics assumes that bad outcomes for African Americans "can only be solved by black people." But no sensible version of respectability politics makes such a broad and unsupportable assumption. Rather, it posits that overcoming oppression is hard work that will require effort from many parties including those who have been grievously injured. Some will object that demanding anything of blacks at all is unfair inasmuch as they are victims of racism. But even if the demand is unfair, responding positively to it may be the fastest way for those victims to attain at least a semblance of the lives they want. A person injured by a drunk driver will have to take it upon herself to participate in the hard work of rehabilitation even if she played no role in her impairment. Similarly, even where a predicament is wholly attributable to white racism, blacks themselves will still have to do the hard work necessary to pull themselves out of it.

Perhaps some of those who denounce the politics of respectability are simply speaking loosely. Maybe what they mean to attack are merely misapplications. Some blacks in the 1960s, for example, were so wedded to a wooden, literalistic allegiance to respectable law-abidingness (and perhaps so dependent on white segregationist sponsors) that they opposed all acts of civil disobedience undertaken on behalf of the black freedom struggle. Among the most ruthless enemies of civil rights activists were black administrators of historically black public colleges who saw black dissidents as disgraceful lawbreakers. The error of these and other black adversaries of the black liberation struggle was failing to recognize that law and order is only *presumptively* legitimate—that under certain circumstances, like those that obtained in the Jim Crow South, "law and order" is undemocratic, oppressive, evil, and thus a suitable target for revolt. In the context of the battle over segregation, lawbreakers such as John Lewis are rightly viewed as heroes.

Seeking desperately to distinguish themselves from "bad" Negroes, some putatively "good" Negroes have wrongly tolerated racist misconduct. While most blacks rightly condemned lynching unequivocally, a few endorsed the theory of lynching's apologists. In 1899, commenting on the rising toll of lynchings, the Seventy-First Annual Conference of the African Methodist Episcopal Zion Church unanimously condemned "those worthless negroes whose shiftlessness leads them into the commission of heinous crimes." Alluding to the lynching of a black man accused of rape, the Reverend George Alexander McGuire stressed the horror of the alleged crime while offering no critique of the lawless violence inflicted upon the supposed miscreant. Speaking to an audience of African Americans at a high school graduation, McGuire declared that they must ruthlessly "ostracize such brutes in their own race."

In *Please Stop Helping Us: How Liberals Make It Harder for Blacks to Succeed,* Jason Riley, a black conservative, describes how he has been repeatedly stopped by police officers. He believes that these officers have racially profiled him—that they have taken his race into account in subjecting him to more intensive surveillance than would befall a white man in like circumstances. Riley, however, steadfastly refuses to chastise the police. Instead, he berates the black criminals who sully the image of the African American male. In Riley's view, it is they, the "bad Negroes"—not the police— who have put a target on his back.

The McGuire-Riley attitude tolerates what ought to be condemned as racist misbehavior perpetrated (or enabled) by police who should be held to a *higher* standard than ordinary citizens. Police are, after all, agents of government endowed with a (quasi) monopoly on the exercise of lawful violence. Failing to discipline wayward police will only exacerbate immoral lawlessness in distressed communities. By disgracing themselves, the putative guardians of law and order subvert what should be their greatest resource: the internalized allegiance of the citizenry.

Misapplications of the politics of respectability, however, should not obscure its essential message: any campaign, espe-

cially one launched by a marginalized group, should be attentive
to how it is perceived. Some claim that for blacks the politics of
respectability is futile because racism is beyond influence, or at
least beyond the influence of attempted good impressions. "Trading our sagging pants for suits and our sometimes foul language
for a newly formed loquacity does nothing to address the systemic
inequities and injustices that plague black bodies," Jared Loggins
declares. "Respectability did little to stop key provisions of the
Voting Rights Act from being stricken and George Zimmerman
from being acquitted of murder." Loggins appears to believe that
a strategy is of negligible value unless it *always* prevails. That is
nonsense. Loggins's cry of futility flies in the face of evidence that,
to an appreciable extent, racist attitudes can be, and are, amenable
to change. Reverend King's effort to touch the latent morality of
white oppressors was not simply a grand gesture of Christian faith
and Gandhian commitment; it was also good politics. The moral
attractiveness of the civil rights movement did convert some people whose negative perceptions of African Americans were altered
by the dignified character of black protests.

It is impossible to quantify precisely the extent to which the
civil rights movement caused or contributed to the evolution of
whites' attitude toward blacks—an evolution, in some instances,
from hard racism to softer racism and in other instances from soft
racism to a belief in racial equality. All one can say with confidence
is that carefully curated protest has contributed to the betterment
of America.

Those who repudiate the politics of respectability also err
in being inattentive to people like me—folks who are primed
for activism but allergic to protesters who are insufficiently concerned about the impressions they convey. I salute the outcry
against excessive use of force by law enforcement, police racism,
and failures to discipline wayward officers. I wince and shudder,
however, upon witnessing demonstrations at which the "I don't
give a fuck" disposition is evident—at which looting and arson
emerge, at which protesters carry themselves as if they were Chris
Rock caricatures, at which participants, by the way they look,
sound, and act, ratify negative stereotypes of black Americans that
are all too pervasive. I do more than wince and shudder; I decline

to participate, fearful of what reckless protesters may do or say. There is, of course, a limit to the order that can be imposed upon a protest. In any sizable crowd there will always be jerks. But what one can and should expect is that the leaders of a protest care about its image and act accordingly.

Such care was shown by most of those who participated in the demonstrations that erupted in the summer of 2020 in the aftermath of George Floyd's murder. Some of those protests were marred by looting and arson. But many activists, displaying commendable discipline and foresight, sought repeatedly to protect their efforts from discreditation by wayward followers, obnoxious thugs, or agents provocateurs. Activists did so by publicly announcing their disavowal of the violence. Some put themselves at risk by personally protecting stores and individuals from hooligans bent on seizing an opportunity to act out destructively. A distressingly numerous cadre of purportedly "woke" commentators justified or excused "rioting"—to surface a word that some progressive editors seem to have put on a "do not use" list. But thoughtful organizers and participants on the ground rejected that spurious line of indulgence. Instead, they insisted upon avoiding situations in which their protests could be made to look bad. They engaged in respectability politics even as they advanced a progressive racial agenda, adding a new chapter to an ongoing chronicle of admirable struggle for social justice.

9

Policing Racial Solidarity[1]

In *Who's Afraid of Post-Blackness? What It Means to Be Black Now*, the journalist Touré assails "self-appointed identity cops" who write "Authenticity Violations as if they were working for Internal Affairs making sure everyone does Blackness in the right way." He aims to "destroy the idea that there is a correct or legitimate way of doing Blackness," arguing that "if there's a right way then there must be a wrong way, and that [that] kind of thinking cuts us off from exploring the full potential of Black humanity." Touré wants African Americans to have the freedom to be black in whatever ways they choose, and he aspires "to banish from the collective mind the bankrupt, fraudulent concept of 'authentic' Blackness."

"Post-Blackness" is the label Touré deploys to describe the sensibility he champions, a "modern individualistic Blackness" that enthusiastically endorses novelty and diversity, fluidity and experimentation. "Post-Blackness," he insists, "is not a box, it's an unbox. It opens the door to everything. It's open-ended and open-sourced and endlessly customizable. It's whatever you want it to be."

Touré is right to be concerned about obsessions over racial disloyalty and compulsions toward racial conformity. The specter of defection occupies a salient place in the African American psyche. It figures in novels (for example, Ralph Ellison's *Invisible Man*), in films (for example, Spike Lee's *Bamboozled*), and in hip-hop (for example, the Geto Boys' "No Sellout"). It also figures in commentary questioning whether blacks have an obligation to reside in "the hood," marry within the race, or decline certain roles such as serving as a prosecutor or as counsel for white supremacists. Fears of abandonment resound in incantations such as "Don't forget where you come from" and "Stay black." They are also glimpsed in the relentless scrutiny trained upon prominent African Americans in searches for evidence of inadequate commitment to black solidarity. Assailed by angst, successful blacks often feel that they must conspicuously signal their allegiance to blackness. This anxiety is exploited by what the journalist John Blake calls the "Soul Patrol," black folk "who impose their definition of blackness on other black people." The Soul Patrol, Blake complains, is not content with choosing your friends. "They want to tell you how to think, where to live, whom to love, how to do your job."

A revealing example of soul patrolling is an obscure volume titled *The American Directory of Certified Uncle Toms: Being a Review of the History, Antics, and Attitudes of Handkerchief Heads, Aunt Jemimas, Head Negroes in Charge, and House Negroes Against the Freedom Aims of the Black Race.* The collective that compiled this *Directory* called itself—no kidding!—the Council on Black Internal Affairs. According to the Council, nothing more impedes blacks' progress than Uncle Toms (and the female equivalent, Aunt Jemimas). The Uncle Tom, the Council asserts, "repudiates strong Black leadership" and, for this service to the white power structure, "is anointed as a 'responsible leader' and praised as 'one of the good ones.'" The Council contends, however, that the Uncle Toms' immunity is ending. According to the Council, Uncle Toms— "non-practicing Black[s]"—will increasingly face sanctions from "practicing Black[s]" who conscientiously fulfill the responsibilities of racial citizenship.

The Council's list of Uncle Toms and Aunt Jemimas was long and varied. It included Julian Bond and John Lewis (too close to white benefactors of civil rights initiatives), Colin Powell and Clarence Thomas (too close to white Republicans), Mary Frances Berry and Vernon Jordan (too close to white Democrats), Harry Belafonte and Henry Louis Gates Jr. (too close to white women), and Oprah Winfrey and Maya Angelou (too close to

white audiences). Given what the Council demands in order to
be considered a practicing black in good standing—isolation from
the perceived contamination of influential whites—updated edi-
tions of the *Directory* would likely list—"blacklist"—almost every
prominent African American in the country.

Touré and other foes of "soul patrols" properly assail judgments that impose *wrongful* constraints. They appropriately
oppose the dogmatism, authoritarianism, and hankering for marginality that blights the thinking of the narrow ideologues who
habitually challenge the racial bona fides of any Negro who wins
widespread acclaim. They err, however, when they adopt a stance
of libertarian absolutism according to which it is *always* wrong
for one black person to question another black person's fidelity
to black America. An example of the absolutism I question can be
found in Stephen Carter's *Reflections of an Affirmative Action Baby*,
where he writes that "loving our people and loving our culture
does not require any restriction on what black people can think or
say or do or be."

No restriction?

Consider the case of William Hannibal Thomas, a black man
born free in Ohio in 1843 who wrote *The American Negro: What
He Was, What He Is, and What He May Become: A Critical and Practical Discussion.* This was one of the most Negrophobic diatribes
ever published, a tract in which Thomas wrote that "negro intelligence is both superficial and delusive"; that the Negro "lives
wholly in his passions, and is never so happy as when enveloped
in the glitter and gloss of shams"; that the Negro "represents an
intrinsically inferior type of humanity"; that Negroes "have not
learned the elementary principles of moral conduct"; and that
Negro men "have an inordinate craving for carnal knowledge
of white women." He recommended that blacks be whipped as
punishment for minor crimes and defended Jim Crow segregation. Demanding "the utter extermination, root and branch, of all
negroid beliefs and practices," he suggested that an optimal way of
handling the "negro problem" would be to remove black children
from their parents and place them in orphanages in which they
could be raised by white guardians.

With virtual unanimity, blacks excoriated *The American Negro* and shunned its author. Blacks in Memphis, living under the threat of lynchings that Thomas implicitly justified, held "an indignation meeting" at which they warned Thomas that he risked physical assault if he ever dared set foot in their city. Charles W. Chesnutt compared Thomas's "traitorous blow" unfavorably to the infamies of Judas and Benedict Arnold. Booker T. Washington concluded his negative review of *The American Negro* by remarking, "It is sad to think of a man without a country. It is sadder to think of a man without a race." J. Max Barber, the editor of *The Voice of the Negro*, declared, "Negro children ought to be taught to spit upon [Thomas's] name." A minister urged Thomas to "go off and hang thyself," while another critic insisted that "death is too good for him."

Was this outraged response wrong? Was this condemnation a regrettable insistence on "political correctness"? Was ostracizing this black white supremacist inappropriate? Should African Americans have accepted Thomas's ranting as just another flavor of blackness—a mere voicing of opinion that must, as a matter of principle, be granted an unimpeded hearing? No. No. No. And no!—at least under the assumption that there is such a thing as "black America," that blacks consider themselves "members" of it, that "black America" has boundaries, and that membership in "black America," like membership in all associations, has governing rules.

I would object to government seeking to ban Thomas's diatribe. Among reasons for protecting even hateful racist speech from governmental oppression is prudent fear of state power. I support, however, private parties and associations of private parties that mobilize to refute, challenge, condemn, shame, and ostracize racism in its manifold guises. In doing so, they are using their rightly protected freedom of expression to articulate a message much in need of voicing.

One should be appalled by the pettiness, bigotry, and dictatorial character of those, like the Council on Black Internal Affairs, who have intermittently afflicted African Americans with destructive bouts of internecine tyranny. Often those who are most militant in insisting upon black unity are those who are most thoughtless in thrusting perceived apostates outside the fold. A befitting response, however, is not to assert, as does Touré (echoing Henry Louis Gates Jr.), that there are as many ways to being "black" as there are black Americans and that therefore the idea of black racial treason ought to be discarded. Every community—be it a family, firm, tribe, denomination, or nation-state—necessarily has perimeters that distinguish members from nonmembers. And to remain a boundary, every perimeter must retain definition by some sort of policing. Any collective action, especially that which is burdensome, will present the seduction of betrayal and free riding—benefiting from the labor of others in the group while shirking one's own dues. "Every people," Martin Luther King Jr. observed, "has its share of opportunists, profiteers, free-loaders, and escapists." He might well have added that every people has its share of traitors. To deter betrayal and free riding, every collective deploys incentives (think of medals for valor) and punishments (think of imprisonment for draft or tax evasion or treason).

One could opt to end "blackness" as a self-conscious collective enterprise. William Whipper (1804–1876) urged African Americans to reject any racial labels that set them apart from other Americans. At a convention in 1835, he proposed a resolution—that passed—which urged his audience to abandon the use of racial classifications. According to Whipper, "We have too long witnessed the baneful effects of distinctions founded in hatred and prejudice, to advocate the insertion of either the word 'white' or 'colored.'" He maintained that for blacks the label "oppressed Americans" was a better tool of self-perception and public presentation than any expressly racial label. Today, numbers of people, from varying perspectives, argue in favor of abandoning racial classifications, racial boundaries, racial identifications.

Assuming the existence of a group that wants to identify itself racially, however, the policing of its boundaries is inescapable. Such policing is part of the unavoidable cost of maintaining a group. That is why all groups have rules that constitute the groups' boundaries. The rules may be implicit, but they are nonetheless rules of some sort. To the extent that one wants to perpetuate community but eschew any rules, one seeks a sociological impossibility. The establishment of boundaries and the threat of expulsion are unavoidable, albeit dangerous, aspects of any collective enterprise.*

Who in black America should be eligible for appropriate ostracism as a race traitor? That baleful designation should require more than a showing that a black person is an outlier—even an extreme outlier. It should require a convincing showing that a person has engaged in conduct that he or she knows, or should know, is deeply threatening to the collective well-being of black America. Merely mistaken, or erroneous, or wrongful conduct is insufficient to qualify as racial betrayal. To qualify, conduct must be of a sort that can properly be deemed unconscionable. But what sort of conduct is that? What, concretely, does racial betrayal look like?

Previously, I referred to William Hannibal Thomas as an African American rightly ostracized as a race traitor. Another is the Reverend H. H. Humes, a black Baptist minister who, for pay, served as the "eyes and ears" of the Mississippi State Sovereignty Commission, an organization that the state legislature established in 1956 to attack antiracist protesters and to defend white supremacy. Reverend Humes attended civil rights meetings so that he could inform his handlers at the Commission about protesters' identities and plans. When journalists exposed him as a paid informant, he was widely shunned. The Ministerial Improvement Association of Mississippi adopted a resolution denouncing Humes as "unworthy of the fellowship of the ministers of the Protestant denomination in Mississippi."

The Mississippi State Sovereignty Commission does not appear to have been highly successful in recruiting "good" Negroes to spy on "bad" Negroes. But, as the career of Reverend Humes attests, it did have some success. It recruited Fred H. Miller of Mound Bayou, Mississippi, who compiled a list of Negroes whom he believed to be members of the NAACP. Then there was B. L. Bell, the principal of a black elementary school in Cleveland, Mississippi, whom white officials lauded as a "white

---

* Bharath Palle made the point crisply in comments addressed to me about this essay: "Solidarity and loyalty are . . . concepts which implicitly rule out certain kinds of conduct. . . . [O]ne cannot do just about anything and still claim to be a loyal friend. . . . [F]or loyalty to be a meaningful concept . . . there *must* be certain actions that are disloyal."

man's Negro." Bell routinely informed the Commission of the identities, addresses, and phone numbers of people he suspected of being members of the NAACP.

Under the direction of the Federal Bureau of Investigation (FBI) and local police departments, black spies and agents provocateurs infiltrated every significant black activist organization during the Second Reconstruction. From 1963 to 1968, Jim Harrison, an accountant working for the Southern Christian Leadership Conference, regularly divulged information about the organization and its leader, Martin Luther King Jr. Between 1958 and 1976, Ernest Withers, a trusted civil rights movement photographer who lived in Memphis, routinely supplied the FBI with information about antiracist activists. Over the course of his eighteen-year career as an informant, he was paid what would amount now to about $150,000. In 1969, William O'Neal, an informant (who had become the chief of security for the Chicago Black Panther Party), relayed information to the FBI and Chicago police that was put to use in a raid that resulted in the killing of Fred Hampton, the young, charismatic leader of the Chicago Panthers. (O'Neal received a $3,000 bonus for this particular item of assistance but paid a high price in return in 1990, when he committed suicide.)

Who else might African Americans rightly exclude from their communion? One candidate is Jesse Lee Peterson, a black denizen of the far right wing whose main accomplishment seems to be his willingness to say just about anything that disparages black people in a way that is conducive to the most current reactionary talking point. In the aftermath of the Hurricane Katrina catastrophe, to undercut protest against governmental indifference and incompetence, Peterson maintained that most of the blacks stranded by the flooding were "welfare pampered," "lazy," and "immoral." In the midst of the outcry over the failed prosecution of George Zimmerman, Trayvon Martin's killer, Peterson parroted the vilification of the teenager that was popular in right-wing circles. In the aftermath of a police killing of a black man in Ferguson, Missouri, Peterson remarked,

> I may be the only one in America who does not grieve for
> Michael Brown's parents. . . . They failed to raise a decent

citizen. . . . Michael Brown's parents should be shunned, they should be made to feel embarrassed for the way that they raised [their son].

During the uproar over a decision to forgo criminal proceedings against a police officer involved in the death of an unarmed black man in Staten Island, New York, Peterson averred that "[Eric] Garner caused his own death by resisting arrest while suffering with pre-existing medical issues. . . . If Garner didn't struggle with police, the altercation wouldn't have escalated—and he'd be alive today!" Criticizing those who charge that racism played a role in the exoneration of the police who killed Brown in Ferguson and Garner in Staten Island, Peterson asserted that "these wicked black leaders are the ones urging a *real* war against the hearts and minds of black Americans."

Peterson gleefully plays the role assigned to him by right-wing propagandists. He invariably castigates those engaged in protests against racial injustice, invariably makes outrageous statements that would be deplored as "racist" were they uttered by a white person, and invariably uses his blackness as a shield against allegations that he is antiblack. Dylann Roof, the man who murdered nine parishioners at the Emanuel African Methodist Episcopal Church in Charleston, South Carolina, in the hopes of igniting a race war, is one of the most villainous criminals in modern American history. To Peterson, however, Roof was merely "angry about black-on-white crime and the false mainstream narrative of white 'racism' (which doesn't exist and never has)." True to form, Peterson blamed antiracist activists for the violence that claimed a life and caused many injuries when armed, belligerent neo-Nazis and adulators of the Ku Klux Klan marched on Charlottesville, Virginia. Later, he proclaimed his support for "white history month" to celebrate "the unsung heroes—whites who helped make this country great."

Some observers reject the idea that an African American can ever properly be dismissed from the race—"de-blacked" to use Professor Kimberly Norwood's memorable term. How one stands on this matter depends on how one conceptualizes racial membership. Some view racial membership as an immutable status: you are born black and that is it. I view the matter differently. I see choice as an integral element of membership. A person (or at least an adult person) should be black by choice with a recognized right of resignation. Carrying through with that contractualist conception, I also believe that a member of the black community should have no immunity from being de-blacked. Any African American should be subject to having his or her membership in blackness revoked if he or she convincingly demonstrates the absence of even a minimal communal allegiance or behaves in a way that is sufficiently adverse to the interests of the group. Touré declares that "Blackness is not a club you can be expelled from." But why should that be so? Religions impose excommunication. Nations revoke citizenship. Parents disown children. Married couples divorce. Why, as a matter of principle, should blacks be disallowed from casting from their community those adjudged to be enemies of it? The power of expulsion is so weighty that prudence should demand extraordinary care in exercising it. Still, the power to exclude and expel is, and should be, part of what constitutes black America.

Unlike the United States of America, black America lacks mechanisms of sovereignty—courts, for example—that can provide bureaucratic, centralized judgments backed by force. In black America only an amorphous public opinion adjudicates such matters, generating inconclusive results. Nonetheless, black public opinion should and does exercise some control over black America's communal boundary, determining in the process a person's standing as member, guest, or enemy.

Racial solidarity will always depend to some extent on self-appointed monitors of racial virtue. Despite occasional invocations of racial anarchism, Touré and his absolutist allies are themselves monitors. Their chiding of black political correctness is itself a variant of black political correctness. Those who want to maintain black community while condemning the peer pressure that makes collective action possible must recognize that solidarity always produces tension between unity and freedom. This dilemma is pervasive and insoluble.

10

Why Clarence Thomas
Ought to Be Ostracized[1]

Clarence Thomas took the oath of office as an associate justice of the Supreme Court of the United States on October 23, 1991. He is the country's second African American justice, having succeeded the first, Justice Thurgood Marshall. Born in Pin Point, Georgia, on June 23, 1948, Thomas grew up poor, experienced antiblack racism, and enjoyed opportunities pried open by the civil rights movement. He attended the College of the Holy Cross and Yale Law School pursuant to admissions programs that expressly sought to assist promising black students. In college and law school he espoused a militant black nationalism nourished by the writings and speeches of Malcolm X. Yet, upon graduating from Yale, he associated himself with the ambitious, well-connected Republican and future Missouri senator Jack Danforth, who became a lifelong mentor and door opener. Enlisting in the Reagan-Bush administrations, Thomas rose up the political ladder. In 1981, he was appointed assistant secretary for civil rights at the U.S. Department of Education; in 1982, chairman of the Equal Employment Opportunity Commission; and in 1990, a judge on the U.S. Court of Appeals for the District of Columbia Circuit. Then, in 1991, President George H. W. Bush tapped Thomas for the Supreme Court, triggering a rancorous battle over confirmation, especially after the future justice was accused of sexual harassment by his former aide Anita Hill.

As a justice, Thomas has developed a distinctive persona. Resolutely silent during oral arguments, he writes bold opinions in which he uninhibitedly repudiates precedent, purporting to propound an originalist understanding of the Constitution. He focuses on the racial consequences of cases more than his colleagues, and he also refers to black thinkers—for example, Frederick Douglass and Thomas Sowell—who are largely ignored by other justices. His voting record places him at the right edge of a conservative court. If Thomas had his way, there would exist no federal constitutional protections against state power aimed at punishing the provision of contraception or abortion; Americans would have no federal constitutional protection against laws punishing consensual sexual relations between adults; the ability of the federal government to regulate industry on behalf of consumers, workers, and the environment would be sharply curtailed; prisoners would have virtually no recourse to federal constitutional redress against abuse; racial affirmative action would be prohibited; and already narrow prohibitions against invidious discriminations would be narrowed even further. In 2000, Thomas cast a decisive vote in *Bush v. Gore*, which guaranteed that George W. Bush would become president. In 2008, he cast a key vote in *District of Columbia v. Heller*, which curtailed governmental authority to regulate firearms. And in 2013, Thomas cast a pivotal vote in *Shelby County v. Holder*, which eviscerated the Voting Rights Act of 1965, opening the door to ill-intentioned changes in election procedures in states with long histories of racial disenfranchisement.

In *The Enigma of Clarence Thomas* (2019), the political theorist Corey Robin sets out to explicate the justice's motivations, writings, and votes. He explores how Thomas "has managed to take his peculiar blend of black nationalism and black conservatism and . . . fit this alien and intransigent politics into that most traditional and stylized genre of the American canon, the Supreme Court opinion." According to Robin, "Race is the foundational principle of Thomas's philosophy and jurisprudence. . . . It is the ground of his thinking about morals and politics, society and the law." Other academics have previously noted this feature of his thinking, but Robin develops the argument for a general audience, updates it, and extends it to a broader range of topics. Robin notes, for example, how Thomas justifies his hostility to the state's power to take private property through eminent domain by reference to episodes in which municipalities callously used that power to demolish black communities. He also notes how Thomas supported his disapproval of campaign finance restrictions by reference to the notorious white supremacist Senator Benjamin Tillman of South Carolina, who authored legislation that banned corporations from contributing to candidates for federal elective office. "For Thomas," Robin notes, "even the seemingly non-racial subject of campaign finance is, like so many constitutional questions, deeply enmeshed in race."

Robin portrays Thomas as self-consciously committed to improving the lot of black people, albeit by means at odds with the prescriptions of many prominent African American politicians and voters, most of whom are liberal Democrats. Convinced that the federal government cannot help black Americans with what he sees as their most pressing problems—internal communal issues of morale—Thomas favors shrinking social welfare programs. Insisting that stringent law enforcement is necessary to save blacks from the depredations of criminality, he favors strengthening policing. In perhaps the most novel feature of Robin's analysis, he argues that Thomas's willingness to countenance disenfranchisement and racially discriminatory punishment derives from Thomas's apparent belief that the best qualities in black America have been elicited in oppressive circumstances and that therefore, paradoxically, those circumstances are good for black Americans. Pursuant to that belief, Robin argues, Thomas has rationalized nearly all of his efforts to maintain the legal architecture under which African Americans have suffered most because "adversity helps the black community develop its inner virtue and resolve." "It's astonishing," Robin observes, "how openly Thomas embraces not just federalism but a view of federalism associated with the slaveocracy and Jim Crow."

To make his case, Robin opts for "interpretation and analysis rather than objection and critique." He abhors Thomas's politics, maintaining that the justice's "beliefs are disturbing, even ugly; his style brutal." But Robin wants readers to engage with Thomas's thinking in detail rather than evading it through summary dismissal. Robin invites this engagement by trying to describe Thomas's beliefs with sufficient equanimity to enable readers to glimpse the world through Thomas's eyes—no matter how troubling that perspective may be. In his determined effort to be coolly analytical and to give Thomas his just due, however, Robin can at times accord the justice an excessive solicitude. Robin depicts Thomas as a figure of impassioned idealism and formidable intellectuality. I view him as a Republican apparatchik skilled in bureaucratic self-promotion and the advancement of retrograde policies.

Thomas routinely portrays himself as an accidental justice whom others elevated without his prompting. That is ridiculous. As Jane Mayer and Jill Abramson showed in *Strange Justice: The Selling of Clarence Thomas*, the justice campaigned assiduously for the post. Then, when he got into trouble in the wake of Anita Hill's allegation that he had sexually harassed her, Thomas cannily manipulated others' decent inhibitions to complete his climb up the political ladder. With appalling effectiveness, he cowed the Senate Judiciary Committee, led by the then senator Joseph Biden, by charging that the public examination of Hill's claim constituted a "high-tech lynching."

Throughout the confirmation hearings, Thomas offered ignorant or evasive answers. That he did so was not wholly his fault, because the Supreme Court confirmation hearing has become a ritual that penalizes candor. Since Robert Bork was defeated in part because of the forthcoming character of his testimony—along with his reactionary politics and Nixonian shadow—nominees have been expected to obfuscate. But Thomas's performance was dismal even by the low standards of the confirmation charade. When Senator Patrick Leahy asked Thomas to name a few important decisions handed down by the Supreme Court during the two preceding decades, the court of appeals judge mustered an embarrassingly halting reply. When asked about *Roe v. Wade*, he acted as though he had hardly even thought about the case.

Robin notes that the two justices who have faced the most complaints of incompetence are Marshall and Thomas. That is not coincidental. Racism plays a role in some of these charges.

But that should not excuse Thomas's lack of legal fluency, nor the evident weakness of Thomas's pre-confirmation legal record (notwithstanding his promotion to high posts), nor his subsequent reluctance to enter into public disputation either at oral arguments or at other unscripted occasions. There is, alas, a strong basis for questioning Thomas's intellectual heft.

Robin accepts at face value Thomas's portrayal of himself as a race man deeply invested in black America. He notes that Thomas quotes approvingly from Frederick Douglass, talks admiringly of black folk who persevered under the brutal reign of Jim Crow, condemns bitterly the continuing prevalence of antiblack racism, and concerns himself with the racial consequences of disputed policies. But Robin fails to explain that much of this is pretense. When Thomas cites Douglass, he does so not to further that great man's challenge to white supremacy but to burnish his own brand. He uses Douglass to signal that beneath his reactionary politics he remains "a brother" who has not forgotten where he came from and that he is no ordinary right-wing Republican but something else more valuable—a *black* right-wing Republican with code-switching capabilities.

Robin is excessively impressed by Thomas's opinions, like his lone dissent in *Virginia v. Black*. In that ruling the Court invalidated on First Amendment grounds a statute criminalizing cross burning. To Robin, Thomas's dissent shows the justice getting his black on. But the position Thomas adopted—supporting the broad criminalization of cross burning—in addition to being misguided as a matter of First Amendment law, posed, in fact, no threat to most white conservatives who are happy to sustain a system of racial hierarchy even as they condemn KKK-style symbolic mayhem.

Thomas gets his black on as a justice only when the stakes are low. When the stakes are high, Thomas's attentiveness to the interests of black Americans is scant. This is best illustrated by his vote in *Shelby County*, the most unjustifiable and hurtful decision imposed upon black America during the past half century. That ruling will go down in history alongside such judicial delinquencies as *Plessy v. Ferguson*, *Giles v. Harris*, and *Korematsu v. United States*. And Thomas provided the crucial fifth vote to cripple legislation for which proponents of racial justice marched, bled, and in some instances died. For Robin, Thomas's vote in *Shelby County* is an expression of belief that the rules of political engagement are so stacked against African Americans that no intervention, including that proffered by the Voting Rights Act, can effectively assist them. Thomas's vote, he contends, was meant to convey the message that for blacks electoral politics is a futile game in which whites will always ultimately call the shots, set the rules, and determine the winners. Albeit creative, this interpretation is also unconvincing. A more familiar and prosaic reading of Thomas's vote in *Shelby County* is far more plausible: that Thomas's partisan motivations and indifference to racial wrongs drove him to aid and abet other Republican justices in crippling a statute that, from their vantage, had been used all too effectively to encourage and protect voters who were likely to support their political enemies.

To a large extent, *The Enigma of Clarence Thomas* falls victim to a talented con artist who has, over the course of his long career, seduced and traduced many observers, allies, and adversaries. Robin maintains that Thomas is authentic, if misguided, in his devotion to advancing the best interests of black America. In support of this view, Robin leans heavily on Thomas's stated idolization of black heroes, particularly the demanding grandfather who raised him, his declared desire to advance African Americans, and his claim that he feels hurt because many black Americans revile him for his pronouncements. An assumption of Thomas's good faith is misplaced. But even an honest belief that a given policy is beneficial ought not insulate a supporter of the policy from condemnation upon a showing that the policy in question harms those it purportedly seeks to help.

At the turn of the twentieth century, a black commentator, William Hannibal Thomas, recommended that black Americans embrace their own racial subordination, even to the extent of permitting the state to divest black parents of authority over their children. He offered this advice with apparent sincerity, honestly believing it to be in the best interest of blacks. Fortunately, though, his sincerity did not assuage the properly outraged sentiments of observers such as the essayist and novelist Charles W. Chesnutt, who denounced William Hannibal Thomas's proposals as a "traitorous blow." Many African American critics of Clarence Thomas have responded similarly. Addressing black Americans in 1993, the writer Pearl Cleage insisted starkly, Thomas "is an enemy of our race." His record as a justice has only accentuated the prescience of her judgment.

I sympathize with those who have been solicitous of Thomas. I am among their number. After Thomas's first year on the Court, he was invited to address the National Bar Association (NBA), an organization created when the American Bar Association was hostile to black lawyers. A stalwart champion of social justice, the court of appeals judge A. Leon Higginbotham, objected, urging the NBA to rescind its invitation. I wrote an article agreeing with the NBA's honoring of Thomas and its effort to engage him in dialogue. I was a sap. Judge Higginbotham was correct. Thomas did not deserve the platform that was offered to him. He had shown little distinction as a jurist and, contrary to his claims, was uninterested in a forthright exchange of ideas.

Subsequently, I erred again. I argued that while Thomas is profoundly mistaken in racial policy, it is wrong to stigmatize him as a "sellout." But if Thomas is not a sellout, then the term has no utility. He is the paradigmatic figure whom many African Americans rightly despise—the black who, from a position of privilege attained by the sponsorship of powerful whites, consistently subverts struggles for African American collective elevation, all the while deploying his blackness as a shield against criticism.

Robin accords Thomas a grudging respect, but alas, the earnestness of his effort to understand an ideological adversary contrasts sharply with the vapidity and opportunism of his subject. This is not to say that Thomas is diabolical in every facet of life. Many who have engaged him personally, including some who disagree strenuously with his politics, report that he is genuinely likable one-on-one. Within the Supreme Court Building, he is widely appreciated for taking time to know and assist members of its workforce who are often ignored—security personnel, secretaries, the food service and janitorial crews. And on occasion he has quietly assisted people whose ideological leanings he opposes.

There is reason to think that he would be a nice neighbor. In his judicial role, however, Thomas's thinking is little more than a distillation of reactionary sentiments, roiling resentments, and a superficial acquaintance with black political thought. He has substantiated the forebodings of those who warned that he would be a disaster as a justice. And he has disappointed those who believed that the circumstances of his upbringing would, with time, make him more attuned to the plight of the disadvantaged. With respect to the most consequential rulings of his career, a far better guide to the thinking of Clarence Thomas than the Constitution or *The Autobiography of Malcolm X* is the platform of the Republican Party and the talking points of Rush Limbaugh.

11

Say It Loud!
On Racial Shame, Pride, Kinship,
and Other Problems[1]

SHAME

In 1968 in the gym at Paul Junior High School in Washington, D.C., I asked a buddy whether he was interested in a certain girl. He told me that he wasn't because she was too dark. Though we were only in our early teenage years, we were aware that society imposed punitive judgments upon us based on the color of our skin.

> *If you're black, get back.*
> *If you're brown, stick around.*
> *If you're white, you're all right.*

At one level of consciousness we objected to this imposition. But at another level, we had internalized the denigration. My friends and I spent hours trading racialized insults, many of which had to do with our mamas (go to the internet and see what pops up when you type "yo mama so black"):

Yo mama so black she blend in with the chalkboard.

Yo mama so black people think she Batman.

Yo mama's so dark when she goes outside streetlights turn on.

In *Soul on Ice*, Eldridge Cleaver noted how, in prison, he and fellow African American inmates played similar rhetorical games that reflected a kindred, albeit grimmer, disparagement of darkness. Recalling a colleague's disdain for African American women, Cleaver remembers the man saying, "I don't want nothing black but a Cadillac." Another inmate reportedly remarked, "If money was black, I wouldn't want none of it."

In August 1968, four months after the assassination of Martin Luther King Jr., James Brown recorded and released "Say It Loud, I'm Black and I'm Proud," which shot to the top of the *Billboard* magazine rhythm and blues singles chart, where it remained for six weeks. Of all of Brown's many hits—"Please, Please, Please," "Try Me," "Papa's Got a Brand New Bag," "Get Up Offa That Thing"—the most influential and resonant is "Say It Loud." Various musicians in the 1960s tapped into and reinforced black assertiveness, defiance, autonomy, solidarity, and pride. Nina Simone sang "Mississippi Goddam." Curtis Mayfield and the Impressions sang "We're a Winner." The Chi-Lites sang "(For God's Sake) Give More Power to the People." Sam Cooke (and Aretha Franklin and Otis Redding) sang "A Change Is Gonna Come." But no entertainer equaled Brown's vocalization of African Americans' newly triumphal sense of self-acceptance.

That Brown created a song popularly associated with the Black Power movement is ironic. He generally stayed away from civil rights activism, endorsed the presidential reelection of Richard Nixon, lavishly praised Ronald Reagan, and consistently lauded Strom Thurmond. In "America Is My Home," also released in the summer of 1968, Brown proclaimed,

> *America is still the best country*
> *And that's without a doubt.*

With panegyrics to the greatness of America and his incessant pull-yourself-up-ism, Brown would have been wholly at home with Clarence Thomas.

The lyrics to "Say It Loud" are not nearly as artful as those that grace "Lift Every Voice and Sing," set to music by James Weldon Johnson and J. Rosamond Johnson in 1905, or "What Did I Do to Be So Black and Blue?," set to music by Fats Waller, Harry Brooks, and Andy Razaf in 1929. "Lift Every Voice" is a magnificent exhortation championing dignity, bravery, and resilience. Known widely as the Negro national anthem, the Johnsons' song has become a staple in the hymnal of American patriotism. "What Did I Do?" is an ironic protest against racist mistreatment that has been performed by a host of remarkable artists, including Ethel Waters and Roy Eldridge. No one performed it with more aching poignancy, however, than the great Louis Armstrong, whose memorable renderings uniquely highlighted the self-loathing that victims of abuse all too often assist in inflicting upon themselves.

The most notable thing about "Say It Loud" is the simple proclamation: "I'm black and I'm proud!" Even though by 1968 uprisings against white supremacism had been erupting for a decade with unprecedented intensity and success—the Montgomery bus boycott, the Children's Crusade in Birmingham, the protest against disenfranchisement in Selma—prejudice against blackness remained prevalent and powerful throughout the country, including among African Americans. In my neighborhood, calling someone "black" was an insult, often the trigger to a fight. Our derogation of "black" derived from a centuries-long campaign of stigmatization that manifested itself in countless ways, including language. "Dirty," "soiled," "sinister," "sad," "sullen," "grim," "tragic," and "miserable" are synonyms for "black." By contrast, "innocent," "pure," "spotless," "fresh," "virginal," "flawless," and "fortunate" are synonyms for "white." "Black magic" refers to the use of supernatural powers for evil. "White magic" refers to the use of supernatural powers for good. A "black lie" is harmful. A "white lie" is harmless.

Champions of African American uplift sought to liberate the image of blackness from the layers of derision, contempt, fear, and hatred with which it had been smeared for centuries. James Brown's anthem was a rousing instance of this attempted rehabilitation. Of course the felt need to proclaim pride in blackness underscored African Americans' vulnerability, the pull of their collective self-negation, the threat posed by the oft-heard accusation "Niggers ain't shit." People secure in their status don't feel compelled to trumpet their pride. It was precisely because of the precariousness of African Americans' confidence in themselves as a people that "Say It Loud" and kindred assertions of racial identity were so exhilarating.

Reclamation of blackness took many forms. After long celebrating light skin, thin lips, and "good" (that is, straight) hair, more African Americans began belatedly to valorize dark skin, thick lips, and "bad" (that is, kinky) hair. For purposes of collective self-identification, African Americans took to calling themselves "black" as opposed to "Negro" or "colored." The *Negro Digest* was renamed *Black World*. Negro History Week was superseded by Black History Month. Students demanded the establishment of black studies programs. Writers such as Amiri Baraka, Nikki Giovanni, Audre Lorde, and Larry Neal created the Black Arts Movement. The ideological heirs of Malcolm X sparked an upsurge in organizing that gave rise to, among other things, the Black Panther Party and the National Black Political Conventions.

The celebration of blackness, however, was not limited to devotees of Black Power. In his final book, *Where Do We Go from Here?*, Martin Luther King Jr. also embraced the reclamation of blackness. "One must not overlook," he insisted, "the positive value in calling the Negro to a new sense of manhood, to a deep feeling of racial pride and to an audacious appreciation of his heritage. The Negro . . . must stand up amid a system that still oppresses him and develop an unassailable and majestic sense of his own value. He must no longer be ashamed of being black."

The reclamation of blackness generated mixed results. By the end of the 1960s, the stigmatization of "black" had ceased among the great majority of African Americans. In my neighborhood, it was no longer a fighting word. To the contrary, at least rhetorically, expressed pride in blackness became wholly conventional. Here, as elsewhere, however, changes wrought by the black liberation movement, though impressive, were only partial. Thirty-nine years *after* the release of "Say It Loud," Professors Jennifer Hochschild and Vesla Weaver, having canvassed the pertinent social scientific literature, declared authoritatively,

Relative to their lighter-skinned counterparts, dark-skinned blacks have lower levels of education, income and job status. They are less likely to own homes or to marry; and dark-skinned blacks' prison sentences are longer. . . . [M]ost Americans prefer lighter to darker skin aesthetically, normatively and culturally. Film-makers, novelists, advertisers, modeling agencies, matchmaking websites— all demonstrate how much the power of a fair complexion, along with straight hair and Eurocentric facial features, appeals to Americans.

The ongoing harm suffered by darker-skinned people stems not only from colorism harbored by whites and other nonblacks; it stems as well from colorism harbored by blacks. Sometimes the message is delivered only inferentially. Consider Stevie Wonder's "Living for the City." Describing the song's protagonist, a young man born in "hard time" Mississippi, Wonder sings, "His sister's black but she is sho 'nuff pretty." *But* she is sho 'nuff pretty? This suggests that the sister is pretty *despite* her blackness. More direct is the searing evidence showcased in the 2011 documentary film *Dark Girls.* There one can hear black men confessing preference for lighter-skinned women and see black women recall the ensuing devastation upon being told by friends and relatives that they would be perceived as more attractive if only they were lighter.

Colorism was part of the drama that featured Barack and Michelle Obama. On the one hand, the fact that a man of color was twice elected to the presidency was an undeniable sign that pigmentocracy has waned. That point was accentuated by the First Lady—not only an African American, but a *dark-skinned* African American. On the other hand, the very delight that many blacks express about the Obamas as a couple—the intense satisfaction that an ambitious black man chose as his partner an accomplished dark woman—arises in part from the rankling impression that frequently such men prefer lighter companions.

Intra-racial colorism in black America is often seen as a topic that should, if possible, be avoided, especially in "mixed company." That sense of embarrassment led officials at historically black colleges in Atlanta to evict Spike Lee from their campuses when they learned that he was exploring and exposing colorism in his film *School Daze*. That impulse toward avoidance remains strong. With racial prejudice against *all* African Americans still a potent force, many blacks would just as soon ditch the discussion of "black on black" complexional bias.

PRIDE

What is the proper role of race in determining how I, an African American, should feel toward other blacks? One response is that although I should not dislike people because of their race, there is nothing wrong with having a racial liking for other black people. Indeed, many would go further and maintain that something would be wrong with me if I did not sense and express racial pride, racial affection, racial kinship, racial patriotism, racial loyalty, racial solidarity—synonyms for that amalgam of belief, intuition, and commitment that manifests itself when, for racial reasons, blacks treat other blacks with more solicitude than they do those perceived to be outside the family of blackness.

Some conduct animated by these sentiments has blended into the background of daily routine, as when blacks who are strangers nonetheless speak to each other—"Hello," "Hey," "Yo"—or hug or give each other a soul handshake or a dap or refer to each other as "brother" or "sister." Other manifestations are more dramatic. The Million Man March, which brought at least 500,000 black men to Washington, D.C., in 1995, was a demonstration predicated on the notion that blackness gives rise to racial obligation and that black people should have a special, closer, more affectionate relationship with their fellow blacks than with others in America's diverse society. The rhapsodic outpouring of black support for Barack Obama is another example. Many African Americans believed that supporting him, and doing so enthusiastically, was an obligatory function of racial pride and kinship.

To a large extent I reject notions of racial pride and kinship. I insert the qualifier—"to a large extent"—not to hedge but simply to acknowledge the inconsistency in my thought and conduct. I often think and act like a conventional left-liberal African American "race man" who situates himself in an imagined black American polity, enjoys racial citizenship, possesses a fanciful "black card," and treats blacks preferentially on grounds of racial kinship. But I view that aspect of myself as problematic.

Sometimes I eschew racial pride because of my conception of what should properly be the object of pride for an individual: something that he or she has accomplished. I can rightly feel pride in a good deed I have done or a good effort I have made. I cannot rightly feel pride in some state of affairs that is independent of my contribution to it. The color of my skin, the width of my nose, the texture of my hair, and the various other signs that prompt people to label me black constitute such a state of affairs. I did not achieve my racial designation. It was something I inherited—like my nationality and socioeconomic starting place and gender—and therefore something for which I should not feel pride or receive credit. In taking this position, I follow Frederick Douglass, who declared that "the only excuse for pride in individuals . . . is in the fact of their own achievements." If the sun has created curled hair and tanned skin, Douglass observed, "let the sun be proud of its achievement."

It is understandable why people have often made inherited group status an honorific credential. Personal achievement is difficult to attain, and the lack of it often leaves a vacuum that racial pride can easily fill. Thus even if a person has little to show for himself, racial pride gives him status.

But maybe I am misconstruing what people mean by racial pride; perhaps it means simply that one is unashamed of one's race. To that I have no objection. No one should be ashamed of the labeling by which she or he is racially categorized, because no one chooses her or his parents or the signs by which society describes and sorts people. (For this very same reason, no one should congratulate herself on her race insofar as it is merely an accident of birth.) I suspect, though, that for many who clutch "racial pride," what they are embracing is more than the idea that they are unembarrassed by their race. They mean, echoing Marcus Garvey, that "to be [black] is no disgrace, but an honor." When they sing "Say it loud / I'm black and I'm proud," they are expressing not just the absence of shame but delight and assertiveness in valuing a racial designation that has long been stigmatized.

There is an important virtue in this assertion of the value of black life. It combats something still eminently in need of challenge: the assumption that because of their race black people are stupid, ugly, and low, and that because of their race white people are smart, beautiful, and righteous. But within some of the forms that this assertiveness has taken are important vices—including the belief that because of racial kinship blacks ought to value blacks more highly than others.

KINSHIP

I reject racial kinship—at least I try to do so when I am thinking about the matter self-consciously. I do so as part of a broad campaign to claim what the political theorist Michael Sandel labels disapprovingly "the unencumbered self." The unencumbered self is free and independent of aims and attachments it does not choose for itself. "Freed from the sanctions of custom and tradition and inherited status, unbound by moral ties antecedent to choice, the self is installed as sovereign, cast as the author of the only obligations that constrain." Sandel believes that the unencumbered self is an illusion and that the yearning for it is a manifestation of a shallow liberalism that "cannot account for certain moral and political obligations that we commonly recognize, even prize"— "obligations of solidarity, religious duties, and other moral ties that may claim us for reasons unrelated to a choice," which are "indispensable aspects of our moral and political experience." Sandel's objection to those who, like me, seek the unencumbered self is that they fail to appreciate loyalties and responsibilities that should be accorded moral force partly because they influence our identity, such that living by these attachments "is inseparable from understanding ourselves as the particular persons we are—as members of this family or city or nation or people, as bearers of that history, as citizens of this republic."

Sandel faults the model of the unencumbered self because, he says, it cannot account for feelings of solidarity and loyalty that most people have not chosen to impose upon themselves but cherish nonetheless. This is a fault, however, only if we believe that the traditional unchosen attachments Sandel celebrates should be accorded moral weight. I am not prepared to do that simply because such attachments exist, have long existed, and are passionately felt. Feelings of primordial attachment often represent mere prejudice or superstition, a hangover of the childhood socialization from which many people never recover.

One defense of racial kinship takes the shape of an analogy between race and family. This position was strikingly advanced by the nineteenth-century black-nationalist intellectual Alexander Crummell, who asserted that "a race *is* a family," that "race feeling, like the family feeling, is of divine origin," and that the extinction of race feeling is thus—fortunately, in his view—just as impossible as the extinction of family feeling.

Analogizing race to family is a potent rhetorical move used to challenge those who, like me, are animated by a liberal, individualistic, and universalistic ethos that is skeptical of, if not hostile to, the particularisms—national, ethnic, religious, and racial—that seem to have grown so strong recently, even in arenas, such as major cosmopolitan universities, where one might have expected their demise. The central point of the challenge is to suggest that the norms I embrace will, or at least should, wobble and collapse in the face of claims on familial loyalty. Blood, as they say, is thicker than water.

One way to deal with the race-family analogy is to question its aptness on the grounds that a race is so much more populous than what is commonly thought of as a family that race cannot give rise to similar circumstances of intimacy or feelings of loyalty. When we think of a family, we think of a small, close-knit association of people who grow to know one another intimately over time. A race, by contrast, is a conglomeration of strangers linked by an imagined attachment. Black men at the Million Man March assuredly called one another "brothers." But if certain questions were posed ("Would you be willing to lend me a thousand dollars?" or "Would you be willing to donate a kidney to me?"), the distance between those "brothers" would have quickly become clear.

But I do not want to rest my argument here. Rather, I want to accept the race-family analogy in order to strengthen my attack on assumptions that privilege status-driven loyalties (the loyalties of blood) over chosen loyalties (the loyalties of will). In my view, many people, including legislators and judges, make far too much of blood ties in derogation of ties created by loving effort. A vivid illustration is provided by the following kind of child-custody decision. It involves a child who has been separated from her parents and placed with adults who assume the role of foster parents. The latter nurture her, come to love her, and ultimately seek legally to become her new parents. If the "blood" parents of the child do not interfere, the foster parents will have a good chance of attaining the adoption. If, however, the blood parents say they want "their" child back, authorities in many jurisdictions will privilege the blood connection and return the child—even if the initial separation is attributable to the fault of the blood parents, even if the child has been with the foster parents for a long time and is prospering under their care, even if the child views the foster parents as her parents and wants to stay with them, and even if there is good reason to believe that the foster parents will provide a more secure home setting than the child's blood parents. Judges make such rulings in large part because they are misled by idolatry of "blood," which is an ideological cousin to the racial beliefs I oppose.

Am I saying that, morally, blood ties are an unsatisfying basis for preferring one's genetic relatives to others? Yes, that is indeed what I am saying. I will rightly give the only life jacket on the sinking ship to my mother as opposed to your mother, because I love my mother (or at least I love her more than yours). I love my mother, however, not because of a genetic tie but because over time she has done countless things that prompt me to love her. She took care of me when I could not take care of myself. She encouraged me. She provided for my future by taking me to the doctor when appropriate, disciplining me, giving me advice, paying for my education. I love her, too, because of qualities I have seen her exhibit in interactions with others—my father, my brother, my sister, neighbors, colleagues, adversaries. The biological connection helped to create the framework in which I have been able to see and experience her lovable qualities. But it is deeds, not blood—doing, not merely being—that is the morally appropriate basis for my preference for my mother over all other mothers in the world.

Some contend, though, that "doing" is what lies at the foundation of black racial kinship—that the reason one should feel morally compelled by virtue of one's blackness to have and show racial solidarity toward other blacks is that preceding generations of black people did things animated by racial loyalty that now benefit all black people. These advocates maintain that the benefits bestowed—for instance, *Brown v. Board of Education,* the Civil Rights Act of 1964, the Voting Rights Act of 1965, and affirmative action programs—impose upon blacks correlative racial obligations. That is what some are getting at when they say that all blacks have a racial obligation to "give back" to the black community.

I agree that one should be grateful to those who have waged struggles for racial justice, sometimes at tremendous sacrifice. But why should my gratitude be racially bounded? Elijah Lovejoy, a white man murdered in Alton, Illinois, in 1837 for advocating the abolition of slavery, participated just as fervently in that great crusade as any person of my hue. The same could be said of scores of other white abolitionists who were hounded, beaten, imprisoned, and killed for radically defying the norms of their time and place. More recently, it was not only courageous black people such as Medgar Evers, Vernon Dahmer, and James Chaney who fought white supremacy in the shadow of death. White people like James Reeb and Viola Liuzzo were there too, as were Andrew Goodman and Michael Schwerner. In light of this history I see no reason why paying homage to the struggle for racial justice and endeavoring to continue that struggle must entail any sort of racially stratified loyalty. One of the most encouraging developments in recent times has been popularization of the slogan "Black Lives Matter." An important aspect of that popularization has involved extending the slogan beyond sponsorship by black people. White people, too, insist that Black Lives Matter. They rightly do so. They rightly do so because *all* people should insist that in light of evidence indicating a continuing devaluation of black lives, special efforts are warranted to underscore that black humanity is fully as precious as all other facets of humanity.

I have argued that there is no obligation for a black person to feel morally bound to prefer blacks to others on the basis of a purported racial kinship. But what do I say to a person who is considering whether to *choose* to embrace racial kinship? In a contribution to an anthology edited by Gerald Early and interestingly titled *Lure and Loathing: Essays on Race, Identity, and the Ambivalence of Assimilation*, Stephen Carter wrote about his racial love for black people, declaring at one point that "to love one's people is to crave a kind of familyhood with them." Carter observed that this feeling of racial kinship affected the way in which he values the opinions of others. "The good opinions of black people . . . matter to me more," he wrote, than the good opinions of white people. "That is my choice, and I cannot imagine ever making another." Previously, in *Reflections of an Affirmative Action Baby*, he offered an illustration of how this choice exhibited itself:

> Each December, my wife and I host a holiday dessert for the black students at the Yale Law School. . . . [O]ur hope is to provide for the students an opportunity to unwind, to escape, to renew themselves, to chat, to argue, to complain—in short, to relax. For my wife and myself, the party is a chance to get to know some of the people who will lead black America (and white America, too). . . . But more than that, we feel a deep emotional connection to them, through our blackness: we look at their youthful, enthusiastic faces and see ourselves. There is something affirming about the occasion—for them, we hope, but certainly for us. It is a reminder of the bright and supportive side of solidarity.

I find this episode troubling. In the mind of a teacher there ought to be no stratification of students such that the instructor feels closer to certain pupils than to others on grounds of racial kinship. No teacher ought to view certain students as his racial "brothers and sisters" while viewing others as, well, mere students. Every student should be free from the worry that because of race he or she will have less opportunity to benefit from what a teacher has to offer.

Friends tell me that I pay insufficient attention to the complexity of the identities and roles that individuals assume in society and that I am thus ignoring or minimizing the ability of a black professor to be both a good teacher who serves all his students well *and* a good racial patriot who feels a special affection for fellow blacks. These friends assert that no one has a valid basis for complaint so long as the professor in his official duties is even-handed in his treatment of everyone. If these duties are met, they see no problem if the black professor, paying homage to his feelings of racial kinship, goes beyond what is officially required in his dealings with black students.

I find it inconceivable, however, that there would be no seepage from the personal into the professional sphere. The students invited to the professor's home are surely being afforded an opportunity denied to those who are not invited—an opportunity likely to be reflected in, for instance, letters of recommendation. The teacher's subjective racial distinctions are almost certain to show themselves somehow, if only indistinctly. I have had the great benefit of being taught by wonderful teachers of various races, including white teachers. I never perceived a racial difference in the way that the best of these teachers treated me in comparison with my white classmates. John McCune, James McPherson, Sanford Levinson, Owen Fiss, and Eric Foner never gave me reason to believe that because of my race I took a backseat to any of my classmates when it came to having a claim on their solicitude. My respect for their conduct is accompanied by disappointment in others who seemed for reasons of racial kinship to invest more in white than in black students—who acted, in other words, in a way that remains, alas, all too "normal."

Am I demanding that teachers be blind to race? No. Teachers should be aware of the ubiquity of racial issues in our society. They should be keenly aware, for instance, that historically and currently the dominant form of racial kinship in American life, the racial kinship that has been best organized and most destructive, is racial kinship mobilized on behalf of whites. This racial kinship has been animated by the desire to make and keep the United States "a white man's country." A teacher should be aware of these and other racial facts of life in order to equip students with essential knowledge about their society. The fact that race matters, however, does not mean that the salience and consequences of racial distinctions are good or that race must continue inevitably to matter in the future. Nor does the brute sociological fact that race matters dictate what one's response to that fact should be.

Assuming that a teacher is aware of the different ways in which race bears down upon his students, how should he react? That depends on the circumstances.

Consider the case of an institution in which white students are receiving considerable attention while black students are being widely ignored. In this setting it would be morally correct for a professor, with eyes focused on race, to reach out especially to the black students. In this circumstance the black students would be more in need than the white students whose needs for mentorship are already being met. This outreach, however, would be based not on racial kinship but on distributive justice. The distinction is significant. Under the rationale of giving priority of attention to those most in need, no racial boundary excuses professors from the obligation to address whatever problems (for example, maldistributions in mentorship) are in need of correction. Furthermore, an appeal to an aspiration untrammeled by race enables any person or group to be potentially the object of solicitude. No person or group is racially excluded from the possibility of assistance, and no person or group is expected to help only "our own." If professors reach out in response to student need, that means that while black students may require special solicitude today, Latino students or Asian American students or white students may require it tomorrow. If Asian American students have a greater need for faculty mentorship than black students, black professors as well as other professors should give them priority.

Some will argue that I ignore or minimize the fact that different groups are differently situated and that it is thus justifiable to impose upon blacks and whites different standards for purposes of evaluating conduct, beliefs, and sentiments. They will maintain that it is one thing for a white teacher to prefer his white students on grounds of racial kinship and a very different thing for a black teacher to prefer his black students on grounds of racial kinship. The former, they will say, is an expression of ethnocentrism that perpetuates racist inequality, whereas the latter is a laudable expression of racial solidarity that is needed to counter white domination.

Several responses are in order.

First, it is a sociological fact that blacks and whites are differently situated in the American polity. Responding in light of that reality is a matter of choice—constrained choice, to be sure, but choice nonetheless. In choosing how to proceed, blacks should insist, as Martin Luther King Jr. urged, that acting with moral propriety is itself a glorious goal. In seeking to attain that goal, blacks should be attuned not only to the all-too-human cruelties and weaknesses in others but also to the all-too-human cruelties and weaknesses in themselves. A good place to start is with the recognition that unless inhibited, every person and group will tend toward self-aggrandizing narcissism. True of those who inherit a dominant status, it is also true of those who inherit a subordinate status. Surely one of the most striking features of human dynamics is the alacrity with which those who have been oppressed will oppress whomever they can once the opportunity presents itself. It is therefore never premature to worry about the possibility of subordinated groups abusing others who are also vulnerable.

A second reason I resist arguments in favor of asymmetrical standards of judgment has to do with reciprocity. I find it difficult to accept that it is wrong for whites to mobilize themselves on a racial basis solely for purposes of white advancement but permissible for blacks to mobilize themselves on a racial basis solely for purposes of black advancement. I propose a shoe-on-the-other-foot test. If a sentiment or practice would be judged objectionable when voiced or implemented by a white person, there ought to be a strong presumption that that sentiment or practice is objectionable when voiced or implemented by a black person. If we would look askance at a white professor who wrote that on grounds of racial kinship he values the opinions of whites more than those of blacks, we should similarly look askance at the black professor who writes that on grounds of racial kinship he values the opinions of blacks more than those of whites.

In some circumstances it is more difficult for blacks to give up the consolations of racial kinship than for whites to do so, insofar as whites typically have more resources to fall back upon. But that should not matter, or at least should not matter decisively. It may be more difficult for a poor person than a rich one to refrain from stealing untended merchandise. But we nevertheless properly expect that person to act rightly.

A third consideration is prudential. It is bad for the country if whites, blacks, or any other group engages in a politics of racial kinship, because racial mobilization prompts racial counter-mobilization, entrenching a pattern of destructive racial competition. But what are blacks to do? How else can they expect to extract concessions from the white power structure other than through hard collective bargaining? Isn't racial unity, racial loyalty, racial solidarity, racial kinship—whatever one wants to call it—absolutely essential for obtaining some measure of justice? If so, isn't my proposal foolhardy idealism, a plan for ruination, a plea for unilateral disarmament in the face of a well-armed foe with a long history of bad intentions?

While I cannot answer these questions fully, I can suggest the beginning of a response, based on two observations. First, it is noteworthy that those who have most ostentatiously asserted the imperatives of black racial solidarity—I think here particularly of Marcus Garvey and Elijah Muhammad—are also those who have engaged in the most divisive and merciless attacks on "brothers" and "sisters" who wished to follow a different path. Although my objection to claims of racial pride and kinship stems from fears of their effect on interracial relations, my objection also stems from fears of their effect on intra-racial relations. More than often recognized, demands for racial pride and kinship stunt individual independence. If racial loyalty is deemed essential and morally virtuous, then a black person's adoption of positions that are deemed racially disloyal will be seen by racial loyalists as a supremely threatening sin, one warranting the harsh punishments that have historically been visited upon alleged traitors.*

Second, if one looks at the most admirable efforts by activists to overcome racial oppression in the United States, one finds people who yearn for justice, not merely for the advancement of a particular racial group. One finds people who ask not whether a given arrangement is good for themselves but whether a given

---

* For a take in obvious tension with this emphasis see "Policing Racial Solidarity" and "Why Clarence Thomas Ought to be Ostracized."

arrangement is good more broadly. One finds people who do not replicate the racial alienations of the larger society but instead welcome interracial intimacy that reconfigures communal boundaries. One finds people who are not content to accept the categories of communal affiliation they have inherited but instead insist upon creating policies that permit the forging of new communal affiliations, ones in which love and loyalty, pride and kinship are unbounded by race.

12

The Struggle for Collective Naming[1]

The name means everything.

—Noble Drew Ali[2]

Few things are more revealing of black Americans' struggle with collective self-identity than debates over the names by which they wish to be known.[3] Along with "Black," "African American" is now the most popular label of collective self-identification. Others, however, are also visible and prevalent. The most important group defense organization among blacks is still the National Association for the Advancement of *Colored* People (NAACP). And the National Council of *Negro* Women and the United *Negro* College Fund continue to make significant contributions. Conflict in racial nomenclature is rife. Millions prefer "African American." But William "Smokey" Robinson does not. "If you go to Africa in search of your race," the legendary singer remarks, "you'll find out quick you're not an African American" but "just a Black American in Africa takin' up space."[4] Albert Murray, the distinguished man of letters, favored "Negro," disliked "black American," and detested "African American."[5] But others have been tolerantly eclectic. "When I write," Harold Cruse declared, "I use 'Negro,' 'Black,' or 'African-American' as the spirit moves me."* Henry

---

* Elaborating on this point, Cruse revealed that, actually, he does harbor strong dislikes when it comes to collective naming:

> I frankly do not favor the term Afro-American at all, because as a writer I find the term cumbersome and awkward despite the claims

Louis Gates Jr. avers, "I don't mind any of the names."[6] Although the historians Karen Fields and Barbara Fields prefer "African American" because it is, in their view, "time-honored, having deep roots in the literary life of American English," they assure readers that they avoid dogmatism regarding the matter and are accepting of a wide range of labels, including "colored" and "Negro."[7] The social critic Stanley Crouch proceeded similarly. "Any [term will] do for me," he wrote. "Negro, Afro-Americans, African-Americans—I don't care."[8]

Some observers condemn debate over racial nomenclature as a wasteful diversion. The pioneering black historian Carter G. Woodson expressed this view in *The Mis-education of the Negro* in an appendix titled "Much Ado About a Name."[9] The Reverend Joseph Lowery, former head of the Southern Christian Leadership Conference, also derided the debate, saying that he preferred "to direct [his] interests and energies toward resisting the assault on our efforts to achieve economic justice."[10] The writer Shelby Steele complained that "self-conscious reaching for pride through nomenclature suggests nothing so much as a despair over the possibility of gaining the less conspicuous pride that follows real advancement."[11] These observers echo Henry Highland Garnet, who stated in 1888, "How unprofitable it is for us to spend our golden moments in long and solemn debate upon the question whether we shall be called 'African,' 'Colored Americans' or 'Africo Americans,' or 'Blacks.'"[12]

Yet many blacks have attached importance to fashioning an appropriate label. W. E. B. Du Bois, Kelly Miller, James Weldon Johnson, George S. Schuyler, and Malcolm X are among those who have devoted extended attention to the matter.[13] "Until we get this racial designation properly fixed in the language and literature of the country," the journalist T. Thomas Fortune declared, "we shall be kicked and cuffed and sneered at."[14]

Some commentators, especially whites who address race matters, strive anxiously to be current in their labeling. On the occa-

---

made for its "ethnic" accord with our African origins. I frankly consider the objections to the word Negro intellectually childish.

Harold Cruse, *Rebellion or Revolution?* (1968), 21.

sion of a new edition of *Simple Justice*, his grand account of *Brown v. Board of Education*, Richard Kluger wrote an "Author's Note" in which he explained why he used the term "Negro" throughout the book's first edition but used the terms "African American" and "black" in a new chapter in a later edition. As he perceived it, by the early twenty-first century, "African American" had become "the preferred form of racial identity of many blacks, connoting a heightened sense of dignity and reminding the rest of the nation of their separate ethnic origin and painful history." In deference to that preference, Kluger noted that his new chapter would use "only the up-to-date term and 'black' still the standard alternative."[15]

It should already be clear that with respect to the labels "black," "African American," "Negro," and so on, consensus is nonexistent. But efforts to create or coerce consensus continue. The *Associated Press Stylebook* directs writers to avoid using "black" as a singular noun but says that "black" is "acceptable as an adjective." It urges using "*Negro* or *colored* only in names of organizations or in rare quotations when essential." It pronounces "African American" to be "acceptable for an American black person of African descent."[16] *"The New York Times" Manual of Style and Usage* says that "Negro" is "acceptable only in the name of an organization or in unmistakable historical contexts." It suggests that "In most United States racial contexts, [colored] is offensive, except in a proper name like National Association for the Advancement of Colored People." It treats "African-American" and "black" as synonyms, but then suggests that writers "try to determine and use the term preferred by the group or person being described." According to the *Manual*, "When no preference is known, the writer should choose."[17]

Believing that choice can be usefully guided by a deeper knowledge of past practices, I offer a tour of pertinent disputes, show how debates over racial nomenclature have mirrored and molded fluctuating racial sentiments, and explain my own usages.

AFRICAN

When the United States was founded, "African" was probably the term preferred by those relatively few blacks in a position to record their preferences, namely the free Negroes who constituted only around 8 percent of the black population. One may infer a preference for the term "African" among free blacks because of the titles they affixed to many of their most cherished institutions: the Free African Society, the African Free School, the African Methodist Episcopal Church, the New York African Society for Mutual Relief, and the Sons of Africa Society.

Professor Sterling Stuckey maintains that the early preference for "African" evinced an effort to retain an inheritance that had been stripped away by kidnapping, enslavement, and forced migration to an alien land in which even the fortunate few who attained freedom faced racial subordination in a society openly committed to white supremacy.[18] By contrast, Professor Patrick Rael contends that blacks "invoked Africa . . . to participate equally in the civic life of the nation. They identified the race with Africa not because they had retained the cultural qualities of the people of that continent but because they sought the public acknowledgment and recognition accorded to those who could claim a legitimate national affiliation." Rael contends that for blacks in the early national era, "African" functioned as "an ethnic identifier, akin to those later employed by European immigrant groups."[19]

Although explanations differ regarding the early preference for "African," there is general agreement that the popularity of that term declined after the founding of the American Colonization Society (ACS) in 1816. The ACS was established by whites who sought to move free blacks in the United States to Africa. Although a few free blacks initially supported the ACS program, most resolved eventually to reject it. In order to make clear their self-identification as Americans and their repudiation of ACS-sponsored emigration, some blacks began to refrain from referring to themselves as Africans. In 1806, a black congregation named itself the African Baptist Church of Boston. In the 1830s, with its officers declaring that "the name African is ill applied to a church composed of American citizens," the congregation renamed itself the First Independent Church of the People of Color.[20]

COLORED

A decided shift toward "colored" is discernible in the linguistic habits of outspoken blacks after the second decade of the nineteenth century. In 1827, in the first issue of *Freedom's Journal*, the nation's first black newspaper, the editors, John Russwurm and Samuel Cornish, announced that it would champion the interests of "free persons of color."[21] In 1837, Cornish renamed another publication *The Colored American*. It had been called the *Weekly Advocate*, but Cornish championed the term "colored," lauding it as "the true term . . . which is above reproach."[22] Between 1830 and 1860, when blacks organized political conventions, they typically described such gatherings as conventions of "colored citizens." David Walker titled his fierce antislavery polemic *David Walker's Appeal to the Coloured Citizens of the World*. Martin R. Delany wrote *The Condition, Elevation, Emigration, and Destiny of the Colored People of the United States*. Frederick Douglass titled a speech "What Are the Colored People Doing for Themselves?"

The abolitionist activist William Whipper objected to "colored" because he rejected designations that racially distinguished African Americans. This position was consistent with his repudiation of *all* "complexional" institutions, including black uplift organizations. In 1835 at the Fifth Annual Convention for the Improvement of the Free People of Colour in the United States, Whipper succeeded in winning passage of a resolution urging blacks to refrain not only from using the term "African" with reference to themselves but also from using "the word 'colored.'" Whipper later argued, "We have too long witnessed the baneful effects of distinctions founded in hatred and prejudice, to advocate the insertion of either the word 'white' or 'colored.'" Through racial labeling, Whipper complained, whites had created an "odious distinction" between people of European ancestry and people of African ancestry. "If we practice the same," he warned, "these distinctions will never cease."[23] Thus Whipper objected when Frederick Douglass referred to his paper, *The North Star*, as a "colored newspaper." In a letter to Douglass, Whipper wrote that drawing racial lines at all, even for well-intentioned purposes of self-description or self-mobilization, would ensure the "perpetuity" of such lines. Instead of racial designations such as "colored Americans," Whipper proposed using a political designation such as "oppressed Americans."[24]

Few blacks joined Whipper's campaign.[25] Here and there,

though, one does find manifestations of his approach. In 1856 a convention of "colored" men in Ohio declared that the appellation "Americans" was the only label they desired. The presence of the term "colored" in practically all of the state and national conventions of blacks in antebellum America, however, attests to the popularity in that era of attaching some sort of racial label to efforts aimed at Negro uplift.

Responding to Whipper's suggestion that blacks refer to themselves as "oppressed Americans," the pioneering journalist Samuel Cornish asked sarcastically, "Oppressed Americans! Who are they?" Answering his own question, Cornish responded, "You are COLORED AMERICANS. The Indians are RED AMERICANS and the white people are WHITE AMERICANS, and you are as good as they and they no better than you." Whipper's way, Cornish warned, would "rob us of our nationality."[26]

Cornish believed that certain names by which blacks were identified had become prohibitively stigmatized by the insults of white supremacists. "We are written about, preached to, and prayed for as Negroes, Africans, and blacks, all of which have been stereotyped, as names of reproach, and on that account, if no other, are unacceptable." He claimed, however, that "colored" had somehow avoided that taint. That is why he embraced it as "the true term . . . which is above reproach."[27]

Others despaired of finding a collective name for blacks that would be spared the consequences of Negrophobia. Some therefore urged blacks to reclaim and use all of the various labels by which they had identified themselves. In 1854, at the National Emigration Convention of Colored People, a resolution posited that "Negro, African, Black, Colored and Mulatto, when applied to us, shall ever be held with the same respect and pride; and synonymous with the terms, Caucasian, White, Anglo-Saxon, and European, when applied to that class of people."[28] This declaration failed, however, to quell continuing debate over the naming of black folk.

After the Civil War, "colored" remained a prominent, respectable, and widely used racial label. In 1874 the black South Carolina congressman Richard Harvey Cain championed civil rights legislation that would offer equal rights to "the colored people of this country."[29] In 1886 the African American John R. Lynch, a former congressman from Mississippi, maintained that "it is the duty of the colored people of the present generation [to have their sons and daughters join] reputable and intelligent labor organizations."[30] In 1896, John Hope, later the first black president of Atlanta University, declared that he "regard[ed] it as cowardly and dishonest for any of our colored men to tell white people or colored people that we are not struggling for equality."[31] That same year the National League of Colored Women and the National Federation of Colored Women combined to form the National Association of Colored Women.[32]

At some point in the first third of the twentieth century the popularity of "colored" waned. It did not receive a frontal, well-articulated, highly publicized attack as has been the case with other labels. The history of, and basis for, its decline is thus indistinct. Probably the demotion stems, at least in part, from an apprehension that "colored" represents an attempted linguistic dilution of blackness, a rhetorical analogue to hair straighteners, nose thinners, and skin lighteners.

Whatever the origins of its decline, the disfavored status of "colored" *now* is clear. Currently any politician—even one speaking at a NAACP convention—would be harshly criticized if he or she referred to "blacks" as "colored" people. "Call a black guy 'colored' today and you'd better run," Jonah Goldberg remarks. "Say 'colored' on TV and your career . . . is over."[33] There are some who give "colored" an airing. Henry Louis Gates Jr. titled his memoir *Colored People* (1994) and "confess[ed]" that he preferred "colored" as a racial label. That he felt called upon to present his preference as a confession, however, signals the discredited niche that "colored" occupies. (Interestingly enough, many who condemn "colored" somehow find it acceptable to describe blacks as "people of color." Although the basis of that distinction is unclear, its presence is certain. "People of color" is generally accepted, while "colored people" is not.) Recall the controversy involving remarks by the British actor Benedict Cumberbatch. He said that "colored" performers in the U.K. are treated unfairly there by an entertainment industry that should be more attentive than it is to the demands and attractions of multiracial diversity. Immediately, some people complained about what they saw as his antiquated vocabulary. This triggered an abject apology. "I'm devastated," Cumberbatch wrote, "to have caused offense by using this outmoded terminology. I offer my sincere apologies. I make no excuse for being an idiot and know the damage is done."[34]

NEGRO

"Negro" has long been a controversial name for African Americans. It is derived from the Latin word for black—*niger*—and seeped into English via Portuguese. Early in the nineteenth century some blacks deployed "Negro" as an alternative to "African." Others, however, eschewed the term because "Negro" and "slave" were frequently used synonymously. "These two words, Negro and Slave," the Reverend Morgan Godwyn wrote in 1680, had "by custom grown homogenous and convertible."[35] Living under the constant risk of being reduced to slavery by mistaken or malicious misidentification, free blacks desired to stay clear of any label that might facilitate confusion regarding their legal status.[36]

Another reason some blacks rejected "Negro" is that, as Professor Rael notes, it "sounded perilously close to a related word that was becoming nothing but a term of extreme disparagement." That related word, of course, was "nigger"*—a term so important to the history of racial nomenclature that it warrants separate and extended treatment. According to Rael, " 'Negro' not only sounded like nigger. Worse, to many Americans there was little difference between the two words."[37] No wonder the influential black businessman James Forten inquired plaintively in 1831, "Why do our friends as well as our enemies call us negroes? We feel it a term of reproach, and could wish our friends would call us by some other name."[38]

Throughout the years following the Civil War, observers with varying perspectives have repudiated "Negro." The outspoken black militant Monroe Trotter disapproved of "Negro" for reasons that echoed the rejection of "African" in the colonial period.

---

* *See* Randall Kennedy, *Nigger: The Strange Career of a Troublesome Word* (2002). *See* also " 'Nigger': The Strange Career Continues."

He believed that "Negro" facilitated the stigmatization of blacks.
Trotter insisted that blacks needed to "overemphasize" their "status as American citizens to the manor born because of the crusade to make [them] aliens." He preferred referring to blacks as
"colored Americans," "colored people," or "Afro-Americans."[39]
Writing in 1937, Professor Kelly Miller remarked that "many of
the off-colored group object to the term . . . because it serves as a
reminder of the humiliation and degradation through which the
race has passed."[40] Twelve years later, in a letter to the editor of
The Washington Post, Mary Church Terrell demanded that that
newspaper stop using the word "Negro" maintaining that it was
"a cruel injustice to call [blacks] by the same name they bore as
slaves." Terrell also objected because "our meanest detractors and
most cruel persecutors insist that we shall be called by that name
so that they can humiliate us by referring to us contemptuously as
'niggers,' or 'Negras.'"*

The most elaborate denunciation of "Negro" is found in
Richard Moore's *The Name "Negro": Its Origin and Evil Use* (1960).
Moore argues for rejecting "Negro" mainly because of its prov-
enance: it was the label unilaterally imposed by the white man.
According to Moore,

> It was in the development of [the] infamous, iniquitous,
> and inhuman slave traffic that the term "negro" was
> foisted as a noun, as a designation, as a name, upon those
> who were unfortunate enough to be caught in the clutches
> of the slave traders. This is the origin of the term "negro."
> Its origin is vile and infamous. It began in indignity. It
> began in immorality, and the consciousness and the dig-
> nity of man must now rise and dispense with it forever.[41]

According to Moore, "Negro" has been "so thoroughly suffused
with the stench of the slave pen . . . so saturated with shame, racial

---

* Terrell also observed, "If a man is a Negro, it follows as the night the day that
a woman is a Negress. 'Negress' is an ugly, repulsive word—virtually a term
of degradation and reproach which colored women . . . can not live down in a
thousand years." *See* Gerda Lerner, ed., *Black Women in White America: A Documentary History* (1972), 549.

inferiority, and foul corruption, that it can neither be cleansed nor deodorized in any foreseeable time."*[42]

In 1960, however, many black intellectuals and activists were continuing to use what Moore condemned as "the slave master's vile appellation." How did he explain the persistence of "Negro" in the speech of such esteemed figures as Roy Wilkins, Thurgood Marshall, Benjamin E. Mays, W. E. B. Du Bois, and Martin Luther King Jr.? Moore explained it in terms of socialization. "What is wrong with some Afroamericans at the present time," he maintained, "is that they have become so conditioned to the smell of this name 'Negro' that they don't recognize the stench anymore. But I can assure you that the ignominy, the indignity, and the stench of the name is very well recognized by those who insist on forcing it upon us."[43]

In the early 1960s, Moore and his Committee to Present the Truth About the Name "Negro" was a small, marginal tendency within the bourgeoning black liberation movement. But Moore anticipated a viewpoint that became increasingly influential. "There is growing resentment of the word 'Negro,'" observed Stokely Carmichael (Kwame Ture) and Charles V. Hamilton in 1967 in their manifesto *Black Power: The Politics of Liberation*. The reason, they maintained, is that "Negro" is "the invention of our oppressor."[44]

The Nation of Islam played a major role in popularizing the repudiation of "Negro." A consistent theme in its eschatology is that the white man—the so-called white devil—has temporarily succeeded in enslaving the black man by, among other things, separating him from his true history and identity and seducing him into embracing falsities such as the group name "Negro" (and

---

* In his poem "Nemesis," Keith E. Baird also gives voice to dissatisfaction with "Negro":

> You snatched me from my land,
> Branded my body with your irons
> And my soul with the slave-name "Negro"
> (How devilish clever to spell it upper case
> And keep me always lower!)

See Keith E. Baird, "Nemesis," *Freedomways* (Spring 1966), quoted in *The Voice of Black America: Major Speeches by Negroes in the United States, 1797–1971*, ed. Philip S. Foner (1972), 1029.

surnames that imitate the names of their former slave masters).
Malcolm X's remarks are representative of the spirit in which the
discrediting proceeded:

> If you call yourself "white," why should I not call myself
> "black"? Because you have taught me that I am a
> "Negro"! . . . [I]f you ask a man his nationality and he says
> he is German, that means he comes from a nation called
> Germany. If he says his nationality is French, that means
> he came from a nation called France. The term he uses to
> identify himself connects him with a nation, a language, a
> culture and a flag. Now if he says his nationality is "Negro"
> he has told you nothing—except possibly that he is not
> good enough to be "American." . . . If Frenchmen are of
> France and Germans are of Germany, where is "Negro-
> land"? I'll tell you: it's in the mind of the white man![45]

Currently "Negro" is widely disapproved. In 2010, journalists
describing Barack Obama's first successful presidential campaign
reported that Harry Reid of Nevada, the Senate majority leader,
had remarked privately that he believed that America was ready to
elect a suitable black candidate such as Obama—a "light-skinned"
African American "with no Negro dialect, unless he wanted to
have one."[46] The feature of this comment that attracted the most
derision was the reference to "Negro" dialect. "It's depressing,"
Joan Walsh observed, "that Democrats have a Senate majority
leader who thinks it's acceptable to use the term . . . even in private, off-the-record conversation. . . . 'Negro' was retired about
40 years ago."[47] "Using that word isn't defensible," Michael
Tomasky intoned. Reid "deserves criticism for it."[48] The editorial page of *The Dallas Morning News* called Reid's words "racially
insensitive."[49] Leonard Pitts Jr. mockingly called for someone to
"please tell Harry Reid there are no Negroes in America" because
in the late 1960s blacks "drove that term out of favor." According
to Pitts, the person who continues to use "Negro" without irony
"paints himself as a geezer out of touch with the last forty years."[50]
Adding legitimacy to the criticism was an apology offered by Reid
and an acceptance of the apology proffered by Obama.[51]

A more consequential example of the devaluation of "Negro" is the decision of the U.S. Census Bureau to abandon it as one of the labels available to Americans for racial self-identification in the census of 2020. The census first used "Negro" as a category of identification in 1930.[52] The Census Bureau dropped "Negro" due to complaints that the term is antiquated (at best) and derogatory (at worst).[53]

Another episode that both mirrors and reinforces the disfavored status of "Negro" is the U.S. Army's response to publicity revealing that until recently army regulations held that "Negro" was an acceptable classification for "a person having origins in any of the black racial groups of Africa." Within days of the revelation, the army backtracked and changed its policy. "The U.S. Army fully recognized, and promptly acted, to remove outdated language [in its regulations] as soon as it was brought to our attention," an army official declared. "We apologize to anyone we offended."[54]

Although "Negro" has been fervently criticized and is now widely disapproved (though not as much as "colored"), it has also been stoutly defended and still retains a place in the vocabulary of an appreciable number of black Americans. The most notable defense was authored by W. E. B. Du Bois in remarks triggered by a letter written to him by a high school sophomore, Roland A. Barton. Why, Barton asked, would the NAACP magazine *The Crisis* "designate and segregate us as 'Negroes' and not as 'Americans.' . . . The word 'Negro,' or 'nigger,' is a white man's word to make us feel inferior. . . . I hope that by the time I become a man, that this word, 'Negro,' will be abolished."

The editor of *The Crisis* answered in an article that appeared in March 1928:

> Do not . . . make the all too common error of mistaking names for things. Names are only conventional signs for identifying things. Things are the reality that counts. If a thing is despised . . . you will not alter matters by changing its name. If men despise Negroes, they will not despise them less if Negroes are called "colored" or "Afro-Americans."

Du Bois asserted that "the feeling of inferiority is in you, not in any name. The name merely evokes what is already there. Exorcize the hateful complex," he continued, "and no name can ever make you hang your head." Du Bois then proceeded to champion "Negro" as against alternatives (though the logic of his argument counsels toleration of virtually all racial labels):

> "Negro" is a fine word. Etymologically and phonetically it is much better and more logical than "African" or "colored" or any of the various hyphenated circumlocutions. Of course, it is not "historically" accurate. No name ever was historically accurate: neither "English," "French," "German," "White," "Jew," "Nordic," nor "Anglo-Saxon." They were all at first nicknames, misnomers, accidents, grown eventually to conventional habits and achieving accuracy because, and simply because, wide and continued usage rendered them accurate. In this sense, "Negro" is quite as accurate, quite as old and quite as definite as any name of any great group of people.[*][55]

Not only did Du Bois use "Negro" without embarrassment throughout his long career. So, too, did Marcus Garvey. After all, he titled his organization the Universal Negro Improvement Association. So, too, did Booker T. Washington, James Weldon Johnson, A. Philip Randolph, Walter White, and Charles Hamilton Houston. So, too, did Ralph Ellison. So, too, did three of the twentieth century's most distinguished Negro historians: Carter G. Woodson, John Hope Franklin, and Benjamin Quarles.

---

* Elsewhere Du Bois was even more positive in his assessment of "Negro," declaring,

> Here is a term strong, definite, distinct, and great. There is no doubt whom the user means—that dark and harsh-haired people. . . . How rich and pregnant with history and legend comes the name out of the dark past. It points to something more than a hero history; it points to a human history. . . . What word more clearly shows that this vast people is a human, living, growing, world-spirit, who must and will be free not only in body, but in mind.

Quoted in Fannie Barrier Williams, "Do We Need Another Name?," *Southern Workman* (1904).

"I see nothing wrong with [Negro]," Quarles averred in 1968. "Words change in their context. We have many words historically that once were terms of denigration. For instance, the Friends were sometimes called Quakers in derision. Instead of dodging the word, they adopted it and made it a term of great respect and meaning. . . . [Y]ou will begin to see the same evolution of the word 'Negro' as Americans of African descent move into their rightful place in American society."[56]

"Negro" continues to have defenders. Responding to the Census Bureau's move toward eliminating the term, the *Los Angeles Times* columnist Sandy Banks insisted that "it's not offensive and it's not dead," noting that "more than 36,000 people felt enough allegiance to the label to write it in on their census forms in 2010." It feels, she complains, like the Census Bureau is "trying to scrub a chapter from a story that is uniquely American, and undeniably mine." Expressing gratitude to forebears, Banks declared, "I have the freedom to declare myself unashamedly black because the generation before me navigated overt racism . . . with Negro strength and vision."[57]

THE CAPITALIZATION OF "NEGRO"

A separate conflict involving "Negro" concerned whether it should be capitalized.[58] Throughout the first third of the twentieth century, many of the most prestigious forums in journalism, the bar, and academia insisted that "Negro" should be spelled without a capital *N*. In 1910, W. E. B. Du Bois specifically requested that *The American Historical Review* permit him "as a matter of courtesy" to capitalize "Negro" in an article he had written. The *Review*'s editor, J. Franklin Jameson, refused, asserting that "negro," as the Spanish word for "black," had nothing to do with nationality (unlike German or Hindu), was merely a characterization of a physical trait, and should thus be handled no differently than, say, "white man, brown man, or red man." This response rankled Du Bois. In *The Philadelphia Negro* (1899), Du Bois had insisted upon his preferred style, declaring that "eight million Americans are entitled to a capital letter." Now he complained to Jameson that "mere uniformity in office practice" was an insufficient basis "for inflicting upon a contributor . . . that which he regards as a personal insult."[59]

There were, to be sure, some who spelled "Negro" with a little *n* who were genuine proponents of racial justice. William Lloyd Garrison often used the small *n* in his abolitionist journal *The Liberator*, as did Atticus G. Haygood throughout *Our Brother in Black* (1881), as did the famous orator and freethinker Robert G. Ingersoll. To most black commentators of the time, though, non-capitalization constituted yet another sign of racist disrespect. They believed, as did Irving Lewis Allen, that in the typical case "to deny a capital letter to the name of an ethnic [or racial or religious] group symbolically diminishes the social status of the group. . . . The user concedes the pronunciation and the spelling, but in print the dignity of the name is taken away."[60] Responding editorially to an NAACP request that it change its typographical tradition, a segregationist newspaper in Eatonton, Georgia, candidly declared in 1930 that it would refuse because capitalization would lead to social equality.

A campaign to standardize use of the capital *N* dates from at least 1878, when Ferdinand Lee Barnett (future husband of the pioneering journalist Ida B. Wells) wrote "Spell It with a Capital," an editorial that appeared in his Chicago newspaper, *The Conservator*. This demand resonated across the black American ideological spectrum. W. E. B. Du Bois and Booker T. Washington clashed heatedly over various issues. But regarding the capital *N* they agreed. Both attempted to convince all who would listen that the absence of a capitalized *N* signaled an absence of proper respect for black folk.

Reformers encountered considerable resistance. In 1918, in response to a complaint about *The New York Times*, an editor defended the paper thusly:

> The question has often been discussed. Generally the small letter is used in newspapers. From our point of view, the capitalization of the word would tend to accentuate a separateness of the colored portion of the population. That is just what we should avoid, is it not? Our view is that we should no more capitalize "negro" than "white." It would be calling special attention to the hue of a man's

skin, accentuating a difference among Americans of different colors.[61]

James Weldon Johnson responded in a column in the *New York Age* newspaper in which he scoffed at the notion that racial egalitarianism prompted the *Times*'s policy of non-capitalization. "It brings a smile that hurts our face to think of the editorial staff of the *Times* delicately considering not to do anything that would 'tend to accentuate a separateness of the colored population.'"[62] After all, he might have added, this was a period during which the *Times* accepted, indeed approved of, the color line in its own employment practices and in its coverage (and neglect) of blacks' racial oppression. During the early decades of the twentieth century, *The New York Times* consistently depicted blacks in ways that mirrored and reinforced racist images of blacks as criminals and incompetents. Its refusal to capitalize "Negro" was yet another way of stigmatizing the Negro.

Then, on March 7, 1930, the *Times* reversed itself. After mounting protests from a variety of quarters, it belatedly acknowledged what it had previously denied:

> It . . . seems reasonable that a people who had once a proud designation, such as Ethiopians, reaching back into the dawn of history, having come up out of the slavery to which men of English speech subjected them, should now have such recognition as the lifting of the name from the lower case into the upper can give them. . . . Every use of the capital "N" becomes a tribute to millions who have risen from a low estate into "the brotherhood of the races."[63]

The *Times* credited Major Robert R. Moton, Booker T. Washington's successor as head of the Tuskegee Institute, with persuading it to change. Noting that Moton had informed them that blacks almost universally wished to see "Negro" capitalized, the editors of the *Times* wrote that its conversion to capitalizing *N* was "not merely a typographical change" but also "an act in recognition of racial self-respect for those who have been for generations in 'the lower case.'"[64]

BLACK

A key development of the 1960s was the demotion of "Negro" and the ascendancy of "black." Lerone Bennett Jr.'s *The Negro Mood* became *The Black Mood*. The *Negro Digest* became *Black World*. Negro History Week became Black History Month. "Negro" became something of an insult, an insinuation that one was insufficiently militant, insufficiently assertive, insufficiently black. "Everybody knows what 'Negroes' are," LeRoi Jones (later Amiri Baraka) declared in 1966. They are "strait-jacketed lazy clowns, whose only joy is carrying out the white man's will. But there are some of us," Jones asserted defiantly, "who will not be Negroes, who know that indeed we are something else, something stronger . . . there are some of us who know we are black people."[65]

The validation, indeed valorization, of "black" constituted one of the key achievements of African American activism during the latter half of the 1960s. Previously "black" had connoted inferiority to many African Americans and was used by them to express contempt for complexions or fashions or ways of acting deemed inferior. Taylor Branch reports that in 1963 in Toledo, Ohio, high school students organized a mass protest after an assistant principal referred to them over the school intercom as "black students."[66] An illustration of Negroes' contempt for blackness was the well-known saying

> *If you're black, get back.*
> *If you're brown, stick around.*
> *If you're white, you're all right.*

In *Soul on Ice* (1967), Eldridge Cleaver recounted how he and fellow Negro male convicts in the 1950s laughingly disparaged the prospect of loving or marrying Negro women, particularly those with dark skin. As one inmate put it, "I don't want nothing black but a Cadillac." A stock feature of the ritualized wordplay known as "the dozens" involved quips that began "Yo mama so black . . ."—as in "Yo mama so black her nickname is evening."

The Black Power movement substantially changed that mindset. It persuaded African Americans to challenge more forcefully than ever before the habitual association of whiteness with good traits—innocence, happiness, cleanliness—and blackness with bad ones: evil, sadness, filth. "Black is beautiful" emerged as a slogan and "Say It Loud, I'm Black and I'm Proud" emerged as an anthem.

Not all blacks were happy with this development. Consider the case of Rayford W. Logan. A distinguished activist and scholar who was a longtime member of the faculty of Howard University, Logan championed the term "Negro" and rejected the term "black." Logan rejected the term "black" because of its use by those he derided as "racial chauvinists who denied that the American Negro also had European roots," " 'prophets of doom' who preached that Negroes could not succeed in America," and demagogues eager to stratify Negroes along color lines that would privilege those who were darker over those who were lighter. Logan did not simply dislike "black"; he fought against its use. He resigned from his fraternity, Alpha Phi Alpha, the oldest African American college fraternity, when it began to describe itself as a "black" fraternity. He quit the advisory committee of the Frederick Douglass Papers because the editor of the project described Douglass as "black." He canceled the planned third edition of a textbook he co-authored rather than agree to have it updated by changing the title from *The American Negro* to *The Black American.* In 1977, when he bequeathed substantial gifts to Williams College and Howard University, he conditioned each with a provision that nothing he left could be used to support any program or person designated as "black" or any scholar who referred to "Negroes" as "blacks."[67] But life is full of ironies. When Logan died in November 1982, the *New York Times* obituary headline read, "Dr. Rayford Logan, Professor Who Wrote Books on Blacks."

THE CAPITALIZATION OF "BLACK"

After "black" emerged as a preferred racial label, there arose the issue of whether, or in what circumstances, it should be capitalized. There was less acrimony in this debate than that which attended the earlier capitalization controversy. Many who disagreed with non-capitalization did not seem to perceive that choice to be as rank an expression of racial disrespect as little-*n* "negro." Still, for some the issue rankled. In a 2014 essay titled "The Case for Black with a Capital B," Professor Lori L. Tharps remarked that non-capitalization was one of her "greatest frustrations as a writer and a Black woman."*[68] Some publications, usually those aimed at African American audiences, like the *Chicago Defender*, capitalized "Black." A few others eventually followed suit. Then, in July 2020, during the cultural upheaval that attended nationwide protests against racist police brutality in the aftermath of the killing of George Floyd, *The New York Times* announced that it had decided to "start using uppercase 'Black' to describe people and cultures of African origin." This style, it declared, "best conveys elements of shared history and identity, and reflects our goal to be respectful of all people and communities we cover." That seems rather anodyne. But anything having to do with race is controversial, and so it was with this initiative as well, partly because of what the *Times* went on to say:

> We will retain lowercase treatment for "white." While there is an obvious question of parallelism, there has been no comparable movement toward widespread adoption of a new style for "white," and there is less of a sense that "white" describes a shared culture and history. Moreover, hate groups and white supremacists have long favored the uppercase style, which in itself is reason to avoid it.[69]

Although many readers applauded the *Times*'s reform, some disagreed with aspects of it. Kwame Anthony Appiah concurred with the *Times*'s decision to capitalize "Black," but objected to its decision to forgo capitalizing "white." He maintained that

---

* Elsewhere Professor Tharps argued that while "black" in lowercase denoted merely a color, "Black" in uppercase denoted "a group of people whose ancestors were born in Africa, were brought to the United States against their will, spilled their blood, sweat and tears to build this nation into a world power and along the way managed to create glorious works of art, passionate music, scientific discoveries, a marvelous cuisine, and untold literary masterpieces." Thus, in her view, "when a copyeditor deletes the capital 'B,' they are in effect deleting the history and contributions of my people." *See* Lori L. Tharps, "I Refuse to Remain in the Lower Case," *My American Meltingpot*, June 2, 2014.

that non-capitalization encouraged a tendency to view whiteness as inert, neutral, standard—something discovered rather than made. He wanted "White" to be understood as a created, blood-stained label forged in history just as "Black" is a created blood-stained label forged in history. As for the concern that capitalizing "White" would reinforce white supremacists insofar as they prefer that spelling, Appiah suggested that the effect could be just the opposite. "If the capitalization of white became standard among anti-racists," he posited, "the [White] supremacists' gesture would no longer be a provocative defiance of the norm and would lose all force. [White] supremacists would have to find another way to enable themselves."[70]

AFRICAN AMERICAN

An influential recent development in the history of American Negroes' collective self-naming was Jesse Jackson's campaign to make "African American" the preferred name for blacks. In 1988, at a meeting of organizations gathered to establish a national black agenda, Jackson maintained that "to be called African American has cultural integrity. It puts us in our proper historical context. Every ethnic group in this country has a reference to some land base, some historical cultural base. African Americans have hit that level of cultural maturity."[71] Jackson's effort to link Africa to the black American experience by dint of labeling was by no means unprecedented. As noted previously, "African" was a favorite term of self-identification among blacks in the colonial and early national period. In the 1880s the journalist T. Thomas Fortune championed "Afro-American," a term that became widely used in the 1960s and 1970s. Malcolm X founded the Organization of Afro-American Unity. At the eulogy that Ossie Davis delivered after Malcolm's assassination, he stressed the significance of this nomenclature:

It is not in the memory of men that this beleaguered, unfortunate, but nonetheless proud community [Harlem] has found a braver, more gallant young champion than this Afro-American who lies before us—unconquered still. I say the word again, as he would want me to: Afro-

American. . . . Nobody knew better than he the power words have over the minds of men. Malcolm had stopped being "Negro" years ago. It had become too small, too puny, too weak a word for him. Malcolm was bigger than that. Malcolm had become an *Afro-American*, and he wanted—so desperately—that we, that all his people would become Afro-Americans too.[72]

Also indicative of the popularity of the term was its use in the titles of numerous programs and departments in colleges and universities that offered "Afro-American" studies.

Reverend Jackson's insistence on the "African American" label pushed it and its variants to a new level of popularity among people of all races. His initiative made "African American" what it is today: perhaps the leading conventional designation for American-born descendants of African slaves.

Jackson's campaign in favor of "African American" has not been without detractors. Some of the criticism is procedural, charging that Jackson acted high-handedly in presuming, without consultation, to speak on behalf of blacks. Numbers of blacks silently agree with the historian Stephan Thernstrom's quip that perhaps the name Jackson really cared most about was his own.[73] Some of the criticism is substantive. "African American obscures more than it illuminates or explains," complains the sociologist Phillip T. Gay, who rejects the notion that "African American" is a good label because it accentuates American Negroes' connection with their supposed "homeland." "A homeland is a place to return to," Gay maintains. But "most black Americans can't return home to Africa, because they were never there in the first place, culturally or otherwise." Echoing the defiant response of blacks to the American Colonization Society in the early nineteenth century, Gay asserts, "America is the black American homeland."[74]

The linguist John McWhorter has also expressed dissatisfaction with labeling American-born descendants of slaves as "African American." Like Gay, McWhorter believes that that appellation exaggerates American blacks' association with Africa. A working-class black man in Cincinnati, McWhorter asserts, has more in common with a working-class white man in Providence than with a black Ghanaian. A second basis of McWhorter's position has to do with the presence in the United States of increasing numbers of African-born newcomers. "With the number of African immigrants . . . nearly tripling since 1990," he writes, "the use of African Americans is becomingly increasingly strained."[75] McWhorter and others argue that as a matter of prudent generosity it would make sense for the descendants of slaves in the United States to leave "African American" free for use by African-born immigrants.

THE FUTURE

What is the future of the debate over blacks' self-naming? Debate rages with no end in sight because the conflict has been useful. It has been deployed for purposes of intra-racial stratification (for instance, distinguishing supposedly authentic blacks from supposedly inauthentic Negroes), intra-racial group therapy (for example, purging Negroes of ingrained antipathy toward blackness), interracial struggle (for instance, critiquing a concept of American uniformity with demands for recognition of African American distinctiveness), and securing and displaying individual leadership (for example, Jesse Jackson's advocacy on behalf of the "African American" label). Fashions, preferences, and usages evolve and will continue to do so. Seven years after describing the label "black" as "baseless" and proclaiming "African American" as the label with "cultural integrity," Reverend Jackson delivered a speech at the Million Man March in Washington, D.C., in which he never referred to "African Americans" but repeatedly referred to "Black men," "Black women," and "Black voters."[76]

Blacks are, and for a long time will continue to be, acutely aware that they have been subjected to a massive, long-standing, and ongoing campaign of denigrating insult that has besmirched their image in America and indeed the world. During the Middle Passage—the traumatic sojourn from Africa to America—the individuality of blacks was almost wholly negated as they were identified and treated as human *things*—nameless animate machines. Later, as slaves born in America, blacks suffered the indignity of being named or renamed by white masters, some of whom inflicted upon their servants names that oozed mockery: Caesar, Apollo, Pompey, Cato. After the abolition of slavery, the great mass of Negroes finally became able to name themselves and their children authoritatively in the way that people born free had long taken for granted. But assaults against the dignity of Negroes continued. Blacks were subjected to a barrage of racially derogatory insults: "nigger," "coon," "jigaboo," "porch monkey." Their degraded place was also inscribed into the American imagination by innumerable representations of grinning black Sambos, scowling Mammies, and fawning Stepin Fetchits. Not only were blacks long denied the capital N in "Negro"; they were also denied courtesy titles—"Mr." or "Mrs."—that others took for granted. And in many areas prior to the 1960s, it was normal practice to call a Negro man "boy" or a Negro woman "girl" regardless of the age or status of the black person in question. Still in the grip of their traumatic experience as a people long deprived of the authority to name themselves individually or collectively, many blacks savor their ability to do so today. So long as that exercise delivers a pleasurable sense of power, one may expect periodic bouts of naming and renaming to recur.

What about my own preferences? I am eclectic. I regularly use all of the terms I have described. I do so for three reasons. The first is aesthetic, to reduce monotony. The second is ideological. I use a wide range of terms to refer to "blacks," "Negroes," "colored folk," and "African Americans" to signal a commitment to a politics of expression that rejects the tyranny of unreflective fashion. I am simply unwilling to defer to arbiters of opinion who, armed with superficial knowledge, rigidly insist that this or that term is correct or incorrect in the face of a rich and complicated historical record that reveals a wide pattern of usages.

My third reason is sentimental. Some of the people whom I have most loved and respected used terms that are now widely disparaged. My grandmother Lillian Spann, "Big Mama," an indomitable black woman who magnificently raised splendid children, preferred "colored." And for most of his career, my former boss, "Mr. Civil Rights," the great Thurgood Marshall, referred to blacks as "Negroes." I pay homage to them in using their preferred terminology. If the labels "Negro" and "colored," "black" and "African American" were good enough for Big Mama and Thurgood Marshall, W. E. B. Du Bois and Martin Luther King Jr., these labels—*all of them*—are certainly good enough for me.

13

The Struggle for Personal Naming

Let me tell you somethin', baby. Niggers get their names the way they get everything else—the best way they can.

—Toni Morrison, *Song of Solomon* (1977)

In the names of African Americans are salutes to ancestors, expressions of creativity, declarations of independence, strategies of elevation, assertions of defiance, bouts of whimsy, narratives of oppression, and yearnings for belongingness.[1]

NAMING IN SLAVERY

Let's start with a story of subordination.[2] During an annual visit to a plantation in Mississippi in the late 1850s, white ministers could hardly contain themselves as they laughingly christened enslaved black children "Alexander de Great," "General Jackson," "Napoleon Bonaparte," "Queen Victoria," "Pharaoh," "Nicodemus," "Jupiter," and "Mars." This "scandalous naming" had originated, according to a governess, in the "merry brain" of the plantation owner's sister.[3]

There were countless episodes in which slave catchers, slave owners, and slave traders imposed names upon their captives. A surgeon on an English slaving vessel wrote in 1787, "The first slave that was traded for . . . was a girl of about fifteen who was promptly named Eve, for it was usual on slave ships to give the names of Adam and Eve, to the first men and women brought aboard."[4] A sailor on another vessel observed, "I suppose [the slaves] . . . all had names in their own dialect, but the effort required to pronounce them was too much for us, so we picked out our favorites and dubbed them 'mainstay,' 'cats head,' 'Bull's eye,' 'Rope-yarn,' and various other sea phrases."[5]

As denigrating as this imposition of names was, it represented an advance over perceived namelessness. After all, as Professor Newbell Puckett observes, "to name a person is to recognize his existence."[6] African captives who had yet to be made into marketable commodities were seen by some captors as nameless bodies with only a mere potential for attaining personality. Prior to reaching the market for bonded labor, they had no identities in the eyes of some traders and thus were given no names.[7]

The extent to which slave masters named and renamed slaves and enforced their preferences changed over time and varied by locale. It seems, however, that owners generally exercised a taken-for-granted authority to impose names on their human chattel if they so chose. One captive recalls enduring several namings: "In this place I was called Jacob; but on board a ship, I was called Michael. . . . [Later] my captain and master named me Gustavus Vasa. . . . [W]hen I refused to answer to my new name, which I at first did, it gained me many a cuff; so [at] length I submitted."[8] Another slave remembered being forced to surrender the name "William"—the name given to him by his mother. His master ordered him to adopt another name because the master's nephew, who had recently joined the household, was also named William. When the slave resisted, he was punished: "I received several severe whippings for telling people that my name was William after orders were given to change it."*

Masters were motivated by a variety of factors. One was a need to track valuable property for purposes of bookkeeping. Given that objective, similarities in the naming of livestock and slaves should not be surprising. When Professor Puckett compared the names of mules and slaves in 1858 in Lowndes County, Mississippi, he found considerable overlap.[9]

For some the naming of slaves might have presented an

---

* That boy gained his freedom by running away. He renamed himself and became the country's first black novelist: William Wells Brown. *See* Leon F. Litwack, *Been in the Storm So Long: The Aftermath of Slavery* (1979), 247.

opportunity to display an awareness of classical or mythical figures—hence the imposition of monikers such as "Caesar" and "Pompey," "Phoebe" and "Venus."[10] The discrepancy between the mightiness of a "Caesar" and the subservience of a slave also leads to a suspicion that in at least some instances the resort to classical names reflected a malevolent mischievousness.*

That masters expressed condescension and contempt does not mean that slaves viewed their names negatively. Nor does a slave's classical name necessarily mean that it was imposed by an owner. One former slave recalled that his mother named him Cicero because she liked its sound. Another, George Cato, proudly claimed to be the great-great-grandson of a Cato who had helped lead the Stono Rebellion in South Carolina in 1739. He recalled that his father, grandfather, and great-grandfather had all been named Cato in honor of their rebellious ancestor and that, when emancipated, he had adopted the name as his surname to perpetuate it.[11]

Although English names predominated among American slaves, African names maintained a presence as well, though their prominence diminished over time. One example of a retained Africanism was the tradition of naming a child for the day of the week on which he or she was born: Cudjo or Juba for Monday; Cubbenah or Beneba for Tuesday; Kwaco or Cuba for Wednesday; Quao or Abba for Thursday; Cuffee or Pheba for Friday; Quame or Mimba for Saturday; Quashee or Quasheba for Sunday.[12] Some Africans named children for the weather or other circumstances that accompanied their births, a custom imprinted on names such as Rainy, Freeze, Starry Night, Stormy, and Eartha.[13] An African tradition of memorializing a child's place of birth likely figures

---

* Fanny Kemble wrote in her famous diary, "Venus . . . is a favorite name among these sable folk, but, of course must have been given originally in derision." Stephen Wilson, *The Means of Naming: A Social and Cultural History of Personal Naming in Western Europe* (1998), 309. Students of Jamaican slavery have uncovered slaves named "Monkey," "Villain," "Strumpet," and even "Whore." See Trevor Burnard, "Slave Naming Patterns: Onomastics and the Taxonomy of Race in Eighteenth-Century Jamaica," 31 *Journal of Interdisciplinary History* 325, 336 (2001). Stressing the rarity of names imposed upon Jamaican slaves that were "clearly intended to demean," Professor Burnard suggests that out of a sense of prudence masters showed "a modicum of respect for slaves' dignity" (325).

in names such as Carolina and Richmond.[14] Another Africanism was the practice of commemorating by name the birth order of children. Sambo, for instance, was a name that some tribes used to denote a second son (though in other tribes "Sambo" meant disgrace and subsequently became a well-known racial insult).[15]

Documents reflecting the nomenclature of the enslaved bear an extensive array of African names: Koma, Zeke, Mingo, Zango, and so on. One place where such names appeared were advertisements for runaway slaves in eighteenth-century newspapers. These ads featured notices such as this—a plea for the capture of "TWO NEW NEGRO YOUNG FELLOWS; one of them . . . calls himself GOLAGA, the name given him here ABEL; the other a black fellow . . . calls himself ABBROM, the name given him here BENNET."[16] Impressed by "the high percentage of African names among those fugitives identified by name," one historian speculates that the captives most likely to have kept African names were those most inclined to "resist . . . in whatever way they could efforts to enslave them and assign them new identities."[17]

NAMING IN EARLY FREEDOM

The clearest indication that many slaves felt dissatisfied with their names is reflected in their conduct upon attaining freedom. After buying his freedom, April Ellison petitioned a South Carolina court for permission to change his name to William Ellison.[18] After gaining her liberty through litigation, Mum Bett changed her name to Elizabeth Freeman.[19] After fleeing slavery, Fred Bailey claimed the name Frederick Douglass.[20]

Slaves who obtained freedom by dint of the Union's victory in the Civil War engaged in a widespread effort to undergird their new status with new names. The most striking feature of this massive re-identification was the search for surnames. Sheer practicality played some role in this drama insofar as slaves needed to obtain surnames to enlist in the Union army, obtain federal aid, and vote.[21] But bureaucratic imperatives alone do not explain this development. According to Professor John Inscoe, the "speed and completeness with which almost all freedmen, once emancipated, took surnames was a dramatic indication of their transformed self-image. It reflected their eagerness to demonstrate their new status and affirm the dignity and self-esteem that accompanied their independence."[22] As a plantation overseer in Louisiana put it, "No man thought he was perfectly free unless he had changed his name and taken a Family name."[23]

Prior to the abolition of slavery, some captives seem to have adopted surnames inconspicuously or even covertly, afraid of attracting attention from owners or other whites.[24] It was only after the Civil War that the taking of surnames became open and widespread. Some former slaves chose to adopt the surnames of former masters. They did so for various purposes. One was to win goodwill and the protection of people who might be able to assist them in the uncertain days ahead.[25] Another purpose was to memorialize familial ties. The surnames of former owners were often associated with the names of the parents and grandparents of the newly freed.

More often former slaves rejected the names of their former owners. A Union army recruiter in Tennessee urged a former slave to adopt his former master's surname. The newly minted freeman demurred: "No suh. . . . I'se had nuff o' ole massa."[26] Explaining his desire for a different surname, a young black man in South Carolina remarked that the name he rejected was "my old rebel master's title. Him's nothing to me now. I don't belong to he no longer, an' I don't see no use in being called for him."[27] An emancipated woman offered a different explanation: "When us black folks got set free, us'n change our names, so effen the white folks change their minds and don't let us be free any more, then they have a hard time finding us."[28]

The names of southern blacks on voter registration lists and marriage records in the late 1860s were notably different from those that appeared on the slave lists of the 1850s. "Romeo Jones" became "Romey O. Jones," "Pericles Smith" became "Perry Clees Smith," "Polly's Jim" became "Apollos James." Joe, Ben, Sam, and Willie became Joseph, Benjamin, Samuel, and William.[29] When former slaves reached for surnames other than those of their former masters, they often embraced names they associated with emancipation—Lincoln, Grant, Sherman—names they associated with high status—Duke, Prince, King—names that expressed pride in their new situations—Freeman, Freeland,

Liberty, Justice—names that advertised skills or occupations: Taylor (as in tailor), Smith (as in blacksmith), Carpenter, and Boatswain.

Blacks' efforts to elevate themselves were met with stiff resistance. Taking on surnames, adopting more formal given names, objecting to being called "boy" or "girl," "uncle" or "auntie" (not to mention "nigger" or "sambo"), insisting upon being addressed as "Mr." or "Miss" or "Mrs."—these and kindred demands were often seen by resentful whites as mere effrontery. During the Civil War, a Union soldier in Alabama asked a slave to identify herself. She recalled responding, "Jest Liza. I ain't got no other names." She said that the soldier then found out the name of her owner and told her, "Next time anybody call you nigger you tell 'em dat you is a negro and your name is Miss Liza Mixon." Soon afterward she encountered her owner, and he addressed her as he had done in the past: "What you doin', nigger." She repeated what the soldier had urged her to say: "I ain't no nigger. I'se a Negro and I'm Miss Liza Mixon." Outraged, and free from the Union soldiers who had departed, the owner proceeded to whip Miss Mixon, who later remarked ruefully, "I jest said dat [my full name] to de wrong person."[30] Other masters also sought to reimpose what the historian Leon Litwack aptly terms "linguistic relics of bondage."[31] A former slave recalls her mistress teasingly telling her, "Come here, you li'l old free nigger."[32]

Developments in black America colored developments elsewhere. The new freedom enjoyed by blacks in the South after emancipation brought black and white naming patterns closer than ever before as blacks discarded names they associated with their former degraded status and embraced names that they associated with freedom—names that largely conformed to the patterns of their white neighbors. Far from feeling flattered, however, some whites felt insulted. "I used to be proud of my name," Caroline Ravenel declared in a letter to a friend. "I have ceased to be so. I fear it will no longer [be] spotless, as the two meanest negroes on the place have appropriated it."[33] Discomfort with the new closeness between white and black names likely prompted some whites to distance themselves by selecting for their children the whitest names available—the names least used by Negroes—an early instance of white flight.[34]

"WHAT'S MY NAME?"

Racial struggles over personal nomenclature continued. The cruel etiquette of Jim Crow insisted that whites refrain from calling Negro adults "Mr." or "Mrs.," that they refer to blacks of any age as "boy" or "girl," and that they address blacks by their first names regardless of the relationship between the parties. Blacks challenged racist codes of address just as they challenged every outcropping of white supremacy. Some did so indirectly by identifying themselves only by their surnames. One man gave a daughter the first name "Miss" in order to outflank racist etiquette.[35] Others challenged racist practices frontally. When the civil rights activist Mary Hamilton was charged with trespass for ignoring Jim Crow restrictions, a prosecutor addressed her in open court by her first name, though he addressed whites by their last names. Miss Hamilton refused to answer unless spoken to properly. The trial judge held her in criminal contempt of court, a ruling eventually reversed by the Supreme Court.[36]

The Nation of Islam (NOI) has articulated an elaborate critique of what it sees as conformist concessions to Anglo-European hegemony in naming. According to its theology, whites stole from blacks their proper names. In its view, the names that most blacks select and use are actually nothing more than counterfeit "slave names." To signal the loss of blacks' real identities, the NOI leader Elijah Muhammad directed followers to substitute an X for their "slave" surnames. The most famous of these followers changed his name from Malcolm Little to Malcolm X. To honor conspicuously devoted followers, Elijah Muhammad conferred what he called "completed" names. The most famous of these was bestowed upon Cassius X, formerly Cassius Clay, after he won the world heavyweight boxing championship. That name, of course, was Muhammad Ali.

According to Ali,

Changing my name was one of the most important things that happened to me in my life. It freed me from the identity given to my family by slavemasters. . . . I was honored that Elijah Muhammad gave me a truly beautiful name.[37]

Others blacks, too, changed names in accordance with NOI protocols. Elijah Robert Poole became Elijah Muhammad. Louis Eugene Walcott became Louis Haleem Abdul Farrakhan.

Additional influences also prompted name changing among blacks in the 1960s and 1970s. One was the rising popularity of traditional Islam. Hence, Malcolm X became El-Hajj Malik El-Shabazz and Ferdinand Lewis Alcindor Jr. became Kareem Abdul-Jabbar. Important, too, were various sorts of secular black nationalism. That was the impetus behind Ronald McKinley Everett becoming Ron Ndabezitha Everett-Karenga, then Ron Karenga, then Maulana Ron Karenga, and finally Maulana Karenga.[38] Don L. Lee became Haki R. Madhubuti. JoAnne Chesimard changed her name to Assata Olugbala Shakur. Stokely Carmichael renamed himself Kwame Ture.[39] Everett LeRoi Jones reidentified himself as Ameer Barakat, then Amiri Baraka, then Imamu Amiri Baraka, before settling again on Amiri Baraka.[40] In giving himself a new name, he felt as if he were "literally being changed into a blacker being. I was discarding my 'slave name' and embracing blackness."[41]

People who changed their names sometimes encountered intra-racial resistance. Disapproving parents felt slighted; after all, they had selected the names that their children were now rejecting. Friends and relatives expressed concern that linguistic signs of rebellion would alienate potential employers and attract unwanted attention from authorities.[42]

The metamorphosis of Cassius Clay into Cassius X into Muhammad Ali provoked opposition from a wide range of observers, blacks as well as whites. "The new name," a biographer observes, "stuck in the public's collective craw." Some people, including journalists, refused to refer to the new boxing champion by his chosen name. At a boxing match that Ali attended in 1964, the president of Madison Square Garden forbade the ring announcer to use the new name to introduce Ali to the crowd. When he was introduced as "Cassius Clay," Ali angrily left the arena amid widespread booing.[43] Reflecting on the controversy, Ali remarked,

> People change their names all the time, and no one complains. Actors and actresses change their name. The pope

changes his name. Joe Louis and Sugar Ray Robinson changed their names. If I changed my name from Cassius Clay to something like Smith or Jones because I wanted a name that white people thought was more American, nobody would have complained.[44]

Another person who refused to recognize Ali's name change was Ernie Terrell,[45] a black boxer who fought Ali for the heavyweight title in 1967. Throughout the fight, which Ali won handily, he would hit Terrell and then yell, "What's my name?"

DISTINCTIVELY BLACK NAMES

Even more far-reaching than the name changing of adults in the Black Power era was the massive, grassroots change in customary preferences regarding the naming of newborns. In the late 1960s and early 1970s "a profound shift in naming conventions took place."[46] African Americans increasingly bestowed upon their offspring names perceived as distinctly black—LaKeisha, DeAndre, Shaniqua, Shanice, Kiara, Deja.

The flowering of distinct or unique black names is part of a long tradition of creative onomastics. "There is no part of the world," Robert Louis Stevenson declared, "where nomenclature is so rich, poetical, humorous and picturesque as the United States of America."[47] In his learned and entertaining treatise on the American language, H. L. Mencken introduces readers to Delphia ("'cause she . . . went to Philadelphia once"), to Vest (because when she was newborn her father wrapped her in his vest), and to Zannis, Avaline, Weeda, Olouise, and Birdene.[48] Writing in the 1930s, Mencken also notes among blacks a special "reaching out for striking and unprecedented names": Utensil Yvonne Johnson, Munsing Underwear Johnson, Slaughter Bugg, and Matthew Mark Luke John Acts-of-the-Apostles Son-of-Zebedee Garden-of-Gethsemane Hill.[49]

JUDGING NAMING?

Black names are seen by some as negative symbols, emblems that prompt cautious, if not fearful, antagonistic, or contemptuous responses. Two enterprising social scientists, Marianne Bertrand and Sendhil Mullainathan, sought to study how labor markets respond to various sorts of job seekers. They sent nearly five thousand résumés to employers who had placed help-wanted advertisements in Chicago and Boston newspapers. The experimenters varied certain features of the putative job seekers—for instance, where they lived, their levels of education, and their employment experience. The experimenters also varied the job seekers' names. When they created a certain résumé for a person with a prototypical white-sounding name—Allison or Anne, Brad or Brendan—they created the identical résumé for a person with a prototypical black-sounding name: Aisha or Ebony, Darnell or Hakim. The researchers found

> large racial differences in callback rates. Applicants with White names need to send about 10 resumes to get one callback whereas applicants with African-American names need to send about 15 resumes. This 50-percent gap in callback is statistically significant. A White name yields as many more callbacks as an additional eight years of experience on a resume.[50]

Some observers view distinctively black names as avoidable burdens that retard upward mobility and racial integration.[51] This reflects a widely held anxiety, perhaps present in all societies, that certain names are disfavored and thus disabling. In the face of prejudice against a particular sort of name, how should one react? Some people abandon disfavored names and substitute other, more acceptable monikers and feel no guilt in doing so. After all, disapproval of names sometimes stems from mere unfamiliarity and inconvenience. "Like stones at the seashore," observe Justin Kaplan and Anne Bernays, "foreign and difficult names yield their roughness and irregularity to the tidal wash of American convenience and usage."[52] Hence "Pfoersching" turns into "Pershing," "Roggenfelder" into "Rockefeller," "Bjorkegren" into "Burke," "Schmitz" into "Smith," "Pappadimitracoupoulos" into "Pappas," "Siminowicz" into "Simmons."[53] Frequently, though, the reason behind name avoidance or name changing arises from uglier sources. Anti-Semitism frames one of the most notable episodes of name changing in American history. To better position themselves to "make it," many Jews in the 1940s and 1950s camouflaged the most obvious signs of their religio-ethnic affiliation.[54] They abandoned Jewish-sounding names and substituted gentile-sounding names. That is why, as Kristen Fermaglich details in her history of Jewish name changing, Allan Stewart Konigsberg became Woody Allen, why Betty Joan Perske became Lauren Bacall, why Bernard Schwartz became Tony Curtis, why Emmanuel Goldenberg became Edward G. Robinson, why Belle Silverman became Beverly Sills, why Jill Oppenheim became Jill St. John, why Benjamin Kubelsky became Jack Benny, and why Nathan Birnbaum became George Burns.[55]

Some viewed name changing as a variant of "passing" and denounced it as a cowardly capitulation. Many others accepted it as a creative adaptation. Charles Silberman notes that some Jewish elders in the 1940s and 1950s virtually demanded that Jewish youngsters adopt names that would facilitate social mobility. He recalls an aunt who was enraged when he and his siblings declined to change their surname.* Here we can see a manifestation of benefit bestowed by whiteness in America. White skin offered a safe harbor for those willing to suppress other indicia of "otherness." The name changing that was common among Jews in mid-twentieth-century America has been far less prevalent among colored marginalized peoples. Why? Maybe because "while aspiring middle-class Jews with white skin and stigmatized names could see in name changing a ticket to upward mobility . . . people of color . . . have not seen economic promise in new names."[56]

What does law say about naming? The answer depends on where you live. Portugal requires parents to choose from an approved list, thus negating the creation of new names. Spain expressly bars names that are "extravagant" or "improper." Argen-

---

* There was a unique twist to the Silbermans' refusal. A paternal grandfather whose name was Zarkey settled in Des Moines. Friends told him that to move up the ladder, he would have to Americanize his name. On the lookout for an American name, he selected one that he saw in the window of a haberdashery: Silberman. He liked its sound, apparently unaware of its association with Jewishness. *See* Charles E. Silberman, *A Certain People: American Jews and Their Lives Today* (1985), 60.

tina prohibits "names signifying ideological or political tendencies," "ridiculous" names, or those "contrary to good morals."
France authorizes officials to reject first names deemed "contrary
to the welfare of the child." In the United States, parents have
broad latitude in naming. But there are some limits. A Louisiana
law allows parents to choose only surnames directly connected
to their own. Hawaii requires that a married couple give a child
at least two names, "a family name and a given name chosen by
one of the child's parents." Several states prohibit using as names
numerical symbols, obscenities, or monikers that exceed a certain
length. Still, relative to some other countries, America is strikingly libertarian.[57]

Believing that parents should have a broad freedom of
choice, however, does not entail liking or even approving of the
selections they make. Surveying the names chosen by celebrity
entertainers—Bronx Mowgli (chosen by Pete Wentz and Ashlee
Simpson), Pilot Inspektor (chosen by Jason Lee), Blanket (chosen
by Michael Jackson), Jermajesty (chosen by Jermaine Jackson),
Kyd (chosen by David Duchovny and Téa Leoni)—Laura Ingraham inveighs against what she sees as "stupid kid names." "Today's
little ones," she complains, "are saddled with some of the most
ridiculous names ever—it's as if the parents are trying to force the
kids to hate them early."[58]

While celebrities who engage in nonconformist naming draw
a bit of disapproval, ordinary folk who do so—especially if they
are black and poor—receive a far more contemptuous censure.
And not just from whites. The journalist Cathy Jackson chastised
black parents in the pages of *Essence* magazine for "sadd[ling]"
their offspring with "burdensome" names.[59] Bill Cosby (before
his criminal disgrace) infamously derided African Americans who
name their children "Shaniqua, Taliqua . . . *Muhammad* and all
that crap."[60] His disdain is by no means isolated. I know a distinguished African American physician who referred to distinctively
black names as "trash names."

Professor Michael Eric Dyson responds that "we have learned
to love and admire" people with such unique names as Oprah,
Shaquille, Keyshawn, and Condoleezza.[61] But learning of this sort
is itself an expense that many people will avoid. Instead of taking

the time and investing the effort to evaluate without prejudgment, many people will take a shortcut and assess others based only on easily accessible signals, including names. Associating certain names not merely with blackness but with lower-class blackness, many onlookers almost automatically disprefer "Lakisha" and "Jamal" to "Jane" and "John."

Given this negative reaction—wrong as it may be—should parents nonetheless name their children Lakisha or Jamal if they so desire? Is refraining from doing so a cowardly capitulation? Or is refraining from doing so a prudent action that displays a mature and loving solicitude for vulnerable children?

No negative judgment should fall upon parents who consciously attach moral, religious, ideological, or aesthetic value to a certain name or certain types of names even if the parents' choice will elicit adverse reactions. Professor Dyson is right to applaud blacks who "have truly cast care for what others think of them to the wind and embraced with courage their freedom to . . . create the meanings of their own names and fulfill their own destinies as best they can." That "is a freedom all Americans . . . should enjoy."[62] Parents should be deemed negligent, however, if they name their children with little or no attention given to the matter of social prejudice. That formula puts a burden on a parent—the burden of at least considering the invidious discrimination that will likely attend a distinctively black-sounding name. It might seem wrongful to insist that those taxed by prejudice have a responsibility to at least consider evading it. Acting accordingly, however, might lessen avoidable injuries inflicted by prejudice. Under this view, a parent is subject to criticism only for inexcusable ignorance or negligently indulging whim. If a parent is intent upon bestowing a given name after sensibly considering consequences, so be it. Obviously, there are African Americans with distinctively black names who are faring well across the social landscape. And what appears to be a burden may actually be an opportunity as the very impediments triggered by prejudiced responses sometimes occasion exertions that lead to remarkable accomplishment.

The race line is found in every aspect of American life—from the most public to the most private, from the most significant to the most trivial. It should thus come as no surprise that the race line marks our naming practices. That it does so is evidenced not only in distinctive black names. It is manifested, too, in the remarkable extent to which blacks figure disproportionately in the ranks of those bearing the most iconic of American surnames. According to the 2000 census, 90 percent of the 163,036 people with the surname "Washington" were African American, making it the blackest surname in the country.[63] The second blackest, at 75 percent, was "Jefferson."[64] Ongoing collective struggles affect even our most intimate efforts to shape individuality.

14

"Nigger": The Strange Career Continues

Dear Colleagues:[1]

I am writing about an issue that has arisen at a number of law schools and is latent in all of them: Is it acceptable to enunciate for pedagogical purposes a racial epithet that some find to be deeply upsetting?[2] The epithet is "nigger." Contexts in which its airing has come into question include the following: a teacher enunciates the word in the course of exploring language from which courts have withdrawn the protection that the First Amendment typically accords to speech; a teacher mentions the word in the course of discussing a hate speech prosecution; a teacher quotes out loud a passage in which "nigger" appears in a Supreme Court opinion; a teacher quotes a statement attributed to a Founding Father who reportedly referred to blacks as "niggers" during debate over the ratification of the Constitution.

In these and kindred cases, instructors have been targeted for investigation, subjected to official censure, banished from campus, suspended from teaching, and threatened with dismissal. Their detractors assert that, given the toxicity of "nigger," enunciating it is wrongful no matter the context or the intention of the speaker. They argue that giving voice to the epithet is so hurtful to some listeners that no pedagogical aim is worth the pain inflicted.*

---

* Apologizing for the pedagogical "use" of the n-word by Eugene Volokh, a member of her faculty, the dean of the University of California at Los Angeles

This controversy interests me for several reasons including the fact that when teaching, I enunciate "nigger" for pedagogical purposes. I do not "use" the term in the sense in which its use is rightly condemned. I do not bandy it about gratuitously, much less to taunt, threaten, demean, or insult anyone. I am well aware that "nigger" continues to be put to terrible purposes. Every few months I check reported court opinions in which "nigger" appears. Doing so forces me to confront anew the horrific animus that often propels and surrounds the epithet. These cases in their thousands reveal antiblack harassment, violence, and hatred in work sites, courtrooms, and homes. The unfiltered specificity of these opinions gives a glimpse as to why "nigger" became the American language's most notorious racial insult.

I enunciate "nigger" in full to drive home to audiences the way in which this troublesome word has been an integral part of the soundtrack of American racism. "Nigger" is thus an item in the lexicon of American culture about which people, especially lawyers, need to be aware.

Several professors have stated that going forward, in light of protest, they will no longer vocalize "nigger." I think here especially of the University of Chicago law professor Geoffrey Stone, an eminent scholar of constitutional law and a stalwart champion of academic freedom. For years in his course on the First Amendment, he vocalized "nigger" to dramatize the controversial doctrine of "fighting words"—the notion that some words, in certain circumstances, should receive no First Amendment protection because, when spoken, they provoke immediate violence. In March 2019 members of the Black Law Students Association (BLSA) detailed objections to his usage. The BLSA president argued that Stone's vocalization of the slur "damages and disrupts and distracts students. . . . Anyone can understand the impact

School of Law, Jennifer Mnookin, remarked that in her view "he could achieve his learning goals more effectively and empathetically without repeating the word itself. . . . The n-word is inextricably associated with anti-Black prejudice, racism, and slavery. . . . I am deeply sorry for the pain and offense the use of this word has caused." Professor Volokh emphatically declines to apologize, stating that professors and students ought to mention what actually happens in a case or incident, without euphemism or expurgation. *See* Eugene Volokh, "UCLA Law Dean Apologizes for My Having Accurately Quoted the Word 'Nigger' in Discussing a Case. I, However, Do Not Apologize," Reason.com, April 14, 2020.

of the N-word without explicitly saying it." The appeal moved Stone. "I never appreciated, before," he said, "the extent to which [hearing the slur] was disconcerting and painful." He announced that he would no longer vocalize the slur because, in his view, it was inessential to do so. "It's the distinction between useful or . . . essential. There are lots of things that you don't do in a classroom as a teacher which might be useful, but you don't do them for whatever reasons."[3]

Stone's new stance defers to the proposition that in these circumstances a feeling of hurt upon hearing "nigger" is a reaction warranting accommodation. I disagree. First, some of the claims of hurt are learned strategic responses as opposed to expressions of spontaneous feelings of alarm or distress. It is well known that in certain settings, particularly those that strive to be socially enlightened (like colleges and universities), you can effectively challenge speech to which you object by claiming that it is socially abhorrent (racist, sexist, transphobic, and so on) and makes you feel insulted, offended, or endangered. The reason that some object to any vocalizing of "nigger"—even when it is obviously being enunciated only for pedagogical purposes—is that saying the word has become, in the eyes of objectors, a symbol of either obtuseness or defiance: a sign that the (white—more about that later) instructor is unaware of the widespread belief that he ought never ever vocalize the term, or a sign that the instructor is disobeying that injunction. In a substantial number of instances these fights are not really over hurt feelings. They are struggles over status and power. Objectors have made avoidance of vocalizing "nigger," even in the guarded circumstances of classroom instruction, a matter of taboo, a matter of quasi-religious observance in which failure to abide by the rule of avoidance is taken as a sign of disrespect.* It is not the word or the circumstances of its

---

* At Princeton University reality mirrored parody. Professor Lawrence Rosen offered an anthropology course titled "Cultural Freedoms: Hate Speech, Blasphemy, and Pornography." In the opening class he asked, "What is worse, a white man punching a black man, or a white man calling a black man a nigger?" A number of students protested, with one reportedly stating that he was uncomfortable "with a white professor using the n-word." To his discredit, the professor proceeded to cancel the course. *See* Breanna Edwards, "Princeton Students

deployment in the classroom that cause anger. What causes anger is the failure of the teacher to submit to the objectors' demand for avoidance regardless of the circumstances.

Second, my position remains the same even in the case of the objector who is spontaneously overcome emotionally upon hearing the n-word. That is because of my view of "feelings." Feelings are not unchangeable givens untouched and untouchable by the ways in which their expression is received. Feelings are, at least in part, influenced by the responses of others. The more that schools validate the idea that hurt is justified in the circumstances pertinent here, the more that feelings of hurt will be expressed, and the more that there will be calls to respect expressed feelings of hurt by avoiding, prohibiting, or punishing what is said to trigger them. I insist upon pushing in another direction, advancing the message that in circumstances in which "nigger" is aired for pedagogical purposes, there is no good reason to feel hurt.

It is doing no favor to students to spare their feelings if doing so comes at the expense of valuable education. Even if hearing "nigger" does cause spontaneous, unmediated, authentic hurt, the slur should nonetheless be enunciated if, in the reasonable judgment of an instructor, doing so furthers the instruction at hand. One could, of course, avoid vocalizing the infamous slur. One could substitute some euphemism, say, "the n-word." But I find that alternative unsatisfactory. It veils or mutes an ugliness that, for maximum educational impact, ought to be seen or heard directly. Professor Stone concluded that vocalizing the n-word was "useful" but inessential. In my view, though, "useful" instruction should be pursued. Lawyers and judges frequently encounter distressing sights and sounds as part of their professional responsibilities. Every year in hundreds of cases "nigger" is heard in courts. It figured prominently in the most infamous murder trial of the twentieth century—the O. J. Simpson case.* A lawyer who

---

Walk Out of Lecture After Professor Allegedly Used the N-word: Report," *Root*, Feb. 8, 2018.

* In 1994–1995 prosecutors in Los Angeles sought to prove that the former football star O. J. Simpson had committed a double murder. An important witness for the prosecution was Officer Mark Fuhrman, who testified that he had

becomes distracted or depressed upon hearing "nigger" or any other slur is a lawyer with a gaping vulnerability. I would hope that part of what a law school would impart to students are techniques of self-mastery that will enable them to manage their feelings in order to optimally assist the people and institutions that will rely upon them for guidance.

I have yet to encounter any difficulties because of my own deployment of "nigger" in the classroom. I hope that my good fortune continues. If a conflict does arise, my position will be that conscientiously vocalizing "nigger" or any other epithet for legitimate pedagogical purposes ought not give rise to any belief or insinuation that the statement displays racism or racial insensitivity. Moreover, I will reject demands for silence, avoidance, or bowdlerization.* My remarks are not the result of a transient, ethe-

---

found incriminating evidence traceable to Simpson. To discredit Fuhrman, Simpson's attorneys moved to reveal to the jury that Officer Fuhrman had a penchant for referring to blacks derogatorily as "niggers." The prosecution urged the trial judge to prevent inquiry into Fuhrman's linguistic habits because references to the n-word would, it contended, "blind [the jury] to the truth" and "impair their ability to be fair and impartial." After all, the prosecutor Christopher Darden declared, "nigger" is the "filthiest, dirtiest, nastiest word in the English language." The lead defense attorney, Johnnie Cochran, countered, on the other hand, that it was "demeaning" to suggest that black jurors—"African Americans [whose forebears] have lived under oppression for two hundred–plus years" and who themselves had lived with "offensive words, offensive looks, [and] offensive treatment every day of their lives"—would be unable to assess the facts fairly. Officer Fuhrman denied the charge but was shown to be lying; unearthed recordings showed that he used "nigger" frequently and with relish. Whether the n-word and the false denial of using it significantly affected the outcome of the trial is difficult to determine. In any event, the jury delivered a controversial (and probably erroneous) acquittal. See Randall Kennedy, Nigger: The Strange Career of a Troublesome Word (2002), 85–87.

* I will certainly offer no apology. A demoralizing aspect of the fight over the n-word is the now familiar spectacle in which a person wrongly under fire issues a false, debasing apology hoping that that will appease protesters. The comedian Bill Maher wrote an op-ed ridiculing spurious ceremonial apologies. See "Please Stop Apologizing," New York Times, March 22, 2012. Yet five years later, Maher found himself apologizing for a joke in which he used the term "house nigger." Maher's apology was not an expression of authentic remorse. It was the formulaic statement of a man who felt he was a hostage and therefore entitled to tell the sorts of lies that hostages tell without fear of internal revulsion because, after all, they are speaking under duress. Various celebrities suggested boycotting Maher.

real concern. They stem in part from a deep well of study nourished by experience. I am an African American, born in 1954 in the Deep South (Columbia, South Carolina). My parents of blessed memory were refugees who fled Jim Crow oppression. They were branded as "niggers." And I have been called "nigger" too.

Should my race make a difference, cloaking me with more leeway than my white colleagues? No. I abjure such a "privilege." In the domain of culture there ought to be no boundaries that fence out people based on their racial identification. There ought to be no words that blacks are permitted to say but that whites are prohibited from saying. Racist use of "nigger" should be condemned no matter the racial identity of the speaker. Non-racist use of "nigger" should be accepted no matter the racial identity of the speaker. This belief in linguistic racial symmetry cuts against the belief in linguistic racial asymmetry that has, in some quarters, become a virtual axiom. It is not accidental that in all of the controversies noted at the outset of this letter, the embattled speaker was a white instructor. Although the racially discriminatory assessment of white speakers is sometimes kept quiet, it is often openly proclaimed: black instructors (singers, comedians, directors, authors) can enunciate the n-word absent condemnation in circumstances in which white instructors (singers, comedians, directors, authors) cannot—no matter what!

Decisions undertaken pursuant to racial double standards of this sort offend federal antidiscrimination law.[4] They are also antithetical to the openness, freedom, and creativity that enliven the domain of teaching and learning.

They harm *all* participants in the creation of culture. Nothing better illustrates this point than the bowdlerization of James Baldwin. He insisted that "nigger" was the creation of white racism and that the term said more about its creators than its targets. He declared that he was not a "nigger." Yet, an acclaimed documentary film transformed his statement into "I am not your Negro." A

Fearing those threats, he apologized and got into line. Pathetic. And frightening. *See* Dave Itzkoff, "Bill Maher Apologizes for Use of Racial Slur on 'Real Time,'" *New York Times*, June 3, 2017; Doreen St. Felix, "Bill Maher's Weird, Effortful Apology for Saying the N-Word," *New Yorker*, June 12, 2017.

white teacher at the New School, Laurie Sheck, pointed this out, quoting Baldwin directly. She referred her students to one of his essays in which he complained about the suppressions and lies that had covered up "the darker forces in our history" and in which he urged "an unflinching assessment of the record." Months later Sheck was called to the office of an administrator because of a student's complaint that her remarks might have violated the university's discrimination policy. The university belatedly "cleared" Sheck after intervention on her behalf by various organizations, including the Foundation for Individual Rights in Education. That there was thought to be a substantial matter to "clear," however, is indicative of antiracism gone awry.[5]

I am well aware that racial oppression and its manifold legacies continue to haunt American life, sometimes in forms that are lethal. I believe that racism is a looming, destructive force that we must resist. Vigilance is essential. But so, too, is a capacity and willingness to draw crucial distinctions. There is a world of difference that separates the racist use of "nigger" from the vocalizing of "nigger" for pedagogical reasons aimed at enabling students to attain important knowledge.

Sincerely,

Randall Kennedy

15

Should We Admire Nat Turner?[1]

How should one view Nat Turner?[2] Should he be lauded as a hero, dismissed as a lunatic, condemned as a criminal, or categorized in some other fashion?

Turner was born enslaved in 1800—the same year as John Brown[3]—in Southampton County, Virginia, where he resided for his entire short life. In August 1831 he initiated an uprising eventually joined by sixty to eighty enslaved and free blacks. The rebellion lasted less than forty-eight hours before it was repressed. Though brief, it was bloody. Turner and his followers marched from house to house in a corner of Southampton, shooting, stabbing, slicing, and bludgeoning as they went. They killed fifty-five white men, women, and children. The killing began with an assault on the household in which Turner lived as a slave. According to *The Confessions of Nat Turner . . . as Fully and Voluntarily Made to Thomas R. Gray*, "The murder of this family . . . was the work of a moment, not one of them awoke; there was a little infant sleeping in a cradle, that was forgotten, until we had left the house and gone some distance, when Henry and Will [fellow rebels] returned and killed it."[4]

The Confessions is a document in which a white lawyer, Thomas R. Gray, claims to set forth in writing a statement conveyed verbally by the jailed Nat Turner as he awaited trial—a statement in which Turner describes his upbringing, religious

visions, relations with owners and fellow slaves, and the planning
and execution of the uprising. In *The Confessions*, Turner purportedly described other acts of the rebellion:

> We started . . . for Mrs. Reese's maintaining the most
> perfect silence on our march, where finding the door
> unlocked, we entered, and murdered Mrs. Reese in her
> bed, while sleeping; her son awoke, but it was only to
> sleep the sleep of death, he had only time to say who is
> that, and he was no more. From Mrs. Reese's went to Mrs.
> Turner's. . . . Will [Turner's chief lieutenant] immediately
> killed Mrs. Turner, with one blow of his axe. I took Mrs.
> Newsome by the hand, and with the sword I had . . . I
> struck her several blows over the head, but not being able
> to kill her, as the sword was dull. Will turning around and
> discovering it, dispatched her also.[5]

Turner continued the narration:

> 'Twas my object to carry terror and devastation wherever
> we went, I placed fifteen or twenty of the best armed and
> most to be relied on, in front, who generally approached
> the house as fast as their horses could run; this was for two
> purposes, to prevent their escape and strike terror to the
> inhabitants. Having murdered Mrs. Waller and ten chil-
> dren, we started for Mr. William Williams'. . . . Mrs. Wil-
> liams fled and got some distance from the house, but she
> was pursued, overtaken, and compelled to get up behind
> one of the company, who brought her back and after
> showing her the mangled body of her lifeless husband, she
> was told to get down and lay by his side, where she was
> shot dead.[6]

Turner and his followers appear to have wanted to march upon
the capital of the county, a village named, remarkably, Jerusalem.
But before they could do so, they were overwhelmed by militia-
men. While many of the rebels were apprehended quickly, Turner
eluded capture for two months.

The aftermath of the rebellion saw an escalation of bloodletting, with a turnabout in the racial demographics of death. Frightened and enraged, whites summarily killed scores of blacks, whether or not evidence tied them to complicity in the rebellion. A cavalry company decapitated as many as fifteen suspected rebels and put their heads on poles for display.[7] One militiaman told a newspaper that he had seen "the slaughter of many blacks without trial, and under circumstances of great barbarity." Another witness related the following regarding the fate of a slave captured by state authorities: "They burnt him with red hot irons—cut off his ears and nose—stabbed him, cut his hamstrings, stuck him like a hog, and at last cut off his head."[8]

Opinion regarding Turner varies widely. Some see him as a criminal. That was the view of the court that convicted him of "making insurrection, and plotting to take away the lives of divers free white persons."[9] That court told Turner,

> You have been convicted of plotting in cold blood, the indiscriminate destruction of men, of helpless women, and of infant children. The evidence before us leaves not a shadow of a doubt, but that your hands were often embrued with the blood of the innocent. . . . [You deprived] us of many of our most valuable citizens; and this was done when they were asleep, and defenceless; under circumstances shocking to humanity.[10]

Appalled by what it deemed a barbaric, inexcusable crime, the court imposed upon Turner its harshest sentence: "The judgment of the court is, that you be taken hence to the jail from whence you came, thence to the place of execution, and . . . be hung by the neck until you are dead! dead! dead!"[11] On November 11, 1831, Turner was hanged, his body dissected, his remains scattered.

Many observers over the years have concurred in condemning Turner as, in the words of the *Norfolk Herald*, a "wretched culprit."[12] Gray says of the rebels,

> No cry for mercy penetrated the flinty bosoms. No acts of remembered kindness made the least impression upon these remorseless murderers. . . . Never did a band of savages do their work of death more unsparingly. Apprehen-

sion for their own personal safety seems to have been the only principle of restraint in the whole course of their bloody proceeding.[13]

The editors of the *Richmond Enquirer* condemned the "horrible atrocity of these monsters. They remind one of a parcel of blood-thirsty wolves . . . or, rather, like a former incursion of the Indians upon the white settlements. Nothing is spared; neither age nor sex is respected—the helplessness of women and children pleads in vain for mercy."[14] Even the destructiveness and cruelty of the Civil War failed to dim the indignation with which some observers recalled Turner's uprising. Writing soon after the war's end, the editors of the Richmond *Dispatch* averred,

> Nat Turner's massacre was the most barbarous and brutal of all the human butcheries of the century. . . . It was a horror of horrors, a brutal and phrensied shedding of human blood, such as has never been exceeded in its unprovoked and brutal character.[15]

Some of Turner's harshest detractors complain that he should have seen that his revolt was obviously futile and that to proceed in the face of certain defeat was deplorable, a waste of the lives of those he killed as well as a waste of the lives of those he led. *The New York Journal of Commerce* expressed this view. Calling the uprising "a savage atrocity," the *Journal* exclaimed, "We cannot imagine what infatuation could have seized the minds of these negroes, that they should even dream of success in attempting to recover their freedom by violence and bloodshed."[16]

Perhaps Turner and his followers, however, had a different mission in mind. According to *The Confessions*, Turner believed that he was being directed by a divine force:

> I heard a loud noise in the heavens, and the Spirit instantly appeared to me and said the Serpent was loosened, and Christ had laid down the yoke he had borne for the sins of men, and that I should take it on and fight against the Serpent, for the time was fast approaching when the first should be last and the last should be first.[17]

If Turner believed that the Holy Spirit was urging him and his comrades to kill slaveholding whites and their kin, he *succeeded* in carrying out what he saw as a religious duty. Pre–Civil War America was awash in the rhetoric and sentiments of apocalypticism, particularly as it pertained to slavery. Thomas Jefferson wrote of trembling for his country when he reflected on how God is just.[18] Abraham Lincoln spoke of God making it so that every drop of blood drawn with the lash would be paid by another drawn with the sword.[19] Perhaps Nat Turner saw himself as God's messenger and his death-dealing rebellion as God's message. That motivation would fit with the impression of Turner that Gray conveys:

> He is a complete fanatic, or plays his part most admirably. . . . The calm, deliberate composure with which he spoke of his late deeds and intentions, the expression of his fiend-like face when excited by enthusiasm, still bearing the stains of helpless innocence about him; clothed with rags and covered with chains; yet daring to raise his manacled hands to heaven, with a spirit soaring above the attributes of man; I looked on him and my blood curdled in my veins.[20]

The *Journal* scoffs at what it portrays as the rebels' *unthinking* martyrdom. But perhaps Turner and his comrades courted martyrdom thoughtfully, preferring to end their lives with a dramatic and instructive flourish. History is full of examples of collective martyrdom in which people chose a course leading to certain and early death with the hope that their sacrifice would usher forth a better future. Some emphasize that Turner's rebellion prompted the slaughter of slaves during the repression of the uprising and provoked Virginia authorities to tighten the policing of enslaved and free blacks subsequently. It is also the case, however, that Turner's rebellion sparked a serious debate in Virginia over the wisdom of perpetuating slavery.[21]

There are other ambitions that Turner and his comrades might have had in mind. The record offers little hard evidence on this point. Here as elsewhere observers are left to draw inferences from documentation generated mainly by the slaves' adversaries.

A plausible speculation, though, is that at least some of the rebels sought revenge.[22] Prior to the rebellion, a slave owner named Thomas Barrow had refused to allow an enslaved man to marry. During the uprising that enslaved man impaled Barrow upon a spit.

A second strand of commentary lauds Turner and his comrades. According to the distinguished African American journalist T. Thomas Fortune, Turner was "a black hero. He preferred death to slavery,"[23] exhibiting "in the most abject conditions the heroism and race devotion which have illustrated in all times the sort of men who are worthy to be free."[24]

Marking the centennial of Turner's execution, *The Liberator*— a publication of the communist League of Struggle for Negro Rights—asserted that

> Nat Turner, in deeds, was a revolutionary leader of the enslaved Negroes. With the utmost courage and determination he led the slaves of Virginia with sword and musket against the slaveowners. . . . He fought for freedom. . . . He lost . . . but his revolt added new strength to the revolutionary traditions of the Negro people.[25]

Around the same time, the black activist-intellectual Rayford Logan declared that African Americans should take pride in Turner because he "kept his 'Rendezvous with Death' rather than live a bondsman. His simple courage surpassed the comprehension of his executioners."[26]

The most concerted praising of Turner occurred in the 1960s. This stemmed, in part, from the heightened interest in black history and culture that was an outgrowth of the civil rights movement.[27] The hagiography also stemmed more particularly from opposition to the Pulitzer Prize–winning novel by William Styron—*The Confessions of Nat Turner*. Leading figures in American culture admired Styron's crafting of an angst-ridden, self-doubting rebel who loved and loathed his fellow enslaved blacks and who hated and lusted after the whites who surrounded him.[28] Detractors, however, perceived Styron to be desecrating Turner's memory. "No event in recent years," John Henrik Clarke observed, "has touched and stirred the black intellectual com-munity more than this book." Black opinion was by no means monolithic; James Baldwin praised Styron's novel. But Baldwin was an outlier. Most of the blacks who published writings on the controversy denounced Styron. "The Nat Turner created by Wil-liam Styron," Clarke complained, "has little resemblance to the Virginia slave insurrectionist who is a hero to his people."[29]

According to Lerone Bennett Jr., "The real Nat Turner was a virile, commanding, courageous figure."[30] According to Ernest Kaiser, Turner "led a heroic rebellion against the dehumanization of chattel slavery."[31] According to Charles V. Hamilton,

> Nat Turner is our hero, unequivocally understood. He is a man who had profound respect and love for his fellow blacks. . . . Nat Turner was a success because he perpetu-ated the idea of freedom—freedom at all cost. He will not be denied his place in the revolutionary annals of black people by white people who—through the guise of art or otherwise—feel a conscious or subconscious need to belittle him.[32]

The fight over Styron's novel contributed to a popularization and elevation of Nat Turner. In many settings he is now accepted as an uncontroversial hero by people who know little about the particulars of his rebellion. In 2009, when Newark, New Jersey, unveiled its largest municipal public park, the Nat Turner Park, all sorts of political dignitaries joined in the celebration. None intimated, at least not publicly, that the naming of the park might be problematic.* They lauded unequivocally the Nat Turner of

---

* *See* "Newark Opens Nat Turner Park in Central Ward After 30 Years," nj.com, July 28, 2009. Though this news account makes no mention of conflict over Turner's reputation, some of the online responses are clearly aware of the con-troversy and take sides with respect to it. One correspondent writes, "North Bergen needs to name a park for Hal Turner, a Turner who didn't enter a home and decapitate 10 children. This is all you need to know about Newark and its feral population." By contrast, another correspondent writes, "Unlike these folks who kill for nothing nowadays . . . Mr. Turner had a cause. . . . [P]ut yourself in his shoes."

black oral tradition, the man who waged war against slavery, the "martyred soldier of slave liberation who broke his chains and murdered whites because slavery had murdered Negroes."[33]

Asserting that Turner was willing to make a full and free confession, Gray writes,

> I determined for the gratification of public curiosity to commit his statements to writing, and publish them, with little or no variation, from his own words. That this is a faithful record of his confessions, the annexed certificate of the County Court of Southampton will attest. They certainly bear one stamp of truth and sincerity. He makes no attempt . . . to exculpate himself, but frankly acknowledges his full participation in all the guilt of the transaction.[34]

There is reason, however, to be extra careful in mining Gray's handiwork. Turner had incentive to misportray his own situation. He never mentions his wife. Perhaps he was trying to protect her. Gray, too, had incentives that might have prompted him to omit certain facts or to exaggerate others. A former slave owner, he sympathized with the whites killed in the rebellion and detested the blacks who did the killing. As a failed lawyer in desperate need of money, moreover, Gray might well have embellished *The Confessions* to make it more salable.[35]

Many blacks' assessments of Turner are rooted in a complex welter of attitudes. Some feel pride in ancestors who, unlike Turner, managed to live out their natural lives despite the awful mistreatment they encountered. Others, however, are haunted by a racial shame that springs from a recognition of all that their ancestors accommodated in order to live. For many of Turner's admirers, his rebellion is an antidote to that humiliation. That is why, at least with respect to the portrayal of violence, Turner's partisans offer little or no complaint against either Gray or Styron. They do not dispute that during the uprising the rebels deliberately killed children. The extremity of the violence is of little concern. What matters is that Turner was willing to kill the whites who purported to own him and other black people. Turner devotees are thrilled by his willingness to attack slavery by any means.

Even in the twenty-first century many black Americans feel mortified by their ancestors' enslavement. They are deeply ashamed that their forebearers were enslavable, that their ancestors submitted to a regime under which they were subjected to having their mothers and fathers, sisters and brothers torn asunder by sale, reduced to witnessing their womenfolk sexually preyed upon by white men who acted with impunity, reduced to a station in which they could mockingly be named anything by their white owners—"Caesar," "Pompey," "Cleopatra"—and exploited incessantly as laboring machines.

Blacks must also continue to grapple with the fact that defenders of slavery argued that Negroes preferred enslavement to freedom because blacks were natural slaves as indicated by their accommodation to bondage. The U.S. senator from South Carolina James Henry Hammond defended slavery, stating,

> In all social systems there must be a class to do the menial duties, to perform the drudgery of life. . . . Its requisites are vigor, docility, fidelity. . . . It constitutes the very mudsill of society. . . . Fortunately for the South she found a race adapted to that purpose. . . . A race inferior to her own but eminently qualified in temper, in vigor, in docility.[36]

The image of the docile Negro was a staple of pro-slavery apologists. Writing in the aftermath of Turner's rebellion, a pro-slavery politician in Virginia dismissed it as an anomaly. "Our slave population," he observed, "is not only a happy one, but it is contented, peaceful and harmless. . . . During all this time [the last sixty years] we have had one insurrection."[37] Writing decades later, Thomas R. R. Cobb remarked that "the negro race" is peculiarly fitted to be a servile, laboring class because their "moral character renders them happy, peaceful, contented, and cheerful in a status that would break the spirit and destroy the energies of the Caucasian and the native American."*[38] The idea of the docile

---

* Abused throughout the history of the United States, Native Americans have enjoyed one advantage over blacks: their reputation as unenslavable. The belief that Native Americans would perish rather than survive in bondage added to the allure of the "noble savage."

Negro, moreover, outlived slavery. In an important text published in 1927, E. B. Reuter claimed that blacks "are patiently tolerant under abuse and oppression and little inclined to struggle against difficulties. These facts of racial temperament and disposition make the Negroes more amenable to the condition of slavery than perhaps any other racial group."[39] Around that time a report of the Army War College claimed that "in physical courage . . . the American Negro falls well back of the white man and possibly behind all other races."[40] A decade later the War College reiterated the point: "The Negro is docile, tractable, lighthearted, care free and good natured."[41]

The image of the submissive Negro slave has long been intertwined with the idea of enslavement as a dishonorable fate worse than death. It is an idea that runs deep in American culture. "Is life so dear," Patrick Henry asked, "as to be purchased at the price of chains and slavery?" His famous response was unequivocal: "Give me liberty or give me death!"[42] The black abolitionist David Walker voiced this same sentiment: "Now, I ask you, had you not rather be killed than to be a slave to a tyrant, who takes the life of your mother, wife, and dear little children?"[43] Behind the question is the insinuation that to live as a slave is to live without any claim to respect.

A hint of shame is found even in one of the great anthems of the civil rights movement:

> *Oh freedom, Oh freedom*
> *Oh freedom over me*
> *And before I'd be a slave*
> *I'll be buried in my grave*
> *And go home to my Lord and be free.*

These lyrics, too, suggest that death is preferable to slavery, a belief that is only a step away from the judgment that those who choose to live as slaves did something dishonorable. Or consider the memoir by the civil rights activist Dorothy Cotton: *If Your Back's Not Bent: The Role of the Citizenship Education Program in the Civil Rights Movement* (2012). The title plays upon the adage "no one can ride you if your back's not bent." The adage puts the onus of blame squarely on the victim by insisting that no one can dominate you if you resist sufficiently. One could resist unto death. But faced with overwhelming force, most people will bend their backs in submission.

The valorization of death over enslavement burdens victims morally by making their choice for survival seem cowardly. There is, however, nothing shameful in choosing to live even if doing so entails enslavement. Eschewing submission, even at the price of death, is easy now on this side of abolition. Prior to 1865, however, the question posed a real, agonizing dilemma.

The idea of the submissive Negro was used to rationalize the enslavement of African Americans. The evil of slavery would be much mitigated if bondage was imposed on beings who did not much mind it. That is why some pro-slavery propagandists maintained that blacks *flourished* under bondage and preferred it to freedom. Such arguments have no purchase on modern observers, especially those inclined to praise Nat Turner. More problematic, however, is the historical record that provides some ballast to the idea of the submissive Negro. A key feature of that record is the relative paucity of violent mass uprisings among slaves in the United States. There were some conspiracies to be sure— Gabriel Prosser's planned uprising in Richmond in 1800 and Denmark Vesey's planned uprising in Charleston in 1822. There were also rebellions that actually erupted, some of which were hushed up to deprive the enslaved of role models.[44] There was also an ongoing stream of low visibility, day-to-day resistance—the broken plow, the "accidental" fire, the spit in the soup, the stolen animals, the withheld labor, the feigned sickness, and all manner of other ways in which slaves deployed the "weapons of the weak."* But with all due respect to Herbert Aptheker and others

---

* Lampooning the notion of the docile Negro, John Oliver Killens writes,

> The slaves were so "contented" the slavemasters could not afford the astronomical cost of fire insurance. Dear old Dixieland was in a constant state of insurrection. Thousands of rapturous slaves killed their mistresses and masters, put spiders in the Big House soup, broke their farming implements accidentally-on-purpose, set fire to the cotton patches, and, all in all, demonstrated their contentedness in most peculiar ways.

John Oliver Killens, "The Confessions of Willie Styron," in John Henrik Clarke, *William Styron's Nat Turner: Ten Black Writers Respond* (1968), 42.

See also James C. Scott, *Weapons of the Weak: Everyday Forms of Peasant Resis-*

who have searched antebellum history for any and every hint of resistance, the fact remains that there were notably few instances in which enslaved blacks rose violently en masse to challenge the slave regime.* That is why Nat Turner stands out so strikingly. What he did was rare.

In an anthology of critical responses to Styron, Loyle Hairston asks the question, "Can a man commit a crime against slavery?"[45] He seems to have asked his question rhetorically, believing that the obvious answer is in the negative, as did Addison Gayle when he declared, in defense of Turner, "No victim has a moral responsibility to recognize the laws of the oppressor."[46] Similarly, Michael Walzer posited that "there is a sense in which oppression makes men free, the more radical the oppression the more radical the freedom. Thus slaves have a right to kill their masters. . . . They are set loose from the normal restraints of social life, because any violence they commit against masters . . . can plausibly be called defensive."[47]

That slaves have no obligation to observe the moral code of their masters† does not mean that it is acceptable for enslaved persons to have no moral obligations. Slaves, like all beings, have some moral obligations. They have a moral obligation, for example, to refrain from informing on other slaves for purely self-interested purposes. Slaves also have a moral obligation to forgo inflicting excessive injury in fighting for freedom. They can rightly resist enslavement. They can rightly resist violently. They can rightly resist violently even if that entails causing inadvertent injury to bystanders. But should they be able to do *anything* to masters or the allies of masters without moral condemnation? Did slaveholders have no rights that slaves were bound to respect?‡

---

tance (1987); Raymond A. Bauer and Alice H. Bauer, "Day to Day Resistance to Slavery," 27 *Journal of Negro History* 388 (1942).

* I refer to Herbert C. Aptheker's scholarship with admiration. *See especially American Negro Slave Revolts* (1943).

† The Commonwealth of Virginia itself recognized this to some extent when it dismissed an indictment for treason against a slave rebel who took part in Turner's insurrection. The reasoning seems to have been that a slave, as a totally alienated outsider, could not betray a polity that was not his in any meaningful sense.

‡ This is an inversion, of course, of Chief Justice Roger B. Taney's observation that in antebellum America blacks had no rights that whites were bound to

Nat Turner and his followers committed no rapes during the insurrection. Thomas Wentworth Higginson wrote tellingly about this matter:

> These negroes had been systematically brutalized from childhood; they had been allowed no legalized or permanent marriage; they had beheld around them an habitual licentiousness, such as can easily exist under slavery; some of them had seen their wives and sisters habitually polluted by the husbands and brothers of these fair women who were now absolutely in their power. Yet I have looked through the Virginia newspapers of that time in vain for one charge of an indecent outrage on a woman against these triumphant and terrible slaves.[48]

Suppose Turner and his men had committed rapes and explained that they did so to punish and terrorize the slave owners? Would *that* conduct be properly immunized against moral censure?

Slaves are accountable to some moral code. Such a code should require even the most oppressed person to forgo cruelty, or inflicting gratuitous injury, or deploying means whose destructiveness clearly outweighs any valid ends. On the assumption that rape would have violated such norms, slaves perpetrating rape would be morally culpable. By the same logic, any gratuitous killings perpetrated by Turner and his followers make them morally culpable. Again: one must be careful here regarding supposed "facts." Documentation of the rebellion was created mainly by those who opposed it. The master class and its allies were certainly willing to vilify slaves by attributing to them all manner of objectionable traits and conduct. But what if it is true that the Turner rebels killed the infant and the fleeing wife (after showing her the lifeless body of her husband)? Such killings seem hard to justify or excuse in terms of defending the insurrection. But just

---

respect. *See Dred Scott v. Sandford,* 60 U.S. 393 (1857). Ralph Waldo Emerson maintained during the Civil War that the Confederate rebel "has no rights which the Negro . . . is bound to respect." Quoted in David S. Reynolds, *John Brown, Abolitionist* (2005), 483.

suppose the impetus behind the killings was pent-up anger, a taste for revenge? Satisfying such a desire ought not to justify or excuse the taking of lives.

Admirers of Turner invoke an analogy to war. They argue that the conduct of the rebels should be assessed similarly as soldiers in combat (with perhaps a bit more leeway in that slave insurrectionists were untrained). Warfare is brutal and ugly and occasions actions that would otherwise be unacceptable. War is hell. But even warfare against the most dastardly of foes should have rules. The specter of mass rape probably did demoralize and intimidate Nazi soldiers and civilians on the eastern front in Germany near the end of World War II. And the Soviet soldiers on hand to commit those rapes had certainly suffered terribly. Still, we properly condemn the Soviet rapists despite the extremity in which they found themselves.[49]

How should one view Nat Turner? If he did what admirers laud him for doing—if his conduct was substantially in accord with the events related in his *Confessions*—he warrants our sympathy but not our praise.* He ought not be celebrated as a hero. He and his comrades rightly sought freedom and the demise of the slave regime even if those aims required a resort to violence. In pursuing those aims, however, Turner was obligated to minimize injury. The historical record suggests that he took no such care.

Empathy for the rebels, abhorrence of slavery, and dedication to struggles for justice do not require praising Nat Turner despite the moral deficits of his insurrection. And withholding such praise is a useful discipline. Consider an article published on September 22, 1831, in the Albany, New York, *African Sentinel and Journal of Liberty*, an antislavery newspaper. Reflecting on the Turner rebellion, the *Sentinel* observed that "the slaves have a perfect right

---

* *Cf.* Paul Butler, "Foreword: Terrorism and Utilitarianism: Lessons from, and for, Criminal Law," 93 *Journal of Criminal Law and Criminology* 1, 10 ("Viewed through contemporary eyes, men like Nat Turner . . . may not exactly be heroes, but they are not exactly 'terrorists' either. They occupy a more nuanced space in our moral universe. As a descendant of slaves, and a witness to the scars slavery left, I am unwilling to condemn, categorically, private violence that sought to hasten its abolition.").

derived from God Almighty to their freedom." But it then stated that Turner and his followers "have done vastly wrong . . . in killing women and children." Affirming the legitimacy of the slaves' strivings, the *Sentinel* maintained that "their struggle for freedom is the same in principle as the struggle of our [founding] fathers in '76." It hoped that the slaves would be able to achieve their liberty eventually by "fair and honorable means." But the *Sentinel* insisted that the slaves "refrain from assailing women and children" and conduct themselves "on the true principles of heroism."*[50]

Demanding exacting standards is difficult in a political culture that routinely celebrates figures guilty of horrifying moral crimes. President Andrew Jackson is a much-honored slave owner and slave seller who ruthlessly dispossessed Native Americans, pursuing a policy of "Indian removal" that would now be called "ethnic cleansing." Those championing Turner might well argue that if America can overlook the bad Jackson did in order to appreciate his good, then America should also overlook the bad Turner did in order to appreciate his good. They are justifiably angry at the biases that allow for the canonization of an Andrew Jackson alongside the minimization or demonization of a Nat Turner. The proper response, however, is not to become less attentive to Turner's failings but to become more attentive to Jackson's. Neither should be offered as subjects of emulation.

Seeking to reach an appropriate assessment of Turner, the great abolitionist William Lloyd Garrison refused to praise him. A pacifist, Garrison objected to deploying violence even against slavery. Yet he also found himself unable to denounce Turner. Instead, he derided as hypocrites those who condemned Turner but praised other purveyors of violence. According to Garrison, Turner and the other rebels "deserve no more censure than the Greeks in destroying the Turks, or the Poles in exterminating

---

* The former slave William Wells Brown was unwilling to laud Nat Turner unequivocally, describing his "strike for liberty" as the "outburst of feelings of an insane man—made so by slavery." *My Southern Home; or, The South and Its People* (1880), 243–44. Earlier, Brown had asserted that Turner's "acts and his heroism live in the hearts of his race." Even then he remarked, however, that Turner was "a victim of his own fanaticism." *The Black Man: His Antecedents, His Genius, and His Achievements* (1863), 59–75. *See also* Eric Foner, *Nat Turner* (1971), 141–45.

the Russians, or our fathers in slaughtering the British. Dreadful, indeed, is the standard erected by worldly patriotism!"[51]

I agree with Garrison that Turner deserves no more critical moral scrutiny than a George Washington, a Thomas Jefferson, a James Madison, or an Andrew Jackson. But he also deserves no less. One's ultimate assessment may vary given the different contexts these figures occupied; these statesmen had access to far greater resources, and thus more choice, than did rebellious slaves. For that reason, the statesmen might appropriately be judged more harshly. But slaves ought not be denied ethical examination. By demanding that Turner and his fellow insurrectionists meet minimal standards of decency, we morally elevate slaves who are all too often unwittingly demeaned by their champions.

16

Frederick Douglass: Everyone's Hero[1]

It is difficult to imagine a more remarkable story of self-determination than the life of Frederick Douglass. Emblematic of the depths from which he rose is the pall of ignorance about his beginnings that long enshrouded him. For many decades he believed that he had been born in 1817. Then, in 1877, during a visit to a former master in Maryland, Douglass was told that he had actually been born in 1818. Douglass could barely recall his mother, who was consigned to different households from the one where her baby lived. And he never discovered the identity of his father, who was likely a white man. "Genealogical trees," Douglass mordantly observed, "do not flourish among slaves."

Douglass fled enslavement in 1838 and, with the assistance of abolitionists, cultivated his prodigious talents as an orator and a writer. He produced a score of extraordinary speeches. The widely anthologized "What to the Slave Is the Fourth of July?," delivered in 1852, is the most damning critique of American hypocrisy ever uttered:

> What, to the American slave, is your 4th of July? . . . a day that reveals to him . . . the gross injustice and cruelty to which he is the constant victim. To him, your celebration is a sham . . . your shouts of liberty and equality, hollow mockery. . . . There is not a nation on the earth guilty of

practices, more shocking and bloody, than are the people of these United States, at this very hour.

He wrote analyses of court opinions that deservedly appear in constitutional law casebooks. He published arresting columns in newspapers, including three that he started. He also wrote three exceptional memoirs, *Narrative of the Life of Frederick Douglass, an American Slave* (1845), *My Bondage and My Freedom* (1855), and *Life and Times of Frederick Douglass* (1881). The most celebrated black man of his era, he was the first African American appointed to an office requiring senatorial confirmation; in 1877, President Rutherford B. Hayes nominated him to be the marshal of the District of Columbia.

Throughout his life Douglass fell victim to the brutalizations and insults commonly experienced by African Americans of his time. As a slave, he suffered at the hands of a vicious "nigger breaker" to whom he was rented. He fled to the "free" North, only to have his work as a maritime caulker thwarted by racist white competitors. As a traveling evangelist for abolitionism, he was repeatedly ejected from whites-only railroad cars, restaurants, and lodgings. When he died, an admiring obituary in *The New York Times* suggested that Douglass's "white blood" accounted for his "superior intelligence." After his death, his reputation declined precipitously alongside the general standing of African Americans in the age of Jim Crow.

Now everyone wants a piece of Frederick Douglass. When a statue memorializing him at the U.S. Capitol was unveiled in 2013, members of the party of Paul Ryan and Mitch McConnell sported buttons that read, "Frederick Douglass Was a Republican." More recently, the Republican National Committee issued a statement joining Donald Trump "in honoring Douglass' lifelong dedication to the principles that define [the Republican] Party and enrich our nation." Across the ideological divide, Barack Obama has lauded Douglass, as has Cornel West. New books about Douglass have appeared with regularity, the most impressive of which is David W. Blight's magnificently expansive and detailed *Frederick Douglass: Prophet of Freedom*.

A history professor at Yale who has long been a major contributor to scholarship on Douglass, slavery, and the Civil War, Blight portrays Douglass as a hero while also revealing his subject's weaknesses. He illuminates important facets of nineteenth-century political, social, and cultural life in America, including the often-overlooked burdens borne by black women. At the same time, he speaks urgently to the Black Lives Matter moment of today. Given the salience of charges of cultural misappropriation, gripes about Blight's achievement would be unsurprising: he is a white man interpreting the most outstanding African American of the nineteenth century. Fortunately, though, I have heard no such complaints, which is good because it should be clear to any reader that Blight's exploration of Douglass's life is admirably sensitive, careful, learned, creative, and soulful.

In the wake of Douglass's death in 1895, it was African Americans who kept his memory alive. Booker T. Washington wrote a biography in 1906. The historian Benjamin Quarles wrote an excellent study in 1948. White historians on the left also played a key role in protecting Douglass from oblivion, none more usefully than Philip Foner, a blacklisted Marxist scholar (and uncle of Eric Foner) whose carefully edited collection of Douglass's writings remains essential reading. But in "mainstream"—that is, white politically conventional—circles, Douglass was widely overlooked. Edmund Wilson's *Patriotic Gore: Studies in the Literature of the American Civil War* (1962) exemplified this problem, receiving lavish praise from the most esteemed historians and cultural critics in the country despite its egregious snubbing of Douglass and virtually all of the other black literary figures of the period.

Keenly attuned to the politics of public memory, Blight shows that the current profusion of claims on Douglass's legacy bears close scrutiny: claimants have a way of overlooking features of his complex persona that would be embarrassing for them to acknowledge. Conservatives praise his individualism, which sometimes verged on social Darwinism. They also herald Douglass's stress on black communal self-help, his antagonism toward labor unions, and his strident defense of men's right to bear arms. They tiptoe past his revolutionary rage against the United States during his early years as an abolitionist. "I have no patriotism," he thundered in 1847. "I cannot have any love for this country . . . or for its

Constitution. I desire to see it overthrown as speedily as possible."
Radical as to ends, he was also radical as to means. He justified
the killing of a deputy U.S. marshal when a group of abolitionists
tried to liberate a fugitive slave from a Boston jail. Similarly, he
assisted and praised John Brown, the insurrectionist executed for
murder and treason in 1859.

Many conservatives who claim posthumous alliance with
Douglass would abandon him if forced to associate publicly with
the central features of his ideology. After all, he championed the
creation of a strong post–Civil War federal government that would
extend civil and political rights to the formerly enslaved; protect
those rights judicially and, if necessary, militarily; and undergird
the former slaves' new status with education, employment, land,
and other resources, to be supplied by experimental government
agencies. Douglass objected to what he considered an unseemly
willingness to reconcile with former Confederates who failed to
sincerely repudiate secession and slavery. He expressed disgust,
for example, at the "bombastic laudation" accorded to Robert E.
Lee upon the general's death in 1870. Blight calls attention to a
speech by Douglass resonant with current controversies:

> We are sometimes asked in the name of patriotism to for-
> get the merits of [the Civil War], and to remember with
> equal admiration those who struck at the nation's life, and
> those who struck to save it—those who fought for slav-
> ery and those who fought for liberty. . . . May my tongue
> cleave to the roof of my mouth if I forget the difference
> between the parties to that . . . bloody conflict.

The progressive tradition of championing Douglass runs
deeper, unsurprisingly, than the conservative adoption. As an abolitionist, a militant antislavery Republican, and an advocate for
women's rights, Douglass allied himself with three of the greatest
dissident progressive formations in American history. Activists on
the left should feel comfortable seeking to appropriate the lus-
ter of his authority for their solicitude for refugees, elevation of
women, and advancement of unfairly marginalized racial minorities. No dictum has been more ardently repeated by progressive

dissidents than his assertion that "if there is no struggle there is no progress. . . . Power concedes nothing without a demand. It never did and it never will."

But certain aspects of Douglass's life would, if more widely known, cause problems for many of his current admirers on the left, a point nicely made in Blight's biography, as well as in Waldo E. Martin Jr.'s *Mind of Frederick Douglass.* A Republican intra-party contest in an 1888 Virginia congressional election pitted John Mercer Langston, a progressive black jurist (who had served as the first dean of the Howard University Law School), against R. W. Arnold, a white conservative sponsored by a white party boss (who was a former Confederate general). Douglass supported Arnold, portraying his decision as high-minded. "The question of color," he said, "should be entirely subordinated to the greater questions of principles and party expediency." In fact, what had mainly moved Douglass was personal animosity; he and Langston had long been bitter rivals. Langston was hardly a paragon, but neither was Douglass. Sometimes he could be a vain, selfish, opportunistic jerk, capable of subordinating political good to personal pique.

Douglass promised that he would never permit his desire for a government post to mute his antiracism. He broke that promise. When Hayes nominated him to be D.C. marshal, the duties of the job were trimmed. Previously, the marshal had introduced dignitaries on state occasions. Douglass was relieved of that responsibility. Racism was the obvious reason, but Douglass disregarded the slight and raised no objection. It is possible that he thought that the benefit to the public of seeing a black man occupy this post outweighed the benefit that might be derived from staging yet another protest. But especially as he aged, Douglass lapsed into the unattractive habit of conflating what would be good for him with what would be good for blacks, the nation, or humanity. In this instance, detractors were likely correct in concluding that he had permitted himself to be gagged by the prospect of obtaining a sinecure.

Douglass was also willing to be complicit in imperialism. He accepted diplomatic missions under Presidents Ulysses S. Grant, in 1871, and Benjamin Harrison, in 1889, that entailed pressuring

Santo Domingo (now the Dominican Republic) to allow itself to become annexed and Haiti to cede territory. Douglass acted with at least partially good intentions, aiming to stabilize and elevate these black Caribbean countries by tying them to the United States in its slavery-free, post–Civil War incarnation. He liked the idea of Santo Domingo becoming a new state, thereby adding to the political muscle in America of people of African descent, a prospect that frightened or disgusted white supremacists. When Douglass realized that Washington was exploiting his solicitude for people of color in the Caribbean, he belatedly resigned. But here again, in temporarily serving the needs of United States diplomacy, Douglass demonstrated (along with a condescending attitude toward his Caribbean hosts) a yearning for power, prestige, and recognition from high political authorities that confused and diluted his more characteristic ideological impulses.

Douglass is entitled to, and typically receives, an honored place in any pantheon dedicated to heroes of black liberation. He also poses problems, however, for devotees of certain brands of black solidarity. White abolitionists were key figures in his remarkable journey to national and international prominence. Without their assistance, he would not have become the symbol of oppressed blackness in the minds of antislavery whites, and without the prestige he received from his white following, he would not have become black America's preeminent spokesman. That whites were so instrumental in furthering Douglass's career bothers black nationalists who are haunted by the specter of white folks selecting or controlling blacks who are putative "leaders."

Douglass's romantic life has stirred related unease, a subject Blight touches on delicately, exhibiting notable interest in and sympathy for his hero's first wife. A freeborn black woman, Anna Murray helped her future husband escape enslavement and, after they married, raised five children with him and dutifully maintained households that offered respite between his frequent, exhausting bouts of travel. Anna never learned to read or write, which severely limited the range of experience that the two of them could share. Two years after Anna died in 1882, Douglass married Helen Pitts, a Mount Holyoke College–educated white former abolitionist twenty years his junior. They tried to keep the marriage quiet; even his children were unaware of it until the union was a done deal. But soon news of it emerged, and controversy ensued. The marriage scandalized many whites, including Helen's father, who rejected his daughter completely. But the marriage outraged many blacks as well. The journalist T. Thomas Fortune noted that "the colored ladies take [Douglass's marriage] as a slight, if not an insult, to their race and their beauty." Many black men were angered, too. As one put it, "We have no further use for [Douglass] as a leader. His picture hangs in our parlor, we will hang it in the stable." For knowledgeable black nationalists, Douglass's second marriage continues to vex his legacy. Some give him a pass for what they perceive as an instance of apostasy, while others remain unforgiving.

That Douglass is celebrated so widely is a tribute mostly to the caliber of his work as an activist, a journalist, a memoirist, and an orator. It is a testament as well, however, to those, like Blight, who have labored diligently to preserve the memory of his extraordinary accomplishments. Ironically, his popularity is also due to ignorance. Some of his champions might lessen their support if they knew more about him. Frederick Douglass was a whirlwind of eloquence, imagination, and desperate striving as he sought to expose injustice and remedy its harms. All who praise him should know that part of what made him so distinctive are the tensions—indeed the contradictions—that he embraced.

17

Anthony Burns and the Terrible Relevancy
of the Fugitive Slave Act

In the files of the Library of Congress is a document that speaks volumes about the status of African Americans during the age of slavery. It is a handbill, dated April 24, 1851, that warns,

> Colored People of Boston, One & All, You are hereby respectfully CAUTIONED and advised, to avoid conversing with the Watchmen and Police Officers of Boston. . . . [They have been] employed in KIDNAPPING, CATCHING, AND KEEPING SLAVES. Therefore, if you value your LIBERTY, and the Welfare of the Fugitives among you, Shun them in every possible manner, as so many HOUNDS on the track of the most unfortunate of your race.[1]

The warning stemmed from fear exacerbated by a federal law that aided slave owners in the recapture of their desperately fleeing human property. Hundreds were re-enslaved pursuant to the Fugitive Slave Act of 1850.[2] One of the most notorious episodes of this ghastly use of law in the service of tyranny involved Anthony Burns, a fugitive slave who was captured in Boston in 1854. The struggle over his fate invites reflection on the ethical limits of the rule of law, the liberatory potential of states' rights, and the moral status of resorts to violence on behalf of freedom. It also invites reflection on the conduct of Americans today as federal agents scour cities and towns in search of desperately fleeing refugees, subjecting them to the terrifying possibility of being separated from their loved ones and returned to jurisdictions in which they will likely face deprivation and danger.

The Fugitive Slave Act of 1850[3] superseded a prior fugitive slave law, the origins of which are darkly ironic. It stemmed not from the demands of slaveholders but rather from a call for legislation that would regulate interstate extradition of fugitives from justice. The incident that highlighted the need for such legislation involved white Virginia fugitives accused of kidnapping a Negro in Pennsylvania with the intent of selling him as a slave. When Pennsylvania's governor demanded that his counterpart surrender the three white men, the Virginia governor declined. This controversy led to the enactment of the federal Fugitive Slave Act of 1793 "respecting fugitives from justice, and persons escaping from the service of their masters."[4] In *Prigg v. Pennsylvania* (1842),[5] the Supreme Court upheld the constitutionality of the act but indicated that the federal government lacked the authority to compel state officials to effectuate it. To the great annoyance of the slaveholding states, many northern jurisdictions enacted "personal liberty laws" that, among other things, prohibited local officials from carrying out the federal legislation.[6] This severely limited the number of officials left to enforce it because, in antebellum America, the federal bureaucracy was skeletal. Slaveholders were forced to engage in self-help to recapture their human property—an expensive and sometimes dangerous business given the militancy with which some communities rebuffed slave hunters whom they viewed as nothing other than "kidnappers" or "manstealers." As the Virginia legislature complained,

> No citizen of the South can pass the frontier of a non-slaveholding state and there exercise his undoubted constitutional right of seizing his fugitive slave, with a view to take him before a judicial officer and there prove his right of ownership, without imminent danger of being prosecuted criminally as a kidnapper, or being sued in a civil action for false imprisonment—imprisoned himself for want of bail, and subjected in his defence to an expense

exceeding the whole value of the property claimed, or finally of being mobbed or being put to death in a street fight by insane fanatics or brutal ruffians.[7]

The Fugitive Slave Act of 1850 sought to remedy the deficiencies slaveholders identified. As Justice John Marshall Harlan observed retrospectively, Congress omitted from the new Act "nothing which the utmost ingenuity could suggest as essential to the successful enforcement of the master's claim to recover his fugitive slave."[8] The Act of 1850 increased the number of officials authorized to enforce it by granting such authorization to commissioners appointed by federal circuit courts and by instructing these courts that they should "from time to time enlarge the number of commissioners."[9] These commissioners were empowered to appoint deputies to execute warrants and to "call to their aid bystanders, or *posse comitatus* of the proper county, when necessary to ensure a faithful observance" of the Act.[10] The Act stipulated that a commissioner would be entitled to a fee of $5 in each case in which he determined that a slave master was not entitled to a certificate authorizing removal of an alleged fugitive slave, and entitled to $10 in each case in which he determined that a slave master was entitled to such a certificate.[11]

To encourage diligence, the Act provided that a $1,000 fine could be imposed upon U.S. marshals who either refused or neglected to execute arrest warrants issued by commissioners.[12] Similarly, to encourage vigilance, the Act provided that a marshal would be liable for the full value of slaves who escaped from custody after arrest.[13] Finally, to streamline the process, the Act commanded commissioners "to hear and determine [cases] in a summary manner."[14] That meant that "upon satisfactory proof" of the identity of an accused person, he could be remanded to a claimant's custody without a jury trial, without access to habeas corpus, and without the opportunity to testify on his own behalf; indeed, the Act specifically prohibited the admission of testimony from accused fugitives.[15]

Antislavery activists, of course, condemned the law. According to Charles Sumner, the Act not only "set[s] at naught the best principles of the Constitution"; it was also "most cruel, unchristian, devilish," and a repudiation of "the very laws of God."[16] Detractors asserted that the Act was invalid because the federal Constitution did not empower Congress to regulate reclamation of fugitive slaves, because the Act purported to delegate judicial power to commissioners appointed without senatorial approval and without life tenure, and because accused fugitive slaves were deprived of the right of habeas corpus.[17]

Detractors also stressed two other features of the law that they perceived as illegitimate and sought to make notorious.[18] The first had to do with the fact that commissioners received compensation through fees rather than salary and that, as noted above, the fees varied: a $10 fee when the commissioner remanded an alleged fugitive to the custody of a claimant but only a $5 fee when he freed an accused. According to critics, this differential amounted to a bribe that vitiated due process.[19] The defense of this provision was that it simply paid commissioners more money for more labor: additional paperwork was required when commissioners remanded an accused fugitive to the custody of a claimant.[20]

A second area of contention had to do with deprivations imposed by the Act's narrow and rigid process for reclaiming alleged fugitive slaves. To initiate the process, an aggrieved master simply needed to go to any court of record in his own state and make out an affidavit describing his slave and declaring that the slave had run away. If the local judge was satisfied that this declaration was true, he would give the owner a document that essentially certified the affidavit. When that document was presented to a commissioner, the Act commanded that it be received as conclusive evidence that the slave described had escaped and owed service to the claimant. The only thing left for the commissioner to do was to decide the identity of the alleged fugitive. If a commissioner determined that the person brought before him was the slave described in the affidavit, he was required to issue a certificate remanding the accused to the custody of the claimant.

Throughout this entire process, the Act completely silenced alleged fugitives, depriving them of the right to confront witnesses and to testify on their own behalf. It also deprived them of an opportunity to have their legal status adjudicated by a jury. These deprivations affronted a broad range of northern sensibilities. The antebellum North was, to be sure, profoundly racist. At the same time, even many racists believed that all persons—even persons of an inferior race—were entitled to elementary safeguards of due process specifically guaranteed by the Bill of Rights.

The defense of this aspect of the Act was that the proceedings it designed were merely for the purpose of effectuating extradition and not for the purpose of making a final settlement of the legal status of the accused. A final settlement would be for the courts in the home state of the claimant to determine. Defenders argued that accused fugitive slaves were put in no worse a position by the Act than accused fugitives from justice; in neither case was extradition tried before a jury, though in both cases courts back home would presumably render justice.[21] The Act did not provide, however, that those remanded under it were entitled to trials in the claimant's home state. During the debate leading up to passage of the Act, some of its backers had proposed such an entitlement in an effort to conciliate northern opinion. But their proposal was defeated. Moreover, to the extent that southern courts were open to alleged fugitive slaves, they appear to have been open only on the terms available to Negroes in general, meaning access on a profoundly prejudicial basis. While an accused remanded white fugitive from justice could count on at least the formal rule that he was innocent until proven guilty, an accused remanded black fugitive from labor faced the formal rule in the antebellum South that all blacks were presumed slaves.

In most cases posing constitutional challenges, judges upheld the Act.[22] That did not save it, however, from ongoing challenges, not only in courts of law, but also in the court of public opinion. One of the most spirited of those challenges occurred in Boston in 1854.

That spring Anthony Burns fled to Boston from Richmond, where he had lived as a relatively privileged, urban slave who hired himself to various employers on behalf of his owner, Charles Suttle.[23] Soon after escaping, Burns obtained a job with a black clothing dealer, Coffin Pitts, and wrote to his brother who remained enslaved in Virginia. This letter proved his undoing. Although Burns sought to disguise his whereabouts by having the letter mailed from Canada, he apparently noted somewhere on it that he was living in Boston. Suttle intercepted the letter, obtained from a Virginia court certification of Burns's status as a slave, enlisted the help of William Brent (a friend and merchant to whom Suttle had leased Burns on several occasions), and then ventured north to reclaim his human property.

In Boston, Suttle sought and obtained an arrest warrant* for Burns from Commissioner Edward G. Loring, a well-respected jurist who spent most of his time serving as a probate judge and lecturer at Harvard Law School. Deputies of the U.S. marshal in Boston traced Burns to his place of employment and on Wednesday evening, May 24, 1854, placed him under arrest. Initially they told him that he was being arrested on suspicion of robbery. At the courthouse, however, he learned of the real reason for his arrest when he was confronted by Suttle. Incriminating himself, Burns acknowledged Suttle by name, answered questions about the conditions under which he had lived as a slave, and offered Suttle an explanation as to how he had come to find himself in Boston.

The next morning, Thursday, May 25, Burns was brought before Commissioner Loring. By then, however, antislavery forces, including several distinguished lawyers, had already begun to mobilize a defense. The alacrity and strength of response stemmed from various sources. The home of Wendell Phillips, William Lloyd Garrison, Charles Sumner, and the American Antislavery Society, Boston was a major center of the abolitionist movement. It was also the home of a vigilant, articulate, and organized black community that was keenly attentive to the plight of fugitive slaves. Moreover, by the time of Burns's arrest, antislavery activists in Boston had attained considerable experience with the Fugitive Slave Act and means of opposing it. In 1851, a group of blacks burst into a courtroom and rescued a fugitive slave named Shadrach Minkins who, having been apprehended pursuant to the Act, would almost certainly have been remanded to his master's custody.[24] That same year, a runaway from Georgia

---

* The warrant begins, "In the name of the President of the United States of America, you are hereby commanded forthwith to apprehend Anthony Burns, a negro man, alleged to be in your District, charged with being a fugitive from labor . . . if he may be found in your precinct." *See Boston Slave Riot, and the Trial of Anthony Burns* (1854), 1–2.

named Thomas Sims was returned to slavery after an intense and highly publicized legal battle.[25]

Fighting the Fugitive Slave Act energized the abolitionist movement. Resisting enforcement, the historian Larry Gara observed, enabled the abolitionists "to link their cause with that of civil liberties and to reach large numbers of people untouched by the purer antislavery arguments."[26] The fugitive slave law brought slavery home to northern communities not as an abstraction, but in the form of a person, a runaway who by his very exertions vividly dramatized what antislavery propagandists labored mightily to show—that slavery was a hateful condition, so horrible as to prompt men and women to go to all lengths to flee it.[27]

Although three prominent antislavery attorneys—Robert Morris, Charles M. Ellis, and Richard Henry Dana—offered their assistance to Burns the morning of his first appearance before Commissioner Loring, he considered forgoing any representation at all thinking that his cooperation might help to mollify his master's anger. He calculated whether by lessening the trouble he caused in Boston, he might also lessen the punishment awaiting him in Alexandria. In the end, he decided to fight removal and thus accepted the lawyers' proffered aid.

Burns's attorneys resorted to a wide range of strategies and arguments. One was delay. Dana succeeded in twice persuading the commissioner to postpone the proceedings. Thus, instead of the case going forward on Thursday, May 25, a full hearing of the case did not begin until Monday, May 29. This delay provided Burns's attorneys with time to hone a defense and to engage in various flanking maneuvers. Dana sought from the federal district court a writ *de homine replegiando*,[28] which was between a writ of habeas corpus and a plea for bail. Unsurprisingly, the request was denied. Burns's attorneys then proceeded to state court where they requested a writ of replevin. Although a judge issued the writ, a U.S. marshal ignored it, refusing to surrender Burns to state officials.

A very different tack was taken by Lewis Hayden, a leading member of Boston's black community and himself a fugitive slave.[29] Hayden filed suit against Suttle and Brent, charging them with having wrongfully conspired to have Burns arrested.

While this suit does not appear to have substantially affected the proceedings against Burns, it did increase the cost of seeking to recapture him because it caused both Suttle and Brent to post a $5,000 bond.

The most extraordinary effort undertaken to free Burns occurred on Friday, May 26. That evening, an agitated, overflow crowd at Faneuil Hall listened to abolitionist firebrands repeatedly emphasize two themes.[30] The first was that the fugitive slave law entailed more than an attack upon runaway slaves (and free blacks who stood in constant terror of being confused with runaways). The law, they argued, also constituted an attack upon the rights and sensibilities of jurisdictions in which the majority of the people had voted to prohibit slavery. In Reverend Theodore Parker's speech that evening, he vividly expressed this theme by referring to his listeners as "vassals of Virginia." Pressing the same point, Parker stated mockingly that while Boston once existed, it existed no longer but was merely "a North suburb to the city of Alexandria [Virginia]."[31] Portraying himself and his neighbors as victims of tyranny, Parker declaimed,

> Slavery tramples on the Constitution; it treads down State Rights. Where are the Rights of Massachusetts? A fugitive slave bill Commissioner has got them all in his pocket. Where is the trial by jury? Watson Freeman has it under his Marshal's staff. Where is the great writ of personal replevin, which our fathers wrested, several hundred years ago, from the tyrants who once lorded it over Great Britain? Judge Sprague trod it under his feet! Where is the sacred right of habeas corpus? Deputy Marshal Riley can crush it in his hands, and Boston does not say any thing against it. Where are the laws of Massachusetts forbidding state edifices to be used as prisons for the incarceration of fugitives? They too are trampled underfoot.[32]

The second theme repeatedly sounded at Faneuil Hall was the righteousness of freeing fugitives. Calling for direct action, Parker said to his audience that a law higher than the law of slavery "is in your hands and your arms, and you can put it into execution, just when you see fit."[33] Wendell Phillips also called for action, asking rhetorically whether Boston would "adhere to the result of Shadrach or the case of Sims."[34] The resolutions adopted by the assembly echoed Parker and Phillips:

> Resolved, That the time has come to declare and to demonstrate the fact that no slavehunter can carry his prey from the Commonwealth of Massachusetts.

> Resolved, That in the language of Algernon Sydney, "that which is not just is not law, and that which is not law ought not to be obeyed."

> Resolved, That, leaving every man to determine for himself the mode of resistance, we are united in the glorious sentiment of our Revolutionary fathers—"resistance to tyrants is obedience to God."[35]

Some activists sought to liberate Burns forcibly. One of their problems, however, was disorganization. The Boston Vigilance Committee decided to attempt a rescue at the courthouse on Saturday morning and suggested as much in various statements made during the Friday evening rally. But during the rally, several leading antislavery militants, most notably Thomas Wentworth Higginson, decided that a rescue effort undertaken right then would have the best chance for success. Without adequately communicating this change of plans to their colleagues, they proceeded to storm the jail where Burns was being held, assuming wrongly that they would soon be reinforced by substantial numbers of those who had attended the rally at Faneuil Hall. They were rebuffed, but not before drawing blood; during the melee, a deputy marshal, James Batchelder, was stabbed to death.[36] Frederick Douglass saw this action as posing a question of "the rightfulness of killing a man who is in the act of forcibly reducing a brother man who is guilty of no crime to the horrible condition of a slave." Douglass's answer repudiated his previous stance of Garrisonian pacificism. He declared it right and wise to kill anyone seeking to enforce the fugitive slave law.[37]

While some sought to rescue Burns through force, others sought to rescue him through purchase. Suttle indicated that he would be willing to sell Burns for $1,200. Throughout Saturday, May 27, the Reverend Leonard A. Grimes—a free black man who had himself fled slavery and been imprisoned for helping others to flee[38]—pleaded for money to meet Suttle's demand. The response was instructive. Some refused on the grounds that doing so involved immoral acquiescence to a slave master.[39] Others refused on the grounds that it would be bad for the country to believe that enforcement of federal law was impossible in Boston. On the other hand, some gave out of a desire to thwart the law. Others gave out of simple humanitarianism. Still others contributed because they wanted to rid the city of disruption. Two of the most notable contributors were Suttle's own attorneys—Edward G. Parker and Seth J. Thomas—who raised a hefty $400.

This effort, too, however, ultimately came to naught. Acting at the behest of President Franklin Pierce, who wanted to make an example of Burns, the U.S. district attorney Benjamin F. Hallett did all that he could to undo the deal that Suttle had made. After stalling the transaction once by arguing that it violated Massachusetts's prohibition against the buying and selling of slaves, he delayed the deal again by maintaining, at the stroke of midnight, that the state's blue laws forbade doing business on Sunday. By Monday Suttle had changed his mind, the result of importunings by fellow slaveholders who demanded that he demonstrate the South's insistence that the Fugitive Slave Act be enforced everywhere in the nation including the headquarters of abolitionism. As his attorney put it, "The claimant being advised thereto by many lovers of law and order, declines to negotiate further until it is first established that the supremacy of the law can be maintained."[40]

After two postponements, the hearing to decide whether Burns should be remitted to the custody of Suttle was begun on Monday, May 29, and lasted three days. The case for Suttle was advanced quickly and without frills. It rested mainly on three bases. The first was a certificate from the Virginia court, describing Burns, finding that he was a slave owned by Suttle, and stating that he had wrongly fled. The second was testimony by Brent to the effect that he had long known Suttle and Burns and that the man under arrest was indeed the latter. Brent also testified that Burns addressed by name both himself and Suttle when they first encountered him soon after his arrest. The third basis of Suttle's case was supplied by deputy marshals who also testified to Burns's apparent familiarity with Suttle and Brent when brought face to face with them after his arrest.

Three aspects of Burns's defense are particularly noteworthy. First, Burns's lawyers attempted to dispel any sense that Commissioner Loring was without choice or that respect for law compelled a judgment for the slave master. They sought to prevent him from embracing what Professor Robert Cover called "the judicial can't"—the comforting belief that a judge cannot properly be blamed for reaching a given judgment when legal duty would admit of no other result.[41] This strategy can be seen in Ellis's opening statement when he describes Commissioner Loring as "judge and jury . . . without any accountability, without any right of challenge."[42] Ellis is to some extent complaining about Loring's power, bemoaning the fact that this official is all that stood between Burns and slavery. But he is simultaneously appealing to Loring to use his power to do that which he believes to be morally right. Ellis presses this same point later, emphasizing to Loring that in terms of considering the constitutionality of the Fugitive Slave Act, he need not defer to precedent. "You are subordinate to no power whatever," Ellis insisted. "The law has not been settled for you."[43]

Second, Burns's attorneys were clearly more interested in saving their client than in castigating slavery or the Fugitive Slave Act. Indeed, in pursuit of his release, his attorneys made certain arguments that surely made some antislavery stalwarts wince. Ellis objected, for instance, to the admission of testimony regarding incriminating statements that Burns made to Suttle after his arrest. Ellis did so on the basis of one of the most hated features of the Fugitive Slave Act—the provision that prohibited accused fugitives from testifying.[44]

Third, although Burns's attorneys did ultimately challenge the Fugitive Slave Act on constitutional grounds, that was not the primary thrust of their defense. They raised most of the familiar antislavery constitutionalist arguments. But they did so only per-

functorily, virtually certain that in light of previous rulings upholding the Act—particularly one handed down three years before by
Lemuel Shaw, the venerable chief justice of the Supreme Judicial Court of Massachusetts[45]—there was no real possibility that
Commissioner Loring would find it to be unconstitutional. Their
primary line of defense was that their client was the victim of a
false allegation. "We shall offer proof," Ellis declared, "that this
atrocious charge . . . [has] no foundation in fact."[46] Burns's attorneys presented witnesses who swore that they had either worked
with him or seen him in Boston prior to the time when he was
alleged to have fled Virginia. They reminded the commissioner of
cases in which false or mistaken identifications of alleged fugitives
had been uncovered. And they argued that Suttle should have to
shoulder a heavy burden of proof in order to prevail. While the
Act indicated that masters needed to muster merely "satisfactory
proof," Burns's lawyers maintained that a claimant must be made
to establish the material facts "beyond any reasonable doubt."[47]

Loring decided in favor of Suttle. First, he dispatched with
the constitutional challenges, making reference to Chief Justice
Shaw's resolution of the arguments.[48] Second, he addressed an
argument that was not advanced by Burns's attorneys but that was
articulated by abolitionists outside the courtroom. According to
that argument, any morally decent person should either refuse to
become a Fugitive Slave Act commissioner or resign the post. As
Loring observed, "It is said that the statute is so cruel and wicked
that it should not be executed by good men." His response took
the form of rhetorical questions: If those demanding resignation had their way, "into what hands shall its administration fall,
and . . . what is to be the protection of the unfortunate men who
are brought here within its operation? Will those who call the
statute merciless commit it to a merciless judge?" His response
was clear: "If any men wish this they are more cruel and wicked
than the statute, for they would strip from the fugitive the best
security and every alleviation the statute leaves him."[49]

Finally, Commissioner Loring faced the defense's claim that
Burns was a victim of mistaken identity. He rejected the "out"
that Burns's attorneys had tried so assiduously to give him—the
alternative of granting freedom to Burns on the grounds of mis-

taken identity while still formally enforcing the Act. Instead, he recognized the obvious—that the Burns before him was the same person identified in the papers of the Virginia court. The evidence that convinced him was that which came from Burns's own mouth the evening of his arrest.[50] Loring does seem to have used the standard of proof proposed by Burns's attorneys, declaring that he was "satisfied beyond a reasonable doubt" that "on the law and facts of the case . . . the claimant was entitled to the certificate" sought.[51] With that, the hearing was ended, and Anthony Burns was marched to the docks—flanked by several detachments of heavily armed soldiers—and put aboard a steamer that carried him, with his master, back to Virginia.

The struggle over Burns did not end with his extradition. Federal officials sought to punish those who had caused them such extraordinary trouble. A federal grand jury indicted some of the leading activists who participated in the events that led to the botched rescue attempt that ended with the death of Deputy Marshal Batchelder. That effort came to naught, however, when, on a technicality, the indictment was quashed and the government, perhaps fearing jury nullification, decided to drop the prosecution.[52] For their part, abolitionists sought to punish those who had thwarted efforts to liberate Burns. Targeting Commissioner Loring, they succeeded in ousting him from his lectureship at Harvard Law School and removing him from his seat as a local probate judge.[53]

As for Burns, three weeks after his re-enslavement, his master, Suttle, wrote to one of the Boston merchants who had previously expressed an interest in purchasing the fugitive. Now, however, the merchant was no longer interested. Fortunately for Burns, his fate continued to concern blacks in Boston. They purchased his freedom for $1,300 (about $43,000 today). Burns went on to obtain a college education at Oberlin and became a clergyman, settling in St. Catharines, Canada, as the pastor of a Baptist church. There he died on July 27, 1862.

For years I offered this account of the battle over Anthony Burns as a lecture to judges who participated in symposia at Harvard

Law School sponsored by the Federal Judicial Center. My aim was to make them confront a conflict between law and justice. It did not require much prompting for them to recognize that distinction as an all-too-familiar presence. Several judges confessed, for example, to feeling disgust, including self-disgust, when sentencing defendants to outrageously excessive punishments required by legislation. A notable feature of the judges' response was their nearly uniform rejection of judicial nullification as a permissible mode of resistance to the Fugitive Slave Act. They applauded hiding runaways, purchasing their freedom, or even forcibly seizing runaways from owners or federal authorities. They drew a line that they refused to cross, however, when I asked them about the permissibility of a commissioner lying to foil the Fugitive Slave Act. They rejected the propriety of a commissioner deciding deceitfully that a runaway did not match an owner's description. They eschewed the morality of judicial nullification. Were their renunciations of the permissibility of judicial sabotage candid expressions of their actual position? Or were they also seeking to signal to one another (and all other onlookers) the depth and intensity of their fidelity to conventional notions of judicial integrity, even in the grip of an extreme crisis such as that brought about by the Fugitive Slave Act? Our discussions into that terrain did not venture as deeply as I would have liked.

Largely absent, too, from those discussions was the recent controversy most strikingly analogous to that generated by the federal fugitive slave laws: the dilemma posed by U.S. immigration policy.[54] Federal immigration law requires or permits treating refugees fleeing horrific circumstances in their home countries in ways that are morally unacceptable. The worst manifestation of this mistreatment thus far has been the notorious separation of children from their parents. Just as antislavery activists rejected the legitimacy of federal laws that criminalized efforts to assist slaves seeking to flee bondage, so, too, are activists rejecting the legitimacy of federal laws that criminalize efforts to aid migrants in fleeing political oppression, economic misery, and social chaos. Harriet Tubman and other conductors of the Underground Railroad self-consciously defied federal law to spirit runaways to freedom in northern states, Canada, or England, calling upon a higher law to justify their defiance of federal authority. Today the Sanctuary Movement invokes "God's law" or secular equivalents to justify actions that also violate federal statutes. Congregants in hundreds of houses of worship across the country have offered shelter and other sorts of support to fleeing migrants. In 1984 federal authorities pursued an undercover investigation, named in appallingly bad taste Operation Sojourner, that nabbed priests, a nun, and a minister for violating criminal anti-harboring provisions. In 2018, forty-five hundred people were prosecuted for such infractions.

In antebellum America, "free" jurisdictions enacted "personal liberty laws" that were designed to offer some protection to people at risk of being apprehended by slave catchers. They also ordered the withholding of local assistance from enforcement of federal fugitive slave law, thereby preventing local police from assisting in hunts for slaves (though many did so anyway) and local jails from being used to cage captured fugitives. Now such actions are replicated in "sanctuary" jurisdictions that withhold cooperation from federal immigration authorities.

In antebellum America, humanitarianism galvanized by the fugitive slave law prompted a small but alert and impassioned sector of the population to engage in all manner of resistance. Now humanitarianism galvanized by reaction against a cruel anti-refugee policy is also impelling Americans to rethink automatic allegiance to "the rule of law." In 2019, a Massachusetts judge, Shelley M. Richmond, was indicted for violating federal law when she allegedly assisted a migrant facing likely deportation. According to federal authorities, the judge told this man, a defendant in her courtroom, to exit using a back door in order to evade U.S. Immigration and Customs Enforcement agents who were seeking to apprehend him. In assessing the character of her conduct, observers ought to recall the controversy surrounding Anthony Burns. The resisters of that earlier era are widely viewed now as heroes. One hopes the resisters of today will not have to wait so long before receiving their due.

18

Eric Foner and the
Unfinished Mission of Reconstruction[1]

Justice Thurgood Marshall delivered a hugely controversial speech in May 1987 in the midst of festivities marking the two hundredth anniversary of the U.S. Constitution. Noting the quasi-religious reverence with which the Founding Fathers are lauded, Marshall expressed skepticism about proclamations of their "wisdom, foresight, and justice." The Founding Fathers, he noted, could not have been but so enlightened and farsighted; after all, the slavery they tolerated caused untold suffering and ended with a civil war that claimed some 600,000 lives. "While the Union survived the Civil War," he said, the Constitution occasioning the celebrating did not. "In its place arose a new, more promising basis for justice and equality." That new, more promising regime was "Reconstruction," an array of reforms undertaken between 1863 and 1877 to refashion the fractured nation.

The year 1863 witnessed the promulgation of President Abraham Lincoln's Emancipation Proclamation, which freed all slaves then residing in jurisdictions in rebellion against the federal government of the United States. Prior to the Emancipation Proclamation, Lincoln had gone out of his way to indicate that in resorting to arms, the federal government sought merely to suppress the uprising of the Confederacy, the eleven states that attempted to secede in 1861 to ensure the perpetuation of their "peculiar institution"—racial slavery. Repudiating the idea that "all men are created equal," the leaders of the Confederacy committed themselves expressly to racial hierarchy. "Our new government... rests," the Confederate vice president, Alexander Stephens, observed, "upon the great truth that the negro is not equal to the white man; that slavery subordination to the superior race is his natural and normal condition."

Lincoln did not believe that under ordinary circumstances the federal government had authority to touch slavery in the states. He maintained, however, that as commander in chief of the armed forces he possessed constitutional authority to free slaves as a war measure to quell rebellion. Because a sentimental glow surrounds the Emancipation Proclamation, many rhapsodize about it without having actually read the two-page document. The historian Richard Hofstadter quipped that it possessed all the "moral grandeur of a bill of lading." It contained no criticism of slavery and did not free all slaves; it left unaffected the legal status of at least 800,000. The Emancipation Proclamation did not free those held in bondage in the four slave states that remained loyal to the Union—Missouri, Delaware, Kentucky, and Maryland. Nor did it free slaves in certain southern territories already under Union control. These rather large exemptions moved the London *Spectator* to observe that the underlying principle of the Emancipation Proclamation was "not that a human being cannot justly own another, but that he cannot own him unless he is loyal to the United States." Still, the Emancipation Proclamation did free more than 3 million slaves, moving many observers to perceive it as an inspirational charter that transformed the war for Union into a war for Union and freedom. When news of Lincoln's signing arrived in South Carolina, slaves recited prayers and sang songs including "My Country, 'Tis of Thee."

The Emancipation Proclamation announced that freedmen would now be received into the U.S. military. Many enlisted. By the end of the Civil War, 180,000 had served—a number that represented about one-fifth of the country's black male population under age forty-five. In the Revolutionary War, when the thirteen American colonies sought to secede from Britain, most African Americans who took up arms did so on behalf of King George (having been promised emancipation for doing so). By contrast, in the Civil War, the overwhelming majority who took up arms fought for the United States (the Confederacy having stubbornly resisted proposals to arm slaves until the very eve of its collapse).

After the Union's victory, the South experienced a whiplash-inducing series of jolting developments. Lincoln planned to re-admit the Confederate states into the Union quickly on generous terms. But in a speech he suggested an openness to granting the vote to some black men—"the very intelligent and . . . those who serve our cause as soldiers." When the actor John Wilkes Booth heard that remark, he warned, "That means nigger citizenship! Now, by God, I'll put him through. That is the last speech he will ever make." Four days later, Booth made good on his threat, shooting Lincoln to death at Ford's Theatre in Washington, D.C., on the evening of Good Friday.

Lincoln's successor, Andrew Johnson, was a rabid racist who, though abhorring secessionism, militantly opposed those who wanted to promote African Americans to a legal status equal to that of whites. He supported the ending of slavery but wanted blacks to be confined to a subordinate caste. That is one of the reasons Radicals in the Republican Party—the party of Lincoln—despised Johnson (a member of the Democratic Party) and attempted to remove him from office through impeachment. Although Johnson survived ouster—he escaped conviction by one vote—the Repub-licans succeeded in enacting civil rights legislation over his oppo-sition. The Republicans also put the former Confederate states under military rule with the understanding that they would not be permitted to become self-governing and rejoin the Union until they permitted black men to participate in politics on the same basis as white men. The pariah states acceded to this demand, gen-erating remarkable results. "You never saw a people more excited on the subject of politics than are the negroes of the South," observed one planter. "They are perfectly wild." Blacks enrolled in organizations like the Union League that encouraged political education through speeches and debates. They petitioned local authorities. They attended Republican rallies and conventions. They voted and ran for office even in the face of violent opposi-tion from resentful whites who were appalled by the prospect of blacks, including former slaves, engaged in governance. Between 1870 and 1877, sixteen blacks were elected to Congress, eighteen to positions as state lieutenant governors, treasurers, secretaries of state, or superintendents of education, and at least six hundred to state legislatures. Blacks never exercised decisive control of any state government, not even in Mississippi or South Carolina, where they held voting majorities. But for a short period in substantial parts of the South they wielded sufficient power to insist upon the establishment of public education, laws relatively favorable to workers, debtors, and tenants, and prohibitions against various sorts of racial discrimination.

The most durable and consequential achievements of Reconstruction were three amendments to the federal Constitution that remain in force. The Thirteenth Amendment went beyond the Emancipation Proclamation by abolishing slavery everywhere in the United States (except as a punishment for crime). The Fourteenth Amendment created a constitutional definition of citizenship, declaring that anyone born in the United States (under its jurisdiction) automatically becomes a citizen. That amendment, the wordiest in the Constitution, also imposed a new set of duties upon states. It required states to refrain from abridging the privileges or immunities of citizens, or from depriving any person of life, liberty, or property without due process of law, or from denying to any person the equal protection of the laws. The Fifteenth Amendment declares that the right of citizens of the United States to vote shall not be denied by the United States or by any state "on account of race, color, or previous condition of servitude." Each of these amendments contained a provision authorizing Congress to enforce the new constitutional entitlement by "appropriate legislation."

Reconstruction was under attack from its origins. Never did it attain a comfortable, consensus legitimacy. Its fortunes sank under the weight of racism, war fatigue, indifference, administrative weakness, the ebbing of humanitarian commitments, the debilitating consequences of economic depression, and a heavy toll exacted by terrorism. Enemies of Reconstruction resorted to rape, mutilation, beating, and murder to intimidate blacks and their white allies. In 1870, when Andrew Flowers, an African American, prevailed over a white candidate for the position of justice of the peace in Chattanooga, he received a whipping at the hands of white supremacists affiliated with the Ku Klux Klan. "They said they had nothing particular against me," he testified, "but they did not intend any nigger to hold office in the United States." That same year in Greene County, Alabama, armed whites broke up a Republican campaign rally, killing four blacks and wounding fifty-four. In 1873 in Colfax, Louisiana, black Republicans and white Democrats each claimed the right to govern. When the whites prevailed in battle, they massacred some fifty blacks who sought to surrender. That era is densely dotted with such episodes.

By 1877 every southern state had been "redeemed"—that is, fallen under the control of those who openly sought to reimpose the norms of white supremacy. Within a quarter century they had succeeded overwhelmingly. Enemies of Reconstruction removed blacks as a factor in politics and consigned them to a degraded position within a rigid pigmentocracy. The constitutional amendments survived untouched. But at least with respect to racial matters, the amendments were narrowly construed if not ignored altogether. By 1900, Reconstruction had been thoroughly demolished, an experiment almost wholly repudiated.

For the first half of the twentieth century, many white historians, commentators, and politicians portrayed Reconstruction as a calamity that stemmed from a mistaken effort to elevate African Americans to civil and political equality. Arguing that Reconstruction ruined African Americans, Claude Bowers wrote in *The Tragic Era* (1929),

> Its crusade of hate and social equality . . . [played] havoc with a race naturally kindly and trustful. Through the [Civil] War, when [white] men were far away on the battle-fields, and the women were alone on far plantations with slaves, hardly a woman was attacked. Then came the scum of Northern society, emissaries of the politicians, soldiers of fortune, and not a few degenerates, inflaming the negroes' egotism, and soon the lustful assaults began. Rape is the foul daughter of Reconstruction.*

---

* This remark is probably the most disgusting in a book filled with misleading observations. The state of bondage had made the enslaved vulnerable to rape on a grand scale. Emancipation and Reconstruction substantially diminished the incidence of sexual abuse in the territory of the Old South.

Bowers's sensational, popular rendition mirrored the depiction of Reconstruction posited by leading academics such as William A. Dunning of Columbia University, who served as president
of both the American Historical Association and the American
Political Science Association. Dunning wrote in his classic *Reconstruction, Political and Economic, 1865–1877* (1907),

> The negro had no pride of race and no aspiration or ide-
> als save to be like the whites. With civil rights and politi-
> cal power, not won, but almost forced upon him, he came
> gradually to understand and crave those more elusive
> privileges that constitute social equality. A more intimate
> association with the other race than that which business
> and politics involved was the end toward which the ambi-
> tion of the blacks tended consciously or unconsciously to
> direct itself. The manifestations of this ambition were infi-
> nite in their diversity. It played a part in the demand for
> mixed schools, in the legislative prohibition of discrimina-
> tion between the races in hotels and theatres, and even in
> the hideous crime against white womanhood which now
> assumed new meaning in the annals of outrage.

This pejorative interpretation of Reconstruction performed
important ideological work. It justified keeping blacks in their
place by painting a frightening picture of what occurred when
blacks last enjoyed civic equality and were permitted to participate
in governance.

Racial liberals, which included most black historians and, in
the 1920s, 1930s, and 1940s, a small number of white ones, rebut-
ted the vilification of Reconstruction. They stressed that under the
aegis of Reconstruction democracy was enlarged, public schooling
enhanced, and labor rights strengthened. They refuted allegations
that black politicians and their white "carpetbagger" and "scala-
wag" allies had been unusually corrupt and incompetent. They
emphasized the illegality and immorality of the means used to topple Reconstruction. The outstanding effort was W. E. B. Du Bois's
sweeping, Marxian revisionist account, *Black Reconstruction in
America, 1860–1880* (1935). Thirty years later the white historian

Kenneth Stampp published *The Era of Reconstruction, 1865–1877*, which marked the end of the dominance of Reconstruction disparagement in the mainstream of academic historians. It is more than happenstance that Stampp's important volume was published the very year of passage of the Voting Rights Act, which removed many racist impediments to suffrage. The increasing legitimacy of revisionist accounts of Reconstruction was reflected in and reinforced by the increasing legitimacy of the civil rights movement. When a federal court ruled in favor of black plaintiffs challenging racial segregation on buses in Birmingham, Alabama, a white supremacist judge, Ben F. Cameron, citing Bowers's *Tragic Era*, urged his colleagues to recall the lessons of Reconstruction, that "period which all Americans recall with sadness and shame." By then, however, a transformation in values was already prompting growing numbers of Americans to reconsider Reconstruction with new respect and hope.

In 1988, Eric Foner published *Reconstruction: America's Unfinished Revolution, 1863–1877*, a grand narrative built upon ground that had largely been cleared of the racist litter left by previous scholars. It is a stupendous scholarly achievement—eloquent, accessible, punctiliously accurate, marvelously detailed, bristling with insight, regardful of broad economic, social, and cultural forces, alert to consequential personal quirks, and attentive to the ideas and activities of actors—often women and racial minorities—whom historians often marginalize and ignore. For three decades it has stood atop Reconstruction historiography despite professional competitiveness, changes in methodological fashions, and ideological disputation.

Now, in *The Second Founding: How the Civil War and Reconstruction Remade the Constitution*, Foner narrows his focus to the key legal monuments of that era. He argues that the Reconstruction Amendments "should be seen not simply as an alteration of an existing structure but as a . . . 'constitutional revolution' . . . that created a fundamentally new document with a new definition of both the status of blacks and the rights of all Americans." Much of American history has been shaped by struggles over the extent to which the Reconstruction Amendments should be seen as either mere "alterations" or a fundamental reordering of the original handiwork of the eighteenth-century Founding Fathers. Conservatives tend to embrace the former view; liberals the latter. One reason this struggle has been so intense is that each side can lay hold to facts, ideas, sentiments, and developments that support their contending positions.

Foner supports the liberal position. He emphasizes the gulf that distinguishes American life, particularly in its racial dimensions, *before* as opposed to *after* the Reconstruction Amendments. Prior to Reconstruction, the Constitution was interpreted as mainly placing limits upon the federal government, not the states. The federal government was prohibited from restricting freedom of religion or abridging freedom of speech or engaging in unreasonable searches and seizures. But no such limits constrained the states. Prior to Reconstruction, the Constitution sought primarily to prevent the federal government from encroaching upon individual liberty, including the freedom to own slaves. With Reconstruction, reformers sought to empower the federal government to guarantee the rights afforded by the three new constitutional amendments, including older rights that were now seen by some as incorporated into the new regime. These older rights were contained in the first ten amendments to the federal Constitution. Sometimes referred to as the Bill of Rights, these amendments, ratified in 1791, provided for (among other things) freedom of religion, freedom of speech, press, and assembly, freedom to bear arms, a prohibition against quartering soldiers in homes, a right against unreasonable searches and seizures, and a right to speedy trial by impartial juries.

Foner refrains from embracing Thurgood Marshall's claim that the Civil War extinguished the constitutional regime of 1787. That assertion—perhaps a projection of wishful thinking—goes too far. For good and for bad—mostly bad—the initial constitutional regime displayed a striking resilience, imposing limitations that constricted efforts to elevate the status of the former slaves, protect them against resentful whites, and undergird their new freedom with socioeconomic support. Like Marshall, however, Foner seeks to redistribute public esteem, elevating the regard with which the second founding is held. The Founding Fathers of the Constitution of 1787—including George Washington, Benjamin Franklin, James Madison, and Alexander Hamilton—enjoy a widespread, albeit superficial, public recognition and esteem. By comparison, key framers of the Reconstruction Amendments—John A. Bingham, James M. Ashley, Henry Wilson, Charles Sumner, Lyman Trumbull, and Thaddeus Stevens—are notably obscure figures in American political culture. Unfamiliar as well are the origins and backstories of their constitutional handiwork. Missing from the curriculums of courses in constitutional law at even elite law schools in the United States is essential information about the Reconstruction Amendments that Foner ably conveys.

Throughout his career Foner has focused sympathetic attention upon progressive strains within the American political tradition. In a 2015 open letter, he praised Senator Bernie Sanders for challenging inequities that thwart the pursuit of happiness in America. But he chided the senator for suggesting that only abroad could one find a usable radical tradition. He argued that Sanders should look to the radical tradition in America for sustenance and inspiration, invoking such figures as Frederick Douglass, Abby Kelley, Eugene Debs, and A. Philip Randolph. In the *Second Founding*, Foner returns to this theme, stressing the innovativeness and exceptionality of the Reconstruction Amendments. He notes, for example, that the Thirteenth Amendment compelled emancipation without compensation and marked the first occasion on which the Constitution expanded the power of the federal government, creating "a new fundamental right to personal freedom, applicable to all persons in the United States regardless of race, gender, class, or citizenship status." Few countries, he observes, "and certainly none with as large a slave population, have experienced so radical a form of abolition." Regarding the Fourteenth Amendment's creation of birthright citizenship, Foner maintains that it represents "an eloquent statement about the nature of American society, a powerful force for assimilation . . . and a repudiation of a long history of racism."

Foner notes the quickness with which the constitutional amendments elevated four million black slaves from bondage to citizenship to formal equality with whites. He quotes James G. Blaine, Speaker of the U.S. House of Representatives during much of the Reconstruction era, declaring that before the Civil War only "the wildest fancy of a distempered brain" could have envisioned the Congress conferring upon blacks "all the civil rights pertaining to a white man." Foner similarly highlights the velocity of the change that the Fifteenth Amendment reflected and reinforced. "It affirmed," he observes, "that only a few years after the death of slavery African Americans were now equal members of the body politic." Illustrating the exuberance with which many longtime antiracist activists greeted the Fifteenth Amendment, Foner cites William Lloyd Garrison, the editor of the abolitionist paper *The Liberator.* Rejoicing, the veteran journalist asserted that "nothing in all history" equaled "this wonderful, quiet, sudden transformation of four millions of human beings from the auction block to the ballot-box."

The Second Founding, however, is far from a triumphalist celebration. It offers a sobering tale containing at least three layers of tragedy. The first has to do with the enmity that the Reconstruction Amendments encountered from birth. Even after the defeat of the Confederacy, opposition to emancipation, much of it fueled by Negrophobia, was sufficiently strong to prevent congressional approval of the Thirteenth Amendment the first time it was considered. Railing against the proposed amendment, Representative Fernando Wood, the former mayor of New York City, warned apocalyptically that it "involves the extermination of the white men of the southern states, and the forfeiture of all the land and other property belonging to them." Foner emphasizes as well that the former Confederate states (except Tennessee) refused initially to ratify the Fourteenth Amendment. It would not have gained a sufficient number of state approvals to become part of the Constitution but for the coercion applied by the Republican Party, which made ratification a prerequisite for the regaining of congressional representation.

The second layer of tragedy has to do with the amendments' deficiencies. Consider Section 2 of the Fourteenth Amendment, which provides that, with certain exceptions, when the right to vote is denied to adult males, the basis of a state's congressional representation is to be reduced. Foner points out that some reformers viewed this provision as a double betrayal. They saw it as betraying blacks by continuing to permit states to exercise racial disenfranchisement, albeit at the cost of suffering a diminution in representational strength. Some reformers also saw the Fourteenth Amendment as betraying women by etching a gender line into the text of the Constitution for the first time. While Section 2 supposedly penalized states for excluding men from the franchise (with black men especially in mind), Section 2 expressly permitted states to exclude women from the franchise with no penalty whatsoever. "If that word 'male' be inserted," Elizabeth Cady Stanton warned, "it will take us a century at least to get it out."

Nowadays in America at public commemorations of the Fourteenth Amendment, celebration ensues with little or no awareness of its compromises. In the debates that surrounded that amendment, however, some Radical Republicans expressed keen disappointment. "It falls far short of my wishes," Thaddeus Stevens remarked, "but . . . I believe it is all that can be obtained in the present state of public opinion." Outraged by the failure to guarantee black male suffrage, the stalwart abolitionist Wendell Phillips denounced the Fourteenth Amendment as "a fatal and total surrender" and urged states to withhold ratification. When the Fourteenth Amendment was voted on by the Massachusetts legislature, its two black members rejected ratification!

The Fifteenth Amendment expressly barred the states from using race as a criterion for voting. But Foner underscores that the amendment ultimately approved was among the narrowest of the alternatives considered. One senator proposed an amendment that would have prohibited states from denying the right to vote to any adult male citizen whose record was clear of conviction for crime or participation in rebellion. Another proposed an amendment featuring a uniform set of voting requirements nationally. But because of hostility toward the prospect of unbounded manhood suffrage, the framers of the Fifteenth Amendment designed an exceedingly narrow instrument that foreseeably permitted the disenfranchisement of all sorts of perceived "undesirables," including immigrants from China and Ireland. In 1870, with the abolition of slavery only five years distant, it was evident that literacy, property, and kindred voting requirements could do much of what an outright racial exclusion could accomplish. Henry Adams observed mordantly that the Fifteenth Amendment was "more remarkable for what it does not than for what it does contain." Complaining that the version of the Fifteenth Amendment that eventually prevailed was "the weakest" considered, Senator Willard Warner maintained that it was "unworthy of the great opportunity now presented to us."

The third layer of tragedy took a while to reveal itself. Racism encumbered the Reconstruction project from the outset and throughout its duration. But after a brief interlude of egalitarian enthusiasm that yielded impressive advances, the always fragile commitment to racial justice embraced by the Reconstruction coalition precipitously weakened. While presidents and legislators contributed ignobly to the retreat from Reconstruction, the judiciary is the branch of government that Foner faults most. He notes ruefully that the Supreme Court constricted the potential reach of the Thirteenth Amendment, limiting it to addressing the problem of forced labor and not to the train of racially stigmatizing policies that continued after slavery's demise to mark blacks as a despised minority. The Court dismissed as frivolous, for example, the argument that the racial exclusion of blacks from places of public accommodation—for example, trains, hotels, theaters—constituted a badge or incident of slavery that Congress should be empowered to prohibit pursuant to the Thirteenth Amendment.

The Fourteenth Amendment bars states from making or enforcing "any law which shall abridge the privileges or immunities of citizens of the United States"—a formulation that might have served as the platform for recognizing a broad array of individual rights. The Court, however, interpreted this new provision crabbily, construing it as protecting only a narrow range of activities such as running for federal office. The Fourteenth Amendment provides that no state shall deny to any person "the equal protection of the laws." The Court insisted that this new prohibition banned racially discriminatory *state* action but not racially discriminatory *private* action. When Congress enacted legislation to punish racial aggressions by private parties, the Court invalidated such laws, ruling that they went beyond the authority bestowed by the Fourteenth Amendment. The Court struck down, for example, a federal law that prohibited private owners of "public accommodations" from engaging in racial discrimination.

Then there was the issue of what "equal protection of the law" entails. In *Plessy v. Ferguson* (1896), the Supreme Court upheld the validity of a Louisiana statute that required the separation of white and black passengers aboard trains. Opponents of the law charged that it was racially discriminatory and thus a violation of the equal protection clause of the Fourteenth Amendment. In lonely dissent, Justice John Marshall Harlan asked rhetorically, "What can more certainly arouse race hate, what more certainly create and perpetuate a feeling of distrust between these races, than state enactments which, in fact, proceed on the ground that colored citizens are so inferior and degraded that they cannot be allowed to sit in public coaches occupied by white citizens?" The majority ruled, however, that the law in question was constitutionally inoffensive because it promised separate but equal accommodations for the races. If blacks felt insulted, the Court declared, their grievance stemmed from oversensitivity.

Similarly disappointing to proponents of racial justice was the Supreme Court's early administration of the Fifteenth Amendment. In *Giles v. Harris* (1903), plaintiffs claimed that the State of Alabama had participated in a conspiracy to disenfranchise African Americans. In an opinion written by Justice Oliver Wendell Holmes Jr., the Court concluded that even if the allegation was true, there was nothing that it could do to redress the wrong. No wonder the *Harvard Law Review* published an article in 1910 titled "Is the Fifteenth Amendment Void?"

Foner acknowledges that some of the ground lost in the long retreat from the First Reconstruction was regained during the Second Reconstruction—the span between approximately 1950 and 1970 that witnessed an all-out challenge to white supremacism. During those years legislation was enacted to prohibit racial discrimination across wide swaths of social activity, racial disenfranchisement was attacked by a series of increasingly effective laws, and the Supreme Court invalidated governmental racial segregation across the board, from schools (*Brown v. Board of Education*) to the marriage altar (*Loving v. Virginia*). "The country," Foner writes, "has come a long way toward filling the agenda of [the First] Reconstruction."

Foner emphatically qualifies his seemingly upbeat appraisal, however, with a disturbing list of dissatisfactions. The Thirteenth Amendment, he complains, remains largely truncated. "Its latent power," he laments, "has almost never been invoked as a weapon against the racism that formed so powerful an element of American slavery." He bemoans that the Fourteenth Amendment's promise has "never been truly fulfilled." He objects that wrongheaded rulings have made it increasingly difficult for racial minorities to obtain fairness. "When it comes to racial justice," Foner declares disapprovingly, "the Court has lately proved more sympathetic to white plaintiffs complaining of reverse discrimination because of affirmative action policies than to blacks seeking assistance in overcoming the legacies of centuries of slavery and Jim Crow." Most distressing, according to Foner, is the current perilous situation of the Fifteenth Amendment. "To this day," he notes, "the right to vote remains the subject of bitter disputation." The single most disturbing recent episode of diminished respect for voting rights was *Shelby County v. Holder*, in which the Supreme Court eviscerated unwarrantedly a key provision of the Voting Rights Act. Since that ruling, acting strictly along party lines in states it controls, the Republican Party has enacted legislation making it more difficult for people to register to vote. Asserting that such laws are required to stem fraud (a claim that has been repeatedly discredited), the Republicans impose new requirements that invariably and invidiously disqualify racial minorities in disproportionate numbers. They also reduce early voting, eliminate state-supported voter registration drives, and systematically purge people from registration lists for spurious reasons. Reflecting on *Shelby County*, Foner notes that when conservative jurists discuss the allocation of authority between the central and the state governments, "they almost always concentrate on the ideas of eighteenth-century framers, ignoring those of the architects of Reconstruction."

The Second Founding exhibits sterling qualities that have now become expected of scholarship by Eric Foner, particularly the making of nuanced, balanced judgments regarding subjects that provoke volatile emotional reactions. He highlights the subtleties of a remarkable episode in which progressive change erupted unpredictably. Who could have imagined in 1860 that in a decade an African American would represent Mississippi in the U.S. Senate? But he insists upon recognizing, too, the ever strong pull of racism in American affairs. "Rights can be gained," Foner observes, "and rights can be taken away. A century and a half after the end of slavery, the project of equal citizenship remains unfinished."

Eric Foner is an earnest educator who seizes upon whatever forum is available to share his knowledge and insight, be it books, articles in the *London Review of Books* and *The Nation*, letters to the editor of *The New York Times*, television programs, museum exhibitions, or Gilder Lehrman Institute programs for outstanding high school teachers. I have had the good fortune to know him personally. We met in 1976. I sought him out because my undergraduate senior thesis was a biography of his dissertation adviser, Richard Hofstadter. I would camp out at his office—he was a visiting professor at Princeton that year—and occasionally after office hours we would play tennis. One afternoon he invited me to join him for dinner. I could not have been more thrilled. In the years since, he has been unfailingly supportive and gracious. My experience is by no means singular. His generosity is attested to by scores of faculty colleagues, undergraduates, and, most especially, graduate students.

Foner propounds the centrality of freedom of expression to any attractive conception of social life. "Civil liberties," he remarks, "are the inheritance of a long history of struggles: by abolitionists for the ability to hold meetings and publish their views in the face of mob violence; by labor leaders for the power to organize unions . . . ; by feminists for the right to disseminate birth-control information without violating the obscenity laws." His attentiveness to the vulnerability of open, robust, uninhibited debate stems, in part, from personal experience. His father, Jack D. Foner, and his uncle Philip S. Foner, both formidable historians, were dismissed from faculty positions at the City University of New York after being named as members of the Communist Party at New York state legislative hearings aimed at ostracizing radicals. His mother, Liza Foner, a high school art teacher, was similarly targeted. They were all blacklisted and prevented from teaching for many years.

Foner is a passionate champion of racial justice who has invested his talents in education as a means of social reform. He wants everyone to learn about the depth, pervasiveness, and continuing influence of racial oppression. Aware of the many layers of ignorance, denial, prejudice, and delusion that hinder an appropriate understanding of what has transpired, Foner deploys language meant to uproot complacency. He describes the destruction of Native American nations as "our home-grown holocaust" and slavery as "our home-grown crime against humanity." He rails against the amnesia, evasions, and misrepresentations that remain evident in popular history. He disapproves of tours of plantations at which guides focus on furniture and gardens to the exclusion of whips and chains.

Well aware that he has been benefited by his male whiteness, Foner has strongly defended sensible affirmative action policies. To those who allege that such programs must inevitably undercut the self-confidence of their supposed beneficiaries, Foner retorts (in an article nicely titled "Hiring Quotas for White Males Only"), "I have yet to meet the white male in whom special favoritism (getting a job, for example, through relatives . . . or because of racial discrimination . . .) fostered doubt about his own abilities." To those who allege that affirmative action is the great impediment to the triumph of meritocracy, Foner declares, "Let us not delude ourselves . . . into thinking that eliminating affirmative action will produce a society in which rewards are based on merit. Despite our rhetoric, equal opportunity has never been the American way. For nearly all our history, affirmative action has been a prerogative of white men."

A stalwart progressive, Foner declines to pander to the "woke." He does not pretend to agree when he actually disagrees, and he does not fall silent when the situation requires intervention. He rightly abjures the notion that whites are characteristically unreliable allies to black activists, noting that throughout American history "countless whites have fought for a society in which all citizens enjoyed equal rights and equal opportunities." Similarly, he rejects categorical denunciations of "integration." He renounces "integration" that means the mere "absorption of blacks into the pre-existing white social order." But he embraces "genuine integration" that entails "the *transformation* of American society so as to give real meaning to the principle of equality." "Properly understood," he writes, "integration means not only the removal of economic, social and political obstacles to full participation in every area of American life but changes in the contours of personal life so that friendship, comradeship and intimacy between the races can become far more common than is possible today." The time has come, Foner asserts, "to reintroduce integration into our political vocabulary—not as a code for whites dictating to blacks or as 'color blindness,' a term appropriated from the civil rights movement by conservatives and made into an empty slogan, but as a vision of a nation transformed, one in which equality is a reality for all Americans."

19

Charles Hamilton Houston:
The Lawyer as Social Engineer[1]

For decades, Charles Hamilton Houston was virtually unknown beyond the ranks of civil rights lawyers and aficionados of African American history. That has changed on account of biographers, historians of the black bar, and commemoration by his alma mater, Harvard Law School.[2] In 2003, Harvard University created a chaired professorship in Houston's honor and appointed to it the newly selected dean of the law school, Elena Kagan (who has subsequently become, of course, an associate justice on the U.S. Supreme Court). In 2005, Harvard Law School professor Charles Ogletree founded the Charles Hamilton Houston Institute for Race and Justice. Nowadays, at Harvard and elsewhere, law students are made aware that Houston was an accomplished educator and attorney who shaped litigation into a vehicle of social protest, designing strategies not only to address a client's need but also to forward the mission of a grand cause—removing impediments to racial decency.

Houston was born September 3, 1895. While his maternal grandparents were free blacks, his paternal grandparents were fugitive slaves. One of them, Thomas Jefferson Houston, was a "conductor" on the Underground Railroad who helped his mother and three brothers to escape bondage. Houston's father was an attorney. His mother was a hairdresser whose clientele included the wives of senators, cabinet officers, and diplomats. An only child, Charles attended Washington's famed M Street High

School (renamed Dunbar High School), the first public high school for black Americans, an institution whose eminent alumni included Charles Drew, the pioneering physician; Benjamin O. Davis, the first African American general; Robert C. Weaver, the first black member of the cabinet; and William H. Hastie Jr., the first black federal appellate judge. Houston then attended Amherst College, where he was the only African American in the class of 1915. Inducted into Phi Beta Kappa, he graduated magna cum laude and delivered a commencement address.

During World War I, Houston helped organize the Central Committee of Negro College Men, which lobbied officials to establish a reserve officer training camp for blacks. He had to fight for inclusion in a Jim Crow army in which a negligible number of blacks were allowed only to become officers in all-Negro units. Houston's encounters with racism while trying to serve his country were profoundly sobering. Whites opposed to elevating blacks to the officer corps attempted to sabotage the experiment by assigning African American soldiers to tasks for which they had not been trained. Black soldiers trained for the infantry, for instance, were sent without further instruction to artillery units. When the foreseeable failures occurred, racists pointed to them as evidence of racial inferiority.

In France, Houston faced a situation in which he and three other black officers were surrounded by white American soldiers who called them "niggers" and threatened to lynch them, alleging that they had been fraternizing with white Frenchwomen. Only the intervention of military police forestalled an injury potentially greater than fright. Recalling his army experiences, he later wrote, "I made up my mind that I would never get caught again without knowing something about my rights; that if luck was with me, and I got through this war, I would study law and use my time fighting for men who could not strike back."[3]

In September 1919, Houston entered Harvard Law School, amassed excellent grades, and was selected as the first black editor of the *Harvard Law Review*. He thrived despite routine bigotry on campus. Excluded from social clubs that barred blacks and Jews, Houston took the lead in establishing the Dunbar Law Club, named after a Jewish lawyer in Boston.

A letter Houston wrote to his parents on January 8, 1922,

offers a glimpse into the complexity of his experience. While he perceived his fellow *Review* editors to have been initially unwelcoming, he sensed that over time they came to accept him. "My stock is pretty high around these parts." Always, though, there remained the anxiety that accompanied his role as a racial pioneer. "God help me against a false move."[4]

Upon graduating, Houston returned to Washington, D.C., and with his father established Houston & Houston, a firm that provided counsel on a wide range of nuts-and-bolts legal problems—wills, estates, contracts, torts, and divorces. He also became involved in teaching at Howard University's law school— the country's leading provider of legal education to blacks: three-fourths of the 950 African American attorneys practicing in the United States during the 1920s were trained there. Although the law school was accredited neither by the American Bar Association nor by the Association of American Law Schools, and although some observers disparaged Howard as the "dummies' retreat," the training it offered was similar to that provided by many run-of-the-mill law schools that featured part-time evening programs for students with full-time jobs. The authorities at Howard, however, wanted an outstanding, fully accredited law school.

Houston was deputized to obtain Howard's accreditation and improve its quality. He succeeded by methods that provoked strong opposition. He raised standards for admission, expelled students who failed to meet elevated academic expectations, ousted faculty members judged to be inadequate, and, most controversially, phased out the night division. These measures shrank the school. In 1922 its graduating class numbered fifty-eight; in 1933 only eleven. Some alumni complained that Houston was a naive, insensitive, rigid elitist wrongly bent on "Harvardizing" Howard. This objection carried weight. After all, Howard had trained scores of people, like Houston's father, who worked during the day and would have been unable to obtain a legal education but for a night division and other accommodations for working folk. Others, however, including Mordecai Johnson, Howard's first black president, and Justice Louis Brandeis, one of Johnson's advisers, embraced Houston's reforms. They, like him, perceived the night school to be siphoning scarce resources from the day school and concluded that abandoning the former would be necessary to increase the value of a Howard Law School diploma.

For Houston reform meant more than increasing the marketability of Howard graduates. It meant creating an institution that could produce a vanguard of talented attorneys who could spearhead black America's struggle against racist oppression. Toward that end he worked ceaselessly and creatively to educate and inspire. He made sure that students met leading figures, inviting to the law school such guests as Clarence Darrow and Felix Frankfurter. He supplemented book knowledge with expeditions to the Federal Bureau of Investigation, penitentiaries, insane asylums, and courtrooms. He constantly reminded his charges that as a practical matter black attorneys had to be better than their white counterparts in order to offset racial prejudice.

The efforts that Houston made on Howard's behalf and the ethos that he embodied continue to be appreciated. On its website presentation of its history, Howard Law School proudly maintains, citing Houston, that it is dedicated to producing jurists who are social engineers—lawyers who are willing and able to design and implement solutions that better the condition of the maltreated and needy.

There was about Houston an aristocratic austerity. From his associates he elicited more admiration than fondness. He "did nothing with levity," recalled James Nabrit, an outstanding attorney who became president of Howard. Houston's work, Nabrit remarked, "was his only real interest in life, and he brought the full force of his personality to it."[5] Thurgood Marshall said of him, "He was hard-crust. First off, you thought he was a mean so-and-so. He used to tell us that doctors could bury their mistakes but lawyers couldn't. . . . He was so tough we used to call him 'Iron Shoes' and 'Cement Pants' and a few other names that don't bear repeating. But he was a sweet man once you saw what he was up to. He was absolutely fair, and the door to his office was always open. He made it clear to all of us that when we were done, we were expected to go out and do something with our lives."[6]

Throughout his career Houston was keenly concerned with nurturing skilled black attorneys. It bothered him that during its first two decades, the National Association for the Advancement of Colored People (NAACP) relied mainly on white attorneys to pursue its legal agenda. That reality occasioned resentment on the part of some black lawyers. After all, most white individuals or businesses did not even consider hiring Negro attorneys. Blacks, too, often discriminated against Negro lawyers, believing that white ones—free from the ostracism that burdened African Americans—would be better positioned to protect their interests. When black attorneys complained that even the National Association for the Advancement of Colored People was slighting colored lawyers, NAACP officials responded testily, asserting that the problem resided not in bias but in the inadequacy of all too many black attorneys. Houston's initial response was to demand that black attorneys prepare themselves so thoroughly as to put their competence beyond question. He pushed them to do just that at Howard. However, when the NAACP continued to display reluctance to engage black attorneys, Houston objected. He maintained that there had arisen a cadre of black lawyers who were fully the equals of their white peers and that the NAACP should make use of their talents.

In 1933 the NAACP selected Houston to defend George Crawford, a black man apprehended in Boston after being charged with the murder of two white women in Virginia. Houston resisted extradition on the grounds that his client would be unable to obtain a fair trial in Virginia because African Americans there were systematically excluded from juries in violation of the federal Constitution. Although Houston persuaded a federal district court judge to rule in Crawford's favor, a court of appeals disagreed.

When Crawford was remanded to Virginia to stand trial, NAACP officials suggested that a white lawyer be hired to represent him or at least assist Houston. Though no one doubted Houston's abilities, many observers believed the presence of a white attorney at the defense table to be essential. Houston, however, refused to use any white tokens. Instead, he turned for assistance to Howard-related associates—alumni, a fellow professor, and a precocious third-year law student named Thurgood Marshall. There was good reason to suppose that the all-black defense team would encounter hostility. Not only was its client a black man accused of murdering two white women. He was on trial in an area of Virginia in which local blacks felt so cowed that none of them would rent living accommodations to defense counsel—a problem that prompted Houston and his team to commute daily from Washington.

As it turned out, Crawford was in fact complicit in a burglary that went murderously awry. An all-white jury sentenced him to life imprisonment. That he escaped the death penalty was widely attributed to Houston's effective advocacy.

Houston's most jurisprudentially significant cases were three that he argued at the federal Supreme Court. *Missouri ex rel. Gaines v. Canada* (1938) arose from an effort by a twenty-five-year-old St. Louis resident, Lloyd Gaines, to attend the University of Missouri Law School. The law school denied Gaines admission solely because he was black. It suggested that he apply for funds set aside for blacks to attend law school outside the state. Houston charged that this arrangement violated the Constitution's equal protection clause (reprising the argument that he and Thurgood Marshall had successfully advanced in Maryland courts two years previously). The Supreme Court agreed. Although the Court did not question the constitutionality of segregation, the majority did rule that if legal education was offered within a state to white citizens, an equal educational opportunity must be offered within the state to black citizens.

In *Steele v. Louisville & Nashville Railroad Company, et al.* (1944), Houston's client was a black locomotive fireman. In 1941 the Brotherhood of Locomotive Firemen and Enginemen amended its collective-bargaining agreement with the L&N Railroad in such a way as to ensure that all Negro firemen would eventually be replaced by white ones. The all-white, racially exclusive union did so without notifying or consulting affected black workers. The federal Railway Labor Act authorized the union to serve as the exclusive bargaining representative of all locomotive firemen, whether or not they were permitted to be members of the union. Houston argued, and the Court unanimously agreed, that by granting unions authority as exclusive bargaining agents, Congress implicitly imposed upon unions a duty of fair representation, which meant at least a duty to forgo discriminating against workers that the unions represented, including workers who were not members of the union.

In 1948, Houston argued a case, *Hurd v. Hodge*, that posed the question whether a federal court could enforce a restrictive covenant in a private agreement stipulating that a given property could never be transferred to "any Negro or colored person." The party seeking to enforce the covenant argued that inasmuch as the clause represented the will of private as opposed to governmental actors, nothing in the Constitution precluded a court from enforcing it in the same way as any other private contract. By contrast, Houston argued, and the Court concluded, that constitutional values prohibit judges from enforcing racially restrictive covenants with equitable remedies because doing so invests racist contracts with a governmental imprimatur.

Several other cases highlight Houston's stature among his contemporaries, the bigotry that surrounded him, and his willingness to leap to the defense of civil rights and civil liberties. One involved Bernard Ades, a white communist Maryland attorney who turned to Houston in 1933 for representation in disbarment proceedings. Ades worked for the International Labor Defense (ILD), a left-wing advocacy organization that was affiliated with the American Communist Party. Ades represented black defendants charged with murder or rape in proceedings attended by threats of lynching, police brutality, and racially prejudiced juries and judges. Ades took it upon himself to represent poor, ignorant, bereft defendants, elbowing aside court-appointed counsel who failed to offer zealous defense. In one case, for example, he forced the state to try his client three times, raising issues—fairness of the venue and racial exclusions in jury selection—that court-appointed counsel declined to raise. Ades's efforts were largely unavailing; his clients were typically convicted and sentenced harshly.

Furthermore, hostile judges sought his disbarment. They claimed that his license to practice law should be revoked because he had, in violation of professional ethics, improperly foisted himself on defendants, made false statements to judges, and dealt improperly with a prosecution witness. The most striking charge was that Ades had acted unethically when he visited a client on death row the day before his execution and obtained a bequest of the client's corpse in the absence of full disclosure. Ades wanted to transport the corpse to New York City for a memorial service organized by the ILD. The organizers believed that the corpse would vivify their claim that the deceased had fallen victim to a "legal lynching."

It is noteworthy that Ades, a white lawyer, turned to Houston for assistance in a Jim Crow state in the 1930s. Ades's ideological orientation certainly had something to do with his engaging Houston. White communists were typically far ahead of other whites in terms of their relationships with blacks. White communists often welcomed blacks into their ranks, intermarried with them, supported blacks as party officials, and appreciated black talent outside party circles. But given what was at stake—Ades's law practice—it is also sensible to infer that the outreach to Houston (Thurgood Marshall was again his junior associate) was indicative of his reputation for effective advocacy.

Noteworthy, too, was Houston's willingness to take the case. Many lawyers in his position would have avoided it. Representing an obscure communist facing disbarment did not seem to be an auspicious vehicle for personal professional advancement or advancing the cause of blacks. Howard's president asked Houston why he wanted to get mixed up with such unsavory company. Houston answered that Ades had "rendered significant service . . . in exposing certain discriminations which Negroes used to suffer in Maryland courts."[7] Houston was well aware of the risks that his client had braved in rendering that "significant service." Ades was twice forced to flee mobs of irate white Marylanders.

In addition to admiration and gratitude for Ades's stand on behalf of due process, Houston voiced another consideration. He maintained that Ades's confrontation with bar disciplinary authorities affected the position of *all* lawyers who represented ostracized clients: "It is a matter of principle vitally affecting the rights of any lawyer who espouses an unpopular cause that he be freed from the threats of arbitrary pressure of the Court."[8]

At the disbarment hearing Houston maintained that the real basis behind the call to end Ades's career was his "insistence on exposing officials with a dual standard of public morality—one for whites and one for blacks."[9] Luckily for Houston and Ades, they drew a capable, conscientious, fair judge, Morris Ames Soper, who rejected the call for disbarment. The judge instead imposed a public reprimand—the very penalty that Houston had suggested as an appropriate response to the gambit with the corpse and certain false and disparaging comments that Ades had leveled against local judges and other officials.

Another of Houston's cases served as the basis of a short story by Richard Wright, "The Man Who Killed a Shadow." On March 1, 1944, Julius Fisher, a black janitor at the National Cathedral in Washington, D.C., complained to a white librarian, Catherine Cooper Reardon, about a statement she had made to his boss. She had accused him of performing his job poorly. In response to his complaint, Reardon, according to Fisher, called him "nigger." He slapped her. She screamed. To stifle her screaming he beat, choked, and stabbed her. Houston conceded that Fisher killed Reardon and that the killing constituted a crime. He argued, though, that the effect of the n-word on his client should be seen as a mitigating factor. He asserted that at most the crime amounted to second-degree murder, to which the death penalty was inapplicable, and *not* first-degree murder, to which the death penalty did apply. Houston succeeded in winning a hearing for Fisher before the Supreme Court. He succeeded also in winning over three justices. The majority, however, affirmed the court below, clearing the way to a death sentence that was eventually carried out.

Houston was an antiracist social democrat committed to the protection of political pluralism. Espousing a view in the early 1930s that he seems to have retained for the remainder of his life, Houston remarked,

> The Negro shall not be content simply with demanding an equal share in the existing system. . . . [H]is fundamental responsibility and historical challenge is . . . to make sure that the system which shall survive . . . shall be a system which guarantees justice and freedom for everyone. The way I usually put it is, "Sure we're being invited [in now] to take a front seat, but there's no particular honor in being invited [in now] to take a front seat at one's own funeral."[10]

Around the same time he refused to endorse an American Civil Liberties Union resolution condemning the Communist Party:

> I must say in fairness that the Communists are working in many fields of special interest to me: anti-lynching, anti-poll tax, anti-segregation, integration of Negroes in the labor movement, etc. I appreciate their activities and I believe that in many ways their work will bring about a broader base of democratic participation by the common people, although the pattern which our economic structure may take may be foreign to their design.[11]

In 1947, Houston railed against the House Un-American Activities Committee's campaign against "subversion" in Hollywood:

> If the Committee is able to stifle independence on the screen, it will move on to radio, to newspapers and periodicals, to books, to the Sunday pulpit, and even to private conversations in the home. . . . I do not trust the House Committee on Un-American Activities . . . and will not trust it until it investigates lynching, disfranchisement, segregation and discrimination.[12]

Later, after several Hollywood screenwriters were convicted of contempt of Congress for refusing to answer questions about their political beliefs and associations, Houston served on the legal team that tried unsuccessfully to reverse the conviction on appeal.

One cannot know confidently the precise character of Houston's commitment to political pluralism. He never seems to have discussed freedom of expression for Klansmen or Nazis. And he died before the acme of McCarthyism and liberals' response to it. The very year of his passing, 1950, the NAACP amended its constitution to bar communists from membership. Ostracism of the communists stemmed partly from ideological revulsion and partly from self-defense. Liberals wanted to stay clear of the massive repression besetting the Communist Party. With respect to African American liberals, the common saying was that it was difficult enough being black; being "red" or even merely "pink" was just too much to bear. Houston's most outstanding apprentice, Thurgood Marshall, declined to oppose the anticommunist repression, even when it ensnared such highly esteemed antiracist activists as W. E. B. Du Bois and Paul Robeson. Perhaps Houston would have acted similarly. But I doubt it. Given his ideological proclivities, the strength of his pre-1950 protests against anticommunist repression, and his penchant for personal independence, I suspect that, had he lived, Houston would have declined to accommodate McCarthyism.

While Houston's record as an attorney is the principal basis for the high esteem to which he is entitled, he did much else besides. As Professors Chris Myers Asch and George Derek Musgrove note in *Chocolate City*, their excellent history of racial struggles in Washington, D.C., Houston was "ubiquitous."[13] He wrote a column for the newspaper *The Afro-American*. He walked picket lines. He gave speeches. He served on the D.C. Board of Education. He testified before Congress. He chaired the Marian Anderson Citizens Committee when the Daughters of the American Revolution, pursuant to its racial policy, barred the world's outstanding contralto from performing at Constitution Hall. He sat on the National Committee on Segregation in the Nation's Capital. He helped found the Washington Bar Association in response to the exclusion of blacks from the Bar Association of the District of Columbia. He served as an officer of the National Lawyers Guild.

Characteristic of Houston's integrity, independence, and attentiveness to collective advancement was his experience with the Fair Employment Practices Commission (FEPC). About a year after being appointed to the FEPC in 1944, he encountered a case involving complaints lodged against the Capital Transit Company in Washington, D.C., which refused to hire Negro bus operators or streetcar conductors. At Houston's urging, the FEPC was about to issue a directive demanding that the company desist from its discriminatory practices when the Truman administration ordered the FEPC to back off. Houston requested a meeting with the president. When his request went unanswered, Houston resigned. He registered the indignation that many African Americans felt as they watched their government show more solicitude for oppressed minorities abroad than for oppressed minorities at home. He declared that "the failure of the Government to enforce democratic practices and to protect minorities in its own capital makes its expressed concern for national minorities abroad somewhat specious, and its interference in the domestic affairs of other countries very premature."[14]

Houston died of a heart attack on April 22, 1950, four years before the watershed event toward which much of his life was directed: the ruling in *Brown v. Board of Education* in which the Supreme Court belatedly invalidated racial segregation in public primary and secondary schooling. Among the talented crew of attorneys who led the charge against segregation were several graduates of Houston's Howard Law School. Among the precedents to which they adverted were several that Houston had helped to establish. And among the threads of public opinion that they wove into a strong argument for constitutional decency were several that Houston had helped to spin. "He guided us through the legal wilderness of second-class citizenship," observed Judge William Hastie Jr. "He was truly the Moses of that journey. He lived to see us close to the promised land of full equality under the law, closer than even he dared hope when he set out . . . and so much closer than would have been possible without his genius and his leadership."[15]

20

Remembering Thurgood Marshall[1]

My impressions of Thurgood Marshall are mainly based on my experience clerking for him in the 1983 Supreme Court term. He was an exacting employer, often gruff, seldom congratulatory. Schooled professionally in an unforgiving environment, he was a stickler for detail who abhorred tardiness. Early on he told me and my three co-clerks that if he got angry at any one of us, he would be angry at *all* of us—an effective strategy for prompting collective monitoring. But his demands were never petty; they were focused solely on getting the work done—examining each petition seeking Supreme Court review, advising on which cases warranted a hearing, preparing for oral arguments by writing memoranda that summarized contending positions, and drafting opinions.

Unlike many big shots, Marshall did not encourage sycophancy and was free from tiresome, self-regarding affectations. His unpretentiousness sometimes lured people into slighting him. But every time I took Justice Marshall lightly, he brought me up short. Late in the term I wrote a draft of a dissenting opinion in which, in a footnote, I showered attention on an article by one of my favorite professors. I thought for sure that the justice would overlook this little item of puffery. A few hours after I submitted the draft, I got it back with a big red *X* scrawled across the offending text. He was minding the store more than he let on.

A benefit (though some considered it a bane) of the Marshall clerkship was that the justice liked to tell stories—lots of them.

They were seldom sweet. One involved Marshall confronting a "moderate" white supremacist politician in the Jim Crow South with the fact that, contrary to the segregationist promise of separate but equal facilities, the whites in the state had a school for nursing while the blacks had none. The politician told Marshall that he could get the state to build a school for blacks but that Marshall had to allow him to use his own methods. Marshall agreed, whereupon the politician immediately called a press conference and announced that he had just witnessed a most sickening spectacle: a white female nurse washing the back of a black man. The politician then demanded that the state legislature immediately appropriate money for "a nigger school" for nursing so that this sort of thing would never happen again. The money was appropriated, the school was built, and some good was accomplished, albeit by foul means.*

Justice Marshall also regaled his colleagues with stories. Justice Sandra Day O'Connor remembers being "particularly moved" by one Justice Marshall recounted while the Court was considering a case in which a black man maintained that racial bias rendered illegitimate the death sentence imposed upon him. "You know," Marshall said,

> "I had an innocent man once. He was accused of raping a white woman. The government told me if he would plead guilty, he'd only get life. I said I couldn't make that decision; I'd have to ask my client. So I told him that if he pleaded guilty, he wouldn't get the death sentence.
>
> "He said, 'Plead guilty to what?'
> "I said, 'Plead guilty to rape.'
> "He said, 'Raping that woman? You gotta be kidding. I won't do it.'
> "That's when I knew I had an innocent man.

---

* This story puts me in mind of the Thurgood Marshall School of Law. That historically black institution was conceived in segregationist sin as an effort to outflank the campaign to desegregate public law school education in Texas, a campaign that involved one of Marshall's most important victories at the Supreme Court, *Sweatt v. Painter*, 339 U.S. 629 (1950). *See* Marguerite L. Butler, "The History of Texas Southern University, Thurgood Marshall School of Law: 'The House That Sweatt Built,'" 23 *Thurgood Marshall Law Review* 45 (1997).

"When the judge sent the jurors out, he told them that they had three choices: Not guilty, guilty, or guilty with mercy. 'You understand those are the three different possible choices,' he instructed. But after the jury left, the judge told the people in the courtroom that they were not to move before the bailiff took the defendant away. I said, 'What happened to "not guilty"?' The judge looked at me, and said, 'Are you kidding?' Just like that. And he was the 'judge.'"

As he neared the end of his tale, Justice Marshall leaned forward, pointed his finger at no one in particular, and said with his characteristic signal of finale, "E-e-e-end of the Story. The guy was found guilty and sentenced to death. But he never raped that woman." He paused, flicking his hand. "Oh well," he added, "he was just a Negro."*

Justice O'Connor recalled that another of Marshall's stories stuck in her memory:

"S-a-a-a-n-d-r-a-a, . . . did I ever tell you about the welcome I received in Mississippi?" It was early evening in a small town in Mississippi in the early 1940s and he was waiting to hop the next train to Shreveport. "I was starving," he told me, "so I decided to go over to this restaurant and see if one of the cooks would let me in the back to buy a sandwich. You know, that's how we did things then; the front door was so inconvenient!" Before he could go over, Justice Marshall recounted, "a man of your race holding a pistol sidled up. 'Boy,' he said, 'what are you doing around these parts?' I said, 'I'm waiting to catch the next train.' He said, 'Listen up boy because I'm only gonna tell you this once. The last train through here is at 4 p.m. and you

* Although Justice O'Connor praised Justice Marshall's storytelling, she notes no instance in which his remarks swayed her vote. With respect to claims of racial discrimination and the death penalty, O'Connor joined the Court in turning such claims aside. *See, e.g., McCleskey v. Kemp*, 481 U.S. 279 (1987). *See* Sandra Day O'Connor, "Thurgood Marshall: The Influence of a Raconteur," 44 *Stanford Law Review* 1217, 1218 (1992).

better be on it cuz niggers ain't welcome in these parts after dark.'"

"Guess what," Justice Marshall added, a twinkle creeping into his eye, "I was on that train."[2]

Although Justice Marshall felt sufficiently secure in his own skin to relish vigorous debate, he was also willing to pull rank when he felt the time for finality nigh. In one instance a clerk made the mistake of telling him that he "had" to do something. The justice offered a quick correction. The only things that he "had" to do, he said, were to stay black and die. On another occasion he called a halt to a long, heated discussion by pointing to the judicial commission on the wall and saying, "*I'm* the one who was nominated by President Lyndon B. Johnson and confirmed by the Senate of the United States. When you get a commission, you can call the shots." Then there was the time I repeatedly advised the justice to vote a certain way because he had done so in similar circumstances previously. After I needled him one time too many about inconsistency, he looked at me with mock exasperation and shouted, "Do I have to be a damn fool *all* of my life!"

MR. CIVIL RIGHTS

Marshall was born July 2, 1908, in Baltimore.[3] He was originally named Thoroughgood. He shortened it himself. His parents were literate, energetic, public-spirited members of the black upper working class. His father worked as a steward at a country club, while his mother worked intermittently as a schoolteacher. Neither attended college. But they sent Thurgood Marshall and his older brother, Aubrey, not only to college but to professional schools. Both attended Lincoln University in Pennsylvania as undergraduates (Thurgood Marshall's classmates included Langston Hughes and Cab Calloway), and both attended Howard University for additional training, Aubrey for medical school, and Thurgood for law school. He would have preferred attending the University of Maryland Law School to minimize travel time and expenses. But the state's exclusionary racial policy discouraged him from even applying. This was, in a way, fortuitous because, by

attending Howard, he gained access to an extraordinary mentor—
Charles Hamilton Houston. Under Houston's tutelage, Marshall excelled as a student and participated in litigating cases that
enabled him to advocate not only on behalf of individual clients
but on behalf of a broader, daunting, exciting, and elusive cause:
racial justice.

Marshall graduated from Howard Law School in 1933 and
returned to Baltimore to start a law practice in the teeth of the
Great Depression. He handled all sorts of cases, including
landlord-tenant disputes and divorce actions, and represented all
sorts of clients, including a laundry, an association of black funeral
directors, and an Afro-American newspaper. He kept afloat professionally but showed little passion or aptitude for moneymaking.
Indeed, a secretary later observed that Marshall "had a genius for
ignoring cases that might earn him any money."[4] Like many black
lawyers handicapped by race in the market for legal services, Marshall resorted to other means to make ends meet. For a while he
worked two nights a week and on Saturdays as a file clerk at a city
health clinic.

In 1935, Marshall embarked upon the first civil rights case
for which he was principally responsible. It involved Donald
Murray, a black graduate of Amherst College who applied to the
University of Maryland Law School, only to be rejected pursuant
to the same Jim Crow policy that had dissuaded Marshall from
applying. Although Maryland offered blacks no facilities for legal
education, the state asserted that it satisfied the equality part of
the segregation formula by offering qualified black Marylanders a small stipend they could use to obtain legal training out of
state. Marshall argued that the scholarship assistance for education elsewhere did not suffice to meet the state's obligation to
provide equal, albeit separate, educational facilities to blacks. He
obtained a decree from a local judge ordering Murray's admission
to the white school in the absence of a black one. In proceedings before the Maryland Court of Appeals, he declared, "What's
at stake here is more than the rights of my client. It's the moral
commitment stated in our country's creed." The state, Marshall
charged, "confuse[d] the issue of segregation and exclusion. . . .
Donald Murray was not sent to a separate school of the University

of Maryland. . . . Donald Murray was excluded from the University of Maryland entirely."[5] The court agreed.

Marshall long savored his first big win as a civil rights attorney. I heard him call it "sweet revenge." The comment arose in a conversation in which I asked him whether he felt discouraged insofar as he was consigned as a justice to dissenting in many of the cases that meant the most to him. He told me that while he sometimes felt frustrated, he did not feel discouraged. He then reminded me that throughout much of his time as a practicing attorney, *Plessy v. Ferguson*, albeit deplorable, was the leading precedent with which he had to work. He persuaded courts to decree, for example, that black public school teachers be paid the same as separately placed but similarly situated white ones.[6] He won a host of such cases citing *Plessy*, wringing out as much equality as he possibly could from the "separate but equal" delusion.

In 1936, Marshall moved to New York to join Houston at the national headquarters of the NAACP. Two years later, Houston returned to private practice in D.C., opening up space for Marshall to become the NAACP's principal lawyer—a post he held for two remarkably busy decades, leading the most extensive and effective campaign of social reform litigation in American history.

Marshall always understood segregation to be oppressive. But pragmatism demanded that he play by its rules even as he disputed the game's legitimacy. He demanded that segregationist jurisdictions live up to their obligation to provide ostensibly "equal" albeit "separate" facilities and services. As conditions changed, so, too, did the tenor of his objections to Jim Crow. After extracting as much equality as possible from the separate but equal regime, Marshall increasingly attacked the legitimacy of segregation per se, arguing that governmentally supported racial separation constituted a policy of caste that deprived racial untouchables of the equal protection of the laws. He maintained that segregation always created racial underlings branded as inferior in the eyes of society.

Looking back, it seems obvious that segregation constituted an invidious and thus impermissible racial discrimination. During much of Marshall's career, however, most whites, including leading jurists, perceived segregation to be constitutionally tolerable.

Through a tireless campaign of public education, much of it in the form of litigation, Marshall and a cadre of remarkable colleagues succeeded slowly in unmasking segregation and revealing its oppressiveness. The most well-known monument to this effort was *Brown v. Board of Education*,[7] the landmark decision in 1954 in which the Supreme Court invalidated segregation in public primary and secondary schooling.

At the same time that Marshall led the attack in the courtroom against Jim Crow segregation, he also participated in legal assaults against other bulwarks of white supremacy, prompting rulings in which the Supreme Court prohibited political parties from excluding blacks from party primaries (*Smith v. Allwright* [1944]),[8] barred judges from enforcing racially restrictive covenants (*Shelley v. Kraemer* [1948][9] and *Hurd v. Hodge* [1948]),[10] disallowed segregation in interstate transportation (*Morgan v. Virginia* [1946]),[11] prevented confessions extracted by duress from being used against criminal defendants at trial (*Chambers v. State of Florida* [1940]),[12] and forbade convictions by juries from which blacks had been racially excluded (*Patton v. Mississippi* [1947]).[13]

I say that the Supreme Court "prohibited" this and "barred" that, which is true—to a point. The Court decided the cases before it and offered reasons for conclusions reached. Whether that reasoning would be subsequently followed depended upon the willingness of other officials to comply. Marshall and his colleagues spent prodigious amounts of time and energy monitoring compliance with Supreme Court decisions. Consider the aftermath of *Smith v. Allwright*, which Marshall described to me as the appellate case of which he was most proud. The Court ruled that the racially exclusionary Texas Democratic Party primary involved state action subject to federal constitutional standards. In response, South Carolina's governor, Olin Johnston, called an extraordinary session of that state's legislature at which it repealed all laws regulating primary elections. He and the legislature were attempting to prevent a court from employing the *Allwright* reasoning. "White supremacy," Governor Johnston announced, "will be maintained in our primaries. Let the chips fall where they may!"[14]

Marshall journeyed to Columbia, South Carolina, to represent a black businessman, George Elmore, who successfully challenged the constitutionality of the new arrangement. Invalidating South Carolina's attempted evasion of the *Allwright* decision, Judge J. Waties Waring declared that it was time "for South Carolina to rejoin the Union" and "to adopt the American way of conducting elections."[15]

Growing up, I often heard about the oral argument in that case. My father witnessed it. What he remembered was not arcane disputation over the contours of the state action doctrine. Rather, what he recalled was a repudiation of Jim Crow etiquette. Back then in South Carolina whites typically refused to address a black man by the honorific title "Mr." Judge Waring, however, addressed Elmore's lawyer as *Mr.* Marshall.*

In addition to appellate advocacy, Marshall plied his trade as a trial attorney, representing clients in places where the very appearance of a colored lawyer was seen by some as an affront. In November 1946, he participated in the defense of two black men in Columbia, Tennessee, who were charged with attempted murder during a riot in which a white mob, backed by police, terrorized a black community. Tried before an all-white jury, one of the defendants was convicted, the other acquitted. Following the trial, police officers stopped the car in which Marshall was riding, put him into a police vehicle, and sped off. The other lawyers desperately followed. Marshall later credited those attorneys with saving his life. He believed that had they abandoned him the police would have handed him over to a Ku Klux Klan lynching party. Eventually, the police drove Marshall back to Columbia, where they took him to a magistrate on charges of drunkenness. Upon smelling Marshall's breath, the magistrate ordered him released! (Marshall enjoyed telling and retelling this story, adding that upon safely reaching Nashville that night, he did take a drink, indeed several.)[16]

Marshall advanced racial reform through more than litiga-

---

* Judge Waring's nephew, a racist editor at the *Charleston News and Courier* newspaper, urged his even more rigidly racist boss to refer to black women in print by the courtesy title "Mrs." His superior grudgingly accepted the suggestion but added, "Don't go too far with it. No Misters." *See* Tinsley E. Yarbrough, *A Passion for Justice: J. Waties Waring and Civil Rights* (1987), 54, 77.

tion. In June 1943 a race riot erupted in Detroit, killing twenty-
five blacks and nine whites. Amid an outcry about the conduct
of the city police the NAACP dispatched Marshall to investigate. He shared his findings in *The Crisis* in an article titled "The
Gestapo in Detroit." "The trouble," Marshall said, "reached riot
proportions because the police once again enforced the law with
an unequal hand. They used 'persuasion' rather than firm action
with white rioters, while against Negroes they used the ultimate
in force: night sticks, revolvers, riot guns, submachine guns, and
deer guns." The police killed seventeen blacks but *no* whites, stok-
ing "the certainty of Negroes that they will not be protected by
police, but instead will be attacked by them."[17]

A decade later, the NAACP dispatched Marshall to Korea to
investigate complaints of racial mistreatment of Negro soldiers.
He quoted white officers telling black soldiers, "I despise nigger
troops. I don't want to command you or any other niggers. . . .
You don't know how to fight."[18] He noted the exclusion of blacks
at General Douglas MacArthur's massive compound, remarking
puckishly that "there wasn't even a Negro in the headquarters'
band."[19] He found that Negro soldiers were being treated unfairly
in disciplinary proceedings, citing a court-martial that lasted all of
forty-two minutes ending with a sentence of life imprisonment.
"I have seen many miscarriages of justice," Marshall wrote. "But
even in Mississippi a Negro will get a trial longer than 42 minutes,
if he is fortunate enough to be brought to trial."[20]

Letter writing was yet another way in which Marshall—
popularly dubbed Mr. Civil Rights—contributed to the struggle.
This long-overlooked feature of his career is captured vividly
in *Marshalling Justice: The Early Civil Rights Letters of Thurgood
Marshall*, edited by Michael G. Long. This compendium of correspondence reflects the wide range of issues with which Marshall
grappled, the crushing needs of the people who reached out for
his assistance, the knowing cruelty or negligent ignorance of influential bureaucrats and politicians, and the extraordinary patience,
energy, and persistence with which he attempted to redress injustice on a retail scale, letter by letter by letter. Responding to an
anonymous note about horrific conditions in a Texas prison, Marshall wrote to Texas's governor, James Allred:

We are informed that the Negro prisoners [at the Ramsey State Farm, Camp #1, near Houston, Texas] are beaten and, in many cases, killed for trivial reasons. . . . We cannot too strongly urge upon you the seriousness of such offenses which, even though committed by persons in charge of a prison, are, nevertheless, brutal murders. . . . [W]e urge you to immediately cause an investigation to be made.[21]

Responding to a racist cartoon, Marshall wrote to the editor of the *New York Herald Tribune*, "Your cartoon . . . 'Topsy Didn't Just Grow' is insulting to Negroes and mischievous in its every implication and probable consequence. It is entirely unworthy of a major national newspaper and goes far toward undoing in one shocking and inexcusable transgression the reputation for fairness and decency which the Herald Tribune has been building."[22] A magazine in Michigan published an item in an advice column that suggested a pretext by which a motel proprietor could exclude black travelers using a nonracial excuse. A reader forwarded the item to Marshall, who wrote to the magazine, complaining that this advice violated state antidiscrimination law.[23]

Marshall's anger was not always directed outward against white supremacists. Occasionally he got salty with allies. Responding to complaints that he and his staff had "let down" activists in a schooling case in Lumberton, North Carolina, Marshall replied, "I, personally, get sick and tired of people in our branches who wait 81 years to get to the point of bringing legal action to secure their rights and then want the lawyers to prepare the case, file it, [and] have it decided . . . in fifteen minutes."[24]

The most moving of Marshall's letters was one he wrote to the mother of a youngster he was unable to help. NAACP officials tried to save two young black men, Arthur Mack and Oscar Perry, who were sentenced to death in Georgia for killing a white night watchman under circumstances suggesting that they had acted in justified self-defense. When Marshall received word that pleas for clemency had been denied and that the youngsters would be executed, he took it upon himself to write a note of condolence to Perry's mother. He wrote tenderly, "I think you should face the situation with the feeling that you did all in your power . . . and that we did the very best we could to save the boys. . . . We join with you in your sorrow."[25]

CONTROVERSIES

Although Marshall's career at the NAACP and the NAACP Legal Defense Fund (LDF)* has been ably chronicled, certain controversies warrant more exploration and discussion. Several involve Marshall's activities during World War II. In September 1942, after the United States had entered the war, Winfred W. Lynn, a black American in New York City, refused induction into the army on the grounds that the racial quota that it used violated the government's own draft law and the federal Constitution. A judge ruled that Lynn's claims would not be adjudicated unless he submitted to induction. Determined to make his case, Lynn submitted to induction, only to witness courts continue to avoid deciding the merits of his complaint. Throughout his ordeal, Winfred Lynn was advised by his brother Conrad Lynn, who subsequently built a career as a formidable left-wing attorney. In *There Is a Fountain: The Autobiography of Conrad Lynn*, the lawyer alleges that Marshall refused to have anything to do with Winfred Lynn's case and indeed prevailed on the American Civil Liberties Union to withhold assistance.[26] On several occasions, I have recounted this allegation and implicitly validated it without substantiating the charge. That was a bad error on my part for which I apologize. It is true that Marshall did not participate in the case before the trial court or the court of appeals. The basis for his absence, however, appears to have been very different from

---

* The NAACP Legal Defense and Educational Fund was incorporated in New York in 1940. Donors to the LDF were allowed to make tax-exempt contributions, a tax advantage denied to the parent NAACP because of its lobbying activities. For a long period, the NAACP and the LDF overlapped fully in terms of personnel and governance. In 1957, however, due to pressure from the U.S. Treasury Department and segregationist foes, the organizations became truly independent of each other, working cooperatively but also becoming rivals. In the 1980s the NAACP unsuccessfully sued the NAACP LDF to prevent it from continuing to use the "NAACP" initials. *See NAACP v. NAACP Legal Defense and Educational Fund*, 753 F.2d 131 (D.C. Cir. 1985).

what Lynn charges. In his autobiography, Conrad Lynn writes, "I contacted the NAACP the day before argument was to take place [at a hearing for habeas corpus relief]. That organization refused to have anything to do with the case." If Marshall and the NAACP were contacted that belatedly—"the day before argument"—their absence is justified. No one could reasonably expect participation to follow such a tardy invitation. When Winfred Lynn (unsuccessfully) petitioned the Supreme Court to review the case, the NAACP supported him with an amicus curiae brief co-written by Marshall. The brief declared that "this case is of central importance to the more than thirteen million members of the Negro race in the United States."[27]

Although the mistreatment of African Americans as part of the mobilization for World War II was disgraceful, that was not the only shameful instance of racism perpetrated by the federal government. In a series of actions initiated or justified by leading figures including Franklin Delano Roosevelt, Earl Warren, and Hugo L. Black, the federal government unjustifiably subjected American citizens of Japanese ancestry to curfews, removals, and detentions. These outrages led to a number of Supreme Court decisions that ratified the government's conduct. The NAACP did not participate in this litigation. It would be useful to know more about the reticence of Marshall and the NAACP in the face of this massive racial injustice.[28]

Some observers charge that after World War II Marshall and his NAACP colleagues focused too narrowly on invalidating de jure segregation in public secondary and primary schooling while paying insufficient attention to the broader context in which black Americans found themselves marginalized and subordinated. This is the critique posited by Professor Risa L. Goluboff in *The Lost Promise of Civil Rights*.[29] She argues that Marshall paid too high a price for the flawed prize of *Brown v. Board of Education* and suggests that he might have accomplished more by pressing alternative claims. She charges that Marshall and the NAACP underestimated the massive racial obstacles that loomed over black America, particularly those stemming from private as opposed to governmental sources, wrongly abandoned assertiveness on behalf of black workers, and excessively distanced themselves from political tendencies on the left that were deemed "subversive" in Cold War America.

One can never know for sure whether Marshall might have been more successful had he pursued a different path. The unavoidable indeterminacy of counterfactualism suggests, to some, that "what if" thinking can never be of much scholarly utility. That is not my position. We are constantly, albeit implicitly, indulging in counterfactualism. In making a criticism of a given action we are conjecturing that it would have been better to have done something else. My problem with Goluboff is that she offers little basis for believing that her preferred alternative course of conduct would have had a better outcome than that which Marshall in fact pursued. She complains that Marshall and company were all too conventional doctrinally, that they should have made more use of the Thirteenth Amendment, and that they should have attacked the state action doctrine more broadly. She offers no sturdy predicate for believing, however, that Marshall could have been successful persuading courts to rule in favor of more ambitious demands. After all, the modest demands he made encountered stiff opposition and reaped limited advances. Armed with meager resources as he faced off against white supremacism nationwide, Marshall battled intelligently and heroically in every sort of judicial venue, including places in which the very presence of dissident black lawyers triggered open, vocal, ugly hostility. That in such circumstances he was able to accomplish as much as he did was extraordinary. Considering alternatives is a worthwhile endeavor. But counterfactualism should always be disciplined by a keen appreciation of the plausible.

A raw conflict that continues to produce hurt feelings has to do with the circumstances under which Jack Greenberg rather than Robert L. Carter succeeded Marshall as the boss of the LDF after Marshall left to become a judge on the U.S. Court of Appeals. Greenberg was white; Carter black. Carter was senior to Greenberg and had served with distinction as Marshall's deputy. But in 1956, Carter was named general counsel of the NAACP, a dubious "promotion" that handicapped him in the competition to succeed Marshall. The LDF had a larger legal staff than the general counsel's office at the NAACP, and its attorneys enjoyed comparatively greater independence insofar as the NAACP attorneys were subject to the oversight of the organization's nonlawyers. When Marshall resigned, Greenberg was named the LDF's new boss. Whereas Marshall was deferred to as the chief attorney for both the NAACP *and* the NAACP LDF, Greenberg and Carter proceeded independently as the chief executives of their respective fiefdoms. They were allies, but their relationship was competitive and testy. Greenberg appears to have wanted Carter to serve solely as in-house counsel to the NAACP, attending to internal organization issues, while the LDF handled all of the cases stemming from struggles against segregation and other racial wrongs. Carter refused to be cabined and instead built a rival staff that handled a variety of key cases, including school desegregation controversies in the North and the defense of activists, including lawyers, in the South. Greenberg remained at the helm of the LDF until 1984. Carter headed the NAACP general counsel's office only until 1968. He resigned in protest against the NAACP Board of Directors' firing of a staff attorney who published a critique of the Supreme Court in *The New York Times* under the provocative title "Nine Men in Black Who Think White."[30]

Opinions conflict over the decision to appoint Greenberg. The governing board of the LDF made the appointment, but there is little doubt that Marshall facilitated it. According to biographer Juan Williams, Marshall did not want Carter to head the LDF and worked to thwart him.[31] Marshall told me a different story. He said that Greenberg got the nod because he was the most senior attorney on the staff at the LDF after Carter's exit to the NAACP and that he thought that Greenberg would do an excellent job. Greenberg's account is similar to Marshall's: the appointment was mainly a function of seniority and hard-earned trust.[32] Carter offered two explanations. One is that Marshall had grown to dislike him. Another is that Marshall wanted Greenberg to succeed him because doing so would demonstrate an absence of bitterness toward white people—a demonstration that might come in handy in a potential confirmation struggle if racial conservatives claimed (as some in fact did) that Marshall would be unable to judge whites fairly.[33]

My impression is that Marshall exiled Carter mainly out of

personal pique. Carter's memoir reveals that he (justifiably) thought well of himself, believed that he had received too little appreciation for behind-the-scenes work for which his boss was lavishly credited, and had grown impatient with what he perceived to be an overly worshipful aura surrounding Marshall. To Carter, "Mr. Civil Rights," though admirable, was also blemished: he drank excessively, hobnobbed too much, and had allowed his attentiveness to his duties to wane. Carter was not the sort of person who could camouflage his feelings, and Marshall undoubtedly picked up on his dissatisfactions. Carter, moreover, imprudently shared his views, which, translated into gossip, undoubtedly got back to Marshall.*

Greenberg's elevation to the top position at the LDF elicited criticism from some who viewed it as an insult to the black bar. The argument went like this: Charles Hamilton Houston had had to prod the NAACP to give black lawyers a chance to litigate on its behalf. Now its offshoot, the LDF, was neglecting to do what Houston had done for Marshall. Instead, an enterprise mainly devoted to black uplift was installing as its head a white man. Greenberg's commitment was indisputable. He had shared unflinchingly the privations and dangers that his black comrades encountered. Still, Greenberg was not black and thus lacked a symbolic significance, the pertinence of which was on display whenever African Americans ventured into forbidding courthouses just to get an inspiriting glimpse of a *black* lawyer plying his trade.

A critical take on Marshall might view the choice of Greenberg over Carter not as an isolated occurrence but as part of a larger pattern, maybe even the inauguration of a pattern, in which Mr. Civil Rights neglected to do what he could and should have

* Constance Baker Motley, an outstanding LDF attorney and later a federal judge, offered a rather damning interpretation of Marshall's motivation in the succession struggle. She maintained that Marshall's preference for Greenberg stemmed from his "feud" with Carter. She also stated that Marshall preferred Greenberg to other plausible candidates, virtually all of whom were black, because he viewed them as having sided with Carter. Finally, she posited that "Thurgood also had difficulty with the idea of a woman in a leadership role in a male world." Constance Baker Motley, *Equal Justice Under Law* (1998), 150–54. As a Supreme Court justice, Marshall consistently and passionately supported antisexist policies.

done to advance the careers of black jurists. At the LDF he did hire several black attorneys in whom he reposed trust. One thinks here of Constance Baker Motley, Derrick Bell, and Franklin Williams. The number of black attorneys who can be identified as Marshall protégés, however, is strikingly small. I know of no blacks who served as his law clerk during his four-year stint (1961–1965) on the court of appeals. I know of no blacks who served on his staff during his two-year stint (1965–1967) as solicitor general. For the first six years of his tenure on the Supreme Court, Marshall had no black law clerks. His first, his goddaughter Karen Hastie Williams, worked for him in the 1974 Supreme Court term. Another six years passed before he hired another (in fact two in the 1980 term—Stephen L. Carter and Adebayo Ogunlesi). He never hired a law clerk from his alma mater, the Howard Law School. True, Marshall hired more black law clerks than his colleagues. But that constitutes a low bar.* I am not concluding that the paucity of blacks in Marshall's inner circle was all his fault.† I am suggesting that this is a neglected and potentially revealing subject that has been overlooked and warrants further exploration.

Another controversy again involves Carter and Marshall. Stung by the success of the drive against segregation in the 1950s, southern segregationists sought ways to hobble or eliminate the NAACP. In Alabama authorities charged that it had failed to comply with a law governing corporate filing requirements. An antagonistic segregationist judge enjoined the NAACP from operating within the state and ordered the organization to surrender its membership list to the state attorney general. There was little doubt that if the lists were disclosed, the identities of members would be publicized, subjecting them to intimidation and vilification and deterring others from becoming members. Carter and

---

* *See* Tony Mauro, "Diversity and Supreme Court Law Clerks," 98 *Marquette Law Review* 361 (2014). Justice Brennan, for example, never had a black law clerk. *See* Stephen Wermiel, "Justice Brennan and His Law Clerks," 98 *Marquette Law Review* 367, 373–74 (2014).

† When I worked for Marshall in 1983–1984, I examined the file of applicants for clerkships, specifically searching for black candidates. I found vanishingly few. But did Marshall publicize the possibility of obtaining a clerkship in his chambers? Or did a well-founded sense of futility discourage potential candidates?

Marshall differed over how to respond. Carter urged the NAACP to fight the order. Marshall counseled obedience. Professor Mark Tushnet, the leading student of Marshall's career as litigator, accepts the rationale that Marshall himself voiced: prudence dictated compliance because legal precedent disfavored the NAACP and it was impolitic to appear to flout the law.[34] In his memoir, published subsequent to Marshall's death, Carter posited a different, rather ugly motivation—stark self-interestedness:

> Thurgood's problem was that he felt he had reached his ultimate goal as NAACP-LDF head counsel. He was looking beyond the NAACP and the LDF, using his political influence to secure a court appointment, and he did not want his record marred by being guilty of contumacious conduct.[35]

If this account is accurate, it should be known. A full rendering of the historical record—no matter the hurt—is more important than protecting a contrived image. Carter offers, however, nothing beyond assertion in support of his reputation-mangling claim.

The NAACP rejected Marshall's advice. It fought the order successfully in litigation directed by Carter, culminating in a landmark decision in which the Supreme Court recognized the idea of constitutionally protected organizational privacy.[36]

What lessons are imparted by this controversy? Two come to mind. First, Carter's remarks highlight another neglected topic: the anger, envy, resentment, and distrust among peers that highly successful people like Marshall often face and surmount. Second, Carter's successful strategy shows that Marshall was not always right. In this case, Carter's counsel appears to have been the better advice.[37]

THE FIRST BLACK JUSTICE

The centerpiece of the second half of Marshall's long career was his service as the first black Supreme Court justice (1967–1991). His nomination by President Lyndon B. Johnson came as no big surprise. At Johnson's urging he had resigned his judgeship on the U.S. Court of Appeals (he had been elevated to that court by President John F. Kennedy in 1961) to serve from 1965 to 1967 as the first black solicitor general. Still, the nomination to the high court was by no means in the bag. Marshall recalled that LBJ expressly disclaimed promising a nomination if a Supreme Court vacancy arose. Moreover, alternatives to Marshall were bruited about from time to time. Clearly, though, Marshall enjoyed the inside track. Johnson's biographer Robert Dallek recounts that when an aide offered the name of A. Leon Higginbotham, a black federal district court judge, Johnson leaned forward and said that "the only two people who ever heard of Judge Higginbotham are you and his momma. When I appoint a nigger to the bench, I want everyone to know he's a nigger."[38]

In discussing Marshall's judicial record, admirers often take a defensive posture. This stems from combating a long train of unfair assessments. At Marshall's various confirmation hearings, racist senators smeared him. They charged or insinuated that he was "soft" on crime and communism, that he was prejudiced against southern whites, and, most galling, that he was insufficiently learned in the law to merit high judicial office. Even at several decades removed, it is stomach turning to read the transcripts of hearings in which Strom Thurmond, Sam Ervin, and John McClellan—senators who repeatedly showed flagrant disregard for constitutional rights—attempted to belittle one of the titans of the American bar. Others of a better mold also unfortunately questioned Marshall's abilities. Archibald Cox, whom Marshall had replaced as solicitor general (and who attained immortality as the intrepid initial special prosecutor in the Watergate scandal), remarked thoughtlessly to a reporter in 1976, "Marshall may not be very bright or hard-working, but he deserves credit for picking the best law clerks in town."[39]

The notion that Marshall was intellectually mediocre and lazy—deficiencies that resonate with centuries of allegations about Negro inferiority—became part of a derogatory portrayal disseminated by his detractors. On April 21, 1989, *National Review* published on its cover a caricature of Marshall asleep on the bench. That unflattering image was reinforced by the muckraking best seller by Bob Woodward and Scott Armstrong, *The Brethren:*

Inside the Supreme Court.[40] Largely based on information drawn from law clerks, *The Brethren* portrayed Marshall as a garrulous, inattentive, ineffective, undisciplined has-been. That view, or at least major parts of it, is held not only by Marshall's enemies; it is also held by some of his admirers.

How did Marshall perform as a justice?

In my estimation he performed outstandingly well.

There are competing theories of what should count as merit in a justice. Some give priority to a justice's influence as exemplified in Justice Antonin Scalia's success in popularizing originalism and textualism. Some give priority to eloquence, a quality for which Justice Robert Jackson is frequently praised. Some give priority to the virtues of the common-law judge—precision, subtlety, self-discipline, humility—attributes for which some canonize Justice John Marshall Harlan II.[41]

I see justices as, first and foremost, judicial policy makers acting in concert and tension with legislative and executive branch policy makers. I assess whether a justice has sensibly advanced key (small *r*) republican precepts and essential (small *d*) democratic values. These include an insistence that government is obligated to offer certain resources (for example, education, security, and freedom from impoverishment), that government is prohibited from indulging in invidious discrimination, that government is authorized (if not required) to take reasonable efforts to redress past or present communal wrongs, that in the absence of compelling circumstances government is barred from repressing expression, that government must be restrained by checks and balances, that government must respect fundamental zones of privacy, that government must be deterred from overreaching in its effort to identify criminality, and that government must accord robust constitutional protections to prisoners and must be restrained from deliberately extinguishing life as a punishment for even the most heinous offenses. Viewed through that prism, Justice Marshall's record is exemplary.

I know of no decision Marshall made as a justice that is rightly viewed as a profound moral blot.* The same cannot be said of

---

* Justice Marshall consistently supported the right of women to govern their bodies through abortion. *See*, for example, *Roe v. Wade*, 410 U.S. 113 (1973), and

Chief Justices John Marshall and Roger Taney (look at their complicity with slavery), Justices Oliver Wendell Holmes and Louis Brandeis (look at their complicity with Jim Crow), or Justice Hugo Black (the author of the egregious *Korematsu v. United States*[42]), Justice Byron White (the author of the cruel *Bowers v. Hardwick*[43]), or Justice Lewis Powell (the author of the execrable *McCleskey v. Kemp*[44]). Marshall refused to condone the purposeful killing of human beings by government, dissenting in every case in which the Supreme Court rebuffed final appeals from convicts on death rows seeking to avoid execution.

Marshall wrote 322 opinions for the Court.*[45] Two of the more notable are *Police Department of the City of Chicago v. Mosley*[46] and *Emporium Capwell Co. v. Western Addition Community Organiza-*

Harris v. McRae, 448 U.S. 297 (1980). Some will view that support as immoral. I view it as yet another indication of his wise commitment to the enlargement of human freedom.

* To what extent were Marshall's writings actually "his" writings? The question arises because much of what went out of Marshall's chambers was drafted by his law clerks. The question is pertinent to all who rely upon staff to produce the opinions, speeches, rulings, proclamations, and orders by which they carry out their duties. It is well known that Peggy Noonan played a major part in drafting speeches attributed to President Ronald Reagan, that Theodore Sorensen played a major part in drafting speeches attributed to President John F. Kennedy, that Richard Goodwin played a major part in drafting speeches attributed to President Lyndon B. Johnson, and that Jon Favreau played a major part in drafting speeches attributed to President Barack Obama. Obscurity continues to surround the identity of law clerks in the drafting of Supreme Court opinions. Clearly, though, clerks are the wordsmiths of much of what is attributed to the justices. Justice Louis Brandeis once quipped that the Supreme Court justices were "almost the only people in Washington who do their own work." But that day is long past. With commendable candor, Chief Justice William Rehnquist acknowledged, "The clerks do the first draft of almost all cases to which I have been assigned to write the Court's opinion." Artemus Ward and David L. Widen, *Sorcerers' Apprentices: 100 Years of Law Clerks at the United States Supreme Court* (2006), 224. He was no outlier. Students of the law clerk regime have estimated that some 30 percent of Supreme Court opinions issue with little or no editing by the justices. *Id. See also* Todd C. Peppers, *Courtiers of the Marble Palace: The Rise and Influence of the Supreme Court Law Clerk* (2006); Stuart Taylor Jr. and Benjamin Wittes, "Of Clerks and Perks," *Atlantic*, Aug. 15, 2006, www.theatlantic .com.

The convention is to credit with authorship the figure who gives authority to a given writing or speech. There is no reason why that convention ought not to apply to Justice Marshall. *See* Mark Tushnet, "Thurgood Marshall and the Brethren," 80 *Georgetown Law Journal* 2109 (1992).

tion.[47] *Mosley* brought into question the constitutionality of a city ordinance that prohibited picketing within 150 feet of a school except peaceful picketing related to a labor dispute. On behalf of the Court, Marshall wrote an opinion striking down the ordinance because it impermissibly privileged, based on content, one type of expression—peaceful picketing involving a labor dispute—over another type of expression: picketing involving other subjects. "Above all else," Marshall declared, "the First Amendment means that government has no power to restrict expression because of its message, its ideas, its subject matter, or its content." There is, he insisted, "'an equality of status in the field of ideas,' and government must afford all points of view an equal opportunity to be heard. Once a forum has been opened up to assembly or speaking by some group, government may not prohibit others from assembling or speaking on the basis of what they intend to say."[48] Enthusiastically lauded by leading commentators on constitutional law, *Mosley* articulated powerfully an equality principle within First Amendment jurisprudence.[49]

Emporium Capwell arose from a labor dispute in which black workers complaining of racial discrimination picketed an employer outside the procedures agreed to by their union through collective bargaining. The workers went outside those procedures because, in their view, the union was failing to represent them adequately. The workers claimed that the employer violated their rights under the National Labor Relations Act (NLRA) by punishing them for the picketing. The employer argued that the workers forfeited protection under the NLRA when they acted on their own outside the union's authorization. The National Labor Relations Board ruled against the picketing workers. A U.S. Court of Appeals reversed. At the Supreme Court two organizations representing interests and traditions that resonated deeply with Marshall found themselves at odds with each other. The AFL-CIO, insisting that workers fared better when they recognized the primacy of union sovereignty, urged reversal. The NAACP, by contrast, urged affirmance, insisting that black workers should not be divested of a right to self-help in battling racial discrimination, especially given the long record of racial prejudice within American unionism.

Writing for the Court, Justice Marshall concluded that the

lower court had erred, that the dissidents should have conducted themselves within the protocols determined by their union, that employers ought to be relieved of the burden of bargaining with several, perhaps competing, bands of workers, and that the NLRA was best understood as respecting union solidarity absent circumstances irrelevant to this case. His resolution of *Emporium Capwell*, one of the few disputes in which Marshall rejected the pleas of the NAACP, displayed a deeply ingrained skepticism toward anything that approximated what he perceived as separatist, Black Power racial politics.* It also manifested his strong inclination to support unions because he viewed worker solidarity—even at the expense of black workers' independence—as essential in struggles between labor and capital. Of all of Marshall's opinions, none has been more pointedly criticized by many of his usual allies.[50]

More celebrated than his opinions for the Court are Marshall's many dissents—363, along with 83 concurrences.[51] Three of the most important dissents involve public education. In *San Antonio Independent School District v. Rodriguez*,[52] the issue was whether it was a violation of the federal Constitution for public education to be financed via local property taxes that create massive disparities in expenditure between poor and rich districts. Reversing a lower court, the Supreme Court, 5 to 4, upheld the constitutionality of this widespread practice. In the course of

---

* Taking a position at variance with Marshall's, Judge Charles Edward Wyzanski Jr. wrote,

> To leave non-whites at the mercy of whites in the presentation of non-white claims which are admittedly adverse to the whites would be a mockery of democracy. Suppression, intentional or otherwise, of the presentation of non-white claims cannot be tolerated in our society even if, which is probably at least the short-term consequence, the result is that industrial peace is temporarily adversely affected. In presenting non-white issues non-whites cannot, against their will, be relegated to white spokesmen, mimicking black men. The day of the minstrel show is over.

Western Addition Community Organization v. NLRB, 485 F.2d 917, 940 (D.C. Cir. 1973) (Wyzanski, J., dissenting), *rev'd sub nom. National Labor Relations Board v. Western Addition Community Organization*, 419 U.S. 816 (1974), and *rev'd sub nom. Emporium Capwell Co. v. Western Addition Community Organization*, 420 U.S. 50 (1975). Justice Marshall, of course, was neither a minstrel nor a patron of minstrelsy.

reaching its conclusion, the Court rejected the claim that socio-economic class discrimination should receive heightened judicial scrutiny. Marshall excoriated what he portrayed as "a retreat from [the Court's] historic commitment to equality of educational opportunity."*[53] The Court did this, he complained, "despite the absence of any substantial justification for a scheme which arbitrarily channels educational resources in accordance with the fortuity of the amount of taxable wealth within each district."[54]

In *Milliken v. Bradley*,[55] the question was whether a federal court had exceeded its authority by ordering suburbs to participate in a busing program to remedy racial segregation in the public schools of Detroit. The Supreme Court, 5 to 4, ruled that the lower court did indeed exceed its authority. The Court held that if suburbs were not at fault for segregation in the Detroit schools, suburbs could not be enlisted as part of a remedy. The Court was declaring, in essence, that the judiciary was unauthorized to subject "innocent" white suburbanites involuntarily to busing for purposes of racial desegregation. Criticizing the Court, Marshall wrote that its holding was "more a reflection of a perceived public mood that we have gone far enough in enforcing the Constitution's guarantee of equal justice than it is the product of neutral principles of law."[56] He observed that "in the short run, it may seem to be the easier course to allow our great metropolitan areas to be divided up each into two cities—one white, the other black—but it is a course, I predict, our people will ultimately regret."[57]

In *Regents of the University of California v. Bakke*,[58] the question was whether a public medical school violated the Constitution when, engaging in "affirmative action," it set aside sixteen out of one hundred places for applicants deemed to be disadvantaged members of racial minority groups. In one of the Court's most controversial post-1960s decisions, it invalidated the admissions set-aside. Justice Marshall maintained, by contrast, that the defendant's affirmative action program was consistent with the Constitution. He argued that seeking to remedy past racial wrongs

---

* Here Marshall was imagining a prior judicial commitment in order to create the predicate for bemoaning its putative abandonment. Sadly, there existed little in the way of a "historical commitment to equality of educational opportunity" on the part of the Supreme Court. Its holding in *San Antonio Independent School District* was not a "retreat" but the Court's default position.

ought to be seen as a justifiable reason for using race as a factor in selecting candidates for a scarce number of seats in a university. "It must be remembered," he admonished, "that during most of the past 200 years the Constitution as interpreted by this Court did not prohibit the most ingenious and pervasive forms of discrimination against the Negro. Now, when a state acts to remedy the effects of that legacy of discrimination, I cannot believe that this same Constitution stands as a barrier."[59]

Like his fellow Marylander the former slave Frederick Douglass, Marshall (who attended Frederick Douglass High School) was a feminist, though I never heard him refer to himself as such. He championed the advancement of women and vigilantly opposed legalized sexism. In *Personnel Administrator of Massachusetts v. Feeney*,[60] the Court reviewed a state statute which provided that all veterans who qualified for civil service positions must be considered for appointment ahead of any qualifying nonveterans. This strong preference for veterans, a large majority of whom were men, had a dramatic adverse impact on women. Because less than 2 percent of women in Massachusetts were veterans, the preference resulted in a state civil service that was overwhelmingly male except in certain exempted categories of lower-grade clerical and secretarial positions traditionally relegated to women.* The Court upheld the constitutionality of the preference, noting that it was formally gender neutral; female veterans received a heavy preference, as did male veterans. Most important to the Court, while the record indicated that lawmakers were aware that the preference would have the effect of disadvantaging women, the record did not show that the purpose of lawmakers was specifically to disadvantage women. That women on the whole were collaterally disadvantaged was unfortunate, the Court maintained, but in and of itself amounted to no constitutional violation.

Justice Marshall, on the other hand, inferred "purposeful gender-based discrimination" in the state's choice of a preference

---

* The female plaintiff in the case, Helen B. Feeney, a nonveteran, was repeatedly bumped downward on lists of prospective candidates as veterans, always men, were placed ahead of her despite her superior performance on standardized competitive civil service examinations. In 1973 she was placed in a position behind twelve male veterans, though her scores were better than all of theirs. *Personnel Administrator of Massachusetts v. Feeney*, 442 U.S. 256, 264 (1979).

scheme that adversely affected women so dramatically.* Marshall
believed that if the gender shoe had been on the other foot—if
the preference at issue had hurt men as much as this one hurt
women—the state would surely have resorted to some other, less
burdensome alternative, and that therefore its decision to maintain the veterans preference was an invidious discrimination.

A dissent of Marshall's frequently cited by fans of the justice
arises from *United States v. Kras*,[61] in which he argued that people
should be excused from having to pay a fee to file for bankruptcy
if they lack the means to do so. The Court's opinion (written by
Justice Harry Blackmun) made light of the petitioner's asserted
inability to pay, stating that saving up to pay the filing fee in weekly
installments would have cost "less than the price of a movie and
little more than the cost of a pack or two of cigarettes."[62] Marshall
objected. While it was "perfectly proper for judges to disagree
about what the Constitution requires," he wrote, it "was disgraceful for an interpretation of the Constitution to be premised upon
unfounded assumptions about how people live."[63] According to
Marshall, the Court had no clue how close Kras and others like
him live "to the margin of survival. The desperately poor almost
never go to see a movie, which the [Court] seems to believe is
almost a weekly activity."[64]

Justice Marshall was not a systematic thinker seeking to further a given methodology or propound a particular theory of law
or justice. He was an eclectic, pragmatic realist who did what
he could to advance a liberal, egalitarian ethos in opinions that

* Although neutral in form, Marshall declaimed, "the statute is anything but
neutral in application. It inescapably reserves a major sector of public employment to 'an already established class which, as a matter of historical fact, is 98%
male.' . . . Where the foreseeable impact of a facially neutral policy is so disproportionate, the burden should rest on the State to establish that sex-based considerations played no part in the choice of the particular legislative scheme. . . .

"Clearly, that burden was not sustained here. The legislative history of the
statute reflects the Commonwealth's patent appreciation of the impact the preference system would have on women, and an equally evident desire to mitigate
that impact only with respect to certain traditionally female occupations. . . .

"Particularly when viewed against the range of less discriminatory alternatives available to assist veterans, Massachusetts' choice of a formula that so
severely restricts public employment opportunities for women cannot reasonably be thought gender-neutral." *Id.* at 284–85 (Marshall, J., dissenting).

occasionally pushed to the leftward margin of conventional legal thought. His opinions, though, sometimes lapsed into familiar but unpersuasive and mythologizing tropes. Consider his dissent in *Payne v. Tennessee*, which was issued the day he announced his retirement.[65] In that case, the Court ruled, reversing itself, that the Eighth Amendment did not bar a sentencing jury in a capital trial from considering "victim impact" evidence relating to the victim's personal characteristics and the effect of the murder on the victim's family. Dissenting, Justice Marshall fervently championed *stare decisis*, asserting that "fidelity to precedent is part and parcel of a conception of the 'judiciary as a source of impersonal and reasoned judgments.' "[66] It was, of course, a bit ironic for Justice Marshall to issue a formalistic paean to the virtues of judicial deference to inherited case law. He became Mr. Civil Rights by undermining and then smashing precedent. But he was not above appealing to conservative arguments if such were all he thought he could turn to for the purpose of attaining humane ends.

THE JUSTICE AS REFORMER

From time to time Justice Marshall succeeded in creating openings, sustaining initiatives, and building support that enabled him to effectuate beneficent reforms from within the Supreme Court. One of those campaigns changed the federal constitutional law governing peremptory challenges. A peremptory challenge is a device that allows attorneys to exclude a certain number of prospective jurors from a jury without having to offer a justification. Peremptory challenges give attorneys a method by which they can use their intuitions to strike certain prospective jurors who they believe will have an adverse effect on their cause. Without regulation, peremptory challenges also give attorneys a device with which they can freely impose racial discrimination in the seating of jurors.

On May 31, 1983, Justice Marshall, joined by Justice William Brennan, dissented from the Court's denial of certiorari*

---

* Most parties seeking review in the Supreme Court do so by petitioning for a writ of certiorari. This writ is granted or denied at the discretion of the justices.

in three cases in which criminal defendants challenged the constitutionality of their convictions on the grounds that prosecutors had used peremptory challenges in a racially invidious way.[67]
One of the cases the Court refused to review was *McCray v. New
York*.[68] McCray had been prosecuted for robbery. He was black.
His alleged victim was white.[69] McCray's first trial ended with a
hung jury. In a second trial, he was convicted by an all-white jury.
In the process of selecting this jury, the prosecutor used peremptory challenges to exclude all seven of the Negroes who sat on
the panel of prospective jurors. Charging that a racial purpose
prompted the prosecutor's action and that such conduct violated
the federal Constitution, McCray's attorney sought a hearing to
examine the prosecutor's motivation.[70] This motion, however, was
denied, on the basis of the Supreme Court's 1965 ruling in *Swain
v. Alabama*.[71]

Swain involved the prosecution of a black man convicted and
sentenced to death by an all-white jury for raping a white woman
in Talladega County, Alabama.[72] Although 26 percent of the people eligible to sit on juries in this county were black, no African
American had ever sat on a trial jury in Talladega County.[73] Typically just one black or a small number of blacks sat on grand juries
or on the jury panels from which trial juries were chosen. But
when it came time to select the jury that would ultimately decide
a defendant's fate at trial, blacks were always excluded pursuant to
peremptory challenges, sometimes at the behest of the defense,
but more often at the behest of the prosecution. In Swain's case,
the prosecution struck all six of the potential Negro jurors.[74]
Swain's attorneys objected. The trial court ruled against the defendant's constitutional challenge, as did the Supreme Court of Alabama.[75] The case was then appealed to the U.S. Supreme Court.

The Court, speaking through Justice Byron White, concluded
that there was nothing in the federal Constitution that required a
court to examine the motives behind a prosecutor's use of peremp-

---

Four justices must vote to grant the petition in order for a case to be reviewed
by the Court. For an excellent review of the history of the Court's certiorari
jurisdiction and the practice of dissents from denial of certiorari, *see* Peter Linzer,
"The Meaning of Certiorari Denials," 79 *Columbia Law Review* 1227 (1979).

tory challenges in any given case.[76] According to Justice White, "The presumption in any particular case must be that the prosecutor is using the State's challenges to obtain a fair and impartial jury to try the case before the court." He went on to say that this "presumption is not overcome and the prosecutor therefore subjected to examination by allegations that in the case at hand all Negroes were removed . . . because they were Negroes. Any other result," Justice White maintained, "would establish a rule wholly at odds with the peremptory challenge system as we know it."[77] Therefore, Justice White concluded, "we have decided that it is permissible to insulate from inquiry the removal of Negroes from a particular jury."[78] One explanation was deference to tradition, a fear that subjecting the prosecutor's challenge to the demands of the equal protection clause in any particular case would entail "a radical change in the nature and operation of the challenge. The challenge . . . would no longer be peremptory, each and every challenge being open to examination."[79] Another explanation was that striking jurors on the basis of race in pursuit of a winning litigation strategy posed no equal protection violation because, presumably, members of any group are similarly vulnerable. In one case, trial strategy might dictate using peremptory challenges to get rid of as many black prospective jurors as possible. But then in the next case, trial strategy might dictate getting rid of as many whites as possible. Because everyone would be subject to the vagaries of trial tactics, no one could complain of being singled out for exclusion.

The Court did recognize the danger that prosecutors might use peremptory challenges to exclude blacks from juries "for reasons wholly unrelated to the outcome of the particular case on trial," namely purposefully denying to Negroes as a class "the same right and opportunity to participate in the administration of justice enjoyed by the white population."[80] This, the Court concluded, would constitute a violation of the equal protection clause and ought not to be permitted.[81] In outlining what would signal an impermissible use of peremptory challenges, however, the Court set forth a strikingly heavy burden. A constitutional problem might arise, Justice White wrote, only if a prosecutor "in case after case, whatever the circumstances . . . is responsible for the removal of Negroes . . . with the result that no Negroes ever serve on petit juries."[82] The Court found that the defendant in *Swain* did not meet this burden.[83]

Eighteen years later, in his dissent from denial of certiorari in *McCray*, Justice Marshall pointed out that "since it was decided, *Swain* [had] been the subject of almost universal and often scathing criticism."[84] He set forth several objections, two of which are particularly significant. First, he questioned why the prosecutorial exercise of peremptory challenges should be allowed episodic exemptions from constitutional scrutiny—why a prosecutor should *ever* be allowed to purposefully exclude a person from a jury on the basis of race. As Marshall put the matter, "Since *every* defendant is entitled to equal protection of the laws and should therefore be free from the invidious discrimination of state officials, it is difficult to understand why several must suffer discrimination . . . before any defendant can object."[85] Second, he emphasized that, in his view, the standard of proof the Court demanded for identifying the illegitimate use of peremptory challenges "imposes a nearly insurmountable burden on defendants."[86]

Justice Marshall therefore urged his colleagues to grant certiorari "to reexamine the standard set forth in *Swain*."[87] To attract the votes of those justices who might be repulsed by *Swain* but anxious about the prospect of directly overruling precedent, Justice Marshall set forth an alternative: making an end run pursuant to the Sixth Amendment. Noting that *Swain* was decided under the equal protection clause of the Fourteenth Amendment, Justice Marshall suggested that the Sixth Amendment right to be tried by an impartial jury drawn from a fair cross section of the community provided a basis for subjecting prosecutorial peremptories to the sort of scrutiny that *Swain* rejected.[88] Furthermore, to allay concerns about the practicability of what he was suggesting, Marshall noted that two state supreme courts, interpreting state constitutions, had rejected the *Swain* approach and created workable alternatives.[89]

Justice Marshall needed to convince two other justices besides himself and Justice Brennan in order for the Court to review *McCray* and reexamine *Swain*. He failed to do this, but he did obtain something for his efforts. Justice John Paul Stevens, joined by Justices Blackmun and Powell, stated that their vote to deny certiorari did not reflect disagreement with Justice Marshall's appraisal of the importance of the underlying issue, but was simply a judgment that the issue was not yet ripe for reexamination.[90] Observing that there existed no conflict of decisions within the federal system and that only two state court systems had charted a different course, Justice Stevens concluded that in his view "it is a sound exercise of discretion . . . to allow the various States to serve as laboratories in which the issue receives further study before it is addressed by this Court."[91]

That Justice Stevens publicly expressed sympathy for Justice Marshall's position was noteworthy. Justice Stevens had recently chastised colleagues for publishing dissents from denial of certiorari, a complaint that fell most heavily on Justice Marshall, who had dissented from denials of certiorari most frequently and with the greatest amount of elaboration. After 1973, Justice Marshall, along with Justices Brennan, Stewart, and William O. Douglas, routinely issued dissents from denial of certiorari in cases arising from obscenity prosecutions.[92] After 1976, Justice Marshall, along with Justice Brennan, issued dissents from denial of certiorari in every petition arising from the imposition of a death sentence.[93]

Most of Justice Marshall's dissents from denial of certiorari arising from the obscenity and capital punishment cases expressed a defiant unwillingness to bow to precedent with which he disagreed. By contrast, his dissent from denial of certiorari in *McCray* was infused with more hopefulness of achieving an immediate goal. It was aimed at encouraging others to press for the reexamination of *Swain* by signaling that he was actively sympathetic to that cause.

At the beginning of the new Supreme Court term in 1983, Justice Marshall again urged his colleagues to reconsider *Swain*. On October 3, 1983, he dissented from the Court's denial of certiorari in a capital punishment case, *Gilliard v. Mississippi*.[94] In *Gilliard* the prosecution used all eight of its peremptory challenges to remove all of the prospective Negro jurors.[95] Justice Marshall directly addressed Justices Stevens, Blackmun, and Powell. He wrote that although he appreciated the reasons behind their "inclination to delay until a consensus emerges on how best to deal with misuse of peremptory challenges," he believed that in this instance that inclination was "inappropriate and ill-advised":

> When a majority of this Court suspects that ... rights are being regularly abridged, the Court shrinks from its constitutional duty by awaiting developments in state or other federal courts. Because abuse of peremptory challenges appears to be most prevalent in capital cases, the need for immediate review in this Court is all the more urgent. If we postpone consideration of the issue much longer, petitioners in this and similar cases will be put to death before their constitutional rights can be vindicated. Under the circumstances, I do not understand how in good conscience we can await further developments, regardless of how helpful those developments might be to our own deliberations.[96]

Justice Marshall declared that he could abide no further delay. But, alas, the fact that he was dissenting meant, of course, that he had no choice in the matter. Again he was joined only by Justice Brennan.

Seven months later, on May 14, 1984, Justice Marshall published a dissent involving three death penalty cases from Illinois.[97] Despite the desperate circumstances, however, he rejected the temptation to indulge in empty rhetorical blasts. Instead, he continued carefully to build a record for the position he advocated. He set forth legal arguments that attorneys and judges might use in other forums to attack *Swain*. And he methodically recorded the dismal facts animating his determination to see *Swain* undone.[98] He noted that in two of the Illinois cases, a black defendant had been sentenced to death after prosecutors used peremptory challenges to remove all of the blacks who might have sat on the defendant's jury.[99]

His frustration growing, Justice Marshall took this opportunity to remind his colleagues that over the preceding twelve months he had twice urged the Court to reconsider the issues implicated by *Swain*. "These petitions," he wrote, "present the Court with three more opportunities to protect criminal defendants against jury-selection procedures that are clearly racially discriminatory. Again today," he pleaded, "I urge my colleagues to grant certiorari on what I believe to be one of the gravest and most persistent problems facing the American judiciary today."[100]

A little over a month later, on June 25, 1984, Justice Marshall again dissented from denial of certiorari. This time he dissented in a Texas case that, in his view, further illustrated the proposition that "prosecutorial abuse of peremptory challenges [had] grown to epidemic proportions."[101]

At the end of the October 1983 term it might have seemed that Marshall's elaborate dissents from denial of certiorari had borne little fruit. Even though Justices Stevens, Blackmun, and Powell had previously indicated some degree of sympathy for his desire to revisit *Swain*, they all kept quiet on this issue throughout the term, despite Justice Marshall's repeated, and increasingly agitated, entreaties. The dissents, however, had not been in vain. Lawyers and judges had already begun to use them to prod the Court into revisiting *Swain*.

After the Supreme Court denied certiorari in *McCray* on direct review, the defendant's lawyers sought habeas corpus relief from the federal district court.[102] These attorneys emphasized the arguments made by Justice Marshall and pointed to the Stevens opinion, representing the views of three other justices.[103] This prompted Judge Eugene H. Nickerson to break away from the grip of *Swain*. In an opinion handed down on December 19, 1983, he noted that "it is unusual, to say the least, for a district court to reexamine a Supreme Court case squarely on point. . . . But surely," Judge Nickerson continued, "there is some invitation implicit in Justice Stevens' opinion for the lower courts to engage in such reconsideration."[104] Addressing the merits of *Swain*, and explicitly tracking Justice Marshall's dissent, Judge Nickerson ruled that *Swain* should be modified, that "the equal protection clause should be construed to prohibit a prosecutor's exercise of peremptory challenges to exclude blacks solely on the basis of race in any case," and that McCray should therefore be granted habeas corpus relief.[*105]

* Seven years earlier, another federal district court judge had tried to reform the law governing peremptory challenges. In *United States v. Robinson*, 421 F. Supp. 467 (D. Conn. 1976), Judge Jon O. Newman invoked the supervisory power of

Judge Nickerson's ruling was affirmed, creating a conflict within the federal system that moved additional justices to vote in favor of reconsidering *Swain*. That reconsideration finally took place during the Supreme Court's 1985 term. *McCray*, however, was not chosen as the vehicle for this task. Instead, the Court decided to revisit *Swain* by adjudicating a case that was appealed from the Supreme Court of Kentucky, a case titled *Batson v. Kentucky*.[106]

In *Batson*, in a 7-to-2 decision written by Justice Powell, the Court overturned the principal holding of *Swain*.[107] It ruled that the equal protection clause is violated when a prosecutor strikes a prospective juror because of that juror's race.[108] This is so, the Court ruled, even if the challenge to the prosecutor's action is limited to a single case without evidence of racially discriminatory peremptory strikes in other cases.[109]

Batson was an important personal triumph for Justice Marshall. Yet, after having toiled so strenuously to have *Swain* overruled, he declined to bask in the glory of vindication. In a concurrence, he noted the limits of the Supreme Court's new position. He congratulated the Court on taking "a historic step toward eliminating the shameful practice of racial discrimination in the selection of juries."[110] He went on to say, however, that the Court's decision would "not end the racial discrimination that peremptories inject into the jury-selection process."[111] That goal, he averred, could be accomplished only by eliminating peremptory challenges entirely, a conclusion he reached by investigating the experience of jurisdictions that had already experimented with the policy the Court was prescribing. One problem was that "defendants cannot attack the discriminatory use of peremptory challenges at all unless the challenges are so flagrant as to establish a prima facie case. . . . Prosecutors are left free to discriminate against blacks in jury selection provided that they hold that discrimination to

---

the district court over federal criminal trials to rule against the U.S. Attorney's office in Connecticut. At that time, eleven years after *Swain*, no other federal or state judge had ever upheld a challenge to a prosecutor's use of peremptories. Judge Newman's intervention, however, was short-lived. Three months after his decision, a panel of the Second Circuit issued a sharply worded writ of mandamus vacating his order. *United States v. Newman*, 549 F.2d 240 (2d Cir. 1977).

an 'acceptable' level."[112] A second problem was that even "when a defendant can establish a prima facie case, trial courts face the difficult burden of assessing prosecutors' motives. . . . Any prosecutor can easily assert facially neutral reasons for striking a juror, and trial courts are ill equipped to second-guess those reasons."[113] A third problem was that "even if all parties approach the Court's mandate with the best of conscious intentions, that mandate requires them to confront and overcome their own racism on all levels"—a challenge he doubted prosecutors could meet.[114] He argued that a prosecutor's *unconscious* racism would often lead him or her to strike a prospective black juror on the grounds that that person appears to be "sullen" or "distant" or possessed of some other troubling trait—characterizations that would not have come to mind if a white juror had acted identically.[115]

Justice Marshall's conclusion—that erasing invidious discrimination in the selection of juries requires the abolition of peremptory challenges—constituted a critique of a position he had previously held. He had previously suggested that opening peremptories to challenge in individual cases would suffice. But he changed his mind, perhaps because of what he himself had learned from his series of dissents from denial of certiorari. He thus demonstrated characteristics that made him special: willingness to modify a previous position, recognition of the depth of the racial crisis confronting the nation, attentiveness to the difference between the law on paper and the law in action, and commitment to speaking his mind even at the price of isolation in the short run.*

---

* Another example of Marshall's effectiveness at changing colleagues' minds is *Ake v. Oklahoma*, 470 U.S. 68 (1985). Glen Burton Ake was sentenced to death after a trial at which he pleaded not guilty by reason of insanity but was deprived by lack of money to access to a psychiatric expert witness of his own who might have been helpful in answering the state's psychiatric expert witness. When Ake sought review, the Supreme Court initially denied his petition for certiorari. Marshall took several weeks to write an extensive dissent from the denial. That dissent prompted several justices to change their minds and vote to hear the case. The next term the case was heard, and in an opinion written by Justice Marshall, the Court held that in capital cases in which indigent defendants raise an insanity defense, states must make available to them some access to a psychiatric expert witness.

THE TRAGIC RETIREMENT

Marshall used to say to us clerks that if he died, we should just prop him up and keep on voting. That was one of his typical jokes—funny with a dark side. The reality, though, was darker still. For Marshall was forced to witness the seating of a successor whom he knew to be hostile to values he cherished. It must have been painful for him to see Clarence Thomas occupy the position he had held for twenty-four years. It must have been even more painful for him to realize that if he had held on for just five more months, he would have enabled a new president, Bill Clinton, to nominate a liberal replacement. As it turned out, he announced his retirement in June 1991, acknowledging that he was old and "coming apart." He thereby armed President George H. W. Bush with an opportunity to push the Court further to the right.

Is Marshall properly criticized for waiting too long to retire? This question takes on added poignancy in the aftermath of Justice Ruth Bader Ginsburg's death, President Trump's selection of a right-wing successor, and criticism of Ginsburg's refusal to retire when President Obama could have ensured the selection of a liberal replacement.[116] It is a fair question. A justice ought to be attentive to the consequences of his or her death or retirement and, to the limited extent possible, try to affect the Court's trajectory by influencing its makeup. For a justice to be inattentive to the timing of his or her exit is to be naive, delusional, or selfish. Given the gulf that separates Marshall's progressive jurisprudence from Thomas's reactionary commitments, it is all but impossible to avoid wondering (though this issue has been submerged) whether Marshall bears some fault for this regrettable declension.

Marshall did not suddenly become old and infirm in 1991. In 1976, after suffering a series of heart attacks, he was asked about retiring and responded that he had no such plans.* That was when Gerald Ford was president. A few years later, during Jimmy Car-

---

* Justice Marshall enjoyed recounting the following story. According to the justice, after falling ill and being sent to a hospital, he received a visit from an aide to President Richard Nixon, purportedly for the purpose of conveying best wishes. Marshall declined to speak to the aide but did write a message for the president. The message was "Not Yet."

ter's presidency, Marshall is reported to have received hints from the White House that retirement would be welcome insofar as it would enable a Democratic president to appoint a successor who would carry on the justice's legacy or at least refrain from dismembering it.* Marshall rebuffed the suggestion. The surrounding circumstances are unclear. But if the hint was delivered with anything other than utmost delicacy, one can understand how Marshall would take offense. When Marshall declined to retire, he was "only" in his late sixties and had sat on the Court for only a bit more than a decade. By contrast, when some observers unsuccessfully urged Justice Ruth Bader Ginsburg to retire during President Barack Obama's first term, she was in her late seventies and had served for more than fifteen years. There was no way that Marshall could have known that Carter was destined to be a one-term president and that the Republican hold on the White House would last so long.

CODA

On a cold, wet, windy day in January 1993, from ten in the morning until midnight, a steady flow of people filed into the Great Hall of the Supreme Court to pay their respects to Thurgood Marshall, who had just died. They somberly passed his cas-

---

* The person who stood the best chance of being tapped by President Carter as Justice Marshall's replacement was Wade McCree, an African American who was then serving as solicitor general. *See* "Uncle Sam's Attorney," *Time*, Oct. 23, 1978, content.time.com.

A graduate of Fisk and Harvard Law School, McCree had comported himself ably as a federal trial and appellate judge. It seems, though, that McCree and Marshall were not especially friendly toward each other and that on at least one occasion Marshall angrily (and mistakenly) perceived the younger man to have disrespected him. *See* Juan Williams, *Thurgood Marshall: American Revolutionary* (1998), 362–64.

Given that the door of what-if counterfactualism has been opened, it should be noted that Marshall outlived McCree, who died in 1987. *If* Carter had nominated McCree and *if* the Senate had confirmed him and *if* he had voted as expected, the ideological makeup of the Supreme Court might not have been substantially altered even *if* Marshall had retired sooner. Still, what happened after Marshall's forced retirement was a cautionary tale to which Justice Ginsburg should have paid more attention.

ket, which was draped with a flag and supported by the same bier on which Abraham Lincoln's coffin had rested. By evening, the number of mourners had reached nearly twenty thousand.

The justice would have been surprised. I had heard him grumble that people seemed to have forgotten the civil rights champions of the 1940s and 1950s: figures such as Walter White, William Hastie, and Charles Hamilton Houston. I got the impression that Justice Marshall felt that he, too, had been eclipsed by those who led the protests of the 1960s, particularly Martin Luther King Jr. As mourners filed past his coffin, however, people from all walks of life showed their appreciation. Beneath a portrait of the justice, one mourner placed a copy of the Supreme Court's opinion in *Brown v. Board of Education*. At the bottom of the first page, the anonymous admirer wrote, "You shall always be remembered."

As I stood with clerks and family members to pay homage to the justice, I recalled his delightfully unfashionable dress (he often wore white socks with black shoes); his insistence upon using the word "Negro" (though at the end of his tenure he had begun to use the term "Afro-American"); the singularity of his questioning of attorneys at oral argument (in a case involving the constitutionality of a regulation prohibiting people from sleeping in public parks, Marshall asked the deputy solicitor general of the United States whether *he* had ever been homeless). I remembered the thrill of being able to talk with him daily and felt anew how lucky I had been to know him.

21

Isaac Woodard and
the Education of J. Waties Waring[1]

On February 12, 1946, at Camp Gordon, Georgia, Isaac Woodard was honorably discharged from the army. A poor black rural southerner, he had served in World War II as a longshoreman, loading and unloading military ships that were sometimes under fire. Three citations honoring his military service graced the uniform that Woodard wore as he boarded a Greyhound bus headed to Winnsboro, South Carolina, where he was to be reunited with his wife. During the bus ride, Woodard requested a toilet break. The bus driver responded with cursing. The veteran cursed back, exclaiming, "I am a man just like you." For that assertion of equality, he paid dearly. The driver reported Woodard, and upon exiting the bus, the veteran was hit over the head with a blackjack by Lynwood Shull, the chief of police in Batesburg, South Carolina. Woodard had done nothing to provoke Shull, yet Shull proceeded to whack Woodard with the blackjack several more times as he dragged him to jail. One of those assaults occurred after Shull asked Woodard whether he had been discharged from the army. When Woodard answered "yes," Shull immediately struck him, admonishing him to respond, "yes, sir." After further beating Woodard, Shull jabbed his baton into the veteran's eyes, one after the other, blinding him. Following a night in jail, Woodard was taken before a local judge who fined him $50. The veteran was then transported to a hospital where physicians determined the full, terrible extent of his injuries.

Shull's assault was part of a postwar pattern of racially motivated atrocities. Two weeks after Woodard's blinding, a riot had
erupted in Columbia, Tennessee, following an altercation featuring a black veteran who had had the temerity to defend himself
when slapped by a white radio repairman. Blacks rallied to his aid
to ward off a lynching, whereupon state police reacted wildly, van-
dalizing black businesses (for example, writing "KKK" on coffins
in a mortuary), stealing jewelry and cash, and beating, shooting,
and arresting scores of blacks indiscriminately. In Georgia, when
a black veteran, Maceo Snipes, dared to vote in the Democratic
primary—the only African American to do so in his rural county—
white men shot him dead in retribution. Elsewhere in Georgia, a
black farmhand, Roger Malcolm, got into a dispute with his white
employer who had reportedly made sexual advances on Malcolm's
pregnant wife. Malcolm stabbed the man in a fight. A white mob,
including police officers, captured Malcolm, his wife, and another
black couple. As the mob prepared to murder the two black men,
one of their wives, pleading for mercy, called the name of a white
man she recognized. Rather than heeding her entreaties, the
mob decided to leave no black witnesses. It shot all four captives
execution-style and castrated Malcolm. In Minden, Louisiana,
John C. Jones, a black veteran, and his seventeen-year-old cousin,
Albert Harris, were subjected to the wrath of a mob because of
an unlucky confluence of two facts: they had both been seen in a
white woman's backyard, and Jones had previously complained of
unfairness in a land transaction, conduct that had marked him as
"an uppity nigger." Harris was pistol-whipped but survived. Jones
was killed with a meat cleaver and blowtorch.

The National Association for the Advancement of Colored
People (NAACP) made the attack on Woodard the centerpiece
of a campaign to combat racially motivated violence. It organized
a tour that brought Woodard to pulpits and auditoriums nationwide to publicize the police brutality that had maimed him. Addi-
tionally, the campaign sought to raise desperately needed funds to
supplement Woodard's paltry veterans' benefits; because he had
been discharged hours before he was injured, the government
took the position that he was ineligible for full disability assistance. The NAACP also affiliated itself with other groups to cre-

ate the National Emergency Committee Against Mob Violence, which succeeded in conveying to President Harry S. Truman the dire situation on the ground. A directive from Truman himself prompted an indictment of officer Shull.

The prosecution, however, failed miserably. Hostile agents at the Federal Bureau of Investigation declined even to obtain a copy of Woodard's hospital records. The prosecutors, based in the U.S. Attorney's office in South Carolina, were incompetent and indifferent. They paid no attention to jury selection and failed to subpoena key witnesses. The lead prosecutor did not even ask the jury to convict. Instead, his insipid closing argument ended with his saying that the government would be satisfied with "whatever verdict you gentlemen bring in."

By contrast, the defense was aroused and vehement and prepared to use every available argumentative weapon, including open appeals to regional resentment and racial prejudice. "If a decision against the government means seceding, then let South Carolina secede again," thundered Shull's defense counsel. Continuing, he maintained that Woodard belonged to "an inferior race that the South has always protected" and that Woodard's back talk to the bus driver indicated that the veteran must have been intoxicated because "that's not the talk of a sober niggra in South Carolina." The all-white jury acquitted Shull after deliberating for less than half an hour.

In a peculiar twist, the farcicality of the trial prompted the presiding judge to reset the course of his life. The U.S. district court judge J. Waties Waring was a South Carolina blue blood, an eighth-generation Charlestonian. After stints as an assistant U.S. Attorney, a private attorney, and corporation counsel for Charleston, Waring had been elevated to a judgeship in 1942 by President Franklin Delano Roosevelt. Judge Waring presided over the case involving Woodard's assailant four years into his judicial tenure. At that point, he seemed to be solidly attached to white racial orthodoxy, which meant, among other things, being reliably loyal to segregation and black disenfranchisement. Even early on, however, he displayed an unusual willingness to recognize inconvenient facts that other judges in the Deep South were prone to ignore. In 1944, Waring ruled in favor of African American plaintiffs who accused the Charleston, South Carolina, school board of violating their rights under the Fourteenth Amendment by paying white teachers more than similarly situated black teachers. The black teachers' lawyer, Thurgood Marshall, recalled that that was "the only case I ever tried with my mouth hanging open half the time." He was struck that "Judge Waring was so fair." Waring had not questioned the validity and wisdom of racial segregation. He had insisted, however, that local authorities heed their legal obligation to offer blacks "equal" services and facilities, even if they were separate.

By the time the Shull prosecution reached him in 1946, Waring's personal circumstances had changed substantially. He had divorced his wife of thirty years, a fellow Charlestonian, with whom he had a child. South Carolina did not permit divorce, so parties seeking one had to leave the state. At Judge Waring's insistence, his wife had moved for a brief period to Florida, where she divorced him. As if that were not scandal enough for the tightly knit highest echelon of Charleston upper-crust white society, Judge Waring had then proceeded to marry a twice-divorced, rich northerner who had proven herself quite willing to defy social conventions. She attended Shull's trial, was shocked by what she witnessed, and, along with the judge, undertook to educate herself more fully about the racial facts of life in the Jim Crow South. Together they read books such as W. J. Cash's *Mind of the South* and Gunnar Myrdal's *An American Dilemma*.

Following the failed prosecution of Chief Shull, Judge Waring handed down the two signature decisions of his judicial career. In *Elmore v. Rice* (1947), Judge Waring invalidated the state Democratic Party's white primary. Because virtually all elected officials in South Carolina were Democrats, the Democratic Party effectively disenfranchised blacks by excluding them from voting in its primary. Responding to the 1944 Supreme Court decision in *Smith v. Allwright* invalidating the white primary in Texas, South Carolina's governor, Olin Johnston, had persuaded the state legislature to erase from its statute books all laws regulating primaries in order to buttress the claim that the Democratic Party was a private organization beyond the reach of the federal Constitution. Insisting that "we must keep our white Democratic primaries pure and unadulterated," the governor declared that once all of the statutes were repealed, "we will have done all within our power to guarantee white supremacy in our primaries." Judge Waring, however, blocked the attempted evasion of *Smith*. He noted that, regardless of its form, the primary of a major party performs an essential governmental function that should be subject to constitutional standards. "It is time," Judge Waring wrote, "for South Carolina to rejoin the Union. It is time to fall in step with the other states and to adopt the American way of conducting elections."

Influential white supremacists denounced Waring's ruling, even though it was upheld by a conservative court of appeals. *The Charleston Evening Post*, which was edited by Judge Waring's nephew, condemned the decision, maintaining that it "arbitrarily" encroached upon "the rights of private citizens" and arrogated to the courts "the power to amend the Constitution by judicial fiat." Such a response was gentle, however, in comparison with the reaction against Judge Waring's most daring opinion: his dissent in *Briggs v. Elliott*.

In *Briggs*, poor, rural South Carolina blacks accused officials of violating their federal constitutional rights by relegating black children to separate school facilities that were unequal to those afforded to white children. Clarendon County served some 6,531 black students and 2,375 white ones. Yet, exclusive of salaries, the county spent $395,000 on the white schools but only $282,000 on the black schools. Officials offered bus transportation to white children but not to black children. White schools enjoyed running water and indoor toilets, whereas black schools did not.

Thurgood Marshall's initial complaint on behalf of his clients focused on the contrast between the educational facilities; he challenged the constitutionality of segregation only obliquely. Judge Waring urged privately, and rather aggressively, that Marshall rescind the initial pleading and file a new complaint, this time expressly challenging the constitutionality of segregation per se. Judge Waring's advice stemmed partly from his recent conversion to anti-segregationism; he had come to believe that Jim Crow arrangements constituted a dire social evil that should be eradicated immediately. The advice also reflected a strategic calculation. Attacking the constitutionality of the state law requiring segregation would trigger the convening of a three-judge federal district court panel whose ruling would proceed directly to the Supreme Court for review.

Marshall followed Judge Waring's advice, but the defendants surprised everyone by confessing that they had failed—inadvertently, of course!—to provide equal resources to black and white students. They sought to preclude proceedings that would have shown in stark detail the extent to which local and state officials had shortchanged African American children. The local federal court unsurprisingly accommodated that strategy. One member of the panel was Chief Judge John J. Parker, whose nomination to the Supreme Court by President Herbert Hoover had been scuttled by opposition from organized labor and the NAACP. Another member was Judge George Bell Timmerman Sr., the head of an influential political family; his son would become the state's governor in 1955. Outvoting Waring, Parker and Timmerman found in favor of the plaintiffs but did not question segregation. Taking refuge in a mountain of judicial precedent, they ordered the local authorities to provide equality within the confines of "separate but equal."

Judge Waring took a dramatically different tack in his dissent. First, he deplored the "judicial evasion" that allowed the *Briggs* court to avoid grappling with the constitutionality of racial segregation in public schooling. Second, he lauded the bravery and public-spiritedness of black plaintiffs suing state officials in a suit seeking racial justice. He wrote that the plaintiffs had "shown unexampled courage in bringing . . . this cause at their own expense in the face of the long established and age-old pattern of the way of life which the State of South Carolina has adopted and practiced and lived in since and as a result of the institution of human slavery." The plaintiffs and their supporters had been fired from jobs, threatened with violence, deprived of essential emergency assistance, and subjected to trumped-up criminal charges. Judge Waring, to his everlasting credit, bestowed upon these heroic dissidents the recognition that they had too often been denied.

Third, Judge Waring let loose with a full-throated denunciation of racism embodied in law. "The whole discussion of race," he asserted, "has been intermingled with sophistry and prejudice. . . . What possible definition can be found for the so-called white race, Negro race or other races?" He excoriated "the sadistic insistence of the 'white supremacists' in declaring that their will must be imposed irrespective of rights of other citizens." He denounced "the false doctrine and patter called 'separate but equal,'" declaring that racial segregation in education "can never produce equality." Insisting that Jim Crow education "is an evil that must be eradicated," and that "segregation is *per se* inequality," Judge Waring maintained that segregation in South Carolina public schools "must go and must go now."

There were a few other judges at the time who outspokenly condemned racism in American law: Justice Frank Murphy at the U.S. Supreme Court (see his indictment of state harassment of Japanese Americans in *Oyama v. California* [1948]), Justice Roger J. Traynor at the Supreme Court of California (see his castigation of a state law prohibiting interracial marriage in *Perez v. Sharp* [1948]), and Judge Henry W. Edgerton at the U.S. Court of Appeals for the District of Columbia Circuit (see his objection to judicial enforcement of racially restrictive housing covenants in *Hurd v. Hodge* [1948]). None of those jurists, however, resided in the Deep South, and none outdid Waring in rhetorical ferocity.

Waring was already persona non grata among the ruling figures of the state, his conduct having attracted intense disapproval. He had desegregated his courtroom, positioning prospective black jurors on the same benches as prospective white jurors. He had hired a black bailiff. He had entertained blacks at his home and permitted them to enter through his front door. But his dissent in *Briggs* provoked a whole new level of enmity. Previously perceived as something of an obnoxious oddball crank, he was now regarded as a dangerous enemy—indeed, the worst of all enemies: a traitor. The Charleston *Post and Courier* warned ominously that the ascendency of Waring's views would lead to "mixed race schools," which would in turn lead to "the extermination of the white race."

White Charleston reviled Waring. Friends deserted him, and strangers threatened him. A cross was burned on his lawn, and a brick was thrown through a window of his home. He became the target of a campaign seeking his impeachment. Most politically engaged blacks, however, praised him. A local leader of the NAACP told Waring, "The people of my group have thanked God for you in the past. America will thank God for you in the future and at some later date the South will raise a monument to you."*

Soon after handing down his dissent in *Briggs*, Judge Waring retired and moved to New York City, where he spent the remainder of his life. President Truman lauded him as "a very great judge." *The New York Times* observed that he had served with "courage, integrity and intelligence." Even his hometown adversary, the *News and Courier*, complimented him, albeit equivocally, writing that but for his "crusading on the Negro question," Waring had made "an excellent record on the bench."

Judge Waring lived to see the Supreme Court follow his lead in finding racial segregation in public schooling to be unconstitutional in a bundle of cases known as *Brown v. Board of Education*. Although one of those cases was *Briggs*, Chief Justice Earl Warren's famous opinion in *Brown* made no mention of Waring's prescient dissent.

There is a feature of Judge Waring's conduct in *Briggs* that is difficult to square with ordinary understandings of judicial propriety. Recall that he had "advised" Thurgood Marshall to attack segregation head-on. In so doing, he had violated ethical norms and generated a conflict of interest. After all, as a sitting judge he was assessing the legal validity of the very advice he had offered to plaintiffs' counsel. Admirers of Judge Waring can take the position that, despite his breach of judicial ethics, he is nonetheless entitled to praise because of the good that he attempted to accomplish. Alternatively, they can opine that in extreme circumstances judicial propriety should be subordinated to other priorities and

---

* One memorial to Waring is the DeLaine Waring African Methodist Episcopal Church in Buffalo, New York. Established in 1956, the church is named after Judge Waring and the Reverend Joseph Armstrong DeLaine, the church's founding pastor. Reverend DeLaine was a leader in the effort to challenge racial discrimination in schooling in Clarendon County, South Carolina. An upshot of his activism was the *Briggs* litigation. Reverend DeLaine had to flee South Carolina to escape trumped-up criminal charges. Like Judge Waring, he was turned into a refugee by white supremacism in his home state.

that this was one such case. Whatever the ultimate moral calculation, it is clear that Waring transgressed conventional norms under which judges are typically expected to forgo advocacy in the very cases they adjudicate.

Judge Waring died on January 11, 1968. For years obscurity shrouded his heroic judgments and fascinating life. Then, in 1987, Professor Tinsley E. Yarbrough wrote a biography, *A Passion for Justice: J. Waties Waring and Civil Rights.* In 2011, the South Carolina Supreme Court Historical Society sponsored a two-day conference on Waring. In 2015, a statue was erected outside the federal courthouse in Charleston to memorialize him. The next year, the federal courthouse itself was named in his honor as a result of a remarkable turnabout. The courthouse had already been named in honor of Ernest "Fritz" Hollings, a former South Carolina governor and U.S. senator. Hollings himself asked that his name be removed from the building and replaced by Waring's. Displaying humility rarely seen in a politician, Hollings explained that he had simply raised the money for the courthouse, whereas Waring had "made history in it."

Another milestone in the rehabilitation of Waring's legacy was the publication of Judge Richard Gergel's *Unexampled Courage: The Blinding of Sgt. Isaac Woodard and the Awakening of President Harry S. Truman and Judge J. Waties Waring,* the principal source of facts for this essay.* Gergel's account offers a rich compendium of sharply drawn profiles: Isaac Woodard, who lived a difficult, scuffling life and died apparently unaware of his own historical significance; President Truman, who, though a lifelong racist,

---

* Gergel is himself a notable figure in the history of the Deep South. He and his wife, Belinda Gergel, played major roles in organizing remarkable commemorations of significant but neglected African American jurists in South Carolina, including Jonathan Jasper Wright, the first black to sit on any state supreme court, and Matthew J. Perry, a leading civil rights attorney who became the first black to sit on a federal court in South Carolina. Judge Gergel also presided over the 2017 trial of Dylann Roof, the white supremacist who killed nine black parishioners at a Charleston church in an effort to start a race war. *See* William Lewis Burke Jr. and Belinda Gergel, eds., *Matthew J. Perry: The Man, His Times, and His Legacy* (2004); Schuyler Kropf, "Judge: Pioneering Justice Deserves Notice," *Post and Courier,* March 15, 2011; Jelani Cobb, "Inside the Trial of Dylann Roof," *New Yorker,* Jan. 30, 2017.

surprised many with the strength and sincerity of his support for African Americans' civil rights; George Elmore, the hero of black enfranchisement in South Carolina who died penniless because of his lawsuit; Walter White, the multitalented, effervescent executive secretary of the NAACP who could pass for white but identified as a black man; and Lynwood Shull, Woodard's unrepentant assailant who died at the age of ninety-two and was remembered in his community "as a kindly and faithful elderly usher at the local Methodist church." Judge Waring, however, is the figure to whom Judge Gergel pays the most attention, memorably bringing to life a privileged outcast who magnificently betrayed his clan.

22

J. Skelly Wright: Up from Racism[1]

Judge J. Skelly Wright's principal claim to historic prominence is found in rulings he made to promote racial justice. Over the course of his thirty-seven years on the bench, he made notable contributions in many areas of law, including the protection of fairness in commercial transactions and the protection of federal constitutional civil liberties in disputes involving the press, protesters, and criminal defendants. But the decisions for which he is most highly esteemed are those in which he advanced the frontiers of racial decency in his home state of Louisiana.[2]

Born on January 14, 1911, in New Orleans, Wright grew up in a large family of modest circumstances. He attended Loyola University for college with the help of a scholarship. He took law school courses at Loyola at night while teaching high school during the day. After serving in the Coast Guard during World War II, practicing law privately, and snagging an appointment as a U.S. Attorney, Wright was seated as a federal trial court judge in New Orleans in 1950. No reliable detailed evidence is available about his racial attitudes at that time. It can be assumed, however, that he had said or done nothing that would lead key local political figures to think that he harbored heterodox views that conflicted significantly with prevailing white supremacist assumptions. Otherwise he would not have been appointed.

For a long time, white supremacist attitudes and federal constitutional law were compatible because of the Supreme Court's maiming of the Reconstruction Amendments. The Court had created an array of doctrines that permitted courts to overlook obvious invidious racial discriminations. In the 1930s and 1940s, however, the Court changed course, interpreting the Reconstruction Amendments with ever-increasing solicitude for racial minorities. By the 1950s a stark conflict had become unavoidable: southern judges had to ally themselves with either local segregationist custom or national desegregationist reformism. Wright chose the latter.

In 1950 the Louisiana Constitution dictated that "separate public schools shall be maintained for the education of white and colored children." Statutes criminalized interracial marriage; prohibited interracial adoptions; decreed that ticket offices could not be less than twenty-five feet apart at circuses admitting whites and blacks; prohibited the renting of dwellings "to a negro person or negro family when such building is already in whole or in part in occupancy by a white person or white family"; and insisted upon equal but separate accommodations aboard intrastate buses and trains.[3]

Enforcing the Fourteenth and Fifteenth Amendments, Judge Wright issued rulings that undermined Louisiana's pigmentocracy. Finding that the registrar of voters in Washington Parish had refused to register Negroes "solely on account of their race and color," Judge Wright prohibited the continuation of that practice.[4] Later he ordered that same registrar to desist from participating in a new scheme of racial disenfranchisement pursuant to which the White Citizens' Council was systematically challenging the eligibility of prospective black voters. Refusing to be misled by pretextual explanations, Judge Wright wrote that "a court need not . . . shut its mind to what all others can see and understand."[5]

After the Supreme Court belatedly repudiated the "separate but equal" doctrine in *Brown v. Board of Education* and subsequent decisions, Judge Wright followed suit resolutely.* In 1957 he

---

* Even before *Brown*, when the baleful concept of "separate but equal" remained "good" federal constitutional law, Judge Wright issued rulings that hastened desegregation in Louisiana higher education. Writing in *Wilson v. Board of Supervisors*, 92 F. Supp 986 (E.D. La. 1950), *aff'd per curiam*, 340 U.S. 909 (1950), Judge Wright (joined by Judge Wayne Borah and Judge Herbert Christenberry)

struck down laws requiring racial segregation in the New Orleans public parks and transit system.[6] Soon thereafter he invalidated the law that barred blacks and whites from competing against one another athletically.[7]

By far the most controversial of Judge Wright's decisions were those in which he became the first federal judge to order school desegregation in a major city in the Deep South. He applied *Brown v. Board of Education* to the public schools of New Orleans. He must have known that ordering desegregation would trigger militant resistance. According to historian Neil R. McMillen, "Louisiana moved with rapidity second to none in establishing an official attitude of defiance [to *Brown*]."[8] Three days after Chief Justice Warren announced the landmark holding, both houses of the Louisiana Assembly ratified a resolution censuring the Supreme Court for what the lawmakers termed an "unwarranted and unprecedented abuse of power."[9] The legislature then promulgated a new constitutional provision that reiterated Louisiana's commitment to racial segregation in public schooling. Segregation was required, the legislature insisted, "not because of race" but rather "to promote and protect public health, morals, better education and the peace and good order in the State."[10] The legislature, moreover, established the Joint Legislative Committee to Maintain Segregation; enacted provisions directing the Louisiana State Board of Education to disregard graduation certificates issued by any racially desegregated public school; withheld from any racially desegregated public school books, supplies, and lunches; and criminalized the conduct of any person, firm, or corporation that violated the new legislation.

These anti-*Brown* enactments were held to be unconstitutional by a three-judge panel that included Judge Wright.[11] Subsequently, sitting alone, Judge Wright enjoined the Orleans Parish School Board from continuing racial segregation. He did not order immediate desegregation. Indeed, he intimated that actual desegregation might not be forthcoming "even in a year or more."[12] Echoing the Supreme Court's invocation of "all deliberate speed"

---

concluded that state authorities had failed to satisfy the requirements of *Plessy v. Ferguson*, 163 U.S. 537 (1896), by consigning blacks to a law school that was separate and *un*equal.

in *Brown*, he directed local officials only to begin making arrangements for racially nondiscriminatory education, stressing the need for circumspection:

> The problems attendant desegregation in the deep South are considerably more serious than generally appreciated in some sections of our country. The problem of changing a people's mores, particularly those with an emotional overlay, is not to be taken lightly. It is a problem which will require the utmost patience, understanding, generosity and forbearance from all of us, of whatever race.[13]

Judge Wright insisted, though, that ultimately *Brown* would be enforced.

For the next four years the school board ignored the new constitutional dispensation, wholly rejecting the black community's demands, even though the majority of the school system's pupils were African American. Eventually, the school board polled parents about whether they would prefer to "see the schools closed rather than integrated" or "kept open, even though a small amount of integration is necessary." The school board conceded that it considered only the wishes of the whites, 82 percent of whom voted for closure rather than integration. "I will abide by the wishes of the white people," the board president declared, "because they are the people who support the school system and elect us."[14]

On May 16, 1960, Judge Wright announced his own plan for desegregation pursuant to which first-grade students at the start of the next school year would be permitted to attend "at their option" the school nearest their residence.* Though the order's

---

* The plan, in whole, reads as follows:

> A. All children entering the first grade may attend either the formerly all-white public school nearest their homes or the formerly all-Negro public school nearest their homes at their option.
> B. Children may be transferred from one school to another, provided such transfers are not based on considerations of race.

See *Bush v. Orleans Parish School Board*, 187 F. Supp. 42, 43n2 (E.D. La. 1960).

scope was quite limited in that it applied only to first graders, the Louisiana white power structure reacted hysterically. The state legislature enacted yet another battery of laws that renewed the requirement that white and Negro schoolchildren be separated, again barred state assistance to desegregated schools, and again criminalized conduct violating the prohibition of desegregation. The legislature also authorized the governor to close any school in the state that was ordered to desegregate, and to close *all* schools in the state if even one should be integrated.

Characterizing these and kindred laws as nothing more than "additional weapons in the arsenal of the State for use in the fight on integration," Judge Wright enjoined officials from enforcing them.[15] The Louisiana legislature, however, defiantly declined to desist. Lawmakers made it a criminal offense for agents of the federal government, including judges, to attempt to enforce *Brown;* required the Louisiana State Board of Education to revoke the license of any teacher who instructed a class in violation of the constitution and laws of Louisiana (that is, a desegregated class); required the board to terminate the employment of any principal who allowed a teacher to instruct a desegregated class; and denied promotion or graduation credits to any student who attended a desegregated class. All of these provisions were eventually annulled by Judge Wright and his colleagues.

The Orleans Parish School Board belatedly submitted a plan of its own. That plan relied upon the state's pupil placement law, which, by being purposefully cumbersome, was intended to discourage blacks from seeking transfers to "white" schools. The law was also intended to provide officials with nonracial pretexts for denying transfer requests. In a move that disappointed the activists spearheading desegregation, Judge Wright accepted the board's proposal. He also pushed back by ten weeks his deadline for initiating desegregation. November 14, 1960, became the new, historic day for a twentieth-century breaching of the race bar in public education in New Orleans.*

---

* Judge Wright stated later that he pushed back the date for desegregation in order to secure a commitment for backup from the Department of Justice in the event that Louisiana officials disobeyed court orders and to spare the Eisen-

Under the school board's direction, only four black girls were allowed to attend "white" schools. But even that minuscule amount of "race mixing" generated widespread apocalypticism. The governor called the legislature into a special session at which it hurriedly enacted twenty-nine new laws for the purpose of delaying or preventing desegregation. The session was, as two historians of the episode observe, "a legislative carnival unique in the annals of American lawmaking."[16] Then, on November 12, the state superintendent of schools declared November 14 to be a statewide school holiday. Judge Wright immediately cited him for contempt of court. The legislature then replicated the superintendent's order. Judge Wright enjoined the governor and the entire legislature, directing the Orleans Parish School Board to proceed to desegregate regardless of the actions of state officials.

On November 14, 1960, federal marshals escorted the four black first graders to schools whose identities had been kept secret to minimize the likelihood of disruption. Marshals accompanied three of the girls to the McDonogh No. 19 Elementary School and the fourth to the William J. Frantz Elementary School. Two days later white segregationists held a rally sponsored by the White Citizens' Council. "Let's don't be cowed," William Rainach, a leading state politician, declared. "Let's use the 'scorched-earth' policy. Let's empty the classrooms where they are integrated."[17] Not to be outdone, Leander Perez, the most influential of the hard-core segregationists, railed against communists, "Zionist Jews," that "weasel, snake-head mayor of yours," and that "smart-alec mulatto lawyer," Thurgood Marshall. He urged his listeners to take their case more forcefully to the school board. "Don't wait for your daughter to be raped by these Congolese. Don't wait until the burr-heads are forced into your schools. Do something about it now."[18]

For hundreds of white high school students, doing "something" included engaging in hooliganism in downtown New Orleans, where they ran in and out of public buildings, banged

---

hower administration from having potentially to deal with a crisis right before a presidential election. *See* Adam Fairclough, *Race and Democracy: The Civil Rights Struggle in Louisiana, 1915–1972* (1995), 238.

on the locked doors of the mayor's office, and harassed blacks. For many white segregationist parents, doing "something" meant boycotting the desegregated schools. The boycotters not only withdrew their children from these schools; they also put pressure on others to maintain white segregationist solidarity. Boycotters created a gauntlet of shrieking mothers that had to be run twice daily by whites who took their children to school. These nonconformists also suffered by having their tires slashed, their home windows shattered, and their porches bespattered with paint. One white family that had a child at Frantz attempted to defy the boycott but then encountered financial difficulties when the father quit his position as a municipal gas-meter reader following taunting from coworkers. Unable to find another job, he moved to Rhode Island with his wife and six children. It is no wonder that by the end of November only two white children continued to attend the Frantz School while none continued to attend McDonogh No. 19.

Despite the boycott and the state government's hostility to Judge Wright's enforcement of *Brown*, desegregation in the New Orleans public schools survived, if only tenuously. Judge Wright's refusal to retreat had resounding importance. His stand changed the parameters of legitimacy, of what was right and wrong in the eyes of the law. As a practical matter, however, racial separation remained the dominant practice, sustained by authorities who deployed the pupil placement law to minimize transfers. In 1961, only twelve blacks were permitted to attend previously "white" schools where they faced racist affronts at every step.

Judge Wright occupies a place among the pantheon of judges who helped to advance the frontiers of racial justice in the 1950s and 1960s, joining a cadre that includes Earl Warren, William J. Brennan, J. Waties Waring, Henry W. Edgerton, Elbert P. Tuttle, and John Minor Wisdom.[19] Three points of supplementation are in order. First, while the efforts of Judge Wright and his colleagues warrant recognition, so, too, do the efforts of those, often overlooked, who brought their cases to courthouses. What enabled Judge Wright to become a heroic jurist was the courage of plaintiffs who braved intimidation to vindicate their rights and those of their children. Honor is certainly due to Judge Wright. But honor is also due to the plaintiffs who, guided by their attorneys, insistently knocked on courthouse doors until they received at least some semblance of appropriate relief.[*]

Second, Judge Wright and his family suffered much on account of his anti-segregationist rulings. A cross was burned on his lawn. He and his family received countless threatening and obscene letters and phone calls. Former friends shunned the Wrights.[20] At the same time, Judge Wright retained his racial prestige as a white man and also enjoyed the extra protection afforded by his status as a judicial officer of the United States—privileges that did not extend to those whose petitions he adjudicated.

Finally, it should be noted that the relationship between judicial decision making and judges' own beliefs about race is more ambiguous than their rulings may suggest. Repudiating the constitutional legitimacy of de jure segregation did not necessarily require believing that blacks are the intellectual, moral, and cultural equals of whites. Justice John Marshall Harlan, for example, was a white supremacist, even though his dissent in *Plessy v. Ferguson* was an eloquent, comprehensive, and prescient condemnation of Jim Crow segregation. With respect to Judge Wright, it is clear that he was unequivocally committed to carrying out the anti-segregationist orders of the Supreme Court. It is unclear, however, whether at the time of the *Bush v. Orleans Parish* litigation he was fully committed to the proposition that blacks are as capable as whites and as deserving of every consideration bestowed upon white citizens. It is true that when he invalidated de jure racial segregation in the New Orleans public schools, Judge Wright

---

* Richard Kluger makes this point beautifully in the opening pages of his magisterial history of *Brown v. Board of Education*, where he rightly begins the story not with the justices of the Supreme Court but with the plaintiffs and the people who stood with and behind them. *See* Richard Kluger, *Simple Justice: The History of Brown v. Board of Education and Black America's Struggle for Equality* (1975, 2004), 3–25. In her history of the New Orleans school desegregation struggle, Liva Baker is similarly mindful of the special racial burden that the plaintiffs and their black attorneys shouldered. *See* Liva Baker, *The Second Battle of New Orleans: The Hundred-Year Struggle to Integrate the Schools* (1996). She recognizes that "parties to legal suits against the white establishment risked heavy losses." *Id.* at 153. For information regarding the principal local attorney representing the *Bush* plaintiffs, *see* Rachel L. Emanuel and Alexander P. Tureaud Jr., *A More Noble Cause: A. P. Tureaud and the Struggle for Civil Rights in Louisiana* (2011).

movingly averred that "we are, all of us, freeborn Americans with a right to make our way, unfettered by sanctions imposed by man because of the work of God."[21] One must also contend, however, with evidence that the pervasive racism that surrounded him for so long tainted his perceptions, intuitions, and habits.[22] "When I shake hands with a Negro," he remarked in 1960 to a British journalist, "I have a different feeling than when I shake hands with a white." He added that he did not "intend to associate personally with Negroes."[23]

Yet, in that same interview, Judge Wright related an anecdote that he would subsequently draw on time and time again. Looking out a window at Christmastime, he glimpsed a party being held in a neighboring building, the House for the Blind. The party-goers were being sorted by race into different rooms. He then realized that left on their own without the external imposition of an artificial divide, the sightless partygoers would have recognized no racial differences. At that moment, he said, he understood the cruel silliness of segregation. As Judge Wright spoke, the journalist observed, he became "so moved that he could not complete the story for several minutes."[24] Obviously Judge Wright was conflicted.

It is to his credit that Judge Wright invested himself so personally in puzzling over the requirements of racial justice. Although he was already an imposing, influential figure, he allowed himself to be corrected and instructed. Through this process of ongoing education he grew, infusing later phases of his career with lessons hard won in the ferocious battles he fought in Louisiana. In 1962, pursuant to nomination by President John F. Kennedy, Judge Wright moved to the U.S. Court of Appeals for the District of Columbia Circuit, where he became even more of a crusading jurist, pushing the limits of legal liberalism.*

---

* His most important racial case after moving north was *Hobson v. Hansen*, in which he invalidated putatively race-blind policies that, in his view, perpetuated racial segregation in the District of Columbia public schools. *See* 269 F. Supp. 401 (D.D.C. 1967) aff'd sub. nom., *Smuck v. Hobson*, 408 F. 2d 175 (D.C Cir. 1969). For commentary on this controversial decision, *see* Donald L. Horowitz, *The Courts and Social Policy* (1977); "*Hobson v. Hansen*: Judicial Supervision of the Color-Blind School Board," 81 *Harvard Law Review* 1514 (1968); Beatrice A.

· · ·

I clerked for Judge Wright in 1982–1983. Receiving an offer to work for him was a thrill. He was highly esteemed in legal academia, particularly at my alma mater, Yale Law School, where there is now a chaired professorship named in his honor. I recall reading opinions by Judge Wright in law school casebooks (most notably his now-classic invocation of the contracts doctrine of unconscionability in *Williams v. Walker-Thomas Furniture Company*) and hearing debates among professors regarding the character of his decision making. As he aged, Judge Wright became increasingly adventurous jurisprudentially, doing what he perceived justice required notwithstanding the inhibitions of law. Many liberals praised his opinions on behalf of the poor, racial minorities, consumers, protesters, criminal defendants, and environmentalists. Many conservatives were appalled. During the year that I worked for him, he wrote an opinion for the court that directed the Food and Drug Administration to regulate the use of drugs in executions by lethal injection. The case stemmed from an effort to throw a wrench into the gears of capital punishment. The law clerk assigned to the case had advised Judge Wright to reconsider his position because, if he proceeded, the Supreme Court would surely reverse his judgment. Judge Wright declined to change course. The prospect of reversal by his superiors at the Supreme Court did not faze him. He remarked with a laugh, "They cannot catch me every time." While the Court did indeed reverse Judge Wright,[25] I suspect that its disapproval failed to convince him that he had acted wrongly. He had a deep and abiding antipathy to capital punishment. In 1946 he had represented a man on death row, Willie Francis, who survived a botched execution by an electric chair that malfunctioned. Attorney Wright argued that it would be a violation of due process to allow Louisiana a second try. The Court rebuffed that argument, 5 to 4, and Francis was subsequently killed by a "successful" execution.[26]

Moulton, "*Hobson v. Hansen:* The De Facto Limits on Judicial Power," 20 *Stanford Law Review* 1252 (1968). *See also* Louis Michael Seidman, "J. Skelly Wright and the Limits of Liberalism," 61 *Loyola Law Review* 69 (2015).

Whatever one's opinion of Judge Wright's methodology, the fact is that he was a major jurist who figured importantly in the key struggles of his time. Who could be more attractive professionally to a newly minted lawyer? Judge Wright, moreover, was known to place virtually all of his clerks with justices at the Supreme Court. Obtaining a clerkship with Judge Wright thus meant access to a valuable twofer: an opportunity to work with a distinguished, liberal, crusading judge and an increased likelihood of receiving a subsequent offer from one of the justices. (This pattern held for me: after working for Judge Wright, I clerked for Justice Marshall, while my co-clerks proceeded to work for Justice Sandra Day O'Connor.)

My year with Judge Wright was difficult. My co-clerks (one of whom had attended Harvard Law School and the other of whom had attended Stanford) were, at that time, much more knowledgeable and skilled than me. The difference was clear and the gap in performance sometimes embarrassing. I am not ashamed to acknowledge that reality. I perceived it at the time and worked hard to catch up. There was, however, a racial aspect to the situation. I was the only black clerk in Judge Wright's chambers, one of only two whom he hired over the course of his long career, and the only African American law clerk that year at the Court of Appeals for the District of Columbia Circuit (just as I would be the only black law clerk the next year at the Supreme Court). I have called upon that experience on many occasions. I tell students to beware of misplaced pride and debilitating self-protectiveness. There is no disgrace whatsoever in recognizing that a peer or group of peers may be superior to you in some way at a given moment in time. It is regrettable if, out of willed pretense, you overlook the need for and means of self-improvement. Where you are on day 1 is not nearly as important as where you are on day 365 or on day 1,000 or on day 2,000.

Judge Wright treated me with respect and cordiality. He criticized my shortcomings sharply but fairly. We were never close emotionally. But I knew that he had bestowed upon me a distinct privilege by inviting me into his juridical family. My appreciation of the good that he did for me, for Louisiana, and for America has only increased over time.

23

On Cussing Out White Liberals:
The Case of Philip Elman

Years ago I wrote a critique of a lawyer named Philip Elman who had published an account of his role in *Brown v. Board of Education.*[1] I asserted that his portrayal was contaminated by an all-too-prevalent strain of white liberal racism. I believe that much of what I wrote was accurate. I also believe, though, that I wrongly diminished the important contributions that Elman made to the campaign for racial decency at a key phase in its development. He deserved a critical response. But he did not deserve scorn. He is entitled to respect and gratitude.

Philip Elman was born in 1918 to Jewish immigrants from Poland. He attended New York's City College during its radical leftist heyday. He recalls being viewed as a "conservative" by classmates, even though he was a Norman Thomas socialist. He then attended Harvard Law School, where he ascended to the student aristocracy by becoming an editor of the *Harvard Law Review*. He served as a law clerk to the Supreme Court justice Felix Frankfurter and occupied a number of significant posts, including a seat on the Federal Trade Commission, where he served with distinction.

Between 1944 and 1961, Elman worked in the office of the Solicitor General (SG), the figure in the Department of Justice (DOJ) who represents the United States before the Supreme Court. Elman became known as "the civil rights man" in the SG's

office. He pushed the DOJ to put its weight behind the growing movement for progressive racial change that followed World
War II. He urged friends associated with the NAACP, the ACLU,
the American Jewish Congress, and other organizations to write
to him, to his superiors, and to other government officials to voice
their desire for the federal government to side with civil rights
plaintiffs. He then used those letters as ammunition in making the
case for federal intervention.

On occasion he even persuaded the Department of Justice to
reverse direction. In 1949 the department originally supported
the Interstate Commerce Commission (ICC) when it was sued
by a black man, Elmer W. Henderson, who had objected to the
racially discriminatory treatment he received while riding on the
Southern Railway. The mistreatment encountered—he was prevented from dining alongside whites—was authorized by ICC
regulations that embraced and extended *Plessy v. Ferguson*, the
notorious 1896 Supreme Court decision that upheld the constitutionality of racial segregation.

When the challenge to the regulations came to Elman's attention, he convinced the SG that he should not only refrain from
backing the ICC's policy but oppose it. The SG did so using an
aggressive, thoughtful, and innovative brief written by Elman. At
a time when racial segregation was still viewed by the Supreme
Court as an innocent, or at least constitutionally permissible,
racial distinction (as opposed to an invidious, impermissible racial
discrimination), Elman forthrightly condemned it. "Segregation
of Negroes," he wrote, "is universally understood as imposing
upon them a badge of inferiority. . . . This message of humiliation comes not as a single voice but with all the reverberations
of the entire pattern of segregation and discrimination of which
it is part. . . . It is bad enough for the Negro to have to endure
the insults of individuals who look upon him as inferior. It is far
worse to submit to a formalized and institutionalized enforcement
of this concept, particularly when as in this case it carries the sanction of an agency of government."

Elman argued that the ICC regulations authorizing racially
segregated accommodations violated both federal statutes and
the Constitution. Addressing himself to the constitutional issue,

Elman contended (four years before *Brown v. Board of Education*) that "the legal and factual assumptions upon which [*Plessy v. Ferguson*] was decided have been demonstrated to be erroneous and that the doctrine of that case should now be overruled. 'Separate but equal' is a constitutional anachronism which no longer deserves a place in our law. It is neither reasonable nor right that colored citizens of the US should be subjected to the humiliations of being segregated." The Court responded by ruling that the ICC regulations violated the statute that the agency was charged with enforcing. The justices agreed with Elman that both the railroad's segregation policy and the regulations that permitted it subjected blacks to "unreasonable prejudice."

Elman's self-portrayal of his role in the SG's office came to widespread public attention in 1987 when the *Harvard Law Review* published an excerpt drawn from an oral memoir based upon conversations between Elman and the Hofstra law professor Norman I. Silber that were transcribed and edited under the auspices of the Columbia University Oral History Research Office. Professor Silber later oversaw the production of an enlarged and annotated version of Elman's oral memoir.[2] In it Silber does far more than serve as Elman's stenographer. He identifies individuals to whom Elman refers, explains events to which Elman alludes, substantiates claims that Elman makes, and assesses controversies in which Elman figured. Although Silber presents his subject, friend, and hero in a decidedly positive light, he also laudably offers due attention to contending perspectives.

One of the most controversial aspects of Elman's memoir is suggested by its title *With All Deliberate Speed*. That phrase has become a key term in the glossary of race relations. It was used most famously in the decision often referred to as *Brown II*, the 1955 ruling in which the Court sketched its framework for enforcing the desegregation of public primary and secondary schools. In its landmark 1954 ruling in *Brown v. Board of Education* (*Brown I*), the Court invalidated de jure segregation in public schooling but expressly withheld judgment regarding the implementation of its ruling. In *Brown II*, the Supreme Court stressed that local school boards, including those that had insisted upon segregation, would remain the primary superintendents of public schooling and that they would not be required to effectuate immediately a transition to nonracial schooling but only to make a "prompt and reasonable start." The Court, in other words, opted for a gradualist strategy—desegregation "with all deliberate speed."

Criticism attended Elman's reflections on "all deliberate speed" two reasons. The first involves charges of unethical conduct. While Elman was an attorney in the SG's office and while *Brown* and its companion cases were pending before the Supreme Court, Elman and Justice Frankfurter discussed the litigation informally, relaying to each other information pertinent to the cases, including confidential internal deliberations within the Court and the SG's office. Elman maintains that he did not discuss the case with Frankfurter *after* the United States had formally entered the litigation on the side of the plaintiffs (eventually submitting briefs largely written by Elman). But he also asserts that information relayed by him to Frankfurter assisted the justice in forging a unanimous ruling.

When Elman detailed these conversations in the *Harvard Law Review*, some observers harshly rebuked him and the deceased justice Frankfurter. *The New York Times* found Elman's revelations to be "deeply disturbing" and condemned him and his mentor for having "crossed a clear ethical line."[3] Anticipating such criticism, Elman took the position that an extraordinary case permitted the taking of extraordinary measures. In *Brown*, Elman states, "I didn't consider myself a lawyer for a litigant. I considered it a cause that transcended ordinary notions about propriety in litigation. . . . I don't defend my discussions with Frankfurter; I just did what I thought was right, and I'm sure he didn't give it much thought. I regarded myself, in the literal sense, an *amicus curiae.*"

Many observers now deride as a blunder the compromise Elman lauds. Characteristic is an observation by Robert L. Carter, a key lieutenant of Thurgood Marshall's who later became a federal judge. The compromise, Carter argues, was "a grave mistake." The Court "apparently believed that its show of compassion and understanding of the problem facing the white South would help develop a willingness to comply [with *Brown*]. Instead, the 'all deliberate speed' formula aroused the hope that resistance to the constitutional imperative would succeed." By contrast,

Elman credits himself and Frankfurter for concocting a formula for gradualism that coaxed anxious justices into voting for invalidating segregation, a step that they might have refused to take in 1954 had they faced the prospect of an immediate end to Jim Crow schooling.

Elman describes the brief he drafted for the SG as "the one thing I'm proudest of in my whole career." He notes that he did not use the famous phrase "all deliberate speed" in the brief. But he insists that it is his brief that initially voiced the concept behind the phrase, a concept that he and his mentor had shaped in their discussions and that Frankfurter subsequently planted in the *Brown* opinions. Elman declares that the reason he is so proud of his idea is that "it offered the Court a way out of its dilemma, a way to end racial segregation without inviting massive disobedience, a way to decide the constitutional issue unanimously without tearing the Court apart. For the first time the Court was told that it was not necessarily confronted with an all-or-nothing choice between reaffirming separate but equal . . . and requiring immediate integration of public schools." Elman avers that the compromise he sketched was "entirely unprincipled" and "simply indefensible" as a matter of constitutional law. Yet he celebrates the compromise as a matter of statesmanship that "broke the logjam. It was the formula that [the] Court needed in order to bring the justices together to decide the constitutional issue on the merits correctly. Without all deliberate speed, in the remedy, the Court could never have decided the constitutional issue in the strong, forthright, unanimous way that it did."

Elman's boastful embrace of "all deliberate speed" might be a bit less grating had it been voiced contemporaneously with *Brown* and launched hopefully toward an unknowable future. But that was not the case. Elman was speaking in the 1980s, three decades after *Brown*. In that time, he had witnessed inspiring breakthroughs to be sure but also violence, evasion, delay, defiance, attempts to intimidate the Supreme Court, efforts to crush the NAACP, campaigns to close rather than desegregate schools, and white segregationist adults spitting on Negro schoolchildren from New Orleans to Boston. Given the depth and bitterness of the reaction against *Brown*, even with its compromise, Elman's cheerful certainty about the rightness and efficacy of "all deliberate speed" is, or should be, off-putting.

Similarly off-putting are Elman's consistently belittling comments about Thurgood Marshall, Robert Carter, and the other attorneys at the NAACP Legal Defense Fund (LDF). According to Elman, they "made the wrong arguments at the wrong time in the wrong cases." He asserts that they erred in pressing too quickly to invalidate segregation, that they erred in bringing cases from the Deep South where the justices were most nervous about the prospect of white supremacist backlash, and that they erred in introducing as evidence social science that purported to demonstrate psychological harms inflicted by de jure segregation. According to Elman, Marshall's "whole strategy [was] unwise." Elman concedes, as he must, that Marshall won on the main substantive point in *Brown*. But, in his view, that victory emerged despite and not because of Marshall's exertions. Marshall won, Elman asserts, "thanks to God and luck" and the insight of Frankfurter and his "law clerk for life" (namely Elman himself).

No part of Elman's oral history is more unbecoming than that in which he makes invidious comparisons between himself and the attorneys who represented plaintiffs in the leading race relations cases of the 1940s and 1950s. On the one hand, he congratulates himself excessively for being a pioneer in directly attacking segregation per se. Describing the wonderful brief that he wrote for the SG's office in *Henderson v. United States*, Elman states that "for the first time, a party before the Court asked it to overrule *Plessy v. Ferguson*." In so doing, he overlooks Henderson's attorneys (particularly Belford V. Lawson Jr.) and others (including the National Lawyers Guild and the American Jewish Committee), who had also directly attacked the constitutionality of the separate but equal doctrine. "Segregation is discrimination," Lawson had argued, "because the very idea of enforced separation by race casts [an unjustified] stigma upon persons."

On the other hand, Elman unduly chastises the attorneys for the plaintiffs in *Brown* for what he saw as an impatient and imprudent decision to seek too quickly a decision on the constitutionality of segregation per se in public schooling. Elman claims that when Marshall began in the early 1950s to attack segregation per se, the Court was badly divided, with a bare majority leaning toward maintaining the Jim Crow status quo. According to Elman, a catastrophic reaffirmance of *Plessy v. Ferguson* had been avoided only because of Frankfurter's stalling tactics and the providential death of Chief Justice Fred Vinson.

Even assuming that Elman's speculations are accurate, none of them should cast a cloud over the remarkable achievement of Marshall and his colleagues. Yes, they took a calculated risk in pushing the Court to rule on the question of whether state-mandated racial separation as such harmed black schoolchildren. But the civil rights crusaders had prepared the ground well for the new doctrine they hoped to establish. Through bringing successful lawsuits that had resulted in desegregation orders for public graduate and professional schools, they had, by the time of *Brown*, already brought the Court close to invalidating segregation per se in education.

Contrary to Elman's suggestion, there was no sloppiness or rashness in Marshall's decision making. He proceeded with due caution, weighing each of his important tactical moves with a cadre of some of the most impressive legal minds in the country. But no amount of thoughtfulness could negate the uncertainties with which Marshall had to grapple as best he could. Unlike Elman, Marshall had no access to inside information about the justices' reservations. Nor did Marshall always have the power to orchestrate the timing and placement of the litigation campaign. Attorneys sometimes disagreed with Marshall and pursued their own strategies. Such was the case, for example, in *Bolling v. Sharpe*, the case that challenged the constitutionality of segregated public schooling in Washington, D.C. Believing that Marshall was proceeding too slowly, James M. Nabrit Jr. decided independently to attack segregation per se. And then there were the additional pressures imposed by the Court itself. On its own motion, the Supreme Court expedited review of certain school segregation cases while delaying review of others. Explaining the Court's rationale, Justice Tom Clark later noted, "We felt it was much better to have representative cases from different parts of the country and so we consolidated them and made *Brown* [the Kansas case] first so that the whole [segregation] question would not smack of being a purely Southern one."

Elman derides the decision of the LDF attorneys to proffer expert testimony by Kenneth and Mamie Clark which purported to show that segregation in education lowered the self-esteem of Negro students. The most famous part of their testimony stemmed from experiments in which the Clarks asked black children to select their favorite dolls. The Clarks concluded that the preference of many black children for white dolls indicated an inferiority complex created or reinforced by state-imposed racial isolation. There is good reason to doubt the methodological rigor behind the Clarks' testimony; indeed, many scholars today disparage it as "junk social science," and even at the time it was viewed with unease by some within the LDF camp. Contrary to Elman's claims, however, the use of the Clarks' testimony did not evidence any absence of "good sense." Having met mixed results with other efforts to unmask the reality of segregation, Marshall was understandably drawn to the Clarks' attention-grabbing doll experiments. Elman notes that John W. Davis, the most prominent attorney for the segregationists, "poured ridicule" on the LDF attorneys and their social scientific evidence. But, of course, Marshall was not attempting to gain Davis's favor. He was attempting to capture the minds, imaginations, and sentiments of the justices. He and his associates were at least partially successful in doing just that. The Court paid respectful attention to the Clarks' testimony and other social science cited by the LDF attorneys. *Brown* was not based on the social scientific evidence that Chief Justice Warren referred to in his famous footnote 11.[4] But he and his colleagues did evidently derive some degree of reassurance from noting these studies. Whatever one thinks of the merits of the social science evidence, Marshall's deployment of it seems to have been efficacious.

It is important to rebut Elman's self-aggrandizing grab for historical credit and his belittlement of Marshall and his colleagues. Ignorance of blacks' contributions to American history remains appallingly pervasive. This ignorance creates fertile ground for misimpressions to take root. Elman conveys the gross misimpression that the plaintiffs in *Brown* and kindred cases were ill-served by their legal counsel. Such a view is profoundly wrong. Thurgood Marshall and his cadre of superb colleagues waged a remarkably successful campaign of social reform litigation (the efficacy of which is reflected in the lengths to which segregationists went to stifle the civil rights crusaders who challenged them).

To be sure, blacks did not monopolize the ranks of the lawyers who represented plaintiffs in *Brown* and similar cases. White attorneys, including Jack Greenberg, Jack Weinstein, Charles L. Black, and Louis Pollak, played important roles as well. That black attorneys were predominant, however, suggests yet another reason to rebut Elman's aspersions. Millions grew up laughing at Calhoun, the bumbling blowhard Negro lawyer featured in the popular radio and television series *Amos 'n' Andy*. For many Americans, the Calhoun figure, along with other denigrating imagery that questions the ability or even capacity of blacks to excel in demanding professional roles, makes the prospect of imagining, much less hiring, a first-rate black lawyer all too difficult. Consequently, it remains useful to remind people that among the most accomplished attorneys in American history were the black jurists who skillfully undermined the Jim Crow regime.

Elman's reticence regarding the skill of these attorneys is all the more regrettable in light of the difficulties his black colleagues faced because of their race. The American Bar Association (ABA), for example, participated fully in ostracizing black attorneys. Beginning in 1919 and for several decades thereafter, blacks were informally barred from ABA membership. Yet despite these and other impediments, black attorneys found a way to ply their trade, sometimes conspicuously outpacing their racially privileged white colleagues.

Although Elman makes several disparaging comments about these black attorneys, he never acknowledges their professional competence, notwithstanding the fact that during the period he chronicles, he encountered an impressive array of remarkable figures including Charles Hamilton Houston, Thurgood Marshall, Robert L. Carter, Constance Baker Motley, William T. Coleman, Louis L. Redding, James M. Nabrit Jr., James M. Nabrit III, Spottswood Robinson, and Oliver Hill. Elman does compliment George L. Vaughn, who argued one of the restrictive covenant cases in *Shelley v. Kraemer*, crediting him with making "the most moving plea in the [Supreme] Court" that he had ever heard. But even that compliment is backhanded insofar as it refers to the emotionality of Vaughn's argument rather than his professional workmanship, which Elman ranked as "poor."

When the *Harvard Law Review* published the excerpt from Elman's memoir, I was called by Julius Chambers, who then headed the LDF. Chambers requested that I write a rebuttal. He was angry at Elman's disrespectful remarks about Marshall and his colleagues, all of whom had been closely affiliated with the LDF. I, too, was angry and directed a blow at Elman's moral solar plexus:

> There may be some innocent explanation for Elman's seeming unwillingness to recognize professional excellence when demonstrated by black attorneys. But any legal historian who intends to use the Elman memoir responsibly must also consider the possibility that, even more than is usually so, his recollections reflect biases that can tell us more about the observer than he wants observed.[5]

Elman responded by saying that the answer to my charge of bias was his "entire life." I did not let that go. Instead, I replied that "this complacent, above-it-all attitude pose[d] an obstacle to deeper inquiry into the complicated reality of social conflict in the United States. In a society still saturated with racist practices, ideas, and intuitions, it is foolhardy for any person—white or black and no matter what their personal background—to proclaim himself completely immune from racial bias."

I regret pressing that line of argument. Absent more incriminating evidence, I should have refrained from ascribing Elman's remarks to racial prejudice. I should have been more charitable, just as Elman should have been more respectful of Marshall and his colleagues. I continue to object to Elman's self-discrediting effort to push himself to center stage in the drama of *Brown v. Board of Education*. But I would like to conclude by accentuating something I wrote in my initial rebuttal: Elman "should be applauded for the stand he took, the vision he demonstrated, and the decency he exhibited." Elman actively fought Jim Crow segregation during a period when many Americans avoided the race question, embraced indifference, or supported a racist status quo. For those efforts he deserves praise and thanks.

24

The Civil Rights Act Did Make a Difference![1]

When I was a kid, my mother and father meticulously prepared our car for holiday journeys from our home in Washington, D.C., to my birthplace, Columbia, South Carolina. They packed coolers filled with sodas, deviled eggs, chicken wings, sandwiches of all varieties, cookies, and candy. I thought of this at the time as an effort to make the eight-hour ride into a party for me and my brother. Only later did I learn that their preparations stemmed from fear. Having fled the Jim Crow South in the 1950s, my parents were seeking to limit our contact with filling stations, restaurants, motels, or other public accommodations where their children might be snarled at by racially prejudiced cashiers and attendants. As I matured, I saw that once we crossed the Potomac River and ventured into Virginia, we encountered a terrain that filled my parents with dread.

My father was particularly burdened by the drive. He became noticeably nervous, trembling at the sight of police officers. Over the years several of them pulled him over. They did not charge him with any infraction. Rather, they stopped him seemingly out of curiosity and a desire to test his willingness to accept the etiquette of white supremacy. Their colloquies went something like this:

"That's a nice car you're driving, boy."
"Thank you, Officer. Have I done something wrong?"
"Not from what I can see just yet. I notice you've got

out-of-state plates. You know, we do things different down here. You do know that?"

"Yes, sir."

"Boy, you *do* know that, right?"

"Yassuh."

"Okay. You're free to go."

The drive took us into a territory that featured signs distinguishing "colored women" from "white ladies," signs indicating whether a business served blacks, signs designating which toilets or water fountains or entrances African Americans were permitted to use. In those days it was legal throughout the Deep South for privately owned places of public accommodation to exclude people on the basis of race—"colored not allowed"—or to discriminate against them in other ways—"colored served only in the rear." This reality prompted Victor H. Green, of Harlem, to publish *The Negro Motorist Green Book*, a guide to establishments that served black travelers. He understood the anxiety that beset African Americans as they sought to obtain elementary decencies on the nation's highways.

How did law burden African Americans in the Jim Crow South, particularly as customers or potential customers at businesses? Two doctrines were especially significant: the state action doctrine and segregation.

To effectuate segregation, southern states and municipalities required businesses to separate customers along racial lines. In 1963, for instance, an ordinance in Greenville, South Carolina, decreed that "it shall be unlawful for any person owning, managing or controlling any hotel, restaurant, café . . . or similar establishment to furnish meals to white persons and colored persons in the same room, or at the same table, or at the same counter. . . ." The ordinance did provide, however, "that meals may be served to white persons and colored persons in the same room where separate facilities are furnished." What did "separate facilities" entail? It meant "separate eating utensils and separate dishes . . . all of which shall be distinctly marked by some appropriate color scheme"; "separate tables, counters, or booths"; and "a distance of at least thirty-five feet . . . between the area where white and colored persons are served."

The legal theory that rationalized segregation posited that, assuming an equivalence in the facilities provided, everyone was being treated equally: for the sake of public peace and morale, whites who wanted to dine with blacks were being deprived just as much as blacks who wanted to dine with whites. That was, of course, a lie. There was no equivalence, no symmetry, no mutuality. Governments monopolized by whites segregated blacks. African Americans were the ones being targeted. They were the ones being treated as if they were infectious. They were the ones being excluded from proximity with whites in any setting that might signal equal status. This arrangement, moreover, was by no means reciprocal. Having been removed from participation in politics by skulduggery or intimidation, blacks played no substantial role in designing or implementing segregration. Their role was simply to endure it.

The state action doctrine freed private parties from federal constitutional restraint. It allowed owners of filling stations or hotels or restaurants to segregate blacks or banish them altogether without regard to federal constitutional inhibitions. Actually, though, the perniciousness of the state action doctrine stretched even further, as indicated by the outcome of the Civil Rights Cases decided in 1883. In those cases the Supreme Court invalidated a key provision of the Civil Rights Act of 1875, which had sought to grant African Americans the "full and equal enjoyment" of public accommodations. The Court held that provision to be unconstitutional because it supposedly exceeded the new powers granted to the federal government by the Fourteenth Amendment. The statute prohibited discrimination by private parties without reference to state action. But according to the Court, the Fourteenth Amendment authorized federal legislation only insofar as it corrected "state action" not private conduct. What this meant is that in states without local antidiscrimination laws, private owners of public accommodations and other businesses were largely free to discriminate on a racial basis since private discrimination was beyond the reach of the equal protection clause of the Fourteenth Amendment, and also beyond the reach of legislation properly enforcing the Amendment.

Behind the wall erected by the judiciary's interpretation of segregation and state action, arose laws, policies, and customs that expressed an obvious judgment that African Americans were inferior and that white people needed to be protected from their contaminating presence. Hence governments consigned blacks to the back of the bus, directed them to use distinct drinking fountains and telephone booths, excluded them altogether from white schools and hospitals, permitted them to visit zoos and museums only on certain days, confined them to designated areas in courtrooms, and elicited oaths from them as witnesses on racially differentiated Bibles. Pursuant to segregationist etiquette, whites routinely declined to bestow upon blacks courtesy titles such as "Mr." and "Mrs." and referred to them simply as "boy" or "girl" regardless of age. Stores prohibited African Americans from trying on clothes before purchase. Telephone directories racially identified black residents. Newspapers refused to carry notices for black weddings.

Of these calculated racial insults, few, if any, were more galling than the ones my parents anticipated on those trips to the South: anti-black discrimination at places of amusement and relaxation and facilities for travel, eating, and sleeping. It was at those places and facilities that African American dissidents focused the world's attention on the injustice at the heart of the so-called southern way of life. On February 1, 1960, four black freshmen at the North Carolina Agricultural and Mechanical College for the Colored Race in Greensboro, North Carolina, sat down at a whites-only lunch counter in a local Woolworth's. They were denied service but remained until the store closed. The next day they returned, bringing more students along with them. Within weeks, sit-ins had spread to towns and cities across the South.

The protesters were guided more by moral intuition than by any carefully reasoned legal strategy. "We want to state clearly and unequivocally," a group of Atlanta students declared in a political advertisement that ran in several local papers in March,

> that [we] cannot tolerate . . . the discriminatory conditions under which the Negro is living today. . . . We plan to use every legal and non-violent means at our disposal to secure full citizenship rights as members of this great Democracy of ours.

Exactly what their rights consisted of, however, was far from clear. In 1954, in *Brown v. Board of Education*, the Supreme Court had delivered African Americans and their allies a major victory by declaring that "in the field of public education, the doctrine of 'separate but equal' has no place. Separate educational facilities are inherently unequal." This ruling, though, important as it was, went only so far. Courts held repeatedly that the Constitution prohibited racial segregation and other forms of racial discrimination imposed by public authorities but not private parties, though such conduct by private parties inflicted major injuries in the markets that allocate employment, housing, and other amenities of daily existence. While those arrested for protesting racial exclusion at a government-sponsored establishment (say, a coffee shop whose premises were leased from a municipality) typically prevailed when they challenged their arrests, those arrested at private establishments were more vulnerable because owners of such businesses were deemed to have a right to select customers on whatever basis they chose.

When a group of African American students entered an S. H. Kress store in Greenville, South Carolina, and seated themselves at the lunch counter, the manager called the police and told the protesters that the counter was closed because serving Negroes there was "contrary to local customs" and in violation of a city ordinance. When the protesters refused to move, they were arrested and prosecuted for violating the state's trespassing law. The South Carolina Supreme Court affirmed the convictions, but the U.S. Supreme Court overturned them, stating that even if the manager had barred the black activists independently of the city ordinance, the presence of the ordinance amounted to state action that made federal constitutional standards applicable.

This conclusion was by no means self-evident. But in this case and others, the Court seized on the slightest hints of state action to trigger federal constitutional standards that could then be used to prohibit racial discrimination and shelter protests against it. In *Lombard v. Louisiana*, the Court reversed the convictions of four students who'd staged a sit-in at a five-and-dime in New Orleans. Although the management could have lawfully excluded the students on its own volition, the Court held that, as actually effectuated, the exclusion was the result of state action. What rendered the exclusion constitutionally illicit were public statements made by the mayor and superintendent of police. Both of them had asserted that sit-ins were prohibited and would be punished. "As we interpret the New Orleans city officials' statement," wrote Chief Justice Earl Warren in the majority opinion,

> they here determined that the city would not permit Negroes to seek desegregated service in restaurants. Consequently, the city must be treated exactly as if it had an ordinance prohibiting such conduct.

The Supreme Court, however, stopped short of embracing the argument, put forth by civil rights activists, that the Constitution ought to prohibit *any* racial exclusion or segregation at commercial establishments, regardless of its sponsorship, private or public. Invoking precedent, federalism, and personal autonomy, a majority of the justices continued to maintain that private racial discrimination should remain exempt from federal constitutional constraint.

Although thirty-two states and the District of Columbia prohibited private racial discrimination in public accommodations, the states of the former Confederacy offered no such legislation. Progress therefore depended on persuading Congress and the president to pass a federal statute. It was with this goal in mind in early 1963 that Martin Luther King Jr. and others set about organizing a series of mass protests in the Deep South's most notoriously racist city: Birmingham, Alabama.

Some white "moderates" chastised King, complaining that he was falling victim to the vice of impatience and that his mass rallies, though peaceful in themselves, risked provoking segregationist violence. In a magnificent defense of civil disobedience, "Letter from Birmingham Jail," King tried to explain why blacks were demanding "Freedom Now!" "I guess it is easy," he remarked, "for those who have never felt the stinging darts of segregation to say 'Wait.' But when you have seen vicious mobs lynch your mothers and fathers at will and drown your sisters and brothers at whim," King continued,

when you suddenly find your tongue twisted and your
speech stammering as you seek to explain to your six-
year-old daughter why she can't go to the public amusement park that has just been advertised on television . . .
when you take a cross-country drive and find it necessary
to sleep night after night in the uncomfortable corners of
your automobile because no motel will accept you . . . ;
when you are harried by day and haunted by night by the
fact that you are a Negro, living constantly at tiptoe stance,
never quite knowing what to expect next, and are plagued
with inner fears and outer resentments; when you are forever fighting a degenerating sense of "nobodiness"—then
you will understand why we find it difficult to wait.

President John F. Kennedy was among those who initially criticized King. Although Kennedy is widely perceived now as having
been a friend of the civil rights movement, for much of his brief
presidency he evinced little commitment to the crusade for racial
justice. He sympathized with the dissidents, but he was also keenly
attuned to the obstructive power of southern congressmen. Chairs
of key committees in the Senate and the House of Representatives were alert defenders of segregation. Primarily concerned
with managing the Cold War and reforming tax policy, Kennedy
avoided taking positions that they would perceive as hostile.

Kennedy's stance changed dramatically, however, after events
in Birmingham forced his hand. On one side were protests against
the institutions, symbols, and practices of white supremacy. Hundreds of black people, including schoolchildren, marched to signal
their disapproval of segregation. On the other side, Birmingham's
commissioner of public safety, Eugene "Bull" Connor, jailed
hundreds, ordered in canine units, and directed firemen to shoot
water at protesters with high-pressure hoses whose streams could
knock over grown men and strip the bark from trees.

Captured by television crews and photojournalists, images
of brutality traveled across the country and around the globe,
prompting many observers to demand a presidential response.
On the evening of June 11, 1963, Kennedy delivered a nationally
televised address in which he announced legislation that would

address racial mistreatment in voting, education, and employment. The most controversial feature of the envisioned legislation, however, was prohibitions against racial discrimination in privately owned places of public accommodation.

When Kennedy sent his civil rights bill to Congress, many observers supposed that it would either expire altogether or survive as mere decoration. In 1957 and 1960, Congress had enacted the first civil rights bills since Reconstruction, but only after southern congressmen succeeded in extracting concessions that substantially undercut the legislation's effectiveness. There was also an important bloc of conservative Republicans who were largely indifferent to the plight of oppressed racial minorities and opposed antidiscrimination measures out of a general antipathy toward federal regulation.

Four months after introducing his civil rights bill, Kennedy was assassinated in Dallas. Within a few days, a new president, Lyndon B. Johnson, delivered a speech to a joint session of Congress in which he invoked Kennedy's martyrdom to heighten the emotional appeal of the legislation. It is arguable that Johnson's southern background, parliamentary experience, and powers of persuasion made him a better shepherd than his predecessor for this particular bill.

The congressional proceedings included more than eighty days of debate, the longest filibuster in Senate history, and a rare invocation of cloture to clear the obstruction. No African Americans sat in the Senate at this time, and only 5 were among the 435 who considered the bill in the House. The insistent voices of African Americans had made civil rights a congressional priority, but those voices emerged only intermittently in the hearings on the legislation. Notably absent from the witness list was Martin Luther King Jr., though other leading activists, including Roy Wilkins, executive secretary of the NAACP, did testify. Wilkins reminded everyone that "while we talk here today . . . Negro Americans throughout our country will be bruised in nearly every working hour by differential treatment in, or exclusion from, public accommodations of every description. From the time they leave their homes in the morning . . . until they return at night, humiliation stalks them."

Senator Hubert H. Humphrey was similarly impassioned:

It is difficult for most of us to fully comprehend the monstrous humiliations and inconveniences that racial discrimination imposes on our Negro fellow citizens. If a white man is thirsty on a hot day, he goes to the nearest soda fountain. If he is hungry, he goes to the nearest restaurant. If he needs a restroom, he can go to the nearest gas station. If it is night and he is tired, he takes his pick of the available motels and hotels.

But for a Negro the picture is different. Trying to get a glass of iced tea at a lunch counter may result in insult and abuse. . . . He can never count on using a restroom, on getting a decent place to stay, or buying a good meal. These are trivial matters in the life of a white person, but for some 20 million American Negroes, they are important considerations that must be planned for in detail. They must draw up travel plans much as a general advancing across hostile territory would establish his logistical support.

On the other side, Mississippi's governor, Ross Barnett, charged that "minority groups . . . have taken to the streets . . . to blackmail this Congress" and that the bill was part of a communist conspiracy "to divide and conquer from within." Alabama's governor, George Wallace, was similarly apocalyptic, denouncing the bill as "a long step in a socialistic scheme . . . which will bring the total destruction of private property rights."

Proponents of the bill pointed to statutes compelling racial separation to impugn the good faith of segregationists who complained that antidiscrimination laws infringed upon property rights and personal autonomy. Where was the libertarianism of the segregationists when the states dictated the color schemes of plates or the precise distance by which entrances to restaurants must be separated? When Senator Strom Thurmond of South Carolina complained that the proposed bill encroached upon private parties' right to use their property as they saw fit, Attorney General Robert F. Kennedy shot back, "Was that point raised when South Carolina . . . ruled that an establishment could not serve a Negro?"

Segregationists charged racial liberals with hypocrisy. Liberals, Wallace claimed, have

> invited the Negro to come North to a land of milk and honey. They have accepted the proposition, and instead of finding this utopia, they have found unemployment. They have been stacked in ghettos on top of one another, to become a part of every city's Harlem.

Wallace had a point. Although racial mistreatment was most open, pervasive, and formalized in the South, it existed throughout the country; at least in the South "the Negro knows where he can go. We are not hypocritical about it."

Segregationists also attacked the bill on legal grounds, citing the Civil Rights Cases. They argued that if it was unconstitutional in 1883 for the federal government to tell private businesses whom they must serve, the same remained true in 1964.

Instead of addressing that objection head-on, the bill's proponents outflanked it, invoking the Commerce Clause (which gives Congress the power "to regulate Commerce . . . among the several States") as the principal source of constitutional authority (as opposed to the equal protection clause of the Fourteenth Amendment). The Supreme Court had offered no opinion on Commerce Clause authorization in 1883 and had interpreted it broadly since upholding New Deal legislation in the 1930s. Attorney General Kennedy maintained that the inhibitions on travel imposed by segregation detrimentally affected interstate commerce. If, under the Commerce Clause, "Congress can, and does, control the service of oleomargarine in every restaurant in the Nation," he noted, "surely it can insure our nonwhite citizens access to those restaurants."

Segregationists complained that the Commerce Clause justification was a sham. Others complained as well. One was the Republican senator John Sherman Cooper of Kentucky:

> I do not suppose that anyone would seriously contend that the administration is proposing legislation, or the Con-

gress is considering legislation, because it has been suddenly determined, after all these years, that segregation is a burden on inter-state commerce. We are considering legislation because we believe . . . that all citizens have an equal right to have access to goods, services, and facilities which are held out to be available for public use and patronage.

On July 2, 1964, after the Senate approved the civil rights bill, 73 to 27, and the House approved it 289 to 126, President Lyndon B. Johnson signed it into law. All persons, Title II of the new legislation declared, "shall be entitled to the full and equal enjoyment of . . . any place of public accommodation . . . without discrimination or segregation on the ground of race, color, religion, or national origin . . ."

While the scope of Title II is broad (though it omitted any mention of gender), its enforcement weaponry is slight compared with the 1875 Act and various analogous state laws. It provides only injunctive relief—a court order directing a defendant to stop violating the statute. Other laws criminalized violations, making defendants liable to misdemeanor convictions carrying jail time and substantial fines and damages (though typically these laws were woefully underenforced). The Civil Rights Act's milder remedial scheme was touted as a virtue by proponents who sought to accentuate the legislation's moderation.

The debate over the Civil Rights Act has reverberated throughout the subsequent decades. Its rejection by Barry Goldwater, the Republican presidential candidate in 1964, played a major role in severing ties between African Americans and the party of Lincoln. Franklin Delano Roosevelt's New Deal attracted many blacks to the Democratic Party, as had Harry S. Truman's order in 1948 to desegregate the armed forces. But in the 1950s, African Americans still voted Republican in substantial numbers. In 1960, Richard Nixon received 32 percent of the black vote. By contrast, in 1964, Goldwater received only 6 percent. (Since then no Republican presidential candidate has received more than 15 percent.)

Opposition to the Act has also had other consequences. The

successful campaign to stop Robert Bork's 1987 Senate confirmation for the Supreme Court drew intense energy from those who recalled his condemnation of the public-accommodations provision of the Civil Rights Act back in the days when he was a professor at Yale Law School. The principle behind the legislation, Bork maintained,

> is that if I find your behavior ugly by my standards . . . and if you prove stubborn about adopting my view of the situation, I am justified in having the state coerce you into more righteous paths. This is itself a principle of unsurpassed ugliness.

Bork conceded that the Act sprang from a "justifiable abhorrence of racial discrimination," and he bemoaned the fact that most of the law's opponents were politicians who had previously defended segregation. In opposing the bill, Bork was probably acting as an authentic (not an opportunistic) libertarian. The difficulty is distinguishing non-racist libertarianism from its fraudulent, pretextual look-alikes. There is good reason to be skeptical of those who, in the name of liberty, condemn a law that has rescued millions from the tyranny of unchecked racial ostracism.

The struggle for racial equality in access to public accommodations has been considerably more successful than struggles on other fronts. Title IV of the Civil Rights Act authorizes the U.S. attorney general to initiate and intervene in public school desegregation cases. But the results have been disappointing. Title VII of the Act bars racial discrimination in many employment markets and established the Equal Employment Opportunity Commission. Employment discrimination, however, remains prevalent. The Civil Rights Act of 1968 and subsequent amendments have banned racial discrimination in a wide range of housing transactions. Yet racial discrimination in that sphere remains notoriously common.

In the aftermath of Title II's passage, however, there was no analogue to the massive resistance that confronted school desegregation. No troops had to be called in to force hoteliers to open their establishments to black travelers. Although Title II had been the provision in the Civil Rights Act about which emotions ran highest, it rather quickly faded in prominence after enactment.

To be sure, Title II encountered some resistance, as has every initiative aimed at elevating the status of racial minorities. There were instances of naked refusal to follow the law. One involved Lester Maddox, the owner of the Pickrick Restaurant, a small, cafeteria-style establishment in Atlanta that became a rallying point for die-hard segregationists. Reacting to the onset of the sit-in movement, Maddox started Georgians Unwilling to Surrender, a loosely organized group of whites that sought to put pressure on politicians and business executives who were perceived as capitulating to the civil rights movement. When the Civil Rights Act became law, Maddox vowed to resist, declaring, "Never! Never! Never!" When blacks sought service at his restaurant the day after President Johnson signed the civil rights bill, Maddox and his son barred them from entering, wielding a pistol and brandishing an ax handle. When judges ordered Maddox to comply with the new law or face charges of contempt of court, he closed his restaurant and reopened it under a new name with a new admissions policy. He announced that he had discontinued excluding people on account of race and had instead begun to bar them on political grounds. "Integrationists," he said, were prohibited. Whites flocked to Maddox's cafeteria. When blacks appeared, however, he ran them away. "I'm not ever going to integrate," he said. "I'd be committing an act of treason against my country, a sin against God and a crime against man if I did." Barring another group of blacks, Maddox exclaimed, "If you live one hundred years, you'll never get a piece of fried chicken here." When a judge ruled that Maddox would be assessed hefty fines for future disobedience to court orders, he shuttered his business, posting on the door a sign that read, "Closed. Out of business resulting from an act passed by the U.S. Congress, signed by Pres. Johnson and inspired and supported by deadly and bloody communism." Maddox's defeat, however, was only partial. His outlandish defense of the prerogative to racial exclusion earned him admiration among many whites. In 1967 he became Georgia's first governor subsequent to passage of the Civil Rights Act.

Moreton Rolleston engaged in a different form of resistance.

A lawyer and the owner of the Heart of Atlanta Motel, Rolleston challenged the constitutionality of the Civil Rights Act. He argued that Congress exceeded its authority to regulate interstate commerce, violated the Fifth Amendment's prohibition against taking property without due process and just compensation, and disobeyed the Thirteenth Amendment's ban on involuntary servitude by requiring him to rent available rooms to Negroes.

The Supreme Court ruled against Rolleston, concluding that evidence sufficiently supported Congress's judgment that racial discrimination in places of public accommodation impinged upon interstate commerce. As for the Act's alleged infringements on constitutionally protected individual rights, the Court noted that thirty-two states had analogous antidiscrimination laws, that prior to those the common law had imposed similar duties upon innkeepers, and that precedent overwhelmingly disfavored the plaintiff's claims. "It may be argued," the Court observed, that "Congress could have pursued other methods to eliminate the obstruction it found in inter-state commerce caused by racial discrimination. But this is a matter of policy that rests entirely with the Congress not with the courts."

The Supreme Court's validation of Title II did not dissuade all diehards from continuing to resist it. When a group of blacks sought admittance to Farr's Café in Bessemer, Alabama, the owner turned them away, shouting angrily, "Get out. We don't serve niggers here." When an interracial couple tried to enter Bek's Fro-stop in Prattville, Alabama, the owner barred them, saying that "the restaurant is closed as of this minute." When judges told the owner of Moore's Barbecue in New Bern, North Carolina, that he would have to accede to the Act now that the Supreme Court had upheld it, he bulldozed his restaurant rather than open it to blacks. When a black army major sought service at Virginia's Drive-In Restaurant in Anniston, Alabama, employees told him to go to the back. In rural areas in the Deep South, pockets of disregard for Title II openly surfaced for decades. *The New York Times* reported in 1985 that in Terrell County, Georgia, "there are bars where blacks know that they cannot buy drinks, restaurants in which they cannot eat," and "motels in which they cannot get a room."

Still, despite all of that, throughout the South, the overwhelming majority of formerly "white" lunch counters, soda fountains, skating rinks, bowling alleys, amusement parks, restaurants, motels, and hotels quietly and quickly shed their racial exclusivity. Ollie McClung of Birmingham, Alabama, maintained initially that the Act did not apply to his place, Ollie's Barbecue, because it was so local in character, catering almost wholly to an in-state clientele. When the Supreme Court disagreed, ruling that the eatery's use of interstate produce made it subject to the legislation, Ollie assumed a stance that many white southerners embraced: "As law-abiding Americans we feel we must bow to the edict of the Supreme Court."

Why has the struggle against racism been more effective in public accommodations than in schooling, housing, and employment? The principal explanation is that Title II attacks a more vulnerable target. By the 1960s, discrimination in public accommodations was largely confined to the South, whereas many of the other issues addressed by antidiscrimination legislation affected states nationwide. Reforming race relations in public accommodations, moreover, did not appear to entail the same redistribution of valuable opportunities that was feared elsewhere. The presence of blacks as consumers in motels, theaters, restaurants, and the like is simply less threatening to many whites than black participation in other activities and venues—for instance, as coworkers or managers. Unlike desegregation at the workplace, where the erosion of white privilege costs white workers real jobs, the desegregation of public accommodations did not require from whites more than psychic sacrifices. Indeed, the new antidiscrimination prohibitions gave many white businesspeople cover to do what market forces would have eventually nudged them to do anyway.

There has long existed a tendency to underestimate the importance of the struggle against racial mistreatment in places of public accommodation. A Mississippi restaurateur who opposed the new law claimed defiantly in December 1964 that "desegregation of public accommodations does not basically alter the pattern of social life anywhere." That is why, he asserted, "it has been accomplished as easily as it has." Some supporters of the legislation have also downplayed its significance. "What is the value," civil rights activist Bayard Rustin once asked, "of winning access to public accommodations for those who lack money to use them?"

Rustin's skepticism is misplaced. People lacking money one day might have it another. More to the point, the struggle was not primarily about this or that individual being able to enjoy the consumer market. It was about historically oppressed racial groups demanding equal respect. It was about the symbolism of inclusion. The student dissidents who sat in would have done so even if the managers of lunch counters had tried to pay them to stay away or had promised them double helpings if they would just go around back to the colored peoples' "place."

"Symbolism" is often contrasted with and subordinated to "substance." But symbolism can be of transcendent importance and was in this instance, as reflected in the lengths to which opponents and proponents of the Civil Rights Act were willing to go to deny or gain the legal authority to be free from racial discrimination in places of public accommodation. Many of the key accomplishments of the civil rights revolution were symbolic—invalidating segregation even if facilities were in some sense equivalent, elevating the meaning of "black," and transforming the terms on which whites and blacks interact (no more demeaning references to "boy" or "girl" when addressing adult African Americans).

The Civil Rights Act and its entailments made a difference in my family's trips to South Carolina. After 1964, my parents continued to feel burdened by a perceived need for extra vigilance. Police officers still made my father nervous. But the signage of Jim Crow segregation rather quickly disappeared and some places from which we had recently been barred became openly welcoming. White attendants and cashiers started calling my father "sir" and my mother "ma'am." Although *The Negro Motorist Green Book* ceased publication, we continued to dine out of those lovingly packed coolers. But we began to shed the sense that we were traveling through enemy territory. My family started to feel that we, too, had a right to enjoy the highway.

25

Black Power Hagiography[1]

African Americans have sought liberation from racial oppression by deploying virtually every form of protest imaginable. Appeals to law elicited rulings such as *Brown v. Board of Education* (1954), while appeals to public opinion elicited legislation such as the Civil Rights Act of 1964 and the Voting Rights Act of 1965. Directed by racial integrationists such as Thurgood Marshall, Roy Wilkins, and Martin Luther King Jr. (though near the end of his life he became decidedly more radical), this exhortatory strand of protest implored the white establishment to live up to the aspirations proclaimed in America's foundational documents—the Declaration of Independence and the Constitution. This camp of activism avoided drawing into question the legitimacy of authority as practiced in the United States and tried to refrain from alienating the white public, or at least those sectors of it amenable to liberal racial reformism. A competing strand of protest, by contrast, pledged to use "any means necessary" to gain and exercise black self-determination. The most influential champions of this approach sought a radically reconfigured society, not one in which blacks are merely assimilated into existing hierarchies. They were, moreover, willing to deploy rhetoric that displayed indifference to, if not contempt for, the sensibilities of whites. The white man's heaven, Malcolm X maintained, was the black man's hell. African Americans, Stokely Carmichael insisted, had become impatient with integration; they now wanted Black Power. Huey Newton and Bobby Seale were no longer willing to turn the other cheek. They asserted a right to defend themselves with armed violence even if that meant confronting "the pigs."

In terms of public memorialization, figures like Marshall, King, and now John Lewis occupy pride of place in terms of holidays, stamps, names on buildings and streets, portraiture in popular culture, allusions in the speeches of politicians, and other markers of public esteem. Figures in the more rhetorically disruptive tradition have not fared nearly so well in American culture as a whole. But in certain niches their memories are revered, and they are viewed with equal, if not more, admiration as their more widely acclaimed peers. A cadre of scholars have worked productively to de-center the old guard of civil rights lore and to revise the narrative of the Second Reconstruction. Their revisions have sought to spotlight Old Left figures who were marginalized by Cold War anticommunism (see, for example, Glenda Elizabeth Gilmore's *Defying Dixie: The Radical Roots of Civil Rights, 1919–1950* and Gerald Horne's *Black Revolutionary: William Patterson and the Globalization of the African American Freedom Struggle*), to highlight women marginalized by sexism (see, for instance, Barbara Ransby's *Ella Baker and the Black Freedom Movement* and Jeanne Theoharis's *The Rebellious Life of Mrs. Rosa Parks*), and to focus on lesser-known activists, especially those who worked outside the southern locales that have received the bulk of attention in the literature of the civil rights movement (see, for example, the collection of papers edited by Brian Purnell and Jeanne Theoharis, with Komozi Woodard, *The Strange Careers of the Jim Crow North: Segregation and Struggle Outside of the South*, and Thomas Sugrue's *Sweet Land of Liberty: The Forgotten Struggle for Civil Rights in the North*).

Revisionists have also written major works on the leading Black Power radicals of the 1960s. Among the most important are *Malcolm X*, by the late Manning Marable, *Stokely: A Life*, by Peniel Joseph, and *Black Against Empire: The History and Politics of the Black Panther Party* by Joshua Bloom and Waldo E. Martin Jr. These books excavate essential information and generate fruitful angles for further study. They are marred, though, by an excessive protectiveness toward their subjects that lapses into hagiography.

MALCOLM X

Named Malcolm Little by his parents, the man later dubbed Malcolm X was born in Omaha on May 19, 1925. He suffered a traumatic childhood. At the age of two, he moved with his parents to a house on the outskirts of Lansing, Michigan. Perhaps unbeknownst to the Littles, the house was encumbered by a racially restrictive covenant—a contract in which a previous owner of the property had promised not to sell it to blacks. White neighbors sought and obtained a court order evicting the Littles. Before the order could be carried out, other whites adopted a more aggressive means of driving the Littles away: they burned the house down.

When Malcolm was only six, his father was run over by a streetcar. Maybe the death was an accident. But Malcolm perceived the matter differently, and not without justification. Earl Little might well have been murdered by white supremacists who were angered by his independence and racial pride; he was a stalwart and vocal supporter of Marcus Garvey's Universal Negro Improvement Association. After her husband's death, Louise Little broke down mentally and was institutionalized for the remainder of her life. Consigned to foster care or the loose supervision of older siblings, Malcolm was eventually expelled from school. He supported himself with menial employment in New York City and Boston, took illicit drugs, and eventually turned to crime. At twenty-one he was sentenced to prison in Massachusetts for burglary and larceny.

In the course of his six-year incarceration, Malcolm was introduced to the Nation of Islam (NOI). His older siblings extolled the virtues of the sect. Its autocratic leader, "the Messenger" Elijah Muhammad, preached a unique theology that synthesized some of the nomenclature and symbolism of Islam with a cosmology that refracted the peculiar experience of blacks in America. While American culture, secular and religious, has typically privileged whiteness and derogated blackness, the NOI reversed this paradigm.

According to Elijah Muhammad, blacks were the earth's "original" people. An evil scientist, Dr. Yakub, created whites, who succeeded for centuries in enslaving and otherwise exploiting and oppressing blacks. Whites, whom Elijah Muhammad called "devils" and "archdeceivers," succeeded in divesting blacks of virtually everything valuable, including their very names. The surnames of most blacks, Elijah Muhammad asserted, were shameful "slave names" that obscured their true identities. Elijah Muhammad, named Elijah Poole at birth, assured his followers that it was God's will for blacks to regain their initial and rightful ascendancy. He insisted, though, that in preparation for that glorious and fast-approaching turnabout, blacks should separate themselves from whites, develop economic self-sufficiency, and cleanse themselves physically and morally by forsaking liquor, drugs, swine, and fornication.

Upon leaving prison in 1952, Malcolm X showed himself to be a driven, resourceful, and charismatic disciple. He drew converts, resuscitated failing temples, established new ones, and delivered countless speeches differentiating what he depicted as the dignified separatism of Black Muslims from the craven integrationism of Uncle Toms and other "so-called Negroes" who begged the white man for acceptance. While civil rights activists encouraged blacks to vote and otherwise participate in every sphere of American life, Malcolm X, following the teachings of Elijah Muhammad, eschewed voting and protest, reasoning that the United States was unchangeable and irredeemable. While civil rights activists repudiated the notion that the United States was a white man's country, Malcolm X insisted it was and would always be so.

With his provocative speeches, military bearing, forbidding countenance, and biting wit, Malcolm X captured the attention of curious whites, such as the television journalist Mike Wallace, who aired a show, *The Hate That Hate Produced*, that both disparaged the Black Muslims and elevated their public profile. While Malcolm X expressed contempt for whites, deriding them as "blue-eyed devils," it was the fascination of white journalists and academics that made him into a minor celebrity on television, radio, and college campuses. That very fascination, however, contributed to his undoing. It brought to him prestige and prominence that exceeded the notice accorded others in the Black Muslim leadership. Envious of his protégé, Elijah Muhammad first muzzled and then hounded Malcolm X, prompting him to leave the NOI in March 1964.

In the last year of his life, Malcolm X conducted himself with the whirlwind energy of a man who intuited that he had little time left. He embraced orthodox Islam, completed the hajj (the pilgrimage to Mecca that Muslims are obligated to undertake if possible at least once in their lifetime), renamed himself El-Hajj Malik El-Shabazz, traveled widely in Africa and the Middle East, renounced the NOI's antiwhite theology, threw himself into political activism that had previously been off-limits, founded the Organization of Afro-American Unity, and collaborated with Alex Haley in writing *The Autobiography of Malcolm X*. Some Black Muslims accused Malcolm of betrayal. "Such a man as Malcolm is worthy of death," Louis X, now known as Louis Farrakhan, proclaimed in December 1964. Weeks later, on February 21, 1965, assailants affiliated with the NOI assassinated Malcolm X in Harlem.

Malcolm X has been the subject of several biographies, the most comprehensive of which is Marable's portrait (a judgment that obtains despite the subsequent publication of Les and Tamara Payne's *The Dead Are Arising: The Life of Malcolm X*). Marable's mission was to "go beyond the legend; to recount what actually occurred in Malcolm's life." He pursued that aim earnestly, probing the whole of his subject's story, personal and public, no matter how embarrassing the findings. He recounts Malcolm X's secret 1961 meeting with representatives of the Georgia Ku Klux Klan to discuss their shared insistence on racial separation. He notes that at several NOI rallies Malcolm X and Elijah Muhammad hosted George Lincoln Rockwell of the American Nazi Party. In Marable's telling, Elijah Muhammad believed himself divinely omniscient, directed Malcolm X to pay tribute, prohibited him from working with civil rights activists, and even prevented him from confronting Los Angeles police who had maimed and killed members of the NOI. Elijah Muhammad's manipulations and impositions extended to all his deputies. He insisted that ministers desist from buying life insurance so that they would be all the more subservient out of fear for their families in the event of their incapacitation or death.

According to Marable, jealousy, enmity, pettiness, and corruption poisoned the upper ranks of NOI leadership. He describes NOI officials beating followers as a mode of discipline and demanding increased tithes to pay for personal extravagances, such as luxury automobiles. He also confirms Malcolm X's allegations that Elijah Muhammad, while married, seduced young followers, got them pregnant, and then abandoned them and their children, all the while preaching the virtue of chastity and patriarchal duty.

Marable provides abundant resources from which to draw for purposes of castigating Elijah Muhammad, the NOI, and Malcolm X. While many of these facts had been previously uncovered by other researchers, none of them had Marable's academic stature or political credentials. Marable was the founding director of the Columbia University Institute for Research in African-American Studies and was an important, well-respected figure among left black activist intellectuals. His candor is impressive; he must have known it would provoke accusations of rank betrayal. He certainly understood that some admirers and apostles of Malcolm X and Elijah Muhammad would berate him for publishing material that hurts the reputation of twentieth-century black nationalism, and would claim that he was doing so opportunistically while feeding off white elite institutions—Columbia University and the Viking publishing house—that are largely unaccountable to black folk.

These and other allegations and insinuations can be found in two compilations of essays, *A Lie of Reinvention: Correcting Manning Marable's Malcolm X* (2012), edited by Jared A. Ball and Todd Steven Burroughs, and *By Any Means Necessary: Malcolm X: Real, Not Reinvented: Critical Conversations on Manning Marable's Biography of Malcolm X* (2012), edited by Herb Boyd, Ron Daniels, Maulana Karenga, and Haki Madhubuti. While the latter collection contains several instructive essays, the former is uniformly tendentious, with piece after piece asserting not just that Marable is mistaken or negligent but that he *knowingly* spread falsehoods. "More than merely viewing Marable's reinvention of Malcolm as false," Ball writes, "we have, beginning with our choice of book title, unapologetically laid down our claim that it is a lie."

These overheated ad hominem attacks lack substantiation. Those who accuse Marable of lying fail to adduce credible evidence. They cavalierly fling charges that should only be made with care. They are also wrong in another way. They maintain that Marable fails to accord Malcolm X sufficient credit. Actually, though, he gives the man too much credit.

Marable remains enmeshed in the Malcolm X legend. He declares in the final sentence of his biography that "Malcolm embodies a definitive yardstick by which all other Americans who aspire to a mantle of leadership should be measured." Yet Marable's narrative indicates that Malcolm X was actually a poor leader, subject to all manner of bad ideas, who constantly misjudged people and events. For most of his post-prison life, he was the mouthpiece for a theocrat who, claiming access to divine revelation, propagated a socially conservative (for example, anti-birth-control) black nationalism that was escapist in its rejection of civil rights activism, sexist in its subordination of women, and racist in its condemnation of whites.

Elijah Muhammad's racial teachings must be recalled with particularity. To him, not *some* whites but *all* whites were "devils," doomed by their race to be evildoers. In *Message to the Blackman in America* (1965), he insists, "The origin of sin, the origin of murder, the origin of lying are deceptions originated with the creators of evil and injustice—the white race." Whites, he writes, "cannot produce good for they are without the nature of good." "None of them are righteous—no not one." "They are ever seeking to do harm to [blacks] every second of the day and night." Angered and disgusted by "the most wicked and deceiving race that ever lived on our planet," he foresaw and eagerly anticipated the destruction of whites. Nothing else could bring relief because "as long as the devil is on our planet we will continue to suffer injustice and unrest and have no peace." But deliverance is coming, the Messenger prophesies: "The guilty who have spread evilness and corruption throughout the land must face the sentence wrought by their own hands."

Malcolm X dutifully echoed his spiritual master, albeit with élan and greater attentiveness to current events, domestic and international. A good example of Malcolm X's oratory as an NOI minister is his address "Message to the Grassroots," delivered in Detroit at the King Solomon Baptist Church in November 1963. In it he expressed his disgust at the government's broken promises with an uninhibited candor that many blacks found thrilling.

The speech was one of the last Malcolm X delivered prior to leaving the NOI, and in it he voiced signature themes. One is the need to recognize that the white man constitutes a danger to all black people: "Once we all realize that we have a common enemy, then we unite. . . . And what we have in common is that enemy—the white man. He's the enemy to us all." A second theme is the importance of a united black front free from white influence. "We need," Malcolm X declared, "to stop airing our differences in front of the white man, put the white man out of our meetings, and then sit down and talk shop with each other." Railing against what he saw as the dilutive effect of white participation in the civil rights movement, he turned to mockery: "It's just like when you've got some coffee that's too black, which means it's too strong. What do you do? You integrate it with cream, you make it weak." He charged that it was because of the need to accommodate whites that the March on Washington had "lost its militancy. It ceased to be angry, it ceased to be hot, it ceased to be uncompromising. Why, it even ceased to be a march. It became a picnic, a circus. Nothing but a circus, with clowns and all. . . . [I]t was a sellout."

A third theme is the absence of authentic black leaders accountable to black folk. According to Malcolm X, the white man takes "a so-called Negro, and makes him prominent, builds him up, publicizes him, makes him a celebrity," and then foists him upon blacks as a leader. The white man then uses these manufactured Negro leaders "against the black revolution":

> Just as the slavemaster . . . used Tom, the house Negro, to keep the field Negroes in check, the same old slavemaster today has Negroes who are nothing but modern Uncle Toms, twentieth-century Uncle Toms, to keep you and me in check, to keep us under control, keep us passive and peaceful and nonviolent.

What caused the most excitement and attracted the most denunciation were Malcolm X's observations regarding violence. "If violence is wrong in America," Malcolm X thundered, "violence is wrong abroad. If it is wrong to be violent defending black women and black children and black babies and black men, then it is wrong for America to draft us and make us violent abroad in defense of her." Before King critically related domestic race relations to U.S. foreign policy, Malcolm X did so. He also reproached blacks for what he saw as their failure to defend themselves adequately. "You bleed for white people," he said. "But when it comes to seeing your own churches being bombed and little black girls murdered, you haven't got any blood. . . . How are you going to be nonviolent in Mississippi, as violent as you were in Korea?" As for the philosophical nonviolence insisted upon by King and others, Malcolm X was downright contemptuous. "Whoever heard of a revolution where they lock arms . . . singing 'We Shall Overcome'? Just tell me. You don't do that in a revolution. You don't do any singing, you're too busy swinging."

While Malcolm X and other followers of Elijah Muhammad put on cathartic performances in relatively safe surroundings, King, Carmichael, Medgar Evers, John Lewis, Fannie Lou Hamer, James Farmer, Julian Bond, Bob Moses, Diane Nash, James Lawson, and others risked their lives repeatedly in face-to-face confrontations with armed, trigger-happy white supremacists. While Malcolm X was taunting King and company for rejecting violence, the tribunes of the civil rights movement were successfully pressuring the federal government to bring its weight to bear against the segregationists through the Civil Rights Act of 1964 and the Voting Rights Act of 1965. While Malcolm X talked tough—"if someone puts his hand on you, send him to the cemetery"—he and the NOI did little to redress effectively racist police brutalization of Black Muslims. While Malcolm X spoke with apparent knowingness about racial uplift, at no point did he communicate a cogent, realistic strategy for elevating black America. Farmer, of the Congress of Racial Equality, unmasked the emptiness of Malcolm X's thinking during a debate in 1962. "We know the disease, physician," he said, "what is your cure? What is your program and how do you hope to bring it into effect?" At a loss for anything pertinent to say, Malcolm X chastised Farmer for having married a white woman.

Marable emphasizes that Malcolm X displayed a remarkable capacity for growth and reinvention, especially during his final year of life. Tragically, however, he was murdered by former comrades before his transformation could fully develop. In subsequent decades, propagandists, activists, politicians, rappers, and film-makers have remade Malcolm X, portraying him as a figure who rivaled King in vision and achievement. By downplaying Malcolm X's complicity in supporting a morally bankrupt and socially backward sect, by exaggerating the significance of that final year, and by failing to examine more searchingly Malcolm X's proposals, Marable contributes to this mythology. He accords to his hero a stature in memory that he lacked in history.

STOKELY CARMICHAEL

While Malcolm X is the most celebrated figure in the Black Power line of African American protest, Stokely Carmichael occupies a unique place as the person who popularized the "Black Power" slogan.

His key intervention came on June 16, 1966, during the March Against Fear, which had been initiated by James Meredith, the black man who broke the color barrier at the University of Mississippi. Meredith had planned to walk alone from Memphis to Jackson to dramatize the determination of blacks to exercise freedoms long denied them. After a white man shot and wounded Meredith on the second day of his trek, Carmichael joined with other activists to resuscitate the effort. Along the way, Carmichael was jailed for defying an order against raising tents to shelter marchers on the grounds of a black public school. Upon release, he declared, the "only way we gonna stop them white men from whuppin' us is to take over. We been saying 'freedom' . . . and we ain't got nothin'. What we gonna start sayin' now is 'black power'!" The crowd responded with exhilaration: "Black Power! Black Power! Black Power!"

Carmichael joined the March Against Fear as the newly elected chair of the Student Nonviolent Coordinating Committee (SNCC). Born in Trinidad in 1941, raised in New York City, and introduced to serious political activism at Howard University, Carmichael was part of that remarkable cadre of reformers whom the historian Howard Zinn called "the new abolitionists" and whom the journalist Jack Newfield dubbed the "prophetic minority." He joined in Freedom Rides, sit-ins, and voter registration drives. He canvassed places in the Deep South where "uppity

Negroes"—that is, blacks who sought to take advantage of their rights as American citizens—were harrassed and worse. On his twentieth birthday he found himself incarcerated in Mississippi's infamous Parchman prison for entering a white waiting room in a train station in Jackson. When he and his associates climbed out of a paddy wagon, an officer drawled, "We got nine: five black niggers and four white niggers." By the time of the March Against Fear, Carmichael had been jailed at least two dozen times.

Peniel Joseph's biography, *Stokely: A Life*, is an admiring depiction of a brave, handsome, talented, well-spoken man who gave himself unstintingly to the civil rights movement during its most glorious years in the early 1960s. The key moment for Carmichael, Joseph agrees, is the evening he shouted "black power" to that crowd in Mississippi. After that Carmichael became a celebrity. He was invited onto television programs such as *Meet the Press* and *Face the Nation* and was profiled in *Time*. He was vilified by politicians seeking the support of anxious or angry white voters and lionized by devotees of the newest sensation.

Working in the Deep South with his comrades in SNCC prior to Black Power—figuring out how to present to the nation the lawless oppression that blacks endured and experimenting with methods for raising the political consciousness of African American serfs—Carmichael distinguished himself as an inspiring organizer. His colleagues admired his dedication, persistence, idealism, loyalty, and courage. As he rose in prominence, however, the quality of his character, political and personal, deteriorated.

Although SNCC was already in decline when Carmichael was elected to head it in 1966, he failed to slow its descent and probably accelerated it. Carmichael's predecessor was the remarkable John Lewis, whose reelection as chair initially appeared pro forma. But some in SNCC complained that he was insufficiently militant and too much of an interracialist. They wanted to assert a right to respond to violence with violence; they thought SNCC should be run by and for blacks only. Though Lewis was at first reelected, opponents challenged the ballot, and Carmichael prevailed in a recount. The awkward reversal poisoned Lewis's relationship with Carmichael. And soon the triumphant faction banished the remaining whites on SNCC's staff.

According to Joseph, "Carmichael used his one-year tenure as SNCC chairman to thrust himself into the stratosphere of American politics." He hobnobbed with the heads of the other leading civil rights organizations—Farmer, Roy Wilkins of the National Association for the Advancement of Colored People (NAACP), Whitney Young of the National Urban League, and, of course, King. He socialized with activist-entertainers such as Harry Belafonte and Miriam Makeba, whom he later married. He interacted, too, with important white politicians, often refusing to abide by conventional standards of decorum: he spurned a White House invitation and declined to shake the outstretched hand of Atlanta's mayor.

The more defiant Carmichael's actions, the more provocative his rhetoric, the more attention he received. This fed his ego but did little to buoy SNCC's sagging fortunes, a fact that did not escape the notice of colleagues who began to deride him as "Stokely Starmichael." "SNCC's organizational strength seemed to decline," Joseph maintains, "in proportion to Carmichael's growing fame." Rather than seek a second term as chair, Carmichael turned the leadership of SNCC over to H. Rap Brown, who fecklessly presided over the organization's quickening slide. In an ugly spectacle, SNCC tore itself apart, pathetically betraying the racial unity its leaders trumpeted. In the summer of 1968, it expelled Carmichael.

After a dalliance with the Black Panther Party (BPP), including as its honorary prime minister, Carmichael journeyed abroad, where in some quarters he was acclaimed as a revolutionary. He established the All-African People's Revolutionary Party, but it never amounted to much. Eventually he settled in Guinea, where he changed his name to Kwame Ture in homage to Kwame Nkrumah, the deposed first president of Ghana, and Sekou Touré, Guinea's dictatorial president. Stricken by prostate cancer, Carmichael/Ture died in Guinea on November 15, 1998.

Joseph has studied Black Power deeply, producing a series of well-regarded articles and books including *Waiting 'til the Midnight Hour: A Narrative History of Black Power in America* and *The Sword and the Shield: The Revolutionary Lives of Malcolm X and Martin Luther King Jr.* His biography of Carmichael, however, is not nearly as informative as it should be. Joseph stresses that Car-

michael was a skillful and effective organizer in the Deep South
during his early days with SNCC. Missing, however, is a detailed
rendering of what being an organizer meant. What did Carmichael say to vulnerable black farmers he sought to bring into the
political process? How did he earn their confidence and respect?
What did he do day by day?

Joseph relies upon confidently asserted adjectives, usually flat-
tering ones, to do what should be done by detailed exposition.
He describes Carmichael's 1966 *New York Review of Books* essay
"What We Want" as "brilliant." According to Joseph, "'What We
Want' intellectually disarmed some of Carmichael's fiercest critics
and in the process announced SNCC's chairman as a formidable
thinker." Joseph neglects, however, to explain why an observer
ought to agree with the attribution of brilliance. He quotes a passage from Carmichael's essay:

> For too many years, black Americans marched and had
> their heads broken and got shot. They were saying to the
> country, "Look, you guys are supposed to be nice guys
> and we are only going to do what we are supposed to
> do—why do you beat us up, why don't you give us what
> we ask, why don't you straighten yourselves out?" After
> years of this, we are at almost the same point—because we
> demonstrated from a position of weakness. We cannot be
> expected any longer to march and have our heads broken
> in order to say to whites: come on, you're nice guys. For
> you are not nice guys. We have found you out.

Is this brilliant? Not self-evidently so.

Joseph spends less than two pages on the most important of
Carmichael's writings: *Black Power: The Politics of Liberation in
America* (1967), co-authored by the political scientist Charles V.
Hamilton. According to Joseph, *Black Power* is a "still-powerful
diagnosis of America's tortured racial history" and "an intellectually rigorous and theoretically subtle political treatise whose
unexpected breadth and depth surprised critics." Joseph, however,
offers no detailed and sustained description and analysis of *Black
Power*. "Carmichael and Hamilton offered an alternative reading
of American history," Joseph writes. "They replaced optimistic

narratives of democratic ascent with the reality of racial oppression, white violence, and a national failure on racial matters." But a summary so abstract offers readers little insight into *Black Power*'s contribution to the literature produced by the civil rights revolution. Joseph notes that *Black Power* was reviewed in several magazines and newspapers upon publication. That is useful. But what have commentators said about *Black Power* over the past four decades? And how does the book look in comparison with the writings of others and in light of subsequent developments? Answers are not to be found in *Stokely*.

Joseph discusses Lewis's ouster from the chairmanship of SNCC all too briefly. Devoting less than a page to this episode, he alludes to it as if readers will be sufficiently familiar with the dispute that further elaboration isn't needed. I have my doubts. Moreover, whether or not readers are familiar with it, the contest between Lewis and Carmichael was so important and remains sufficiently divisive that it warrants comprehensive evaluation. In *Walking with the Wind: A Memoir of the Movement*, Lewis spends an entire chapter on the disputed election. In his autobiography, *Ready for Revolution: The Life and Struggles of Stokely Carmichael*, Joseph's hero offers a very different story. Which account is more credible? Is there a synthesis superior to both? Again, Joseph offers no guidance.

HUEY NEWTON

In 1966, in Oakland, Huey Newton and Bobby Seale set in motion what became the Black Panther Party. Newton was a child of the Great Migration. He was born in 1942 in Monroe, Louisiana, the youngest of seven, and moved to Oakland in 1945. His parents were drawn by the prospect of economic opportunities stemming from the World War II industrial boom. In the early 1960s, Newton attended Merritt College, where he met Seale. Seale was also a migrant—born in Dallas in 1936 and raised in Oakland in a working-class family. He did a stint in the U.S. Air Force before enrolling at Merritt, where, along with Newton, he immersed himself in roiling debates about black history, socialism, black nationalism, integration, and anticolonialism.

Frustrated by continuing racial subordination notwithstanding the apparent victories of the civil rights movement, Newton and Seale decided to express themselves in a fashion that would appeal first and foremost to the "brothers on the block." Their audience comprised working- and lower-class blacks who were impatient with appeals to the conscience of the white establishment and who hungered instead for a more assertive, defiant politics, a politics that expressed demands for Black Power not only in rhetoric but in deed. Newton and Seale objected to the entire gamut of disabilities that burdened the poor urban black. The scope of their discontent, the depth of their ambition, and the radicalism of their methods can be seen in the most impressive writing they produced—the "Ten-Point Program" that served as a platform for the newly formed Panthers. "To those poor souls who don't know Black history, the beliefs and desires of the Black Panther Party may seem unreasonable," Newton and Seale wrote. But "to Black people, the ten points covered are absolutely essential to survival." Echoing calls for "Freedom Now," the program complained that blacks "have listened to the riot producing words 'these things take time' for 400 years." Newton and Seale itemized "what we want":

1. We want freedom. We want power to determine the destiny of our Black Community. We believe that Black people will not be free until we are able to determine our destiny.
2. We want full employment for our people.
3. We want an end to the robbery by the White man of our Black community.
4. We want decent housing, fit for the shelter [of] human beings.
5. We want education for our people that exposes the true nature of this decadent American society. We want education that teaches us our true history and our role in the present-day society.
6. We want all Black men to be exempt from military service.
7. We want an immediate end to police brutality and murder of Black people.
8. We want freedom for all Black men held in federal, state, county, and city prisons and jails.

9. We want all Black people when brought to trial to be tried in court by a jury of their peer group of people from their Black communities. As defined by the Constitution of the United States.
10. We want land, bread, housing, education, clothing, justice, and peace.

In a following section titled "What We Believe," Newton and Seale demanded "the overdue debt of forty acres and two mules" as reparations for "slave labor and mass murder of Black people," asserted that the Second Amendment of the Constitution of the United States "gives us a right to bear arms," and closed by invoking the prologue to the Declaration of Independence.

Early in the history of the BPP, Newton and Seale chose as their key issue police misconduct, especially the use of excessive force. Police brutality was a frequently mentioned problem in litanies of complaint voiced by activists. Periodically it emerged as a focal concern in local controversies. But the Panthers were alone among national black political organizations in making a priority of protest against racist police malfeasance. Their signature move was to follow and observe Oakland cops, all the while carrying loaded firearms publicly, which state law then permitted them to do. Although this tactic prompted confrontations with police, Newton and Seale refused to back down. They believed that routine humiliation and brutalization by police epitomized blacks' racial subordination, and they insisted that blacks had a right to defend themselves against police misconduct.

Three confrontations with police in 1967 forged the Panthers' reputation. In January a contingent led by Newton entered the lobby of the San Francisco airport. In *Black Against Empire*, Bloom and Martin write that the Panthers were "dressed in uniform—waist-length leather jackets, powder blue shirts, and black berets cocked to the right." The men displayed shotguns and pistols—again, legally. They had come to the airport to receive Betty Shabazz, the widow of Malcolm X, and to escort her to an interview with an ex-convict journalist writing for *Ramparts* magazine, Eldridge Cleaver. At the *Ramparts* office, Newton got into an altercation with a reporter. According to Bloom and Martin,

Police officers reacted, several flipping loose the little straps that held their pistols in their holsters. One started shouting at Newton, who stopped and stared at the cop. Seale tried to get Newton to leave. Newton ignored him and walked right up to the cop. "What's the matter," Newton said, "you got an itchy finger?"

The cop made no reply and simply stared Newton in the eye, keeping his hand on his gun and taking his measure. The other officers called out for the cop to cool it, but he kept staring at Newton. "O.K. you big fat racist pig, draw your gun," Newton challenged. The cop made no move. Newton shouted, "Draw it, you cowardly dog!" He pumped a round into the shotgun chamber.

The other officers spread out, stepping away from the line of fire. Finally, the cop gave up, sighing heavily and hanging his head. Newton laughed in his face as the remaining Panthers dispersed.

A second episode, in May, earned the Panthers their first brush with national media attention. A group of uniformed Panthers entered the California capitol with their firearms in full view to denounce proposed legislation that, if enacted, would outlaw the carrying of loaded guns in public. Bloom and Martin portray this demonstration as profoundly significant:

> The Sacramento protest attracted a wider movement audience and established the Black Panther Party as a new model for political struggle. Soon students at San Francisco State College and the University of California, Berkeley flocked to Panther rallies by the thousands. Countless numbers of young blacks—looking for a way to join the "Movement," or just to channel their anger at the oppressive conditions in which they lived—now had a political organization they could call their own.

Finally, on the morning of October 28, Newton killed an Oakland police officer, John Frey. Newton was charged with murder and convicted of manslaughter, though his conviction was overturned on appeal. Two retrials ended with hung juries. The "Free Huey" campaign made Newton one of the most publicized prisoners of the 1960s.

Bloom and Martin maintain that "from 1968 through 1970, the Black Panther Party made it impossible for the U.S. government to maintain business as usual, and it helped create a far-reaching crisis in U.S. society." For substantiation, they turn to a witness on the left, the Students for a Democratic Society, which called the Panthers the "vanguard in our common struggles against capitalism and imperialism." They also turn to a witness on the right, the FBI director, J. Edgar Hoover, who in 1969 declared, "The Black Panther Party, without question, represents the greatest threat to the internal security of the country." Indeed, according to Bloom and Martin, the Panthers' impact did not stop at the border: the party "forged powerful alliances, drawing widespread support . . . from anti-imperialist governments and movements around the globe." "Without the Black Panther Party," Bloom and Martin insist, "we would now live in a very different world."

The authors are unabashed in their admiration. They praise the Panthers' revolutionary aspirations—their demand for a new, postcapitalist, antiracist social order—as opposed to the comparatively modest entreaties of integrationist reformers who merely wanted a larger piece of the American pie. They laud the Panthers' willingness to confront police in word and practice. They applaud the party's efforts to suppress homophobia and sexism within its own ranks. They acclaim the Panthers' efforts to feed children through a much-heralded breakfast program and to make accessible to poor people much-needed medical care. They commend the Panthers for having been more cosmopolitan and open to interracial coalitions than were other champions of Black Power in the late 1960s, for having been more radical than the establishment's favorite organs of civil rights protest, and for having opposed U.S. foreign policy even in a time of war. They rightly note that the party was the victim of a ruthless campaign of suppression by local, state, and federal police. Making a mockery of legal protections for freedom of expression and association, the FBI sought to turn local constituencies against the Panthers and tried, sometimes with deadly effectiveness, to turn Panthers against themselves and other radicals.

As they go about correcting what they perceive as misimpressions that minimize the Panthers' significance and sully their character, Bloom and Martin accuse several historians of having "effectively advanced J. Edgar Hoover's program of vilifying the Party and shrouding its politics." These detractors "omit and obscure the thousands of people who dedicated their lives to the Panther revolution, their reasons for doing so, and the political dynamics of their participation, their actions, and the consequences."

But Bloom and Martin's effort to burnish the Panthers' reputation founders on tendentious advocacy. Read again their description of the confrontation at the *Ramparts* office. It wholly indulges the Panthers' own uncorroborated portrayal of what transpired. In another depiction of Newton and Seale facing down Oakland cops, Bloom and Martin have Newton pushing a policeman out of a parked car, leaping out of the vehicle with shotgun in hand, and shouting, "Now, who in the hell do you think you are, you big rednecked bastard, you rotten fascist swine, you bigoted racist? . . . Go for your gun and you're a dead pig." This reads like a script from a Melvin Van Peebles film—in other words, a fantasy in which Newton is the swashbuckling hero who mouths all of the baddest lines. But how do Bloom and Martin know that, in fact, Newton pushed the cop and then called him a "rednecked bastard"? "The description of the event," they declare in their endnotes, "comes from Bobby Seale, *Seize the Time: The Story of the Black Panther Party and Huey P. Newton* . . . and from Joshua Bloom's tour of the site of the incident with Bobby Seale." Seale's memoir is certainly a pertinent source, but one that should have been handled more carefully. Bloom and Martin make little effort to look beneath the swaggering veneer of Panther reminiscences. In *Reviews in American History*, the historian Jama Lazerow notes that in *Black Against Empire* "it is not clear just what constitutes historical proof." Writing in the *Los Angeles Times Book Review*, Héctor Tobar observes that Bloom and Martin's "most dramatic failing" is "their lack of critical distance from their subjects. . . . Many passages read as if they were written in the pages of the Panthers' official publication, 'The Black Panther,' circa 1970."

Bloom and Martin also produce little evidence or sustained argument to support their assertions of the Panthers' significance. Here is a characteristic formulation: "For a few years, the Party seized the political imagination of a large constituency of young black people." What do they mean by "large"? Thirty percent of black people between the ages of eighteen and fifty in the late 1960s or early 1970s? Forty percent? Twenty percent? In the United States? In California? In Oakland? They don't say.

They further maintain that by 1970 "what was once a scrappy local organization was now a major international political force, constantly in the news, with chapters in almost every major city." It is true that the Panthers were "constantly in the news." But was that media presence an accurate reflection of their activity and influence, or a reflection of journalists' hunger for the sensational (albeit marginal)? Perhaps it was both, but Bloom and Martin fail to examine either hypothesis carefully.

At one point, they do attempt to inject some quantitative specificity into their narrative. By 1970, they write, the Panthers "had opened offices in sixty-eight cities," "the Party's annual budget reached about $1.2 million (in 1970 dollars)," and the "circulation of the Party's newspaper . . . reached 150,000." While this is an improvement over vague adjectives ("large," "major"), Bloom and Martin never subject their evidence to rigorous analysis. What constituted an "office"? A post office box, two conveners, and a casual nod from party authorities in Oakland? Or something more substantial? As for the $1.2 million budget, that figure would be more meaningful if compared with the budgets of, say, the SCLC, NAACP, and other black defense and uplift organizations. The sociologist Herbert Haines generated useful insights by pursuing such comparisons in *Black Radicals and the Civil Rights Mainstream, 1954–1970* (1988). He found that the NAACP and kindred organizations were even more attractive to donors thanks to militant activism: "Moderate groups . . . profited immensely from the pressure created by more radical groups and rebellious ghetto-dwellers." In light of Haines's research, one might investigate whether the Panthers exerted a notable influence as a threat even when their own activity was negligible. Yet here, as elsewhere, Bloom and Martin fail to pursue potentially fruitful inquiries. As Fabio Rojas writes acidly in *The American Historical*

Review, Black Against Empire "shies away from the most important
question about the Black Panther Party."

Bloom and Martin rightly criticize writings that one-
sidedly assail the Panthers, paying little heed to the inequities they
sought to remedy, the repression they faced, and the benefits they
bestowed. Bloom and Martin especially loathe the work of David
Horowitz, a progressive who turned reactionary in part out of disgust with the BPP. They also cite *The Shadow of the Panther: Huey
Newton and the Price of Black Power in America*, by Hugh Pearson, who was an editorial writer for *The Wall Street Journal*. *The
Shadow of the Panther* chronicles a long and lurid list of legal and
moral crimes, including extortion, drug trafficking, and murder.
To Bloom and Martin, Horowitz and Pearson simply continued
Hoover's vilification of the Panthers.

Detractors, however, would be hard-pressed to sow more suspicion of the Panthers than do Bloom and Martin, albeit inadvertently. They write, for example, that Newton's "street knowledge
helped put him through college, as he covered his bills through
theft and fraud." Nothing is said more specifically about the "theft
and fraud," the identities of those hurt, or the extent of their
losses. Bloom and Martin even leaven their description with a hint
of esteem, noting, "When Newton was caught, he used his book
knowledge to study the law and defend himself in court, impress-
ing the jury and defeating several misdemeanor charges." Later,
Bloom and Martin consign to obscurity the killing of Officer Frey,
a key event in the history of the Panthers. "There are conflicting
accounts of what happened," they say, but they do not describe
those competing portrayals, thus leaving readers without guidance as to which ought to be believed. Bloom and Martin mention
that Newton fled to Cuba after being indicted in 1974 for killing
a seventeen-year-old prostitute and beating a man. But again they
forgo exploring the circumstances surrounding these allegations,
insinuating that the charges were meant to demonize Newton and
the Panthers. On the other hand, they concede, albeit grudgingly,
that there is reason to believe that "for much of the 1970s, Newton ruled the Party through force and fear and began behaving
like a strung-out gangster."

If Bloom and Martin refer to Newton as a "gangster," his misdoings must have been awful indeed, for they hold to a minimum any information or conclusions that reflect badly on the Panthers. They relegate to a mere clause in a sentence the sensational fact that in 1973 Newton expelled Seale from the party. Excessively condensed, as well, is their rendition of the sad story of Newton's end. With conspicuous terseness, they note simply that on August 22, 1989, he was killed by "a petty crack dealer from whom he was likely trying to steal drugs."

In assessing Malcolm X, Stokely Carmichael, Huey Newton, and Bobby Seale, we should keep in mind that they tried to act against the racial injustice that has befouled America. That alone entitles them to some respect. It is important to acknowledge the daunting obstacles they encountered within and outside black communities. It is imperative to recall the devious and illicit machinations of Hoover and other enforcers of "law and order." It is also important to note that Carmichael was only twenty-five when he shouted "black power!" and that Newton was only twenty-four when, with Seale, he founded the BPP. It should come as no surprise that young people sometimes display bad judgment. But none of this lessens the responsibility of scholars to be exacting. Neither the art of scholarship nor the struggle for social justice is advanced when intellectuals are anything less than punctilious in confronting inconvenient realities.

26

The Constitutional Roots of "Birtherism"

Donald J. Trump has shown an appalling capacity to exploit American weaknesses. This extends to a flaw in the Constitution that facilitated his takeover of the Republic Party.[1] Article II, Section 1, Clause 5 of the Constitution declares, "No Person except a natural born Citizen, or a Citizen of the United States, at the time of the Adoption of this Constitution, shall be eligible to the Office of President."* By charging that Barack Obama had been born outside the United States and was thus ineligible for the presidency, Trump became the darling of millions of Americans now known as "birthers."

Trump's accusation has rightly triggered denial. The allegation is inaccurate and demagogic. Trump was obviously uninterested in the facts of the matter. But an appropriate response should go further and include a critique of the eligibility proviso itself, for that criterion is an invidious discrimination.

Many observers laud America for its openness, its freedom from feudalistic stratifications, its aspiration to reward good conduct as opposed to mere status, its privileging of loyalty to republican values over immutable claims of parentage. Yet the

---

* The qualification clause also provides, "Neither shall any Person be eligible to that Office who shall not have attained to the Age of thirty-five Years, and been fourteen years a Resident within the United States."

presidential qualification proviso, by barring from consideration for the presidency millions of naturalized citizens, puts an unjustifiable nativist exclusion into the very core of American democracy. The provision wrongly diminishes potential candidates it disqualifies as well as voters who might prefer a naturalized citizen to those who are eligible. The natural born citizen qualification elevates to governance a rank superstition, an idolatry of place of birth.*

John Jay, a future chief justice of the U.S. Supreme Court, is the progenitor of the natural born citizen requirement. He wrote a letter to George Washington during the Constitutional Convention in which he suggested that "it would be wise and seasonable to provide a strong check to the admission of Foreigners into the administration of our national Government" by declaring "expressly that the Command in Chief of the American army shall not be given to nor devolve on, any but a natural born citizen."[2]

Jay and other Founding Fathers apparently believed that the risk of elevating to the presidency a hidden subversive under foreign influence would be substantially diminished by reserving that singular position to one born on this soil. In *Commentaries on the Constitution of the United States*, Justice Joseph Story approvingly observed that the natural born citizen proviso "cuts off all chances for ambitious foreigners, who might otherwise be intriguing for the office; and interposes a barrier against those corrupt interferences . . . which have inflicted the most serious evils upon the elective monarchies of Europe."[3]

Two criticisms have dogged the natural born citizen proviso. One is that it invites potentially paralyzing disagreement over a candidate's eligibility. Is a person born in Puerto Rico, Guam, the U.S. Virgin Islands, or the Northern Mariana Islands a natural born citizen of the United States? (Probably not.) What about

---

* While Article II is the wellspring of the reservation of the presidency to "a natural born Citizen," other constitutional and statutory interventions have reinforced that mischief. The Twelfth Amendment extends the discrimination to the vice presidency: "No Person constitutionally ineligible to the office of President shall be eligible to that of Vice-President of the United States." The Presidential Succession Act (1947) provides that presidential authority can be vested only in an official "eligible to the office of President under the Constitution."

a person born in the District of Columbia? (Probably so.) What about a person born abroad to U.S. citizens who were merely on a temporary sojourn? What about children of citizens born abroad in embassies or military bases? What about a person whose birthplace is unknown?

A second and more fundamental objection is that the proviso wrongly elevates people born in the United States (however defined) over those born elsewhere. Some observers try to minimize the importance of the disqualification by citing the extreme unlikelihood of any given person attaining the presidency no matter what his or her background. They contend, in effect, that ineligibility for the presidency is like ineligibility for a lottery—an exclusion from a fanciful possibility. Actually, though, the natural born proviso creates, literally, a category of second-class citizenship because it declares that only the native born are suitable for the country's highest post. All others are unsuitable—no matter their demonstrated patriotism. Hundreds of veterans awarded the Congressional Medal of Honor have sacrificed their lives in service to the United States. Yet because of where they were born, they were barred from consideration for the presidency.

The natural born citizenship requirement ought to be abolished. That it adds substantially to our security is highly unlikely. No individuals in American history have been more traitorous than natural born citizens, including Robert Philip Hanssen (the Chicago-born FBI operative who spied for Soviet intelligence), Aldrich Ames (the River Falls, Wisconsin–born CIA counterintelligence officer who betrayed the United States), and Ronald Pelton (the Benton Harbor, Michigan–born National Security Agency officer who sold secrets to the Soviets). Place of birth is no secure proxy for loyalty.* It indicates nothing about a person's

---

* Noting the arbitrariness of the eligibility proviso, Professors Duggin and Collins observe that "an infant born in one of the fifty states but raised in a foreign country by non–United States citizens could serve as President, while a foreign born child adopted by United States citizens at two months of age and raised in the United States would be ineligible to become President." Sarah Helene Duggin and Mary Beth Collins, "Natural Born in the U.S.A.: The Striking Unfairness and Dangerous Ambiguity of the Constitution's Presidential Qualifications Clause and Why We Need to Fix It," 85 *Boston University Law Review* 137 (2005).

willed attachment to a government, nation, community, or way of life. It describes only an accident of fate over which an individual has no control.

Of course Americans want to protect themselves against Manchurian candidates. That is at least part of the function of careful, informed, skeptical, intelligent scrutiny through journalism, debates, party primaries, and the other rigors of general elections. The natural born citizen proviso offers a spurious filter.

Without a strong justification, then, the natural born citizenship proviso stigmatizes a substantial portion of the American political family—naturalized citizens. The requirement brands them by declaring that unlike fellow citizens born in America, they are permanently barred from serving in the nation's highest office. This is, or should be, a big deal. As Professor Robert Post declares,

> At the very heart of the constitutional order, in the Office of the President, the Constitution abandons its brave experiment of forging a new society based upon principles of voluntary commitment; it instead gropes for security among ties of blood and contingencies of birth. In a world of ethnic cleansing, where affirmations of allegiance are drowned in attributes of status, this constitutional provision is a chilling reminder of . . . a fate we have struggled to avoid.[4]

There are reasons neither Henry Kissinger nor Arnold Schwarzenegger should have been president. But disqualification based on place of birth—Germany and Austria—should not have been one of them. Naturalized citizens have served ably in the highest echelons of the military—for example, John Shalikashvili, chairman of the Joint Chiefs of Staff (1993–1997), born in Warsaw, Poland; the highest echelons of law—for instance, Felix Frankfurter, associate justice of the U.S. Supreme Court (1939–1962), born in Vienna, Austria-Hungary; and the highest echelons of diplomacy—for example, Madeleine Albright, secretary of state (1997–2001), born in Prague, Czechoslovakia. There is no good reason for disqualifying naturalized citizens as a matter of law from bringing their skills to bear on the presidency. Excluding them not only stigmatizes naturalized citizens. It also hurts the American polity by unjustifiably removing from consideration individuals whom voters might prefer. Applauding the foreign-born citizens "who run companies, teach classes, work two shifts, comfort the sick, command platoons, find cures, and make laws," Scott Simon of National Public Radio rightly asks, "Can we afford a clause that excludes some of our most talented Americans?"[5]

An amendment is needed to address the invidious discrimination against naturalized citizens that is presently lodged in the American Constitution. It should remove from the criterion of eligibility for the presidency any distinction based on how individuals attain their citizenship. It should reinforce the idea that within the American political family *all* persons are truly equal before the law.*

---

* A useful model has been drafted by Professors Duggin and Collins:

> Any citizen of the United States who has attained to the age of thirty-five years and who has been fourteen years a resident within the United States shall be eligible to the Office of the President, provided that any person elected to the office of President who is also a citizen of any other country shall renounce any such citizenship under oath or by affirmation prior to taking the oath of the office of President. *Id.* at 152.

27

Inequality and the Supreme Court[1]

The Supreme Court occupies an exalted place in the American imagination that is associated with all sorts of quasi-religious overtones. Its members, nine justices dressed in black robes, are widely portrayed as fundamentally different from other people who deploy power in that they have supposedly undergone some purification that makes them attentive only to "law" and not to "politics." These oddly priestly figures swear an oath to "administer justice without respect to persons, and to do equal right to the poor and to the rich." They conduct their business in a marble temple, engage in arcane rituals hidden from public view, and interpret a delphic text, the U.S. Constitution, in the course of settling searing controversies that divide the country.

Americans shower the justices of the Supreme Court with a deference that is different from that shown to "political" figures. Power based on electoral results is the source of the authority that prompts many people to kowtow to presidents, senators, and the like. With justices, the kowtowing stems not only from obeisance to power but also from a notion that the justices exhibit an elevated quality of thought that endows them with a deserved special aura. This added element of deference is evident even in law schools where one might expect to find more resistance to juridical hagiography. After being selected as a Supreme Court nominee, a person whose ideas had heretofore been ignored or even scoffed at is suddenly transformed into a deep thinker with a "jurisprudence." Prior to his nomination to the Supreme Court, Judge Anthony Kennedy would not have been considered a plausible candidate for a professorship at any of the most elite law schools. He had a perfectly respectable career but not one that would have captured the interest of legal academia's leading talent scouts. After Kennedy ascended to the Supreme Court, however, faculties at these same schools fell all over themselves genuflecting to him. The same is true with respect to most of the other justices.

Many Court watchers, academic and journalistic, suppress acknowledging that to an overwhelming extent the justices are lawyers who occupy coveted positions of prestige and authority merely by dint of political connections and fortuity. A few are truly learned in the law. But for most, luck is their main distinction. Yet Court watchers insistently endow the justices with a meritocratic gloss as if the quality of their thought and craft explained their ascension to the top of the legal profession. Such cultivated delusion is what prompted Judge Richard Posner to lash out at what he saw as ridiculous sycophancy in assessments of the justices: "I sometimes ask myself [whether the Supreme Court justices] are the nine best-qualified lawyers to be justices," he remarked splenitically in 2016. "Obviously not. Are they nine of the best 100? Obviously not. Nine of the best 1,000? I don't think so. Nine of the best 10,000? I'll give them that." Posner was overstating his point. But as Richard Hofstadter once observed, any good point should be able to bear the strain of overstatement. And this one does. Posner's put-down, albeit bilious, is preferable to the mythologizing he skewers.

Fortunately, there are some commentators who are attempting to convey to the public a realistic understanding of the justices, the Court, and its role in American life. One is Adam Cohen, who argues in *Supreme Inequality* that for fifty years the Supreme Court has repeatedly hurt the poor while helping the rich. The Court, he laments, has "expanded the rights of wealthy individuals and corporations to use their money to gain influence over government." Simultaneously, in rulings on voter ID, the Voting Rights Act, and voter roll purges, the Court has diminished the ability of those with relatively little money to use the one thing they have at their disposal to influence government: their votes. Cohen goes on to argue that "the Court's decisions involving the rights of workers ... have had a devastating impact on the economic standing of low- and middle-income Americans," denying damage awards when workers are treated unfairly and leaving workers bereft of the wage and benefit premiums that come with union membership. The Court's rulings, Cohen charges, are "a major reason that the poorest workers have not seen an increase in the minimum wage in a decade," have "little recourse when their wages are stolen," and suffer unnecessarily high rates of death and injury on the job. Moreover, while the Court shows little solicitude for those charged with "street" crime, it displays keen sympathy for white-collar malefactors, bending over backward to shield them from criminal liability and civil punitive damages.

Cohen designates *Dandridge v. Williams* (1970) as the case in which, after a brief period of progressive rulings during the 1960s, the Court began again to turn against citizens of color, workers, and the poor. The issue in *Dandridge* was whether a state violated the equal protection clause of the Fourteenth Amendment by capping welfare payments at $250 per month regardless of a family's size or need. Reversing judgments in lower courts, the Supreme Court concluded that "the intractable economic, social, and even philosophical problems presented by public welfare assistance programs are not the business of [the federal judiciary]."

In subsequent rulings the Court's aversion to judicial redistributionist interventions only deepened. In *San Antonio Independent School District v. Rodriguez* (1973), the Court determined that there is no violation of federal constitutional law when children in poor districts, limited by constricted tax revenues, receive less funding for public schooling than children in more affluent districts. The plaintiff in the case attended schools in San Antonio that received 40 percent less funding than schools in a wealthier district that was, Cohen notes, nearby but "a world away" in terms of opportunity. According to Cohen, this case, "more than any since *Brown v. Board of Education*, had the potential to transform the nation's education system and create a more equal America." Although a lower court sided with the plaintiff, the Supreme Court reversed this ruling. At least where wealth is involved, Lewis Powell declared, "the Equal Protection Clause does not require absolute equality or precisely equal advantages."

In cases on racial inequality, the Court also put the brakes on judicial intervention. In *Milliken v. Bradley* (1974), the question was whether predominantly white suburbs could be enlisted to remedy racial discrimination in the predominantly black public schools of Detroit by busing. Lower courts thought that such a remedy ought to be permissible. After all, the state as a whole was responsible for the unconstitutional infractions of its subdivisions, cities, and suburbs alike. Four justices agreed. But the same five who determined *Rodriguez* ruled against the plaintiff, holding that federal courts lack authority to order "innocent" white suburbs to contribute to desegregation in metropolitan areas.

In *Buckley v. Valeo* (1976), the Court decided, Cohen tells us, "a case that was as important to equality in elections as [*Rodriguez* and *Milliken*] were to equality in education." Striking down provisions that would have limited the amount of money that individuals can expend in supporting a candidate, it invalidated major portions of campaign finance legislation enacted to address problems brought to light by the Watergate scandals. In the course of doing so, the Court posited two key propositions. One is that spending money in support of a candidate is tantamount to speaking out on behalf of the candidate, thus equating the spending of money with speech. The other is that when it comes to speech, leveling down on behalf of equal opportunity is impermissible. "The concept that government may restrict the speech of some elements of our society in order to enhance the relative voice of others is wholly foreign to the First Amendment."

In rulings that followed, the Court further limited governmental authority to regulate the deployment of wealth in elections. Most significantly, in the 2010 case *Citizens United v. Federal Election Commission*, it ruled that the McCain-Feingold campaign finance law overstepped constitutional boundaries by prohibiting corporations and unions from expending funds from their treasuries on electioneering speech. Objecting to the Court's bestowal of First Amendment rights upon corporations, John Paul Stevens noted in dissent that firms have "no consciences, no beliefs, no feelings, no thoughts, no desires." Corporate personhood is a useful legal fiction in certain contexts, he added, but corporations "are not themselves members of 'We the People' by whom and for whom the Constitution was established." For the five-justice majority, however, what mattered was not the source of the "speech"—namely, money—but its content. "Political speech," Anthony Kennedy intoned, "is indispensable to decision-making in a democracy and this is no less true because the speech comes from a corporation rather than an individual."

Elsewhere in the law of elections, the Court repeatedly facilitated impediments to voting. In the 2008 case *Crawford v. Marion County Election Board*, the Court upheld an Indiana voter identification law in the absence of any showing that it was needed to thwart actual voter fraud and even though it foreseeably and disproportionately burdened black prospective voters and other groups that Republican lawmakers view and treat as unlikely supporters. In its 2013 *Shelby County v. Holder* ruling, the Court invalidated a key provision of the Voting Rights Act that had effectively monitored and restrained jurisdictions with long records of racial disenfranchisement, and in the 2018 *Husted v. A. Philip Randolph Institute* decision, the Court permitted Ohio to purge from its voter rolls persons who had not voted for a number of elections and been unresponsive to notices from boards of elections—an action undertaken with the obvious hope of getting rid of as many minority and other Democratic-leaning voters as possible.

Cohen's catalog also includes cases in which the Court has displayed antipathy toward organized labor, indifference toward workers seeking recourse through antidiscrimination lawsuits, and solicitude for wrongdoing business corporations facing the wrath of justifiably outraged juries. In 2018, in the *Janus v. American Federation of State, County, and Municipal Employees* ruling, the Court held that it was unconstitutional for a state to require workers to pay a fee to unions to defray costs associated with collective bargaining. The main justification for requiring the payment of such fees was to prevent free riding from workers who benefited from the union's bargaining even if they refrained from becoming members of the union. But in *Janus*, in an opinion written by Samuel Alito for a 5–4 majority, the Court held that forcing workers to pay such fees amounted to coerced expression, violating First Amendment rights by compelling workers to subsidize speech with which they disagree and would otherwise refrain from supporting.

In the 2007 case *Ledbetter v. Goodyear Tire and Rubber Company*, the Court added to its litany of antilabor rulings, erasing a jury award of damages in favor of a woman who had sued her employer under Title VII of the 1964 Civil Rights Act for gender discrimination. The Court held that she sued too late even though there was no feasible way for her to have known earlier that she was being paid less than similarly situated men. In the 2008 case *Exxon Shipping v. Baker*, the Court added to its run of pro-business rulings by reducing a jury award of punitive damages for the catastrophic oil spill that attended the grounding of a supertanker on an Alaskan reef. The captain of the tanker, absent when the grounding occurred, was found to have a high level of alcohol in his blood. At trial, it was revealed that Exxon allowed this person to captain a supertanker even after becoming aware that he had a record of alcohol abuse. A court of appeals assessed punitive damages of $2.5 billion, remitting a jury's assessment of $5 billion. The Supreme Court, however, thought that even that amount was impermissibly excessive. It limited punitive damages to no more than a bit over $500 million.

Cohen notes that while the Court protected corporations from what it saw as excessive penalization for grossly negligent conduct, the Court declined to protect convicts from what many see as excessive punishment for relatively trivial criminal violations. In the 2003 case *Lockyer v. Andrade*, the Court upheld the application of California's "three strikes" law in a decision that condemned a man with prior convictions to a prison term of twenty-five years to life after he was caught stealing $150 worth of videotapes from two stores. Four dissenting justices remarked that if that sentence was not impermissibly disproportionate, "the principle has no meaning." Yet the majority, in an opinion by Sandra Day O'Connor, concluded that the sentence was allowable, or, in the Court's peculiar phrasing, "not objectively unreasonable."

Cohen's book offers a damning indictment. With a disciplined fury, he patiently collates and dissects cases whose connective tissues are often neglected, effectively bringing to light a subject that should receive more attention than it does—the Supreme Court's *inequality* jurisprudence. Many Americans repose more faith in the judiciary than the other branches of the federal government. According to Gallup, in 2020, 81 percent of those polled expressed at least some confidence in the Supreme Court (as opposed to 62 percent in the presidency and 55 percent in Congress). Some mistakenly believe that the judiciary is the one branch of government in which the rules apply evenly to all, rich and poor alike. Part of the excitement that surrounds the legal misfortunes of the high and mighty—for instance, the celebrity parents caught up in the college admissions scandal—is a sublimated yearning for a forum in which class privileges do not matter. Citizens and judges alike intone the mantra that no one—no matter how wealthy or prestigious or powerful—is above the law. Cohen's analysis belies the myth: at the Supreme Court, wealth and its absence do indeed make a difference.

Though definitely worth reading, *Supreme Inequality* does have deficiencies to which we ought to be attentive.

Eager, it seems, to leaven his withering narrative of Supreme Court knavery with something more positive, Cohen offers an overly cheery depiction of the Supreme Court presided over by Earl Warren between 1953 (when the former governor of California was named to be chief justice by Dwight Eisenhower) and 1969 (when Warren unhappily retired at the beginning of the presidency of Richard Nixon). Warren's arrival, Cohen maintains, "launched a progressive legal revolution" with a "mission" of "uplifting the poor and the weak, and of building a more equal and inclusive society." "The Warren Court," he declares, "systematically looked for ways in which the poor were unfairly disadvantaged." Cohen does temper his assessment, recognizing that the Warren Court was a "historical outlier," lasting only briefly before being overrun with Nixon appointees who steered the Court to a resumption of "its traditional role in national life: protector of the rich and powerful." Still, his celebration of the Warren Court is excessive.

It is true that the Warren Court issued an array of holdings that began to create a predicate for a jurisprudence more helpful to "the other America." In *Griffin v. Illinois* (1956), the Court struck down a state's procedures for appellate review in criminal cases because they severely disadvantaged indigent defendants. "There can be no equal justice," Justice Hugo Black declared, "where the kind of trial a man gets depends on the amount of money he has." In *Gideon v. Wainwright* (1963), the Court ruled that the state must provide an attorney to a defendant charged with a felony if he cannot afford to retain counsel himself. In *Harper v. Virginia Board of Elections* (1966), the Court ruled that a state violates the federal Constitution by conditioning the right to vote on the payment of a tax. Yet these decisions and the surrounding juridical infrastructure—the state courts and lower federal courts, the bar, and legal academia—failed to create a momentum sufficient to disrupt habits of interpretation that are far more attuned to negative as opposed to positive duties: rights against governmental interference as opposed to governmental obligations to assist people in need.

The Warren Court's most consequential, controversial, equalitarian, and esteemed decision was its 1954 ruling in *Brown v. Board of Education*, in which it invalidated racial segregation in public primary and secondary schooling. But celebration of *Brown* has exaggerated the Court's role in racial desegregation. Pushed by the NAACP and other civil rights activists, the Truman and Eisenhower Justice Departments called for the invalidation of racial segregation before Warren's arrival at the Court. Prior to *Brown*, moreover, all of the branches of the armed forces announced that they were abandoning segregation. The justices were nowhere nearly as pioneering as they are frequently portrayed as being.

Cohen's account—which follows the dominant narrative in

many constitutional law courses—also obscures how *Brown* and associated rulings assuaged segregationist sentiment by assuring white supremacists that they would be permitted to desegregate "with all deliberate speed." Cohen writes that "the Court did not back down" from enforcing *Brown* despite powerful opposition. He is right in lauding the Warren Court for declining to retreat from its decision. But in the decade after *Brown*, in the context of schooling, the justices tried as much as possible to stay out of the way of segregationists, even in locales in which litigants tried to challenge conspicuous nullifications of the Court's famous ruling.

In other contexts, too, the Warren Court conducted itself in ways that belie the rapturous praise often bestowed upon it. In 1965, at the height of the Second Reconstruction, the Supreme Court (with Warren in dissent) handed down one of the most retrograde race law decisions of the twentieth century. The Court ruled in *Swain v. Alabama* that the use of racially discriminatory peremptory challenges for purposes of tactical advantage in a trial gives no offense to the equal protection clause of the federal Constitution. The Court emphasized the venerable lineage of the peremptory challenge. It also maintained that inasmuch as racially discriminatory peremptory challenges were available to all parties, blacks as well as whites, they were susceptible to equal application. That thinking, which smacked of the perverse formalism of *Plessy v. Ferguson*, legitimated a device used repeatedly to exclude blacks from juries virtually anytime a prosecutor or defense attorney saw fit to do so. The consequence was a baleful record of racial exclusion in jury trials all over the United States until *Swain* was belatedly reversed in 1986.[*]

I revisit this history not to denigrate the Warren Court; it did indeed take significant steps toward racial equity that warrant acknowledgment. But we need to be clear-eyed: the Warren Court was no egalitarian Valhalla.

With respect to other subjects, too, Cohen's analysis is questionable. In his treatment of *Dandridge v. Williams*—the case involving the constitutionality of a cap on state aid regardless of

---

[*] For discussion of Justice Marshall's campaign to reverse *Swain*, *see* pages 315–323.

family size—Cohen scoffs at the Court's unwillingness to declare certain levels of welfare payments unconstitutionally stingy. This case, however, poses a difficult problem. How should a court go about determining whether a given amount of state assistance is impermissibly penurious? The cap at issue was $250 per month. If that was too little, would $300 suffice? What about $400? What about $500? What about $1,000? On what basis, in this context, should line drawing by judges be entitled to more deference than line drawing by legislators? It is important for those supportive of Cohen's judicial egalitarianism to be able to respond to this question. He arms them plenty with indignation; he ought to have armed them more with argumentation.

There are still other difficulties that Cohen slights. He excoriates the Court's ruling in *Citizens United v. FEC*, complaining that it has negatively "transformed American politics," facilitating a situation in which "the wealthiest Americans now play an extraordinarily large role in funding electoral politics." He derides as ridiculous the Court's argument equating money with speech. Although many astute observers agree, some do not, including people with progressive politics. The American Civil Liberties Union (ACLU) has consistently opposed parts of the campaign finance legislation that Cohen champions (though opinion within the organization is divided). These ACLU opponents of campaign finance restrictions are hardly reactionary plutocrats. They are strong liberals, typically inclined toward egalitarian reforms. But they are also militantly skeptical of any governmental action that might plausibly constrict freedom of expression, particularly political dissent. One might well reject their position. But it deserves a hearing and careful consideration. Cohen regrettably omits discussing the progressive libertarian critique of campaign finance laws. Missing from his pages is mention of the important, fascinating, and provocative fact that the ACLU occupies, on this issue, a position that is largely aligned with the Koch brothers and Senator Mitch McConnell.

Throughout *Supreme Inequality*, Cohen shows how the Supreme Court has reflected and effected racial inequities. He is considerably less attentive to gender relations and overlooks almost entirely struggles on behalf of equality for people with lesbian, gay, bisexual, and transgender identities. Discussing these subjects complicates Cohen's thesis because with respect to gender and especially sexual orientation, the Court's trajectory has been positive from a progressive vantage—keeping in mind that the starting place was low. Prior to the confirmation of Sandra Day O'Connor in 1981, there had never been a woman on the Court. O'Connor has been followed by four additional female justices—Ruth Bader Ginsburg, Sonia Sotomayor, Elena Kagan, and Amy Coney Barrett. Alongside the breakup of the male monopoly at the Court has been the emergence of a jurisprudence that has become, in some contexts, increasingly feminist. In *United States v. Virginia* (1996), a case unmentioned in *Supreme Inequality*, the Court had to decide whether Virginia violated the equal protection clause of the Fourteenth Amendment when it maintained a military institute that was reserved exclusively for men. In an opinion written by Justice Ginsburg, the Court invalidated the exclusion of women, notwithstanding the state's insistence that it had created an alternative educational opportunity for women that was substantially equal to that afforded to men. In this case, as in similar controversies, the Court expanded constitutional norms of gender equality.

The past half century has also witnessed a striking elevation of the legal status of people with heterodox sexual orientations. In *Baker v. Nelson* (1971), a gay couple that wanted to marry challenged a state law that restricted marriage to "persons of the opposite sex." When the couple appealed a judgment from the Minnesota Supreme Court that upheld that law, the U.S. Supreme Court dismissed the appeal "for want of a substantial federal question." In *Bowers v. Hardwick* (1986), in an opinion written by Justice Byron White that oozed with contempt for gays, the Supreme Court upheld the authority of the State of Georgia to criminalize consensual sodomy. Within half a century, both of those holding were overruled. In *Lawrence v. Texas* (2003), in an opinion by Justice Kennedy, the Court overruled *Bowers*. Then, in *Obergefell v. Hodges* (2015), in another opinion written by Justice Kennedy, the Court invalidated state laws that restricted marriage to unions between one man and one woman. The Court decreed, essentially, that for purposes of matrimony government had to treat same-sex couples the same as opposite-sex couples.

Thus, during the same period that the Supreme Court was facilitating inequality in certain key forums of social life—education, elections, labor, corporate regulation—it was undermining inequality in others: gender relations and the regulation of sexual orientation. Cohen shines no light on this fascinating disjunction.

Finally, Cohen is ensnared by the difficulty of distinguishing "law" from "politics." But that is no disgrace because it is true of practically everyone who seeks to make sense of the Supreme Court. Robert Dahl once observed that "as a political institution, the Court is highly unusual, not least because Americans are not quite willing to accept the fact that it *is* a political institution and not quite capable of denying it." Like many journalists, Cohen sharply distinguishes the Court from the "political" branches of the federal government. He complains that the Court over which Chief Justice John Roberts presides "seems more like a political body than a legal one." But the Court has always been political and is inescapably so given, among other things, the way it is constituted. How can the Court not be substantially "political" when the justices are selected and confirmed by electoral politicians.

Uncomfortable with assessing the Court through a thoroughly politicized lens, Cohen vacillates in his criterion of judgment, sometimes prioritizing craft, sometimes prioritizing outcome. When he lambastes *Citizens United*, he begins with a criticism about craft, complaining that the Court's majority "was almost lawless in its rush to overturn well-established law." That procedural craft complaint, however, is a cover for a political substantive objection. Surely Cohen would have had no objection had the cases targeted for a rushed overruling been deplorables such as *Dred Scott v. Sandford* (1857) or *Plessy v. Ferguson* (1896) or *Korematsu v. United States* (1944).

We need to become more realistic in our estimation of the Court, recognizing that the justices *are* politicians in robes. They pursue their agendas differently than the politicians in the White House and Congress. Teasing out those differences and similarities is a task that no one has thus far accomplished satisfactorily. But the "political" character of the Supreme Court is evident notwithstanding their and others' strenuous efforts at obfuscation.

Chief Justice Roberts chastised Donald Trump for referring to judges by the presidents who nominated them. "We do not have Obama judges or Trump judges," the chief justice declared. "What we have is an extraordinary group of dedicated judges doing their level best to do equal right to those appearing before them." But Trump, awful as he is, has the better of this dispute. There *were* "Nixon judges"; they bequeathed *Rodriguez* and *Milliken*. There were "Reagan judges"; they bequeathed *Bush v. Gore*. Similarly, there *are* Trump judges. What they bequeath only the future will tell, though their provenance and early decisions hardly inspire confidence.

Cohen argues persuasively that Republicans have managed the politics of the judiciary much more effectively than Democrats. Throughout *Supreme Inequality* he recurs to an obvious but important point: Supreme Court decisions are determined by who sits on it, which is determined by presidents who nominate, senators who ratify, and citizens who vote. This largely explains the trajectory of the Court since the 1960s. In 1967 liberal justices held a slim majority. But then the first of a series of disasters struck. Earl Warren announced his retirement while Lyndon Johnson was still president, trying to ensure that a liberal would succeed him on the bench. But Johnson miscalculated. When he nominated Justice Abe Fortas to succeed Warren as chief justice, the Senate rebelled. In the face of a filibuster, Johnson withdrew his nomination of Fortas (who later resigned his associate justiceship under a cloud of scandal). Johnson's misjudgment opened the door for his successor to nominate a new chief justice. That president was Richard Nixon, who, over four years, got to nominate four justices who received confirmation (Warren Burger, Harry Blackmun, Lewis F. Powell Jr., and William Rehnquist), creating a conservative majority that has held sway ever since.

A difficulty that has haunted liberals who have made it to the Supreme Court is the problem of knowing when to leave. In 1990, in his thirty-fourth year on the Court, William J. Brennan, the leader of the Court's liberal wing, retired at age eighty-four on account of poor health. President George H. W. Bush thought that he was nominating a conservative to succeed Brennan. In naming David Souter, however, the president erred inasmuch as Souter turned out to be quite moderate. Conservative Republicans noted the mistake. They organized under the banner of "No More Souters!" and vowed to avoid miscues in the future. They have succeeded all too well.

In 1991, in his twenty-fourth year on the Court, Thurgood Marshall at eighty-three was forced to retire because of poor health. If he could have held on for just five more months, he could have retired after the election of President Bill Clinton, who would surely have nominated someone favorably disposed to Marshall's jurisprudence. Instead, "Mr. Civil Rights" was replaced by "Mr. Anti–Civil Rights"—Clarence Thomas, the Court's most reactionary member.

In September 2020, in her twenty-seventh year on the Court, Ruth Bader Ginsburg died at eighty-seven after long bouts of serious illness. Her votes were typically smart, humane, and liberal. And some of her opinions were eloquent and moving. The circumstances surrounding her demise, however, will forever cast a shadow upon her reputation. In light of the Marshall-Thomas fiasco and the precarity of her health, Ginsburg's refusal to retire during the first administration of President Barack Obama, when a majority Democratic Senate would have assured a liberal successor, was one of the most irresponsible and selfish acts by a leading public figure in recent memory.

Not only have Republicans dominated the Court through their appointive power, with Republicans outnumbering Democrats twenty to five among justices seated between 1968 and 2020. Republicans have also dominated ideologically. Republican presidents have straightforwardly declared, when nominating judges, that they mean to appoint conservatives. Democratic presidents, by contrast, have blurred the ideological complexion of their choices, as if there were something disreputable about being liberal.

To forge a better future, this will have to change: Democrats need to be more candid about their reasons for opposing Supreme Court nominees. They should not be at all reluctant about voting to reject nominees on ideological grounds. Just because someone is smart and knowledgeable, hardworking and honorable—like Amy Coney Barrett—does not mean that that person should be elevated to the Supreme Court. If that person is likely to advance policies that are politically unacceptable, then he or she ought to be opposed. That Antonin Scalia was confirmed with no dissenting votes (98–0) despite a record that gave ample cause for alarm reflects poorly on the senators who judged him, especially the liberals among them (including Joe Biden, John Kerry, and Ted Kennedy).

Democrats also need to be much more intently focused on pushing the judiciary in a more progressive direction. That will require study, debate, and the identification and encouragement of prospective nominees. Liberals should have rolling lists of favorite candidates who are assessed in terms of their potentiality for refashioning the judiciary such that it can contribute to the making of a more just America. Above all, liberals need to recognize that the Supreme Court is inescapably political. The key is to ensure that a judicial politics of equitable fairness prevails.

28

Brown as Senior Citizen[1]

Brown v. Board of Education attained on May 17, 2019, that notable landmark in American life—the age of sixty-five. One of the Supreme Court's most esteemed decisions became a senior citizen. *Brown* is a ruling that people tend to think they know even if they have not actually read it. This contributes to a fate that often bedevils celebrities. Observers project their yearnings upon *Brown*, neglecting its particularities. They sanctify *Brown*, make it an icon, and invoke its constitutional authority to impose preferred policies. Liberals have done this. And so, too, have conservatives.

I proceed in five stages. First, I define what I mean by *Brown*. Second, I recall its painful birth and traumatic childhood. Then I reject prominent claims said to be justified by *Brown*. Next I rebut frequently heard charges of "betrayal," noting that the Supreme Court, throughout *Brown*'s adulthood, has never retreated from the invalidation of segregation in public schooling. Finally, I assert that we should acknowledge *Brown*'s limits, and, renouncing ancestor worship, look to ourselves to fashion fresh ideas that suitably address the new challenges we face.

I

When I refer to *Brown v. Board of Education*, I refer to three rulings of the Supreme Court in 1954–1955, all of which were authored by Chief Justice Earl Warren.[2] These rulings constitute the historical *Brown*—not an allegory, not a metaphor, not an emblem, but rather a cluster of discrete though related opinions that announced decisions in three cases. The first case is a collection of disputes that arose in states. *Brown v. Board of Education* arose from the state of Kansas. The other disputes arose in Delaware, Virginia, and South Carolina. At issue was the legitimacy of state constitutional and statutory law that authorized or required officials to separate students on a racial basis for primary and secondary schooling. The South Carolina Constitution, for instance, declared, "Separate schools shall be provided for children of the white and colored races, and no child of either race shall ever be permitted to attend a school for children of the other race."[3] The companion to the *Brown* cases, *Bolling v. Sharpe*, arose from the District of Columbia, where a policy superintended by the federal government separated students on a racial basis.

In the cases from the states, plaintiffs challenged segregation pursuant to the Fourteenth Amendment to the federal Constitution, which declares that no *state* shall deny to any person within its jurisdiction the equal protection of the laws. In the case from the District of Columbia, the plaintiff challenged segregation pursuant to the Fifth Amendment, which declares that no person shall be deprived of liberty without due process of law.

Officials defended segregation by saying it was a long-established tradition that diminished social frictions and protected "racial integrity." They denied that segregation was an invidious discrimination. They insisted that separate but equal facilities satisfied federal constitutional requirements because insofar as segregation was implemented such that racially separated services and facilities were equal, no one had a basis for justified complaint.

On May 17, 1954, the Supreme Court ruled in the state cases that "in the field of public education the doctrine of 'separate but equal' has no place. Separate educational facilities are inherently unequal." The Court held that "the plaintiffs and others similarly situated . . . are, by reason of the segregation complained of, deprived of the equal protection of the laws."[4] In the companion case, the Court ruled that with respect to the District of Columbia "segregation in public education is not reasonably related to any proper governmental objective, and thus [imposes] . . . a burden that constitutes an arbitrary deprivation of . . . liberty in violation of the Due Process Clause."[5] The Court addressed the issue of remedy in a third decision a little more than a year later. On May 31, 1955, the Court remanded all of the cases to the trial courts from which they had arisen. The Court determined that local officials should continue to exercise primary authority over schooling and that the trial courts should appraise the good faith of these officials in implementing admission to public schooling on a nondiscriminatory basis. The Court also decreed that while the new dispensation could not be permitted to yield to popular disagreement, a variety of obstacles could justify permitting local officials additional time to carry out the ruling in an effective manner. *Brown*, the Court concluded, required officials "to admit to public schools on a racially nondiscriminatory basis with all deliberate speed the parties to these cases."[6]

II

Most Supreme Court rulings are rendered after one round of oral arguments. *Brown* needed three. To elicit the unanimous holdings that followed required a feat of diplomacy inasmuch as views diverged markedly on a bench filled with strong-willed personalities.[7] Essential to the success of that diplomacy was securing the votes of at least five justices. Crucial to securing those votes was writing an opinion that would be acceptable to racial conservatives and proponents of "judicial restraint" while nonetheless satisfying the aim of racial liberals to invalidate racial segregation in primary and secondary public schooling.

Given the reverence with which some commentators discuss *Brown*,[8] one might expect it to contain a searing denunciation of racist deprivation or a thrilling call for a new birth of racial equality. If eloquence is your expectation, however, Warren's opinion will bring disappointment. *Brown* is strikingly wan, studiously restrained.* It says next to nothing about segregation's origins,

---

* "A schoolboy of the twenty-first century reading back and expecting to find a Declaration of Independence or Gettysburg Address will likely be deflated."

purpose, ideology, or implementation. A reader of *Brown* alone, with no knowledge of American race relations, might well be mystified by the depth of the feelings surrounding the case. The opinion offers little explanation for what the fighting is about.

Warren says that "to separate [blacks] from others of similar age and qualifications solely because of their race generates a feeling of inferiority as to their status in the community that may affect their hearts and minds in a way unlikely ever to be undone." He embraces the finding of a lower court that "the policy of separating the races is usually interpreted as denoting the inferiority of the negro group."[9] In his strongest negative aside, he says that "segregation in public schooling is not reasonably related to any proper governmental objective."[10] But Warren omits explaining why segregation generated a feeling of inferiority or was usually interpreted as denoting the inferiority of the Negro group or was devoid of any proper governmental purpose.

In 1896, in *Plessy v. Ferguson*,[11] the Supreme Court upheld the constitutionality of racial segregation in intrastate rail transportation, a policy of racial separation that metastasized into every crevice of southern society. Dissenting, Justice John Marshall Harlan wrote, "What can more certainly arouse race hate . . . than state enactments which, in fact, proceed on the ground that colored citizens are so inferior and degraded that they cannot be allowed to sit in public coaches occupied by white citizens?"[12] Appropriately mocking segregation's "thin disguise" of delusive symmetry—the cunning lie of separate but equal—Harlan remarked that "everyone knows that [segregation] had its origin in the purpose, not so much to exclude white persons from railroad cars occupied by blacks, as to exclude colored people from coaches occupied by . . . white persons."[13] Harlan pointed out that segregation was some-

J. Harvie Wilkinson III, *From Brown to Bakke: The Supreme Court and School Integration, 1954–1978* (1979), 29. Wilkinson, a shrewd observer, understood that the dullness of the opinion was purposeful. "If the price of unanimity was a lack of language to anthologize, then that price, sensed Warren, would have to be paid." *Id.* at 31. On the other hand, the great civil rights advocate Jack Greenberg maintained that *Brown* "proved to be the Declaration of Independence of its day." Jack Greenberg, "The Supreme Court, Civil Rights, and Civil Dissonance," 77 *Yale Law Journal* 1520, 1521 (1968).

thing done by whites to blacks, that segregation was a deliberate negation of racial equality, that segregation was a proclamation of white superiority, that segregation was meant to protect whites from the supposedly contaminating influence of colored people. Harlan's blunt exposure of segregation's ugliness is absent from Warren's narrative, and Harlan's dissent is never even cited in *Brown*.

Warren's diffidence was neither negligent nor inadvertent. It was part of his diplomacy. Warren wrote privately that he sought to craft an opinion that was "short, readable by the lay public, non-rhetorical, and, above all, non-accusatory."[14] He did just that. Warren's *Brown* managed to invalidate segregation without castigating the officials who designed and imposed Jim Crow oppression. It depicted stigma without stigmatizers, injustice without perpetrators. It struck down school segregation policies in twenty-one states and the District of Columbia without setting forth clearly the basis for this momentous action. Judicial opinions are typically lauded for clarification as well as resolution. *Brown* is a testament to delphic ambiguity.

Perhaps the chief justice was right to engage in obfuscation. Perhaps he was prudent to avoid candor. Perhaps he was sensible in eschewing immediate compliance and permitting instead the gradualism of "all deliberate speed." Perhaps he was wise to be evasive for the purpose of securing unanimity behind the Court's ruling.[15]

We should, however, be aware of the realities attending *Brown*'s birth. As with other positive developments in the American law of race relations, *Brown* was conceived in compromise. The Emancipation Proclamation left unaffected the legal status of around 800,000 slaves.[16] The Fourteenth Amendment permitted the states to continue racial exclusion at the ballot box, imposing only a penalty for doing so.[17] The Fifteenth Amendment was among the narrowest of the voting rights provisions considered during the First Reconstruction and was promulgated despite the foreseeability of easy evasion.[18] Perceiving a need to compromise, Warren omitted from *Brown* central aspects of the segregation story, most notably white supremacists' rationale for racially separating children pursuant to the coercive force of state power.

Largely absent from the most honored race relations decision in American constitutional law is a candid reckoning with racism.

Despite Warren's effort to soften the blow that the Court delivered to the white supremacist "southern way of life," *Brown* triggered an extraordinary negative reaction. Echoing Confederate ancestors, lawmakers in several segregationist states promulgated resolutions of interposition that proclaimed the authority of states to disregard the federal Supreme Court's ruling. Nineteen senators and eighty-two members of the House of Representatives endorsed the Declaration of Constitutional Principles, better known as the Southern Manifesto, which denounced *Brown* as "a clear abuse of power" and voiced an intention to resist and reverse it.[19] Mississippi's governor, Hugh L. White, called *Brown* "the most unfortunate thing that ever happened" and said that his state was "not going to pay any attention to the Supreme Court."[20] Repudiating the Court's gradualism, Georgia's governor, Marvin Griffin, declared that "no matter how much the Supreme Court seeks to sugarcoat its bitter pill of tyranny, the people of Georgia and the South will not swallow it."[21]

Over the next several years, states moved from rhetoric to action. Louisiana enacted school segregation statutes anew that denied credits to any student who attended desegregated instruction, decertified any teacher who delivered instruction in a desegregated class, fired any principal who permitted desegregated schooling, and threatened prosecution of any agent of the federal government who attempted to implement *Brown*. Several jurisdictions rescinded laws requiring mandatory school attendance. Others enacted laws empowering officials to close schools that were ordered to desegregate. In a county in Virginia officials did away with public schooling altogether for five years in order to avoid any desegregation (and would have continued the shutdown even longer in the absence of judicial intervention).[22] In Little Rock, Arkansas, Governor Orval Faubus called out the state's National Guard to prevent the court-ordered desegregation of a high school and subsequently closed all of the city's high schools for a year rather than see any of them desegregated. Voicing a sentiment consistent with the governor's conduct, a white teenager bluntly announced why she would prefer no schooling to schooling governed by *Brown*. The teen said that she would "rather be stupid than go to school with a nigger."[23]

III

Seldom, if ever, has a Supreme Court ruling met with as much sustained, outspoken, defiant, and intermittently violent resistance as the backlash against *Brown v. Board of Education*. Yet, as a matter of law, the Supreme Court's invalidation of Jim Crow segregation in schooling has never been rescinded. To the contrary, the Court supported the champions of the civil rights movement with rulings that enabled them to spread anti-segregationism beyond schooling to recreation, housing, employment, transportation, seating in courtrooms, prisons, matrimony, and just about every other conceivable facet of social life.[24] Jim Crow was routed. Nothing like the segregation provision of the South Carolina Constitution exists in the United States anymore as an effective law-giving force. This is not to say that racial injustice in all its manifold incarnations has been overcome. In many domains, whiteness continues to elicit privilege, while coloredness continues to attract deprivation. But the type of racial oppression that *Brown* specifically targeted has been vanquished.

After Heman Sweatt, an African American, applied for admission to the University of Texas School of Law in 1947, state officials, confidently reliant upon the validity of segregation, openly rejected him on a racial basis, admitting that "he possessed every essential qualification for admission, except that of race."[25] Fourteen years later, when James Meredith, another African American, applied for admission to the University of Mississippi, a profound change had occurred that prevented racist officials from confidently relying upon the validity of segregation. That change was *Brown*. It had moved the needle of legitimacy. Now the segregationists could no longer be honest. *Brown* forced them abjectly to lie. The state claimed now that it no longer maintained a policy of segregation at the university, an obviously untrue assertion at which a court of appeals scoffed. Deprived of the legal high ground they had long enjoyed, the segregationists resorted to violence, fraud, and corruption of the judicial process.[*] But eventually, albeit after frustrating delay, Meredith did enroll at Ole Miss, a step forward that could not have been achieved without *Brown*. Meredith's advance has now been replicated on innumerable occasions. Now nowhere in the United States can an official say without fear of legal repercussion that he or she is using governmental authority to separate pupils on a racial basis to create or maintain racially homogeneous "white" schools. Officials said that loudly and assuredly prior to May 17, 1954. No more.

For a decade after *Brown*, segregationist defiance succeeded impressively. By 1964 only a little bit more than 1 percent of black children in Dixie attended schools with whites.[26] Then, by dint of private litigation initiated by brave plaintiffs who refused to back down even in the face of frightening intimidation, by dint of federal legislation, and by dint of nudging by the Johnson and even the Nixon administrations, the situation on the ground was transformed. The dam broke and desegregation even in the Deep South flowed. Black children crossed the race line to enter schools regarding which segregationists had vowed, "Never!"

Reflective of that profound change in American life and law was the trajectory of *Brown's* reputation. Segregationists who vilified *Brown* at its birth and during its early years received a degree of succor from others who distanced themselves from the Court's ruling or spoke of *Brown* skeptically, sometimes even with disdain, because of objections to Warren's ruling, including its theoretical

---

[*] U.S. District Court judge Sidney Mize, forsaking his obligation to be truthful, sought to ratify the deceitful claim of state educational officials who swore that they rejected Meredith's application for nonracial reasons. Judge Mize "found" that the University of Mississippi no longer engaged in racial segregation and that its rejection of Meredith's application had nothing to do with race. *See Meredith v. Fair*, 202 F. Supp. 224 (S.D. Miss. 1962). Reversing Judge Mize in a sardonic opinion penned by Judge John Minor Wisdom, the Fifth Circuit Court of Appeals noted "that from the moment the defendants discovered Meredith was a Negro they engaged in a carefully calculated campaign of delay, harassment, and masterly inactivity. It was a defense," the court observed, "designed to discourage and to defeat by evasive tactics which would have been a credit to Quintus Fabius Maximus." 305 F. 2d 343, 344 (CA 5 1962), *cert. denied*, 371 U.S. 828 (1962). All too little attention has been paid to the corruption of the legal process that occurred when segregationist judges lied repeatedly in order to avoid the conclusions demanded by *Brown v. Board of Education*.

thinness and allusions to ill-supported social science. Over time, however, *Brown*'s prestige grew and solidified to the place where its justifiability ascended to the rank of an unquestionable assumption. Its acclaim grew as millions were transfixed and transformed by the morally resplendent oratory of Martin Luther King Jr., the disciplined militancy of the Student Nonviolent Coordinating Committee, the heroic persistence of the National Association for the Advancement of Colored People, the exposure of injustice that led to the civil rights bills of 1957, 1960, 1964, 1965, and 1968, and the shocking sacrifice of brave activists such as Medgar Evers, Andrew Goodman, Michael Schwerner, James Chaney, Jimmie Lee Jackson, Viola Liuzzo, James Reeb, and Vernon Dahmer. As the civil rights movement won influence and admiration, so, too, did *Brown*.

By the late 1960s, former declared enemies of *Brown* were abandoning open opposition. In 1952 a law clerk to the Supreme Court justice Robert Jackson wrote a memo titled "A Random Thought on the Segregation Cases" in which he posited that *Plessy v. Ferguson* ought to be reaffirmed. Nineteen years later, that attorney, William Hubbs Rehnquist, came before the U.S. Senate for confirmation as President Richard Nixon's nominee as an associate justice of the Supreme Court. Rehnquist insisted that in that memo he had articulated not his own thinking but that of his boss. Fifteen years after that, when he was nominated to become chief justice, Rehnquist again distanced himself from the memo. Both times he realized that his chances for confirmation would be seriously diminished were he to admit what is almost certainly true: that as a young attorney he saw no constitutional infirmity in racial segregation and that as a mature attorney he had continued to doubt *Brown*'s justifiability. So he pinned the substance of the memo upon his deceased boss and engaged in a belated confirmation reassessment: "I wish to state unequivocally that I fully support the legal reasoning and the rightness from the standpoint of fundamental fairness of the *Brown* decision."[27]

By offering ratification from the right wing of the legal establishment, Rehnquist and other conservatives grudgingly completed *Brown*'s canonization. Since the late 1960s few ambitious jurists have been willing to dispute publicly the rightness of *Brown*. It is, as Professors Jack Balkin and Sanford Levinson observe, "normatively canonical. . . . [O]ne establishes oneself as a properly acculturated lawyer by affirming *Brown's* correctness."[28]

IV

Brown's beatification has prompted advocates of all sorts to enlist it in support of their causes. They want to associate its aura with their aims. Racial liberals did this in the 1970s and 1980s when they successfully invoked *Brown* as a justification for requiring authorities not simply to desist from segregating schools but also to take affirmative steps to ensure that schools be racially mixed. While *Brown* had initially declared, "Thou shalt not segregate," reformers came to interpret it as declaring, "Thou shalt integrate." The original *Brown* prohibited racial segregation in schooling as a matter of governmental policy. *Brown* as later recast required authorities to create racially heterogeneous schools even if doing so required burdensome busing.[29] In retrospect, this recasting is remarkable given the modesty of the original *Brown*. Warren's rulings in 1954–1955 offer an implausible predicate for the sweepingly affirmative actions taken in its name subsequently.

Political and judicial reverses undercut the ability of racial liberals to implement some of their plans.[30] But ideas that animated those plans have persisted. They manifest themselves in efforts to revise the meaning of certain highly emotive terms, most notably "segregation." Many racial liberals now erase the distinction between the "segregation" of the pre-*Brown* era, when law expressly required racially homogeneous institutions, and the "segregation" of today, when that term is often used to refer to institutions that are said to be "racially imbalanced," having populations that do not mirror the racial demographics of the surrounding community.[31] While for some this usage is merely imitative habit, for others this usage is part of a strategy to discredit those institutions by tarring them with a label associated with the state-sanctioned racial stratification that was openly and unapologetically practiced prior to *Brown*.

If schools are bad or unjustly organized, they should be exposed and made better or fairer. "Segregation" with its accompanying connotations, however, is a misleading term to use in seeking to understand and remedy some of the problems we currently face, including circumstances under which, in the absence of current state-sanctioned efforts to separate students on racial grounds, students of color nonetheless suffer strikingly poorer educational outcomes in comparison with white peers. "Segregation," properly understood, means racial separation in schools that has been deliberately engineered by public authorities. Typically, though, this is not what is at play as dissension erupts among whites, blacks, Latinos, Native Americans, people of Asian ancestry, and still others over optimal or permissible ways to organize public schooling. Rather, at play is a mosaic of contending forces battling over charter schools, Afrocentric schools, race-conscious integrationism, selection schemes based on standardized testing, and other contested initiatives. These conflicts are marked in unprecedented ways by crosscutting fissures of class, culture, and ideology as well as race—a situation much more complicated than that which *Brown* addressed.

Overlooking complication will lead us awry. But that is the fate to which we consign ourselves when we apply terminology that suitably illuminated the problems of an earlier time but that is unsuitable to the illumination of looming difficulties today. The problem of the school from which blacks are racially excluded categorically notwithstanding grades or test scores or anything else should be viewed differently from the problem of the selective school in which the black population is disproportionately small because relatively few blacks have applied and a large number of those who have applied are outperformed by peers of different races.[32] While the former school should be labeled "segregated," the latter school ought not. By hypothesis, the rules pursuant to which the latter school is organized are racially unbiased in design and implementation. The racial demographics of the school do not stem from efforts by officials to deter, exclude, or in any way diminish the presence of students of color on account of race. Rather, the racial demographics of the student body almost certainly reflect the obstructive power of debilitating disadvantages left by vestiges of racial injustice, including historically victimized parents who, relative to others, have fewer resources to impart to their children. These and other difficult-to-remedy problems will be obscured by portraying the school as "segregated" when, in fact, its problems lie elsewhere.

Commentators who wield loosened definitions of "segregation" invoke the specter of "the New Jim Crow." The outstanding articulation of this concept is Michelle Alexander's influential critique of the administration of criminal justice.[33] But invocations of "the New Jim Crow" have now reached to other domains as well, indeed to apply to American society in general. The central theme of the New Jim Crow is that the racial hierarchy that gave rise to old-style segregation remains intact. Social reforms (for example, Jackie Robinson breaking the color bar in baseball or Vanessa Williams breaking the color bar at the Miss America pageant), judicial reforms (for instance, *Smith v. Allwright* and *Shelley v. Kraemer*), and legislative reforms (for example, the Civil Rights Act and the Voting Rights Act) have etched significant changes into the fabric of American life. A few blacks are CEOs of major corporations. Colin Powell was the most admired military officer since World War II. Every presidential cabinet since 1964 has featured at least one African American. Barack Obama was elected and reelected president of the United States. An African American woman, Kamala Harris, has been elected vice president of the United States, while an African American man, Raphael Warnock, has been elected to serve as a U.S. senator from Georgia. But despite these indicia of change, analysts who propound the idea of the New Jim Crow insist that America remains a pigmentocracy. They assert that racial hierarchy manifests itself in educational regimes in which, systematically and predictably, whites fare far better than people of color. They argue that these circumstances are the result of decisions in which officials have chosen, with varying degrees of self-awareness, to privilege policies advantageous to whites over policies that would be advantageous to nonwhites. An example, they say, is the Supreme Court's choice to condemn as unconstitutional de jure segregation while putting de facto segregation beyond the reach of constitutional regulation.

The New Jim Crow analogy taps into the memory of a notorious, older regime of racial injustice. Those who deploy it are
determined to make vivid the current situation in which blacks
continue to be relegated to the bottom tiers of American society
as measured by all manner of indicia of well-being—from longev-
ity and wealth to access to employment, housing, health care, and
education. Purveyors of the New Jim Crow analogy, however, use
it for more than exegesis; they also use the analogy for purposes
of political mobilization. They implore audiences to resist assur-
ances of mission accomplished and to reject claims that we have
overcome. It was sure to happen, as it has, that a law professor was
going to assert that "the new Jim Crow is the old Jim Crow."[34]

There is much that is laudable about the aims and tactics of
those sounding alarms about the supposed New Jim Crow. The
analogy has assisted in triggering indignation that has fueled
new activism challenging formidable problems. Purveyors of the
New Jim Crow analogy, however, tend to erase its crucial distinctions, insisting upon a continuous, unchanging narrative of white
supremacist ascendancy. Although proponents of the New Jim
Crow analogy decry triumphalism, their central rhetorical trope
derives its power from the fact that, overwhelmingly, Americans condemn the (old) Jim Crow system. The widely perceived
unacceptability of *that* system prompts and undergirds the effort
to associate it with contemporary policies and conditions also
deemed to be unacceptable. This strategy, however, holds dangers
of its own. One is relying too much on the intellectual and political labors of precursors—echoing overmuch imagery that is now
overused. If nothing much has changed between the segregation
regime and what exists today, it would seem that no harm will
ensue from continuing to use the same old vocabulary of protest.
If much has changed, however, deploying obsolescent terminology is bound to mislead.

A far more troubling example of anachronism is supplied by
the Supreme Court, particularly Chief Justice John Roberts. In
2007, in *Parents Involved in Community Schools v. Seattle School District No. 1*,[35] in a set of cases arising from Kentucky and the state
of Washington, the Court invalidated policies undertaken voluntarily by local school boards that used race as one of several pos-

sible factors in determining placements for students in primary and secondary schools. The school boards' purpose was to sustain as much racial heterogeneity as possible.

At the end of his plurality opinion for the Court in *Parents Involved*, the chief justice wrapped himself in *Brown*. Because *Brown* required admission to public schools on a nondiscriminatory basis, Roberts reasoned, it should be impermissible for school boards on their own, absent judicial compulsion, to take race into account in making student assignments, even if maintaining racial integration was the aim. "The way to stop discrimination on the basis of race," Roberts concluded, "is to stop discriminating on the basis of race."[36]

Chief Justice Roberts's equation of the racial discrimination at issue in *Brown* and the racial discrimination at issue in *Parents Involved* is obtuse. It is an awful example of myopic formalism. The segregation challenged in *Brown* was a regime that oppressed blacks. It categorically disadvantaged them with a policy signaling that in the estimation of officials African Americans were an inferior group that should be publicly labeled as such. The policy challenged in *Parents Involved* can hardly be said to have oppressed whites. The upshot of predominantly white school boards, those policies contained nothing that could plausibly be seen as signaling a belief that whites are racial inferiors. *Brown* featured officials separating the races in order to quarantine all blacks. *Parents Involved* featured policies that adversely affected some whites—not all, but some—for the purpose of securing racially mixed schooling. Roberts says that drawing racial distinctions to create segregation and to create integration are both similarly violative of the Constitution's directive to government to offer to all persons equal treatment before the law. This position is ridiculous and ought to be rejected. It purports to erase the difference between the policies in question in *Brown* and those in *Parents Involved*. That polarity is the difference between a sign that says "People of Color Are Welcome!" versus a sign that says "People of Color Are NOT Welcome!"* Both signs draw racial distinctions. But the

_____

* Justice John Paul Stevens made the point nicely: "There is no moral or constitutional equivalence between a policy that is designed to perpetuate a caste

424 Say It Loud!

first is a benign, positive racial discrimination, while the second is a malign, negative racial discrimination. *Brown* addressed the latter, which was all too prevalent in the United States of 1954. The former—positive discrimination aimed at fostering integration or rectifying past injustices or enhancing diversity—hardly had a presence in American life back then. *Brown* simply did not speak to the permissibility or wisdom of such policies. When Chief Justice Roberts justifies his views on the matter by reference to *Brown*, he is engaging in bamboozlement.

V

We would do well, now, to appreciate the historical *Brown*, and continue to deploy it to invalidate any governmental action undertaken for the purpose of separating people on a racial basis to signify and accomplish racial hierarchy. We should also acknowledge *Brown*'s boundaries and retool ourselves to confront a very different racial landscape than that confronting Americans in 1954. The creators of *Brown*—the brave plaintiffs, their justly celebrated lawyers, the justices who allowed themselves to break from tradition—all warrant congratulations and gratitude. *Brown* is a vehicle that carried essential freight. But it should not be looked to longingly as a vehicle that can carry *all* of the burdens of racial justice. To adequately address the crises we confront now requires more than habitual incantations of *Brown*. It requires forging *new* law, *new* ideas, and a *new* vocabulary pertinent to current demands.

---

system and one that seeks to eradicate racial subordination." To ignore the gulf that should be seen as separating positive from negative racial distinctions, he rightly complains, is to "disregard the difference between a 'No Trespassing' sign and a welcome mat." *Adarand v. Peña*, 515 U.S. 200, 243–47 (1995) (Stevens, J. dissenting).

29

Racial Promised Lands?

What do people mean when they call for "racial justice"? What competing aspirations are embedded in such calls? Should we be more ambitious in our planning, or is modesty the better policy? In seeking to address these and kindred questions, I will consider different visions of racial justice articulated since the mid-twentieth century. One is white supremacism as embodied by George Wallace. Another is black separatism as embodied by Elijah Muhammad. A third is the Black Power initiative embodied by Stokely Carmichael, Bobby Seale, and Huey Newton. A fourth, the most influential, is color blindness, which has generated the idea of the race-blind Constitution. I then address the abolition initiative that has become prominent recently. I conclude with observations about the way in which grappling with this subject has moved my thinking toward a more cautious posture than the one I had at the outset of this exercise.

I

Certain racial aspirations have been given short shrift in legal academia and elsewhere as topics of study. One is a vision of society in which people of different races know their places and stay in them. It is the dream of a pigmentocracy in which whites are on top and people of color subordinate. This desire has been embraced by leading intellectuals, politicians, and jurists for most of American history—the champions of racial slavery in the United States (for instance, John C. Calhoun), the proponents of racial slavery in the Confederate States of America (for example, Alexander Stephens), the promoters of racial hierarchy pursuant to segregation, imperialism, and racially discriminatory immigration policies (for instance, Madison Grant). This conception of racial justice suffered from a substantial loss of prestige in the 1930s, 1940s, and 1950s partly as a result of opposition from people of color, fallout from the atrocities of the Nazi regime, and the Cold War struggle for international hegemony between the United States and the Soviet Union. Still, devotion to racial hierarchy—or, more specifically, commitment to white supremacism—remained quite popular and powerful in the 1960s.

On January 14, 1963, forty-three-year-old George C. Wallace propounded a white supremacist version of racial justice in his inaugural address as governor of Alabama. Speaking from Montgomery, which he called the "very Heart of the Great Anglo-Saxon Southland," he denounced federal tyranny, which he saw manifested in *Brown v. Board of Education* and other efforts to enforce the Reconstruction Amendments on behalf of African Americans. Assailing the civil rights movement that he abhorred, Wallace maintained that liberals seek "to persecute the international white minority" for the benefit of "the international colored majority." Acknowledging that he viewed himself as the representative of white but not black Alabamians, Wallace declared, "We invite the negro citizens . . . to work with us from his separate racial station . . . as we will work with him . . . to develop, to grow, in individual freedom and enrichment. We want jobs and a good future for BOTH our races." In Wallace's view that happy future was only possible, however, under racial separatism directed by whites and secured by states' rights. "If we amalgamate . . . as advocated by the communist philosophers," Wallace warned, "the freedom of our development . . . is gone forever. We become . . . a mongrel unit of one under a single all powerful government . . . and we stand for everything . . . and nothing." Championing a vision of America as a white man's country, Wallace announced his commitment in a flourish that would become infamous: "Segregation today . . . segregation tomorrow . . . segregation forever."[1]

. . .

Two years later, a very different vision of an ideal racial future was offered by sixty-seven-year-old Elijah Muhammad, the person who, more than any other, made the Nation of Islam an influential force in black America. In *Message to the Blackman in America*, he set forth a platform for his organization in which he listed ten aims. Several were similar to goals identified by many others devoted to the defense and uplifting of black Americans. "We want a full and complete freedom," Muhammad declared. "We want equality of opportunity." "We want equal justice under law . . . [and] an immediate end to . . . police brutality." Other features of his platform, however, were unusual. He demanded "freedom for all Believers of Islam now held in federal prisons"* and "freedom for all black men and women now under death sentence in innumerable prisons in the North as well as the South."† He also sought a wholly separate racial territory for blacks. "We want our people in America whose parents or grandparents were descendants from slaves, to be allowed to establish a separate state or territory of their own—either on this continent [North America] or elsewhere." Muhammad explained that "since we cannot get along with [whites] in peace and equality, after giving them 400 years of our sweat and blood and receiving in return some of the worst treatment human beings have ever experienced, we believe our contributions to this land and the suffering forced upon us by white America, justifies our demand for complete separation in a state or territory of our own." Reflecting the strict dictates governing gender and race in the Nation of Islam, Muhammad insisted in the near term upon "equal . . . but separate schools" for boys and girls and education in which black children would be

* It is unclear whom he is referring to when he references "Believers of Islam." Does he mean all Muslims or only those who adhered to the unique theology propounded by the Nation of Islam? Nor is it clear why he singled out inmates in federal prisons as opposed to inmates in all prisons, including state prisons, especially in light of the fact that the latter population is much larger than the former.

† It is also unclear why he demands freedom for inmates under sentence of death in nonfederal custody but refrains from demanding freedom for other inmates. Satisfaction of Minister Muhammad's demand would result in a murderer under sentence of death being freed while a convicted forger would remain imprisoned.

taught by "their own teachers." Finally, in accord with the Nation of Islam's teaching that whites are, literally, "devils," a strain of humanity created by a renegade scientist, Minister Muhammad demanded the prohibition of "intermarriage or race mixing."[2]

II

In 1966, a cadre of young African Americans voiced their vision of a better racial future. Their thinking, unlike Muhammad's, was secular. They launched two interventions. One was a declaration by twenty-five-year-old Stokely Carmichael (later Kwame Ture), whose call for Black Power during the resumption of the March Against Fear in the summer of 1966 had marked a new stage in the civil rights movement. In "What We Want," an article published in *The New York Review of Books*,[3] Carmichael defended the Black Power slogan, rebutting denunciations of it by many in the civil rights movement establishment, including both white liberals and leading black figures. Roy Wilkins of the National Association for the Advancement of Colored People scoffed at Black Power as "a reverse Mississippi, a reverse Hitler, a reverse Ku Klux Klan."[4] But black people, Carmichael retorted, "are going to use the words they want to use—not just the words whites want to hear. And [blacks] will do this no matter how often the press [and other forces try] to stop the use of the slogan by equating it with racism or separatism."

Carmichael was careful to acknowledge that he had not worked out a detailed blueprint: "We have no infallible master plan and we make no claim to exclusive knowledge of how to end racism." But he did set forth certain propositions. He stated that in the political sphere Black Power means "the creation of power bases from which black people can work to change state-wide or nationwide patterns of oppression through pressure from strength. . . . [It means] the coming together of black people to elect representatives and to force those representatives to speak to their needs." He stated that in the economic sphere the ambition of Black Power was to liberate the black colonies of America. Positing that "the economic foundations of this country must be shaken if black people are to control their lives," he complained that "a powerful few have been maintained and enriched at the expense of the poor and voiceless colored masses." Accordingly, he insisted, "this pattern must be broken. . . . For racism to die, a totally different America must be born."

One of the most striking features of "What We Want" was its stance on racial integration. Carmichael's organizational home was the Student Nonviolent Coordinating Committee (SNCC). Founded in 1960, SNCC had been an interracial group of activists whose logo featured a white and a black hand clasped in solidarity. After Carmichael assumed the leadership of SNCC, however, whites were pushed out of the organization. And in "What We Want," Carmichael expressly repudiated liberal integrationism as antithetical to black independence, solidarity, and self-respect. Integration, he charged, "speaks to the problem of blackness in a despicable way. As a goal, it has been based on complete acceptance of the fact that in order to have a decent house or education, blacks must move into a white neighborhood or send their children to a white school. This reinforces the idea . . . that 'white' is automatically better and 'black' is by definition inferior. This is why integration is a subterfuge for the maintenance of white supremacy."[5]

Perhaps to assuage fears swirling around his Black Power message, Carmichael concluded his essay by stating that African Americans "do not want to 'take over' this country. They don't want to 'get whitey'; they just want to get him off their backs." According to Carmichael, then, the essential characteristic of the Black Power racial promised land was both profoundly simple and profoundly complicated: it was a polity in which blacks no longer felt the suffocating weight of white oppression on their minds and bodies.

Less than a month after the publication of Carmichael's declaration, thirty-year-old Bobby Seale and twenty-four-year-old Huey Newton wrote the Black Panther Party Platform and Program. It echoed much of what Muhammad and Carmichael had demanded:

We want freedom. . . . We want full employment for our people. . . . We want an end to the robbery by the white man of our Black Community. . . . We want decent housing. . . . We want education for our people. . . . We want all black men to be exempt from military service. . . . We want an immediate end to POLICE BRUTALITY and MURDER of black people. . . . We want freedom for all black men held in federal, state, county and city prisons and jails. . . . We want all black people when brought to trial to be tried in court by a jury of . . . people from their black communities. . . . We want . . . a United Nations supervised plebiscite to be held throughout the black colony in which only black colonial subjects will be allowed to participate, for the purpose of determining the will of black people as to their national destiny.

The BPP Platform, however, took a notably different rhetorical tack from kindred radical black nationalist manifestos in expressly invoking an iconic (white) American foundational document: the Declaration of Independence. The Panthers reminded readers that it was America's revolutionary Founding Fathers who had declared that "when a long train of abuses and usurpations . . . evinces a design to reduce [the people] under absolute Despotism, it is their right, it is their duty, to throw off such Government, and to provide new Guards for their future security."[6]

One reason for mentioning these various figures is that in many settings, including legal academia, commentators often truncate the spectrum of thinking on race that Americans have entertained, omitting perceived "extremists" and thereby obscuring appropriate attentiveness to socially significant ideas. This deficiency has certainly been evident in my own writing and teaching. In my books, articles, and classes I have paid insufficient attention to figures such as Wallace and Muhammad. This is due in part to abhorrence for the racisms that Wallace and Muhammad propagated. Wallace's racism had behind it far more power than Muhammad's and reached much further. Still, both racisms demeaned large swaths of humankind and, on that basis, warrant moral condemnation. I abjure them. But moral objection to ideas ought not distort one's perception and presentation of their significance. Often consigned to historiographical marginality, Wallace and Muhammad and the ideas they propounded exerted an influence that warrants more attention than it often receives.

Wallace articulated white racism in its Deep South guise and shrewdly discerned its non-southern variants. He helped to southernize national politics, turning "law and order" into a potent racial dog whistle before Richard Nixon did so.[7] The triumphs of Nixon, Ronald Reagan, George H. W. Bush, and Donald Trump are attributable in part to insights, strategies, and legacies that Wallace bequeathed. A consequential offshoot of those victories is the character of the federal judiciary that has held sway for more than half a century. Counterfactualism, of course, is always a complicated, indeterminate enterprise. But it is at least conceivable that had Wallace's brand of white racial resentment been less politically potent as channeled especially by Nixon and Reagan, the composition of the federal judiciary and thus the law it generated would have differed considerably from what has, in fact, ensued.

Though often marginalized in recollections of the 1960s, Elijah Muhammad and the Nation of Islam also exercised a far-reaching influence. Minister Muhammad played a central role in the political and spiritual rehabilitation of Malcolm X, who went on to become a major figure in modern American political culture in his own right. Minister Muhammad was also the mentor of the remarkable boxer and activist Muhammad Ali, who enjoyed immense international standing. Moreover, the Nation of Islam, under Minister Muhammad, played a role in the development of American law in the 1960s akin to that which was played by the Jehovah's Witnesses in the 1940s.[8] Members of the Nation of Islam, insisting upon rights to religious observance, initiated pioneering suits that belatedly brought federal constitutional requirements into prisons.[9] The ongoing influence of Minister Muhammad can be seen in our own time in the career of Minister Louis Farrakhan, who has been a substantial fixture on the African American landscape for decades.

III

The most celebrated American racial visionary is Martin Luther King Jr. On April 3, 1968, the night before he was assassinated, King announced in his final speech at the age of thirty-nine that he had been to the mountaintop and glimpsed the racial promised land. But he disclosed little about its borders and topography and omitted telling us what we could expect to see and feel there. Nor did he provide a map to guide us to the promised land. Indeed, he left us unaware of a way to decipher whether we are close or far from arrival. Five years before he was murdered, King had spoken longingly in "I Have a Dream" of a nation in which his children would be judged not by the color of their skin but by the content of their character. Of the many statements he made in his lifetime, none has been more cited or lauded. It is widely perceived as voicing the ideal of a race-blind society: a polity in which no one is treated better or worse because of race, in which race has receded to the social insignificance of eye color, in which the weightiness of race has evaporated.

Inspired by this ideal, activists have sought through suasion, litigation, and legislation to remove from American life race-dependent decision making. They have challenged laws and practices that, for racial purposes, segregated or otherwise burdened racial minorities. They have also challenged laws and practices that, for racial purposes, preferred racial minorities. "One gets beyond racism," Professor William Van Alstyne declared, "by getting beyond it now: by a complete, resolute, and credible commitment *never* to tolerate in one's own life—or in the life or practices of one's government—the differential treatment of human beings by race."[10] Some champions of a race-blind ethos eschew any practice that involves organizing people by reference to their race; they oppose the creation of racially defined affinity groups or racially defined political organizations. Some go so far as to oppose the collection of racial data and to attack altogether the very idea of "race."[11]

Although some observers embrace the idea of racelessness, others find the prospect unwelcome if not downright oppressive. Among them are people for whom a cultivated racial identity is a key feature of their persona. They think of themselves—and *like* thinking of themselves—as white, black, Latino, Asian American, Native American (or affiliated with a particular tribe), and so forth.[*]

---

[*] In their amicus curiae brief for the Supreme Court in *Fisher v. University of Texas at Austin*, Dean Robert Post of Yale Law School and Dean Martha Minow

They affiliate themselves with organizations defined expressly by race. Some are organizations that many would be willing to bar from a racial promised land without much regret, such as the National Association for the Advancement of White People (NAAWP), the White Aryan Resistance, and the White Patriot Party. But what about the Black Law Students Association, or the National Association of Black Journalists, or the Congressional Black Caucus, or the Congressional Hispanic Caucus, or the Society of Hispanic Engineers, or the National Association of Asian American Professionals, or the Asian American Writers' Workshop, or the National Native American Bar Association?

Some readers will reject what they see as an implied and unfounded moral equivalence. They will resist any suggestion of parity between the NAAWP and, say, the National Conference of Black Lawyers (NCBL). So let me say expressly that I am making no claim of parity. The NAAWP is a racist organization; the NCBL is an antiracist organization. People of color established organizations of "their own" in response to being excluded from or made to feel unwelcome in organizations dominated by whites. But organizations established as a reaction to racism have taken on identities independent of the circumstances of their birth. They have become, for many, much more than temporary refuges that may be readily dispensed with upon the emergence of wider opportunities. They have become beloved institutions that many devotees are unwilling to abandon and are committed to sustaining and enjoying even *after* the revolution. Here it is well to recall Alexander Pekelis's "Full Equality in a Free Society: A Program for Jewish Action."[12] Writing on behalf of the American Jewish Congress (AJC), Pekelis asserted that freedom is even more important than equality and that "no society is free unless it assures . . . the freedom of individual and collective self-expression." The AJC,

of Harvard Law School argued against a rule that would prohibit a public university from taking race into account in making admissions decisions on the ground, among others, that doing so would wrongly disable applicants from discussing their racial identity, a feature of their persona that some applicants perceive to be an important and valuable attribute. Post and Minow assert that "an individualized admission process that excluded consideration of race would demean the dignity of applicants." *See* Brief for Dean Robert Post and Dean Martha Minow as Amicus Curiae Supporting Respondents, *Fisher v. University of Texas at Austin,* 570 U.S. 297 (2013) (No. 11-345).

he announced approvingly, "would reject individual equality if its price were renunciation of our collective individuality."[13] Many blacks (and others who affiliate themselves with racial groups) also adopt this position. They renounce equality offered on the condition that they relinquish their racial identity. They refuse to allow their racial loyalties to be incinerated in the American melting pot.

A related objection to the idea of a race-blind society stems from apprehension about what would be required to reach and sustain this state of changed consciousness. Opponents fear that extinguishing race-dependent decision making in *all* areas of life would require an unacceptable level of intrusion upon individuals' freedom. It would involve, for example, the policing of choices regarding dating, marriage, assisted reproduction, and adoption. Such choices are highly consequential.[14] They affect intimate relations, the self-understanding of individuals and groups, the allocation of property, and the distribution of valuable knowledge regarding business, employment, and other endeavors facilitated by social networks. Many would find it utterly repellent to try to prohibit, punish, or even merely discourage race-dependent decision making in these innermost precincts.[15] To be sure, some who adopt this view believe racially discriminatory dating, marriage, or adoption to be silly, self-defeating, or even immoral. But they object even more to any governmental encroachment upon this intimate sphere.*

---

* Of course, for a long period, many jurisdictions did prohibit, indeed some criminalized, sex and marriage across racial boundaries. Antimiscegenation laws, however, have been thoroughly (though not universally) repudiated. *See Loving v. Virginia*, 388 U.S. 1 (1967). Revulsion against such laws would contribute to opposition to permitting direct governmental regulation in this area if a proposal for such regulation was ever to be seriously put forward.

Professor Brendan O'Flaherty notes that nowadays "people looking online or in print for partners or spouses often proclaim their race . . . and often specify what they are looking for (or not looking for) in their partners. This is discrimination: race matters in how decisions are made. But it's legal, and almost nobody believes it should be illegal (not even the explicit public declaration of discriminatory intent) or that an affirmative action program should be established." Brendan O'Flaherty, *The Economics of Race in the United States* (2015), 229. *But see* R. Richard Banks, "The Color of Desire: Fulfilling Adoptive Parents' Racial Preferences Through Discriminatory State Action," 107 *Yale Law Journal* 875

Another conception of race blindness is more modest; it does not demand race blindness throughout society but does demand it of government. Proponents of this view assert that the federal Constitution requires officials to be race blind. The idea of the race-blind Constitution has attracted near-consensus support in the Supreme Court. But the justices have divided sharply on the best strategy for achieving this ideal. One camp contends that the best way to perfect race-blind constitutionalism is to prohibit the government from taking race into account in decision making, effective immediately. This camp condemns not only invidious racial discrimination (for example, segregation) but also positive racial discrimination (for instance, affirmative action). Another camp contends that the best way to perfect race-blind constitutionalism is to prohibit invidious racial discrimination immediately but to permit positive racial discrimination temporarily.* This conflict runs deep, but note that both of these camps describe as their ultimate aim a state of affairs in which race, finally, plays no role in governmental decision making.

Race-blind constitutionalism is vulnerable to important objections. One is directed at those who contend that we will have reached the racial promised land as soon as all public institutions are prohibited from taking race into account in decision making. For some in this camp, the existence of large gaps between the power, wealth, status, and opportunities enjoyed by whites and those enjoyed by people of color does not, by itself, preclude the attainment of the racial promised land—so long as government desists, going forward, from making racial distinctions. These proponents maintain that the realization of constitutional race blindness does not depend on diminishing racial disparities. In their view, the racial promised land can coexist with social conditions under which, across a range of domains, blacks consistently,

---

(1998); Emens, "Intimate Discrimination"; Camille Gear Rich, "Contracting Our Way to Inequality: Race, Reproductive Freedom, and the Quest for the Perfect Child," 104 *Minnesota Law Review* 2375 (2020).

* Justice Harry Blackmun memorably advanced this position, maintaining that "in order to get beyond racism, we must first take account of race." *Regents of the University of California v. Bakke*, 438 U.S. 265, 407 (1978) (Blackmun, J., concurring in part and dissenting in part).

even uniformly, fare poorly in comparison with whites—so long as those outcomes are not attributable to some contemporary, direct, purposeful racial discrimination undertaken with governmental authority.

Somehow proponents of this view miss the moral significance of the stubborn fact that with respect to practically every indicator of well-being—life expectancy, health, wealth, employment, education, and housing—whites on average fare better, lots better, than blacks. That African Americans face a much greater risk than Euro-Americans of suffering from a range of social catastrophes— unemployment, malnourishment, poverty, incarceration, eviction, and vulnerability to infectious disease—is not accidental. It is the consequence of indefensible present or past discrimination based on race.[16] Unworthy of support is any vision of the racial promised land that accommodates complacently such pervasive harms stemming from racial wrongs.

A second objection is directed at race-blind constitutionalists who want gradually to do away with all governmental race-dependent decision making. This gradualist camp comprises people willing to accept affirmative action as a transitional measure, one that must be retired when unjust conditions have been suitably ameliorated. The ground, however, has shifted beneath this camp's feet. Precluded by a bloc of Supreme Court justices from successfully justifying affirmative action on the basis of reparative justice, advocates for affirmative action had to resort to other justifications. Thus, while initially conceived as a *transitory* device to redress the debilitating scars of past racial wrongs, affirmative action is now primarily justified on grounds of "diversity" or creating institutions that "look like America." The diversity rationale is the belief that racial heterogeneity enhances universities, firms, and organizations of all sorts by contributing to a cross-pollinating synthesis of perspectives and experiences that will produce more knowledge and insight and generate better decision making than would otherwise be possible. The "looks like America," or social-mirroring, rationale is the belief that ensuring racial heterogeneity is essential for promoting distributive justice. But affirmative action based on these rationales is not transitory but permanent. As long as America is composed of discrete racial groups, the aim of capturing the benefits of diversity will always justify race-conscious selectivity. Similarly, as long as America is composed of discrete racial groups, the goal of promoting distributive justice for disadvantaged racial groups will prompt gatekeepers to be race observant rather than race blind. As a result, proponents of race-blind constitutionalism who support temporary positive racial discrimination find themselves in an awkward position. The affirmative action they support has turned into a practice that is at odds with the gradualist version of their race-blind aspiration.

The diversity conception of affirmative action received a big boost in 1978 in the landmark case of *Regents of the University of California v. Bakke*. In the pivotal opinion in that case, Justice Lewis F. Powell endorsed the diversity rationale as the only valid basis on which public universities could take race into account in selecting among candidates for admission. It should come as no surprise that following *Bakke* proponents of affirmative action programs accentuated the diversity rationale undergirding their initiatives. In 2003, in a case involving the University of Michigan, sixty-five leading American businesses including American Express, Coca-Cola, and Microsoft submitted an amicus curiae brief to the Supreme Court in support of the university's affirmative action program. They declared that in their experience individuals who have been educated in "a diverse setting" are more likely to have attained skills and experiences valuable to business enterprises:

> First, a diverse group of individuals educated in a cross-cultural environment has the ability to facilitate unique and creative approaches to problem-solving, arising from the integration of different perspectives. Second, such individuals are better able to develop products and services that appeal to a variety of consumers. . . . Third, a racially diverse group of managers with cross-cultural experiences is better able to work with business partners, employees, and clientele in the United States and around the world.[17]

Nearly a decade later, in a case involving the University of Texas, the deans of the law schools at Yale and Harvard University also vouched for the diversity justification for affirmative action. They declared that in their view "diversity is associated with better educational outcomes."[18]

Acceptable to a sufficient number of justices to secure approval from the Supreme Court in the context of higher education, the diversity rationale has also attained acceptance in other forums of American political culture. Approval of it stems from various sources, some acknowledged, some not. At least in theory, the diversity preference is open to all. While in many contexts it will operate to the advantage of racial minorities, in others it could operate to the advantage of whites. A white candidate seeking admission to a historically black institution might well receive a boost based on the diversity rationale. The diversity justification for affirmative action depends on no predicate of misconduct. It thus avoids or tamps down anger ignited when whites are accused of complicity in wrongdoing as the heirs of oppressors, the beneficiaries of racial privilege, or the perpetrators of their own misdeeds. Another attraction is that the diversity justification explains affirmative action not as a special aid to racial minorities or a requirement of distributive fairness but rather as a prerequisite for better goods and services that will presumably benefit society as a whole. Unlike other justifications for affirmative action, the diversity rationale is consistent with meritocratic premises. It does not concede that for reasons extrinsic to the mission of an institution minority candidates should be chosen who are less capable and accomplished than white competitors. Rather, the diversity justification maintains that conventional indicia of talent, achievement, and potential must be supplemented by other indicators of potential contribution that have heretofore been overlooked.

Though the diversity justification has enjoyed considerable popularity, it has also confronted strong criticism. Some doubt whether, in fact, racial diversity per se generates pedagogical or related benefits or, if it does, whether the benefits generated are anywhere near the extent advertised by proponents of affirmative action. Others doubt whether claims of benefit have been made in good faith. The diversity rationale has long been dogged by allegations of fraud. The most damning of such charges have come from liberals sympathetic to affirmative action. "I am increasingly dismayed," Professor Sanford Levinson reports, by "the costs to intellectual honesty of the felt need to shoehorn one's arguments [in support of affirmative action] into the language of 'diversity.'"[19]

President William Jefferson Clinton invoked the social-mirroring conception of diversity in 1992 when he promised to select a cabinet that "looks like America." Now it is commonplace for people to assert that police departments, university faculties, the ranks of Academy Award nominees, corporate CEOs, doctors, lawyers, accountants, and other professions ought to mirror the racial composition of the communities in which they are situated. Behind such assertions is the belief that, ideally, every important social domain—high (for example, the U.S. Senate) to low (for example, the prison population)—should mirror the racial demographics of the country so that all of these spheres "look like America."

One reason that some observers prefer the "looks like America" model to the race-blind model is that the former, with its latent proportionalism, *guarantees* the presence of people of color in forums that have long been monopolized by whites. Race blindness, fully matured, is indifferent to the racial demographics generated by any given process of selection or allocation. The "looks like America" model, by contrast, demands the inclusion of blacks and other people of color and consequently assuages lingering distrust of the administration of facially raceless rules and standards. Another attraction, for some, of the "looks like America" motif is that it, like the diversity rationale, presents racial difference as a potential virtue to be lauded and utilized rather than a problem to be minimized or merely tolerated. The racial-mirroring model of a racial promised land embraces positive racial recognition and makes it permanent, enabling coloredness to be seen as a valuable credential.[20]

The "looks like America" model, however, also confronts serious objections. For one, it only guarantees the presence in key forums of persons associated with sufficiently large minority groups; smaller minority groups may be eclipsed in the struggle for group recognition. A racial minority group constituting 10 percent of the American population might well argue that under a norm of rough proportionalism it is entitled to at least one seat in a presidential cabinet of twelve. But what about a racial minority group constituting only 2 percent of the American population?

That group cannot plausibly claim entitlement to a seat in any particular cabinet on the basis of demographic proportionality. Furthermore, there is the difficulty of determining which groups count in assessing whether a cabinet looks like America. Should we ask whether it contains a Chinese American, Japanese American, or Thai American? Or should we ask whether it contains anyone who has any aspect of a pan-Asian identity? Then there is the further difficulty of determining whether a given person is a suitable representative of a group. In the racial promised land will the son of, say, a white mother and a black father be a suitable representative for "blacks"? Or should he be designated as the representative for "whites" or "multi-racials"? These questions are not unanswerable; we are already responding to them with varying results. But for some observers, these questions are sufficiently obnoxious that any polity that requires posing them should be disqualified as a racial promised land.

Finally, the "looks like America" model normalizes practices that inevitably subordinate claims of individual merit to claims of racial group pluralism. The call for proportionality must grapple with the flip sides of its demands: the situations where there are said to be "too many" members of racial minorities as a matter of proportional representation (for example, law school faculties said to include too many Jews or scientific laboratories said to include too many people of Asian descent). In a society rigorously governed by an imperative for racial representativeness, some black players in the National Basketball Association (NBA) might well be benched in order to create teams that "look like America."*

IV

A white man's country, a vision of a separate black territory, race blindness, the "looks like America" motif, "assimilation,"

---

* Describing how the managers of NBA franchises have sought to make their teams look more like their ticket-buying customers, Professor John Skrentny writes that "filling the bench . . . with white players was a common NBA practice in the 1990s; though only 27.6 percent of the league's players were white, 52.6 percent of the players who scored the fewest points on each team were white." John D. Skrentny, *After Civil Rights: Racial Realism in the New American Workplace* (2014), 192.

"integration," "affirmative action," "diversity," and metaphors of rainbows, salads, mosaics, and orchestras are among the ideas and images used over the past several decades to orient aspirations for a racially just society. One will find versions of them, sometimes scrambled together, in state and federal constitutional, statutory, and administrative law as well as in juridical and political commentary.

A salient feature of American race law that is in tension, sometimes strikingly so, with some of these aspirations is a strong tendency toward acting negatively as opposed to positively. *Anti*-discrimination, *anti*-classification, and *anti*-subordination are the key legal concepts in this area.[21] The Thirteenth Amendment prohibits slavery; it does not designate the essentials of freedom. The Fourteenth Amendment prohibits states from denying persons the equal protection of the law; it does not elaborate on what equality means in terms of a positive entitlement.[22] The Fifteenth Amendment prohibits states from denying persons the vote on the basis of race; it does not arm citizens with a right to vote. Much is written about what we repudiate. Much less is written about what we desire.

Lately, though, a literature brimming with desire has risen to prominence. It seeks to supersede familiar aims and expand conceptions of acceptable means for attaining new ambitions. It sounds an original idiom and radiates a distinctive sensibility. It is self-consciously maximalist and proudly "radical" (though it, too, makes much of what it rejects). It brandishes the rhetoric and tenor of what was the most defiant and vilified movement in American history—the forces of antislavery immediatism in the antebellum period. This is the literature of "abolition."[23]

Much of this literature focuses on racial injustice in the administration of criminal law. This focus is its entry point, the area it has discussed most extensively, and the topic that has brought it the most attention. But the proponents of abolition have a larger ambition than transforming the administration of criminal law. Maintaining that such a transformation cannot be accomplished without broader change, the proponents of abolition call for nothing less than revolutionary renewal in every sphere of American life—political, socioeconomic, and cultural. They envision, says Professor Amna Akbar, "fundamentally transforming the relationships among state, market, and society."[24] They seek, according to Professor Allegra McLeod, "a new conception of justice."[25] She writes that

> justice in abolitionist terms involves at once exposing the violence, hypocrisy, and dissembling entrenched in existing legal practices, while attempting to achieve peace, make amends, and distribute resources more equitably. Justice for abolitionists is an integrated endeavor to prevent harm, intervene in harm, obtain reparations, and transform the conditions in which we live. This conception of justice works, for example, to eliminate the criminalization of poverty and survival while addressing the criminality of a global social order in which the eight wealthiest men own "the same amount of wealth as" fifty percent of all people on earth.[26]

What is the "new conception of justice" envisioned by abolitionists, the theoreticians of Black Lives Matter, the architects of the Movement for Black Lives, and the other organizers and supporters of initiatives across the country that seek "fundamental," "systemic," "transformational" change? Opinions vary. The abolitionist movement is far-flung and decentralized. It hosts internal debates over aims and strategies. The abolitionists, however, do hold in common certain key tenets. They believe that racism is a dominant force in every significant aspect of American life and that white supremacism is reinforced by drivers and manifestations of what they see as other social wrongs, including, most especially, capitalism, male supremacism, and the privileging of conventional heterosexuality. They generally disavow compromise aimed at winning over adversaries or fence-sitters. They harbor a thoroughgoing disgust toward the status quo and a profound disappointment with previous efforts at racial reform that, in their view, attained only cosmetic change, such as elevating "acceptable" blacks to high places (for example, positions as mayors, police chiefs, a president of the United States) while consigning large portions of the African American population to deteriorating circumstances. As concerns the administration of criminal justice, abolitionists "are not simply arguing the state has created a fundamentally unequal criminal legal system. They are identifying policing, jail, and prison as the primary mode of governing Black, poor, and other communities of color in the United States. . . . They are working to build another state—another world even—organized differently than the one . . . inherited." Convinced that policing and prisons are inextricably and ineluctably connected to white supremacism, abolitionists are committed to turning away from policing and prisons and ultimately doing away with those institutions. Abolitionists insist that this is "a moment calling for a radical imagination, where the scale of deep critique is matched with a scale of grand vision."[27]

The abolitionist intellectual uprising attacks antiblack racism comprehensively and intensively, focusing upon an area that has proven to be singularly resistant to progressive change. Abolitionists did not discover the scandalous state of law enforcement. Critics have long been sounding alarms.[28] But the abolitionists have highlighted its wrongs with striking vigor, capturing imaginations.

The abolitionist literature has documented the extent to which local governments have subsidized the ever-increasing budgets of police departments. It has exposed the bipartisanship that underwrote the incarceration binge. It has spotlighted the limitations of widely touted reforms that, as typically implemented, fall far short of what is needed to satisfactorily resolve deep-seated problems. For decades, for example, increasing the number of black personnel in police departments has been posited as a remedy for racist policing. Abolitionists, however, have been at the forefront of those noting that for various reasons black police are often unable to play an ameliorative role insofar as they are captured or overcome by the imperatives of police bureaucracies.

Abolitionist intellectuals have collaborated with organizers in ways that have been mutually beneficial, teaming up to move ideas to the center of popular as well as elite discourse. Commentators of all stripes now take seriously such slogans as "Abolish the police!" and "Abolish prisons!" Figures who would heretofore have avoided proclaiming "Black Lives Matter!" now do so with enthusiasm. Abolitionists have provoked and informed an untold number of discussions in journals, lecture halls, and classrooms.

If the abolitionist literature displays certain virtues, it also manifests certain vices. As used by the activist-intellectuals under discussion, the term "abolition" is in itself a problem. Death penalty abolitionists demand an end to the state-administered killing of individuals immediately and unconditionally. Similarly, anti-slavery abolitionists demanded the immediate and unconditional cessation of enslavement. They sought its prohibition because slavery was unequivocally evil and served no good social function. The same cannot be said of prisons or the police. They are both institutions that can and do serve useful social functions. Slavery cannot be put to any just use. Prisons can. Prisons house convicted inmates who have hurt society by injuring victims absent justification or excuse. They are confined to prevent further criminality, to deter others who might be inclined to transgress the boundaries of criminal law, and to impose punishment.

Now, it is true that far too many people are imprisoned in the United States, that the process by which people are incarcerated is shot through with unfairness, that an appreciable number of prisoners are wrongly convicted, and that cruel, inhumane, and dangerous conditions are far too prevalent in American prisons. America is disgraced by the barbarity, the hyper-punitiveness, and the obvious inequities in its system of criminal justice. But it is not improper for society to protect itself from individuals who rape, murder, assault, or rob others in violation of laws that set bounds that, if crossed, make one vulnerable to imprisonment. To the contrary, it is morally imperative for a polity to maintain agencies of collective self-defense, including police and prisons. Justice requires that arbitrariness, prejudice, and cruelty be removed from such agencies. But that is a project of reform, not abolition.

Some abolitionists insist that the number of people who can properly be confined against their will for the safety of the community is much smaller than is usually realized. Let's grant that that is true. Even so, it proves only that some fraction of the incarcerated population is unjustifiably imprisoned. What about the rest—the several thousands (probably the tens of thousands) of prisoners who did in fact engage in serious, violent criminal encroachments—murder, robbery, assault, rape?[29] Is it wrong to detain them for at least some period of time? Even the most stalwart abolitionist is likely to concede that it is acceptable to confine a violent sociopath. In other words, almost everyone will concede that at least under some circumstances confining someone against their will is required for the social good—a tragedy, to be sure, but an acceptable response in light of the circumstances. By contrast, in no circumstance is slavery a social good.

Many prison abolitionists themselves recognize the disanalogy that haunts their efforts to demonstrate a moral equivalence between their position and the position of antislavery immediatists. They awkwardly admit that they do not actually favor unlocking all prison gates right away. Rather they want to shrink, dramatically, the overblown presence of incarceration in American life. Fine. But if massive shrinkage is what they really seek, as opposed to total erasure, as opposed to abolition, why not say so? The answer lies partly in considerations of public relations. "Abolition" has a dramatic, absolutistic ring to it. "Shrinking" the imprint of prisons is less alluring. It is also partly a matter of wanting to avoid conceding openly that at least to some extent prisons do serve a useful social function.

A similar argument obtains with respect to police abolition. The nationwide protests against police misconduct are thoroughly justified. All too often, police humiliate, intimidate, injure, and kill under circumstances in which such conduct is unwarranted and in violation of civil rights, not to mention criminal codes. It is imperative that police be regulated more effectively. But some agency cloaked with the authority to use force in support of legitimate social norms is required to protect people against marauders, to apprehend criminal predators, and to perform other essential tasks. Need is especially acute among those dependent upon public as opposed to private protective services. Some abolitionists who insist that they really do want to eliminate police altogether regrettably deny or minimize the very real problem posed by violent criminality, especially in vulnerable neighborhoods.[30] Other abolitionists, when pressed, concede that they do not actually mean that they want to get rid of police altogether; instead, they clarify, they aim to diminish the presence, expense, and power of police. They also advocate alternative methods of community response to criminality that they claim to be superior to existing practices.

They point to promising, small-scale experiments in "restorative" or "transformative" justice in which community norms supplant alienating formalities, permitting the victims of criminality, the peers of the accused, and defendants themselves to become far more involved in the resolution of cases than is possible under conventional practices of criminal law. All too often, however, these alternatives are shrouded under the rhetoric of abolition as some activists continue to opt for the catchy slogan over the more accurate, the more reformist, description of their vision.

As I noted, abolitionists differ. Some adamantly insist that they *really* do seek the complete removal of all carceral institutions. They stress that they are invoking abolition not for shock value but out of a sincere belief that society would be better off without any police or prisons. They have in mind "a society based on principles of freedom, equal humanity and democracy—a society that has no need for prisons."[31] In the polity they envision, police and prisons are "unimaginable."[32]

This aspiration is so far-fetched that it lacks the plausibility needed to gain substantial political traction. No political movement can do away with human evil and thus moot the necessity for protection against it. I, for one, am repulsed by the prospect of a polity in which serious criminality (for instance, rape, murder, robbery) faces no credible threat of containment, deterrence, and punishment. I am not claiming that police and prisons can ensure our safety. They do not. They cannot. There are limits to what any system of criminal law enforcement can accomplish. Much crime does and will go unpunished (and that is likely to remain so in any society that enjoys a considerable amount of liberty). Moreover, when crime is punished, the victim of criminality is never made whole. He or she cannot be fully vindicated by the law even when it is efficient and fair. That is a big part of what makes crime tragic. But by seeking to apprehend, detain, deter, and punish lawbreakers, society at least signals a profound disapproval of criminal encroachment upon others. That signal is rendered all too indistinct by abolitionist theorists.

Localities across the country are already benefiting from reforms in the administration of criminal law that abolitionists spurred, including a greater willingness to discipline wayward officers quickly, cuts to swollen police budgets, an increased appetite for exercising civilian control over police departments, the outlawing of excessively aggressive tactics by police, and an insistence on greater transparency in police operations. Those are notable achievements. More and deeper reforms will, one hopes, ensue. Abolitionism has erred, however, in choosing to target for erasure (actually or even only rhetorically) public institutions that are essential. If the racial promised land for abolitionism is a polity devoid of police or prisons, it is a prospect that has no likelihood of realization and a great likelihood of generating a retrograde reaction.

V

At the outset of writing these comments, I felt embarrassed by the undeveloped state of my own imaginings. Even after years of study, I am bereft of a satisfactory answer to the question, what racial order do I want? I was abashed by the absence of a map in my own mind detailing a racial promised land. But my sentiments have changed. I have become much less enamored of the idea of a grand design. One must think hard about aims in order to provide some sort of guidance for conduct. So I continue to favor assessing competing visions of racial promised lands. But I am also swept up by a chastened caution that has been significantly intensified by the misplaced certainties of the abolitionists. After all, utopianism has a checkered history. Armed with a willingness and ability to impose their conception of the good, utopians of various stripes have engaged in conduct and propounded policies spoiled by hubris, delusion, and coercion.

This caution prompts me to reassess the state of our racial policy. It is, to be sure, a hodgepodge filled with lacunae, tensions, and contradictions. We say that we have no tolerance for racism, but we obviously do. Out of a protectiveness for freedom of expression, American law permits hateful, racist speech to an extent that is singular among advanced democracies. In deference to freedom of association, federal civil rights legislation permits racial discrimination in private clubs. Our federal lawmakers have expressly declared that at the workplace there shall be no bona fide occupational qualification exception to antidiscrimination standards for race (though there is one for gender). Yet, in practice, an exception for race does exist insofar as some employers announce, with little fear of legal liability, that they are seeking only people of a given race for certain positions—as, for example, when film directors openly engage in race-specific casting.[33] Jurists who embrace race-blind constitutionalism of the immediatist variety accept governmental racial selectivity for purposes of addressing an "emergency," and jurists who embrace race-blind constitutionalism of the gradualist variety support race-dependent decision making based on rationales that have no real temporal end point.

I view these conflicted beliefs and fragmented practices more charitably now than I have in the past. Maybe there is something functional about the scrambled state of our race law in light of the complexity and volatility of our racial situation. Maybe it is prudent to forswear strict allegiance to any grand blueprint that would seek to master our unruly racial reality. Maybe the best that can safely be managed are smaller, though significant, interstitial goals that are attentive to the pluralism that infuses American practices: distaste for racial prejudice alongside permission for racial prejudice; aversion to unjustifiable racial distinctions alongside accommodation of desires to identify in racial terms; remedying racial wrongs alongside handling other tasks; yearning for racial promised lands alongside pragmatic acceptance of decent compromises.

ACKNOWLEDGMENTS

It is a joy to give thanks to those who have assisted in creating this book. At the top of the list is the wonderful novelist Mona Simpson, to whom this book is dedicated. Her devotion to her craft, her love for reading, her passion for learning, and her belief in me have been sources of inspiration I have tapped time and time again. I am especially grateful for countless adventurous, instructive, thrilling, and hilarious conversations.

My family has been unstintingly supportive. My children—Henry William, Rachel, and Thaddeus—have patiently and lovingly allowed me to try out on them many of the ideas voiced in these pages. And I continue to feel buoyed by the spirit of my wife of blessed memory, Yvedt Love Matory.

Harvard Law School has provided a marvelous environment for writing. Faculty colleagues have generously shared with me questions, suggestions, corrections, and, yes, objections as well. It would be difficult to exaggerate the number of times that peers at HLS and elsewhere have offered encouragement. What a blessing it has been to receive counsel from John Manning, Martha Minow, Cass Sunstein, Sanford Levinson, John Herfort, Mac McCorkle, Eric Foner, Justin Driver, Stephen Carter, Richard Fallon, John Goldberg, Guy Charles, Ruth Okediji, Terry Fisher, Howell Jackson, Scott Brewer, Michael Seidman, Charles Fried, Conrad Harper, Carole Steiker, Andrew Crespo, Daphna Renan, Todd Rakoff, Michael Klarman, Mark Tushnet, Michael Meltsner, and Adam Shatz. Students, too, have been helpful, particularly those who read the manuscript in the fall of 2020, even though we were prevented from meeting in person because of the pandemic. I am grateful to those "super readers": Adam Aleksic, Aabid Allibhai, Palle Bharath, Sophia Breggia, Christian Carson, Deanna Krokos, Daniel Nathan, Krupa Patel, Celia Reynolds, Nikita James Rumsey, Kyle Skinner, and L. Ashe Smith.

One of the glories of HLS is its cadre of magnificent librarians. I have benefited enormously from their expertise and enthusiasm. Especially helpful have been the reference librarians: Jennifer Allison, Deanna Barmakian, Maya Bergamasco, Catherine Biondo, AJ Blechner, Mindy Kent, Lisa Lilliott, Anna Martin, Rachel Parker, Michelle Pearse, Steven Wiles, Aslihan Bulut, Claire DeMarco, Meg Kribble, Tim McAllister, Heather Pierce, Louise Ragno, and George Taoultsides. Similarly helpful was the staff at the New York University library.

Several of the essays in this book began as pieces commissioned by thoughtful editors, including Robert Kuttner at *The American Prospect*, David Marcus at *The Nation*, Chris Beha at *Harper's*, Len Gutkin at *The Chronicle of Higher Education*, Ann Hulbert at *The Atlantic*, and Paul Mysercough at *The London Review of Books*.

Noah Delwiche ably shepherded the manuscript despite the awkwardness occasioned by extreme social distancing.

My agent, Andrew Wylie, is a paragon of professionalism who somehow, magically, responds to every query quickly and candidly.

I appreciate the care lavished upon me by the staff at Pantheon Books, particularly Altie Karper, Michiko Clark, Ingrid Sterner, and Maria Massey. Then there is Erroll McDonald, who introduced me to writing books, an activity that has immeasurably enriched my life. All of my books have been written under Erroll's editorial aegis. I am thankful for his support over the years—now the many years.

NOTES

1. SHALL WE OVERCOME?
OPTIMISM AND PESSIMISM IN AFRICAN AMERICAN RACIAL THOUGHT

1. The initial iteration of this essay was the 2014 War Memorial Address delivered at Milton Academy. Another version was published as "Black America's Promised Land: Why I Am Still a Racial Optimist," *American Prospect*, Nov. 10, 2014.
2. Peter Osborne, "It Is Time for Us to Be Up and Doing," *Liberator*, Dec. 1, 1832, reprinted in *The Voice of Black America: Major Speeches by Negroes in the United States, 1797–1971*, ed. Philip S. Foner (1972).
3. Paul Beatty, *The White Boy Shuffle* (1996).
4. *See* William Cooper Nell, *The Colored Patriots of the American Revolution* (1855).
5. *See* Douglas R. Egerton, *Death or Liberty: African Americans and Revolutionary America* (2009); Sylvia R. Frey, *Water from the Rock: Black Resistance in a Revolutionary Age* (1991); Gary B. Nash, *The Forgotten Fifth: African Americans in the Age of Revolution* (2006); Henry Wiencek, *An Imperfect God: George Washington, His Slaves, and the Creation of America* (2004).
6. Thomas Jefferson, *Autobiography*, in *Writings*, ed. Merrill D. Peterson (1984).
7. *Id.* at 264. (*Notes on the State of Virginia*). *See generally* John Chester Miller, *The Wolf by the Ears: Thomas Jefferson and Slavery* (1991).
8. Alexis de Tocqueville, "The Present and Probable Future Condition of the Three Races Which Inhabit the Territory of the United States," in *Democracy in America* (1835).
9. Quoted in James T. Campbell, *Middle Passages: African American Journeys to Africa, 1787–2005* (2006), 44.
10. *Id.* at 33. *See also* Lamont D. Thomas, *Paul Cuffe: Black Entrepreneur and Pan-Africanist* (1988).
11. *Id.* at 55.
12. *Id.* at 69–70.

13. *Id.* at 70.

14. Quoted in Manning Marable, *Let Nobody Turn Us Around: Voices of Resistance, Reform, and Renewal: An African Anthology* (2003), 84.

15. 60 U.S. 393 (1857).

16. William E. Cain, ed., *William Lloyd Garrison and the Fights Against Slavery* (1994), 87. *See generally* Henry Mayer, *All on Fire: William Lloyd Garrison and the Abolition of Slavery* (1998), 472–73.

17. R. Dick, *Black Protest: Issues and Tactics* (1974), 44. *See also Liberator,* May 21, 1847.

18. Abraham Lincoln, *Speeches and Writings, 1859–1965: Speeches, Letters, and Miscellaneous Writings, Presidential Messages, and Proclamations,* ed. Don Edward Fehrenbacher (1989), 32.

19. James McPherson, *The Negro's Civil War: How American Blacks Felt and Acted During the War for the Union* (1965; 1982), 29–30.

20. *Id.* at 34.

21. *Id.* at 81.

22. *Id.* at 87.

23. Quoted in John Dittmer, "The Education of Henry McNeal Turner," in *Black Leaders of the Nineteenth Century,* ed. Leon Litwack and August Meier (1988), 255.

24. Quoted in Edwin S. Redkey, *Black Exodus: Black Nationalist and Back-to-Africa Movements, 1890–1910* (1969), 27.

25. Quoted in *The Modern African American Political Thought Reader: From David Walker to Barack Obama,* ed. Angela Jones (2013), 226.

26. *Id.* at 227–29.

27. Quoted in Dittmer, "Education of Henry McNeal Turner," 271.

28. Quoted in Jones, *Modern African American Political Thought Reader,* 238.

29. Quoted in Foner, *Voice of Black America,* 753.

30. W. E. B. Du Bois, *The Souls of Black Folk: Essays and Sketches* (1903).

31. Elijah Muhammad, *Message to the Blackman in America* (1965; 1997), 163–64.

32. *Id.* at 161.

33. *Id.* at 162.

34. *See* Randall Robinson, *Quitting America: The Departure of a Black Man from His Native Land* (2004), 212.

35. *See* Waldo E. Martin Jr., *The Mind of Frederick Douglass* (1984), 73 (stating Douglass was "an inveterate optimist").

36. *See* Frederick Douglass, "The Present and Future of the Colored Race in America," June 1863, quoted in Randall Kennedy, "My Race Problem," *The Atlantic,* May 1997.

37. *See* Imani Perry, *May We Forever Stand: A History of the Black National Anthem* (2018).

38. Quoted in Foner, *Voice of Black America,* 820.

39. Mary McLeod Bethune, "What Does American Democracy Mean to Me?," America's Town Meeting of the Air, New York City, Nov. 23, 1939, in *Say It*

Plain: A Century of Great African American Speeches, ed. Catherine Ellis and Drury Smith (2005), 13.

40. *Id.*

41. Ralph J. Bunche, "Nothing Is Impossible for the Negro," in *Ralph J. Bunche: Selected Speeches and Writings*, ed. Charles P. Henry (1995), 265.

42. *Id.* at 268.

43. Quoted in Foner, *Voice of Black America*, 901–2.

44. *Id.* at 953.

45. Martin Luther King Jr., *Testament of Hope: The Essential Writings and Speeches of Martin Luther King Jr.*, ed. James M. Washington (1986), 217.

46. *Id.*

47. Barack Obama, "A More Perfect Union" (speech at the National Constitution Center, March 18, 2008).

48. *Id.*

49. Barack Obama, Presidential Victory Speech at Chicago's Grant Park, Nov. 4, 2008.

50. 570 U.S. 529 (2013).

51. *Id.* at 590.

52. Ta-Nehisi Coates, "Barack Obama, Ferguson, and the Evidence of Things Unsaid," *Atlantic*, Nov. 26, 2014.

53. *See* Dana Canedy, "The Talk: After Ferguson, a Shaded Conversation About Race," *New York Times*, Dec. 14, 2014. *See generally* Keeanga-Yamahtta Taylor, *From #BlackLivesMatter to Black Liberation* (2016).

54. Geoffrey Skelley, "Just How Many Obama 2012–Trump 2016 Voters Were There?," Sabato's Crystal Ball, University of Virginia Center for Politics, June 1, 2017.

55. Quoted in Theodore Draper, *The Rediscovery of Black Nationalism* (1970), 24.

56. *See* Kriston McIntosh et al., "Examining the Black-White Wealth Gap," Brookings, Feb. 27, 2020; Eileen Patten, "Racial Gender Wage Gaps Persist in U.S. Despite Some Progress," Pew Research Center, July 1, 2016. *See also Grutter v. Bollinger*, 539 U.S. 306 (2003) ("The Court expects that 25 years from now, the use of racial preferences will no longer be necessary to further the interest approved today."); Jennifer A. Richeson, "Americans Are Determined to Believe in Black Progress," *Atlantic*, Sept. 2020 ("[Grutter's] prediction seems at best naive.").

57. Kim Parker et al., "Amid Protests, Majorities Across Racial and Ethnic Groups Express Support for the Black Lives Matter Movement," Pew Research Center, June 12, 2020.

58. *See* election exit polls 2020, *New York Times*, Nov. 3, 2020.

2. DERRICK BELL AND ME

1. Writings on Bell from which I have derived much benefit include Mary E. Becker, "Racism and Legal Doctrine," review of *And We Are Not Saved*, by

Derrick Bell, 67 *Texas Law Review* 417 (1988); LeRoy D. Clark, "A Critique of Professor Derrick A. Bell's Thesis of the Permanence of Racism and His Strategy of Confrontation," 73 *Denver University Law Review* 23 (1995); Justin Driver, "Rethinking the Interest-Convergence Thesis," 105 *Northwestern University Law Review* 149 (2011); Alan D. Freeman, "Race and Class: The Dilemma of Liberal Reform," 90 *Yale Law Journal* 1880 (1981); John A. Powell, "Racial Realism or Racial Despair?," 24 *Connecticut Law Review* 533 (1992). Three chroniclers of Professor Bell's work and legacy warrant special attention. While my views differ sharply from theirs in important respects, I admire their collegial fidelity. *See* Kimberlé Crenshaw, *Critical Race Theory: The Key Writings That Formed the Movement* (1995); Richard Delgado and Jean Stefancic, *The Derrick Bell Reader* (2005).

2. For biographical background, *see* Derrick Bell, *Silent Covenants: Brown v. Board of Education and the Unfulfilled Hopes for Racial Reform* (2004); Derrick Bell, *Confronting Authority: Reflections of an Ardent Protester* (1994). *See also* Eleanor Kerlow, *Poisoned Ivy: How Egos, Ideology, and Power Politics Almost Ruined Harvard Law School* (1994), 72–96; Fred A. Bernstein, "Derrick Bell, Pioneering Harvard Law Professor and Civil Rights Advocate, Dies at 80," *New York Times*, Oct. 6, 2011, www.nytimes.com; Fox Butterfield, "Old Rights Campaigner Leads a Harvard Battle," *New York Times*, May 21, 1990, www.nytimes.com; interview by the History Makers with Derrick A. Bell Jr., Dec. 1, 2004, www.thehistorymakers.org; Janet Dewart Bell and the Geneva Crenshaw Society, Derrick Bell Official Site (2014), professor derrickbell.com/.

3. Derrick Bell, "Black Students in White Law Schools: The Ordeal and the Opportunity," 2 *University of Toledo Law Review* 539, 545 (1970).

4. *See* Derrick Bell, "Legislation: Pennsylvania Fair Employment Practices Act," 17 *University of Pittsburgh Law Review* 438 (1955); Derrick Bell, Note, "The Girard Will Case—a Charitable Trust Faces the Fourteenth Amendment," 18 *University of Pittsburgh Law Review* 620 (1956).

5. Bell, *Confronting Authority*, 17.

6. *See, e.g., Swann v. Charlotte-Mecklenburg Board of Education*, 369 F.2d 29 (4th Cir. 1966); *City of Jackson v. Bailey*, 376 U.S. 910 (1964); *Goss v. Board of Education, City of Knoxville*, 305 F.2d 523 (6th Cir. 1962); *Meredith v. Fair*, 305 F.2d 341 (5th Cir. 1962); *Dixon v. Alabama State Board of Education*, 294 F.2d 150 (5th Cir. 1961); *Morrow v. Mecklenburg County Board of Education*, 195 F. Supp. 109 (W.D.N.C. 1961). For an incisive description of work life at the NAACP LDF in the 1960s, *see* Michael Meltsner, *The Making of a Civil Rights Lawyer* (2006).

7. Bell, *Silent Covenants*, 99.

8. *See* Bell, *Confronting Authority*, 21–22.

9. Bell, *Silent Covenants*, 102–4.

10. *See* Bell, *Confronting Authority*, 20.

11. *Id.* at 25.

12. *Id.* at 31–33.

13. Derrick A. Bell Jr., "The Western Center on Law and Poverty," *Los Angeles Bar Bulletin*, Oct. 1968.

14. *Id.* at 513.

15. *Id.* at 515.

16. *See* Bell, *Confronting Authority*, 33.

17. *Id.* at 34.

18. *Id.* at 43.

19. Bell to George Lefcoe (professor, Yale Law School), Dec. 17, 1969, box 1, folder 18, Derrick Bell Papers, New York University Library.

20. Bell to Hastie, Feb. 27, 1970, box 2, folder 2, Bell Papers.

21. *See* "Black Law Students Face Disciplinary Decision," *Harvard Law Record*, Jan. 29, 1970.

22. *See* "Law School Faculty Discipline Blacks," *Harvard Law Record*, March 12, 1970.

23. Bell, *Confronting Authority*, 35.

24. *Id.*

25. *Id.* at 34.

26. Derrick Bell, *Race, Racism, and American Law*, 1st ed. (1970), xl.

27. 85 *Yale Law Journal* 470 (1976).

28. Derrick Bell, *Shades of Brown: New Perspectives on School Desegregation* (1980), ix.

29. *Id.*

30. Derrick A. Bell Jr., "*Brown v. Board of Education* and the Interest-Convergence Dilemma," 93 *Harvard Law Review* 518 (1980).

31. *Id.* at 523.

32. *See* Driver, "Rethinking the Interest-Convergence Thesis."

33. *See, e.g.*, Richard Delgado, "Rodrigo's Roundelay: *Hernandez v. Texas* and the Interest-Convergence Dilemma," 41 *Harvard Civil Rights–Civil Liberties Law Review* 23 (2006); Rhonda V. Magee, "The Master's Tools, from the Bottom Up: Responses to African-American Reparations Theory in Mainstream and Outsider Remedies Discourse," 79 *Virginia Law Review* 863, 908–9 (1993); Steven A. Ramirez, "Games CEOs Play and Interest Convergence Theory: Why Diversity Lags in America's Boardrooms and What to Do About It," 61 *Washington and Lee Law Review* 1583 (2004); David A. Singleton, "Interest Convergence and the Education of African American Boys in Cincinnati: Motivating Suburban Whites to Embrace Interdistrict Education Reform," 34 *Northern Kentucky Law Review* 663 (2007); Stephanie M. Weinstein, Note, "A Needed Image Makeover: Interest Convergence and the United States' War on Terror," 11 *Roger Williams University Law Review* 403 (2006).

34. Bell, *Confronting Authority*, 38. *See also* Susan Chira, "At Lunch with Derrick Bell: The Charms of a Devoutly Angry Man," *New York Times*, Oct. 28, 1992, www.nytimes.com (profile noting that Bell "says he never felt accepted" at Harvard).

35. Bell, *Confronting Authority*, 39–44.

36. *See* Linda Greene, "A Short Commentary on the Chronicles," 3 *Harvard BlackLetter Law Journal* 60 (1986) ("The *Harvard Law Review*'s decision to publish the Chronicles in the Supreme Court Foreword deserves recognition as an important confirmation of Professor Derrick Bell's stature . . . as a scholar and teacher.").

37. Derrick Bell, Foreword, 99 *Harvard Law Review* 4 (1985).

38. *Id.* at 13.

39. *Id.* at 41–42.

40. *Id.* at 42.

41. *Id.* at 54.

42. Bell, *Confronting Authority*, 45.

43. *See* David A. Kaplan, "Letter Calls for Harvard Probe; Academic Freedom in Peril?," *National Law Journal*, Aug. 10, 1987; Jennifer A. Kingson, "Harvard Tenure Battle Puts 'Critical Legal Studies' on Trial," *New York Times*, Aug. 30, 1987, www.nytimes.com.

44. *See* Bernstein, "Derrick Bell, Pioneering Harvard Law Professor and Civil Rights Advocate, Dies at 80"; Keith Boykin, "Remembering Derrick Bell," *Huffington Post*, Dec. 6, 2011, www.huffingtonpost.com.

45. "Derrick Bell," *New York Times*, June 30, 1992 ("Derrick Bell . . . received notice today that his teaching days [at HLS] are over because of the university's two-year limit on leaves of absence.").

46. Derrick Bell, *Faces at the Bottom of the Well: The Permanence of Racism* (1992), 12.

47. *Id.*

48. *See, e.g.*, Willie Abrams, "A Reply to Derrick Bell's Racial Realism," 24 *Connecticut Law Review* 517 (1992). "A mindset or philosophy that demands that black Americans acknowledge the permanence of their subordinate status . . . is no solution at all. . . . Black Americans have not been defeated in the struggle for justice and equality." *Id.* at 523–24. *See also* Clark, "Critique of Professor Derrick A. Bell's Thesis of the Permanence of Racism and His Strategy of Confrontation"; Powell, "Racial Realism or Racial Despair?"

49. *See* Randall Kennedy, "Black America's Promised Land: Why I Am Still a Racial Optimist," *American Prospect*, Nov. 10, 2014, prospect.org.

50. Bell, *Faces at the Bottom of the Well*, ix.

51. Derrick Bell Jr., "What's Diversity Got to Do with It?," 6 *Seattle Journal for Social Justice* 527, 528 (2007).

52. Bell, *Faces at the Bottom of the Well*, x, 97, 198.

53. *Id.* at ix.

54. *Id.* at 10.

55. *Id.* at 12.

56. *Id.* at 23.

57. Gerald David Jaynes and Robin M. Williams Jr., *A Common Destiny: Blacks and American Society* (1989), 4.

58. *Id.* at 155.

59. *Compare* Derrick A. Bell Jr., "Racial Remediation: An Historical Perspective on Current Conditions," 52 *Notre Dame Law Review* 5, 11–12 (1976), *with* Bell, "*Brown v. Board of Education* and the Interest-Convergence Dilemma," *and with* Derrick A. Bell Jr., "The Unintended Lessons in *Brown v. Board of Education*," 49 *New York Law School Law Review* 1053–54 (2005).

60. Derrick A. Bell, "Humanity in Legal Education," 59 *Oregon Law Review* 243, 247 (1980).

61. Bell, "*Brown v. Board of Education* and the Interest-Convergence Dilemma," 518.

62. Bell, "Unintended Lessons," 1054.

63. *Id.* at 1061.

64. *Id.* at 1053.

65. Quoted in James T. Patterson, *Brown v. Board of Education: A Civil Rights Milestone and Its Troubled Legacy* (2001), 68.

66. Derrick A. Bell Jr., dissenting, in *What Brown v. Board of Education Should Have Said*, ed. Jack M. Balkin (2001), 196.

67. Derrick A. Bell Jr., Foreword, 61 *Oregon Law Review* 151 (1982).

68. Michael Klarman, "*Brown v. Board of Education:* Facts and Political Correctness," 80 *Virginia Law Review* 185, 186 (1994).

69. *See, e.g., Loving v. Virginia*, 388 U.S. 1 (1967) (marriage); *Gayle v. Browder*, 352 U.S. 903 (1956) (buses); *Holmes v. City of Atlanta*, 350 U.S. 879 (1955) (golf course); *Mayor and City Council of Baltimore v. Dawson*, 350 U.S. 877 (1955) (swimming pools).

70. *See* Randall Kennedy, "The Civil Rights Act's Unsung Victory and How It Changed the South," *Harper's*, June 2014.

71. *See, e.g., Griggs v. Duke Power Co.*, 401 U.S. 424 (1971).

72. *See* Gavin Wright, *Sharing the Prize: The Economics of the Civil Rights Revolution in the American South* (2013). *See also* John J. Donohue III and James Heckman, "Continuous Versus Episodic Change: The Impact of Civil Rights Policy on the Economic Status of Blacks," 29 *Journal of Economic Literature* 1603 (1991).

73. *See Shelby County v. Holder*, 570 U.S. 2, 15 (2013). *See also* Chandler Davidson and Bernard Grofman, *Quiet Revolution in the South: The Impact of the Voting Rights Act, 1965–1990* (1994).

74. Derrick A. Bell Jr., "On Celebrating an Election as Racial Progress," *Human Rights* (Fall 2009).

75. *Id.*

76. Bell to McCree, Dec. 3, 1971, box 2, folder 28, Bell Papers.

77. Ferguson to Bell, July 19, 1973, box 20, folder 1, Clarence Clyde Ferguson Papers, Harvard Law School Library.

78. Wanda Payne, "Bell Toasted by 200 at Farewell Tribute Dinner," *Harvard Law Record*, Nov. 26, 1980.

79. Bell to Charles Duncan, Sept. 8, 1971, box 2, folder 28, Bell Papers.

80. Bell to Areeda, Nov. 16, 1971, box 2, folder 28, Bell Papers.
81. Bell, "Black Students in White Law Schools," 541.
82. *Id.* at 548.
83. *Id.*
84. *Id.* at 552.
85. *Id.* at 553.
86. For another example of clear-eyed, commonsensical pragmatism in Bell's writing, *see* Derrick A. Bell Jr., "Law School Exams and Minority-Group Students," 7 *Black Law Journal* 304 (1981).
87. Bell, *Confronting Authority*, 76.
88. Quoted in *id.* at 63; Fox Butterfield, "At Rally, Jackson Assails Harvard Law School," *New York Times*, May 10, 1990, www.nytimes.com.
89. Bell, *Confronting Authority*, 82–83.
90. *See* "Portions of the C.C.R. Lawsuit," *Harvard Law Record*, Nov. 30, 1990.
91. *See, e.g.*, David Snouffer, "Bok Vetoes Trubek, Reviews Dalton Bid," *Harvard Law Record*, Sept. 18, 1987.
92. *See* "Complaint on Harvard Law's Hiring," *New York Times*, March 4, 1992.
93. *See* Laura A. Murray, "HLS Hiring to Come Under Federal Scrutiny," *Harvard Law Record*, Oct. 30, 1992.
94. Bell, *Confronting Authority*, 76.
95. *See* Elizabeth Bartholet, "Application of Title VII to Jobs in High Places," 95 *Harvard Law Review* 945 (1982).
96. Bell, *Confronting Authority*, 76.
97. *Id.* at 79.
98. *See* G. Vincent, "Guinier Says Yes to Tenure at HLS," *Harvard Law Record*, Feb. 6, 1998.
99. *See* Bell, Foreword, 99 *Harvard Law Review* 4 (1985). Bell subsequently included this part of his *Harvard Law Review* Foreword in his book *And We Are Not Saved: The Elusive Quest for Racial Justice* (1987).
100. Bell, *And We Are Not Saved*, 158.
101. Derrick A. Bell Jr., "Application of the 'Tipping Point' Principle to Law Faculty Hiring Policies," 10 *Nova Law Review* 319, 325 (1986).
102. Jacqueline Goggin, "Countering White Racist Scholarship: Carter G. Woodson and the *Journal of Negro History*," 68 *Journal of Negro History* 355, 359 (1983) (quoting a letter from Franklin to Goggin, Sept. 14, 1981). "Indeed, the generation before me had stronger scholars who were at home both in the black groups and the white groups. . . . [T]he papers in the *Journal of Negro History* for that period reflect that high standard." *Id.*
103. *See* Thomas Sowell, *Black Education: Myths and Tragedies* (1972).
104. Cornel West, "The Crisis of Black Leadership," *Zeta Magazine*, Feb. 1987, 25.
105. Rennard Strickland, "Scholarship in the Academic Circus or the Balancing Act at the Minority Side Show," 20 *University of San Francisco Law Review* 491, 500 (1986).

106. *See* Gerald Frug, "McCarthyism and Critical Legal Studies," 22 *Harvard Civil Rights–Civil Liberties Law Review* 665 (1987); Robert W. Gordon, "Law and Ideology," 3 *Tikkun* (1998); Mark Tushnet, "Critical Legal Studies: A Political History," 100 *Yale Law Journal* 1515 (1991).

107. *See* Bell to Robert Clark (dean, Harvard Law School), in Delgado and Stefancic, *Derrick Bell Reader,* 206–7.

108. Derrick Bell, "The Strange Career of Randall Kennedy," 7 *New Politics* 1 (1998).

109. "Racial Critiques of Legal Academia," 102 *Harvard Law Review* 1745 (1989).

110. Bell, "Strange Career of Randall Kennedy."

111. *Id.* (quoting Derrick Bell, letter to the editor, *New York Times,* Jan. 26, 1990).

112. In *People v. Hall,* 4 Cal. 399, 404–5 (1854), the California Supreme Court ruled that state law excluded Chinese, along with blacks and Indians, from testifying against whites. In the course of its decision the Court described the Chinese as "[a people] whose mendacity is proverbial; a race . . . nature has marked as inferior, and who are incapable of progress or intellectual development beyond a certain point." *Id.* at 405. A prominent Chinese merchant responded in the following terms: "[The whites] have come to the conclusion that we Chinese are the same as Indians and Negroes. . . . And yet these Indians know nothing about the relations of society; they know no mutual respect; they wear neither clothes nor shoes; they live in wild places and [in] caves." Charles J. McClain Jr., "The Chinese Struggle for Civil Rights in Nineteenth Century America: The First Phase, 1850–1870," 72 *California Law Review* 529, 550 (1984) (second alteration in original) (footnote omitted). The Chinese merchant argued, in other words, that it was understandable to exclude Indians and blacks from the witness stand but an injustice to do the same to people of Chinese ancestry.

113. *See* Annie Heloise Abel, *The American Indian as Slaveholder and Secessionist* (1992), 1–5; Theda Perdue, *Slavery and the Evolution of Cherokee Society, 1540–1866* (1979), 38–39, 66; Kathryn E. Holland Braund, "The Creek Indians, Blacks, and Slavery," 57 *Journal of Southern History* 601, 601–2, 616–18 (1991); C. Calvin Smith, "The Oppressed Oppressors: Negro Slavery Among the Choctaw Indians of Oklahoma," 2 *Red River Valley Historical Review* 240, 240–41 (1975); William S. Willis, "Divide and Rule: Red, White, and Black in the Southeast," 48 *Journal of Negro History* 157, 168–73 (1963).

114. In 1914, a group of African Americans rightly objected to an Oklahoma statute that authorized railroads to provide first-class service only to whites. They prevailed in the U.S. Supreme Court, which ruled that the statute in question violated the formal equality under which de jure segregation was justified. *See McCabe v. Atchison, Topeka & Santa Fe Railway,* 235 U.S. 151, 161–62 (1914). Unfortunately, in the course of pleading their case, they participated in the unjustified vilification of other oppressed people. Complaining that Indians were protected from exclusion while blacks were not,

the plaintiffs objected that Indians are "far more vicious as well as unclean and unhealthy." Alexander Bickel and Benno C. Schmidt Jr., *The History of the Supreme Court of the United States*, vol. 9, *The Judiciary and Responsible Government, 1910–1921* (1984), 778n146 (quoting Brief for Appellants at 50–51, *McCabe v. Atchison, Topeka & Santa Fe Railway*, 235 U.S. 151 [1914]).

115. In an effort to defend Leo Frank against rape charges, supporters pointed to a black man who should have been a prime suspect. They attempted to foment anger against him by resorting to racist, antiblack stereotypes that depict black men as rapacious sexual beasts. A sign of the extraordinary character of the animus against Frank is that the Negro-baiting tactics of his defenders failed. They "expressed outrage that a white employer was indicted, rather than a black worker with a criminal record, and shock that their appeals to white supremacy failed to rally the jury or the public." Nancy MacLean, "The Leo Frank Case Reconsidered: Gender and Sexual Politics in the Making of Reactionary Populism," 78 *Journal of American History* 917, 925 (1991). Many blacks reacted angrily to this attempt to supersede anti-Jewish prejudice with antiblack bigotry. *See* Eugene Levy, " 'Is the Jew a White Man?': Press Reaction to the Leo Frank Case, 1913–1915," 35 *Phylon* 212 (1974).

116. *See* Kwang Chung Kim and Shin Kim, "The Multiracial Nature of Los Angeles Unrest in 1992," in *Koreans in the Hood: Conflict with African Americans*, ed. Kwang Chung Kim (1999), 17, 34; Heon Cheol Lee, "Conflict Between Korean Merchants and Black Customers: A Structural Analysis," in *id.* at 113, 114; Pyong Gap Min and Andrew Kolodny, "The Middleman Minority Characteristics of Korean Immigrants in the United States," in *id.* at 131, 144–49.

117. Derrick Bell, *Race, Racism, and American Law*, 3rd ed. (1992), 683. It should be noted that in the fourth edition of *Race, Racism, and American Law*, Professor Bell changes "White racism" to "American racism." Derrick Bell, *Race, Racism, and American Law*, 4th ed. (2000), 1029. All things considered, however, one doubts that this emendation signals a significant transformation in his outlook.

118. Bell, *Confronting Authority*, 84.

119. Bell, *Faces at the Bottom of the Well*, 116.

120. *Id.* at 117.

121. *See* Bruce A. Kimball and Daniel R. Coquillette, *The Intellectual Sword: Harvard Law School, the Second Century* (2020), 706–15.

122. Derrick Bell, "A Tragedy of Timing," 19 *Harvard Civil Rights–Civil Liberties Law Review* 277 (1984) (describing the career of his recently deceased colleague Clyde Ferguson, "the Satchel Paige of legal education").

123. *See* Fondren to Bell, Aug. 10, 1967; Memorandum from Bell to Office for Civil Rights, HEW, box 1, file 8, Bell Papers.

124. *See* Bell to Morris Abram, Dec. 18, 1969, box 1, folder 18, Bell Papers ("I provide this report to you as a means of urging whatever further steps are necessary to insure that employees receive the same courtesy and under-

standing direction at the lowest levels of supervision that I know they would receive in your office."). *See also* David S. Squire to Bell, Jan. 27, 1970, box 2, folder 2, Bell Papers.

125. Henry McGee, "A Tribute to Derrick Bell," 36 *Seattle University Law Review* xxxvii (2013).

126. Patricia J. Williams, "Tribute in Memory of Professor Derrick Bell," Derrick Bell Official Site, Oct. 11, 2011, professorderrickbell.com.

127. Patricia J. Williams, "Tribute to Derrick Bell," 69 *New York University Annual Survey of American Law* 7, 8–9 (2013).

128. Adrien K. Wing, "Derrick Bell: Tolling in Protest," review of *Confronting Authority*, by Derrick Bell, 12 *Harvard BlackLetter Law Journal* 161 (1995).

129. Cheryl I. Harris, "Tribute in Memory of Professor Derrick Bell," Derrick Bell Official Site, Oct. 15, 2011, professorderrickbell.com.

3. THE GEORGE FLOYD MOMENT: PROMISE AND PERIL

1. An earlier iteration of this essay appeared as Randall Kennedy, "The George Floyd Moment: Promise and Peril," *American Prospect*, June 19, 2020.

4. ISABEL WILKERSON, THE ELECTION OF 2020, AND RACIAL CASTE

1. An earlier iteration of this essay appeared as Randall Kennedy, "The Ebb and Flow of Racial Progress," *American Prospect*, Dec. 3, 2020.

5. THE PRINCETON ULTIMATUM: ANTIRACISM GONE AWRY

1. An earlier iteration of this essay appeared as Randall Kennedy, "How Racist Are Universities, Really?," *Chronicle of Higher Education*, Aug. 12, 2020.

6. HOW BLACK STUDENTS BROUGHT THE CONSTITUTION TO CAMPUS

1. An earlier iteration of this essay appeared as Randall Kennedy, "The Forgotten Origins of the Constitution on Campus," *American Prospect*, Dec. 28, 2017.

8. THE POLITICS OF BLACK RESPECTABILITY

1. An earlier version of this essay appeared as Randall Kennedy, "Lifting as We Climb: A Progressive Defense of Respectability Politics," *Harper's*, Oct. 2015.

9. POLICING RACIAL SOLIDARITY

1. An earlier version of this essay appeared as Randall Kennedy, "The Fallacy of Touré's Post-blackness Theory," *Root*, Aug. 11, 2011.

10. WHY CLARENCE THOMAS OUGHT TO BE OSTRACIZED

1. An earlier version of this essay appeared as Randall Kennedy, "The Apparatchik," *Nation*, Oct. 29, 2019.

11. SAY IT LOUD! ON RACIAL SHAME, PRIDE, KINSHIP, AND OTHER PROBLEMS

1. This piece draws upon earlier efforts: "How James Brown Made Black Pride a Hit," *New York Times*, July 20, 2018; and "My Race Problem," *Atlantic*, May 1997.

12. THE STRUGGLE FOR COLLECTIVE NAMING

1. An earlier version of this essay appeared as Randall Kennedy, "Finding a Proper Name to Call Black Americans," 46 *The Journal of Blacks in Higher Education* 72 (Winter 2004–2005).
2. Quoted in Garrett Felber, *Those Who Don't Know Say: The Nation of Islam, the Black Freedom Movement, and the Carceral State* (2020), 9.
3. *See* Henry Louis Gates Jr. and Jennifer Burton, *Call and Response: Key Debates in African American Studies* (2011), 86–95, 867–74; Gilbert Thomas Stephenson, *Race Distinctions in American Law* (1910), 20–25; Ben L. Martin, "From Negro to Black to African American: The Power of Names and Naming," 106 *Political Science Quarterly* 83 (1991); Michael C. Thornton, Robert Joseph Taylor, and Tony N. Brown, "Correlates of Racial Legal Use Among Americans of African Descent: Colored, Negro, Black, and African American," *Race and Society* 149 (1999).
4. Advocating use of the label "black," Robinson writes, "Instead of focusing on who we were, let's be proud of who we are." *See* Smokey Robinson, "A Black American," *Def Jam Poetry*, YouTube, Aug. 31, 2014.
5. Albert Murray, *From the Briarpatch File: On Context, Procedure, and American Identity* (2001), 191. Ralph Ellison also disliked the term "black" and referred to himself as a "Negro." *See* "The Emergence of the Term 'African American' at Two Prestigious Institutions: *The New York Times* and the Supreme Court," 16 *Journal of Blacks in Higher Education* 12 (1997).
6. Henry Louis Gates Jr., *Colored People: A Memoir* (1994), xvi.
7. Karen E. Fields and Barbara J. Fields, *Racecraft: The Soul of Inequality in American Life* (2012).
8. Quoted in Phillip Brian Harper, *Are We Not Men? Masculine Anxiety and the Problem of African-American Identity* (1996), 55. W. E. B. Du Bois and Booker T. Washington seem to have shared this view. *See* Washington quoted in Stephenson, *Race Distinctions in American Law*, 22: "I do not think my people should be ashamed of their history, nor of any name that people choose in good faith to give them." *See also* Gates, *Colored People* ("I don't

mind any of the names myself."). After expressing a preference for "Afro-American," Karen E. Fields and Barbara J. Fields write that they "do not take a dogmatic view" and are accepting of a wide range of labels including "colored" and "Negro." Fields and Fields, *Racecraft*, vii.

9. *See* Carter G. Woodson, *The Mis-education of the Negro* (1933; 2000).

10. Harper, *Are We Not Men?*, 55. Smokey Robinson also voices impatience with continued wrangling over nomenclature:

> As a Black man in this country, I think it's a shame that every few years we get a change of name. . . . We are the only people whose name is always a trend. When is this shit gonna end?

11. Shelby Steele, *The Content of Our Character: A New Vision of Race in America* (1990), 47.

12. Quoted in Sterling Stuckey, *Slave Culture: Nationalist Theory and the Foundations of Black America* (1987), 225.

13. In an oft-cited article, the legal scholar Kimberlé Crenshaw explained that she uses "African American" and "black" interchangeably and that she capitalizes the *B* in "Black." Her explanation and approach have generated much notice, reflecting the importance that many observers attach to the matter of racial labeling. *See* Kimberlé Crenshaw, "Race, Reform, and Retrenchment: Transformation and Legitimation in Antidiscrimination Law," 101 *Harvard Law Review* 1331, 1332n1 (1988).

14. Quoted in Mary Frances Berry and John W. Blassingame, *Long Memory: The Black Experience in America* (1982), 389.

15. Richard Kluger, *Simple Justice: The History of Brown v. Board of Education and Black America's Struggle for Equality* (1975; 2004), ix.

16. *The Associated Press Stylebook and Briefing on Media Law*, 55th ed. (2020–2022), 252.

17. Allan M. Seigal and William G. Connolly, revised and updated by Philip B. Corbett, Jill Taylor, Patrick LaForge, and Susan Wessling, *The New York Times Manual of Style and Usage* 5th ed., (2015), 9, 67, 210.

18. Stuckey, *Slave Culture*, 199–200.

19. Patrick Rael, *Black Identity and Black Protest in the Antebellum North* (2002), 90.

20. *See id.* at 91; Stuckey, *Slave Culture*, 202.

21. Rael, *Black Identity and Black Protest in the Antebellum North*, 105.

22. *Id.* at 109.

23. *Id.* at 108.

24. *Id.* at 316n92. *See also North Star*, Feb. 4, 1848.

25. Professor Rael writes that "many" black leaders supported Whipper's position. Rael, *Black Identity and Black Protest in the Antebellum North*, 109. But neither evidence he adduces nor independent research substantiates his assertion regarding the popularity of Whipper's approach.

26. *Id.* at 109–10.

27. *Id.* at 109.
28. *Id.* at 114.
29. Herbert Aptheker, *A Documentary History of the Negro People in the United States* (1951), 2:609.
30. *Id.* at 652.
31. *Id.* at 758.
32. *Id.* at 887.
33. *See* Jonah Goldberg, "Arguments of Color," *National Review Online*, Jan. 21, 2002. An episode illustrating Goldberg's observation is available on You-Tube. It features an apology by a television journalist after he referred to blacks as "colored people." He made this reference in the course of congratulating the president of the NAACP. *See* "MSNBC Anchor Peter Alexander Apologizes After Saying 'Colored People,'" *Huffington Post*, March 15, 2009.
34. Nick Thompson, "Benedict Cumberbatch Apologizes for 'Colored Actors' Remark in U.S. Interview," CNN, Jan. 28, 2015.
35. Thomas D. Morris, *Southern Slavery and the Law, 1610–1860* (1999), 17. Conflating "Negro" and "slave," Samuel Johnson scorned the hypocrisy of the American colonists when he asked, "How is it that we hear the loudest yelps for liberty among the drivers of negroes?"
36. *See* Harold R. Isaacs, *The New World of Negro Americans* (1963), 82.
37. *See* Rael, *Black Identity and Black Protest in the Antebellum North*, 100.
38. *Id.*
39. *See* Stephen R. Fox, *The Guardian of Boston: William Monroe Trotter* (1970), 251.
40. Kelly Miller, "Negroes or Colored People?," *Opportunity: Journal of Negro Life*, May 1937.
41. Richard B. Moore, *The Name "Negro": Its Origin and Evil Use* (1960; 1992), 37.
42. *Id.* at 50.
43. *Id.* at 48.
44. Stokely Carmichael (Kwame Ture) and Charles V. Hamilton, *Black Power: The Politics of Liberation* (1967; 1992), 37.
45. Quoted in Eric Lincoln, *The Black Muslims in America*, 3rd ed. (1994), 64–65.
46. John Heilemann and Mark Halperin, *Game Change* (2010), 36.
47. Joan Walsh, "A Democrat's Gaffe, the GOP's Shame," *Salon*, Jan. 10, 2010.
48. Michael Tomasky, "Harry Reid's 'Negro' Problem," *Michael Tomasky's Blog, Guardian*, Jan. 11, 2010, www.theguardian.com.
49. Editorial, "The Crass Politics of Race," *Dallas Morning News*, Jan. 11, 2010.
50. Leonard R. Pitts Jr., "Criticism of Reid Is Off Base—What He Said Was the Truth," *Press of Atlantic City*, Jan. 14, 2010.
51. Jeff Zeleny, "Reid Apologizes for Remarks on Obama's Color and 'Dialect,'" *New York Times*, Jan. 9, 2010.

52. *See* Melissa Nobles, *Shades of Citizenship: Race and the Census in Modern Politics* (2000), 28, 44.

53. Robert Groves, "The Word 'Negro,'" *Director's Blog*, U.S. Census Bureau, Jan. 19, 2010. *See also* Associated Press, "Census Bureau Surveys to Stop Using 'Negro,'" *Los Angeles Times*, Feb. 26, 2013; Clarence Page, "Our Census Reflects Our Confusion," *Chicago Tribune*, Feb. 3, 2010.

54. *See* Barbara Starr and Jeremy Diamond, "Army Apologizes for Policy Approving Use of Word 'Negro,'" CNN, Nov. 7, 2014.

55. *See* W. E. B. Du Bois, *Writings*, ed. Nathan Huggins (1986), 1219–22.

56. Quoted in Lerone Bennett Jr., "What's in a Name? Negro vs. Afro-American vs. Black," 26 *ETC: A Review of General Semantics* 399, 409 (1969).

57. Sandy Banks, "Long Live the Word 'Negro,'" *Los Angeles Times*, March 12, 2013.

58. *See* Willis N. Huggins and John G. Jackson, *A Guide to Studies in African History* (1935), 31–32; Monroe Work, *Negro Year Book, 1931–1932* (2012), 21; Irving Lewis Allen, "Sly Slurs: Mispronunciation and Decapitalization of Group Names," 36 *Names* 217 (1988); Donald L. Grant and Mildred Bricker Grant, "Some Notes on the Capital 'N,'" 36 *Phylon* 435 (1979).

59. *See* David Levering Lewis, *W. E. B. Du Bois: Biography of a Race, 1868–1919* (1994).

60. *See* Allen, "Sly Slurs."

61. *See The Selected Writings of James Weldon Johnson*, vol. 1, *The "New York Age" Editorials (1914–1923)*, ed. Sondra Kathryn Wilson (1995), 36.

62. *Id.*

63. "'Negro' with a Capital 'N,'" *New York Times*, March 7, 1930.

64. *See* Allen, "Sly Slurs."

65. Imamu Amiri Baraka (LeRoi Jones), *Home: Social Essays* (1966), 235.

66. Taylor Branch, *Parting the Waters: America in the King Years, 1954–1963* (1988), 748.

67. *See* Kenneth Robert Jackson, *Rayford W. Logan and the Dilemma of the African American Intellectual* (1993).

68. *See* Lori L. Tharps, "The Case for Black with a Capital B," *New York Times*, Nov. 18, 2014.

69. *See* "Uppercasing 'Black,'" *New York Times*, June 30, 2020. *See also* Nancy Coleman, "Why We're Capitalizing Black," *New York Times*, July 5, 2020.

70. *See* Kwame Anthony Appiah, "The Case for Capitalizing the *B* in Black," *Atlantic*, June 18, 2020.

71. "Jackson and Others Say 'Blacks' is Passe," *New York Times*, December 21, 1988.

72. Quoted in Philip S. Foner, *The Voice of Black America: Major Speeches by Negroes in the United States, 1797–1971* (1972), 1011.

73. Stephan Thernstrom, "Just Say Afro," *New Republic*, Jan. 23, 1989.

74. Phillip T. Gay, Commentary, "A Vote Against Use of 'African American,'" *Los Angeles Times*, April 2, 1989.

75. John McWhorter, "Why I'm Black, Not African American," *Los Angeles Times*, Sept. 8, 2004.

76. *See* John Heilemann, "Black Is Back," *New Yorker*, Oct. 30, 1995.

13. THE STRUGGLE FOR PERSONAL NAMING

1. The work that introduced me to this topic and prompted me to study it is Stanley Lieberson, *A Matter of Taste: How Names, Fashions, and Culture Change* (2000).

2. *See* Eugene Genovese, *Roll, Jordan, Roll: The World the Slaves Made* (1976), 443–50; Herbert G. Gutman, *The Black Family in Slavery and Freedom, 1750–1925* (1976), 230–56; Iman Makeba Laversuch, "Runaway Slave Names Recaptured," 54 *Names* 331 (2006) ("The naming of enslaved persons . . . was often part of the general dehumanizing process by which self-appointed masters routinely stripped their newly acquired chattel of their original African names and reassigned them new European names, thereby not only marking their constructed legal ownership, but also asserting their perceived racial dominance.").

3. *See* J. H. Ingraham, *The Sunny South; or, The Southerner at Home, Embracing Five Years' Experience of a Northern Governess in the Land of the Sugar and the Cotton* (1860), 68–70. This source was brought to my attention by Kenneth M. Stampp in his landmark *The Peculiar Institution: Slavery in the Ante-bellum South* (1956), 328, 329.

4. George F. Dow, *Slave Ships and Slaving* (1927), 172. *See also* Newbell Niles Puckett, *Black Names in America: Origins and Usage*, ed. Murray Heller (1975), 6.

5. Dow, *Slave Ships and Slaving*, 295; Puckett, *Black Names in America*, 6.

6. Puckett, *Black Names in America*, 6.

7. *See id.* at 6. *See also* John C. Inscoe, "Carolina Slave Names: An Index of Acculturation," 49 *Journal of Southern History* 527, 529 (1983) ("Usually slaves remained nameless entities, only part of a mass of cargo, from the time of their capture in Africa until their final sales to their new masters, with no attempt having been made, or needed, to identify them individually prior to that point.").

8. Peter H. Wood, *Black Majority: Negroes in Colonial South Carolina from 1670 Through the Stono Rebellion* (1974), 181–82n47.

9. *See* Puckett, *Black Names in America*, 11.

10. *See* Inscoe, "Carolina Slave Names," 541.

11. *Id.* at 543.

12. *See* Justin Kaplan and Anne Bernays, *The Language of Names* (1997), 78; *see* Inscoe, "Carolina Slave Names," 532–33.

13. According to Inscoe, "Eartha Kitt has said that her parents gave her that name because they were having a good harvest at the time of her birth." Inscoe, "Carolina Slave Names," 536n27.

14. *Id.* at 537.

15. *See* Leslie Alan Dunkling, *What's in a Name?* (1977), 150–51; Joseph Boskin, *Sambo: The Rise and Demise of an American Jester* (1986).

16. Inscoe, "Carolina Slave Names," 533.

17. *Id.*

18. Michael P. Johnson and James L. Roark, *Black Masters: A Free Family of Color in the Old South* (1984).

19. Johnnetta Cole, "Militant Black Women in Early U.S. History," 9 *Black Scholar* 38, 44 (1978).

20. *See* William S. McFeely, *Frederick Douglass* (1991), 304.

21. *See* Leon F. Litwack, *Been in the Storm So Long: The Aftermath of Slavery* (1979), 248.

22. Inscoe, "Carolina Slave Names," 548.

23. Litwack, *Been in the Storm So Long*, 249.

24. *Id.* at 248.

25. *Id.* at 251.

26. *Id.* at 250; Inscoe, "Carolina Slave Names," 551.

27. Inscoe, "Carolina Slave Names," 551.

28. Julius Lester, *To Be a Slave* (1968), 147.

29. Inscoe, "Carolina Slave Names," 553.

30. Litwack, *Been in the Storm So Long*, 176.

31. *Id.* at 252. According to a former slave in Virginia, "My master would kill anybody who called *any-body* but a white person Missis." *Id.* at 254.

32. *Id.* at 252.

33. *Id.* at 251.

34. *See* Andrew S. London and S. Philip Morgan, "Racial Differences in First Names in 1910," 19 *Journal of Family History* (1994), 261.

35. *See* Isabel Wilkerson, *Caste: The Origins of Our Discontents* (2020), 55.

36. *See Hamilton v. Alabama*, 376 U.S. 650 (1964). *See also* "The Law: Call Her Miss," *Time*, April 10, 1964.

37. Thomas Hauser, *Muhammad Ali: His Life and Times* (1991), 102.

38. *See* Jerry G. Watts, *Amiri Baraka: The Politics and Art of a Black Intellectual* (2001), 312.

39. He named himself after two of his heroes: Kwame Nkrumah and Sekou Touré. *See* Stokely Carmichael, *Ready for Revolution: The Life and Struggles of Stokely Carmichael (Kwame Ture)*, with Ekwueme Michael Thelwell (2003), 626–28.

40. According to Jones/Baraka, "the man who buried Malcolm X," Hajj Heesham Jaaber, gave him the name Ameer Barakat (the Blessed Prince). Later, under the influence of Maulana Karenga, Barakat changed his first name to Amiri, a process he described as "Bantuizing or Swahilizing." Karenga also prompted Baraka to begin his name with the title Imamu. But Baraka dropped that aspect of his name, partly as a way of distancing himself from Karenga's U.S. organization and partly because he learned on

a trip to Africa that that title "is like Reverend. . . . People [there] actually thought you were a preacher and I couldn't take that. . . . So I tried to cut it loose." *Conversations with Amiri Baraka*, ed. Charlie Reilly (1994), 126; Amiri Baraka, *The Autobiography of LeRoi Jones* (1997), 376; Werner Sollors, *Amiri Baraka/LeRoi Jones: The Quest for a "Populist Modernism"* (1978), 263n2.

41. Baraka, *Autobiography*, 376.

42. *See* Scot Brown, *Fighting for US: Maulana Karenga, the US Organization, and Black Cultural Nationalism* (2003), 60.

43. Hauser, *Muhammad Ali*, 102.

44. *Id.*

45. Terrell later claimed that his refusal to recognize Ali's new name was simply a ruse to generate publicity for the fight. *Id.* at 163.

46. Roland G. Fryer Jr. and Steven D. Levitt, "The Causes and Consequences of Distinctively Black Names," 119 *Quarterly Journal of Economics* 767, 770 (2004). Some researchers insist, by contrast, that African American preferences for distinctively black names long predated the 1960s. *See* Lisa D. Cook, Trevon D. Logan, and John M. Parman, "Distinctively Black Names in the American Past" (NBER, Working Paper No. 18802, 2013).

47. H. L. Mencken, *The American Language: An Inquiry into the Development of English in the United States*, 4th ed. (1980), 525.

48. *Id.* at 521–22.

49. *Id.* at 525.

50. Marianne Bertrand and Sendhil Mullainathan, "Are Emily and Greg More Employable Than Lakisha and Jamal? A Field Experiment in Labor Market Discrimination," 94 *American Economic Review* 991, 992 (2004).

51. Albert Mehrabian and Marlena Piercy, "Positive or Negative Connotations of Unconventionally and Conventionally Spelled Names," 133 *Journal of Social Psychology* 445 (1993).

52. Kaplan and Bernays, *Language of Names*, 51.

53. *Id. See also* Mencken, *American Language*, 479–505.

54. For the most comprehensive treatment of this subject, *see* Kirsten Fermaglich, *A Rosenberg by Any Other Name: A History of Jewish Name Changing in America* (2018). *See also* Mencken, *American Language*, 497 ("Of all the immigrant peoples in the United States, the Jews seem to be the most willing to change their names. . . . [Those following the initial immigrants] shrink from all the disadvantages that go with their foreignness and their Jewishness, and seek to conceal their origin, or, at all events, to avoid making it unnecessarily noticeable.").

55. *See* Kaplan and Bernays, *Language of Names*, 55–64. *See also* Charles E. Silberman, *A Certain People: American Jews and Their Lives Today* (1985), 61.

56. Fermaglich, *Rosenberg by Any Other Name*, 162.

57. Carlton F. W. Larson, "Naming Baby: The Constitutional Dimensions of Parental Naming Rights," 80 *George Washington Law Review* 159 (2011).

58. Laura Ingraham and Raymond Arroyo, *Of Thee I Zing: America's Cultural Decline from Muffin Tops to Body Shots* (2011), 9.
59. *See* Cathy M. Jackson, "Names CAN Hurt!," *Essence*, April 1989.
60. Michael Eric Dyson, *Is Bill Cosby Right? Or Has the Black Middle Class Lost Its Mind?* (2005), xii.
61. *Id.* at 137.
62. *Id.* at 139.
63. Jesse Washington, "Washington: The 'Blackest Name' in America," *Huffington Post*, Feb. 21, 2011; David L. Word et al., *Demographic Aspects of Surnames from Census 2000*, Jan. 2008.
64. Word et al., *Demographic Aspects of Surnames from Census 2000*.

14. "NIGGER": THE STRANGE CAREER CONTINUES

1. This essay stems from a letter I wrote to law school colleagues in the summer of 2020. It also derives from other writings of mine on the infamous n-word. *See Nigger: The Strange Career of a Troublesome Word* (2002); "How a Dispute over the N-Word Became a Dispiriting Farce," *Chronicle of Higher Education*, Feb. 8, 2019; "When the N-Word Meets Public Education," *Boston Globe*, April 7, 2019. Useful, too, was an article I had the pleasure of co-authoring alongside Eugene Volokh, "Quoting Epithets in the Classroom and Beyond," *Capital Law Review* (2021).
2. *See, e.g.*, Nick Anderson, "A Stanford Law Professor Read a Quote with the N-Word to His Class, Stirring Outrage at the School," *Washington Post*, June 3, 2020; Tom Bartlett, "A Professor Has Long Used a Racial Slur in Class to Teach Free-Speech Law. No More, He Says," *Chronicle of Higher Education*, March 7, 2019; Joe Patrice, "Stanford Joins List of Law Schools with White Professors Using the N-Word in Class," *Above the Law*, June 1, 2020; "Professor at Wake Forest University Apologizes for Reading the N-Word in Class," *Journal of Blacks in Higher Education*, April 7, 2020; Eugene Volokh, "UCLA Law Dean Apologizes for My Having Accurately Quoted the Word 'Nigger' in Discussing a Case. I, However, Do Not Apologize," Reason.com, April 14, 2020; Eugene Volokh, "Wake Forest Dean Apologizes for Constitutional Law Professor's Quoting the Word 'Nigger' from a Leading Supreme Court Case," Reason.com, March 31, 2020; Debra Cassens Weiss, "Stanford Law Prof Who Used Quote with Racial Slur in Class Says He Won't Do It Again," *ABA Journal*, June 2, 2020; Erin Woo, "Law Professor Criticized After Reading Racial Slur in Class," *Stanford Daily*, May 30, 2020.
3. Elaine Chen, "After Stirring Speeches by Black Law Students, Free Speech Prof to Stop Saying Racial Epithet in Class," *Chicago Maroon*, March 12, 2019.
4. *Cf. Burlington v. Fox*, 759 F. Supp. 2d 580 (E.D. Pa. 2010). *See also* Debra Cassens Weiss, "Law Prof Sues over N-Word Suspension and Says Being White Led to Different Treatment," *ABA Journal*, Aug. 10, 2020.

5. Colleen Flaherty, "New School Drops N-Word Case," *Inside Higher Ed*, Aug. 19, 2019. *See also* John McWhorter, "The Idea That Whites Can't Refer to the N-Word," *Atlantic*, Aug. 27, 2019.

15. SHOULD WE ADMIRE NAT TURNER?

1. For an earlier iteration of this essay, see Randall Kennedy, "On Judging Nat Turner," in *Dixie Redux: Essays in Honor of Sheldon Hackney*, ed. Raymond Arsenault and Orville Vernon Burton (2013).
2. For a comprehensive overview of the Nat Turner rebellion, *see* Patrick H. Breen, *The Land Shall Be Deluged in Blood: A New History of the Nat Turner Revolt* (2015).
3. John Brown's abolitionist violence poses ethical dilemmas similar to some of those posed by Turner's rebellion. *See, e.g.*, Paul Finkelman, ed., *His Soul Goes Marching On: Responses to John Brown and the Harpers Ferry Raid* (1995); Benjamin Quarles, *Allies for Freedom and Blacks on John Brown* (1994); Peggy A. Russo and Paul Finkelman, eds., *Terrible Swift Sword: The Legacy of John Brown* (2005); John Stauffer and Zoe Trodd, eds., *The Tribunal: Responses to John Brown and the Harpers Ferry Raid* (2012).
4. Quoted in *The Confessions of Nat Turner and Related Documents*, ed. Kenneth S. Greenberg (1996), 49.
5. *Id.*
6. *Id.* at 50–51.
7. *Id.* at 19.
8. Both quoted in Tony Horwitz, "Untrue Confessions," *New Yorker*, Dec. 13, 1999.
9. Quoted in Henry Irving Tragle, *The Southampton Slave Revolt of 1831: A Compilation of Source Material* (1971), 318.
10. *Id.* at 319.
11. *Id.*
12. Quoted in *Confessions of Nat Turner*, 90.
13. *Id.* at 41.
14. *Id.* at 67.
15. Quoted in Scot French, *The Rebellious Slave: Nat Turner in American Memory* (2004), 141.
16. The *Journal* went on to say, "Do they not know that in addition to the forces of the white population among whom they are placed, the whole strength of the General Government is pledged to put down such insurrection?" The *Journal* is probably referring here to Article IV, Section 4 of the U.S. Constitution, which declares, "The United States shall . . . protect [each state] against invasion; and an application of the legislature, or of the executive (when the legislature cannot be convened) against domestic violence." The editors declared that "much as we abhor slavery . . . there is not a man of us who would not run to the relief of our friends in the South, when sur-

rounded by the horrors of servile insurrection." Quoted in Eric Foner, *Nat Turner* (1971), 75.

17. Quoted in *Confessions of Nat Turner*, 47–48.

18. *The Portable Thomas Jefferson (Notes on the State of Virginia)*, ed. Merrill D. Petersen (1977), 215.

19. Abraham Lincoln, Second Inaugural Address, March 4, 1865.

20. Quoted in *Confessions of Nat Turner*, 54–55.

21. *See* Alison Goodyear Freehling, *Drift Toward Dissolution: The Virginia Slavery Debate of 1831–1832* (1982); Erik S. Root, *Sons of the Fathers: The Virginia Slavery Debates of 1831–1832* (2010).

22. *See* Patrick H. Breen, "A Prophet in His Own Land: Support for Nat Turner and His Rebellion Within Southampton's Black Community," in *Nat Turner: A Slave Rebellion in History and Memory*, ed. Kenneth S. Greenberg (2003), 116 ("Nothing was a more potent recruiting tool for Nat Turner's army than some slaves' desire for revenge. For a brief moment . . . blacks had a chance to redress some of the wrongs they had endured.").

23. *Washington National Leader*, Jan. 19, 1889, quoted in Foner, *Nat Turner*, 148.

24. "John Brown & Nat Turner," *New York Age*, Jan. 26, 1889, quoted in Foner, *Nat Turner*, 149–50.

25. "Nat Turner Marches On," *Liberator*, Nov. 7, 1831, quoted in Foner, *Nat Turner*, 160.

26. "Nat Turner, Friend or Martyr?," *Opportunity*, Nov. 1931, quoted in Foner, *Nat Turner*, 163.

27. *See* French, *Rebellious Slave*, 233 ("The stature of the rebellious slave rose dramatically in the years between 1960 and 1965 as the civil rights movement, energized by student participation and leadership, took to the streets.").

28. *See* Albert E. Stone, *The Return of Nat Turner: History, Literature, and Cultural Politics in Sixties America* (1992).

29. John Henrik Clarke, *William Styron's Nat Turner: Ten Black Writers Respond* (1968), vii.

30. Lerone Bennett Jr., "Nat's Last White Man," in Clarke, *William Styron's Nat Turner*, 5.

31. Ernest Kaiser, "The Failure of William Styron," in Clarke, *William Styron's Nat Turner*, 57.

32. Charles V. Hamilton, "Our Nat Turner and William Styron's Creation," in Clarke, *William Styron's Nat Turner*, 78.

33. Stephen B. Oates, *The Fires of Jubilee: Nat Turner's Fierce Rebellion* (1975), 145.

34. Quoted in *Confessions of Nat Turner*, 40–41.

35. *See* Breen, "Prophet in His Own Land," 105.

36. Quoted in *Defending Slavery: Proslavery Thought in the Old South: A Brief History with Documents*, ed. Paul Finkelman (2003), 86–87.

37. Quoted in George M. Fredrickson, *The Black Image in the White Mind: The Debate on Afro-American Character and Destiny, 1817–1914* (1972), 57.

38. Thomas R. R. Cobb, *An Inquiry into the Law of Negro Slavery in the United States of America* (1958), 46.

39. E. B. Reuter, "The American Race Problem," 12 *Journal of Negro History* 559 (1927). *See also* Ulrich B. Phillips and Eugene Genovese, eds., *The Slave Economy of the Old South: Selected Essays in Economic and Social History* (1968).

40. Sherie Mershon and Steven L. Schlossman, *Foxholes and Color Lines: Desegregating the U.S. Armed Forces* (1998), 16.

41. *Id.* at 15.

42. Patrick Henry, Speech before the Virginia House of Delegates, March 23, 1775, quoted in John Bartlett, *Bartlett's Familiar Quotations* (1937), 270.

43. David Walker, *David Walker's Appeal to the Colored Citizens of the World*, ed. Peter P. Hinks (1829; 2000), 28.

44. *See, e.g.*, Daniel Rasmussen, *American Uprising: The United States of America's Largest Slave Revolt* (2011).

45. Loyle Hairston, "William Styron's Nat Turner—Rogue Nigger," in Clarke, *William Styron's Nat Turner*, 72.

46. Addison Gayle, *The Black Situation* (1970), 68–70.

47. Michael Walzer, *Obligations: Essays on Disobedience, War, and Citizenship* (1970), 62.

48. Quoted in French, *Rebellious Slave*, 118–19.

49. *Cf.* [Marta Hillers], *A Woman in Berlin: Eight Weeks in the Conquered City: A Diary* (2005).

50. Quoted in Foner, *Nat Turner*, 84.

51. Quoted in *id.* at 82.

16. FREDERICK DOUGLASS: EVERYONE'S HERO

1. This essay is drawn from Randall Kennedy, "The Confounding Truth About Frederick Douglass," *Atlantic*, Dec. 2018.

17. ANTHONY BURNS AND
THE TERRIBLE RELEVANCY OF THE FUGITIVE SLAVE ACT

1. Published in Boston in 1851. Library of Congress, portfolio 60, folder 22. Digital ID http://hdl.loc.gov/loc.rbc/rbpe.06002200.

2. *See* Stanley W. Campbell, *The Slave Catchers: Enforcement of the Fugitive Slave Law, 1850–1860* (1970), 207. Campbell maintains that, pursuant to the law, about three hundred were captured and returned. Professor Daniel Farbman notes, however, that the number was smaller once one takes into account captives who were freed by purchase. He shows persuasively that resistance to the law was much more effective than generally appreciated. *See* "Resistance Lawyering," 107 *California Law Review* 1877 (2019). For

additional commentary on the fugitive slave laws and the issues that surrounded them, *see* R. J. M. Blackett, *The Captive's Quest for Freedom: Fugitive Slaves, the 1850 Fugitive Slave Law, and the Politics of Slavery* (2018); Andrew Delbanco, *The War Before the War: Fugitive Slaves and the Struggle for America's Soul from the Revolution to the Civil War* (2018); Steven Lubet, *Fugitive Justice: Runaways, Rescuers, and Slavery on Trial* (2011).

3. The Fugitive Slave Act of 1850, 9 Stat. 462 (1850).

4. The Fugitive Slave Act of 1793, 1 Stat. 302 (1793). *See* C. W. A. David, "The Fugitive Slave Law of 1793 and Its Antecedents," 9 *Journal of Negro History* 18 (1924).

   Congressional power to enact the fugitive slave acts was said to flow from Article IV, Section 2, Clause 3 of the Constitution, which declares, "No person held to service or labor in one State, under the laws thereof, escaping into another, shall, in consequence of any law or regulation therein, be discharged from such service or labor; but shall be delivered up on claim of the party, to whom such service or labor may be due." U.S. Constitution, art. 4, § 2, cl. 3.

5. 41 U.S. 539 (1842).

6. *See* Thomas D. Morris, *Free Men All: The Personal Liberty Laws of the North, 1780–1861* (1974). According to Morris, "Nearly all the states above the Mason-Dixon line experimented at one time or another with such laws (the only exceptions are Illinois and the far western states that came into the Union in the 1850s)." *Id.* at xi.

7. Quoted in Allen Johnson, "The Constitutionality of the Fugitive Slave Acts," 31 *Yale Law Journal* 161 (1921). *See also* Campbell, *Slave Catchers*, 8.

8. *See* Civil Rights Cases, 109 U.S. 3, 30 (1883) (Harlan, J., dissenting).

9. *See* Fugitive Slave Act of 1850, § 3.

10. *Id.* at § 5.

11. *Id.* at § 8.

12. *Id.* at § 5.

13. *Id.*

14. *Id.* at § 6.

15. *Id.*

16. Quoted in Johnson, "Constitutionality of the Fugitive Slave Acts," 161.

17. Critics of the Act argued that Article IV of the Constitution did not grant Congress authority to regulate reclamation of fugitive slaves, that the act violates Article III of the Constitution by granting judicial power to commissioners appointed without senatorial approval and without life tenure, and that accused fugitive slaves were deprived of the right of habeas corpus in violation of Article I, Section 9, which states that this writ shall not be suspended unless in cases of rebellion or invasion.

    For good discussions of the constitutional questions raised by the Act, *see* Campbell, *Slave Catchers*, 26–47; Johnson, "Constitutionality of the Fugitive Slave Acts." The most thorough judicial explication of the constitutional issues is found in *In re Booth*, 3 Wis. 1 (1854).

18. As Campbell notes, "Arguments that the Fugitive Slave Law of 1850 contravened the Bill of Rights were the most frequently heard and had the most significant effect on public opinion in the North." Campbell, *Slave Catchers*, 42.

19. What this provision meant, according to Sumner, is that "the Commissioner is bribed by a double fee, to pronounce against Freedom." Quoted in Johnson, "Constitutionality of the Fugitive Slave Acts," 172. A modern student of the Act maintains that the variable fee rendered the Act unconstitutional. "To give a commissioner a pecuniary interest in the outcome of a hearing over which he presides and in which he must make findings of fact . . . is a violation of the due process clause of the Fifth Amendment." Julius Yanuck quoted in Campbell, *Slave Catchers*, 42.

20. The Supreme Court justice John McLean expressly articulated this rationale in *Miller v. McQuerry*, 17 F. Cas. 332 (C.C.D. Ohio, 1853). Allen Johnson derided critics of the fee differential, arguing that "to assume that the framers of [the Act] purposed effectively to secure the rendition of fugitive slaves by a paltry bribe of five dollars convicts Sumner and his followers of a want of humor. There may be creatures low enough in the human scale to perjure their souls for five pieces of silver, but the federal judges have not usually been held in such contempt." Johnson, "Constitutionality of the Fugitive Slave Acts," 172.

21. For an elaboration of this defense in the nineteenth century, *see In re Booth*, 3 Wis. 1 at 83–84 (Crawford, J., dissenting); for a twentieth-century affirmation of this view, *see* Johnson, "Constitutionality of the Fugitive Slave Acts," 176–82.

22. The great exception is *In re Booth*, 3 Wis. 1 (1854), *rev'd* 62 U.S. 506 (1859).

23. For biographical information on Burns, *see* Albert J. Von Frank, *The Trials of Anthony Burns: Freedom and Slavery in Emerson's Boston* (1998). *See also* Virginia Hamilton, *Anthony Burns: The Defeat and Triumph of a Fugitive Slave* (1988); Jane H. Pease and William H. Pease, *The Fugitive Slave Law and Anthony Burns: A Problem in Law Enforcement* (1975); Charles Emery Stevens, *Anthony Burns: A History* (1856).

24. *See* Gary Collison, *Shadrach Minkins: From Fugitive Slave to Citizen* (1998). *See also* Thomas P. Slaughter, *Bloody Dawn: The Christiana Riot and Racial Violence in the Antebellum North* (1991).

25. *See* Leonard W. Levy, "Sims' Case: The Fugitive Slave Law in Boston in 1851," 35 *Journal of Negro History* 39 (1950). Like Burns, Sims was traced by correspondence he had with loved ones who remained in the South.

26. *See* Larry Gara, "The Fugitive Slave Law: A Double Paradox," 10 *Civil War History* 229, 234 (1964).

27. Gara quotes an abolitionist who declared that "to make our anti-slavery idea fully understood we must put legs on it." That is precisely what controversies over fugitive slaves allowed abolitionists to do. *Id.* at 241.

28. A writ *de homine replegiando* "lies to replevy a man out of prison, or out of the custody of a private person, upon giving security to the sheriff that the

man shall be forthcoming to answer any charge against him. . . . This writ has been superseded almost wholly, in modern practice, by that of habeas corpus, but it is still used, in some of the states, in an amended and altered form." *Black's Law Dictionary*, 5th ed. (1979), 382.

29. *See* Benjamin A. Quarles, *Black Abolitionists* (1969), 149.

30. A handbill advertising the meeting at Faneuil Hall read as follows:

> A Public Meeting will be held at Faneuil Hall . . . to secure justice for a man claimed by a Virginia kidnapper, and imprisoned in Boston Court House, in defiance of the laws of Massachusetts. Shall he be plunged into the hell of Virginia slavery by a Massachusetts Judge of Probate?

Boston Slave Riot, and the Trial of Anthony Burns (1854), 3 (hereafter cited as Burns Documents).

31. *See* Theodore Parker, *The Trial of Theodore Parker* (1855; 1971), 199–200.

32. *Id.* at 201.

33. *Id.*

34. Quoted in Pease and Pease, *Fugitive Slave Law and Anthony Burns*, 32.

35. *Id.*

36. On the failed rescue attempt and its aftermath in the courts, *see* David R. Maginnes, "The Case of the Court House Rioters in the Rendition of the Fugitive Slave Anthony Burns, 1854," 56 *Journal of Negro History* 31 (1971).

37. *See* "Is It Right and Wise to Kill a Kidnapper?," in *The Portable Frederick Douglass*, ed. John Stauffer and Henry Louis Gates Jr. (2016).

38. On Grimes, *see* Quarles, *Black Abolitionists*.

39. On the debate within antislavery circles over the propriety of purchasing slaves, *see* Aileen Kraditor, *Means and Ends in American Abolitionism: Garrison and His Critics on Strategy and Tactics, 1834–1850* (1969), 220–22.

40. Pease and Pease, *Fugitive Slave Law and Anthony Burns*, 40.

41. *See* Robert M. Cover, *Justice Accused: Antislavery and the Judicial Process* (1975), 119–23.

42. Burns Documents, 44.

43. *Id.* at 49.

44. *Id.* at 41.

45. *See* Thomas Sims's Case, 61 Mass. 285 (1851).

46. Burns Documents, 45.

47. *Id.* at 44.

48. *Id.* at 76–79.

49. *Id.* at 78.

50. According to Loring, "In every case of disputed identity there is one person always whose knowledge is perfect and positive, and whose evidence is not within the reach of error, and that is the person whose identity is questioned, and such evidence this case affords. The evidence is of the conversation which took place between Burns and the claimant on the night of the arrest." *Id.* at 79.

51. *Id.*

52. *See* Maginnes, "Case of the Court House Rioters." This matter clearly needs greater elaboration. *See* Von Frank, *Trials of Anthony Burns.*

53. *See* Charles Warren, *History of the Harvard Law School and of Early Legal Conditions in America* (1908), 188–99. For a commentary on this controversy from the point of view of one who defended Loring, *see* Charles Francis Adams, *Richard Henry Dana: A Biography* (1890), 341–43. Note that Dana was one of Burns's attorneys. For the perspective of Loring's harshest critic, *see* Wendell Phillips, *Speeches, Lectures, and Letters* (1863), 154–212.

54. *See* Christopher N. Lasch, "Rendition Resistance," 92 *North Carolina Law Review* 149 (2013); Karla Mary McKanders, "Immigration Enforcement and the Fugitive Slave Acts: Exploring Their Similarities," 61 *Catholic University Law Review* 921 (2012); Sandra L. Rierson, "Fugitive Slaves and Undocumented Immigrants: Testing the Boundaries of Our Federalism," *University of Miami Law Review* (forthcoming) (Thomas Jefferson School of Law Research Paper No. 3474033, papers.ssrn.com); Jeffrey M. Schmitt, "Immigration Enforcement Reform: Learning from the History of Fugitive Slave Rendition," 103 *Georgetown Law Journal Online* 1 (2014); Kathleen L. Villarruel, "The Underground Railroad and the Sanctuary Movement: A Comparison of History, Litigation, and Values," 60 *Southern California Law Review* 1429 (1987); James A. Kraehenbuehl, Note, "Lessons from the Past: How the Antebellum Fugitive Slave Debate Informs State Enforcement of Federal Immigration Law," 78 *University of Chicago Law Review* 1465 (2011).

18. ERIC FONER AND THE UNFINISHED MISSION OF RECONSTRUCTION

1. This essay is based upon a variety of previous efforts. *See* "Reconstruction and the Politics of Scholarship," 98 *Yale Law Journal* 521 (1989); "Racist Litter: The Lessons of Reconstruction," *London Review of Books*, July 30, 2020; introduction to *Battles for Freedom: The Use and Abuse of American History, Essays from "The Nation,"* by Eric Foner (2017).

19. CHARLES HAMILTON HOUSTON: THE LAWYER AS SOCIAL ENGINEER

1. For an earlier iteration of this essay, see Randall Kennedy, "The Moses of That Journey," *Constitution* (Winter 1993).

2. *See* Genna Rae McNeil, *Groundwork: Charles Hamilton Houston and the Struggle for Civil Rights* (1983); J. Clay Smith Jr., *Emancipation: The Making of the Black Lawyer, 1844–1944* (1993); Symposium on Charles Hamilton Houston, 27 *New England Law Review* (1992–1993); Spottswood W. Robinson III, "No Tea for the Feeble: Two Perspectives on Charles Hamilton Houston," 20 *Howard Law Journal* 1 (1977). *See also* Kenneth W. Mack, *Representing the Race: The Creation of the Civil Rights Lawyer* (2012); Rawn James Jr., *Root and Branch: Charles Hamilton Houston, Thurgood Marshall, and the Struggle to End Segregation* (2010).

3. Quoted in McNeil, *Groundwork*, 42.

4. *Id.* at 52.

5. Richard Kluger, *Simple Justice: The History of Brown v. Board of Education and Black America's Struggle for Equality* (1975; 2004), 128.

6. *Id.* at 127–28.

7. Quoted in McNeil, *Groundwork*, 45.

8. *Id.* at 95.

9. *Id.* at 96.

10. *Id.* at 208.

11. *Id.* at 203.

12. *Id.* at 204.

13. Chris Myers Asch and George Derek Musgrove, *Chocolate City: A History of Race and Democracy in the Nation's Capital* (2017), 298.

14. McNeil, *Groundwork*, 174.

15. Quoted in Juan Williams, *Thurgood Marshall: American Revolutionary* (1998).

20. REMEMBERING THURGOOD MARSHALL

1. Writings of mine on which I draw for this essay include "Doing What You Can with What You Have: The Greatness of Justice Marshall," 80 *Georgetown Law Journal* 2081 (1992); "Thurgood Marshall and the Struggle for Women's Rights," 17 *Harvard Women's Law Journal* 1 (1994); "Fanfare for an Uncommon Man: Thurgood Marshall," *Time*, Feb. 8, 1993, content .time.com; "Mr. Civil Rights," *New Republic*, April 5, 1999; "Thurgood's Coming," *American Lawyer*, Dec. 1999.

2. Sandra Day O'Connor, "Thurgood Marshall: The Influence of a Raconteur," 44 *Stanford Law Review* 1217, 1219 (1992).

3. For the most careful, comprehensive treatment of Marshall's life as a jurist, *see* Mark V. Tushnet, *Making Civil Rights Law: Thurgood Marshall and the Supreme Court, 1936–1961* (1994); Mark V. Tushnet, *Making Constitutional Law: Thurgood Marshall and the Supreme Court, 1961–1991* (1997). For an insightful biography that shines light on Marshall's extralegal activities and controversies, *see* Juan Williams, *Thurgood Marshall: American Revolutionary* (1998). A remarkably detailed account of the justice's early years is found in Larry S. Gibson, *Young Thurgood Marshall: The Making of a Supreme Court Justice* (2012). For an intimate view of the justice from the vantage of a knowledgeable friend, *see* Carl T. Rowan, *Dream Makers, Dream Breakers: The World of Justice Thurgood Marshall* (1993). Excellent descriptions of Marshall's role in various key cases can be found in Gilbert King, *Devil in the Grove: Thurgood Marshall, the Groveland Boys, and the Dawn of a New America* (2012); Richard Kluger, *Simple Justice: The History of Brown v. Board of Education and Black America's Struggle for Equality* (2004); Gary M. Lavergne, *Before Brown: Heman Marion Sweatt, Thurgood Marshall, and the Long Road to Justice* (2010).

   A vivid profile published in March 1956 has the benefit of having been written before Marshall's judicial appointments. It is less influenced by the distortions that almost inescapably taint commentary aware of the celebrity that Marshall eventually attained. *See* Bernard Taper, "A Meeting in Atlanta," *New Yorker,* March 17, 1956, www.newyorker.com.

4. Tushnet, *Making Civil Rights Law,* 10.

5. *Id.* at 14–15.

6. *See, e.g., Alston v. School Board of City of Norfolk,* 112 F.2d 992 (4th Cir. 1940). *See also* Tushnet, *Making Civil Rights Law,* 20–26.

7. 347 U.S. 483 (1954). *See also,* of course, *Bolling v. Sharpe,* 347 U.S. 497 (1954) (invalidating segregation in schooling in the District of Columbia).

8. 321 U.S. 649 (1944).

9. 334 U.S. 1 (1948).

10. 334 U.S. 24 (1948).

11. 328 U.S. 373 (1946).

12. 309 U.S. 227 (1940).

13. 332 U.S. 463 (1947).

14. *Elmore v. Rice,* 72 F. Supp. 516, 520 (E.D.S.C. 1947), *aff'd,* 165 F.2d 387 (4th Cir. 1947).

15. *Elmore,* 72 F. Supp. at 528.

16. *See* "Reminiscences of Thurgood Marshall," in *Thurgood Marshall: His Speeches, Writings, Arguments, Opinions, and Reminiscences,* ed. Mark V. Tushnet (2001), 428–30; Marshall to Maceo Hubbard, Dec. 4, 1946, in *Marshalling Justice: The Early Civil Rights Letters of Thurgood Marshall,* ed. Michael G. Long (2011), 183–84.

17. *See* Tushnet, *Making Civil Rights Law,* 83–84, 89.

18. *Id.* at 135.

19. *Id.* at 136.

20. *Id.* at 133.

21. Long, *Marshalling Justice,* 27–28.

22. *Id.* at 210–11.

23. *Id.* at 296–97.

24. *Id.* at 201.

25. *Id.* at 40–41.

26. Conrad J. Lynn, *There Is a Fountain: The Autobiography of Conrad Lynn* (1993), 93, 104.

27. Brief for the National Association for the Advancement of Colored People as Amicus Curiae Supporting Petitioner, *U.S. ex rel. Lynn v. Downer,* 322 U.S. 756 (1944).

28. The issue arises in none of the Marshall biographies. For the beginnings of instructive excavation of the subject, *see* Mark Brilliant, *The Color of America Has Changed: How Racial Diversity Shaped Civil Rights Reform in California, 1941–1978* (2010); Cheryl Greenberg, "Black and Jewish Responses to Japanese Internment," 14 *Journal of American Ethnic History* 3 (1995).

29. Risa L. Goluboff, *The Lost Promise of Civil Rights* (2007).

30. Robert L. Carter, *A Matter of Law: A Memoir of Struggle in the Cause of Equal*

Rights (2005), 200–202. For an account by the lawyer who was fired, *see* Lewis M. Steel, *The Butler's Child: An Autobiography*, with Beau Friedlander (2016), 154–58.

31. Williams, *Thurgood Marshall: American Revolutionary*, 294.

32. Jack Greenberg, *Crusaders in the Courts: How a Dedicated Band of Lawyers Fought for the Civil Rights Revolution* (1994), 293–98.

33. Carter, *Matter of Law*, 146.

34. Tushnet, *Making Civil Rights Law*, 284–85.

35. Carter, *Matter of Law*, 151.

36. *NAACP v. Alabama*, 357 U.S. 449 (1958).

37. *See generally* Ronald K. L. Collins and Sam Chaltain, *We Must Not Be Afraid to Be Free: Stories of Free Expression in America* (2011), 134–71.

38. Robert Dallek, *Flawed Giant: Lyndon Johnson and His Times, 1961–1973* (1998), 44.

39. Williams, *Thurgood Marshall: American Revolutionary*, 362.

40. Bob Woodward and Scott Armstrong, *The Brethren: Inside the Supreme Court* (1979).

41. For different rankings, *see* Henry J. Abraham, *Justices, Presidents, and Senators: A History of the U.S. Supreme Court Appointments from Washington to Clinton* (1999), 369–72 (noting a listing that ranks Thurgood Marshall as "average"). *See also* Bernard Schwartz, "Supreme Court Superstars: The Ten Greatest Justices," 31 *Tulsa Law Review* 93 (1995).

42. 323 U.S. 214 (1944).

43. 478 U.S. 186 (1986).

44. 481 U.S. 279 (1987).

45. Tushnet, *Making Constitutional Law*, 517.

46. 408 U.S. 92 (1972).

47. 420 U.S. 50 (1975).

48. 408 U.S. at 95.

49. *See* Kenneth L. Karst, "Equality as a Central Principle in the First Amendment," 43 *University of Chicago Law Review* 20 (1975); Geoffrey R. Stone, "Kenneth Karst's Equality as a Central Principle in the First Amendment," 75 *University of Chicago Law Review* 37 (2008). *See also* David L. Hudson Jr., "Justice Thurgood Marshall, Great Defender of First Amendment Free Speech Rights for the Powerless," 2 *Howard Human and Civil Rights Law Review* 167 (2018).

50. *See, e.g.*, William B. Gould, *Black Workers in White Unions: Job Discrimination in the United States* (1977), 249–64; Derrick Bell, "An Epistolary Exploration for a Thurgood Marshall Biography," 6 *Harvard BlackLetter Law Journal* 51, 59–60 (1989).

51. Tushnet, *Making Constitutional Law*, 517.

52. 411 U.S. 1 (1973).

53. *Id.* at 71.

54. *Id.*

55. 418 U.S. 717 (1974).

56. *Id.* at 814.

57. *Id.* at 815.

58. 438 U.S. 265 (1978).

59. *Id.* at 387.

60. 442 U.S. 256 (1979).

61. 409 U.S. 434 (1973).

62. *Id.* at 449.

63. *Id.*

64. *Id.* at 460 (Marshall, J., dissenting).

65. 501 U.S. 808 (1991).

66. *Id.* at 852 (Marshall, J., dissenting).

67. *People v. McCray*, 443 N.E.2d 915 (N.Y. 1982), *People v. Miller*, 437 N.E.2d 945 (Ill. 1982), *State v. Perry*, 420 So. 2d 139 (La. 1982), *cert. denied*, 461 U.S. 961 (1983).

68. *McCray v. New York*, 461 U.S. 961 (1983).

69. *Id.* at 963.

70. *People v. McCray*, 443 N.E.2d 915 (N.Y. 1982), *cert. denied*, 461 U.S. 961 (1983).

71. 380 U.S. 202 (1965).

72. *Id.* at 203.

73. *Id.* at 223, 233.

74. *Id.*

75. *Id.*

76. *Id.*

77. *Id.* at 222.

78. *Id.* at 223.

79. *Id.* at 221–22.

80. *Id.* at 224.

81. *Id.* at 223–25.

82. *Id.* at 223.

83. *Id.* at 226.

84. *McCray v. New York*, 461 U.S. 961, 964 (1983) (Marshall, J., dissenting) (footnote omitted).

85. *Id.* at 964–65 (footnote omitted).

86. *Id.* at 965.

87. *Id.* at 966.

88. *Id.* at 966–67.

89. *Id.* at 962.

90. *Id.* at 961–62.

91. *Id.* at 963.

92. *See* Peter Linzer, "The Meaning of Certiorari Denials," 79 *Columbia Law Review* 1227, 1270 (1979).

93. *Id.* at 1271.

94. 464 U.S. 867 (1983).

95. *Id.* at 868.

96. *Id.* at 869–70 (Marshall, J., dissenting).

97. *See Williams v. Illinois, Dixon v. Illinois, Yates v. Illinois*, 466 U.S. 981 (1984) (Marshall, J., dissenting).

98. *Id.* at 981–82.

99. *Id.* at 981.

100. *Id.* at 983–84.

101. *Harris v. Texas*, 467 U.S. 1261, 1264 (1984) (Marshall, J., dissenting).

102. *McCray v. Abrams*, 576 F. Supp. 1244 (E.D.N.Y. 1983).

103. *Id.* at 1246.

104. *Id.*

105. *McCray v. Abrams*, 576 F. Supp. 1244, 1249 (E.D.N.Y. 1983).

106. 476 U.S. 79 (1986).

107. *Id.* at 90–93.

108. *Id.* at 89.

109. *Id.* at 95.

110. *Id.* at 102 (Marshall, J., concurring).

111. *Id.* at 103.

112. *Id.* at 105.

113. *Id.* at 106.

114. *Id.*

115. *Id.*
   Several judges have expressed agreement with Justice Marshall's conclusion. *See, e.g., Crittenden v. Chappell*, 804 F.3d 998, 1020 (9th Cir. 2015) (McKeown, J., dissenting) ("Justice Marshall was prescient."); *State v. Saint-calle*, 309 P.3d 326, 334 (Wash. 2013) ("Twenty-six years later it is evident that Batson like Swain before it, is failing us."). Academic critics of Batson are legion. *See, e.g.,* Alafair S. Burke, "Prosecutors and Peremptories," 97 *Iowa Law Review* 1467 (2012); Charles J. Ogletree, "Just Say No! A Proposal to Eliminate Racially Discriminatory Uses of Peremptory Challenges," 31 *American Criminal Law Review* 1099 (1944). *But see* Jonathan Abel, "*Batson*'s Appellate Appeal and Trial Tribulations," 118 *Columbia Law Review* 713 (2018).

116. *See* Randall Kennedy, "The Case for Early Retirement," *New Republic*, April 28, 2011; Emily Bazelon, "Why Ruth Bader Ginsburg Refused to Step Down," *New York Times*, Sept. 21, 2020.

21. ISAAC WOODARD AND THE EDUCATION OF J. WATIES WARING

1. This essay is derived from an earlier effort, "The Courage to Defy Brutality," *American Prospect*, Feb. 25, 2019.

22. J. SKELLY WRIGHT: UP FROM RACISM

1. This is a revised version of an essay for a symposium at Loyola Law School honoring Judge J. Skelly Wright. *See* "Judge J. Skelly Wright and the Racial Desegregation of Louisiana," 61 *Loyola Law Review* 57 (Spring 2015).

2. See *United States v. DeCoster*, 487 F.2d 1197 (D.C. Cir. 1973); *Women Strike for Peace v. Morton*, 472 F.2d 1273 (D.C. Cir. 1972); *United States v. Washington Post Co.*, 446 F.2d 1322, 1325 (D.C. Cir. 1971) (Wright, J., dissenting); *Javins v. First National Realty Corp.*, 428 F.2d 1071 (D.C. Cir. 1970), *cert. denied*, 400 U.S. 925 (1970); *Powell v. United States*, 352 F.2d 705, 710 (D.C. Cir. 1965) (Wright, J., dissenting); *Williams v. Walker Thomas Furniture Co.*, 350 F.2d 445 (D.C. Cir. 1965). *See generally* Liva Baker, *The Second Battle of New Orleans: The Hundred-Year Struggle to Integrate the Schools* (1996); Jack Bass, *Unlikely Heroes* (1990), 112–35; Arthur S. Miller, *A Capacity for Outrage: The Judicial Odyssey of J. Skelly Wright* (1984); J. W. Peltason, *Fifty-Eight Lonely Men: Southern Federal Judges and School Desegregation* (1971), 221–43; Michael S. Bernick, "The Unusual Odyssey of J. Skelly Wright," 7 *Hastings Constitutional Law Quarterly* 971 (1980).

3. Pauli Murray, ed., *States' Laws on Race and Color* (1997), 170–95.

4. See *Dean v. Thomas*, 93 F. Supp. 129 (E.D. La. 1950).

5. See *United States v. McElveen*, 180 F. Supp. 10 (E.D. La. 1960), *aff'd in part*, *United States v. Thomas*, 362 U.S. 58 (1960).

6. See *Davis v. Morrison*, No. 16-886 (E.D. La. 1957), *aff'd* 252 F.2d 102 (5th Cir. 1958), *cert. denied*, 356 U.S. 968 (1958); "Transit, City Park Segregation Loses," *New Orleans Times Picayune*, May 15, 1957.

7. See "U.S. Court Voids Louisiana Ban on Mixed Athletics," *New Orleans States-Item*, Nov. 28, 1958. See Bernick, "Unusual Odyssey of J. Skelly Wright," 986n67.

8. Neil R. McMillen, *The Citizens' Council: Organized Resistance to the Second Reconstruction, 1954–64* (1971; 1994), 59.

9. *Id.*

10. Louisiana Constitution art. XII § 1, *amended by* Acts 1974, No. 752. *See also* Vanderbilt University School of Law, *Race Relations Law Reporter* 239 (1956).

11. *Bush v. Orleans Parish School Board*, 138 F. Supp. 336 (E.D. La. 1956). *See also Bush v. Orleans Parish School Board*, 242 F.2d 156 (5th Cir. 1957), *cert. denied*, 354 U.S. 921 (1957).

12. *Bush*, 138 F. Supp. at 337, *aff'd*, *Orleans Parish School Board v. Bush*, 242 F.2d 156 (5th Cir. 1957), *cert. denied*, 354 U.S. 921 (1957).

13. *Bush*, 138 F. Supp. at 342.

14. Adam Fairclough, *Race and Democracy: The Civil Rights Struggle in Louisiana, 1915–1972* (1995), 234, 522n1. *See also* Donald E. DeVore and Joseph Logsdon, *Crescent City Schools: Public Education in New Orleans, 1841–1991* (1991), 236–37; Mary Lee Muller, "New Orleans Public School Desegregation," 17 *Louisiana History* 69 (1976).

15. *Bush v. Orleans Parish School Board*, 187 F. Supp. at 45 (E.D. La. 1960).

16. Frank T. Read and Lisa S. McGough, *Let Them Be Judged: The Judicial Integration of the Deep South* (1978), 139.

17. Quoted in Fairclough, *Race and Democracy*, 244.

18. *Id.*

19. *See Freedom in the Balance: Opinions of Judge Henry W. Edgerton Relating to Civil Liberties,* Eleanor Bontecou, ed. (1960); Anne Emmanuel, *Elbert Parr Tuttle: Chief Jurist of the Civil Rights Revolution* (2011); Joel William Friedman, *Champion of Civil Rights: Judge John Minor Wisdom* (2009); Bernard Schwartz, *Super Chief: Earl Warren and His Supreme Court: A Judicial Biography* (1983); Seth Stern and Stephen Wermiel, *Justice Brennan: Liberal Champion* (2010); Tinsley E. Yarbrough, *A Passion for Justice: J. Waties Waring and Civil Rights* (1987); Tinsley E. Yarbrough, *Judge Frank Johnson and Human Rights in Alabama* (1981). *See also* Bass, *Unlikely Heroes.*

20. Bernick, "Unusual Odyssey of J. Skelly Wright," 986–87; Baker, *Second Battle of New Orleans,* 423–26.

21. *Bush,* 128 F. Supp. at 342.

22. *See* Baker, *Second Battle of New Orleans,* 91–94 ("If there was any strong element of conformity in [Judge Wright's] youth, it was his attitude toward blacks.").

23. Fairclough, *Race and Democracy,* 245.

24. *See* W. J. Weatherby, "A Judge with a Conscience," *Chicago Sun-Times,* Nov. 27, 1960. *See also* Fairclough, *Race and Democracy,* 245.

25. *See Chaney v. Heckler,* 718 F.2d 1174 (D.C. Cir. 1983), *rev'd,* 470 U.S. 821 (1985).

26. *See Francis v. Resweber,* 329 U.S. 459 (1947). *See also* Gilbert King, *The Execution of Willie Francis: Race, Murder, and the Search for Justice in the American South* (2008); Deborah W. Denno, "When Willie Francis Died: The 'Disturbing' Story Behind One of the Eighth Amendment's Most Enduring Standards of Risk," in *Death Penalty Stories,* ed. John H. Blume and Jordan M. Steiker (2009).

23. ON CUSSING OUT WHITE LIBERALS: THE CASE OF PHILIP ELMAN

1. Randall Kennedy, "A Reply to Philip Elman," 100 *Harvard Law Review* 1938 (1987).

2. Norman I. Silber, *With All Deliberate Speed: The Life of Philip Elman: An Oral History Memoir* (2004).

3. Opinion, "With All Deliberate Impropriety," *New York Times,* March 24, 1987.

4. *Brown v. Board of Education,* 347 U.S. 483, 494n11 (1954).

5. Kennedy, "Reply to Philip Elman," 1944.

24. THE CIVIL RIGHTS ACT DID MAKE A DIFFERENCE!

1. For an earlier iteration of this essay, see Randall Kennedy, "The Civil Rights Act's Unsung Victory," *Harper's,* June 2014.

25. BLACK POWER HAGIOGRAPHY

1. For an earlier iteration of this essay, see Randall Kennedy, "Protesting Too Much: The Problem with Black Power Revisionism," *Boston Review*, March 2015.

26. THE CONSTITUTIONAL ROOTS OF "BIRTHERISM"

1. I have railed against the natural born citizen proviso previously. *See* Randall Kennedy, "A Natural Aristocracy?," in *Constitutional Stupidities, Constitutional Tragedies*, ed. William N. Eskridge Jr. and Sanford Levinson (1998). Writings that have provided useful guidance include Sarah Helene Duggin and Mary Beth Collins, "Natural Born in the U.S.A.: The Striking Unfairness and Dangerous Ambiguity of the Constitution's Presidential Qualifications Clause and Why We Need to Fix It," 85 *Boston University Law Review* 53 (2005); Charles Gordon, "Who Can Be President of the United States: The Unresolved Enigma," 28 *Maryland Law Review* 1 (1968); Christina S. Lohman, "Presidential Eligibility: The Meaning of the Natural-Born Citizen Clause," 36 *Gonzaga Law Review* 349 (2000); J. Michael Medina, "The Presidential Qualification Clause in This Bicentennial Year: The Need to Eliminate the Natural Born Citizen Requirement," 12 *Oklahoma City University Law Review* 253 (1987); Robert Post, "What Is the Constitution's Worst Provision?," 12 *Constitutional Commentary* 191 (1995); Jill A. Pryor, "The Natural-Born Citizen Clause and Presidential Eligibility: An Approach for Resolving Two Hundred Years of Uncertainty," 97 *Yale Law Journal* 881 (1988); Akhil Reed Amar, "Natural Born Killjoy: Why the Constitution Won't Let Immigrants Run for President, and Why That Should Change," *Legal Affairs*, April 2004.
2. Quoted in Duggin and Collins, "Natural Born in the U.S.A." 64.
3. Quoted in Duggin and Collins, "Natural Born in the U.S.A.," 70.
4. Post, "What Is the Constitution's Worst Provision?," 193.
5. Scott Simon, "Do Away with 'Natural Born Citizen' Clause," CBSNews .com, Jan. 24, 2016.

27. INEQUALITY AND THE SUPREME COURT

1. For an earlier iteration of this essay, see Randall Kennedy, "Politicians in Robes," *Nation*, Oct. 5, 2020.

28. *BROWN* AS SENIOR CITIZEN

1. This essay derives from a lecture that I prepared for delivery at the New-York Historical Society. I thank Dale Gregory and Alexander Kassl for making the Society one of my favorite venues for trying out new material.
2. *See Brown v. Board of Education*, 347 U.S. 483 (1954); *Bolling v. Sharpe*, 347 U.S. 497 (1954); *Brown v. Board of Education*, 349 U.S. 294 (1955).

3. Pauli Murray, ed., *States' Laws on Race and Color* (1951; 1997), 406.

4. *Brown*, 347 U.S. at 495.

5. *Bolling*, 347 U.S. at 500.

6. *Brown*, 349 U.S. at 301.

7. On the behind-the-scenes diplomacy see Michael J. Klarman, *From Jim Crow to Civil Rights: The Supreme Court and the Struggle for Racial Justice* (2004), 292–320; Mark Tushnet, "What Really Happened in *Brown v. Board of Education*," with Katya Lazin, 91 *Columbia Law Review* 1867 (1991); Dennis J. Hutchinson, "Unanimity and Desegregation: Decisionmaking in the Supreme Court, 1948–1958," 68 *Georgetown Law Journal* 1 (1979).

8. For an illustration of *Brown*-worshipping piety, see Owen Fiss, *Pillars of Justice: Lawyers and the Liberal Tradition* (2017), 1–3. In his first three pages, Fiss mentions *Brown* eleven times, referring to it as "an extraordinary moment in the life of the law, transforming the law into an instrument for realizing the highest ideals of the nation."

9. *Brown*, 347 U.S. at 483, 494.

10. *Bolling*, 347 U.S. at 497, 500.

11. 163 U.S. 537 (1896).

12. *Id.* at 560.

13. *Id.* at 557.

14. Quoted in Richard Kluger, *Simple Justice: The History of Brown v. Board of Education and Black America's Struggle for Equality* (1975; 2004), 699.

15. The unanimity of *Brown* is often portrayed as a key feature of its attractiveness. *See, e.g.*, Wilkinson, *From Brown to Bakke*, 30 (It was precisely the unusualness of unanimity on so divisive an issue that made *Brown* so effective.). Justin Driver bracingly challenges this conventional view, suggesting that "the veneration of *Brown*'s unanimity appears to rest on a severely exaggerated understanding of the Supreme Court's ability to stifle opponents by speaking with one voice." *The Schoolhouse Gate: Public Education, the Supreme Court, and the Battle for the American Mind* (2018), 253.

16. Eric Foner, *The Second Founding: How the Civil War and Reconstruction Remade the Constitution* (2019), 28.

17. *Id.* at 87.

18. *Id.* at 107–9.

19. *See* Waldo E. Martin Jr., *Brown v. Board of Education: A Brief History with Documents* (1998), 220.

20. Quoted in Reed Sarratt, *The Ordeal of Desegregation: The First Decade* (1966), 1, 5.

21. Quoted in Yasuhiro Katagiri, *Black Freedom, White Resistance, and Red Menace: Civil Rights and Anticommunism in the Jim Crow South* (2014), 98.

22. *Griffin v. Prince Edward County*, 377 U.S. 218 (1964).

23. Quoted in Karen Anderson, *Little Rock: Race and Resistance at Central High School* (2010), 195.

24. *See* Greenberg, "Supreme Court, Civil Rights, and Civil Dissonance," 77 *Yale Law Journal* 1520 (1968).

25. *Sweatt v. Painter,* 210 S.W. 2d. 442, 443 (1948), *rev'd* 339 U.S. 629 (1950).

   The Texas Constitution, echoing the South Carolina Constitution, provided that "separate schools shall be provided for the white and colored . . . and impartial provision shall be made for both." The federal Supreme Court ordered that Sweatt be admitted to the University of Texas but only because the state failed to offer to colored applicants a law school that was equal to that offered to whites. The Court made it practically impossible for the state to create racially segregated law schools that could be deemed "equal" under the Court's analysis. Still, as a formal matter the Supreme Court did not extinguish the legal vitality of segregation in *Sweatt v. Painter.*

26. Gerald N. Rosenberg, *The Hollow Hope: Can Courts Bring About Social Change?,* 2nd ed. (1991; 2008), 52.

27. Quoted in Brad Snyder, "How the Conservatives Canonized *Brown v. Board of Education,*" 52 *Rutgers Law Review* 383, 445 (2000).

28. J. M. Balkin and Sanford Levinson, "The Canons of Constitutional Law," 111 *Harvard Law Review* 963, 997 (1999). *See also* Michael J. Klarman, "*Brown v. Board of Education:* Facts and Political Correctness," 80 *Virginia Law Review* 185, 185 (1994) (*Brown* is "politically sacrosanct."). Louis Michael Seidman, "*Brown* and *Miranda,*" 80 *California Law Review* 673, 675 (1992) (Genuflection to *Brown,* according to Professor Louis Seidman, is the "admission ticket for entry into mainstream constitutional dialogue."). It should be noted, though, that some jurists nominated for judgeships by President Trump declined to state their belief that *Brown* specifically was rightly decided. They justified their nonresponse on the ground that sharing their personal view of *Brown* would put pressure on them to share their personal view on other cases, most notably *Roe v. Wade. See* Laura Meckler and Robert Barnes, "Trump Judicial Nominees Decline to Endorse *Brown v. Board* Under Senate Questioning," *Washington Post,* May 16, 2019.

29. *See, e.g., Keyes v. School District No. 1 Denver,* 413 U.S. 189 (1973); *Swann v. Charlotte-Mecklenburg Board of Education,* 402 U.S. 1 (1971).

30. *See, e.g., Milliken v. Bradley,* 433 U.S. 267 (1977).

31. *See Spangler v. Pasadena,* 311 F. Supp. 501 (C.D. Cal. 1970), for an early example of judicial revision of "segregation" that expressly collapsed the distinction between the racial separation of students directly caused by purposeful governmental policy and a condition of racial separateness stemming from a variety of causes. According to the district judge in *Spangler,* "Racial segregation and racial imbalance are two names for the same phenomenon, racial separation." He then notes that he uses the two terms "interchangeably." *Id.* at 506. The Supreme Court ultimately disapproved of much of the district court's ruling. *See Pasadena City Board of Education v. Spangler,* 427 U.S. 424 (1976).

32. *See generally* Joshua Goodman and Melanie Rucinski, "Increasing Racial Diversity in Boston's Exam Schools," Rappaport Institute, Harvard Kennedy School, Oct. 2018; Jelani Cobb, "Back to School Reform," *New Yorker,* Sept. 8, 2019; Eliza Shapiro, "Only 7 Black Students Got into Stuyvesant,

N.Y.'s Most Selective High School, Out of 895 Spots," *New York Times*, March 18, 2019; Susan Dynarski, "Evidence on New York City and Boston Exam Schools," Brookings, July 19, 2018.

33. Michelle Alexander, *The New Jim Crow: Mass Incarceration in the Age of Colorblindness* (2010).

34. Katie Eyer, "The New Jim Crow Is the Old Jim Crow," 128 *Yale Law Journal* 1002 (2018).

35. 551 U.S. 701 (2007).

36. *Id.* at 748.

29. RACIAL PROMISED LANDS?

1. Governor George Wallace, Inaugural Address, Jan. 14, 1963, transcript available in the Alabama Department of Archives and History.

2. Elijah Muhammad, *Message to the Blackman in America* (1965).

3. Stokely Carmichael, "What We Want," *New York Review of Books*, Sept. 22, 1966.

4. Quoted in Clay Carson, *In Struggle: SNCC and the Black Awakening of the 1960s* (1981), 22.

5. Carmichael, "What We Want."

6. *See* Philip S. Foner, ed., *The Black Panthers Speak* (1970).

7. *See* Dan T. Carter, *The Politics of Rage: George Wallace, the Origins of the New Conservatism, and the Transformation of American Politics* (1995; 2nd ed., 2000).

8. *See, e.g., Clay v. United States*, 403 U.S. 698 (1971) (reversing conviction for refusing induction into the military on basis of religious conscientious objection).

9. *See* Garrett Felber, *Those Who Know Don't Say: The Nation of Islam, the Black Freedom Movement, and the Carceral State* (2020).

10. William Van Alstyne, "Rites of Passage: Race, the Supreme Court, and the Constitution," 46 *University of Chicago Law Review* 775, 809 (1979).

11. *See generally* Andrew Kull, *The Color-Blind Constitution* (1992). *See also* Ward Connerly, *Creating Equal: My Fight Against Race Preferences* (2000); Thomas Chatterton Williams, *Self-Portrait in Black and White* (2019).

12. Milton R. Konvitz, ed., *Law and Social Action: Selected Essays of Alexander H. Pekelis* (1950), 218.

13. *Id.* at 219.

14. *See* Randall Kennedy, *Interracial Intimacies: Sex, Marriage, Identity, and Adoption* (2003). *See also* Elizabeth Emens, "Intimate Discrimination: The State's Role in the Accidents of Sex and Love," 122 *Harvard Law Review* 1307 (2009); Russell K. Robinson, "Structural Dimensions of Romantic Preferences," 76 *Fordham Law Review* 2787 (2007); Alan Wertheimer, "Reflections on Discrimination," 43 *San Diego Law Review* 945 (2006).

15. *See, e.g.,* Glenn C. Loury, *The Anatomy of Racial Inequality* (2002), 123

("There is a sphere of intimate social intercourse, governed to some degree by raced perceptions in individuals' minds, that, out of respect for liberty and the dignity of human beings, should not become the object of political or bureaucratic manipulation."). *But see* R. Richard Banks, "The Color of Desire: Fulfilling Adoptive Parents' Racial Preferences Through Discriminatory State Action," 107 *Yale Law Journal* 875 (1998); Emens, "Intimate Discrimination"; Camille Gear Rich, "Contracting Our Way to Inequality: Race, Reproductive Freedom, and the Quest for the Perfect Child," 104 *Minnesota Law Review* 2375 (2020).

16. *See* K. Anthony Appiah and Amy Gutmann, *Color Conscious: The Political Morality of Race* (1996), 107.

17. Quoted in Randall Kennedy, *For Discrimination: Race, Affirmative Action, and the Law* (2013), 95.

18. *Id.* at 96.

19. *Id.* at 102–3.

20. *See* John D. Skrentny, *After Civil Rights: Racial Realism in the New American Workplace* (2014).

21. *See, e.g.*, Paul Brest, "In Defense of the Antidiscrimination Principle," 90 *Harvard Law Review* 1 (1976); Reva B. Siegel, "Equality Talk: Antisubordination and Anticlassification Values in Constitutional Struggles over *Brown*," 117 *Harvard Law Review* 1470 (2004).

22. *Cf. Strauder v. West Virginia*, 100 U.S. 303, 307–8 (1880) (The words of the Fourteenth Amendment "are prohibitory, but they contain a necessary implication of a positive immunity, or right, most valuable to the colored race—the right to exemption from unfriendly legislation against them distinctively as colored—exception from legal discriminations implying inferiority in civil society . . . discrimination which are steps towards reducing them to the condition of a subject race.").

23. *See, e.g.*, Angela Y. Davis, *Are Prisons Obsolete?* (2003); Amna A. Akbar, "Toward a Radical Imagination of Law," 93 *New York University Law Review* 405 (2018); Ruth Wilson Gilmore and James Kilgore, "The Case for Abolition," Marshall Project, June 19, 2019; Rachel Herzing, "Black Liberation and the Abolition of the Prison Industrial Complex: An Interview with Rachel Herzing," *Propter Nos*, Aug. 30, 2016; Mariame Kaba, "Yes, We Mean Literally Abolish the Police," *New York Times*, June 12, 2020; Rachel Kushner, "Is Prison Necessary? Ruth Wilson Gilmore Might Change Your Mind," *New York Times Magazine*, April 17, 2019; Allegra McLeod, "Envisioning Abolition Democracy," 132 *Harvard Law Review* 1613 (2019); Allegra McLeod, "Prison Abolition and Grounded Justice," 62 *UCLA Law Review* 1156 (2015); Dorothy E. Roberts, "Abolitionist Constitutionalism," 133 *Harvard Law Review* 1 (2019); Dylan Rodriguez, "Abolition as Praxis of Human Being: A Foreword," 132 *Harvard Law Review* 1567 (2019); Movement for Black Lives, m4bl.org/.

24. Akbar, "Toward a Radical Imagination of Law," 410.

25. McLeod, "Envisioning Abolition Democracy," 1615.

26. *Id.*

27. Akbar, "Toward a Radical Imagination of Law," 412.

28. *See, e.g.,* David Cole, *No Equal Justice: Race and Class in the American Criminal Justice System* (1999); Ed Cray, *The Enemy in the Streets: Police Malpractice in America* (1972); Randall Kennedy, *Race, Crime, and the Law* (1997).

29. According to the Prison Policy Initiative, in 2020 state prisons incarcerated 183,000 people convicted of murder, 165,000 convicted of rape, and 169,000 convicted of robbery. Prison Policy Initiative, "Mass Incarceration: The Whole Pie 2020," press release, March 24, 2020, www.prisonpolicy .org.

30. For an egregious instance, *see, e.g.,* Madison Pauly, "What a World Without Cops Would Look Like," *Mother Jones,* June 2, 2020 (interviewing Alex Vitale, author of *The End of Policing* [2017]). For an instructive critique of Vitale, *see* Matthew Yglesias, "The End of Policing Left Me Convinced We Still Need Policing," *Vox,* June 18, 2020.

31. Roberts, "Abolitionist Constitutionalism," 110.

32. *Id.* at 121.

33. *See* Skrentny, *After Civil Rights,* 153–215.

INDEX

National Association for the Advancement of Colored People (NAACP), 12, 16, 18, 32, 37, 38, 103, 143–4, 172, 186, 294n, 304, 305, 328, 343, 346, 387, 402, 418; black respectability politics and, 127; LDF relations with, 32n, 294n, 296–7; Lynn case and, 294, 295; Marshall's tenure as principal lawyer of, 289–300; order to submit membership list of, to Alabama authorities, 299–300; racially motivated violence combated by, 322–3; reliant mainly on white attorneys, 275–6, 298

National Association for the Advancement of White People (NAAWP), 433

National Bar Association (NBA), 153

National Basketball Association (NBA), 440

National Council of Negro Women, 17

National Football League (NFL), 80, 93

National Labor Relations Act (NLRA), 304

National Research Council, 45–6

National Review, 301

Nation of Islam (NOI), 12, 13, 101, 116, 427–8, 431; cosmology of, 370–1; Malcolm X and, 370, 371, 372–3, 374, 377; "Negro" repudiated by, 181–2; personal naming and, 202–4, 371

Native Americans, 57n, 89–90, 225, 231, 270, 420, 432

natural born citizen proviso, 390–4

Nazi Germany, 89, 230

"Negress," use of term, 180n

"Negro" (or "negro"), use of term, 172, 173, 174, 177, 179–87, 188, 189–90, 191, 193, 194–5, 462n5, 463n8; capitalization of, 185–7, 189–90, 194

Negro Motorist Green Book, The (Green), 353, 367

Negrophobia, 6, 9, 85, 114, 129, 177, 264

Nell, William, 4

"Nemesis" (Baird), 181

New Deal, 361, 362

New Jim Crow, 421–2

Newman, Jon O., 315–16n

New Orleans: school desegregation in, 333–9; sit-in protests in, 356–7

Newton, Huey, 368–9, 381–9, 425, 429–30; Bloom and Martin's book on BPP and, 369, 383–9; police officer killed by, 384–5, 388

New York Herald Tribune, 293

New York Journal of Commerce, 220, 470–1n16

New York Times, 79, 86, 93, 112, 115, 174, 186–7, 189, 190–1, 234, 297, 328, 345, 365

New York Times v. Sullivan, 103

Nickerson, Eugene H., 315–16

"nigger," use of word, 179, 180, 210–16, 280; in courts, 213–14; formulaic apologies for, 214n; hurt feelings as objection to, 212–13; for pedagogical purposes, 210–13, 214, 216; racial identity of speaker and, 215–16; racist purposes for, 215, 216

Nixon, E. D., 46–7, 91, 123

Nixon, Richard M., 156, 318n, 362, 401, 407, 417, 418, 431

Nobel Peace Prize, 18, 113

Norman, Peter, 37n

Obama, Barack, xi, 20–3, 24, 29, 42, 74n, 160, 182, 234, 303n, 390, 421; birtherism and, 24, 390; colorism and, 159; elections of, 21–3, 25, 51–2, 87, 91, 182; Ginsburg's retirement and, 318, 319; letter written to Bell by, 74n; optimism of, 20–1; origin story of, 87; Supreme Court nominations and, 407, 408

Obama, Michelle, 159

Obergefell v. Hodges, 405

Some of the chapters in this book originally appeared, in different form, in the following publications:

The American Prospect: "Shall We Overcome? Optimism and Pessimism in African American Racial Thought" as "Black America's Promised Land: Why I Am Still a Racial Optimist" (November 10, 2014); "How Black Students Brought the Constitution to Campus" as "The Forgotten Origins of the Constitution on Campus" (December 28, 2017); "The George Floyd Moment: Promise and Peril" as "The George Floyd Moment: Promise and Peril" (June 19, 2020); "Isabel Wilkerson, the Election of 2020, and Racial Caste" as "The Ebb and Flow of Racial Progress" (December 3, 2020).

The Atlantic: "Frederick Douglass: Everyone's Hero" as "The Confounding Truth About Frederick Douglass" (December 2018).

Boston Review: "Black Power Hagiography" as "Protesting Too Much: The Problem with Black Power Revisionism" (March 2015).

The Chronicle of Higher Education: "The Princeton Ultimatum: Antiracism Gone Awry" as "How Racist Are Universities, Really?" (August 12, 2020).

Harper's Magazine: "The Civil Rights Act Did Make a Difference!" as "The Civil Rights Act's Unsung Victory" (June 2014); "The Politics of Black Respectability" as "Lifting As We Climb: A Progressive Defense of Respectability Politics" (October 2015).

Loyola Law Review: "J. Skelly Wright: Up from Racism" as "Judge J. Skelly Wright and the Racial Desegregation of Louisiana" (Spring 2015).

The Nation: "Why Clarence Thomas Ought to Be Ostracized" as "The Apparatchik" (October 29, 2019).

The Root: "Policing Racial Solidarity" as "The Fallacy of Touré's Post-blackness Theory" (August 11, 2020).

"Eric Foner and the Unfinished Mission of Reconstruction" is based on "Reconstruction and the Politics of Scholarship" in *Yale Law Journal* (January 1989); "Racist Litter: The Lessons of Reconstruction" in *London Review of Books* (July 30, 2020); and the introduction to *Battles for Freedom: The Use and Abuse of American History, Essays from* The Nation, by Eric Foner, I.B. Tauris & Co. Ltd. and The Nation Company LLC (2017).

"Say It Loud! On Racial Shame, Pride, Kinship, and Other Problems" first appeared as "My Race Problem" in *The Atlantic* (May 1997) and subsequently in *The New York Times* as "How James Brown Made Black Pride a Hit" (July 20, 2018).

"Should We Admire Nat Turner?" first appeared as "On Judging Nat Turner," originally published in *Dixie Redux: Essays in Honor of Sheldon Hackney*, edited by Raymond Arsenault and Orville Vernon Burton (NewSouth Books, 2013).

"Remembering Thurgood Marshall" is based on "Doing What You Can with What You Have: The Greatness of Justice Marshall" in *The Georgetown Law Journal* (August 1992); "Fanfare for an Uncommon Man: Thurgood Marshall" in *Time* (February 8, 1993); and "Thurgood Marshall and the Struggle for Women's Rights" in *Harvard Women's Law Journal* (Spring 1994).

A NOTE ABOUT THE AUTHOR

Randall Kennedy is the Michael R. Klein Professor at Harvard Law School, where he teaches courses on contracts, criminal law, and the regulation of race relations. He attended St. Albans School, Princeton University, Oxford University, and Yale Law School. He is a member of the bar of the District of Columbia, the American Law Institute, the American Academy of Arts and Sciences, and the American Philosophical Society. His other books are *For Discrimination: Race, Affirmative Action, and the Law* (2013); *The Persistence of the Color Line: Racial Politics and the Obama Presidency* (2011); *Sellout: The Politics of Racial Betrayal* (2008); *Interracial Intimacies: Sex, Marriage, Identity, and Adoption* (2003); *Nigger: The Strange Career of a Troublesome Word* (2002); and *Race, Crime, and the Law* (1997). He lives in Dedham, Massachusetts.

A NOTE ON THE TYPE

This book was set in Janson, a typeface long thought to have been made by the Dutchman Anton Janson, who was a practicing typefounder in Leipzig during the years 1668–1687. However, it has been conclusively demonstrated that these types are actually the work of Nicholas Kis (1650–1702), a Hungarian, who most probably learned his trade from the master Dutch typefounder Dirk Voskens. The type is an excellent example of the influential and sturdy Dutch types that prevailed in England up to the time William Caslon (1692–1766) developed his own incomparable designs from them.

Composed by North Market Street Graphics,
Lancaster, Pennsylvania

Printed and bound by Berryville Graphics,
Berryville, Virginia